Seventeenth Edition

# MINITAB LAB WORKBOOK

Howard S. Kaplon

*Towson University*

McGraw Hill **Learning Solutions**

Boston   Burr Ridge, IL   Dubuque, IA   New York   San Francisco   St. Louis
Bangkok   Bogotá   Caracas   Lisbon   London   Madrid
Mexico City   Milan   New Delhi   Seoul   Singapore   Sydney   Taipei   Toronto

# MINITAB LAB WORKBOOK
Seventeenth Edition

1 2 3 4 5 6 7 8 9 0 QSR QSR 0 9

ISBN-13: 978-0-07-804650-6
ISBN-10: 0-07-804650-5
PART OF:
ISBN-13: 978-0-07-735166-3
ISBN:10: 0-07-735166-5

*Custom Publishing Specialist: Jeff Schmitt*
*Production Editor: Jessica Portz*
*Cover Design: Paul L. Illian*
*Printer/Binder: Quebecor World*

# TABLE OF CONTENTS

# PREFACE

This Minitab Lab Workbook is designed to be used by students taking a one or two semester introductory statistics course. The typical situation is one where the students have access to a microcomputer laboratory. This laboratory may have copies of the Minitab software available either on each computer's hard disk or on a network. The Minitab software may be either the full version or the Student Edition. As an alternative, the students may be expected to purchase their own copy of the Student Edition of Minitab or lease a copy of the full version of Minitab for use in the laboratory and/or at their homes. This workbook is not tied to any specific textbook, and the presentation and examples are purposely written in a way that allows this workbook to be used as a supplement with any statistics textbook. However, the use of this workbook is not limited to students, and may be used by anyone who possesses a knowledge of basic statistical methods and wants to learn how to use the Minitab program. This workbook is not intended to be a complete Minitab manual, nor does this workbook describe all of Minitab's features.

This edition is based on the Full Windows Version of Minitab Release 15, but almost everything presented here may also be done using the Student Edition of Minitab for Windows Release 14. One of these is the ability to save **all** of your work: Session Window, Worksheet Windows and Graphics Windows, together in a single file as a Minitab project. This feature makes it easy to interrupt a Minitab session before its completion, and then to continue later at the point where you left off previously.

The Full Version of Minitab Release 15 is currently available. Most of the changes and improvements in Release 15 are in areas not addressed in this workbook. The interface remains basically the same as in Release 14. There is an Info icon on the button bar of Release 15, and double clicking on this brings up the information about the columns and the active Worksheet Window. Click on the Columns folder to get the information about the worksheet. You may also click on the Constants folder to see what constants are being stored and what their values are. However, there does not seem to be a nice way to print these information windows (as there was in Release 12). If you want to print this information, then click in the Session Window and after the **MTB >** prompt, type in the command info and press the Enter key. The information will then be displayed in the Session Window.

This workbook is divided into chapters and sections with each containing: an explanation of the use of Minitab as related to a statistical procedure, worked out examples, and a lab assignment(s). Each workbook comes with a numbered Data CD containing saved worksheets, raw data files, and macros. Although for different workbooks the data disc's worksheets and data files have the same names, the actual data are slightly different. Therefore, correct answers to the lab assignments will be different for each student. Each lab assignment has a place for the student's name, date, course number, section number, and diskette number

Minitab is designed to perform the many computations needed to solve problems that involve raw data. Many exercises in statistics textbooks contain only the summarized sample statistics and not the raw data. These are exercises where only the results of the sample statistics are given, but no raw data is available. These type of problems are usually solved with a calculator, since the "hard part" of computing the sample statistics has already been done. However, many students still find these problems difficult, and make careless error in computing the p-values. A set of macros that compute confidence intervals and test statistics for problems containing summary statistics is included on the data diskette. The macros on the enclosed data diskette have been written to utilize columns 26 through 49 in their computations. And so when creating new worksheets, you should place all data in columns 1 through 25. Appendix B shows the name of each "Summary Statistics Macro" to use corresponding to each formula discussed in the workbook. This edition of the workbook incorporates the use of macros for completing summary statistic data problems directly in the chapters. With the addition of these summary statistics macros, students should be able to do most textbook problems using Minitab. I encourage all users to take full advantage of these "summary statistics macros," and these should motivate students to see the usefulness of computer software as opposed to being a course requirement that is only good for a few lab assignments.

Chapter 1 is an general introduction and should be read by all users. Chapter 2 contains the procedures for entering, editing, printing, saving and retrieving data. This chapter must be covered next. These two chapters are **very** **important** as they describe the basic procedures for using the Minitab program and computer, and they must be completed before attempting to read any further in this workbook. Chapters 3 and 4 contain procedures for graphically and numerically describing data. These two chapters may be done in either order, but should be covered before any of the remaining chapters are read. Macros for doing some procedures have been stored on the data diskette, and the use of these macros is introduced in Chapter 5; therefore this chapter should be done next. The remaining chapters are fairly independent, and they may be done in any order. Chapter 13 follows naturally after Chapter 12, but could be done without having covered Chapter 12. Chapters 12 and 13 contain analysis of variance tables used within the regression analysis; but the use of the p-value in these tables is explained, and so these two chapters may be done without having covered the Analysis of Variance in Chapter 9.

Appendix A contains descriptions of macros that compute the finite population adjustments for the one sample confidence interval for the population mean or proportion of successes, and for adjusting the optimal sample size when corresponding on sample interval estimation. Appendix B serves as an quick reference guide for the techniques presented in this.

This 17th edition of the workbook includes two new sections in Chapter 7. The first new Section 4 is about how to compute the power of a test for one sample hypothesis testing of the population mean and proportion of "successes." The second new Section 5 describes how to compute the optimal sample size before doing one sample hypothesis testing of the population mean and proportion of "successes."

Most of the graphics in this workbook are screen shots from Minitab running under Windows XP, but in this 17th edition some of the newer screen shots are taken when Minitab is running under under Windows Vista. For the most part, slight changes in shading are the only noticeable differences. But in the three commands under the menu item *File , Other Files* , one more substantial change is in the dialog boxes where you locate a specific file. Under Window XP, there is a *Look in:* or *Save in:* box in where you may navigate to the specific storage device that contains the file. Then in the box below you may navigate to the appropriate directory and then choose the specific file. This is the same method for locating files in all **other** Minitab procedures regardless of which operating system you are running. However, in the menu item *File , Other Files* ; for the three commands of *Import Special Text... , Export Special Text... , and Run an Exec...* , the navigation is slightly different. The dialog box is similar to Vista's Windows Explorer with an address bar with mostly http:// addresses and two, side-by-side windows underneath. You will need to locate the storage device by first clicking on the Computer item in the left window, and then navigating to the specific device and file in the right window. Instructions for both Windows XP and Windows Vista are given in the corresponding chapters where these commands are introduced.

Also typographical errors, incorrect graphics, and example numbering have been corrected. This edition contains only a data CD and **not** a 3½ floppy diskette, and so the users will need to provide their own storage device. This may be a floppy diskette, a flash memory "thumb" drive, a network drive, or their own hard disk. The workbook recommends creating a folder named "Minitab Projects" on whatever storage device is chosen, and saving your Lab Assignments in this folder.

I and several colleagues have used earlier copies of this workbook in a variety of one semester basic statistics courses. The workbook was used as a supplement to the statistics textbook required for the course. In each of the courses very little or no specific instructions on the use of Minitab were given during class time, although occasionally students would ask specific questions during class. I suggest that the students be in front of a computer with the Minitab program active as they read this lab workbook. I tell the students to replicate the worked out examples and compare their results with those given in the examples. Students should try to understand the general purpose of each procedure and dialog box, and then reinforce this understanding by observing the procedure's and dialog box's action in the examples. For the most part this workbook has proven to be self-explanatory in the usage and output of the Minitab procedures described. In addition to the lab assignments in this workbook, I encourage students to use Minitab for doing some textbook homework exercises. I have tried to present the material in a philosophically free manner. For example, some texts suggest using a "Z test" whenever the sample size is greater than 30, while other texts suggest that the "t test" is appropriate when the population is normally distributed regardless of the sample size. Even though the examples were chosen to avoid most of these philosophical differences, some instructors may not always agree. Nevertheless, I believe that most instructors and students will find this workbook a useful supplement.

Minitab is a registered trademark of Minitab, Inc.  The Student Edition of Minitab for Windows is licensed software from Addison-Wesley Publishing Company.  Tampering with or making copies of this software is a violation of U.S. copyright laws and Federal and State laws.  For example, the law in Maryland is: **ABUSES, UNAUTHORIZED ACCESS AND COPYING OF AUTOMATED PUBLIC RECORDS, which includes this software, IS A VIOLATION OF ARTICLE 27, SECTIONS 45A AND 146 OF THE ANNOTATED CODE MARYLAND AND IS PUNISHABLE BY A FINE OF UP TO $1000.00 AND THREE YEARS IMPRISONMENT**. Most states have similar laws.


Finally, I want to thank my colleagues, students, and reviewers of the previous editions for their comments and suggestions; these have helped make this a better workbook.


*Howard S. Kaplon*

# CHAPTER 1:     Introduction


The Minitab Statistical Package is a powerful tool to be used and not a crutch to be leaned upon!  Computers do exactly what their name says, they compute; and so you use a computer in much the same way you use a hand-held calculator.  If you want to compute the square root of 20; you simply enter 20, "push the square root button," and the calculator or computer displays the answer.  However neither tool will tell you that finding the square root of 20 in the solution of your problem was appropriate; this must be your decision based upon the requirements of the problem. As a tool, Minitab has several major advantages over a hand-held calculator. Computers can do the calculations much faster and with less effort on your part.  This advantage becomes more important as the data sets become larger.   Also, Minitab can combine many different computations into one "button push."

Minitab will not tell you which one of its many computations is appropriate for any specific problem; that is, Minitab is not a crutch to replace your analysis of the problem.  You must apply your knowledge of statistics in order to determine which computation is needed to solve the problem, and only then will Minitab give you the correct answer.  A common error is to believe that whatever the calculator or computer displays must be the correct answer, no matter how that answer was obtained.   A student once was positive that the square root of 20 was 400 because "the calculator said so."  The student inappropriately pushed the square button instead of the square root button.   Similar situations often occur when using computers.   Be careful; the answers Minitab provides are only correct if you have "pushed the appropriate button."  This workbook is designed to teach you the relevant Minitab procedures needed to solve most problems contained in a beginning one or two semester course in basic statistics, but it is up to you to use these tools in the appropriate manner to obtain the correct results.

Many of the computations you will need to perform are contained in the Minitab program. However there are some statistical procedures that are not part of the menu system, but require many commands and subcommands to be entered in exactly the correct sequence. Fortunately, Minitab allows these lengthy sequences of instructions to be contained in a **MACRO** and then performed using the *Run an Exec...* menu item (described in Chapter 5). Since macros usually contain a lengthy sequence of commands, the computer seems to  take a longer time to perform macros than to do commands.  These macros have been written for you and are on the data disc that accompanies this workbook.

The Microsoft Windows versions of Minitab have become very popular and incorporate the standard graphical user interface (GUI) features of all Windows applications.  This gives the user the option of using a mouse to access menus and dialog boxes.  The full version of Minitab Release 15 will be used in this workbook.  Students may wish to purchase the Student Edition of Minitab or lease the full version of Minitab for use on their personal computer. The full version of Minitab contains additional features and also allows for larger problems, but almost everything shown in this workbook will also be available in the Student Edition and will work the same way as in the full version. The opening screen of either Windows version will look similar to the picture on the next page.

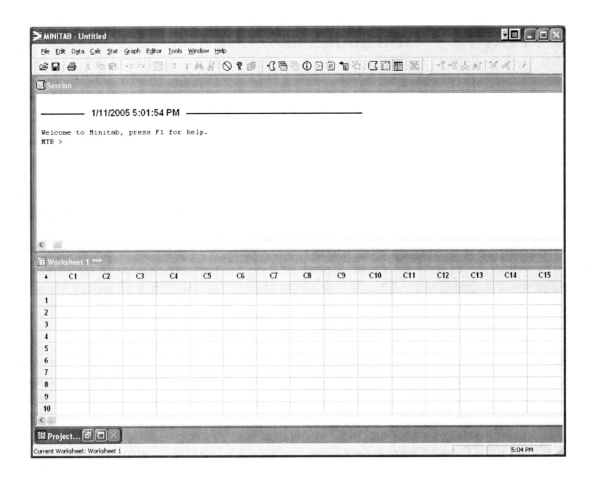

The row at the top which looks like

is called the Menu Bar.   When you click the left mouse button on each of these, a "drop down" menu appears.

The next section which looks like

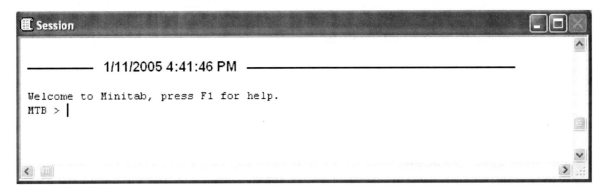

is called the Session Window.  As you use the Menu Bar, the resulting commands and subcommands will be automatically displayed in the Session Window.

If the **MTB >** prompt is not displayed in your Session Window, you will have do the following. Click on *Tools* in the Menu Bar and then click on *Options*. In the Options - General dialog box, click on the ⊞ to the left of *Session Window* and then click on *Submitting Commands*. In the resulting Options - Submitting Commands dialog box and under the *Command Language*, click in the circle to the left of Enable, and then click on the **OK** button.

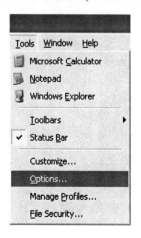
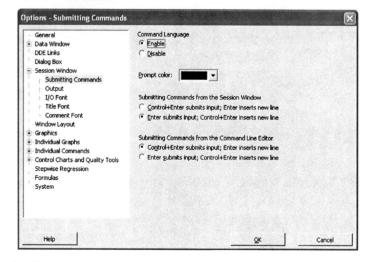

The next section which looks like

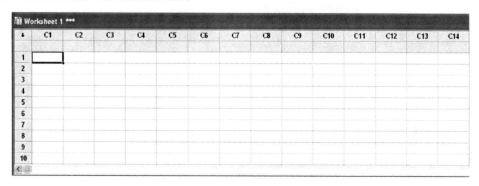

is called the Worksheet or Data Window. You may enter and edit data and name columns directly in this window.

You may or may not see the icon ![Project icon], depending on the window layout configuration of your system. When you click on the double window on the right the Project Manager Window opens and displays pertinent information about the current project. If the icon is not visible, the Project Manager Window is always available from the Window item on the menu bar.

The active window will have its descriptive top bar in a dark blue color, while the other window(s) will have a light blue descriptive top bar. The active window is the one you are currently working with.

When a new Minitab procedure is introduced, the appropriate menu choices in GUI format will be indicated by a "mouse box" on the left and a detailed set of instructions on the right. This will be followed by a series of "screens" that correspond to each instruction (series of mouse clicks). It will be assumed that the user is familiar with the usual Windows interface, conventions and use of drop-down menus.

For example, the Execute a Macro procedure, which is introduced and fully described in Chapter 5, will be shown as

 Click on *File , Other Files , Run an Exec ...*

Make sure that 1 is in the *Number of times to execute* box, and then click on the

    Select File    button.

In the Run an Exec dialog box: click on the Look in icon, scroll to find the *Data Disc* icon (if this is not the default drive shown), and then click on it. Next highlight the Ci-1v.mtb file (you may need to scroll through the file names box), and click on the    Open    button.

Items that appear in the menus and in dialog boxes as buttons or check off boxes will be shown in *italics*.

The "screens" that correspond to these instructions (mouse clicks) are shown next. In this example, *File , Other Files ,Run an Exec ...* are Menu Bar and drop down menu choices to click on, and the corresponding screen is shown below.

After clicking on *Run an Exec ...* you get the "dialog box" shown below.

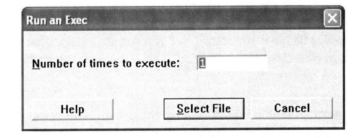

*Select File* is a button in this dialog box. When you click on the *Select File* button, another Run an Exec dialog box appears with a list of macros in the default directory - which may or may not be the data disc. This dialog box will look and act somewhat differently depending on which operating system your computer is running.

| Windows XP | Windows Vista |
|---|---|
| For Windows XP, there is a *Look in* box showing the default directory. Click on the down triangle at the right to navigate to your Data Disc. Once you have *Data Disc* as the default drive in the *Look in:* box, highlight and click on the desired macro name as shown below.  | For Windows Vista there is **no** *Look in* box, instead the navigation starts by clicking on the location of the Data Disc on in the left side of this dialog box. You will probably need to begin by clicking on Computer in the left side. Then you use the right side to navigate to the exact location of you Data Disc. Once you have the Data Disc showing in the top address box and the list of macros in the right panel of the dialog box, highlight and click on the desired macro name as shown below. 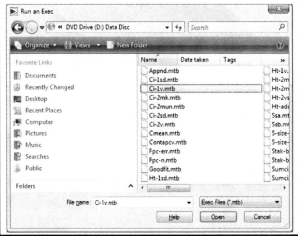 |

In general, you do **NOT** press the [ **Enter** ] key when you finish typing in a dialog box, as that will end the selection process before you have a chance to complete other options. Finally click on the [ **OK** ] button.

The procedures will be explicitly illustrated when first introduced, but usually will not be done so afterwards since the graphical interface will make them obvious to you.

Minitab contains many more procedures than are presented in this workbook. These specialized procedures and the more advanced features of Minitab, such as the actual construction of macros, are beyond the scope and intention of this workbook. The objective is that, upon your completion of this workbook, you will be able to use Minitab and the macros contained on the accompanying data disc as a computational tool when doing statistical analysis. You are not expected to become expert at programming the Minitab Statistical Package.

The next chapter will take you through the basic techniques for working with data in Minitab.

# CHAPTER 2: Basic Procedures for Entering, Editing, Printing, Saving and Retrieving Information

The Minitab Statistical Package is available in both a full version and Student Edition. This workbook will exclusively use the full Windows version of Minitab Release 15. The examples in this workbook were done on a Pentium class microcomputer at Towson University, and this workbook will assume that you are using a similar type of microcomputer. The Windows XP operating system was used and the monitor resolution was 1280 x 1024 pixels. If you are not using Windows XP and the same monitor resolution, then the graphics shown in this workbook may look slightly different than what is displayed on your computer. Also, some of the graphics have been truncated to conserve space.

Take this workbook with you to the computer. After you have begun the Minitab program, the computer will display an opening screen similar to that shown on page 2. An **MTB>** "prompt" in the Session Window indicates the computer is waiting for you to enter information. Whenever you see some letters with a **>** at the end, this is a microcomputer prompt. The convention used in this workbook is to show anything displayed by the microcomputer in a **BOLD ITALIC** font typeface and anything that you type in a regular font typeface.

In general you will be entering procedures via the Minitab Menu Bar, but occasionally you may need to type some information directly into the Session Window. On such occasions, after you enter any line of information, you must press the  Enter . If you notice a typing mistake **before** you push the  Enter  key, you push the backspace key until you have erased all characters including the mistake. Then you continue typing in the correct information. The backspace key has the back arrow symbol, <– , on it and is usually located directly above the  Enter  key. Do **NOT** use the key in the number pad with both a 4 and a <– on it.

Minitab stores all data for computations in a current worksheet in the microcomputer's memory. The data are logically organized as a two dimensional table or worksheet. Each column of the table holds the values of a variable. If there is one variable, then there will be one column; if there are two variables, then there will be two columns; etc. Since the values of a variable are stored in a column, the terms variable and column will be used interchangeably in this workbook. Each different observation of a variable is stored in a different row of the table. For each column (or variable) there will be as many rows as there are observations of that variable.

The first step in any statistical analysis is to enter data into the current worksheet. Data are all values for each variable in the problem. Minitab requires each variable to be set up as a separate column and labeled C#, where the # is replaced with a number. If there is only one variable, it usually is labeled C1. If there are four variables, they are set up as four columns and are usually labeled C1, C2, C3 and C4. Do **not** use the column labels from C26 through C49, since these will be used and/or erased by the MACROs on your data disc.

To enter data into the current worksheet, click on the Worksheet (Data) Window bar and then in the specific row of the column number (variable) where you want to begin entering the data. This is usually row 1 of column 1. There is an arrow in the top left corner of the Worksheet window. If this arrow is not pointing down, click on this arrow and it will change from pointing right to pointing down. This is more convenient, since when you push the ⌨ Enter key, the cursor moves down to the next position of the same column. Then type in the desired value and press the ⌨ Enter key. Continue entering the rest of the data for this column (variable). Then click in the first row of the next column to enter data for a second variable. Enter each value and press the ⌨ Enter key. Continue for each variable in your data set.

Example 2.1: The profit margins of four sporting goods stores are 3.2, 3.4, 3.1 and 3.3 percent. Start a Minitab session as described in Chapter 1 and enter this data as variable C1 into the Minitab current worksheet.

Click in the cell that is in row 1 of the first column. This cell will be outlined. Type 3.2 and press the ⌨ Enter key. Now the cell in row 2 should be outlined. Continue entering 3.4, 3.1 and 3.3 .

| Worksheet 1 *** | | |
| --- | --- | --- |
| ↓ | C1 | C2 |
| | | |
| 1 | 3.2 | |
| 2 | 3.4 | |
| 3 | 3.1 | |
| 4 | 3.3 | |
| 5 | | |

Example 2.2: The profit margins of three toy stores are 12.6, 11.2 and 10.8 . The profit margins of four clothing stores are 12.9, 16.2, 15.1 and 8.6 . Enter this data into two new variables (i.e., not C1) in the current worksheet.

The Worksheet Window should look like the graphic below.

| Worksheet 1 *** | | | | |
| --- | --- | --- | --- | --- |
| ↓ | C1 | C2 | C3 | C4 |
| | | | | |
| 1 | 3.2 | 12.6 | 12.9 | |
| 2 | 3.4 | 11.2 | 16.2 | |
| 3 | 3.1 | 10.8 | 15.1 | |
| 4 | 3.3 | | 8.6 | |
| 5 | | | | |

Changing or correcting a value is particularly easy in the Windows version. First, simply click on the cell that contains the value you want to correct, and this cell will be outlined. Second, just type in the correct value and press the ⌈ **Enter** ⌋ key. The new value will now be in that cell, the next cell down (if the top left corner arrow is pointing down) will be outlined, and, if there is a value in that cell, it will be highlighted.

Example 2.3:      Correct the mistake of 3.4 in the C1 variable to the correct value of 3.5.

Click in row 2 of column 1, type in 3.5 and press the ⌈ **Enter** ⌋ key. The Worksheet Window should look like the graphic below.

| ↓ | C1 | C2 | C3 |
|---|-----|------|------|
|   |     |      |      |
| 1 | 3.2 | 12.6 | 12.9 |
| 2 | 3.5 | 11.2 | 16.2 |
| 3 | 3.1 | 10.8 | 15.1 |
| 4 | 3.3 |      | 8.6  |
| 5 |     |      |      |

**Worksheet 1 ***

If there is a large number in the cell, and you only need to change one or two digits; it is possible to edit the current value in the cell. Double click in the cell you want to edit, use the left and right arrow keys to move around in the value, use the BackSpace or Delete key to delete digit(s), and then type the correct digit(s). Press the ⌈ **Enter** ⌋ key when you have finished.

Adding a new value at the end of a column is done exactly the same as changing an existing value. Click on the empty cell at the bottom of the desired column, and then enter the new score. If there is more than one new score, simply continue entering the new values.

Example 2.4:      The two values of 3.6 and 2.7 were omitted and need to be added to the end of the C1.

Click in row 5 of column 1, type in 3.6 and press the ⌈ **Enter** ⌋ key. Now type in 2.7 and pres the ⌈ **Enter** ⌋ key. The Worksheet Window should look like the graphic below.

**Worksheet 1 ***

| ↓ | C1 | C2 | C3 | C4 |
|---|-----|------|------|----|
|   |     |      |      |    |
| 1 | 3.2 | 12.6 | 12.9 |    |
| 2 | 3.5 | 11.2 | 16.2 |    |
| 3 | 3.1 | 10.8 | 15.1 |    |
| 4 | 3.3 |      | 8.6  |    |
| 5 | 3.6 |      |      |    |
| 6 | 2.7 |      |      |    |
| 7 |     |      |      |    |

You may insert an additional value in a specific position that already contain a value,  but you may insert **only one additional value at a time**.

Click on the cell where you want to insert the additional value.

Click on *Editor, Insert Cells*

This cell will be outlined, a highlighted asterisk will be in the cell, and all of the scores from this position down will be moved down one cell.   Type in the new value and press the ⌞ **Enter** ⌟ key.

To insert more than one score; for **each** additional score, you must repeat the click on *Editor, Insert Cells* and then enter the next score (you should automatically be in the next cell down after you add the previous score).   You may insert one row of scores in **all** columns that have a score in the row the cursor is in by clicking on *Editor, Insert Rows*.   The scores in **all** columns that have a score in that row will be moved down one position, and asterisks will be inserted in those affected rows. Next enter the additional scores in each column.

Example 2.5:   The values 3.6 and 3.7 need to be added to the variable C1 starting in row 3.

Click in row 3 of column 1 in the Worksheet Window, click on *Editor, Insert Cells* , type in 3.6 and press the ⌞ **Enter** ⌟ key.   Repeat click on *Editor, Insert Cells* , now type in 3.7 and press the ⌞ **Enter** ⌟ key.  The Worksheet Window should look like the graphic on the next page.

(continued on the next page)

**Worksheet 1 ***

| ↓ | C1 | C2 | C3 | C4 |
|---|-----|------|------|----|
| 1 | 3.2 | 12.6 | 12.9 | |
| 2 | 3.5 | 11.2 | 16.2 | |
| 3 | 3.6 | 10.8 | 15.1 | |
| 4 | 3.7 | | 8.6 | |
| 5 | 3.1 | | | |
| 6 | 3.3 | | | |
| 7 | 3.6 | | | |
| 8 | 2.7 | | | |

Deleting values is accomplished using standard Windows methods; you block (highlight) the cell or cells you want to delete (click and drag the cursor), and then press the ⌑ **Delete** ⌑ key. You can only delete contiguous and rectangular groupings of cells. To delete non adjacent values in a column or row, you must block and delete them separately.

Example 2.6:  The values 3.3 and 3.6 are to be deleted from the current worksheet variable C1. Also delete the score of 11.2 from variable C2 and delete the score of 16.2 from variable C3.

Click in row 6 of column 1, block the 3.3 and the 3.6 in the next row, and press the ⌑ **Delete** ⌑ key. Then click on the 11.2 in column 2, drag the mouse over to also block the 16.2 in column 3, and press the ⌑ **Delete** ⌑ key. Then the Worksheet Window should look like the graphic below.

**Worksheet 1 ***

| ↓ | C1 | C2 | C3 | C4 |
|---|-----|------|------|----|
| 1 | 3.2 | 12.6 | 12.9 | |
| 2 | 3.5 | 10.8 | 15.1 | |
| 3 | 3.6 | | 8.6 | |
| 4 | 3.7 | | | |
| 5 | 3.1 | | | |
| 6 | 2.7 | | | |
| 7 | | | | |

Since the C# column label is not very informative, Minitab allows variables to be given a descriptive name of up to eight characters. Simply click in the cell directly under the C# column number (above row 1), type in the name you wish to use, and press the ⌑ **Enter** ⌑ key. This attaches the name to the variable, and this name is included on all output produced by Minitab. You may use a name of more than eight characters; but Minitab will display only the first eight characters in the Session Window output.   Once a variable has been named, Minitab will use this name instead of the column number in all of the output.

11

Example 2.7:  Name the variables C1, C2 and C3 as **Sports, Toy** and **Clothing** respectively.

Click in each name cell and enter the respective names; capitalize the first letter of each name.   Then the Worksheet Window should look like the graphic below.

| ↓ | C1 | C2 | C3 | C4 |
|---|------|------|----------|---|
|   | **Sports** | **Toy** | **Clothing** |   |
| 1 | 3.2 | 12.6 | 12.9 |   |
| 2 | 3.5 | 10.8 | 15.1 |   |
| 3 | 3.6 |      | 8.6 |   |
| 4 | 3.7 |      |      |   |
| 5 | 3.1 |      |      |   |
| 6 | 2.7 |      |      |   |
| 7 |     |      |      |   |

Worksheet 1 ***

There are occasions for which you will want to display the data values in the **Session Window** in addition to examining the data in the Worksheet Window.  This is done with the *Display Data* procedure.  For **one** variable, the values will be displayed in horizontal rows. But for **two or more** variables, the data will be displayed in side by side columns with the left most column being the corresponding row numbers.

Click on *Data , Display Data...*

In the Display Data dialog box: click on the column number you want to display, if you want to display more than one column hold down the ⌈ **Ctrl** ⌉ key and click on the other column(s) you want to display, click on the *Select* button (these columns will now be shown in the columns to Display box), and click on *OK*.

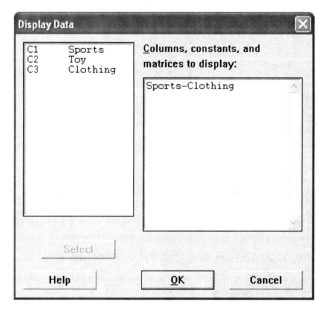

12

Example 2.8:  Display the values of all three variables in the current worksheet

Click on *Data , Display Data...* , and then click on the C1 (Sports) variable in the Display Data dialog box.  Hold down the ⟦ **Ctrl** ⟧ key and click on the C2 and C3 variables.  Click on the *Select* button and then on *OK*.  Then the Session Window should contain the output shown below.

| ROW | Sports | Toy | Clothing |
|-----|--------|------|----------|
| 1 | 3.2 | 12.6 | 12.9 |
| 2 | 3.5 | 10.8 | 15.1 |
| 3 | 3.6 | | 8.6 |
| 4 | 3.7 | | |
| 5 | 3.1 | | |
| 6 | 2.7 | | |

Many times the same data set will be analyzed several different ways and on several different days.  Because of this, you will want to save the current worksheet and all of the work you have done so far so that you do not have to start from the very beginning each time you use the same data set.  You will need a storage device such as a floppy disk, a flash memory "thumb" drive, a network drive, etc.  On this device create a new folder and name it Minitab Projects.  A current worksheet is saved using the *Save Project As* procedure.   Each project that you save must be given a descriptive filename.  The drive where the project is to be saved must also be chosen, and the Minitab Projects folder selected.

Click on *File , Save Project As...*

In the Save Project As dialog box: Minitab.MPJ in the File name box will be highlighted, type in the specific filename you want to use (this will replace the default Minitab.MPJ), click on the *Save in:* drop down icon and select your storage drive and the *Minitab Projects* folder (if it is not already selected); and click on ⟦ **Save** ⟧ .

Do not add a three letter extension to the filename, as Minitab will automatically add the .MPJ extension to your saved file, do not include a period in the filename.  This procedure will save a copy of the **current project** that is in the computer's memory into your *Minitab Projects* folder.  The current project remains intact in the computer's memory.   A current project exists only in the computer's memory and does not have a filename.

If a project with the same name already exists in your Minitab Projects folder, a second Save Project As dialog box, shown below, will tell you that the file already exists and ask you if you want to replace existing file. If you click on the *Yes* button, the project in your Minitab Projects folder will be updated with the contents of the current worksheet in memory. If you click on the *No* button, the saved project in your Minitab Projects folder will not be changed; and then you may either choose a different name, type it in the File Name box and click on the *Save* button, or click on the *Cancel* button to return to the Minitab session.

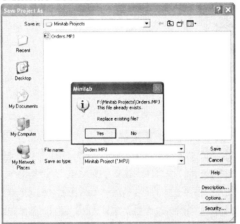

If you have modified a current project and **are sure** that you want to update the existing saved project: click on *File, Save Project* (the item directly above *Save Project As*), and the saved project will be immediately be updated with the contents of the current project. The above dialog box will not appear, and the saved project in your Minitab Projects folder will be immediately updated. This is faster but **dangerous**, since you are **not** given a chance to change your mind if you want to save the modified current project with a different name.

> Example 2.9: Save the current project using the name Orders into your Minitab Projects folder.

> Click on *File , Save Project As...*, and in the Save Project As dialog box type Orders in the File name box; click on the *Save in:* drop down icon, find and click on the *Minitab Projects* folder. Finally click ⌴ **Save** ⌴ . The current project will be saved in your Minitab Projects folder with the name Orders.MPJ and the following confirmation will appear in the Session Window.

**MTB > Save "F:\Minitab Projects\Orders.MPJ";**
**SUBC> Project;**
**SUBC> Replace.**
**Saving file as 'F:\Minitab Projects\Orders.MPJ'**

If the saved worksheet had already existed and you had answered *Yes* to the replace question, the output in the Session Window would also contain the line

**Existing file replaced.**

Note that after you click on *File, Save Project As...*, a list of all saved projects in theMinitab Projects folder will appear in the large center box. If you are updating an existing saved project, you may click on the desired name (you may need to scroll to find the name) instead of typing the name in again. Then click on *Save* and the saved project will be updated.

14

Example 2.10:   Add a new variable in column 4 and name it Return.  Then insert the two scores of 13.7 and -3.2 into the first two rows of this variable.  Finally save this as the updated Orders project.

Click in the name position of C4 and enter the name Return.  Then insert the two scores of 13.7 and -3.2 into the first two rows of this column.  The Worksheet Window should now look as

| ↓ | C1 | C2 | C3 | C4 |
|---|----|----|----|----|
|  | Sports | Toy | Clothing | Return |
| 1 | 3.2 | 12.6 | 12.9 | 13.7 |
| 2 | 3.5 | 10.8 | 15.1 | -3.2 |
| 3 | 3.6 |  | 8.6 |  |
| 4 | 3.7 |  |  |  |
| 5 | 3.1 |  |  |  |
| 6 | 2.7 |  |  |  |

Worksheet 1 ***

Using the safer method; click on *File , Save Project As...*; in the Save Project As dialog Orders.MPJ should be highlighted in the File name box, the *Minitab Projects* folder should be in the *Look in:* box, and then click *Save*.  Then click on *Yes* when asked if you want to replace the file.  The current project will be saved in your Minitab Projects folder as an updated version of Orders.MPJ and the confirmation will appear in the Session Window.

**MTB > Save "F:\Minitab Projects\Orders.MPJ";**
**SUBC>   Project;**
**SUBC>   Replace.**
**Saving file as 'F:\Minitab Projects\Orders.MPJ'**
**Existing file replaced.**

Using the faster (but sometimes dangerous method); click on *File , Save Project* and the worksheet will be immediately updated in your Minitab Projects folder without asking you if you want to replace it.  The exact same confirmation above will appear in the Session Window.

Once you have finished your Minitab session, you will need to exit from the Minitab program.  This is done with the *File , Exit* menu item.  If you have made any changes to the current project after the last time you saved it, Minitab will ask you "Save changes to the project (current project name) before closing?"  You may answer *Yes*, *No*, or *Cancel*; and you should click on whichever is appropriate for the situation.

If you never saved the current project, Minitab will ask you "Save changes to this project before closing?", you will have the same *Yes*, *No*, or *Cancel* options.  If you choose *Yes*; you will get the Save Project As dialog box, and you proceed as shown previously.

Click on *File, Exit*

**If** you have made any changes to or never saved the current project; in the dialog box click on *Yes* to save or update the project in your Minitab Projects folder, click on *No* to exit without saving or updating any further, or click on *Cancel* to cancel the exit and return to Minitab as you were.

(You will only get this dialog box if you have made changes or have never saved the current project.)

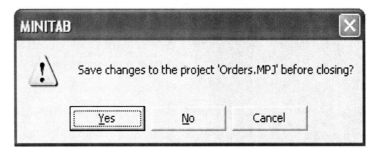

Example 2.11:   Exit from Minitab.

Click on *File , Exit* . Since you have made no additional changed to the current project, you will not be asked if you want to save changes.

So far everything you have done has appeared either in the Session or Worksheet Windows. Many times you will need to have a copy of your work printed on paper (a "hard copy").  There are several ways of getting a printed copy of your work, but the easiest method is to print the contents of the Session and/or Worksheet Windows when you have finished, but **before** you exit from Minitab.  First you **must be in the specific Window you want to print**. The active window is indicated by having is descriptive title bar in a darker color, while the other windows' title bars are shown in a lighter shade of this color.   If a window is shown on the screen, you may activate it by clicking once in the title bar at the top of the window.  To activate any window, whether or not it is showing on the screen, you may click on the menu bar item *Window* and then click on any of the specific windows listed at the bottom of this drop down menu.  Once you have activated the desired window, the *File* drop down menu will contain a *Print Xyz...* , where *Xyz* will be the name of the active window.  For example, if you have the Session Window active,

Click on *File* and *Print Session Window...*

In the Print dialog box: make sure the *All* button in the *Print Range* section is selected, the number in the *Copies* box is 1, and then click on ⬛ **OK** ⬛ . The description of the Printer will depend upon the specific setup of the computer you are working on.

(See the graphics on the next page.)

16

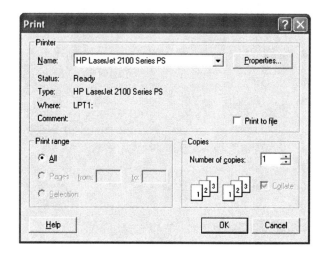

However, if you have the Worksheet Window active, you will see a Data Window Print Options dialog box. If you un-check the Print Grid Lines box (shown below), the printing will be considerably faster. Under Column Names and Labels: , you should click on the circle to the left of Numeric Right Justified; text Left Justified; as this will line up the output correctly. You may add a descriptive title in the Title: box. Also, in the next Print dialog box, the Pages option is not available. If you have the Data Window active,

Click on *File* and *Print Worksheet...*

In the Data Window Print Options dialog box, click in the box to the left of Print Grid Lines to un-check this box, and click on the circle to the left of Numeric Right Justified; text Left Justified. Optionally, you may click in the Title: box and enter a descriptive title.

In the Print dialog box, click on ⬛ **OK** ⬛ . The description of the Printer will depend upon the specific setup of the computer you are working on.

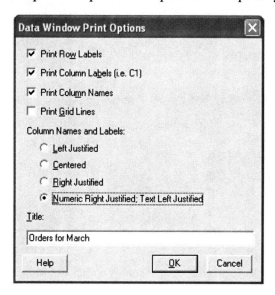

If you want to print the data; it is usually more convenient to first use the *Display Data* procedure, choose exactly those variables you want displayed in the Session Window, and then just print the (active) Session Window at the end of your Minitab computer session.

Example 2.12:  Start a Minitab session.  Enter 4, 3, -6, 3, 2, 7 and 10 into column 1 and name this column Pel. Display the values of this variable in the Session Window.  Then enter 3.5, 2.3 and 5.8 into column 2; enter 23, 21, 25 and 30 to column **4**; name column 4 as Age; and display the values of all three variables in the Session Window.  Print both the Session Window and the Worksheet Window.

The results of the "hard copy" of *Print Session Window...*:

## Data Display

**MTB > Print 'Pel'.**

**Pel**
     4    3   -6    3    2    7   10

**MTB > Print  'Pel'  C2  'Age'.**

## Data Display

| ROW | Pel | C2 | Age |
|-----|-----|-----|-----|
| 1 | 4 | 3.5 | 23 |
| 2 | 3 | 2.3 | 21 |
| 3 | -6 | 5.8 | 25 |
| 4 | 3 | | 30 |
| 5 | 2 | | |
| 6 | 7 | | |
| 7 | 10 | | |

The results of the "hard copy" of *Print Worksheet...*:

| | C1 | C2 | C4 |
|-----|-----|-----|-----|
| | Pel | | Age |
| 1 | 4 | 3.5 | 23 |
| 2 | 3 | 2.3 | 21 |
| 3 | -6 | 5.8 | 25 |
| 4 | 3 | | 30 |
| 5 | 2 | | |
| 6 | 7 | | |
| 7 | 10 | | |

A project that previously has been saved in your Minitab Projects folder may be opened as the current project in Minitab with the *Open Project* procedure. Everything from the saved project; data (Worksheet), Graphs and Session Window will be retrieved as the current Minitab project. If there already is a current project in Minitab that has **not** been saved, you will be given the opportunity to save that project now before Minitab opens the previously saved project.

Click on *File , Open Project...*

In the Open Project dialog box; click on the *Look in:* drop down icon and select *Minitab Projects* folder (if it is not already selected); then a list of previously saved projects will appear in the box below; click on the desired project to highlight the name; and then click on [ **Open** ] .

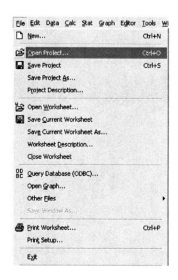

**If** there already is a current project in Minitab that has **not** been saved, Minitab will ask you "Save changes to this project before closing?", you will have the options *Yes*, *No*, or *Cancel*. If you click on *Yes*, this project will be saved and then the new project will be retrieved. If you click on *No*, then this project will not be saved, and the new project will be retrieved. In both cases, the first project will be removed from this current Minitab session. If you click on *Cancel*, then you will be returned the first Minitab project. This dialog box is shown on page 16.

Often you will want to do a new problem, with a fresh current worksheet (Data Window), in the current Minitab Session. To do this, you use the *New, Worksheet* procedure. A second Worksheet Window will be opened and become the active window. Any work done with data in this second worksheet will be indicated in the Session Window as being from the second worksheet.

Click on *File , New...*

In the New dialog box; click on *Minitab Worksheet*; and then click [ **OK** ] .

Then a second Worksheet, titled Worksheet 2 (or higher) will be created and tiled on the screen over the previous worksheet.

(See the graphics on the next page.)

The two Worksheet Windows will look similar to the graphic shown below.

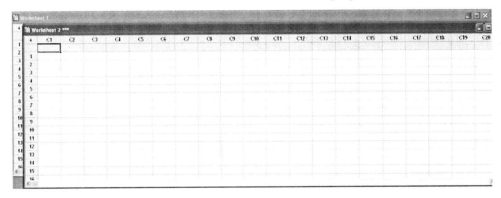

There are situations when only the data and variable names in the Worksheet Window have been saved, and not the Session Window nor any Graph Windows created. This is done to save storage space when the Session Window information is not needed for future use. The data disc (CD) that comes with this workbook contains many such saved worksheets. You may open a new worksheet by retrieving the saved worksheet information from the data disc by using the *Open Worksheet* procedure. Another Worksheet Window containing the saved data will be opened; the name of the saved worksheet will be shown in the title bar; and this will become the active window. Any work done with data in this second worksheet will be indicated in the Session Window as being from this named worksheet.

Click on *File , Open Worksheet...*

In the Open Worksheet dialog box; click on the *Look in:* drop down icon and select *Data Disc* (if it is not already selected); then a list of previously saved worksheets (ending in .mtw) and projects (ending in .mpj) will appear in the box below; click on the desired worksheet to highlight the name; and then click on [ **Open** ] .

A dialog box informing you that "A copy of this file will be added to the current Project." may or may not appear. Click on [ **OK** ] .

(See the graphics on the next page.)

The saved worksheet will be tiled on top of any other worksheets, and they will look similar to the graphic shown below.

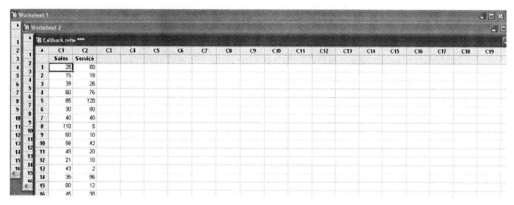

**Note:** If the most current Worksheet Window is completely empty, the saved worksheet will **replace** this Worksheet Window instead of tilling on top of it.

Example 2.13:   Open the saved project Orders.MPJ (do not save any current project). Then display the data of C1 and C3 in the Session Window. Next open a new worksheet and enter the three number: 23, 32 and 15 into column 1 of this new worksheet. Now open the worksheet Callback.mtw that is saved on your data disc. Activate the second worksheet and display the values of C1 in the Session Window. Now activate the Callback.mtw worksheet and display the values of C1 (Sales) in the Session Window.

(continued on the next page)

Click on *File , Open Project*; make sure the *Data Disc* is in the *Look in:* box; click on Orders.MPJ; and click on the ⬚ Open ⬚ button. Next use the *Display Data* procedure to display the values of C1 and C3 in the Session Window. The following will be in the Session Window.

## Data Display

| ROW | Sports | Clothing |
|-----|--------|----------|
| 1 | 3.2 | 12.9 |
| 2 | 3.5 | 15.1 |
| 3 | 3.6 | 8.6 |
| 4 | 3.7 | |
| 5 | 3.1 | |
| 6 | 2.7 | |

Click on *File , New* ; select *Minitab Worksheet* ; and click on ⬚ **OK** ⬚. A new worksheet will open and be titled Worksheet 2. After you open this new Minitab worksheet, the cursor should be in the name row of column 1. Move down 1 cell to be in row 1 of this column and enter 23, 32 and 15 into the first three rows of this second worksheet. The Worksheet Windows should look like the graphic below.

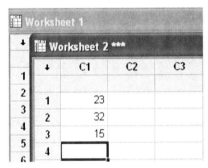

Click on *File , Open Worksheet...* ; the *Data Disc* should be in the *Address:* box; click on Callback.mtw to highlight this worksheet; click on ⬚ Open ⬚ and then ⬚ **OK** ⬚ in the next dialog box. A third Worksheet Window will open and should look like the graphic below.

(continued on the next page)

22

Click in the Worksheet 2 title bar or click on *Window* in the Minitab menu bar and then on Worksheet 2. Notice that this worksheet comes to the front and the Callback.mtw worksheet is hidden from view. Use the *Display Data* procedure to print the values of C1 in the Session Window. You may press the ⌨ **F3** key to clear the previous contents in the dialog box. Next, since you can not see the Callback.mtw window, click on *Window* in the Minitab menu bar and then on Callback.mtw to activate this Worksheet Window. Use the *Display Data* procedure to print the values of C1 (Sales) in the Session Window. The rest of the Session Window should contain the following.

## Results for: Worksheet 2

MTB > WOpen "D:\Callback.mtw".
Retrieving worksheet from file: 'D:\Callback.mtw'
Worksheet was saved on Tue May 16 2000
MTB > Print C1.

## Data Display

C1
  23   32   15

## Results for: Callback.mtw

MTB > Print 'Sales'.

## Data Display

Sales
  25   15   39   60   85   30   40  110   60   56   49   21   43
  35   80   45   47   21

There are situations in which the data have been previously stored in a **raw data** file on a disc. This often occurs when the data has been machine scanned directly into a raw data file, or when the raw data file has been created by another program like the EXCEL spreadsheet program. You will need to know how many variables are in the raw data file. This is done with the *Import Special Text* procedure. You usually will want to open a new worksheet. If you do not open a new worksheet, the data will be imported into the current Active Worksheet Window. In this situation be careful to specify an unused column number, since if you specify an existing column number, the new data may replace the existing data.

When The raw data file contains only numeric data, this data is imported into columns in a worksheet as follows.

Usually click on *File , New* , select *Minitab Worksheet* , and click $\boxed{\textbf{OK}}$ .

Click on *File , Other Files , Import Special Text ...*

In the Import Special Text dialog box: the cursor will be in the *Store Data in Column(s)* box (you may need to press the $\boxed{\textbf{F3}}$ key to clear previous column numbers or formatting), type the column number or numbers that are to contain the imported data and click on $\boxed{\textbf{OK}}$ . If there is more than one column, separate column numbers with a space only; do **not** use a comma. If some columns have been named ahead of time, you may click to highlight the desired column(s) in the box on the left, and then click on $\boxed{\textbf{Select}}$ .

Be careful and do not type in a column number or select a column that already contains data. The *Import Special Text* procedure will erase the current data and replace it with the imported data when the circle to the left of *Replace any existing data in these columns* is selected (looks like ⦿ ). This is the usual situation. But if you do want to add the new data to the existing data in a column, then click on the circle to the left of *Append to any existing data in these columns.* In this case the imported data will be added after the last existing score in the column. Now click $\boxed{\textbf{OK}}$ .

In the Import Text From File dialog box, this dialog box will look and act somewhat differently depending on which operating system your computer is running (see on the next page). Click on the desired raw data filename, and then click on $\boxed{\textbf{Open}}$ .

(The graphic boxes for the first two steps are shown below. On the next page the directions and graphic boxes will be shown for Windows XP and Windows Vista.)

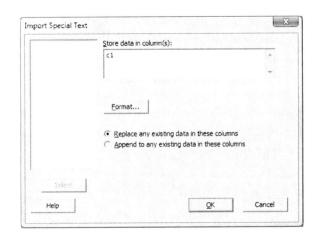

| Windows XP | Windows Vista |
|---|---|
| For Windows XP, there is a *Look in* box showing the default directory. Click on the down triangle at the right to navigate to your Data Disc. Once you have *Data Disc* as the default drive in the *Look in:* box, highlight and click on the desired raw data file as shown below, then click on  Open . | For Windows Vista there is **no** *Look in* box, instead the navigation starts by clicking on the location of the Data Disc on in the left side of this dialog box. You will probably need to begin by clicking on Computer in the left side. Then you use the right side to navigate to the exact location of you Data Disc. Once you have the Data Disc showing in the top address box and the list of macros in the right panel of the dialog box, highlight and click on the desired raw data file as shown below, then click on  Open . |
|  | 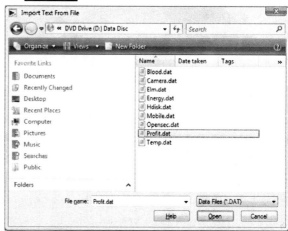 |

Example 2.14: Data for one variable have been stored in a **raw data** file named Profit.dat that is on your data disc. Open a new Worksheet Window and import this data into the C1 variable, name the variable Sports, and display the values of this variable in the Session Window.

Click on *File , New* , select *Minitab Worksheet* , and click  OK .

In general it is better to name a variable (column) **before** you use it rather than afterwards. So click in the name row of column C1 and enter Sports as the name.

Click on *File , Other Files , Import Special Text ...*

In the Import Special Text dialog box: click on the Sports variable and click on  Select . Sports will now appear in the *Store Data in Column(s) box*. Now click on  OK .

In the Import Text From File dialog box: make sure *Data Disc* is in the *Look in:* or *Address:* box; click on the Profit.dat filename (you may need to scroll), and then click on  Open .

(continued on the next page)

The following information will be shown in the Session Window.

*MTB > Read 'Sports';*
*SUBC>   File "D:\Profit.dat";*
*SUBC>   Decimal ".".*
*Entering data from file: D:\PROFIT.DAT*
*6 rows read.*

Click on *Data, Display Data...* In the Display Data dialog box, click on the C1 Sports variable, click on the *Select* button, and then click *OK*. The following will be displayed in the Session Window.

## Data Display

**Sports**
   **3.2     3.5     3.6     3.7     3.1     3.6**


However, when the raw data file contains text data, or a combination of some text and some numeric variables, then the procedure for importing this data requires an additional step. In the Import Special Text dialog box, Minitab needs to know the format of the data, that is which columns in the raw data file contain text data. There also is an option to have the variable (column) names in the first row of the raw data file. In general these raw data files have been created with tabs separating the columns ('tab delimited'), but in some cases the data may be in a specified format. In such a case, one needs to know computer formatting code (which will not be discussed in this workbook). This is done by clicking on the | **Format...** | button in the Import Special text dialog box **before** clicking on the | **OK** | button.

Usually click on *File , New* , select *Minitab Worksheet* , and click | **OK** | .

Click on *File , Other Files , Import Special Text ...*

In the Import Special Text dialog box: the cursor will be in the *Store Data in Column(s)* box (you may need to press the | **F3** | key to clear previous column numbers or formatting), type the column number or numbers that are to contain the imported data and click on | **OK** | . If there is more than one column, separate column numbers with a space <u>only</u>; do **not** use a comma. If some columns have been named ahead of time, you may click to highlight the desired column(s) in the box on the left, and then click on | **Select** | .

(continued on the next page)

Be careful and do not type in a column number or select a column that already contains data. The *Import Special Text* procedure will erase the current data and replace it with the imported data when the circle to the left of *Replace any existing data in these columns* is selected (looks like ◉ ). This is the usual situation. But if you do want to add the new data to the existing data in a column, then click on the circle to the left of *Append to any existing data in these columns.* In this case the imported data will be added after the last existing score in the column. Next click on the │ **Format...** │ button.

In the Import Special text - Format dialog box, under the *Data Format* heading, click on the circle to the left of *Tab delimited.* In the usual case where the raw data file contains only the data and no column names in the first row, click on the square to the left of *Column names in first row* to **un**check this box. In those few cases when the raw data file does have column names in the first row, leave this block checked. If the raw data file contains columns of both text and numeric data, click in the box under the heading of *User-specified text columns:* and type in the column numbers **in the raw data file** that contain text data. Type in only the number and not the C. **If all** columns of the raw data file contain text data, you do not need to enter the column number in this box. Now click │ **OK** │ .

In the Import Special Text dialog box: click on │ **OK** │ .

In the Import Text From File dialog box: navigate so that the *Data Disc* is in either the *Look in* box (Windoes XP) or in the *Address:* box (Windows Vista); click on the desired raw data filename, and then click on │ **Open** │ .

(Only the graphic for the Import Special Text - Format dialog box is shown below.)

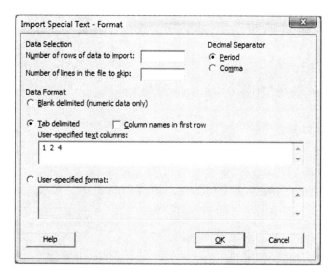

Example 2.15: Data for three variables have been stored in a **raw data** file named Elm.dat that is on your data disc. The first column contain the student's name, the second column contains that student's age and the third column contains the student's grade (First, Second, etc.). In the current worksheet, name three columns as Student, Age and Class. Import the data into these three columns, and then display the values of these three variables in the Session Window.

In general it is better to name a variable (column) **before** you use it rather than afterwards. So click in the name row of columns C3, C4 and C5 and enter Student, Age and Class respectively as the names.

Click on *File , Other Files , Import Special Text ...*

In the Import Special Text dialog box: press the ⬚ F3 ⬚ key to clear previous column numbers or formatting, then block the columns Student, Age and Class (hold the ⬚ Ctrl ⬚ key and click on each variable or drag the mouse over the three consecutive variable names) and click on ⬚ Select ⬚ . Student-Class will now appear in the *Store Data in Column(s) box*. Next click on the ⬚ Format... ⬚ button.

In the Import Special text - Format dialog box, under the *Data Format* heading, click on the circle to the left of *Tab delimited*. Since this raw data file contains only the data and no column names in the first row, click on the square to the left of *Column names in first row* to **un**check this box. Since this raw data file contains columns of both text and numeric data, click in the box under the heading of *User-specified text columns:* and type in the column numbers 1 and 3 that contain text data. Separate with a space and not a comma. Now click ⬚ OK ⬚ .

In the Import Special Text dialog box: click on ⬚ OK ⬚ .

In the Import Text From File dialog box: make sure your *Data Disc* is in the *Look in:* (Windows XP) or *Address:* box (Windows Vista); click on the Elm.dat filename (you may need to scroll), and then click on ⬚ Open ⬚ .

The following information will be shown in the Session Window.

*MTB > Read 'Student'-'Class';*
*SUBC>    File "D:\Elm.dat";*
*SUBC>    Tab;*
*SUBC>    NoNames;*
*SUBC>    Alpha 1 3;*
*SUBC>    Decimal ".".;*
*Entering data from file: D:\PROFIT.DAT*
*6 rows read.*

Click on *Data, Display Data...* In the Display Data dialog box, block the C3 Student, C4 Age, and C5 Class variables, click on the *Select* button, and then click *OK*. The following will be displayed in the Session Window.

(continued on the next page)

28

## Data Display

| ROW | Student | Age | Class |
|-----|---------|-----|-------|
| 1 | Jean | 7.5 | Second |
| 2 | Mark | 8.7 | Third |
| 3 | Sam | 7.2 | Second |
| 4 | Marilyn | 9.6 | Fourth |
| 5 | Deborah | 6.1 | First |
| 6 | Alan | 8.4 | Third |

There is a command that you need to enter directly in the Session Window that will display some basic, but important information about the active worksheet. This **Info** command displays the basic information about the <u>active</u> worksheet. Some or all of the items below will be displayed in the Session Window, depending on whether or not they pertain to the active worksheet:

(1)   the column label (number) for each variable, under the heading Column,
(2)   the number of objects that were measured by each variable, under the heading Count,
(3)   the number of missing values (*) for each variable, under the heading Missing,
(4)   the name for each named variable, under the heading Name,
(5)   the names of any constants used and their values, and
(6)   the names of any matrices used and their dimensions.

Note that the number of <u>valid</u> scores for each variable is the Count minus Missing difference. Also, if any variable (column) contains any non-numeric data, that column is labeled with an **T** on the left to indicate the column is being treated as text data. You can not perform any numeric computations on text variables. If you have more than one Worksheet Window in the current project, the active worksheet is the worksheet that is on top of the rest. To activate a different worksheet; click on the *window* menu item, and then click on the worksheet you want to activate.

The **Project Manager** Window is a relatively new feature. This window contains information about the entire Minitab project. This includes:

(1)   a summary of the Session Window,
(2)   a History of what commands were used in the Session Window,
(3)   a list of Graphs that were done (as will be explained in Chapter 3),
(4)   a Report Pad which may be used to compile information from different windows and user inserted text,
(5)   a list of Related Documents, and
(6)   the worksheets in the project along with information of the columns and any constants and matrices associated with these worksheets.

While this Project Manger can be very useful for the more advanced users, the workbook will not use this feature.

Occasionally you may wish to start a completely new project during the same Minitab session. This could be done by simply exiting from Minitab and then starting Minitab again. However there is an alternative which combines these two steps.

Click on *File* , *New* , select *Minitab Project* , and click [ **OK** ] .

**If** you have made any changes to or never saved the current project; in the dialog box click on *Yes* to save or update the project in your Minitab Projects folder, click on *No* to exit without saving or updating any further, or click on *Cancel* to cancel the exit and return to Minitab as you were.

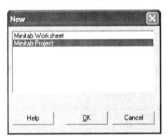

(You will only get this dialog box if you have made changes or have never saved the current project.)

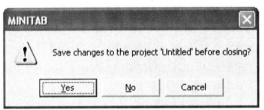

Example 2.15: Start a new Minitab project; do not save the current project. Open the saved worksheet Study4.mtw, and then open a new Minitab worksheet. Enter the numeric data: 2, 21, 17 and 4 in the first four rows of column 1. Then enter the text data: Sam, Mary and Susan into the first three rows of column 2. Now enter the score of 9 into row 6 of column 1 and the name David into row 5 of column 2. Note that the empty skipped cell in column 1 (numeric) now contains an * to indicate missing data in this cell, but the empty skipped cell in column 2 (text) remains blank. Numeric and text data are treated differently by Minitab. Now enter the Info command in the Session Window to display the basic information about this active worksheet, and then about the Study4.mtw worksheet. When done, exit from Minitab without saving the project.

Click on *File* , *New...* , select *Minitab Project*, click on [ **OK** ] , and do not save changes to the current project.

Click on *File* , *Open Worksheet...* ; make sure to choose *Data Disc* in the *Look in:* box; click on Study4.mtw to select this file; and then click on the [ **Open** ] button.

Enter the data into columns 1 and 2 as described in the example. Notice that the label for the second column is now C2 -T to indicate this column contains text data.

(continued on the next page)

Enter the info command in the session window after the **MTB>** prompt.
The following information for Worksheet 2 will appear in the Session Window .

**MTB >** info

| | Column | Count | Missing | Name |
|---|---|---|---|---|
| | C1 | 6 | 1 | |
| T | C2 | 5 | 1 | |

Activate the Study4.mtw Worksheet Window, and then enter the Info command after the **MTB>** prompt in the Session Window.  The following will appear in the Session Window

**MTB >** info

| Column | Count | Missing | Name |
|---|---|---|---|
| C1 | 36 | 2 | Age |
| C2 | 36 | 7 | G.P.A. |
| C3 | 36 | 1 | Work Hrs |
| C4 | 36 | 1 | StudyHrs |

The number of **valid** scores for the four variables are:

C1:   34   (Count - Missing  =  36 - 2  =  34),
C2:   29   (Count - Missing  =  36 - 7  =  29),
C3:   35   (Count - Missing  =  36 - 1  =  35), and
C4:   35   (Count - Missing  =  36 - 1  =  35) .

Lastly, click on *File , Exit* and do not save any changes to the project.

This completes all of the basic data entry procedures you will need to create, save and retrieve Minitab Projects.   The remaining chapters describe the actual analysis of data.

# Lab  Assignment 2.1

**Name:**                                                                          **Date:**

**Course:**                        **Section:**                        **Data CD Number:**


1.      Start a Minitab session.  If you are unable to complete this lab assignment in one Minitab session, save the project as Lab 2-1 . **Never** use a period as part of the project  name; since Minitab uses the period to attach the file type to the file name.  Then at your next Minitab session, you may open this Lab 2-1.MPJ project and continue to work where you left off previously.

2.      Enter the following data into the C1 variable in the current worksheet:
        7 , 3.5 , -2.4 , 1 , 8.3 , 4.2 , -3 , 0.6 , 2.7 and 5.6

3.      Display the values of the C1 variable in the Session Window.

4.      The score of 8.3 is incorrect.   Correct it to become 3.8

5.      Delete the scores 3.5 , 4.2 , -3 , 0.6 and 2.7

6.      Add the three scores 2.4 , 2.9 and -3.7 to the C1 variable between the current scores of -2.4 and 1.

7.      Add the scores of 5.5 and 4.3 to the end of the variable.

8.      Name the variable using your last name.

9.      Display the current values of the variable in the Session Window.

10.     The Temp.dat raw data file is stored on your data disc and contains numeric data for one variable.  Import the data in this raw data file into the C2 variable in the **current** worksheet. Name this variable Day-Temp, and then display the values of this variable in the Session Window.


(lab assignment is continued on the second side of this page)

11. The Blood.dat raw data file is stored on your data disc and contains three columns of data. The first column contains the blood type (text data), the second column contains a one word description of the amount of that blood type that is available (text data), and the third column contains the number of pints of that blood type in inventory (numeric data). This raw data files does **not** have a column names in the first row. Name three unused columns as Blood Type, Level, and Pints Available, and then import the data from this raw data file into these three variables in the **current** worksheet. Then display the values of this variable in the Session Window.

12. Open the worksheet Mailbag.mtw that is on your data disc, and then enter the Info command in the Session Window.

13. How many variables are in this Mailbag.mtw worksheet ? _____

14. How many variables have been named ? _____

15. How many valid observations are there for the second variable ? _____

16. How many of the variables have missing observations ? _____

17. What is the name of the C3 variable, (answer "NONE" if C3 has not been named) ?

_____

18. Activate the Session Window, and then print its contents on the printer.

19. Exit from this Minitab session. This instruction may not be given in other lab assignments; but, of course, you will need to end the Minitab session once you have completed each lab assignment (or if you must stop your Minitab work in the middle of an assignment).

20. Attach your Minitab output (paper) to this sheet and submit both to your instructor.

# Lab Assignment 2.2

Name: Date:

Course: Section: Data CD Number:

1.  Start a Minitab session. If you are unable to complete this lab assignment in one Minitab session, save the project as Lab 2-2 . **Never** use a period as part of the project name; since Minitab uses the period to attach the file type to the file name. Then at your next Minitab session, you may open this Lab 2-2.MPJ project and continue to work where you left off previously.

2.  Enter the following data into the Worksheet Window and name the variables accordingly:

    | Coal | Gas | Oil | Nuclear |
    |------|-----|-----|---------|
    | 27 | 34 | 45 | 50 |
    | 15 | 29 | 27 | 30 |
    | 43 | 56 | 60 | 61 |
    | 37 | 40 | 50 | unknown (missing) |
    | 29 | 26 | 21 | 35 |

3.  Change the second score of 29 in the Gas variable to the value of 19.

4.  Insert the following data after the first position (between the first and second positions):

    | Gas | Oil | Nuclear |
    |-----|-----|---------|
    | 41 | 46 | 51 |
    | 13 | 14 | 20 |

5.  Delete the scores of 27 and 34 from the Coal and Gas variables respectively.

6.  Display the values of all variables (in the current worksheet) in the Session Window.

7.  The Energy.dat raw data file is stored on your data disc and contains numeric data for three variables. Import the data in this raw data file into the C10 , C11 , and C12 variables in the **current** worksheet, and display the values of these variable in the Session Window.

8.  Enter the Info command in the Session Window.

(lab assignment is continued on the second side of this page)

9. How many valid cases there are for each of these three new variables:

C10_____

C11_____

C12_____

10. The Opensec.dat raw data file is stored on your data disc and contains three columns of data about course availability at a local university. The first column contains the number of open sections( numeric data), the second column the department name (text data), and the third column contains the name of the department chairperson (text data). This raw data files also **has the variable (column) labels in the first row** of the data file. Import the data from this raw data file into these three unused variables in the **current** worksheet. Then display the values of this variable in the Session Window.

11. Open the worksheet Homesale.mtw that is on your data disc and then enter the Info command in the Sesssion Window.

12. How many variables are in this worksheet ? _____

13. How many variables have been named ? _____

14. How many valid observations are there for the third variable ? _____

15. How many of the variables have missing observations ? _____

16. What is the name of the C3 variable, (answer "NONE" if C3 has not been named) ?

_____

17. Activate the Session Window, and then print its contents on the printer.

18. Exit from this Minitab session. This instruction may not be given in other lab assignments; but, of course, you will need to end the Minitab session once you have completed each lab assignment (or if you must stop your Minitab work in the middle of an assignment).

19. Attach your Minitab output (paper) to this sheet and submit both to your instructor.

# CHAPTER 3:     Graphical Display of Data

## Section 1:     High Resolution Graphs

There are a number of different methods for graphically displaying data once the data has been entered into a Minitab worksheet. The DOS version of Minitab presented "character graphs"; that is, graphs that are composed of regular keyboard characters. One of the advantages of the Windows version of Minitab is its ability to present some graphs using "high resolution graphics"; that is, graphs that appear to be drawn with a pen and look far superior to character graphs. These graphs appear in a separate Graph window, and they must be printed **separately** from the Session Window. The Windows version also is able to produce the DOS "character graphs" and one of these will be described in Section 2. This chapter will present some of the more common graphical displays of data.

All of the graphs are drawn using the *Graph* choice in the menu bar. Perhaps the most often used graphical display of data for one continuous variable is the histogram. The high resolution histogram is graphed by

Click on *Graph , Histogram ...*

In the Histograms dialog box: the *Simple* graph should be highlighted. Next click on the   OK   button.

In the Histogram Simple dialog box: the cursor will be in the box under *Graph variables:*. Click on the desired variable in the box to the left, and then click on the *Select* button. Then click on the   OK   button.

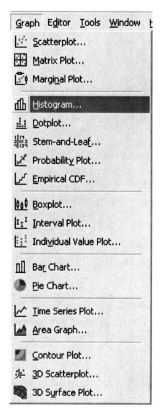

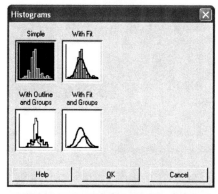

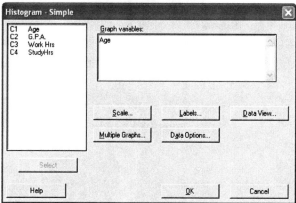

The choice of *CutPoint* in this Histogram Options dialog box produces a histogram with the class boundaries (edges of the rectangle) labeled on the horizontal axis, the usual method for drawing a histogram. Whereas choosing the *MidPoint* labels the midpoints of the rectangles on the horizontal axis.

Example 3.1: Start a Minitab session and open the worksheet Study4.mtb that is on your data disc. Graph a histogram for the variable C1 (Age).

Click on *File , Open Worksheet...* In the Open Worksheet dialog box; click on the *Look in:* drop down icon and select *Data Disc* (if it is not already selected). Then click on the Study4.mtw to highlight the name; and then click on the ⬛ **Open** ⬛ button. A dialog box informing you that "A copy of this file will be added to the current Project." may appear. Click on ⬛ **OK** ⬛ .

Click on *Graph , Histogram*. In the Histogram box: make sure that Simple is chosen and then click ⬛ **OK** ⬛ .

In the Histogram Simple dialog box, slick on the C1 Age variable, click on the *Select* button and then click on the ⬛ **OK** ⬛ button.

The graph below will appear in the Histogram of Age Window.

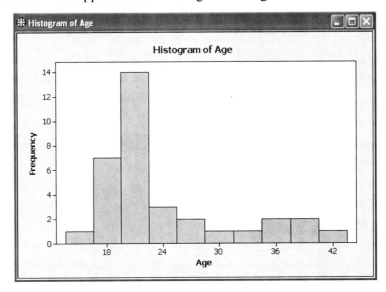

Notice that the bottom left corner of this graph is **not** the origin. Minitab always graphs the smallest bar near the left end of the horizontal axis. Also note that Minitab chooses the interval width and the value of the first endpoint. You may edit many things on this graph just by double clicking on that item. Among these are the title of the graph, the axis labels, the color of the shading inside the bars, and most importantly the width and value of the first endpoint.

To change the title; simply double click on the default title, and you will get an Edit Title dialog box. You may change the font, style, size, and actual text of the title, as well as the alignment (position) of the title.

To change an axis label, just double click on the label you want to change, and you will get an Edit Axis Label dialog box. You may change the font, style, size, and actual text of the axis label. The *Alignment* and *Show* tabs are not very useful for most graphs.

To change the shading color, double click inside one of the histogram bars, and you will get an Edit Bars dialog box. In the *Attributes* tab, click on the circle to the left of *Custom* in the *Fill Pattern* area. Then click on the down triangle to the right of the *Background color:* box, and a palette of colors will appear. Choose the desired color for the shading of the histogram bars. Optionally you may want to insert a pattern of lines such as cross-hatching. To do this, click on the down triangle to the right of the *Type* box, and choose the type of fill pattern you want; such as solid, solid with cross-hatching, and several others. Do **not** choose the type that is at the top with a N inside of a box. This type will block any further editing of the shading.

To change interval width and value of the first endpoint, again double click inside one of the histogram bars, and you will get an Edit Bars dialog box. First click on the *Binning* tab and in the *Interval Type* area, click on the circle to the left of *Cutpoint*. This will cause the tick marks on the horizontal axes to display ant the end points of the intervals instead of the midpoints. Next in the *Interval Definition* area, click on the circle to the left of *Midpoint/Cutpoint Positions:* and click in the box under this label. Now you may either (1) enter the endpoints of the intervals explicitly by typing in each endpoint separated by a space or (2) use the shorthand method by entering the first interval's left endpoint, a colon (:), the last interval's right endpoint, a slash (/) and the interval width. For example method (1) would look like 20 30 40 50 60 70 80 90 100 , while method (2) would be 20:100/10 . Graphics of these changes will be shown in the next example.

Example 3.2:   Use the data in the current Study4.mtb worksheet and graph a histogram of the Age variable. Also add the title of Histogram of 36 College Students, and label the X axis as Ages of Students. Fill in the bars with yellow, but do not add any type of line pattern. The smallest interval is 15 to under 20, and the largest interval is 40 to under 45; so change the graph to indicate these endpoints.

Double click on the default title of Histogram of Age, and change the *text* to Histogram of 36 College Students.

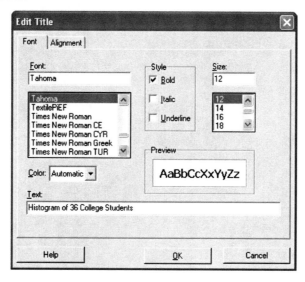

(continued on the next page)

Next double click on the x axis label of Age and change the text to Ages of Students.

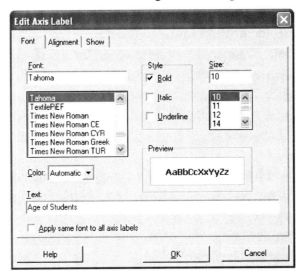

Now double click inside one of the histogram bars, change the color to yellow and change the interval width and values of the endpoints.

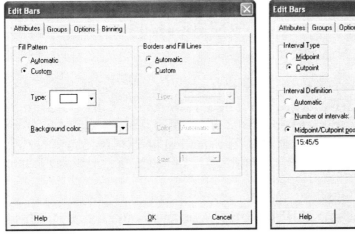 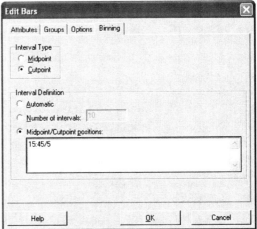

The graph below will appear in the Histogram of Age Window. (Any indicators of what item was being edited will not be printed.)

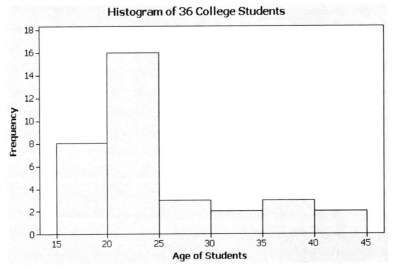

In some cases, you may want to change the x-axis scale numbering. For example, if there are many intervals, the x-axis numbering becomes very cluttered and you may want to only display every other endpoint. Or you may want to try to display the graph so that the y-axis appears to be at zero on the x-axis. To change the x-axis scaling, double click on any number on the x-axis, and you will get an Edit Scale dialog box with the Scale tab showing. Under the *Major Tick Positions* heading, click on the circle to the left of *Position of Ticks* and then click in the box to the right of this label. Erase the current entries in this box, and enter the scaling that you want using the same format as used in binning; either enter the scale numbers explicitly (without commas, or use the (lowest scale number):(highest scale number)/(spacing between numbers) format. If you had a histogram whose intervals were 10 wide and went form 100 to 300, you may want the x-axis to only display every other endpoint, and so you would enter 100:300/20 .

Example 3.3:  Modify the current histogram so that the x-axis scaling goes from 0 to 50 and numbered only by tens.

Double click on any number on the x-axis. In the Edit Scale dialog box, under the *Major Tick Positions* heading, click on the circle to the left of *Position of Ticks*, and then click in the box to the right of this label. Erase the current entries in this box and enter 0:50/10 . Click on the **OK** button and the graph below will appear in the Histogram of Age Window.

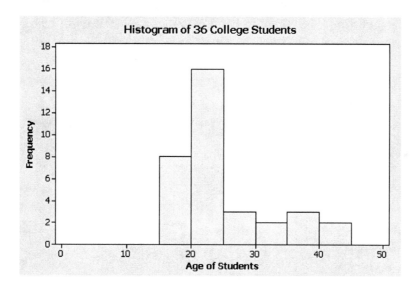

All high resolution graphs may be edited in a similar manner as will be shown in this chapter.

Each new graph is placed in an additional, new graphics window. Once you have viewed the graph and possibly printed the graph, you will usually want to minimize that specific graphics window so as not to clutter the screen. Graphics windows are minimized by clicking on the underscore in the ▣◨☒ at the right end of the Graphics Window title bar. If you want to delete this Graphics Window, click on the X in the ▣◨☒ , and Mintab tells you that the graph will be removed from the project, the action cannot be undone, and asks if you would like to save the graph in a separate file. If you click Yes, you will get a Save As dialog box in which you can choose a name and location for this Minitab graphics file (it will have the three letter extension of .MGF). If you click on No, the graphics window will be removed from the project.

Example 3.4:   Delete the first histogram graph done in Example 3.1. Print the Age histogram done in Example 3.2, and then minimize this Graphics window that contains the Age histogram.

Activate the first Graphics Window and click on the X in the [■□✕] . Click on [ No ] to remove this graphics window from the project.   Activate the remaining Graphics Window. Click on *File , Print Graph...*  In the Print dialog box: make sure that the number 1 is in the *Copies:* box, and then click on the [ OK ] button. After the histogram has been printed, click on the underscore in the [■□✕] .

When two variables have been measured on each object, you are often interested in examining any possible relationship between these two variables.  For example, one may want to determine if there is any relationship between a person's cholesterol level and daily salt intake. The graphical technique used when you are interested in the relationship between two variables is called a scatter plot.   The data is graphed on the standard Cartesian coordinate plane (x-y axis) using the *Plot* procedure.

Click on *Graph , Scatterlot ...*

In the Scatterplots dialog box: the *Simple* graph should be highlighted.  Next click on the [ OK ] button.

In the Scatterplot - Simple dialog box: the cursor will be in the box on the first line under the *Y variables* heading; click on the desired Y variable and click on the [ Select ] button.  The cursor will move to the box in the first line under the *X variables* heading; click on the desired X variable and click on the [ Select ] button. (It is possible to graph another scatter plot by selecting a second set of Y and X variables for second scatterplot graphics window.) Then click on the [ OK ] button.

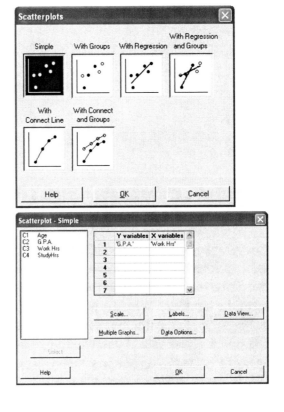

42

Example 3.5: Use the data in the current Study4.mtb worksheet and graph a high resolution (x,y) scatter plot where Work Hrs is the X axis variable and G.P.A. is the Y axis variable.

Click on *Graph, Scatterlot...* then in the Scatterplots dialog box: the *Simple* graph should be highlighted. Next click on the ⬜ **OK** button. In the Scatterplot - Simple dialog box the cursor will be in the box on the first line under the *Y variables* heading; click on the G.P.A. (C2) variable and click on the ⬜ **Select** button. The cursor will move to the box in the first line under the *X variables* heading; click on the Work Hrs (C3) variable and click on the ⬜ **Select** button. Then click on the ⬜ **OK** button.

The graph below will appear in the Scatterplot of G.P.A. vs Work Hrs Window.

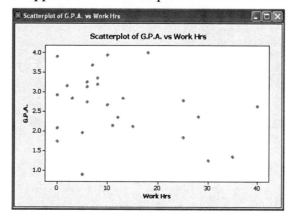

Also note that, as with the histogram, **the intersection of the horizontal and vertical axes is not necessarily the origin (0,0), but is near the minimum of each variable**.

You may edit the title and/or axes labels exactly the same way as described for the Histogram, just double click on the item. You may also add one or more title lines, subtitle lines (smaller font size and not bold), and a footnote to the graph by right clicking in the graphics window. A menu will be displayed, and left click on Add. A second menu will be displayed with 11 choices, and Title... , Subtitle... and Footnote... will be in the middle of these choices. Left click on the desired choice, and a dialog box will appear with the heading corresponding to the choice you selected and a box for entering the desired text. After any titles, subtitles, axis label and/or footnotes have been created, you may click on a specific item and move it to a different location on the graph.

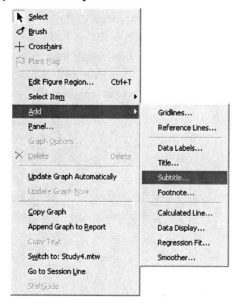

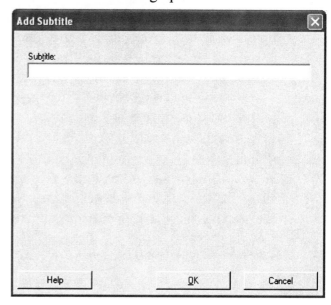

One additional feature Minitab incorporates is the ability to choose from many different plotting symbols; for example, open circle, solid circles of various sizes, triangles, diamonds and others. You may choose an optional plotting symbol and color by double clicking on any of the current plotting symbols on the graph. In the Edit Symbols dialog box, select the Attribute tab at the top, and then click in the circle next to *Custom* in the Symbols area. This will allow you to choose the *Type*, *Color* and *Size* of the graphing symbols for the current graph.

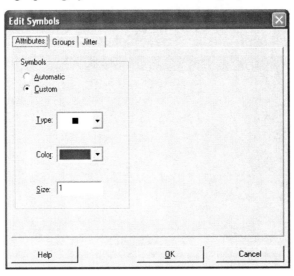

Example 3.6:  Delete the current scatter plot, and then graph a high resolution (x,y) scatter plot where the X axis is StudyHrs and the Y axis is Age. Create a title of **Scatter Plot of 36 College Students**, label the X axis as **Study Hours per Week by Student**, label the Y axis as **Age of Student**, and change the graphing symbol to a solid blue triangle.

Activate the Plot Window and click on the X in the ▢▢▢ and click on No to not save the graph.

Click on *Graph, Scatterplot...* then in the Scatterplots dialog box: the *Simple* graph should be highlighted. Next click on the OK button. In the Scatterplot - Simple dialog box the cursor will be in the box on the first line under the *Y variables* heading. Notice that the 'G.P.A.' and 'Work Hrs' variables are in the boxes on this first line. You may either highlight a different variable and click on the Select button to select a new variable, press the Delete key on the keyboard to empty the box and select a different variable, or press the F3 key on the keyboard to clear all boxes. For this example, press the F3 key on the keyboard to clear all boxes. Then highlight the Age (C1) variable and click on the Select button. The cursor will move to the box in the first line under the *X variables* heading; click on the StudyHrs (C4) variable and click on the Select button. Then click on the OK button. The graph on the next page will appear in the Scatterplot of Age vs StudyHrs Window.

(continued on the next page)

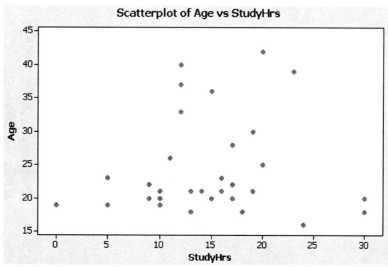

Now double click on the title and change the text to **Scatter Plot of 36 College Students**. Next double click on the current label for the X axis and change the text to **Study Hours per Week by Student**. Then double click on the current label for the Y axis and change the text to **Age of Student**. Now double click on any of the circles on the graph. In the Edit Symbols dialog box, select the Attribute tab at the top, and then click in the circle next to *Custom* in the Symbols area. Click on the drop down triangle button to the right of the symbol in the *Type* box, and click on the triangle symbol (▲). Click on the drop down triangle button to the right of the *Color* box, and click on the blue color box. Leave the *Size* as 1. The modified graph in the Scatterplot of Age vs StudyHrs Window is shown on the next page.

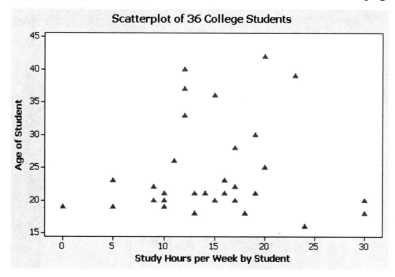

A dotplot has the data values on the x axis and graphs a dot over each value as often as it occurs in the data set. Because most scores only occur once or twice in a sample, the dotplot often is just a series of dots. This graph does indicate: where the center of the data is located, the clustering versus spread of the data, and the range of the scores. However it usually does not give as nice of a picture of the overall nature of the data as a histogram. When the data set is large and there are many repeats of each score, the dotplot begins to resemble a histogram. One main usage of this graph is to be able to quickly graph **two or more** data sets on the same axis, so as to be able to roughly compare these data sets. The dotplot for <u>one</u> variable is graphed by

Click on *Graph*, *Dotplot...*

In the Dotplots dialog box: the *One Y Simple* graph should be highlighted. Next click on the **OK** button.

In the Dotplot - One Y, Simple dialog box: the cursor will be in the box under *Graph variables:*. Click on the desired variable in the box to the left, and then click on the **Select** button. Then click on the **OK** button.

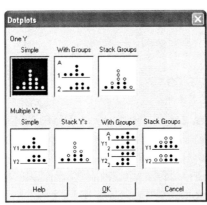

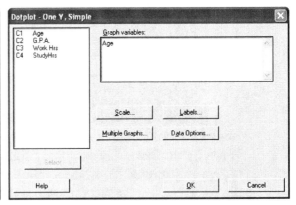

Example 3.7: Use the data in the current Study4.mtb worksheet and graph a dotplot for the Age (C1) variable in this worksheet. Use the title of **Dotplot of 36 College Students**. Then compare this graph to the histogram graphed in Example 3.2

.

Click on *Graph*, *Dotplot...* In the Dotplots dialog box: the *One Y Simple* graph should be highlighted. Next click on the **OK** button. Next in the Dotplot - One Y, Simple dialog box: the cursor will be in the box under *Graph variables:*. Click on the Age (C1) variable in the box to the left, and then click on the **Select** button. Then click on the **OK** button. Once the graph appears, double click on the title and change the text to **Dotplot of 36 College Students**. The graph below will appear in the Dotplot of Age Window.

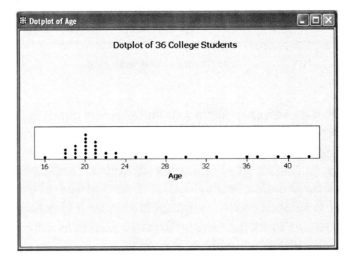

(continued on the next page)

46

Activate the Histogram of Age Window. If you cannot see the Histogram of Age Window, click on the Window item in the menu bar at the top, and then click on Histogram of Age in the resulting drop down menu. Place the mouse in the middle of the title bar of each Graphic Window and drag the windows so that you are able to see both the dotplot and this histogram. You may need to use the Windows method to somewhat resize these two Graphics Windows. Most of the scores are centered around 20 years, with some scores spreading out to past 40 years old. This is the same impression you get from examining the histogram in Example 3.2, but the trend is more attractively and emphatically displayed in the histogram.

You may edit the different parts of the Dotplot graph in the same way as described previously for the Histogram and Scatterplot. Double click on the title, variable or a plotting symbol; and edit them in the manner explained above. Also you may change the scale numbers on the axis by double clicking on a number displayed below the axis. In the Edit Scale dialog box, you may change the *Position of ticks:* by entering the new ticks (scale numbers displayed under the axis) using either method (1) or method (2) as described for the Histogram. In addition, if you right click in the gray area and click on *Add*, then you may add a subtitle and/or footnote.

If you *select* two or more variables in the Dotplots - One Y, Simple dialog box, a separate Dotplot Graphics Window will appear for each variable selected, and each will have a axis scaled to the data for the respective variable. When dotplots for two or more variables are graphed, you usually want them to be on the same reference axis so as to be able to compare the different variables. These multiple vertical dotplots are graphed by

Click on *Graph , Dotplot...*

In the Dotplots dialog box: the *One Y Simple* graph should be highlighted. Click on the picture under *Multiple Y's Simple* and then click on the OK button.

In the Dotplot - Multiple Y's, Simple dialog box: the cursor will be in the box under *Graph variables:*. Hold the Ctrl key and click on the desired variables in the box to the left, and then click on the Select button. Then click on the OK button.

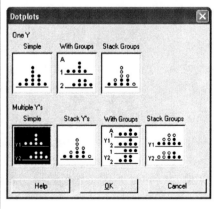

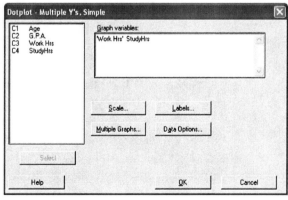

Example 3.8:   Delete the previous Dotplot of Age Graphic Window and now graph a dotplot for both the work hours (C3) and study hours (C4). Compare the location and spread of these two variables.

Click on *Graph , Dotplot...*  In the Dotplots dialog box: the *One Y  Simple* graph should be highlighted.  Click on the picture under *Multiple Y's Simple* and then click on the $\boxed{\textbf{OK}}$ button.  In the Dotplot - Multiple Y's, Simple dialog box: the cursor will be in the box under *Graph variables:.*  You may need to press the $\boxed{\textbf{F3}}$ key to clear all contents of this dialog box.  Now hold the $\boxed{\textbf{Ctrl}}$ key and click on the Work Hours (C3) and StudyHrs (C4) variables in the box to the left, and then click on the $\boxed{\textbf{Select}}$ button. Then click on the $\boxed{\textbf{OK}}$ button. The graph below will appear in the Dotplot of Work Hrs, StudyHrs Window.

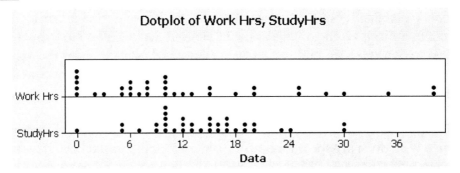

From these two dotplots, you can see that the dots for study hours in the bottom line of the graph are centered about 15 hours, while the dots for work hours center about a smaller value. And so it appears that these students spend more time studying than they work. Next, the spread of the work hours is much larger than the study hours.  Also there are five students who do not work (Work Hrs = 0), but only one student who does not study (StudyHrs = 0).

You may edit and/or add items to the Multiple Y's Dotplot in the same way as for the Simple Y Dotplot. To change the variable labels, you double click on any of the labels on the left side of the graph. In the Edit Scale dialog box that appears, there are six tabs across the top, and you will click on the *Labels* tab. Then click on the button to the left of *Specified* and click inside the box to the right of *Specified.* The labels are listed in top to bottom of the graph order, and they are separated by one or more spaces. Labels that contain a space **in** the label must be enclosed with quotation marks.

Example 3:9:   Edit the Multiple Y Dotplot in the current project so that the title is **Dotplot of Hours Spent by Students**, and the two axes are labeled **Working Hours** and **Studying Hours**.

Double click on the title and enter Dotplot of Hours Spent by Students as the new title. Next double click on one of the current axis labels, click on the *Labels* tab, click on the button to the left of *Specified*, delete the (automatic) labels in the box to the right and type in "Working Hours" "Studying Hours". Then click on the $\boxed{\textbf{OK}}$ button. The modified graph in the Dotplot of Age Window is shown on the next page.

(continued on the next page)

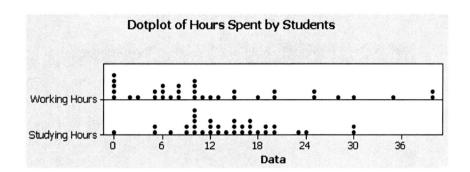

**Dotplot of Hours Spent by Students**

When working with discrete data, the two most common graphical techniques used are the bar chart and the pie chart. The bar chart is the discrete data counterpart to the histogram for continuous data. This graph is used primarily to display the relationships between the different outcomes of the variable.

You usually will want to label the X axis with a descriptive name for the variable and label the Y axis as Frequency. Additionally, most bar charts contain a title at the top of the graph. As its default setting, Minitab draws the bars and shades them in with a grey color. Coloring in the bars makes a major improvement to the presentation of the data, and after the graph has been drawn, you may edit the graph to customize the color of each bar individually. This will be shown after the next example. Minitab arranges the outcomes along the X axis in numerical order for numeric data and in alphabetical order for text data. The bar chart is graphed by

Click on *Graph, Bar Chart...*

In the Bar Charts dialog box: the *Simple* graph should be highlighted. Next click on the ⬚ **OK** ⬚ button.

In the Bar Chart - Counts of unique values, Simple dialog box: the cursor will be in the box under *Categorical variables:*. Click on the desired variable in the box to the left, and then click on the ⬚ **Select** ⬚ button. Then click on the ⬚ **OK** ⬚ button.

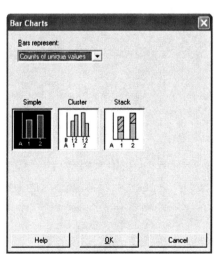

(See third graphic on the next page.)

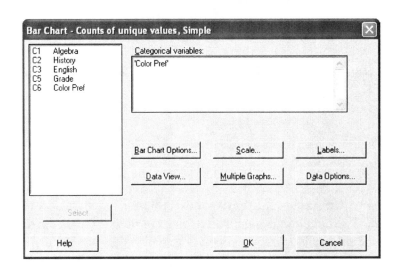

Example 3:10:   Start a new Minitab project; do not save the current project. Open the
                Grades.mtw worksheet and graph a bar chart for the Color Pref variable.
                Label the X axis with **Color Preference of Students in Econ 101**, label the
                Y axis **Frequency**, and title the graph as **Economics 101 Section 8**.

Click on *Graph, Bar Chart...* In the Bar Charts dialog box: the *Simple* graph should be
highlighted. Next click on the | **OK** | button. In the Bar Chart - Counts of unique values,
Simple dialog box: the cursor will be in the box under *Categorical variables:*. Click on the
Color Pref variable in the box to the left, and then click on the | **Select** | button. Then click
on the | **OK** | button.   The graph shown below will appear in the Chart of Color Pref
Window.

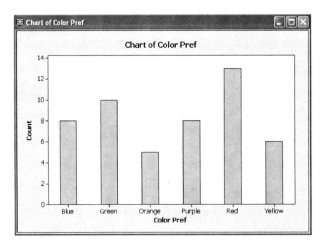

Now double click on the current title and change the text to Economics 101 Section 8, double
click on the current x axes label of Color Pref and change the text to Color Preference of
Students in Econ 101, and double click on the current y axis label of Count and change the text
to Frequency. The modified graph in the Chart of Color Pref Window is shown on the next
page.

(continued on the next page)

50

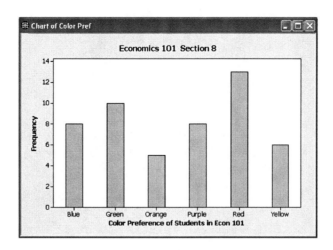

If you want to edit the graph in order to color all of the bars with the same color, just double click on any of the bars in the graph. The Edit Bars dialog box will appear. In the *Attributes* tab click on the circle to the left of *Custom*. The drop down menu for *Type* allows you to choose a type of shading such as solid (the default) or different types of line hatching. The drop down menu for *Background Color* allows you to choose a common color for all off the bars. Now click on the **OK** button.

However if you want to color each individual bar differently, you single slick on any bar so that all bars are selected, wait about one or two seconds and single click in the bar you want to color. That specific bar will now be selected and you double click on that bar. The Edit Bars dialog box will appear. In the *Attributes* tab click on the circle to the left of *Custom*. The drop down menu for *Type* allows you to choose a type of shading such as solid (the default) or different types of line hatching. The drop down menu for *Background Color* allows you to choose a color for the specific bar you clicked on. Now click on the **OK** button. Next double click on a different bar and the Edit Bars dialog box will appear again. Click on the circle to the left of *Custom*, select the color for this specific bar, and click on the **OK** button. Repeat this for each bar you want to color.

Example 3:11:    Use the Bar Chart in the current project and color the bars to match their color label.

Single slick on any bar so that all bar are selected, wait about one or two seconds and single click in the Blue bar. Now double click on that bar and the Edit Bars dialog box will appear. In the *Attributes* tab click on the circle to the left of *Custom*. Click on the down triangle to open the drop down menu for *Background Color*, click on the blue color block, and then click on the **OK** button. That bar will still be selected, but it will be colored blue. Now double click on the Green bar. In the *Attributes* tab click on the circle to the left of *Custom*. Click on the down triangle to open the drop down menu for *Background Color*, click on the green color block, and then click on the **OK** button. Now repeat this process until all bars are colored. The modified graph shown below will appear in the Chart of Color Pref Window (since this workbook is in black and white, your graph will look much better than the graph shown on the next page).

(continued on the next page)

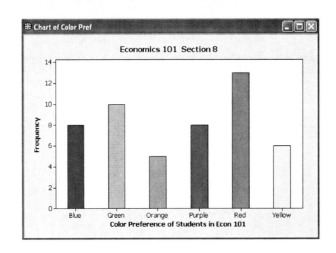

The pie chart is used to illustrate the relationships of each outcome to the entire set of data. Pie charts are often used when displaying budgetary data. There are a few options available with Minitab when graphing a pie chart. These include adding a title, "exploding" one or several slices, the placement order of the slices around the pie, where the first slice begins and how the slices will be labeled. The Minitab default setting for the placement order is to go counter clockwise in either numerical (for numeric data) or alphabetical (for text) data. The default setting is to label the slices with the data value and include the frequency and per cent for each outcome, and this is usually the best choice. An option to add a line pointing to slice will be shown as it makes the information clearer. The first slice starts at zero degrees (the 3 o'clock position), but many people like to change this to 90 degrees (the 12 o'clock position). The slices are consecutively numbered with 1 being the "first" slice. Slices are "exploded" by indicating the slice number. This is often done after the pie chart done the first time, since then it easy to see which number(s) corresponds to the slice(s) you want to "explode". There are options to combine outcomes that are a small per cent of the total, and to omit missing data as a category in the pie chart. Minitab will color the slices using a default color scheme; but you will likely want to change these colors using the editing features described for the bar chart. The pie chart is graphed by

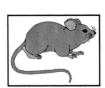

Click on *Graph , Pie Chart...*

In the Pie Chart dialog box: make sure the button to the left of *Chart raw data* is selected, and then click inside the box to the right. Then click on the variable you want to graph and click on the | **Select** | button. Then click on the | **OK** | button.

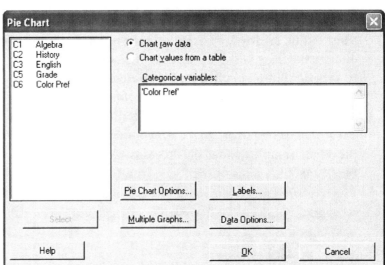

Example 3.12: Use the data in the current Grades.mtw worksheet and graph a pie chart for the Color Pref variable.

*Graph , Pie Chart...*

In the Pie Chart dialog box: make sure the button to the left of *Chart raw data* is selected, and then click inside the box to the right. Then click on the Color Pref variable and click on the ⬚ **Select** button. Then click on the ⬚ **OK** button.

The graph below will appear in the Pie Chart of Color Pref Window.

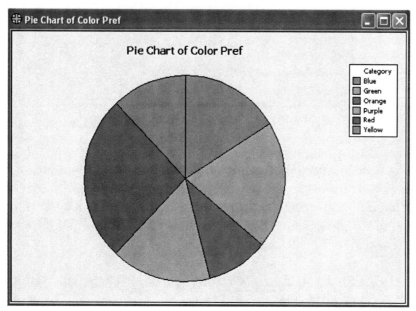

Minitab arbitrarily assigns colors to the different categories of the variable. In most cases these colors will be fine, but occasionally you may want to change the colors. You may edit the colors in exactly the same way the colors are changed for a Bar Chart as follows.

Single click on any pie slice so that all of the pie slices are selected, wait about one or two seconds and single click in the pie slice you want to color. That specific pie slice will now be selected and you double click on that slice. The Edit Pie dialog box will appear. In the *Attributes* tab click on the circle to the left of *Custom*. The drop down menu for *Type* allows you to choose a type of shading such as solid (the default) or different types of line hatching. The drop down menu for *Background Color* allows you to choose a color for the specific bar you clicked on. Now click on the ⬚ **OK** button. Next double click on a different pie slice and the Edit Pie dialog box will appear again. Click on the circle to the left of *Custom*, select the color for this specific bar, and click on the ⬚ **OK** button. Repeat this for each pie slicer you want to color. The color legend will show the current color for each category of the variable (you may have to move the Edit Pie dialog box a little to see the complete legend). After you change the color of the slice, the color legend is automatically updated.

(See graphic on the next page.)

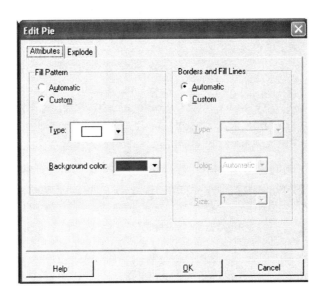

Usually you will want to have the frequency and/or the percent of each category displayed on the graph, and sometimes you may want the category itself displayed on the graph. Often it is easier to read this information if it is connected to the respective slices with a line. This may be done at the very beginning as you are creating the graph, or you may add this information as you edit the graph. At the beginning you may add this information by

In the Pie Chart dialog box: after you have selected the variable to be graphed, click on the | **Labels...** | button.

In the Pie Chart - Labels dialog box: click on the *Slice labels* tab at the top.

In this *Slice labels* tab: click on the box(es) to the left of *Category name*, *Frequency*, *Percent*, and/or *Draw a line from label to slice* to add the feature(s) you want, and click on the | **OK** | button.

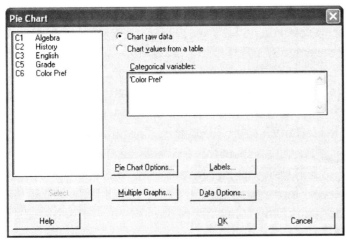 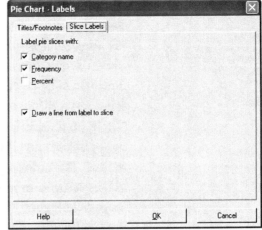

You may add this information after you have created the Pie Chart graph by

Single click in the grey area outside of the Pie Chart to select the entire graph. Double click inside one of the slices and the Edit Pie dialog box will appear. In the Edit Pie dialog box: click on the *Slice labels* tab at the top.

In this *Slice labels* tab: click on the box(es) to the left of *Category name*, *Frequency*, *Percent*, and/or *Draw a line from label to slice* to add the feature(s) you want, and click on the │ **OK** │ button.

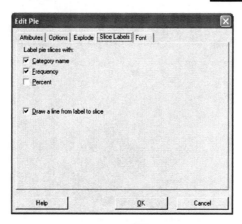

If you include the category names, you may want to delete the color legend from the graph. To delete the legend, just single click in the legend and then press the Delete key on the keyboard.

You may edit the title by double clicking on the current title and changing the text to the new title that you want. Also you may add a second title line, a subtitle, and/or a footnote by using the same technique that applies to all other graphs. Right click in the grey area, a drop down menu will appear, left click on *Add*, and then click on *Title*, *Subtitle*, or *Footnote*. Add the text for the item you chose and then click on the │ **OK** │ button. Repeat for each item you want to add.

Example 3.13: Use the Pie Chart for the Color Pref variable in the current project and change the title to **Color Preference of Students in Economics 101**. Then add a subtitle of **Section 8**. Next add the category names, frequencies and lines from these labels to the slices. Finally change the color of each slice to match the category name.

Double click on the current title. In the Edit Title dialog box delete the current title and insert Color Preference of Students in Economics 101 as the text for the new title, and click on the │ **OK** │ button.

Right click on the grey area of the graph, click on *Add* in the menu. and then click on *Subtitle...* in the next menu. In the Add Subtitle dialog box, add Section 8 as the text for this subtitle, and click on the │ **OK** │ button.

Double click on a pie slice. In the Edit Pie dialog box: click on the *Slice labels* tab at the top.

In this *Slice labels* tab boxes to the left of *Category name*, *Frequency*, and *Draw a line from label to slice*, and click on the │ **OK** │ button.

(continued on the next page)

All of the pie slices should be selected. But if not; click on the grey area outside of the pie, and then single click on one of the slices to select all slices. Now wait two seconds, single click on the slice labeled Blue, and then double click on this blue slice.

The Edit Pie dialog box will appear. In the *Attributes* tab click on the circle to the left of *Custom*. Click on the down triangle to the right of *Background Color* and click on the blue color. Now click on the OK button.

Repeat this for each of the other five colors.

The modified graph shown below will appear in the Pie Chart for Color Pref Window.

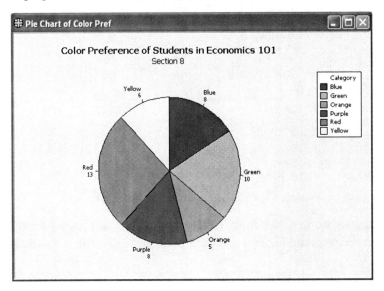

Several other options for the Pie Chart are available. One is the order in which the slices are arranged around the pie, and this is done by

Make sure the entire pie is selected and then double click.

Double click inside one of the slices and the Edit Pie dialog box will appear.

In the Edit Pie dialog box: click on the *Options* tab at the top. In this tab under the heading *Order slices by:* there are three choices. *Default* orders the slices in alphabetical or numerical order. *Increasing volume* orders the slices by increasing frequency order. And *Decreasing volume* orders the slices by decreasing frequency order. Click on the circle to the left of the desired order, and then click on the OK button. Slices are ordered clockwise.

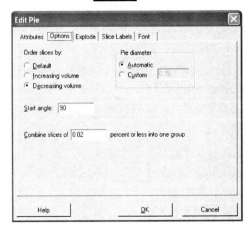

A second option is to combine several small slices into one category which is labeled "Other", and this is done by

Make sure the entire pie is selected and then double click.

Double click inside one of the slices and the Edit Pie dialog box will appear.

In the Edit Pie dialog box: click on the *Options* tab at the top. The last item in this tab is to *Combine slices of* 0.02 *percent or less into one group.* By default, Minitab combines categories which make up 0.02 % or less of the total group. Click in this box, delete the *0.02*, and type in the percent for which you want to define a small categories and want to combine into one "Other" category. You may want to (temporarily) add *Percent* to the slice labels. You will need to do this first and click on the OK button. Then double click inside one of the slices and the Edit Pie dialog box will appear again. The graphic for this is shown above.

A third option is being able to "explode" one or more slices, and this is done by

Make sure the entire pie is selected wait two seconds, then single click on the slice you want to "explode", then double click on this same slice, and the Edit Pie dialog box will appear.

In the Edit Pie dialog box: click on the *Explode* tab at the top.

In this *Explode* tab, click on the box to the left of *Explode slice*. You may change the distance the slice is pulled out from the pie ("exploded") by clicking inside of the box to the right of *Explode length:* and changing the default value of 0.5 to anything between 0.01 to 0.99.

Then click on the OK button.

Repeat this for each slice you want to "explode" from the pie.

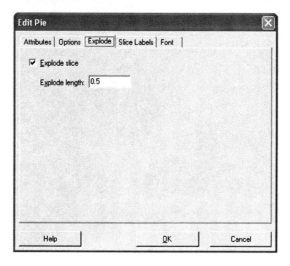

Example 3:14:    Redo the pie chart for the Color Pref variable, but arrange the slices in decreasing frequency order, and explode the Green and Yellow slices to a distance of 0.70.


Double click inside one of the slices and the Edit Pie dialog box will appear.

In the Edit Pie dialog box: click on the *Options* tab at the top. In this tab under the heading *Order slices by:* click on the circle to the left of the *Decreasing volume*, and then click on the ⬛ **OK** ⬛ button.

Make sure the entire pie is selected wait two seconds, then single click on the Green slice, and then double click on this Green slice, and the Edit Pie dialog box will appear.

In the Edit Pie dialog box: click on the *Explode* tab at the top.

In this *Explode* tab, click on the box to the left of *Explode slice*. Now click inside of the box to the right of *Explode length:* delete the value of 0.5, and type in 0.70 .

Then click on the ⬛ **OK** ⬛ button.

Next double click on the Yellow slice, and the Edit Pie dialog box will appear.

In the Edit Pie dialog box: click on the *Explode* tab at the top.

In this *Explode* tab, click on the box to the left of *Explode slice*. Now click inside of the box to the right of *Explode length:* delete the value of 0.5, and type in 0.70 .

Single click on the Legend, and then press the ⬛ **Delete** ⬛ key on the keyboard to remove the legend from the graph..

Then click on the ⬛ **OK** ⬛ button.

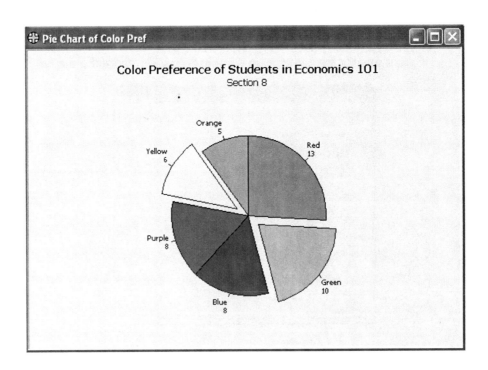

Occasionally a variable will contain missing data (a blank cell for text data and an * for numerical data). This missing data category will be included in the Pie Chart unless you specifically want to omit this category from you graph. Omitting missing data from the graph **must be done before** you create the first version of the Pie Chart. This is done by

Click on *Graph , Pie Chart...*

In the Pie Chart dialog box: click on the **Data Options...** button.

In the Pie Chart - Data Options dialog box click on the *Group Options* tab at the top. Then click in the box to the left of *Include missing as a group* to **un**check this box, and then click on the **OK** button.

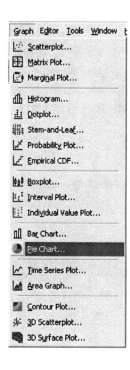

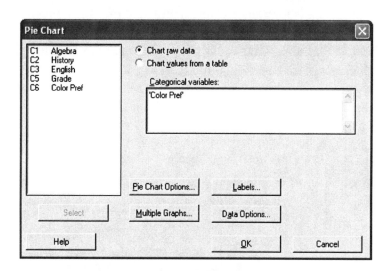

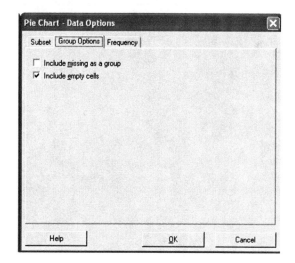

**Section 2:      Character Graphs**

"Character graphs" are drawn using characters that appear on the keyboard as opposed to the nice looking pen on paper look of the "high resolution graphs." The other difference is that the "character graphs" always appear in the **Session Window**, whereas the "high resolution graphs" appear in their own Graphics Window. And so the "character graphs" are printed on paper when the Session Window is printed. The stem-and-leaf is the only "character graph" available on the menu item *Graph* drop down menu.

This graph is for numerical data only and provides information similar to a histogram, but is not as graphically effective. However the stem-and-leaf does supply some additional information about the data that a histogram does not. It is part of "exploratory data analysis"; i.e., where you get several pieces of information quickly but not necessarily in an attractive format.     Since a stem-and-leaf is similar to a histogram, you must decide on the value for the width of each class interval before drawing the graph. This width is called the *increment* in Minitab. The stem-and-leaf graph is plotted by

Click on *Graph , Stem-and-Leaf...*

In the Stem-and Leaf dialog box: click on the desired variable, click on the *Select* button, click in the *Increment:* box, type the value of the desired class interval width, and then click on ▢ **OK** ▢ .

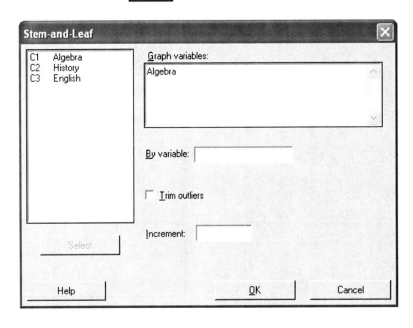

The stem-and-leaf graph output contains the variable name or column number if the variable was not named, the number of valid (N) and missing (N*) observations.  The "Leaf Unit" is automatically computed, based on the value entered for the increment, and displayed.    Then the "stems" and "leaves" are displayed.  The displayed "leaves" are the digits with the "Leaf Unit" place value.  The stems are the digits with a place value that are 10 times the "Leaf Unit." It is usually best to make the *increment* (interval width) either a power of 10 (1, 10, 100, 1000, etc.) or a number that evenly divides into a power of 10 (0.2, 0.25, 0.5, 2, 5, 20, 25, 50, 200 etc.).

For example; suppose the "Leaf Unit" equals 100, the digit in the "stem" column is 7 and the digit in "leaf" column is 3. Then the "stems" have a place value of 10 x 100 = 1000, the "stem" of 7 represents 7000, and the "leaf" of 3 represent 300. So the 7 and 3 combination represents the number 7300.

The number to the left of each stem is the cumulative number of values from the closer end (minimum or maximum score) to and including that stem except for the number in parentheses. The parentheses are used to indicate that this stem is the median (middle) of the data, and the number inside is the number of scores in that one class interval.

Example 3.15:    Open the worksheet Study4.mtw that is saved on your data disc. Graph a stem-and-leaf display for the StudyHrs (C4) variable in this worksheet. Use an class interval width of 10.

Click on *File , Open Worksheet...* In the Open Worksheet dialog box; click on the *Look in:* drop down icon and select *Data Disc* (if it is not already selected). Then click on the Study4.mtw to highlight the name; and then click on the  Open  button.

File , Click on *Graph , Stem-and-Leaf...* In the Stem-and Leaf dialog box: click on the StudyHrs (C4) variable, click on the  Select  button, click in the *Increment:* box, type in 10, and then click on  OK . The output shown on the next page will appear in the Session Window.

## Stem-and-Leaf Display: StudyHrs

**Stem-and-leaf of StudyHrs   N = 35**
**Leaf Unit = 1.0**
**N\* = 1**

```
    6     0   055799
  (23)    1   00000122233455566777899
    6     2   0034
    2     3   00
```

The rightmost column contains the leaves, and since the leaf unit is 1.0, this means that each leaf is a number in the 1's place. The middle column shows the stems. Since the leaf unit is 1.0, the stems are 10's (place value to the left of the 1's place). So, for example, the last 4 on the right of the third row represents the score of 24. The 6 in the left most column of the third row indicates that there are 6 scores from the maximum to and including the scores in the 20's stem. The (23) in the first column of the second row indicates that the 10's stem is the median stem and contains 23 scores. The combination of the stem and leaves displays how many scores are in an interval and the values of these scores accurate to the leaf unit place. By rotating the graph 90 degrees, you see a pattern similar to a histogram graph.

61

Example 3.16: Graph a stem-and-leaf graph for the Age (C1) variable. Use a class interval width of 5.

Click on *Graph ,Stem-and-Leaf...*

In the Stem-and Leaf dialog box: first press the  F3  key to clear the information in all of the dialog boxes. Now click on the Age (C1) variable, click on the  Select  button, click in the *Increment:* box, type in 5, and then click on  OK .

The stem-and-leaf graph below will appear in the Session Window.

## Stem-and-Leaf Display: Age

**Stem-and-leaf of Age      N = 34**
**Leaf Unit = 1.0**
**N\* = 2**

```
   8     1  68889999
 (16)    2  0000000111112233
  10     2  568
   7     3  03
   5     3  679
   2     4  02
```

Since the leaf unit is 1.0, the stems are in the 10's place. And since the width is 5, two stems (10 ÷5 = 2) are needed for each number in the 10' s place. The 1 in the first row is the only stem in the 10's, and the leaves are 5 and above; so this stem corresponds to a class interval of 15 to under 20. There is one leaf of 6, three leaves of 8 and four leaves of 9. These leaves together with the stem of 1 correspond to one score of 16, three scores of 18 and four scores of 19. The next two stems are both 2's. The first 2 corresponds to the class interval of 20 to under 25, and thus its leaves are between 0 and 4. There are sixteen leaves on this first stem, and thus sixteen scores in the class interval of 20 to under 25. The second stem of 2 corresponds to the class interval of 25 to under 30, and its leaves are between 5 and 9. The three leaves of 5, 6 and 8 on this stem represent the three scores of 25, 26 and 28.

The data in the G.P.A. (C2) variable is recorded with two decimal places. The next example illustrates the method that Minitab uses when the data is recorded with more places of accuracy than the leaf unit place value.

Example 3.17: Plot a stem-and-leaf graph for the G.P.A. (C2) variable in the current worksheet using a class interval width of 0.5 .

Click on *Graph ,Stem-and-Leaf...*
In the Stem-and Leaf dialog box: first press the | F3 | key to clear the information in all of the dialog boxes. Now click on the G.P.A. (C2) variable, click on the | Select | button, click in the *Increment:* box, type in 5, and then click on | OK |.
The stem-and-leaf graph below will appear in the Session Window.

## *Stem-and-Leaf Display: G.P.A.*

*Stem-and-leaf of G.P.A.*      *N = 29*
*Leaf Unit = 0.10*
*N\* = 7*

```
   1     0  9
   3     1  23
   6     1  789
  11     2  01133
  (8)    2  56677889
  10     3  112233
   4     3  699
   1     4  0
```

Since the leaf unit is 0.10, the stems are in the 1's place. And since the class interval width is 0.5, two stems (1 ÷0.5 = 2) are needed to represent each number in the 1's place. The 0 in the first row is the only stem in the 1's and, the leaves are 5 and above; so this must be the class of 0.5 to under 1.0. There is one leaf of 9 in the 0.1's place. The combination of the stem of 0 in the 1's place and 9 in the 0.1's place corresponds to a score of 0.9 (0x1 + 9x.1). The next stem is a 1 and has leaves of 2 and 3; so these correspond to the values of 1.2 and 1.3 . These two scores are actually 1.25 and 1.35; but the since the leaf unit is 0.10, the stem-and-leaf graph only displays the digits in the 0.1's place and not in the 0.01 place. Any digits it the 0.01 place and smaller are truncated, and the digit in the "leaf" place is exactly as it appears in the original number. This "leaf" digit is **not** rounded off.

Example 3.18: Print the contents of the Session Window and then exit from Minitab.

Click on the Session Window to make sure that it is the active window. Next click on *File , Print Session Window...* Then in the Print dialog box make sure that the *All* button in the Print Range box is filled in and that the *Copies:* is 1. Then click on the | OK | button. The printed output should contain all of the commands that Minitab places in the Session Window as well as the three stem-and-leaf "character graphs" that you displayed in the previous examples. Lastly click on *File , Exit* to exit from this Minitab Session; do not save the project.

63

Other graphical techniques available in the Minitab Statistical Package include overlays of x-y graphs, and time series graphs. Interested readers are encouraged to consult a Minitab user's manual or the on-line help for further details concerning these and other graphical techniques. The next chapter introduces numerical methods for describing data.

# Lab  Assignment 3.1

**Name:**                                                **Date:**

**Course:**                     **Section:**                           **Data CD Number:**

1. Start a Minitab session. If you are unable to complete this lab assignment in one Minitab session, save the project as Lab 3-1 . **Never** use a period as part of the project  name; since Minitab uses the period to attach the file type to the file name.  Then at your next Minitab session, you may open this Lab 3-1.MPJ project and continue to work where you left off previously.

2. Open the worksheet Acreage.mtw that is on your data disc.

3. Graph a histogram for the C1 variable with class intervals that are 5 wide.  The scores for this variable range from 0 to 40.   Describe the shape of this set of scores.

4. Graph a dotplot for the C1 variable.  Does this graph give you the same information as the histogram you graphed in problem 3?  Which graph is easier to interpret?

5. Display the values of the C1 variable in the current worksheet.

6. Graph a stem-and-leaf for the C1 variable with class intervals that are 5 wide.

7. Open a second worksheet using Trenton.mtw from your data disc.

8. Graph two Multiple Y dotplots for the C1 and C4 variables. Compare the location and spread of these two variables.

9. Open a third worksheet using Homesale.mtw from your data disc.

10. Graph the (x,y) plot with the Asking P variable as the X-axis and the SellingP variable as the Y-axis.  Describe any relationship or lack of relationship among the two variables.

11. Open a fourth worksheet using Grades.mtw from your data disc.

(lab assignment is continued on the second side of this page)

12. Graph a bar chart for the Grade variable. Label the X axis as "Final Exam Grades" and the Y axis as "Frequency". Title this graph as "Economics 101 - Section 8" and add a Subtitle of "Fall Semester 2002". Color the bars as A - Green, B - Blue, C - Yellow, D - Gray, and F - Red. How many students earned a grade of B? Describe this bar chart of grades in words.

13. Graph a pie chart for the Grade variable. Title this graph as "Economics 101 - Section 8" and add the Subtitle of " Final Exam Grades". Color the slices the same as given in problem 12, and explode the D grade slice. What per cent of the students earned a grade of B?

14. Print your Session Window and all Graphic Windows to the printer now, and then exit from the Minitab session.

15. Attach your Minitab paper output and your written descriptions in problems 3, 4, 8, 10, 12 and 13 to this sheet and submit all three to your instructor.

# Lab  Assignment 3.2

**Name:**                                                                  **Date:**

**Course:**                          **Section:**                          **Data CD Number:**

1.    Start a Minitab session.  If you are unable to complete this lab assignment in one Minitab session, save the project as Lab 3-2 . **Never** use a period as part of the project  name; since Minitab uses the period to attach the file type to the file name.  Then at your next Minitab session, you may open this Lab 3-2.MPJ project and continue to work where you left off previously.

2.    Open the worksheet Living.mtw that is on your data disc.

3.    Graph a histogram for the C1 variable with class intervals that are 20 wide.  The scores range from 60 to 220.   Describe the shape of this set of scores.

4.    Graph a dotplot for the C1 variable.  Does this graph give you the same information as the histogram you graphed in problem 3?  Which graph is easier to interpret?

5.    Display the values of the C1 variable in the Session Window.

6.    Graph a stem-and-leaf for the C1 variable with class intervals that are 20 wide.

7.    Open a second worksheet using Homesale.mtw from your data disc.

8.    Graph two Multiple Y dotplots for the SellingP and Asking P variables.   Compare the location and spread of these two variables.

9.    Graph the (x,y) plot with the SellingP variable as the X-axis and the Asking P variable as the Y-axis. Describe any relationship or lack of relationship among the two variables.

10.   Open a second worksheet using Grades.mtw from your data disc.

11.   Graph a bar chart for the Grade variable. Label the X axis as "Final Exam Grades" and the Y axis as "Frequency".  Title this graph as "Economics 101- Section 8" and add the Subtitle of "Fall Semester 2002".  Color the bars as A - Green, B - Blue, C - Yellow, D - Gray, and F - Red. How many students earned a grade of B?  Describe this bar chart of grades in words.

(lab assignment is continued on the second side of this page)

12. Graph a pie chart for the Grade variable. Title this graph as "Economics 101 - Section 8" and add a Subtitle of "Final Exam Grades". Color the slices the same as given in problem 11, and explode the D grade slice. What per cent of the students earned a grade of B?

13. Print your Session Window and all Graphic Windows to the printer now, and then exit from the Minitab session.

14. Attach your Minitab paper output and your written descriptions from problems 3, 4, 8, 9, 11 and 12 to this sheet and submit all three to your instructor.

# CHAPTER 4: Numerical Descriptive Statistics

Graphical displays of data are very useful; however, numerical descriptions are required for a detailed analysis of any set of data. The mean and median are the two most often used measures of central tendency (or position), and the standard deviation is commonly used to describe the variability of the data. These three descriptive statistics, and others, may be computed on any **one** variable (column).

Click on *Calc , Column Statistics...*

In the Column Statistics dialog box: click on the circle of the specific statistic you want to calculate, click inside of the *Input variable:* box, then click on the one variable for which you want to calculate this statistic, and click on the | **Select** | button.

Minitab will allow you to choose **only one variable and one statistic at a time**. To compute other statistics for the **same** variable click on *Calc , Column Statistics...* again, and then click on a different statistic. Also if you want to compute a statistic for a **different** variable (column) and a variable name is already in the *Input variable:* box, you must click in this box and erase the current variable (column) before choosing the **different** variable. Lastly, click on the | **OK** | button.

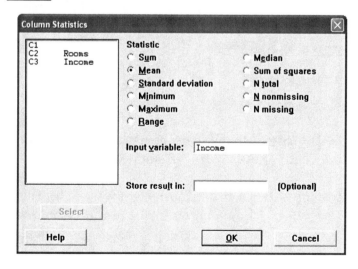

Example 4.1:  Start a Minitab session.  Find the mean, median, standard deviation, sum, maximum and range of the following data: 3, 10, -4, 6, 0 and 2.

Enter these six scores into column 1 directly in the Worksheet Window.  Then click on *Calc , Column Statistics...*  In the Column Statistics dialog box: click on the circle to the left of *Mean*, click inside of the *Input variable:* box, then click on the C1 variable, click on ⊡ **Select** ⊡ , and then click on ⊡ **OK** ⊡ .  Repeat clicking on *Calc , Column Statistics...* and successively choose *median, standard deviation, sum, maximum* and *range*; each time clicking on ⊡ **OK** ⊡ after choosing the desired statistic. The corresponding commands and resulting statistics below will appear in the Session Window.

## Results for Worksheet 1

*MTB > Mean C1.*

## Mean of C1

**Mean of C1 = 2.8333**

*MTB > Median C1.*

## Median of C1

**Median of C1 = 2.5**

*MTB > StDev C1.*

## Standard Deviation of C1

**Standard Deviation of C1 = 4.83391**

*MTB > Sum C1.*

## Sum of C1

**Sum of C1 = 17**

*MTB > Maximum C1.*

## Maximum of C1

**Maximum of C1 = 10**

*MTB > Range C1.*

## Range of C1

**Range of C1 = 14**

Notice that the Minitab computes the standard deviation using the <u>sample</u> standard deviation formula which uses (n - 1) in the denominator.

Example 4.2:  Open the Housing5.mtw worksheet that is saved on your data disc.  Enter the Info command in the Session Window to display the basic information about the contents of this worksheet.  Compute the mean of the Income and Rooms variables, compute the standard deviation and minimum of the Income variable, and compute the median and range of the first variable.

(continued on the next page)

Click on *File , Open Worksheet...* In the Open Worksheet dialog box; click on the *Look in:* drop down icon and select *Data Disc* (if it is not already selected). Then click on the Housing5.mtw to highlight the name; and click on the | Open | button. A dialog box informing you that "A copy of this file will be added to the current Project." will appear. Click on | OK |. Click to the right of the last **MTB >** in the Session Window and enter the info command. The basic information about this worksheet shown below will appear in the Session Window.

## *Results for: Housing5.mtw*

**MTB >** info

### Information on the Worksheet

| Column | Count | Missing | Name |
|--------|-------|---------|------|
| C1 | 25 | 0 | |
| C2 | 25 | 1 | Rooms |
| C3 | 25 | 2 | Income |

Next click on *Calc , Column Statistics...* Press the | F3 | key to clear any information from Example 4.1 . In the Column Statistics dialog box: click on the circle to the left of *Mean*, click inside of the *Input variable:* box, then click on the Income variable, click on the | Select | button, and then click on | OK |. Now click on *Calc , Column Statistics...* again, click inside of the *Input variable:* box, erase the Income variable, click on the Rooms variable, click on | Select | and click on | OK |. Continue successively for the standard deviation and minimum of the **Income** variable, and the median and range of the **C1** variable. The resulting statistics below will appear in the Session Window. (The corresponding commands to the right of the **MTB >** prompts have been omitted below.)

## Mean of Income

**Mean of Income = 33615.5**

## Mean of Rooms

**Mean of Rooms = 6.83333**

## Standard Deviation of Income

**Standard Deviation of Income = 20971.6**

## Minimum of Income

**Minimum of Income = 8648**

## Median of C1

**Median of C1 = 405**

## Range of C1

**Range of C1 = 965**

Instead of computing these statistics separately, you may use the *Descriptive Statistics* procedure to compute eleven measures for **one or several or all variables <u>at the same time</u>**.

Click on *Stat , Basic Statistics , Display Descriptive Statistics...*

In the Display Descriptive Statistics dialog box: click on the variable or variables for which you want to calculate these statistics (hold the $\boxed{\text{Ctrl}}$ key to choose non consecutive variables), click on the *Select* button, and then click on the $\boxed{\text{OK}}$ button.

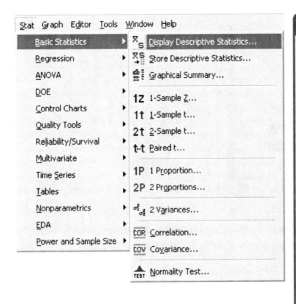
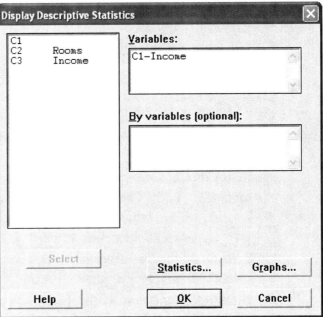

The output of the *Display Descriptive Statistics* procedure contains the variable name or column number if the variable was not named, and:

(1)   N         =   number of valid (non missing) observations,
(2)   N*        =   number of missing observations,
(3)   Mean    =   mean of the variable,
(4)   SE Mean   =   standard error of the mean; i.e., the standard deviation divided by the square root of N,
(5)   StDev    =   standard deviation of the variable,
(6)   Minimum   =   minimum value of the variable,
(7)   Q1         =   25 %-tile of the variable,
(8)   Median   =   median of the variable,
(9)   Q3         =   75 %-tile of the variable and
(10)   Maximum   =   maximum value of the variable.

This output does **not** contain the total number of observations nor the range; but these two and others may be added to the output, and some of the statistics in the default display may be removed by clicking on the $\boxed{\text{Statistics...}}$ button. A Descriptive Statistics - Statistics dialog box appears, and you may add and or remove specific statistics by clicking on the box to the left of each one to check or uncheck that box.

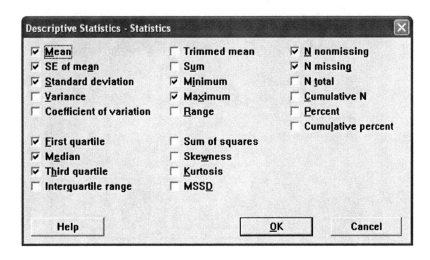

Example 4.3: Compute the descriptive statistics for all variables in the current Housing5.mtw worksheet. Omit the SE of Mean and add the Variance and Range statistics.

Click on *Stat*, *Basic Statistics*, *Display Descriptive Statistics...*

In the Display Descriptive Statistics dialog box: click on the C1 variable and drag the mouse down to the Income C3 variable to highlight all variables (or click on the first variable, hold the | Shift | key and click on the last variable to choose all variables between and including the first one and last one clicked) and click on the | Select | button. Next click on the | Statistics... | button, click on the box to the left of *SE of mean* to **un**check this box, and click on the boxes to the left of *Variance* and *Range* to check these boxes. Then click on the | OK | button and click on the | OK | button back in the Display Descriptive Statistics dialog box..

The results below will appear in the Session Window.

## Descriptive Statistics: C1, Rooms, Income

| Variable | N | N* | Mean | StDev | Variance | Minimum | Q1 | Median | Q3 |
|----------|-----|-----|-------|-------|-----------|----------|-------|--------|--------|
| C1 | 25 | 0 | 419.3 | 211.8 | 44854.5 | 89.0 | 265.0 | 405.0 | 578.0 |
| Rooms | 24 | 1 | 6.833 | 2.408 | 5.797 | 2.000 | 5.000 | 6.000 | 8.750 |
| Income | 23 | 2 | 33616 | 20972 | 439809911 | 8648 | 21242 | 28381 | 42033 |

| Variable | Maximum | Range |
|----------|---------|--------|
| C1 | 1054.0 | 965.0 |
| Rooms | 12.000 | 10.000 |
| Income | 101290 | 92642 |

For the *Display Descriptive Statistics* procedure, one of the options on the Display Descriptive Statistics dialog box is the *Graphs...* button. If you click on this *Graphs...* button, you will be given choices as shown in the graphic below.

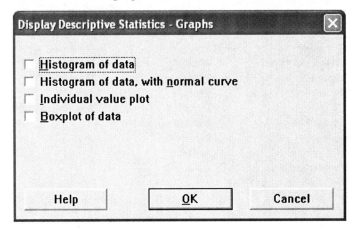

A boxplot (or box-and-whiskers plot) is used to show the Median, 25<sup></sup> percentile (also called the first quartile and symbolized as Q1 by Minitab), 75<sup></sup> (also called the third quartile and symbolized as Q3 by Minitab) percentile, minimum and maximum scores as well as to indicate the symmetry or skewness of the data. In other words, a boxplot is useful for showing the center, spread and shape of a set of data. In addition, boxplots are often used to help identify outliers; i.e., scores that are relatively far away from the rest of the scores in the data. Once an outlier is identified, it needs to be carefully examined. Often an outlier occurs because of an error in the collection or recording of the score. In this case, the score should be corrected if possible, but if it is not possible to obtain the correct value, then the outlier should be deleted from the data. In Minitab you may graph a boxplot for a single set of data, or multiple boxplots for several data sets may be displayed in the same graph. This latter application is very useful for comparing different sets of data to each other. The box plot for a single variable is graphed by

Click on *Graph, Boxplot...*

In the Boxplots dialog box: the *One Y Simple* graph should be highlighted. Next click on the  OK  button.

In the Boxplot - One Y, Simple dialog box: the cursor will be in the box under *Graph variables:*. Click on the desired variable(s) in the box to the left, and then click on the  Select  button. Then click on the  Scale...  button.

In the Boxplot - Scale dialog box: the *Axis and Ticks* tab should be visible. Click on the box to the left of *Transpose value and category scales* to select this option which will graph the boxplot in a more natural horizontal position (instead of the default vertical position that Minitab uses). Then click on the  OK  button.

Back in the Boxplot - One Y, Simple dialog box: click on the  OK  button.

(See graphics on the next page.)

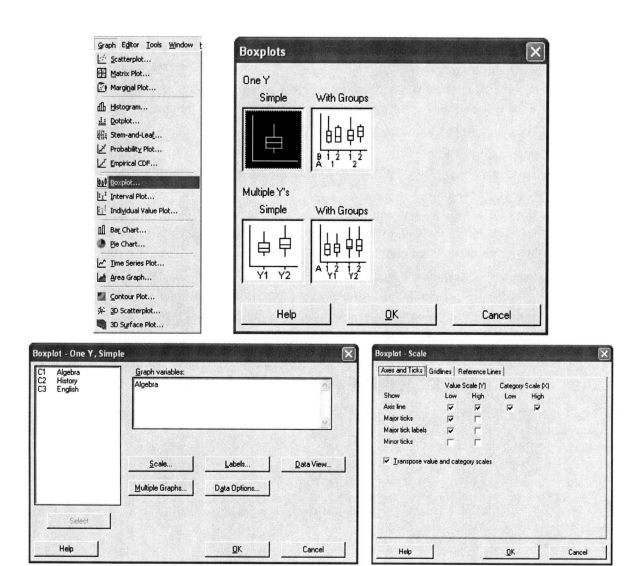

Minitab draws the boxplot as follows. First a rectangle is drawn with the ends located at the 25th and 75th percentile (first and third quartile). These values are labeled Q1 and Q3 and their computations are done by the *Describe Descriptive Statistics* menu item. Then a line located at the middle (median) is drawn between the two ends. Next, the InterQuartileRange (IQR) = Q3 - Q1 is computed, and the length of the "hinge" is calculated as 1.5 times the IQR. The "lower limit" is equal to Q1 - the hinge and the "upper limit" is equal to Q3 + the hinge. A line is drawn from the lower box end (Q1) to the lowest score in the data which is within the lower limit, and from the upper box end (Q3) to the largest score in the data which is within the upper limit. If any scores are beyond the lower or upper limits, these scores are graphed with an asterisk (*); and these are called outliers.

Example 4.4: Start a new Minitab project; do not save the current project. Open the saved worksheet Grades.mtw . Graph a boxplot for the Algebra variable, and title this graph as Grades Example.

(continued on the next page)

Click on File , New... , select Minitab Project , click on ‖ **OK** ‖ , and do not save changes to the current project.

Click on *File , Open Worksheet...* In the Open Worksheet dialog box; click on the *Look in:* drop down icon and select *Data Disc* (if it is not already selected). Then click on the Grades.mtw to highlight the name; and then click on the ‖ **Open** ‖ button.

Click on *Graph, Boxplot...*

In the Boxplots dialog box: the *One Y Simple* graph should be highlighted. Next click on the ‖ **OK** ‖ button.

In the Boxplot - One Y, Simple dialog box: the cursor will be in the box under *Graph variables:*. Click on the Algebra variable in the box to the left, and then click on the ‖ **Select** ‖ button. Then click on the ‖ **Scale...** ‖ button.

In the Boxplot - Scale dialog box: the *Axis and Ticks* tab should be visible. Click on the box to the left of *Transpose value and category scales* and then click on the ‖ **OK** ‖ button.

Back in the Boxplot - One Y, Simple dialog box: click on the ‖ **OK** ‖ button.

Double click on the current title and edit the text to now be Grades Example.

The graph below will appear in the Boxplot of Algebra Window.

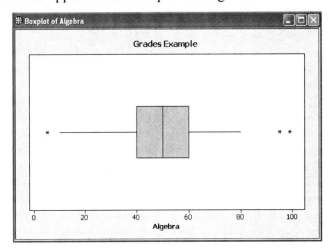

For this data: Q1 = 40, Q3 = 60 and the median = 50. So the IQR = 60 - 40 = 20. The hinge = 1.5 times 20 = 30, and so the lower limit is 10 (Q1 - hinge = 40 - 30), and the upper limit is 90 (Q3 + hinge = 60 + 30). The smallest three scores in the data set are 5, 10 and 20; and the largest three scores are 80, 95 and 99. Since 5 is beyond the lower limit and 95 and 99 are beyond the upper limit, these three scores are graphed with an asterisk (*). The smallest score within the lower limit is 10, and so that is where the line (whisker) to the left ends. And the largest score within the upper limit is 80, and so that is where the line (whisker) to the right ends. From this graph you can see that: (1) the middle score in this data is 50, (2) that the middle 50 % of the scores lie between 40 and 60, and (3) the scores are highly symmetric.

Optionally you may edit and/or add a title, subtitle and footnote. You may change the axis label, axis numerical scaling, box color and type of shading, and the outlier symbol by double clicking on each of these items.

Example 4.5:     Use the data in the current Grades.mtw worksheet and graph boxplots for both the History and English variables.

Click on *Graph , Boxplot...*

In the Boxplots  dialog box: the *One Y Simple* graph should be highlighted.  Next click on the ⬛ **OK** ⬛ button.

In the Boxplot - One Y, Simple dialog box: the cursor will be in the box under *Graph variables:*. in the box to the left click on the History variable, hold the ⬛ **Ctrl** ⬛ key and click on the English variable, and then click on the ⬛ **Select** ⬛ button.  Then click on the ⬛ **Scale...** ⬛ button.

In the Boxplot - Scale dialog box: the *Axis and Ticks* tab should be visible.  Click on the box to the left of *Transpose value and category scales* and then click on the ⬛ **OK** ⬛ button.

Back in the  Boxplot - One Y, Simple dialog box: click on the ⬛ **OK** ⬛ button.

The graphs below will appear in separate Boxplot of History and Boxplot of English Windows.

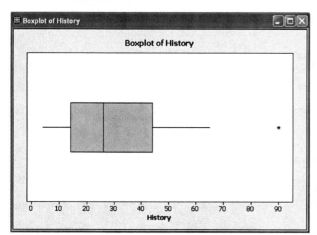

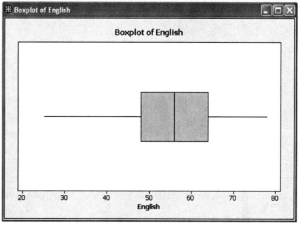

The second (English) graphic window will overlap the first (History) window on your screen. To see both windows at the same time, simply click in the bright blue title bar of the Boxplot of English graphic window and drag it to the right until you can see both graphic windows.

When printing these graphic windows, you must activate the specific window and then print that one graphics window.  And so this will result in each graph being printed on a separate piece of paper.  In order to conserve paper, there is an option to have all graphs displayed in the same graphics window, and this print on one piece of paper.  This is done by following the same steps as show above, inserting on step after checking the box to the left of *Transpose value and category scales* and then clicking on the ⬛ **OK** ⬛ button.

Back in the    Boxplot - One Y, Simple dialog box: click on the ⬛ **Multiple Graphs...** ⬛ button.

In the Boxplot - Multiple Graphs dialog box; directly under the heading *Show graph variables*, click on the circle to the left of *In separate panel of the same graph* and then click on the ⬛ **OK** ⬛ button.

(See graphic on the next page.)

77

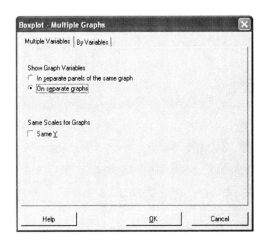

Example 4.6:   Use the data in the current Grades.mtw worksheet and graph boxplots for Algebra, History and English variables to be displayed in one graphics window..

Click on *Graph , Boxplot...*

In the Boxplots  dialog box: the *One Y Simple* graph should be highlighted.  Next click on the | **OK** | button.

In the Boxplot - One Y, Simple dialog box: the cursor will be in the box under *Graph variables:*.  in the box to the left click on the Algebra variable, hold the | **Ctrl** | key and click on the English and History variables, and then click on the | **Select** | button.  Then click on the | **Scale...** | button.

In the Boxplot - Scale dialog box: the *Axis and Ticks* tab should be visible.  Click on the box to the left of *Transpose value and category scales* and then click on the | **OK** | button.

Back in the  Boxplot - One Y, Simple dialog box: click on the | **Multiple Graphs...** | button.

In the Boxplot - Multiple Graphs dialog box; directly under the heading *Show graph variables*, click on the circle to the left of *In separate panel of the same graph* and then click on the | **OK** | button.

Back in the  Boxplot - One Y, Simple dialog box; click on the | **OK** | button.

The graph of all three variable will appear in on graphics window shown below.

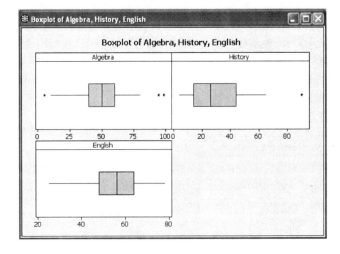

When graphing boxplots for two or more variables, you often want to compare the variable to each other. Displaying the graphs in the same graphics window **and** on using the **same axis scaling** will allow you to easily compare the centers, spreads and shapes of the different variables. This is called Multiple Boxplots for several variables and are graphed by

Click on *Graph, Boxplot....*

In the Boxplots dialog box: the *Multiple Y's Simple* graph should be highlighted. Click on the picture under *Multiple Y's Simple* and then click on OK .

In the Boxplot - Multiple Y's, Simple dialog box: the cursor will be in the box under *Graph variables:*. Click on the desired variables in the box to the left (hold the Ctrl key to choose non consecutive variables), and then click on the Select button. Then click on the Scale... button.

In the Boxplot - Scale dialog box: the *Axis and Ticks* tab should be visible. Click on the box to the left of *Transpose value and category scales* to select this option which will graph the boxplot in a more natural horizontal position (instead of the default vertical position that Minitab uses). Then click on the OK button.

Back in the Boxplot - Multiple Y's, Simple dialog box: click on the OK button.

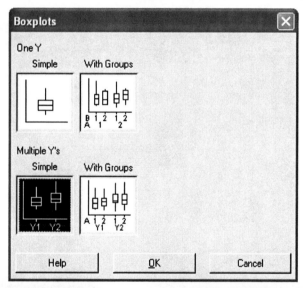

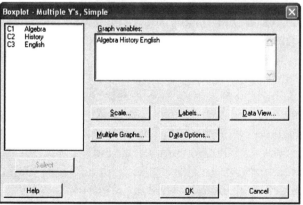

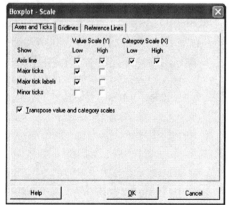

Example 4.7: Use the data in the current Grades.mtw worksheet and graph a multiple boxplots for the Algebra, History and English variables.

Click on *Graph , Boxplot...*

In the Boxplots dialog box: the *Multiple Y's Simple* graph should be highlighted. Click on the picture under *Multiple Y's Simple* and then click on the | **OK** | button.

In the Boxplot - Multiple Y's, Simple dialog box: press the | **F3** | key to clear all contents of this dialog box and any other successive dialog boxes. Now click in the box under *Graph variables:*, click on the desired variables in the box to the left (hold the | **Ctrl** | key to choose non consecutive variables), and then click on the | **Select** | button. Then click on the | **Scale...** | button.

In the Boxplot - Scale dialog box: the *Axis and Ticks* tab should be visible. Click on the box to the left of *Transpose value and category scales* to select this option which will graph the boxplot in a more natural horizontal position (instead of the default vertical position that Minitab uses). Then click on the | **OK** | button.

Back in the Boxplot - Multiple Y's, Simple dialog box: click on the | **OK** | button.

The graph below will appear in the Boxplot of Algebra, History, English Window.

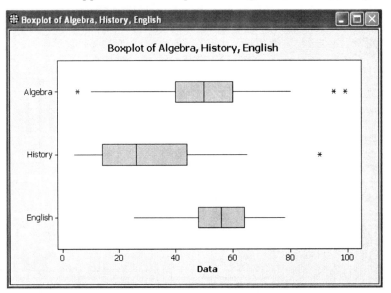

From this graph there are several comparison you can make. The median lines show that the middle of the History grades is the lowest of the three, Algebra is considerably higher, and English is slightly higher than Algebra. The boxes for Algebra and English have similar widths and their whiskers are not too different in length. This tells us that these two variables have a similar spread, while the box for History is wider and thus indicates these scores are more spread than both Algebra and History. The boxes for Algebra and English have the median lines in the middle of the boxes, and the left and right whiskers of each box are somewhat similar in length. This tells you that the Algebra scores and the English scores each have fairly symmetric shape. Whereas the box for History has a longer right "half than its left half, and the right whisker is longer than the left whisker. This indicates that the History scores are skewed to the right. You may want to verify this by graphing a histogram for each of these variables (use the *Options...* of *Number of intervals:* as 6). Also notice that Algebra has three outliers, History has one outlier, and English has no outliers.

You may edit the Boxplot graph in the same manner as was described for the graphs in Chapter 3. To edit the current title, bottom axis label, outlier symbol and numerical scaling of the axis; just double click on those items. You may add/edit the title, subtitle and footnote by right clicking in the grey area, and then click on *Add* in the drop down menu. To color in the boxes, you single slick on any box so that all boxes are selected, wait about one or two seconds and single click in the box you want to color. That specific box will now be selected and you double click on that box. The Edit Interquartile Range Box dialog box will appear. In the *Attributes* tab click on the circle to the left of *Custom*. The drop down menu for *Type* allows you to choose a type of shading such as solid (the default) or different types of line hatching. The drop down menu for *Background Color* allows you to choose a color for the specific box you clicked on. Now click on the $\boxed{\text{OK}}$ button. Next double click on a different box and the Edit Bars dialog box will appear again. Click on the circle to the left of *Custom*, select the color for this specific bar, and click on the $\boxed{\text{OK}}$ button. Repeat this for each bar you want to color. Pastel or light colors are best as they will not mask the median line in side of the box.

Example 4.8: Edit the Multiple Y Boxplot to: change the title to **Boxplot of Three Courses**, change the bottom axis label to **Course Grades**, color the Algebra box very light blue, color the History box light green, color the English box light yellow, and change the Algebra label to **Algebra 2**.

Double click on the current title and change the text to Boxplot of Three Courses.

Double click on the current label (Data) on the bottom axis and change the text to Course Grades.

Click on any box, wait two seconds, single click on the algebra box, and then double click on the algebra box. The Edit Interquartile Range Box dialog box will appear. In the *Attributes* tab click on the circle to the left of *Custom*. Click on the down triangle to the right of *Background Color* and choose the very light blue color block. Now click on the $\boxed{\text{OK}}$ button.

Repeat for light green in the History box and light yellow in the English box.

Double click on the Algebra label, and then click on the *Labels* tab. In the ⊙ to the left of *Specified:* and click inside of the box to the right which contains the current labels. Edit these labels by adding a space and a 2 after the label Algebra and then enclosing Algebra 2 within a set of quotes (since this label has a space inside of the label).

The modified graph below will appear in the Boxplot of Algebra, History, English Window.

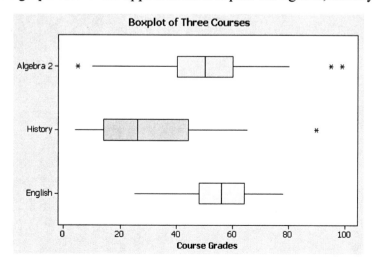

This concludes the chapters dealing with many of the methods that are commonly called descriptive statistics. The remaining chapters in this workbook describe the techniques that comprise the area of inferential statistics.

# Lab Assignment 4.1

**Name:**                                                  **Date:**

**Course:**                     **Section:**                        **Data CD Number:**

1. Start a Minitab session. If you are unable to complete this lab assignment in one Minitab session, save the project as Lab 4-1 . **Never** use a period as part of the project name; since Minitab uses the period to attach the file type to the file name. Then at your next Minitab session, you may open this Lab 4-1.MPJ project and continue to work where you left off previously.

2. Open the worksheet Acreage.mtw that is on your data disc.

3. What is the mean of the variable ? _____

4. What is the median of the variable ? _____

5. What is the standard deviation of the variable ? _____

6. What is the sum of all values of the variable ? _____

7. Enter the Info command in the Session Window to find the sample size. Then use the answer to problem 6, the sample size from the Info command in the Session Window and a calculator to compute the mean of the variable accurate to 4 decimal places. _____

8. Open a second worksheet using Mailbag.mtw that is on your data disc.

9. What is the mean of:

   (a) the first variable ? _____

   (b) the second variable ? _____

   (c) the third variable? _____

10. What is the maximum of:

   (a) the second variable ? _____

   (b) the last variable ? _____

(lab assignment is continued on the second side of this page)

11. What is the 25 %-tile of:

(a) the first variable ? _____

(b) the second variable ? _____

12. What is the sum of all valid values for:

(a) the first variable ? _____

(b) the last variable ? _____

13. Open a third worksheet using Homesale.mtw that is on your data disc.

14. Graph a Multiple Y's boxplot using the **same axis scaling** for the SellingP and Asking P variables. Compare the location and spread of these two variables.

15. Graph three separate boxplots for the SellingP, Asking P and HouseAge variables. To conserve paper, graph these three separate boxplots in the same graphics window. Do any of these three data sets contain any outliers? If so, which variable(s), and what are the approximate values of these outliers?

16. Print your Session Window and Graphics Windows to the printer.

17. Attach your Minitab paper output your written descriptions from problems 14 and 15 to this sheet and submit all three to your instructor.

# Lab Assignment 4.2

**Name:**                                          **Date:**

**Course:**                 **Section:**                     **Data CD Number:**

1. Start a Minitab session. If you are unable to complete this lab assignment in one Minitab session, save the project as Lab 4-2 . **Never** use a period as part of the project name; since Minitab uses the period to attach the file type to the file name. Then at your next Minitab session, you may open this Lab 4-2.MPJ project and continue to work where you left off previously.

2. Open the worksheet Living.mtw that is on your data disc.

3. What is the mean of the Income variable ? _____

4. What is the median of the Income variable ? _____

5. What is the standard deviation of the Income variable ? _____

6. What is the sum of all values of the Income variable ? _____

7. Enter the Info command in the Session Window to find the sample size. Then use the answer to problem 6, the sample size from the Info command in the Session Window and a calculator to compute the mean of the variable accurate to 4 decimal places. _____

8. Open a second worksheet using Trenton.mtw that is on your data disc.

9. What is the mean of:

    (a) the first variable ? _____

    (b) the second variable ? _____

    (c) the third variable? _____

10. What is the maximum of:

    (a) the second variable ? _____

    (b) the last variable ? _____

(lab assignment is continued on the second side of this page)

11. What is the 25 %-tile of:

   (a) the first variable ? _____

   (b) the second variable ? _____

12. What is the sum of all valid values for:

   (a) the first variable ? _____

   (b) the last variable ? _____

13. Graph a Multiple Y's boxplot using the **same axis scaling** for the C1 and C4 variables. Compare the location and spread of these two variables.

14. Graph two separate boxplots for the Junior and Senior variables. To conserve paper, graph these two separate boxplots in the same graphics window. Do either of these two data sets contain any outliers? If so, which variable(s), and what are the approximate values of these outliers?

15. Print your Session Window and all Graphics Windows to the printer.

16. Attach your Minitab paper output your written descriptions from problems 13 and 14 to this sheet and submit all three to your instructor.

# CHAPTER 5:     One Sample Confidence Intervals

**Section 1:     Confidence Interval For The Population Mean**

Estimation of unknown population parameters is one of the primary objectives of statistical inference.   When the variable of interest is continuous, the parameter of most interest is the population mean which is symbolized by $\mu$.   This chapter will describe the Minitab methods for computing confidence intervals for the population mean, $\mu$.

The sample data associated statistical problems is presented as either **raw data** or **summary statistics data**.  Raw data is where all of the individual scores are available, as this is the usual situation when solving real life problems.  However, many statistics textbooks contain exercises which only give summary statistics data and show none of the original raw data.  Summary statistics include the: sample mean, sample variance, sample standard deviation, sample number of "successes", sample proportion of "successes" and sample size.  In many situations, Minitab Release 14 is able to do the statistical computations with either type of data.  But in those cases where Minitab has not been designed to directly deal with the specific situation, macros have been included on the data disc.   Macros are pre-written programs that contain many commands and subcommands in exactly the correct sequence, and these will be introduced in the next section of this chapter.

If there is only one population being analyzed,  the inferential methods are usually called "one sample" techniques.  Depending upon the distribution type and what parameters are known, a confidence interval for the mean of the population is computed using one of the following three formulas:

$$\text{(i)} \quad \bar{x} \mp Z\frac{\sigma}{\sqrt{n}} \qquad\qquad \text{(ii)} \quad \bar{x} \mp Z\frac{s}{\sqrt{n}} \qquad\qquad \text{(iii)} \quad \bar{x} \mp t\frac{s}{\sqrt{n}}$$

The $\mp$ in these formulas emphasize that you should subtract <u>first</u> and add <u>second</u> so as to end up with an interval from the **smaller** value to the **larger** value.  If formula (i) has been chosen as the appropriate confidence interval; the value of the population standard deviation ($\sigma$) will be known, and the *1-Sample Z* confidence interval is computed.

When the problem has raw data, this formula (i) is computed by

Click on *Stat , Basic Statistics , 1-Sample Z...*

In the 1-Sample Z (Test and Confidence Interval) dialog box: you may press the $\boxed{\text{F3}}$ key to clear the contents of this dialog box and reset all options and erase any previous variables. Make sure the button to the left of *Samples in columns* is selected, and then click inside of the box below. The variables (columns) will appear in the large box on the left side of this dialog box. If a previous variable is shown, erase the variable, click on the variable you want to analyze, and click on the $\boxed{\text{Select}}$ button. Next click inside of the box to the right of *Standard deviation:*, erase any current incorrect value, and type in the known value of the population standard deviation (σ). Make sure that the box to the left of *Perform hypothesis test* is **un**checked, and then click on the $\boxed{\text{Options...}}$ button.

In the 1-Sample Z - Options dialog box: if the value in the *Confidence level:* box is not the level you want, erase this value and type in the correct confidence level. Then make sure that the box to the right of *Alternative:* contains *not equal*. If not, click on the down triangle ( $\boxed{\blacktriangledown}$ ), and click on the *not equal* choice. Then click on $\boxed{\text{OK}}$ .

Back in the 1-Sample Z (Test and Confidence Interval) dialog box, click on $\boxed{\text{OK}}$ .

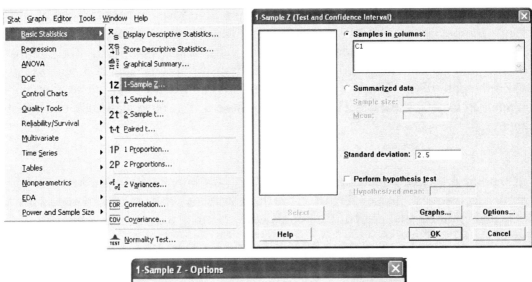

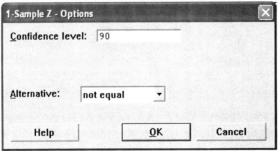

However, when the problem has summary statistics data, this formula (i) is computed by

Click on *Stat , Basic Statistics , 1-Sample Z...*

In the 1-Sample Z (Test and Confidence Interval) dialog box: you may press the [ **F3** ] key to clear the contents of this dialog box and reset all options and erase any previous variables. Make sure the button to the left of *Summarized data* is selected, and then click inside of the box to the right of *Sample size:*. Now type in the value of the sample size. Next click in the next box down that is to the right of *Mean:* and type in the value of the sample mean. Next click inside of the box to the right of *Standard deviation:,* erase any current incorrect value, and type in the known value of the population standard deviation ($\sigma$). Make sure that the box to the left of *Perform hypothesis test* is **un**checked, and then click on the [ **Options...** ] button.

In the 1-Sample Z - Options dialog box: if the value in the *confidence level:* box is not the level you want, erase this value and type in the correct confidence level. Then make sure that the box to the right of *Alternative:* contains *not equal*. If not, click on the down triangle ( [ ▼ ] ), and click on the *not equal* choice. Then click on [ **OK** ] .

Back in the 1-Sample Z (Test and Confidence Interval) dialog box, click on [ **OK** ] .

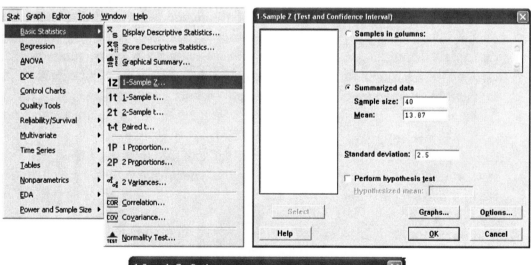

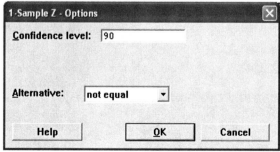

For both raw data and summary statistics data computations, the output of the *1-Sample Z* procedure contains:

(1)     the value you specified for σ, shown as **The assumed standard deviation = xx**,
(2)     the variable column label or name ,
(3)     the number of valid observations, the sample mean, sample standard deviation and standard error of the mean ($s/\sqrt{n}$) and
(4)     the specified confidence interval.

Even though this procedure computes the value of the sample standard deviation, this is done for information purposes only. The confidence interval is calculated using the entered value of sigma.

> Example 5.1:   A random sample of five boxes of cereal were taken from the production line, and each box was weighed with the following results: 23.0, 23.5, 25.0, 23.5 and 24.5 ounces. It is known that the weight of all boxes of this cereal are normally distributed with a population standard deviation of 0.85 ounces. Find a 98% confidence interval for the mean weight of all cereal boxes in the production process.

Enter these five scores into column 1 of the Worksheet Window. For this problem, formula (i) is the appropriate confidence interval.

Click on *Stat , Basic Statistics , 1-Sample Z...*

In the 1-Sample Z (Test and Confidence Interval) dialog box: you may press the $\boxed{\textbf{F3}}$ key to clear the contents of this dialog box and reset all options and erase any previous variables. Make sure the button to the left of *Samples in columns* is selected, and then click inside of the box below. Now the variables (columns) will appear in the large box on the left side of this dialog box. If a previous variable is shown, erase the variable, click on the C1 variable and click on the $\boxed{\textbf{Select}}$ button. Next click inside of the box to the right of *Standard deviation:*, erase any current incorrect value, and type in 0.85. Make sure that the box to the left of *Perform hypothesis test* is **un**checked, and then click on the $\boxed{\textbf{Options...}}$ button.

In the 1-Sample Z - Options dialog box: if the value in the *confidence level:* box is not the level you want, erase this value and type in 98. Then make sure that the box to the right of *Alternative:* contains *not equal*. If not, click on the down triangle ( $\boxed{\blacktriangledown}$ ), and click on the *not equal* choice. Then click on $\boxed{\textbf{OK}}$ .

Back in the 1-Sample Z (Test and Confidence Interval) dialog box, click on $\boxed{\textbf{OK}}$ .

The output below containing the 98% confidence interval will appear in the Session Window.

## One Sample Z: C1

**The assumed standard deviation = 0.85**

| Variable | N | Mean | StDev | SE Mean | 98 % C.I. |
|----------|---|---------|--------|---------|-------------------|
| C1 | 5 | 23.9000 | 0.8216 | 0.3801 | ( 23.0157, 24.7843) |

(continued on the next page)

90

And so the 98% confidence interval for the mean weight of all cereal boxes is from 23.02 to 24.79 ounces. If the cereal boxes are labeled 24 ounces, the production line would be considered in control; that is, working properly.

Example 5.2:  An instructor gave all freshmen at T.H.U. a standardized test for which she knows the value of $\sigma = 6$. A sample of 34 exams were graded and produced a mean score of 78. Compute a 90% confidence interval for the mean test score of all freshmen at T.H.U. Then Exit from Minitab.

With the sample size being greater than 30 and the population standard deviation ($\sigma$) being known, the appropriate confidence interval is computed using

$$\overline{x} \mp Z \frac{\sigma}{\sqrt{n}}$$

which is formula (i). However the data in this problem is summary statistics data.

Click on *Stat , Basic Statistics , 1-Sample Z...*

In the 1-Sample Z (Test and Confidence Interval) dialog box: you may press the | **F3** | key to clear the contents of this dialog box and reset all options and erase any previous variables. Make sure the button to the left of *Summarized data* is selected, and then click inside of the box to the right of *Sample size:*. If a previous value is shown, erase this number; and type in 34. Next click in the next box down that is to the right of *Mean:* and type in 78. Next click inside of the box to the right of *Standard deviation:*, erase any current incorrect value, and type in the known value of 6. Make sure that the box to the left of *Perform hypothesis test* is **un**checked, and then click on the | **Options...** | button.

In the 1-Sample Z - Options dialog box: erase the value in the *confidence level:* box and type in 90. Then make sure that the box to the right of *Alternative:* contains *not equal*. If not, click on the down triangle ( ▾ ), and click on the *not equal* choice. Then click on | **OK** | .

Back in the 1-Sample Z (Test and Confidence Interval) dialog box, click on | **OK** | .

The output below containing the 98% confidence interval will appear in the Session Window.


## One Sample Z

### The assumed standard deviation = 6

| N | Mean | SE Mean | 90 % C.I. |
|---|------|---------|-----------|
| 34 | 78.0000 | 1.0290 | ( 76.3075, 79.6925) |


And so the instructor is 90% confident that the interval from 76.31 to 79.69 contains the mean standardized test grade of all freshmen at T.H.U.

When formula (ii) is the appropriate confidence interval, and you have **raw data**; the sample standard deviation, s, must be calculated before computing the confidence interval. To avoid having to remember the value that Minitab computes for s, it is possible to store this value in a Minitab constant. These constants are labeled K1, K2, K3, etc., and are used to store single pieces of information that can be used later.

First the sample standard deviation is computed and stored into the constant K1 using *Column Statistics*

Click on *Calc , Column Statistics...*
In the Column Statistics dialog box: click on the circle to the left of *Standard deviation*, click inside of the *Input variable:* box, click on the variable that contains the sample data, and click on the | Select | button. Next click in the box to the **right** of *Store results in:*, and type in k1 as the constant name. (Minitab accepts lowercase k1 or uppercase K1 as the same constant.) Then click on the | OK | button.

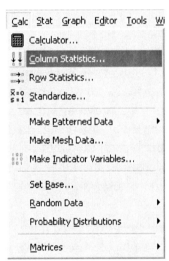
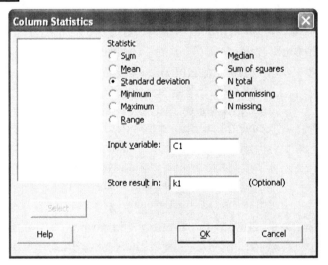

Then the confidence interval itself is computed again using the *1-Sample Z* procedure, but this time inserting the computed sample standard deviation (stored in K1) in the *Standard deviation:* box..

Click on *Stat , Basic Statistics , 1-Sample Z...*
In the 1-Sample Z (Test and Confidence Interval) dialog box: make sure the button to the left of *Samples in columns:* is selected, and then click inside of the box below. Now the variables (columns) will appear in the large box on the left side of this dialog box, click on the variable you want to analyze, and click on the | Select | button. Next click inside of the box to the right of *Standard deviation:,* and the constant K1 will appear in the large box on the left side of this dialog box. click on this K1 and click on the | Select | button (or just type k1 into this box). Make sure that the box to the left of *Perform hypothesis test* is **un**checked, and then click on the | Options... | button.

(Only the graphic for the second step is shown on the next page)

In the 1-Sample Z - Options dialog box: if the value in the *confidence level:* box is not the level you want, erase this value and type in the correct confidence level. Then make sure that the box to the right of *Alternative:* contains *not equal*. If not, click on the down triangle ( 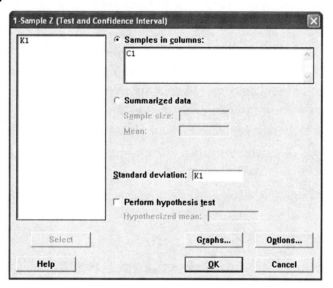 ), and click on the *not equal* choice. Then click on **OK** .

Back in the 1-Sample Z (Test and Confidence Interval) dialog box, click on **OK** .

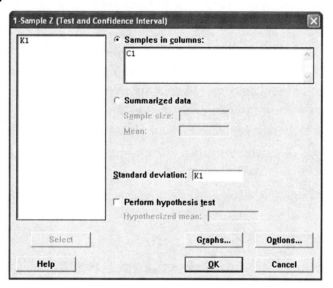

Example 5.3: Open the Study4.mtw worksheet that is on your data disc. Compute a 90% confidence interval for the mean age of the population of all students from which this sample was taken using formula (ii)

Use the *File , Open Worksheet...* to open the Study4.mtw from your data disc into a second worksheet. First the sample standard deviation must be computed and stored into the K1 constant.

Click on *Calc , Column Statistics...*

In the Column Statistics dialog box: click on the circle to the left of *Standard deviation*, click inside of the *Input variable:* box, click on the Age variable, and click on the *Select* button. Next click on the small square to the **left** of *Store results in:* to check this box, then click in the box to the **right** of *Store results in:*, and type in k1 as the constant name. Then click on **OK** .

The resulting output below will appear in the Session Window.

## Standard Deviation of Age

### Standard deviation of Age = 7.16678

Next the 90% confidence interval is computed.

(continued on the next page)

Click on *Stat , Basic Statistics , 1-Sample Z...*

In the 1-Sample Z (Test and Confidence Interval) dialog box: make sure the button to the left of *Samples in columns* is selected, and then click inside of the box below.  Now the variables (columns) will appear in the large box on the left side of this dialog box, click on the Age (C1) variable, and click on the [ Select ] button. Next click inside of the box to the right of *Standard deviation:,* and the constant K1 will appear  in the large box on the left side of this dialog box.  Click on this K1 and click on the [ Select ] button (or just type k1 into this box).  Make sure that the box to the left of *Perform hypothesis test* is **un**checked, and then click on the [ Options... ] button.

In the 1-Sample Z - Options dialog box: if the value in the *confidence level:* box is not 90, erase this value and type in the correct confidence level of 90.  Then make sure that the box to the right of *Alternative:* contains *not equal*.  If not, click on the down triangle ( [ ▾ ] ), and click on the *not equal* choice.  Then click on [ **OK** ] .

Back in the 1-Sample Z (Test and Confidence Interval) dialog box, click on [ **OK** ] .

The 90% confidence interval show below will appear in the Session Window.

## One Sample Z: Age

### The assumed standard deviation = 7.16678

| Variable | N | Mean | StDev | SE Mean | 90 % C.I. |
|---|---|---|---|---|---|
| Age | 34 | 24.0294 | 7.1668 | 1.2291 | ( 22.0077,  26.0511) |

And so you are 90% confident that the interval from 22.01 to 26.05 contains the mean age of all students from which this sample was taken.

If the appropriate confidence interval is computed using $\overline{x} \mp Z \dfrac{s}{\sqrt{n}}$ which is formula (ii),

and the problem has **summary statistics data**; then you do exactly the same as was shown for summary statistics data with formula (i), but you will type the given value of the sample standard deviation (s) in the box to the right of *Standard deviation:.*

When a sample is taken from a population which is normally distributed, but the value of the population's standard deviation ($\sigma$) is <u>not</u> known; a confidence interval for the population mean is based upon the Student's  t distribution, and formula (iii) is used.   The Minitab *1-Sample t* procedure is used to do this, and since this procedure always uses the sample standard deviation (symbolized as s), you do not have to compute the sample standard deviation separately.  When the problem has raw data, this formula (iii) is computed by

Click on *Stat , Basic Statistics , 1-Sample t...*

In the 1-Sample t (Test and Confidence Interval) dialog box: you may press the [ F3 ] key to clear the contents of this dialog box and reset all options and erase any previous variables. Make sure the button to the left of *Samples in columns* is selected, and then click inside of the box below. Now the variables (columns) will appear in the large box on the left side of this dialog box. If a previous variable is shown, erase the variable, click on the variable you want to analyze, and click on the [ Select ] button. Make sure that the box to the left of *Perform hypothesis test* is **un**checked, and then click on the [ Options... ] button.

In the 1-Sample t - Options dialog box: if the value in the *confidence level:* box is not the level you want, erase this value and type in the correct confidence level. Then make sure that the box to the right of *Alternative:* contains *not equal*. If not, click on the down triangle ( ▼ ), and click on the *not equal* choice. Then click on [ OK ] .

Back in the 1-Sample t (Test and Confidence Interval) dialog box, click on [ OK ] .

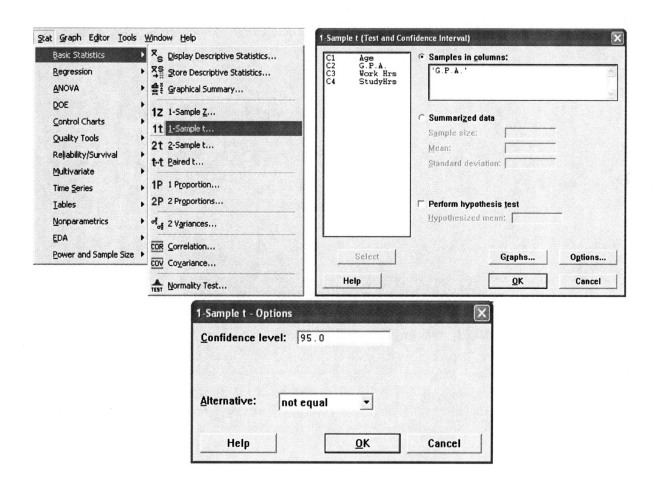

However, when the problem has summary statistics data, this formula (iii) is computed by

Click on *Stat , Basic Statistics , 1-Sample t...*

In the 1-Sample t (Test and Confidence Interval) dialog box: you may press the F3 key to clear the contents of this dialog box and reset all options and erase any previous variables. Make sure the button to the left of *Summarized data* is selected, and then click inside of the box to the right of *Sample size:*. If a previous value is shown, erase this number; and type in the value of the sample size. Next click in the next box down that is to the right of *Mean:* and type in the value of the sample mean. Next click inside of the box to the right of *Standard deviation:*, erase any current incorrect value, and type in the given value of the sample standard deviation. Make sure that the box to the left of *Perform hypothesis test* is **un**checked, and then click on the Options... button.

In the 1-Sample t - Options dialog box: if the value in the *confidence level:* box is not the level you want, erase this value and type in the correct confidence level. Then make sure that the box to the right of *Alternative:* contains *not equal*. If not, click on the down triangle ( ▾ ), and click on the *not equal* choice. Then click on OK .

Back in the 1-Sample t (Test and Confidence Interval) dialog box, click on OK .

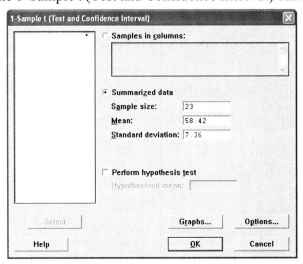

The output of *1-Sample t* is exactly the same as the output of the *1-Sample Z*; with the exception that expression **The assumed standard deviation = xx** is <u>not</u> printed.

Example 5.4:  Assume that the G.P.A. variable in the original population is normally distributed. Compute a 95% confidence interval for the average G.P.A. of the population of all students from which this sample was taken.

Since the population standard deviation is not known, formula (iii) is the correct confidence interval.

(continued on the next page)

Click on *Stat , Basic Statistics , 1-Sample t...*

In the 1-Sample t (Test and Confidence Interval) dialog box: you may press the [ **F3** ] key to clear the contents of this dialog box and reset all options and erase any previous variables. Make sure the button to the left of *Samples in columns* is selected, and then click inside of the box below. Now the variables (columns) will appear in the large box on the left side of this dialog box. If a previous variable is shown, erase the variable, click on the G.P.A. (C2) variable, and click on the [ Select ] button. Make sure that the box to the left of *Perform hypothesis test* is **un**checked, and then click on the [ **Options...** ] button.

In the 1-Sample t - Options dialog box: if the value in the *confidence level:* box is not 95, erase this value and type in the correct level of 95. Then make sure that the box to the right of *Alternative:* contains *not equal*. If not, click on the down triangle ( [▼] ), and click on the *not equal* choice. Then click on [ **OK** ].

Back in the 1-Sample t (Test and Confidence Interval) dialog box, click on [ **OK** ].

The 95% confidence interval show below will appear in the Session Window.

### One-Sample T: G.P.A.

| Variable | N | Mean | StDev | SE Mean | 95 % C.I. |
|----------|-----|---------|---------|---------|---------------------|
| G.P.A. | 29 | 2.65897 | 0.80617 | 0.14970 | ( 2.35232, 2.96561) |

And so you are 95% confident that the interval from 2.35 to 2.97 contains the average G.P.A. of all students in the original population. This confidence interval would lead you to doubt that the average G.P.A. of the population is 3.0 or better.

Example 5.5: The Consumer Safety Commission tested ten Hurvey full size sedans for their front bumper impact capability. Starting at 2 mph and increasing the speed by 1 mph, these automobiles were repeatedly run into a solid wall until the front bumper showed visible damage. The results of this test yielded a mean of 8.4 mph and a standard deviation of 2.31 mph. This data is known to come from a normally distributed population. Compute a 99% confidence interval for the mean impact speed at which all Hurvey full size sedans' front bumper will show visible damage.

The data is normally distributed, but the population standard deviation is unknown and the sample size is small, so the appropriate formula for this confidence interval is $\bar{x} \mp t\dfrac{s}{\sqrt{n}}$

which is formula (iii). Also, this problem has summary statistics data, and so the confidence interval is computed by

(continued on the next page)

97

Click on *Stat*, *Basic Statistics*, *1-Sample t...*

In the 1-Sample t (Test and Confidence Interval) dialog box: you may press the ⎡ F3 ⎤ key to clear the contents of this dialog box and reset all options and erase any previous variables. Make sure the button to the left of *Summarized data* is selected, and then click inside of the box to the right of *Sample size:*. If a previous value is shown, erase the variable, and type10 in this box. Next click in the next box down that is to the right of *Mean:* and type in 8.4. Next click inside of the box to the right of *Standard deviation:*, erase any current incorrect value, and type in 2.31 (the given value of the sample standard deviation). Make sure that the box to the left of *Perform hypothesis test* is **un**checked, and then click on the ⎡ **Options...** ⎤ button.

In the 1-Sample t - Options dialog box: if the value in the *confidence level:* box is not the level you want, erase this value and type in the correct confidence of 99. Then make sure that the box to the right of *Alternative:* contains *not equal*. If not, click on the down triangle ( ⎡ ▾ ⎤ ), and click on the *not equal* choice. Then click on ⎡ **OK** ⎤ .

Back in the 1-Sample t (Test and Confidence Interval) dialog box, click on ⎡ **OK** ⎤ .

The 99% confidence interval show below will appear in the Session Window.

## One-Sample T

| N | Mean | StDev | SE Mean | 99 % C.I. |
|---|------|-------|---------|-----------|
| 10 | 8.40000 | 3.21000 | 0.73049 | ( 6.02604,  10.77396) |

The Consumer Safety Commission is 99% confident that the interval from 6.03 to 10.77 mph contains the mean impact speed upon which the front bumper of all Hurvey full size sedans will exhibit visible damage.

# Lab Assignment 5.1.1

**Name:**                                                      **Date:**

**Course:**              **Section:**                **Data CD Number:**


1.   Start a Minitab session.  If you are unable to complete this lab assignment in one Minitab session, save the project as Lab 5-1-1 . **Never** use a period as part of the project name; since Minitab uses the period to attach the file type to the file name.  Then at your next Minitab session, you may open this Lab 5-1-1.MPJ project and continue to work where you left off previously.


2.   The following **describes** the data in the Tasktime.mtw worksheet saved on your data disc.

   A random sample of "cleaning" workers was taken and the time (in minutes) required to clean the production machine was recorded.   Another sample of "loading" workers was taken and the time (in minutes) to load the raw materials into the machine was recorded. The distribution of load times among all workers is normal.   Then twenty-three workers from the Method A assembly line were randomly selected, and their production times (in minutes) were measured.   Then these **same** workers were moved to the Method B assembly line, and their production times (in minutes) were measured.  It is known that production times by either of these two methods are normally distributed.

   a.   Open the worksheet Tasktime.mtw that is on your data disc.

   b.   Compute a 90% confidence interval for the mean loading time of all "loading" workers (who load the raw materials into the machine).

   c.   Compute a 98% confidence interval for the mean production time by all workers from the Method B assembly line.


3.   The distribution of late arrival times by all Gamma Airlines flights is normally distributed with a population standard deviation of 12 minutes.   A random sample of late Gamma Airline flights was taken, and the results are: 25, 14, 7, 1, 3, 34, 60, 37, 28, 18, 23, 34, 41 and 8 minutes.  Open a new Worksheet Window, enter the data, and find a 95% confidence interval for the mean late arrival time for all late Gamma Airline flights.   If the airline industry standards are:
> (a) Excellent - 0 to under 15 minutes late,
> (b) Good - 15 to under 40 minutes late, and
> (c) Poor - 40 or more minutes late;

how would you describe Gamma Airlines performance (Excellent, Good or Poor)?


(lab assignment is continued on the second side of this page)

4.  In order to justify sample auditing, a test case is designed. A population of sales invoices with a known standard deviation of $35 is constructed. Then an auditor takes a random sample of 50 invoices and computes the mean to be 256.35 dollars. Compute a 90% confidence interval for the population mean. Several weeks after this audit it was found that the actual population mean was $250.00 ; was the sample audit successful?

5.  Weights of new born babies are known to be normally distributed. A random sample of 23 newborn babies was taken and their weights in pounds were measured. The mean is 6.85 and the standard deviation is 1.47 . Compute a 99% confidence interval for the mean weight of all newborn babies.

6.  Print your Session Window to the printer.

7.  For each problem, show **all** of the work you did in determining which formula was the appropriate one to use. In addition to any statement about the confidence intervals, write any conclusion you would make for each problem where appropriate. Include any special discussions assigned by your instructor. This will be referred to as your complete answers in this and all future lab assignments.

8.  Attach both your Minitab output and your complete answers to this sheet and submit all three to your instructor.

# Lab Assignment 5.1.2

**Name:**                                          **Date:**

**Course:**              **Section:**              **Data CD Number:**

1.  Start a Minitab session. If you are unable to complete this lab assignment in one Minitab session, save the project as Lab 5-1-2 . **Never** use a period as part of the project name; since Minitab uses the period to attach the file type to the file name. Then at your next Minitab session, you may open this Lab 5-1-2.MPJ project and continue to work where you left off previously.

2.  The following **describes** the data in the Tasktime.mtw worksheet saved on your data disc.

    A random sample of "cleaning" workers was taken and the time (in minutes) required to clean the production machine was recorded. Another sample of "loading" workers was taken and the time (in minutes) to load the raw materials into the machine was recorded. The distribution of load times among all workers is normal. Then twenty-three workers from the Method A assembly line were randomly selected, and their production times (in minutes) were measured. Then these **same** workers were moved to the Method B assembly line, and their production times (in minutes) were measured. It is known that production times by either of these two methods are normally distributed.

    a.  Open the worksheet Tasktime.mtw that is on your data disc.

    b.  Compute a 90% confidence interval for the mean cleaning time of all "cleaning" workers (who clean the production machine).

    c.  Compute a 98% confidence interval for the mean production time by all workers from the Method A assembly line.

3.  The following **describes** the data in the Cespud.mtw worksheet saved on your data disc.

    The U.S. Department of Labor conducts Consumer Expenditure Surveys about U.S. households and creates data files for public use. A sample from the 1972 survey was taken and the following five variables were recorded:
      (i)   age of head of household,
      (ii)  marital status of head of household,
      (iii) total household income after taxes,
      (iv)  spending on food and clothing, and
      (v)   spending on shelter (rent, utilities, mortgages, etc.).

    (lab assignment is continued on the second side of this page)

a.  Open a second worksheet using Cespud.mtw from your data disc.

b.  Compute a 95% confidence interval for the average age of all heads of households in the United States in 1972.

4.  The Lonco Electric Company is advertising that their new 90 watt Extended Life light bulbs have an average lifetime of 2500 hours.  The Consumer Protection Agency tested a sample of 150 Lonco 90 watt Extended Life bulbs and computed the mean and standard deviation as 2460 and 210 hours respectively.  Compute a 95% confidence interval for the average lifetime of all Lonco Extended Life 90 watt light bulbs, and then say if the Consumer Protection Agency found the Lonco Electric Company in or out of compliance with the Fair Advertising Act.

5.  Soy bean yield (pounds per plant) is normally distributed.  In a controlled experiment, a random sample of 15 soy bean plants were grown under conditions where they received 2 inches of rainfall during the critical first month of growth.  After the first month the plants were placed outside with the rest of the soy bean crop.  The sample harvest produced a mean yield of 6.72 pounds per plant and a standard deviation of 0.74 pounds per plant.  Compute a 98% confidence interval for the mean yield of all soy bean plants grown under the experimental conditions.

6.  Print your Session Window to the printer.

7.  For each problem, show **all** of the work you did in determining which formula was the appropriate one to use.  In addition to any statement about the confidence intervals, write any conclusion you would make for each problem where appropriate.  Include any special discussions assigned by your instructor.  This will be referred to as your complete answers in this and all future lab assignments.

8.  Attach both your Minitab output and your complete answers to this sheet and submit all three to your instructor.

# Section 2: Confidence Intervals For The Variance and Standard Deviation of a Normal Population

The variance, symbolized by $\sigma^2$, and standard deviation, symbolized by $\sigma$, measure the dispersion of scores in a population. When the variable is a continuous type of measurement and has a normal distribution, a confidence interval for the variance of the population is computed using the formula

$$(iv) \quad \frac{(n-1)s^2}{\chi_U^2} \quad to \quad \frac{(n-1)s^2}{\chi_L^2}$$

where $\chi_U^2$ and $\chi_L^2$ are the upper and lower percentiles, respectively, of the Chi-Square distribution with (n-1) degrees of freedom A confidence interval for the standard deviation of the normally distributed population is computed by taking the square root of each term above to get the formula

$$(v) \quad \sqrt{\frac{(n-1)s^2}{\chi_U^2}} \quad to \quad \sqrt{\frac{(n-1)s^2}{\chi_L^2}}$$

For example; if the desired confidence level is 90%, then $\chi_U^2$ is the 95th (.95) percentile and $\chi_L^2$ is the 5th (.05) percentile of the Chi-Square distribution with (n-1) degrees of freedom.

Unlike the statistical procedures for computing confidence intervals for the population mean given in Section 1, Minitab does not provide special procedures to compute the confidence intervals for the population variance and standard deviation. Confidence intervals for $\sigma$ and $\sigma^2$ may be computed by using macros saved on your data disc. The macros for computing confidence intervals prompt you for the needed sample statistics, the sample size, and the desired confidence level. When prompted for the confidence level; enter the percent confidence level as a whole number, but do **not** add the % sign. The procedure for executing Minitab macros is as follows.

Click on *File , Other Files , Run an Exec ...*

In the Run an Exec dialog box: make sure the *Number of times to execute:* box contains the number 1, and then click on the | Select File | button.

In the Run an Exec dialog box: for Windows XP – click on the *Look in:* icon, and then click on the *Data Disc* (if this is not the drive shown), and for Windows Vista – click on computer in the left pane and then click on the Data Disc (if this is not the drive shown in the *Address* box). Next click on the desired macro file name to highlight this macro, and click on the | Open | button.

(See graphics on the next page.)

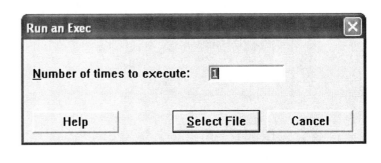

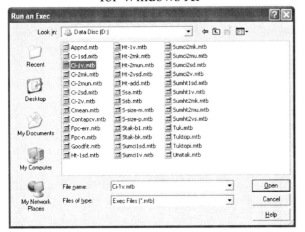

for Windows XP

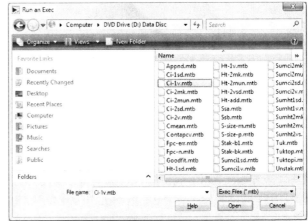

for Windows Vista

Note that Minitab macros may be used with **raw data** as well as with **summary statistics**, but that different macros are used depending upon which type of data you have in the problem. When the macros used with **raw data** prompt you to enter the number of the column that contains the raw data in the Worksheet Window; enter <u>only</u> the number and <u>not</u> the letter C. When prompted for the confidence level; enter the percent confidence as a whole number; **do <u>not</u> add the % sign nor the word percent**. The macro for computing a confidence interval for the variance of a normal population, formula (iv), is **Ci-1v.mtb**. The name of each macro is an indicator of what the macros does. For example, the macro name Ci-1v is short for **C**onfidence **i**nterval for **1 v**ariance. The Reference Guide lists the abbreviated instructions for executing a Minitab macro and the actual macro name for computing the corresponding confidence interval when the problem contains **raw data**. Do not confuse the **raw data** macro with the **summary statistic** macro, but use the appropriate one depending upon the type of data that is in the problem.

The Reference Guide in Appendix B lists all of the formulas used in this workbook that may be computed with Macros. This reference Guide also gives an abbreviated set of instructions for computing these formulas when Minitab has the computation built in to its menu system. Once you have worked through this workbook, the Reference Guide should be all that you need to effectively use Minitab for basic statistics computations. You are encouraged to make full use of this Reference Guide when doing textbook problems.

Example 5.6: Open the Study4.mtw worksheet from your data disc.  In Example 5.4 the G.P.A. variable was given to be normally distributed.  Compute a 95% confidence interval for the population variance of the G.P.A. variable.

Use *File , Open Worksheet...* to retrieve the Study4.mtw Worksheet from your data disc. Since the G.P.A. variable is normally distributed, the appropriate confidence interval is computed using

$$\frac{(n-1)s^2}{\chi_U^2} \quad \text{to} \quad \frac{(n-1)s^2}{\chi_L^2}$$

From the Reference Guide (Appendix B) in the table with the heading **One Sample Confidence Intervals for the Population Variance and Standard Deviation**, the **raw data** instructions say to execute the Ci-1v.mtb macro.  From the Study4.mtw Worksheet Window you see that the G.P.A. data is in column 2.

Click on *File , Other Files , Run an Exec ...*
In the Run an Exec dialog box: make sure the *Number of times to execute:* box contains the
　　number 1, and then click on the 　Select File 　button.
In the Run an Exec dialog box: make sure that the *Data Disc* is in the *Look in:* or *Address*
　　box. Next click on Ci-1v.mtb to highlight the macro file name, and click on the 　Open 　
　　button.

The steps for this macro are shown below.  The **bold italicized** words are displayed by Minitab in the Session Window, and the numbers you are to enter in the Session Window are shown in regular print.

***After the DATA> prompt, enter the column number that contains the data.***
***Enter ONLY the number, but NOT the C !***

***DATA>*** 2 　Enter　 　　　(since the G.P.A. variable is in column 2; i.e., C2)

***After the DATA> prompt, enter the confidence level.***

***DATA>*** 95 　Enter　

## Data Display

　　　***95.0 percent confidence interval for***
　　　　***the population variance of C 2:***

　　　　***0.4093　　to　　　1.1888***

and so you are 95% confident that the interval from 0.41 to 1.19 contains the variance of G.P.A. scores of all students in the original population.

The macro that computes a confidence interval for the standard deviation of a normal population is called **Ci-1sd** (Confidence interval for **1** standard deviation). This is also found in the Reference Guide in the table with the heading **One Sample Confidence Intervals for the Population Variance and Standard Deviation**.

Example 5.7:   Open another worksheet using Housing5.mtw from your data disc. Given that the Income variable is normally distributed, compute a 98% confidence interval for the population standard deviation of the Income variable.

Use *File , Open Worksheet...* to retrieve the Housing5.mtw Worksheet from your data disc. Since the Income variable is normally distributed, the appropriate confidence interval is computed using

$$\sqrt{\frac{(n-1)s^2}{\chi_U^2}} \ \text{to} \ \sqrt{\frac{(n-1)s^2}{\chi_L^2}}$$

From the Reference Guide in the table with the heading **One Sample Confidence Intervals for the Population Variance and Standard Deviation**, the **raw data** instructions say to execute the Ci-1sd macro. From the Housing5.mtw Worksheet Window you see that the Income data is in column 3.

Click on *File , Other Files , Run an Exec ...*

In the Run an Exec dialog box:  make sure the *Number of times to execute:* box contains the number 1, and then click on the | **Select File** | button.

In the Run an Exec dialog box:  make sure that the *Data Disc* is in the *Look in:* or *Address* box. Next click on Ci-1sd.mtb to highlight the macro file name, and click on the | **Open** | button.

The steps for this macro and resulting confidence interval shown on the next page will appear in the Session Window.

**After the DATA> prompt, enter the column number that contains the data. Enter ONLY the number, but NOT the C !**

**DATA>** 3 | **Enter** |        (since the Income variable is in column 3; i.e., <u>C3</u>)

**After the DATA> prompt, enter the confidence level.**

**DATA>** 98 | **Enter** |

## Data Display

**98.0 percent confidence interval for population standard deviation of C 3:**

**15497.0366  to   31842.9237**

and so you are 98% confident that the interval from $15,497.04 to $31,842.92 contains the standard deviation of incomes of all people in the original population.

There are several careless mistakes that you might make when using a saved macro from your data disc with raw data. One such error is to enter the letter C along with the column number. For example, suppose you entered C2 instead of just the number 2. Minitab will display the following error message.

**\* NOTE \* Text found in data line.**

but the macro will use just the number part and continue executing.

Another error is to include a % sign or the word percent after the confidence level. For example, suppose you entered 95% instead of just the number 95. Minitab will display the warning

**\* NOTE  \* Text found in data line.**

but will continue to compute the confidence interval with the correct confidence level. If you enter the confidence level as a decimal instead of a whole number (e.g., 0.95 instead of 95), Minitab will convert the decimal to the corresponding whole number percent and correctly compute the confidence interval.

The next potential error to be discussed is entering the number of a column that does <u>not</u> exist in the current worksheet. For example, suppose that the current worksheet has four variables: C1, C2, C3 and C4, but you entered the number 12 instead of just a 1 at the first **DATA>** prompt. Minitab would continue to prompt you for the confidence level and start the macro. Then several lines from the macro would be displayed in the Session Window followed by the following two error messages:

**\* ERROR \* Empty column , undefined or illegal stored constant at s**

**\* ERROR \* Completion of computation impossible.**

and then some more lines of error messages. If you make this type of mistake, simply start over again by clicking on *File, Other Files, Run an Exec...* and executing the same macro again. And at the **DATA>** prompt, enter the correct column number containing the data to be analyzed.

Finally, if your Session window does **not** have the **MTB >** prompt displayed, you will get an error box displayed that looks like

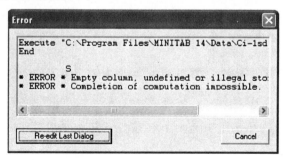

You must click on the    Cancel    button repeatedly until this error box disappears. Then do Options → Session Window → Submitting Commands → Command Language → Enable, as described in Chapter 1, to enable command language and get the **MTB >** prompt displayed in your Session Window. Now the Macro will function properly.

If at any time during a macro, you enter the wrong value and press the [ **Enter** ] key; simply enter a 1 for the rest of the **DATA>** prompts, allow the macro to compute some nonsense answer, execute the macro again, and enter the correct values.

Example 5.8: The commissioner of Minor League baseball is concerned about the disparity of salaries among all of the players. A random sample of 60 players was taken, and the salaries of each player was determined. The resulting mean and standard deviation are $39,450.45 and $8,462.12 respectively. Knowing that the minor league salaries are normally distributed, compute a 90% confidence interval for the standard deviation of all Minor League baseball players.

This problem involves **summary statistics** instead of **raw data** since the 60 individual salaries are not available, but only the resulting sample statistics. Since the Income variable is normally distributed, the appropriate confidence interval is computed using

$$\sqrt{\frac{(n-1)s^2}{\chi_U^2}} \quad \text{to} \quad \sqrt{\frac{(n-1)s^2}{\chi_L^2}}$$

which is formula (iv). From the Reference Guide in the table with the heading **One Sample Confidence Intervals for the Population Variance and Standard Deviation**, and in the Summary Statistics Technique column; the macro to be executed is Sumci1sd.mtb .

Click on *File* , *Other Files* , *Run an Exec ...*

In the Run an Exec dialog box: make sure the *Number of times to execute:* box contains the number 1, and then click on the [ **Select File** ] button.

In the Run an Exec dialog box: make sure that the *Data Disc* is in the *Look in:* or *Address* box. Next click on Sumci1sd.mtb to highlight the macro file name (you may need to scroll through list box), and click on the [ **Open** ] button.

The macro proceeds by asking you to enter the sample standard deviation (remember do **not** include the comma as part of the number), the sample size, and the confidence level. After each **DATA>** prompt, you will enter the requested number and then press the [ **Enter** ] key. The steps for this Summary Statistics macro are shown below. The ***bold italicized*** words are displayed by Minitab in the Session Window, and the numbers you are to enter in the Session Window are shown in regular print.

***After the DATA> prompt, enter the Sample standard deviation.***

***DATA>*** 8462.12 [ **Enter** ]　　　(Remember, you do **not** enter any commas within the number)

***After the DATA> prompt, enter the Sample size***

***DATA>*** 60 [ **Enter** ]

***After the DATA> prompt, enter the confidence level.***

***DATA>*** 90 [ **Enter** ]

(continued on the next page)

### *Data Display*

**90.0 percent confidence interval for the population standard deviation is:**

**7362.9421 to 9989.2598**

And so the commissioner is 90% confident that the interval from \$7,362.94 to \$9,989.26 contains the standard deviation of salaries of all players in Minor League baseball.

The Summary Statistics Macro **Sumcilv.mtb** is used for computing

$$\frac{(n-1)s^2}{\chi_U^2} \text{ to } \frac{(n-1)s^2}{\chi_L^2} ,$$

which is formula (iv) and is given in the Reference Guide in the table with the heading of **One Sample Confidence Intervals for the Population Variance and Standard Deviation**.

# Lab Assignment 5.2.1

**Name:**                                                                                  **Date:**

**Course:**                          **Section:**                                     **Data CD Number:**

1.   Start a Minitab session. If you are unable to complete this lab assignment in one Minitab session, save the project as Lab 5-2-1 . **Never** use a period as part of the project name; since Minitab uses the period to attach the file type to the file name. Then at your next Minitab session, you may open this Lab 5-2-1.MPJ project and continue to work where you left off previously.

2.   Open the worksheet Majorage.mtw that is on your data disc. This worksheet contains the ages of four independent samples of art, economics, mathematics and psychology majors at Bowling Green University.  The ages are normally distributed for the students in each of these four majors at Bowling Green University.

   a.   Compute a 90% confidence interval for the variance of age of all mathematics majors at Bowling Green University. The **standard deviation** of all college students in Ohio is 3.25 years.  Discuss how the variation of ages of mathematics majors at Bowling Green University compares to that of all Ohio college students (i.e., more, less or about the same).

   b.   Compute a 99% confidence interval for the standard deviation of age of all art majors at Bowling Green University.  How does the standard deviation of ages of all art majors at Bowling Green University compare to that of all Ohio college students?

3.   Open another worksheet using Tasktime.mtw from your data disc. As described in Lab Assignment 5.1.1, the distribution of load times among all "loading" workers is normal. Compute a 95% confidence interval for the standard deviation of load times by all "loading" workers.

4.   A random sample of 15 apples from a large shipment were weighed with the following results:  16, 12, 14, 20, 16, 13, 18, 20, 14, 15, 19, 15, 15, 20 and 17 grams.  The weights of this shipment of apples are known to be normally distributed.  Compute a 90% confidence interval for the variance of weights of all apples in the large shipment. The quality control manager wants the apples to look uniform in the store's display case, and the size of the apples to have a variance less than 15 grams$^2$.  Will the manager accept this large shipment of apples (population), or will the shipment be returned to the packing house?  Start a new worksheet (*File , New , Minitab Worksheet*) and enter this data into column C1.

   (lab assignment is continued on the second side of this page)

5.    After one full year of using the phonetic approach to teach reading, the school board wanted to known if the gains in the students' reading scores were consistent. Research has shown that reading score gains are normally distributed. A sample of 35 students was taken and the gain in reading scores was measured. The sample mean and standard deviation were 1.2 years and .35 years respectively. Compute a 90% confidence interval for the standard deviation of reading score gains for all students taught by the phonetic method.

6.    Research is being done concerning the decibel level at which loud noise becomes physically painful to adults with no hearing problems. So far the research has determined that these threshold scores are normally distributed. A random sample of 18 able hearing adults produced a mean threshold value of 135 decibels and a standard deviation of 20 decibels. Compute a 95% confidence interval for the variance of threshold scores for all adults with no hearing problems.

7.    Print your Session Window to the printer.

8.    Attach both your Minitab output and your complete answers to this sheet and submit all three to your instructor.

# Lab Assignment 5.2.2

**Name:**                                                              **Date:**

**Course:**                    **Section:**                    **Data CD Number:**


1.  Start a Minitab session. If you are unable to complete this lab assignment in one Minitab session, save the project as Lab 5-2-2 . **Never** use a period as part of the project name; since Minitab uses the period to attach the file type to the file name. Then at your next Minitab session, you may open this Lab 5-2-2.MPJ project and continue to work where you left off previously.

2.  A precision instrument used to measure the diameter of steel shafts is guaranteed to be accurate. This guarantee is stated that if the same object is measured many times, the standard deviation of all possible readings on that object will be less than 4 mm. The population of all instrument readings is known to be normally distributed. Before purchasing such an instrument, the buyer takes a sample of readings on the same steel shaft with the following results: 356, 352, 357, 358, 354, 353, 356, 355, 359, 356, 353 and 352 mm. Compute a 95% confidence interval for the population standard deviation of all possible readings on that shaft. Would the buyer accept this particular instrument as meeting the guarantee?

3.  Open the worksheet Majorage.mtw that is on your data disc. As described in Lab Assignment 5.2.1, this worksheet contains the ages of four independent samples of art, economics, mathematics and psychology majors at Bowling Green University. The ages are normally distributed for the students in each of these four majors at Bowling Green University. And the **standard deviation** of ages of all college students in Ohio is 3.25 years.

    a.  Compute a 98% confidence interval for the variance of ages of all economics majors at Bowling Green University. Discuss how the variation of ages of economics majors at Bowling Green University compares to that of all Ohio college students (i.e., more, less or about the same).

    b.  Compute a 95% confidence interval for the standard deviation of age of all psychology majors at Bowling Green University. How does the standard deviation of ages of all psychology majors at Bowling Green University compare to that of all Ohio college students?

4.  Open another worksheet using Tasktime.mtw from your data disc. As described in Lab Assignment 5.1.2, the distribution of production times among all workers from the Method B assembly line is normal. Compute a 90% confidence interval for the standard deviation of production times by all workers who from the Method B assembly line.

(lab assignment is continued on the second side of this page)

113

5. When tomatoes are grown in a greenhouse, the weight of these "hothouse" tomatoes is normally distributed. A horticulturist sampled 40 such tomatoes and found their weights to have a mean and variance of 6.32 oz. and 1.3 oz.$^2$ respectively. Compute a 90% confidence interval for the variance of weight of all "hothouse" tomatoes.

6. Bicycle tires come in various sizes, but a common size is 700 x 23. One consumer complaint is that some tires seem easy to mount onto the bicycle rims while others are very difficult to put on. The quality control department has determined that the actual diameters of all of their 700 x 23 tires are normally distributed, and now wants to compute a 99% confidence interval for the standard deviation of diameters of all such tires. A sample of 35 tires was measured. The mean diameter is 699.99 cm and the standard deviation is 0.008 cm. What is the desired confidence interval?

7. Print your Session Window to the printer.

8. Attach both your Minitab output and your complete answers to this sheet and submit all three to your instructor.

**Section 3:    Confidence Interval For The Population Proportion of "Successes"**

The previous two sections considered variables which were of a continuous type of measurement. This section will consider a discrete variable which may have only two possible outcomes, usually labeled "success" and "failure". A variable of this type of measurement is called a Bernoulli variable, and the parameter of interest is the population proportion of "successes". This parameter is usually symbolized by the lower case letter **p** (or sometimes the Greek letter $\pi$). If the sample size is sufficiently large (often interpreted as requiring both $n\hat{p} \geq 5$ and $n(1-\hat{p}) \geq 5$ or equivalently $y \geq 5$ and $(n-y) \geq 5$ ), a confidence interval for the proportion of the population which are "successes" is computed using the formula

$$\text{(vi)} \quad \hat{p} \mp Z\sqrt{\frac{\hat{p}(1-\hat{p})}{n}}$$

where $\hat{p} = \frac{Y}{n}$ is the proportion of the sample that is "success", and Y is the number of "successes" in the sample.

This confidence interval is computed using the *1 Proportion* procedure. The data for a Bernoulli type variable **must** be entered in the Worksheet Window into a variable (column) such that the **exact same** coding is used for each "success" and the **exact same** coding is used for each "failure." If you are entering alphabetic symbols or words, then you must use the exact same upper case and lower case letters each time for each "success" and for each "failure." As an alternative you may code each "success" outcome an one (1) and each "failure" outcome as a zero (0). Furthermore, if you enter alphabetic symbols or words, Minitab **always** assigns "failure" to the one that comes first in alphabetical order, and assigns "success" to the one that comes last in alphabetical order. So if you enter M for male and F for female: (1) you must use all of the same case for the Ms and all of the same case for the Fs, and (2) Minitab will assign "success" to the M (male) outcome.

If you want female to be the "success" outcome, you have two options. One is to code male and female so that the female code comes alphabetically after the male code; for example, code male as X-Male and code the female as Y-Female. A second option is to have Minitab recode the Ms to 0s and the Fs to 1s. This is done using the *Data* item from the menu bar.

Click on *Data, Code , Text to Numeric ...*

In the Code - Text to Numeric dialog box only the columns with alphabetic (text) will be displayed in the box on the left. The cursor should be in the box under the heading *Code data from columns:*, then click on the variable (column) that contains the text you want to code to 0s and 1s and click on ⬛ **Select** ⬛ . Next click in the *Into columns:* box and type in a **new** column number C#. Then click in the first box under the *Original values* heading and type in the alphabetic symbol or word that was used for the "failure" outcome. Next click in the first box under the *New:* heading and type in the number 0. Similarly on the second row enter the symbol or word that was used for the "success" outcome and the number 1. Then click ⬛ **OK** ⬛ .

(See graphics on the next page.)

115

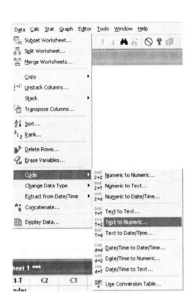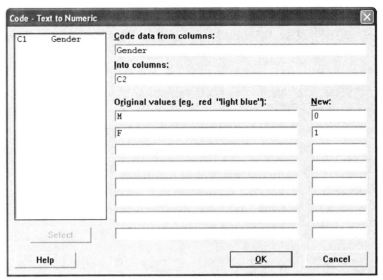

So that before you code the Gender (C1) variable, the Worksheet Window might look like the graphic below on the left; and after you use *Data, Code, Text to Numeric*, the Worksheet Window might look like the graphic below on the right

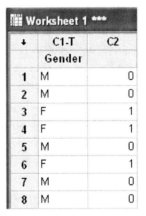

Once the raw data is in the correct format, the confidence interval is computed from formula (vi) on page 105 using the *1 Proportion* procedure as follows.

Click on *Stat , Basic Statistics , 1 Proportion ...*

In the 1 Proportion (Test and Confidence Interval) dialog box: make sure the button to the left of *Samples in columns* is selected, and then click inside of the box below and erase any previous variables. Now the variables (columns) will appear in the large box on the left side of this dialog box, click on the variable you want to analyze, and click on the **Select** button. Then click on the **Options...** button.

In the 1 Proportion - Options dialog box: if the value in the *confidence level:* box is not the level you want, erase this value and type in the correct confidence level. Next make sure that the box to the right of *Alternative:* contains *not equal*. If not, click on the down triangle ( ▾ ), and click on the *not equal* choice. Then make sure that the box to the left of *Use test and interval based on normal distribution* is checked. Then click on **OK** .

Back in the 1 Proportion (Test and Confidence Interval) dialog box, click **OK** .

(See graphics on the next page.)

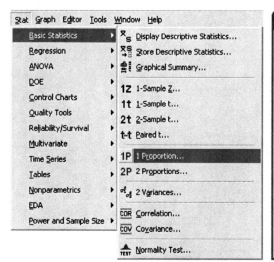 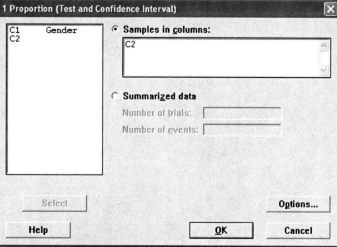

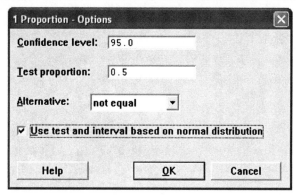

Problems that contain only summary statistics instead of raw data also can be done using the *1 Proportion* procedure. The only change is in the 1 Proportion (Test and Confidence Interval) dialog box where you indicate you are using summary statistics (*Summarized data*) instead of raw data.

Click on *Stat , Basic Statistics , 1 Proportion ...*

In the 1 Proportion (Test and Confidence Interval) dialog box: make sure the button to the left of *Summarized data* is selected, and then click inside of the box to the right of *Number of trials:*. In this box erase any previous value and type in the sample size. Next click inside of the box to the right of *Number of events:*, erase any previous value and type in the number of "successes" in the sample. Then click on the **Options...** button.

In the 1 Proportions - Options dialog box: if the value in the *confidence level:* box is not the level you want, erase this value and type in the correct confidence level. Next make sure that the box to the right of *Alternative:* contains *not equal*. If not, click on the down triangle ( ▼ ), and click on the *not equal* choice. Then make sure that the box to the left of *Use test and interval based on normal distribution* is checked. Then click on **OK** .

Back in the 1 Proportion dialog box, click on **OK** .

(The first and third graphic are exactly the same as shown above, and so only the second graphic is shown on the next page.)

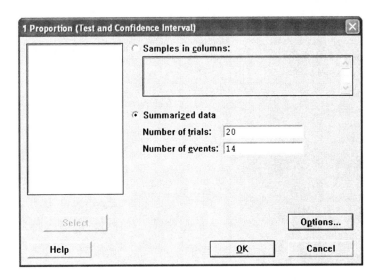

This *1 Proportion* procedure computes both a confidence interval and a hypothesis test (discussed in Chapter 7) for the population proportion of "successes" - p. The output of the *1 Proportion* procedure contains:

(1) the statement of the null and alternative hypotheses (discussed in Chapter 7),
(2) the outcome Minitab assigns as "success" written as **Event = outcome** (only for raw data),
(3) the variable name or column number (for raw data) or the sample number - usually 1 - (for summarized data)
(4) the number of "successes" (which is labeled **X**),
(5) the sample size,
(6) the value of the sample proportion of "successes" - $\hat{p}$ (which is labeled **Sample p**) ,
(7) the specified confidence interval,
(8) the value of the Z test statistic (explained in Chapter 7),
(9) the p-value (explained in Chapter 7), and
(10) a warning if the criteria for using formula (vi) are not met.

Example 5.9: Find a 98% confidence interval for the proportion of males in grade 1. A sample of 30 first graders was taken with the following results:

M, M, M, F, M, M, M, F, F, M, M, M, M, F, M, M, F, M, F, F, M, F, F, M F, M, M, F, F and M.

In this example you are concerned about the proportion of males in the population, therefore the "success" outcome is male and so the outcomes may be entered as M and F.

First enter the data into column 1 directly into the Worksheet Window and name the variable Grade 1.

(continued on the next page)

Since "success" is M and this comes after F in the alphabet, no recoding is needed.; and the confidence interval is computed using formula (vi) on the page 111.

Click on *Stat , Basic Statistics , 1 Proportion ...*

In the 1 Proportion (Test and Confidence Interval) dialog box: make sure the button to the left of *Samples in columns* is selected, and then click inside of the box below and erase any previous variables. Now the variables (columns) will appear in the large box on the left side of this dialog box, click on the Grade 1 (C1) variable, and click on the  Select  button. Then click on the  Options...  button.

In the 1 Proportion - Options dialog box: if the value in the *confidence level:* box is not 98, erase this value and type in the correct level of 98. Next make sure that the box to the right of *Alternative:* contains *not equal*. If not, click on the down triangle ( ▾ ), and click on the *not equal* choice. Then make sure that the box to the left of *Use test and interval based on normal distribution* is checked. Then click on  OK  .

Back in the 1 Proportion (Test and Confidence Interval) dialog box, click  OK  .

The resulting output shown on the next page will appear in the Session Window.

## Test and CI for One Proportion: Grade 1

### Test of p = 0.5 vs p not = 0.5

### Event = M

| Variable | X | N | Sample p | 98.0 % CI | Z-Value | P-Value |
|----------|---|---|----------|-----------|---------|---------|
| Grade 1 | 18 | 30 | 0.600000 | (0.391925, 0.808075) | 1.10 | 0.273 |

and so you are 98% confident that the interval from 0.39 to 0.81 contains the proportion of all first graders who are male.

Example 5.10:   Find a 95% confidence interval for the proportion of females in grade 2. A sample of 30 second graders was taken with the following results: 19 males and 11 females.

In this example, female is the "success" outcome. Since the number of "successes" = 11 and the number of "failures" = 19, and both are $\geq$ 5, the confidence interval is computed using

$$\hat{p} \mp Z \sqrt{\frac{\hat{p}(1-\hat{p})}{n}}$$

(continued on the next page)

Click on *Stat*, *Basic Statistics*, *1 Proportion ...*

In the 1 Proportion (Test and Confidence Interval) dialog box: make sure the button to the left of *Summarized data* is selected, and then click inside of the box to the right of *Number of trials:*. In this box erase any previous value and type in the sample size of 30. Next click inside of the box to the right of *Number of events:*, erase any previous value and type in 11. Then click on the ⬛ Options... ⬛ button.

In the 1 Proportions - Options dialog box: if the value in the *confidence level:* box is not 95, erase this value and type in the correct level of 95. Next make sure that the box to the right of *Alternative:* contains *not equal*. If not, click on the down triangle ( ▾ ), and click on the *not equal* choice. Then make sure that the box to the left of *Use test and interval based on normal distribution* is checked. Then click on ⬛ OK ⬛ .

Back in the 1 Proportion dialog box, click on ⬛ OK ⬛ .

The resulting output shown below will appear in the Session Window.

## Test and CI for One Proportion

### Test of p = 0.5 vs p not = 0.5

| Sample | X | N | Sample p | 95.0 % CI | Z-Value | P-Value |
|--------|----|----|----------|--------------------------|---------|---------|
| 1 | 11 | 30 | 0.366667 | (0.194226, 0.539107) | -1.46 | 0.144 |

and so you are 95% confident that the interval from 0.19 to 0.54 contains the proportion of all second graders who are female.

Note that if the conditions of both $y \geq 5$ and $(n-y) \geq 5$ are **not** met, Minitab will add a line at the bottom of the output warning you that these conditions have not been fulfilled. This warning is displayed as

### The normal approximation may be inaccurate for small samples.

and in such cases you will need to increase the sample size or use the exact binomial technique.

# Lab Assignment 5.3.1

**Name:**                                                 **Date:**

**Course:**                  **Section:**                       **Data CD Number:**

1. Start a Minitab session. If you are unable to complete this lab assignment in one Minitab session, save the project as Lab 5-3-1 . **Never** use a period as part of the project name; since Minitab uses the period to attach the file type to the file name. Then at your next Minitab session, you may open this Lab 5-3-1.MPJ project and continue to work where you left off previously.

2. A study was done to determine the proportion of all Ohio graduate students who plan to remain in Ohio after graduation. A random sample of Ohio graduate students was asked and the responses were:

   L , R , R , L , L , R , L , R , R , R , L , L , R , L , L , L , R , L , R , L , L , R , L ,   L , R , R , L , L , R   and   L.

   where
   > R = plan to remain in Ohio after graduation, and
   > L = plan to leave Ohio after graduation.

   Enter the data into the current Worksheet Window in column 1 using the alphabetic symbols L and R. Compute a 90% confidence interval for the proportion of all graduate students in Ohio who plan to remain in the state after graduation.

3. A psychologist conducted an experiment in which she wanted to find the proportion of all students at her university who, when in a sleep deprived state of mind, prefer the color blue over red. She randomly chose 27 sleep deprived students at her university and asked them to choose between blue and red. Their responses were:

   Blue , Blue , Red , Blue , Red , Blue , Blue , Blue , Red , Red , Blue , Blue , Red , Blue , Blue , Red , Red , Blue , Blue , Blue , Red , Red , Red , Blue, Blue, Red and Blue.

   Enter the data into the current Worksheet Window in column 3 using the alphabetic words Blue and Red. Since Blue is the "success" outcome, code the Red to 0 and the Blue to 1 and place these coded values into column 4. Name this 4th column ColorPrf. Compute a 98% confidence interval for the proportion of all sleep deprived students at the psychologist's university who prefer the color Blue.

   (lab assignment is continued on the second side of this page)

4.    Open a second worksheet using Cespud.mtw from your data disc.  As described in Lab Assignment 5.1.2; the data is a sample of households from the 1972 U.S. Consumer Expenditure Survey.  One of the variables (C2) is the marital status (0=unmarried and 1=married) of the head of the household.  Compute a 99% confidence interval for the population proportion of heads of households who are married.

5.    The Northern Mutual Insurance Company surveyed fifty of its car insurance customers. Fifteen said they had never received a driving ticket, while the rest had at least one citation on their driving record.  Compute a 95% confidence interval for the proportion of all Northern Mutual Insurance Company's car insurance customers who have a clean "lifetime driving record."

6.    First print your **Worksheet 1** Window, but **not** the Cespud.mtw Worksheet Window to the printer, and then print your Session Window to the printer.

7.    Attach both your Minitab output and <u>your complete answers</u> to this paper and submit all three to your instructor.

# Lab Assignment 5.3.2

**Name:**                                                 **Date:**

**Course:**                   **Section:**                            **Data CD Number:**

1.     Start a Minitab session. If you are unable to complete this lab assignment in one Minitab session, save the project as Lab 5-3-2 . **Never** use a period as part of the project name; since Minitab uses the period to attach the file type to the file name. Then at your next Minitab session, you may open this Lab 5-3-2.MPJ project and continue to work where you left off previously.

2.     As the price of gasoline rises, the American Automobile Association (AAA) wants to predict the proportion of people who have changed their commuting means from private automobile to public transportation. They randomly selected 35 people who drove their own car to work in 2007 and asked them if they had switched to public transportation. The results of this survey were:

   D , C , D , D , D , C , D , D , C , D , D , C , D , D , D , C , D , D , D , D , C , D , D , D , D , D , P , C , D , D , D , D , D , C and D

   where
   > C = changed to public transportation and
   > D = still drive private automobile to work.

   Enter the data into column 1 of the current Worksheet Window using the alphabetic symbols C and D. Since C is the "success" outcome, code the D to 0 and the C to 1 and place these coded values into column 2. Name this 2nd column Commuter Choice. Compute a 90% confidence interval for the proportion of all American commuters by private automobile in 2007 who have changed to commuting by public transportation in 2008.

3.     The National Football League's Super Bowl is one of the most watched television programs in the United States. A survey randomly selected homes was taken this past January, and each household was asked if it was watching television, and if so, what program it was viewing. The possibilities were SuperBowl, Heros, Housewives, Bones, Girlfriends and None (television not turned on). The results of this survey are in the Tvsurvey.mtw worksheet that is saved on your data disc. Choose an empty column and name it Survey. Then code any None responses as missing data. For text data, this needs to be an empty cell; and would be done by coding None to "" (two quotes with no space between them). Code all other non SuperBowl responses as Other. Now display the data in this Survey column in the Session Window. Then compute a 95% confidence interval for the proportion of all United States households watching television which were tuned to the Super Bowl.

   (lab assignment is continued on the second side of this page)

4. With the almost universal Salk and then Sabin vaccine inoculation of pre-school children in the last third of the 20<sup>th</sup> Century, many health authorities believed that polio had been eradicated in the United States. And so they suggested that these vaccines no longer be administer to children since the extremely small chance of contracting polio from the vaccine was now larger than the chance (zero percent they now believed) of contracting polio. However in 2008 cases of polio have been diagnosed again in the United States. In a recent survey of departments of health; out of 85,250 randomly selected children, 13 were diagnosed with a form of polio. Compute a 99% confidence interval for the proportion of all United State children who have been diagnosed with a from of polio.

5. Many companies have stopped offering their employees a company based retirement plan, and instead are offering to match the employees contribution (up to a certain limit) to his or her private 401K retirement plan. However many fiscal planners are concerned that the employees will not take advantage of this plan since it means that the employee will have to contribute to the plan and manage it. Instead many employees may opt to get a larger paycheck nor, and not worry about the future. In a random survey of 300 employees of companies with this new policy, 226 took advantage of the employer's contribution and setup private 401K retirement plans. Compute a 98% confidence interval for the proportion of all employees in companies that offer only to contribute to the 401K plans who actually setup such plans for their future retirement.

6. First print your **Worksheet 1** Window, but **not** the Tvsurvey.mtw Worksheet Window to the printer, and then print your Session Window to the printer.

7. Attach both your Minitab output and <u>your complete answers</u> to this paper and submit all three to your instructor.

**Section 4:     Choosing a Sample Size**

All of the examples and lab assignment problems contain data from samples that have already been collected.  However, when one begins a "real world" estimation problem, often the sample does not exist.  One of the first tasks is to choose an appropriate sample size. There are several ways to approach such problems.  One is to take as large of a sample as possible, constrained only by the time and money allocated to the specific problem.  This approach has the advantage that it will produce the smallest error of estimation possible within the constraints of the problem. However, this approach has several disadvantages.  On one hand this error of estimation still may be larger than desired, and thus the resulting confidence interval is of little use.  On the other hand this error of estimation may be smaller than is needed, and thus time and money were wasted in taking such a large sample.

The second approach is to choose an optimal size sample satisfying two predetermined needs.  Before collecting sample data, one must decide upon (1) the confidence level and (2) the size of the error of estimation needed  so that the resulting confidence interval will be satisfactory. The error of estimation is also interpreted as how close one believes that the point estimate is to the true population value, with a certain amount of confidence.  This section will show how to compute such optimal sample sizes in two situations.  One where the data is continuous and the population mean is to be estimated after the sample size is determined, and the second case for Bernoulli data where a confidence interval for the population proportion of "successes" is to be computed after the sample size has been determined.  In either case, once the optimal sample size has been computed, you need to determine if you have enough time and money allocated to take a sample of this size.

In the first situation where the data is continuous and the population mean is to be estimated, the formula for computing the optimal sample size is

$$\text{(vii)} \quad n = \left[ \frac{Z\sigma}{E} \right]^2$$

where the value for Z is replaced with the appropriate percentile from the Z table and the E is replaced with the desired error of estimation.  If the value of the population standard deviation ($\sigma$) is unknown, then $\sigma$ must be replaced with an "estimate."  Choices for this estimate include:

(1)     take a small (less than 30) pilot sample, compute this sample's standard deviation, and use the result as the "estimate";

(2)     use the value of the standard deviation from a previous similar study as the "estimate"; or

(3)     make an educated guess of the typical range for most of the data (about the central 95%), divide this range by 4, and use the result as the "estimate."

The macro that computes the appropriate optimal sample size is **S-size-m.mtb** (Sample **size** for **m**eans), and is executed using *File , Other Files , Run an Exec* from the Minitab menu bar.  This macro will prompt you for the desired confidence level, the size of the error of estimation that is needed, and the value of the population standard deviation ($\sigma$) or an "estimate" of $\sigma$.

Example 5.11:  Grey and Associates, an accounting firm, has been contracted to audit the sales invoices of a large retailer. Since an 100% audit is costly and time consuming, the retailer has agreed to a sampling audit. The retailer requires a 98% confidence interval for the population mean invoice amount with an error of estimation of no more than 35 cents. The auditor from Grey and Associates took a small pilot sample of invoices and computed the standard deviation to be 3.75 dollars. What size sample should be selected by the auditor?

The predetermined confidence level is 98% and the desired error of estimation is 0.35 . Formula (vii) from the previous page is used to compute the optimal sample size. As computed from the pilot sample, the auditor will use the standard deviation of 3.75 as the "estimate" of σ.

Click on *File , Other Files , Run an Exec ...*

In the Run an Exec dialog box:  make sure the *Number of times to execute:* box contains the number 1, and then click on the [ **Select File** ] button.

In the Run an Exec dialog box:  make sure that the *Data Disc* is in the *Look in:* or *Address* box. Next click on S-size-m.mtb to highlight the macro file name, and click on the [ **Open** ] button.

The steps for this macro are shown below. The **bold italicized** words are displayed by Minitab in the Session Window, and the numbers you are to enter in the Session Window are shown in regular print.

**After the DATA> prompt, enter the confidence level.**

**DATA>** 98 [ Enter ]

**After the DATA> prompt, enter the desired Error of Estimation.**

**DATA>** 0.35 [ Enter ]

**After the DATA> prompt, enter the Population Standard Deviation or your best guess of the Population Standard Deviation.**

**DATA>** 3.75 [ Enter ]

## Data Display

**To compute a 98.0 percent confidence interval for the population mean with a      0.35  error of estimation,  the sample size needed is:      622**

and so the auditor determined that a random sample of 622 invoices should be selected in order satisfy the predetermined needs of the retailer.

In the second case for Bernoulli data where a confidence interval for the population proportion of "successes" is to be computed, the formula for computing the optimal sample size is

$$\text{(viii)} \quad n = p(1 - p)\left[\frac{Z}{E}\right]^2$$

where the value for Z is replaced with appropriate percentile from the Z table and the E is replaced with the desired error of estimation. The value of the population proportion of "successes" is unknown, since it is to be estimated after the optimal sample size is computed. Therefore the value of p must be replaced with an "estimate." Choices for this estimate include:

(1) take a small (less than 30) pilot sample, compute this sample's proportion of "successes", and use the result as the "estimate";

(2) use the value of the proportion of "successes" from a previous similar study as the "estimate";

(3) make an educated point guess of the proportion of "successes", and use this guess as the "estimate";

(4) make an educated interval guess of the proportion of "successes", and use the number in this interval that is closest to (or equal to) 0.5 as the "estimate"; or

(5) use 0.5 as the "estimate."

The macro that computes the appropriate sample size in this second case is **S-size-p.mtb** (Sample **size** for **p**roportions). This macro will prompt you for the desired confidence level, the size of the error of estimation that is needed, and an estimate of the population proportion of "successes." Both macros in this section can be found in the Reference Guide in the **Formulas from Chapter 5** section, in the table with the heading "Determining the Optimal Sample Size before One Sample Estimation."

Example 5.12:   The local blood bank wants to estimate the proportion of blood donors whose HIV test was a false negative (i.e. the test result was negative, but on further more comprehensive testing the blood donation was found to be positive for HIV). The administrator of the blood bank wants to estimate this proportion with 90% confidence and to be within 0.01 of the true population proportion of false negatives. He feels certain the actual proportion of false negatives is about 0.06 . What size sample of initial negative HIV blood donations should be taken by the administrator for further comprehensive testing?

The predetermined confidence level is 90% and the needed error of estimation is 0.01 . Formula (viii), given at the top of this, page is used to compute the optimal sample size. The administrator's educated guess of the proportion of false negatives is 0.06 , and this is used as the "estimate" of p.

(continued on the next page)

Click on *File* , *Other Files* , *Run an Exec* ...

In the Run an Exec dialog box: make sure the *Number of times to execute:* box contains the number 1, and then click on the [ **Select File** ] button.

In the Run an Exec dialog box: make sure that the *Data Disc* is in the *Look in:* or *Address* box. Next click on S-size-p.mtb to highlight the macro file name, and click on the [ **Open** ] button.

The steps for this macro and resulting confidence interval shown below will appear in the Session Window.

**After the DATA> prompt, enter the confidence level.**

*MTB* > 90 [ **Enter** ]

**After the DATA> prompt, enter the desired Error of Estimation.**

*MTB* > 0.01 [ **Enter** ]

**After the DATA> prompt, enter your best guess of
the Population Proportion of "successes".**

*MTB* > 0.06 [ **Enter** ]

## Data Display

**To compute a 90.0 percent confidence interval for the population
proportion of "successes" with a 0.010  error of estimation,  the
sample size needed is:     1526**

and so the administrator of the local blood bank would take a random sample of 1526 donations that initially tested negative for HIV, and he would do further comprehensive tests on these to find the false negatives.   Then the computed 90% confidence interval will have an error of estimation of approximately  0.01 .

# Lab  Assignment 5.4.1

**Name:**                                                                        **Date:**

**Course:**                          **Section:**                          **Data CD Number:**

1.    Start a Minitab session.  If you are unable to complete this lab assignment in one Minitab session, save the project as Lab 5-4-1 . **Never** use a period as part of the project name; since Minitab uses the period to attach the file type to the file name.  Then at your next Minitab session, you may open this Lab 5-4-1.MPJ project and continue to work where you left off previously.

2.    Before settling on a National Health Care plan, the senate committee wants to know the additional cost that employers will have to pay.  In order to compute this additional cost, the committee needs to estimate the proportion of the work force that currently does **not** have health insurance.   This estimate should have an error no bigger than .02 and a confidence level of 95%.  A previous similar survey resulted in 23% of the workforce being uninsured.  What size sample should the senate committee take in order to meet their goals when they estimate the current proportion of the work force that do **not** have health insurance?

3.    When automobile companies advertise the gasoline consumption of a particular model, they give the average miles per gallon for that model.  Standards require that the estimate must be within plus or minus 1¼ miles of the true average, with a 95% confidence level.  A new model called the Shark is being marketed, and the advertising director needs to know what average miles per gallon to use in the advertisements.  Prototype testing indicates the Shark typically gets between 13 and 29 miles per gallon, depending upon the type of driving conditions. How large of a sample of Sharks must be tested in order to obtain the average miles per gallon to be used in the advertisements?

4.    Postage due letters cost the Post Office more than the amount due on these letters.  Before changing the policy, the Post Office wants to estimate, within .03, the proportion of the first class mail that is postage due.   The Postmaster guesses that the actual proportion is between 0.10 and 0.15 .   What size sample of first class mail should be taken if the Postmaster is to compute a 98% confidence interval for the proportion of all first class letters that are postage due?

(lab assignment is continued on the second side of this page)

5. For each medical procedure, Blue Shield pays a certain percentage of the average charge for that procedure. Each year Blue Shield needs to re-compute the amount paid to participating doctors. Since surveying all of the doctors is not cost effective, Blue Shield takes a random sample and estimates the average charge. In order to set their payment schedule for a tonsillectomy, Blue Shield wants to estimate the average charge with an error of estimation of no more than $50 and a 99% confidence level. A pilot sample of doctors was taken, and that sample's standard deviation was $175. How large of a sample of doctors should Blue Shield take in order to estimate the average charge for a tonsillectomy?

6. Print your Session Window to the printer.

7. Attach both your Minitab output and <u>your complete answers</u> to this paper and submit all three to your instructor.

# Lab Assignment 5.4.2

**Name:**                                                          **Date:**

**Course:**                    **Section:**                    **Data CD Number:**

1.    Start a Minitab session. If you are unable to complete this lab assignment in one Minitab session, save the project as Lab 5-4-2 . **Never** use a period as part of the project name; since Minitab uses the period to attach the file type to the file name. Then at your next Minitab session, you may open this Lab 5-4-2.MPJ project and continue to work where you left off previously.

2.    When Portland's college bound high school seniors take the SAT test, the population standard deviation is 100. The Portland superintendent of schools wants to know the mean SAT test score for the college bound seniors in Portland's public schools. Since the Educational Testing Service charges to have these results sent, the superintendent will be satisfied to estimate a 90% confidence interval for the mean SAT test score of all of Portland's college bound seniors. The school board directs the superintendent to estimate the mean SAT score within 10 points of the true population mean. How large of a sample should the superintendent have sent to her?

3.    Each year the Department of Labor distributes a list which contains the estimated average beginning salary for different professions. These estimated averages have an error of estimation of no more than $100 and are computed using a 95% confidence level. Last year the survey of first year chemists had a standard deviation of beginning salaries equal to $1,227.34 . Using this figure as an "estimate" of the population standard deviation, how large of a sample should the Department of Labor take for this year's survey of first year chemists?

4.    The Aftco Corporation manufactures precision springs for expensive classic watches. The quality control engineer samples the production run twice a day to determine the proportion of springs that do not meet standards. If more than 20% of the springs are defective, the production process is halted and corrections are made. Otherwise Aftco just includes 15% additional springs in each order, since this is less expensive than shutting down the production process. Twice a day the engineer takes a small pilot sample and then a full quality control sample. Today, the morning pilot sample contains 26% defective springs. How large of a full quality control sample should the engineer take, if he wants to estimate the population proportion of defective springs within plus or minus 0.04 and with a 99% confidence level?

(lab assignment is continued on the second side of this page)

5. The Department of Health and Human Services has been asked to estimate the proportion of "latch-key" children (children who have their own key and come home to an empty house) in New Jersey. This estimate is to be within plus or minus 0.03 of the true population proportion with a 98% level of confidence. The head of the Department's Family Division has no idea of what this proportion might be, so she uses 0.5 as the "estimate" of p. What size sample of New Jersey's children should be taken?

6. Print your Session Window to the printer.

7. Attach both your Minitab output and your complete answers to this paper and submit all three to your instructor.

# CHAPTER 6:     Two Sample Confidence Intervals

**Section 1:**     **Confidence Intervals For The Difference of Two Population Means Using Two**
**Independent Samples**

Comparison of two separate populations is the goal in many research situations, and the methods used are usually called "two sample" techniques. One of these techniques is a confidence interval for the difference of population means $\mu_1$ - $\mu_2$.

The objects in two samples may be chosen independently of each other, or the objects may be paired or matched as they are selected for each sample. Techniques for independent samples are presented in this section, and techniques for paired samples are given in the next section.

When the two populations are normally distributed, but the populations's variances are unknown, the independent sample confidence interval for $\mu_1$ - $\mu_2$ is based upon the Student's t distribution. If the population variances are different (i.e., $\sigma_1^2 \neq \sigma_2^2$), the "separate variance" t formula is used to compute the confidence interval. The formula for the "separate variance" t confidence interval for $\mu_1$ - $\mu_2$ is

$$\text{(i)} \qquad (\bar{x}_1 - \bar{x}_2) \mp t \sqrt{\frac{s_1^2}{n_1} + \frac{s_2^2}{n_2}}$$

However; if the two unknown population variances are equal (i.e., $\sigma_1^2 = \sigma_2^2$), the "pooled variance" t technique is used to compute the confidence interval for $\mu_1$ - $\mu_2$. The formula for this "pooled variance" t confidence interval is

$$\text{(ii)} \qquad (\bar{x}_1 - \bar{x}_2) \mp t \sqrt{s_p^2 \left( \frac{1}{n_1} + \frac{1}{n_2} \right)}$$

$$\text{where} \quad s_p^2 = \frac{(n_1 - 1)s_1^2 + (n_2 - 1)s_2^2}{n_1 + n_2 - 2}$$

If you do not know whether or not these two unknown variances are equal, a "F test" for $\sigma_1^2 = \sigma_2^2$ is given in Chapter 8.

There are two methods of entering **raw data** for two samples. The simplest and most straight forward is to enter each sample in a separate variable (column). However, a second method is to enter all of the data into one variable (column) and to use a second variable (column) to indicate which sample, 1 or 2, each corresponding score came from. This second method has some advantages when doing Analysis of Variance (see Chapter 9), but for all confidence intervals in this chapter the first, simplest method will be used. If formula (i) has been chosen as the appropriate confidence interval, the "separate variance" *2-Sample t* confidence interval is computed.

Click on *Stat , Basic Statistics , 2-Sample t ...*

In the 2-Sample t (Test and Confidence Interval) dialog box: click on the circle to the left of *Samples in different columns*, click in the box to the right of *First:*, click on the variable that contains the data from sample 1, and click on the $\boxed{\textbf{Select}}$ button. The cursor now will be in the box to the right of *Second:*, click on the variable that contains the data from sample 2, and click on the $\boxed{\textbf{Select}}$ button. Make sure that the *Assume equal variances* box is **not** checked; if it is checked, click on that box to un-check this option. Then click on the $\boxed{\textbf{Options...}}$ button. Remember, do **not** press the $\boxed{\textbf{Enter}}$ key after you have typed in anything, but use the mouse to move to another place in the dialog box.

In the 2-Sample t - Options dialog box: if the value in the *confidence level:* box is not the level you want, erase this value and type in the correct confidence level. Leave the 0.0 in the box to the right of *Test difference:*. Then make sure that the box to the right of *Alternative:* contains *not equal*. If not, click on the down triangle ( $\boxed{\blacktriangledown}$ ), and click on the *not equal* choice. Then click on $\boxed{\textbf{OK}}$ .

Back in the 2-Sample t (Test and Confidence Interval) dialog box, click on $\boxed{\textbf{OK}}$ .

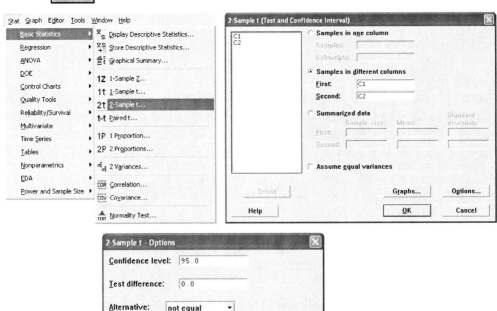

However, when the problem has **summary statistics data**, this formula (i) is computed by

Click on *Stat , Basic Statistics , 2-Sample t ...*

In the 2-Sample t (Test and Confidence Interval) dialog box: click on the circle to the left of *Summarized data*, and then click inside of the box on the *First:* row and underneath of *Sample size:*. If a previous value is shown, erase this number; or you may press the $\boxed{\text{F3}}$ key to clear the contents of this dialog box and reset all options and erase any previous variables. Now type in the value of the first sample size. Click in the next box to the right that is underneath of *Mean:* and type in the value of the first sample mean. Next click inside of the next box to the right that is underneath of *Standard deviation:* and type in the given value of the first sample standard deviation. Then repeat this on the *Second:* row for sample 2. Make sure that the *Assume equal variances* box is **not** checked, if it is checked, click on that box to un-check this option, and then click on the $\boxed{\text{Options...}}$ button.

In the 2-Sample t - Options dialog box: if the value in the *confidence level:* box is not the level you want, erase this value and type in the correct confidence level. Leave the 0.0 in the box to the right of *Test difference:*. Then make sure that the box to the right of *Alternative:* contains *not equal*. If not, click on the down triangle ( $\boxed{\blacktriangledown}$ ), and click on the *not equal* choice. Then click on $\boxed{\text{OK}}$ .

Back in the 2-Sample t (Test and Confidence Interval) dialog box, click on $\boxed{\text{OK}}$ .

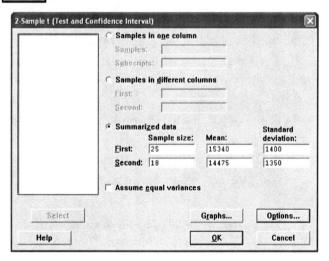

The output of the "separate variance" *2-Sample t* procedure contains:

(1) the column label or name of each variable,
(2) the number of valid observations, the mean, standard deviation and standard error (which is the standard deviation divided by the square root of n) of each variable,
(3) the difference of the specific variables (columns),
(4) the point estimate for the difference $\mu_1 - \mu_2$,
(5) the desired confidence interval for $\mu_1 - \mu_2$ and
(6) a t test of the difference (which will be explained in Chapter 8).

Example 6.1:   Six male and five female junior executives were sampled from the large ABC Corporation.   Their annual salaries were:

| Male | Female |
|------|--------|
| $39,450 | $42,500 |
| 60,275 | 36,400 |
| 43,000 | 41,250 |
| 50,500 | 44,800 |
| 37,200 | 35,000 |
| 48,750 | |

Assuming that the annual salaries of all male and all female junior executives are normally distributed, but the population variances are not equal; find a 95% confidence interval for the difference in the mean annual salaries of all male and all female junior executives.

Enter each sample's data into columns 1 and 2 respectively directly into the Worksheet Window and name the two variables Male and Female.

Click on *Stat* , *Basic Statistics* , *2-Sample t ...*

In the 2-Sample t (Test and Confidence Interval) dialog box: click on the circle to the left of *Samples in different columns*, click in the box to the right of *First:*, click on the Male (C1) variable, and click on the ⬚ **Select** ⬚ button. The cursor now will be in the box to the right of *Second:*, click on the Female (C2) variable, and click on the ⬚ **Select** ⬚ button. Make sure that the *Assume equal variances* box is **not** checked; if it is checked, click on that box to un-check this option.  Then click on the ⬚ **Options...** ⬚ button. Remember, do **not** press the ⬚ **Enter** ⬚ key after you have typed in anything, but use the mouse to move to another place in the dialog box.

In the 2-Sample t - Options dialog box: if the value in the *confidence level:* box is not the level you want, erase this value and type in the confidence level of 95.  Leave the 0.0 in the box to the right of *Test difference:*.  Then make sure that the box to the right of *Alternative:* contains *not equal*.  If not, click on the down triangle ( ⬚▾ ), and click on the *not equal* choice.  Then click on ⬚ **OK** ⬚ .

Back in the 2-Sample t (Test and Confidence Interval) dialog box, click on ⬚ **OK** ⬚ .

The output below containing the 95% confidence interval will appear in the Session Window.

## Two-Sample T-Test and CI: Male, Female

### Two sample T for Male vs Female

| | N | Mean | StDev | SE Mean |
|--------|---|-------|-------|---------|
| Male | 6 | 46529 | 8476 | 3460 |
| Female | 5 | 39990 | 4148 | 1855 |

**Difference = mu (Male) - mu (Female)**
**Estimate for difference:  6539.17**
**95% CI for difference:  (-2744.99, 15823.33)**
**T-Test of difference = 0 (vs not =): T-Value = 1.67  P-Value = 0.140  DF = 7**

(continued on the next page)

In this example the "separate variance" technique was used since the population variances are not equal. You are 95% confident that the interval from -$2,744.99 to $15,823.33 contains the difference in the mean salaries of all male versus all female junior executives in the ABC Corporation. Since the confidence interval contains the value of zero, there is no conclusive evidence that a real difference of average salaries exists between the populations of male and female junior executives. This is so even though the mean salary of the sample of six males is considerably higher than the mean salary of the sample of five females.

Example 6.2: The Congressional Taxation Committee wanted to know the average difference between the tax liability of middle income "married" couples versus two single people "living together". A random sample of 25 "married" couples was taken and it yielded a mean liability of $15,340 and standard deviation of $950. A second sample of 18 "living together" singles was taken and its mean and standard deviation are $14,475 and $1,350 respectively. Previous studies have shown that tax liability in these two populations is normally distributed and the population standard deviations are different. Compute a 90% confidence interval for the difference of the mean tax liability in the two populations.

The information in this example indicates that the appropriate confidence interval is the "pooled variance" formula (i) of

$$(i) \qquad (\overline{x}_1 - \overline{x}_2) \mp t \sqrt{\frac{s_1^2}{n_1} + \frac{s_2^2}{n_2}}$$

Click on *Stat*, *Basic Statistics*, *2-Sample t ...*
In the 2-Sample t (Test and Confidence Interval) dialog box: click on the circle to the left of *Summarized data*, and then click inside of the box on the *First:* row and underneath of *Sample size:*. If a previous value is shown, erase this number; or you may press the $\boxed{\textbf{F3}}$ key to clear the contents of this dialog box and reset all options and erase any previous variables. Now type in the first sample size of 25. Click in the next box to the right that is underneath of *Mean:* and type in the first sample mean of 15340. Next click inside of the next box to the right that is underneath of *Standard deviation:* and type in the first sample standard deviation of 950. Repeat this in the *Second:* row by typing in 18, 14475 and 1350 respectively. Make sure that the *Assume equal variances* box is **not** checked, if it is checked, click on that box to un-check this option, and then click on the $\boxed{\textbf{Options...}}$ button.
In the 2-Sample t - Options dialog box: if the value in the *confidence level:* box is not the level you want, erase this value and type in the confidence level of 90. Leave the 0.0 in the box to the right of *Test difference:*. Then make sure that the box to the right of *Alternative:* contains *not equal*. If not, click on the down triangle ( $\boxed{\blacktriangledown}$ ), and click on the *not equal* choice. Then click on $\boxed{\textbf{OK}}$ .
Back in the 2-Sample t (Test and Confidence Interval) dialog box, click on $\boxed{\textbf{OK}}$ .
The output containing the 95% confidence interval will appear in the Session Window and is shown on the next page.

(continued on the next page)

137

## Two-Sample T-Test and CI

| Sample | N | Mean | StDev | SE Mean |
|--------|-----|-------|-------|---------|
| 1 | 25 | 15340 | 950 | 190 |
| 2 | 18 | 14475 | 1350 | 318 |

**Difference = mu (1) - mu (2)**
**Estimate for difference: 865.000**
**90% CI for difference: (234.548, 1495.452)**
**T-Test of difference = 0 (vs not =): T-Value = 2.33  P-Value = 0.027  DF = 28**

The Congressional Taxation Committee may conclude that with 90% confidence, the interval from $234.55 to $1,495.45 contains the difference between the mean tax liability of the "married" versus the "living together" populations. This implies that the middle income "married" people pay more tax than "living together" people.

If the two unknown population variances are equal (i.e., $\sigma_1^2 = \sigma_2^2$), the "pooled variance" t technique, formula (ii), is used to compute the confidence interval for $\mu_1 - \mu_2$. The procedure for computing this "pooled variance" t formula is exactly the same as for the "separate variance" formula (i); except that in the 2-Sample t dialog box, you now must make sure that the box to the left of *Assume equal variances* **is** checked.

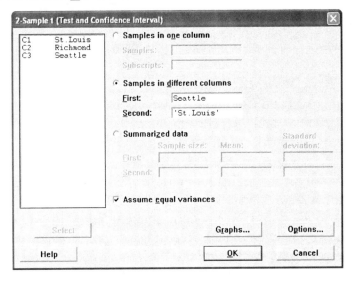

The output of the "pooled variance" *2 Sample t* procedure contains the same information as the "separate variance" output, and additionally, the value of the pooled sample standard deviation ($s_p$) also is displayed.

Example 6.3:  Open the Hospital.mtw worksheet that is saved on your data disc.  These data are samples of daily room rates in hospitals in St. Louis, Richmond and Seattle.  These rates are known to be normally distributed with the three population standard deviations all being equal.  Compute a 90% confidence interval for the difference in mean room rates in Seattle versus St. Louis.

(continued on the next page)

Use the *File , Open Worksheet...* to open the Hospital.mtw worksheet from your data disc. Click on *Stat , Basic Statistics , 2-Sample t ...*

In the 2-Sample t (Test and Confidence Interval) dialog box: click on the circle to the left of *Samples in different columns*, click in the box to the right of *First:*, click on the Seattle (C3) variable, and click on the [ **Select** ] button. The cursor now will be in the box to the right of *Second:*, click on the St. Louis (C1) variable, and click on the [ **Select** ] button. Make sure that the *Assume equal variances* box **is** checked; if it is not checked, click on that box to check this option. Then click on the [ **Options...** ] button. Remember, do **not** press the [ **Enter** ] key after you have typed in anything, but use the mouse to move to another place in the dialog box.

In the 2-Sample t - Options dialog box: if the value in the *confidence level:* box is not the level you want, erase this value and type in the confidence level of 90. Leave the 0.0 in the box to the right of *Test difference:*. Then make sure that the box to the right of *Alternative:* contains *not equal*. If not, click on the down triangle ( [▼] ), and click on the *not equal* choice. Then click on [ **OK** ].

Back in the 2-Sample t (Test and Confidence Interval) dialog box, click on [ **OK** ].

The output below containing the 95% confidence interval will appear in the Session Window.

## Two-Sample T-Test and CI: Seattle, St.Louis

### Two-sample T for Seattle vs St.Louis

|          | N   | Mean  | StDev | SE Mean |
|----------|-----|-------|-------|---------|
| Seattle  | 16  | 130.0 | 21.3  | 5.3     |
| St.Louis | 15  | 117.2 | 16.6  | 4.3     |

**Difference = mu (Seattle) - mu (St.Louis)**
**Estimate for difference: 12.8000**
**90% CI for difference: (1.0907, 24.5093)**
**T-Test of difference = 0 (vs not =): T-Value = 1.86  P-Value = 0.073  DF = 29**
**Both use Pooled StDev = 19.1747**

In this example, the "pooled variance" technique was used since the population standard deviations are equal (which is equivalent to saying that the population variances are equal). You are 90% confident that the interval from $1.09 to $24.51 contains the mean rate of all hospital rooms in Seattle minus the mean rate in St. Louis. Since this confidence interval contains only positive numbers (does not contain the value of zero), you may be reasonably certain (90%) that the average daily hospital room rate in Seattle is higher than in St. Louis.

There are problems for which neither of the t intervals are appropriate; for example, when both population variances are known. If the information concerning the original populations's parameters and types of distribution indicate that a confidence interval based upon the Z distribution is needed, then one of the two formulas shown on the next page are used.

$$\text{(iii)} \qquad (\bar{x}_1 - \bar{x}_2) \mp Z\sqrt{\frac{\sigma_1^2}{n_1} + \frac{\sigma_2^2}{n_2}}$$

$$\text{(iv)} \qquad (\bar{x}_1 - \bar{x}_2) \mp Z\sqrt{\frac{s_1^2}{n_1} + \frac{s_2^2}{n_2}}$$

If the values of $\sigma_1^2$ and $\sigma_2^2$ are known, formula (iii) is used; otherwise $s_1^2$ and $s_2^2$ must be computed and formula (iv) is used.

These two confidence intervals may be computed using macros saved on your data disc. When you have raw data: the macro that computes the confidence interval given in formula (iii) is **Ci-2mk.mtb** (Confidence interval for **2 m**eans with **k**nown population variances), and the macro that computes the confidence interval given in formula (iv) is called **Ci-2mun.mtb** (Confidence Interval for **2 m**eans with **un**known population variances). When the problem has summary statistic data: the macro that computes the confidence interval given in formula (iii) is **Sumci2mk.mtb** , and the macro that computes the confidence interval given in formula (iv) is called **Sumci2mu.mtb**. These are also found in the Reference Guide in the and in the table with the heading **Two Sample Confidence Intervals For The Difference of Two Population Means Using Two Independent Samples**.

An explicit description of executing a macro was given in Chapter 5, so what is shown next is an abbreviated description.

Click on *File , Other Files , Run an Exec...*

In the Run an Exec dialog box: *Number of times to execute:* is 1 and click on *Select File* button.

In the next Run an Exec dialog box: make sure the *Data Disc* is active (if not already done so), click on specific macro, and click on the | **Open** | button .

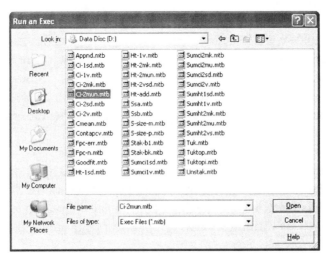

These macros will prompt you for the specific numbers of the columns that contain the data in the two samples. You must be very careful to enter the number that represents population 1 first, and the number that represents population 2 second. These two column numbers should be separated with a comma. Next these macros will prompt you to enter the desired confidence level. The potential careless mistakes and their solutions are discussed at the end of Section 2 in Chapter 5.

When applying any two-sample technique, you must clearly describe population 1 and population 2. The column numbers that correspond to the data from these samples must be carefully identified. The correct numbers **and** correct order are essential to obtain a valid result.

Example 6.4: Retrieve the Ispaint.mtw worksheet from your data disc. This worksheet contains data for three different brands of highway paint. Parallel strips of the BriLite and DayGlo brands were painted on the highway at various test locations. By using parallel lines; different weather, road and traffic conditions are equalized. Then strips of the Everlast brand were painted at highway locations that were randomly chosen independently of the locations for BriLite and DayGlo. The time at which each paint strip was no longer viable was measured, and this score is called the wear time. Compute a 98% confidence interval for the difference between the mean wear times of the populations of all BriLite and all Everlast painted highway lines.

Use the *File , Open Worksheet...* to open the worksheet Ispaint.mtb that is saved on your data disc.

Now click in the Session window to the right of the **MTB >** prompt and enter the info command (type info and press the ⎾ **Enter** ⏌ key) to display the basic information about the variables stored in this worksheet. The information shown below will appear in the Session Window.

## *Results for: Ispaint.mtw*

*MTB >* info ⎾ **Enter** ⏌

### *Information on the Worksheet*

| Column | Count | Missing | Name |
|--------|-------|---------|----------|
| C1 | 40 | 0 | Location |
| C2 | 40 | 1 | BriLite |
| C3 | 40 | 1 | DayGlo |
| C4 | 53 | 0 | Everlast |

The distributions of these two populations are not specified. Since both the BriLite and DayGlow sample sizes are greater than 30 and the population variances unknown, formula (iv) is the appropriate technique for computing a confidence interval for the difference of the two population means. The Ci-2mun.mtb macro will be used.

(continued on the next page)

141

Population 1 is all highway lines painted with BriLite, and so column C2 contains the data in the corresponding sample. Therefore C2 is the "first variable" requested by the macro.

Population 2 is all highway lines painted with Everlast, and so column C4 contains the data in the corresponding sample. Therefore C4 is the "second variable" requested by the macro.

Click on *File , Other Files , Run an Exec ...*

In the Run an Exec dialog box: make sure the *Number of times to execute:* box contains the number 1, and then click on the | Select File | button.

In the Run an Exec dialog box: the *Data Disc* should be selected. Next click on Ci-2mun.mtb to highlight this macro, and click on the | Open | button.

The macro proceeds by asking you to enter the column numbers of the two samples and the confidence level. After the first **DATA>** prompt, you enter the requested column numbers of 2 and 4 separated by a comma and then press the | Enter | key. After the second **DATA>** prompt, you enter the requested confidence level of 98 and then press the | Enter | key. The steps for this macro are shown below. The **bold italicized** words are displayed by Minitab in the Session Window, and the numbers you are to enter in the Session Window are shown in regular print.

**After the DATA> prompt, enter the column numbers that contain the data of the first and second samples. Enter ONLY the numbers, but NOT the C's !**

**DATA>** 2, 4 | Enter |     (since C2 contains the sample data from population 1
                                and C4 contains the sample data from population 2)

**After the DATA> prompt, enter the confidence level.**

**DATA>** 98 | Enter |

## Data Display

**98.0 percent confidence interval for**
**population 1 mean of C 2 - population 2 mean of C 4:**

**-1.7415 to        7.5405**

and so you may be 98% confident that the interval from -1.74 to 7.54 contains the difference in mean wear time of all BriLite minus the mean wear time of all Everlast painted highway lines. This confidence interval does not indicate that one of these brands is superior to the other. Notice that the macro output displays the two variable column numbers in the order in which the macro computed the confidence interval.

Example 6.5: A study comparing Regular Unleaded gasoline against Unleaded gasoline with Ethanol added was done to examine the mileage automobiles get from each type of gasoline. A random sample of 70 family sedans was chosen, and these cars used the gasoline without the additive. A second random sample of 50 family sedans was chosen, and these cars used the gasoline with the ethanol additive. After three months the mileage and number of gallon used were recorded. The cars using the regular gasoline had an average of 21.67 miles per gallon, and the cars using the gasoline with the ethanol additive had an average of 19.32 miles per gallon. The distribution of mileage for these two types of gasoline is unknown, but the respective population standard deviations is known to be 4.31 and 5.86 respectively. Find a 95% confidence interval for the difference in the average mileage between gasoline without versus gasoline with the ethanol additive.

The distributions of these two populations are not specified. Since both sample sizes are greater than 30, and the population variances are known, formula (iii)

$$(\bar{x}_1 - \bar{x}_2) \mp Z\sqrt{\frac{\sigma_1^2}{n_1} + \frac{\sigma_2^2}{n_2}}$$

is the appropriate technique for computing a confidence interval for the difference of the two population means. Since this example uses summary statistic data, the Sumci2mk.mtb macro will be used.

Population 1 is all family sedans using Regular Unleaded gasoline without the ethanol additive.

Population 2 is all family sedans using Unleaded gasoline with Ethanol added.

Click on *File , Other Files , Run an Exec ...*
In the Run an Exec dialog box: make sure the *Number of times to execute:* box contains the number 1, and then click on the Select File button.
In the Run an Exec dialog box: the *Data Disc* should be selected. Next click on Sumci2mk.mtb to highlight this macro, and click on the Open button.

The **bold italicized** words are displayed by Minitab in the Session Window, and the numbers you are to enter in the Session Window are shown in regular print.

**After the DATA> prompt, enter the mean of Sample 1 a comma, and then the mean of Sample 2.**

**DATA>** 21.67, 19.32 Enter

**After the DATA> prompt, enter the respective values of the two Populations' standard deviations (NOT variances).**

(continued on the next page)

143

**DATA>** 4.31, 5.86 [ Enter ]

*After the DATA> prompt, enter the respective sizes of the two Samples.*

**DATA>** 70, 50 [ Enter ]

*After the DATA> prompt, enter the confidence level.*

**DATA>** 95 [ Enter ]

## Data Display

*95.0 percent confidence interval for*
*population 1 mean  -  population 2 mean:*
*0.4375  to         4.2625*

and so you may be 95% confident that the interval from 0.44 to 4.26 miles per gallon contains the difference in mean mileage of all family sedans using Regular Unleaded gasoline minus the mean mileage of all mileage of all family sedans using Unleaded gasoline with Ethanol added. Since this confidence interval contains only positive numbers, this indicates the average mileage obtained with Regular Unleaded gasoline (Population 1) is higher that the average mileage obtained with Unleaded gasoline with Ethanol added (Population 2).

# Lab Assignment 6.1.1

**Name:**                                                          **Date:**

**Course:**                    **Section:**                    **Data CD Number:**


1.   Start a Minitab session. If you are unable to complete this lab assignment in one Minitab session, save the project as Lab 6-1-1 . **Never** use a period as part of the project name; since Minitab uses the period to attach the file type to the file name. Then at your next Minitab session, you may open this Lab 6-1-1.MPJ project and continue to work where you left off previously.

2.   The interest rate on tax free municipal bonds is generally less than the interest rate on taxable corporate bonds. A financial advisor wishes to investigate the net (after tax) return on these two types of investments. He takes a random sample of each type of bond and computes the net return for each bond with the following results.

Municipal Bonds:   8.2 , 4.5 , 6.7 , 7.4 , 6.7 , 8.4 , 10.3 , 9.3 , 5.7 , 6.6 , 7.9 , 7.3 , 6.5 , 7.2
7.2 , 5.8 , 11.2 , 8.8 , 3.9 , 7.5 , 5.9 , 7.3 , 8.2 , 12.4 , 9.3 , 8.2 , 10.7 , 6.1
4.8 , 7.3 , 6.9 , 7.3 , 8.3 , 5.8 and 7.0

Corporate Bonds:   9.3 , 10.3 , 11.3 , 10.2 , 8.5 , 2.5 , 7.3 , 5.9 , 9.5 , 8.3 , 9.5 , 4.6 , 14.1
4.3 , 8.4 , 9.1 , 5.2 , 6.1 , 13.2 , 9.6 , 13.2 , 5.6 , 6.3 , 7.2 , 8.6 , 12.3 , 3.5
18.4 , 3.2 , 7.4 , 5.2 , 8.4 , 11.3 , 9.9 , 3.1 , 7.1 , 9.2 , 13.7 , 7.3 , 8.5 , 8.8
and 10.0

Compute a 95% confidence interval for the difference in the average net returns between these two types of bond investments.

3.   The following paragraph **describes** the data in the Run400.mtw worksheet saved on your data disc.


The local track association wants to have boys and girls compete against each other. However they need to give a "handicap" time to the girls (much like a "handicap" score in bowling or golf). The track officials sampled boys and girls in both the eight and twelve year old age groups and measured their times (in seconds) in a 400 meter race. These times are normally distributed for all four populations. All race times were measured in seconds. It is known that the population standard deviation of 400 meter race times are different for eight year old boys and girls, but that the standard deviations of the 400 meter race times are the same for the twelve year old boys and girls.


(lab assignment is continued on the second side of this page)

a. Open the worksheet Run400.mtw that is on your data disc.

b. Compute a 90% confidence interval for the difference of the mean 400 meter race times for all eight year old boys versus all eight year old girls. What would you conclude from this result?

c. Compute a 98% confidence interval for the difference of the mean 400 meter race times between all twelve year old boys and all twelve year old girls. What conclusion may be made from this result.

4.  The viscosity of two different brands of motor oil were measured and the results are shown in the following table.

| Brand | Sample Size | Mean | Standard Deviation |
|-------|-------------|------|--------------------|
| Alcorn | 21 | 10.45 | 3.53 |
| Shore | 17 | 12.64 | 1.05 |

Compute a 90% confidence interval for the difference between the mean viscosity of all Alcorn and Shore motor oil, assuming that the two populations are normally distributed but that the two population standard deviations are not equal.

5.  The average yield of a sample of 625 hybrid corn plants was 34.6 bushels per acre with a standard deviation of 2.1 bushels per acre. A second sample of 715 pure bred corn plants yielded a mean and standard deviation of 32.8 and 3.6 bushels per acre respectively. Compute a 99% confidence interval for the difference in the mean yields of all hybrid versus all pure bred corn plants.

6.  Print your Session Window to the printer.

7.  Attach both your Minitab output and <u>your complete answers</u> to this sheet and submit all three to your instructor.

# Lab Assignment 6.1.2

**Name:**                                                 **Date:**

**Course:**                     **Section:**                           **Data CD Number:**

1. Start a Minitab session. If you are unable to complete this lab assignment in one Minitab session, save the project as Lab 6-1-2 . **Never** use a period as part of the project name; since Minitab uses the period to attach the file type to the file name. Then at your next Minitab session, you may open this Lab 6-1-2.MPJ project and continue to work where you left off previously.

2. There is a great deal of interest among politicians in the public's attitude towards raising taxes to pay for education. A legislator recently had a survey done on a sample of those voters who favor a tax raise for education. A second survey was given to a sample of voters who are against any tax raise. One of the variables measured was the age of the voter, and the results are shown below.

   For:        23 , 34 , 32 , 32 , 21 , 56 , 43 , 52 , 37 , 44 , 26 , 51 , 24 , 27 , 41 , 27 , 29 , 31 , 39
   54 , 65 , 23 , 71 , 33 , 31 , 26 , 28 , 32 , 42 , 22 , 25 , 41 , 37 , 28 , 23 , 31 , 35 and 26

   Against:  31 , 63 , 42 , 25 , 63 , 54 , 57 , 42 , 27 , 59 , 39 , 42 , 43 , 48 , 26 , 35 , 46 , 52 , 26
   63 , 43 , 52 , 38 , 28 , 41 , 29 , 48 , 57 , 52 , 33 , 29 , 36 , 55 , 33 , 24 , 54 , 23 , 43
   47 , 48 , 25 , 37 , 59 and 39

   The standard deviation of both populations is known to be 12 years. Compute a 98% confidence interval for the difference between the average age of all voters who favor a tax raise for education and all voters who are against such a tax raise.

3. The following paragraph **describes** the data in the Cityidx.mtw worksheet saved on your data disc.

   Cities in the United States were geographically grouped into three regions: East, Central and West. A random sample from each region was taken and the following five variables were measured: (1) municipal bond rating 1 = A or better and 0 = below A, (2) retail sales index, (3) urban unemployment index, (4) rural unemployment index, and (5) construction starts index. These five variables are in columns C1 - C5 for the East region, in columns C6 - C10 for the Central Region, and in columns C11 - C15 for the West region. The four indices are known to be normally distributed in each geographical region.

   (lab assignment is continued on the second side of this page)

a. Open the worksheet Cityidx.mtw that is on your data disc.

b. Compute a 95% confidence interval for the difference between the mean construction start index in all U.S. East and all U.S. West region cities. The population variances of this index are unknown in the two regions, but most experts believe that these two population variances are not equal.

c. Compute a 90% confidence interval for the difference between the mean rural unemployment index in all U.S. Central and all U.S. East region cities. It is thought that the standard deviation of the rural unemployment index is the same in both of these regions.

4. In a random sample of 80 ChargIt Blue Card customers, the mean daily balance for 1996 was $435.67. An independent sample of 75 ChargIt Gold Card customers yielded a mean daily balance $498.52 for 1996. Previous complete audits have convinced the manager that the population standard deviations of the two respective populations are $34.85 and $41.78. Compute a 95% confidence interval for the difference in the mean daily balances in 1996 for these two types of ChargIt Cards.

5. The viscosity of two different brands of motor oil were measured and the results are shown in the following table.

| Brand | Sample Size | Mean | Standard Deviation |
|---|---|---|---|
| Revup | 16 | 11.45 | 2.53 |
| SureSlip | 27 | 13.84 | 2.65 |

Compute a 90% confidence interval for the difference between the mean viscosity of all Revup and SureSlip motor oil, assuming that the two populations are normally distributed and that the two population standard deviations are equal.

6. Print your Session Window to the printer.

7. Attach both your Minitab output and your complete answers to this sheet and submit all three to your instructor.

**Section 2:** **Confidence interval For The Difference of Two Population Means Using Two Paired Samples**

If the two populations of interest are sampled using a paired or matched sampling method, a confidence interval for the difference of population means, $\mu_1 - \mu_2$, is easily computed. Depending upon the sample sizes and what you know about the populations, one of the following two formulas is used.

$$(v) \qquad \bar{d} \mp t\frac{s_d}{\sqrt{n}} \qquad or$$

$$(vi) \qquad \bar{d} \mp Z\frac{s_d}{\sqrt{n}}$$

In both of these formulas, d represents the "difference" variable between each pair of scores in the two samples; that is, $d = x_1 - x_2$. To compute a confidence interval using formula (v), the *Paired t* procedure is used. It is very important to correctly identify which variable contains the data from sample **one** and which variable contains the data from sample **two**. These variables often are **not in columns C1 and C2** respectively. For problems that involve **raw data**, the paired t confidence interval is computed by

Click on *Stat , Basic Statistics , Paired t ...*

In the Paired t (Test and Confidence Interval) dialog box: click on the circle to the left of *Samples in columns*, click in the box to the right of *First sample:*, click on the variable that contains the data from sample 1, and click on the Select button. The cursor now will be in the box to the right of *Second sample:*, click on the variable that contains the data from sample 2, and click on the Select button. Then click on the Options... button.

In the Paired t - Options dialog box: if the value in the *confidence level:* box is not the level you want, erase this value and type in the correct confidence level. Leave the 0.0 in the box to the right of *Test mean:*. Then make sure that the box to the right of *Alternative:* contains *not equal*. If not, click on the down triangle ( ▾ ), and click on the *not equal* choice. Then click on the OK button.

Back in the Paired t (Test and Confidence Interval) dialog box, click on OK .

(See graphics on the next page.)

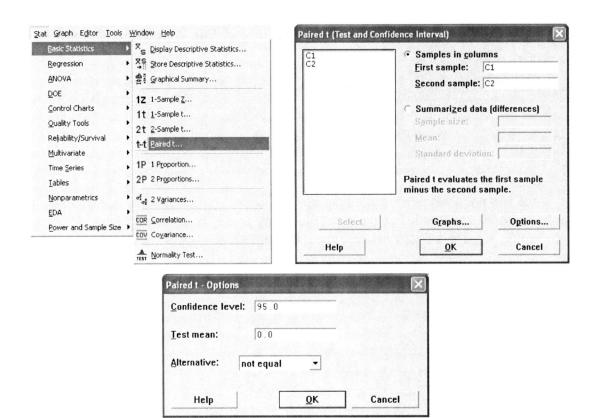

However when the problems only have **summary statistics data**, the paired t confidence interval is computed by

Click on *Stat , Basic Statistics , Paired t ...*

In the Paired t (Test and Confidence Interval) dialog box: click on the circle to the left of *Summarized data (differences)*. Next click in the box to the right of *Sample size:*. If a previous value is shown, erase this number; or you may press the ⬛ **F3** key to clear the contents of this dialog box and reset all options and erase any previous variables. Now type in the value of the common sample size. Next click in the next box down that is to the right of *Mean:* and type in the value of the sample mean of differences. Next click inside of the box to the right of *Standard deviation:*, erase any current incorrect value, and type in the given value of the sample standard deviation of the differences. And then click on the ⬛ **Options...** button.

In the Paired t - Options dialog box: if the value in the *confidence level:* box is not the level you want, erase this value and type in the correct confidence level. Leave the 0.0 in the box to the right of *Test mean:*. Then make sure that the box to the right of *Alternative:* contains *not equal*. If not, click on the down triangle ( ▾ ), and click on the *not equal* choice. Then click on the ⬛ **OK** button.

Back in the Paired t (Test and Confidence Interval) dialog box, click on ⬛ **OK** .

(See graphic on the next page.)

The output of the *Paired t* procedure contains:

(1) the sample size, mean, standard deviation, and standard error of the mean for each sample (only when problem has raw data),

(2) the common sample size, mean, standard deviation, and standard error of the mean for the sample of "difference" scores,

(2) the requested confidence interval for the population mean of the "difference" scores, and

(3) information used in hypothesis testing, which is explained in Chapter 8.

Example 6.6:   Open the worksheet Exam.mtw that is on your data disc.  This contains the results of exam 1 and exam 2 for ten students taken randomly from a large statistics class.  Since the same students took each exam, these two samples are paired.  Compute a 90% confidence interval for the difference between the mean of exam 2 and exam 1 for all students in the statistics class.  The difference scores in these populations are known to be normally distributed, but nothing is known about the population standard deviation.

Use the *File, Open Worksheet...* to open the worksheet Exam.mtw that is saved on your data disc.

Population 1 is all students in the class who took **exam 2**, and so EXAM 2 (C2) contains the data in the corresponding sample.

Population 2 is all students in the class who took **exam 1**, and so EXAM 1 (C1) contains the data in the corresponding sample.

Since the difference scores are normally distributed, but the population standard deviation

is unknown; the formula   **(v)**  $\bar{d} \mp t \dfrac{s_d}{\sqrt{n}}$   is used to compute the confidence interval.

(continued on the next page)

Click on *Stat* , *Basic Statistics* , *Paired t* ...

In the Paired t (Test and Confidence Interval) dialog box: click on the circle to the left of *Samples in columns*, click in the box to the right of *First sample:*, click on the EXAM 2 (C2) variable that contains the data from sample 1, and click on the | **Select** | button. The cursor now will be in the box to the right of *Second sample:*, click on EXAM 1 (C1) variable that contains the data from sample 2, and click on the | **Select** | button. Then click on the | **Options...** | button.

In the Paired t - Options dialog box: if the value in the *confidence level:* box is not 90, erase this value and type in the correct confidence level of 90. Leave the 0.0 in the box to the right of *Test mean:*. Then make sure that the box to the right of *Alternative:* contains *not equal*. If not, click on the down triangle ( ▼ ), and click on the *not equal* choice. Then click on the | **OK** | button.

Back in the Paired t (Test and Confidence Interval) dialog box, click on | **OK** | .

The following results will appear in the Session Window.

## Paired T-Test and CI: EXAM 2, EXAM 1

### Paired T for EXAM 2 - EXAM 1

|            | N | Mean    | StDev    | SE Mean |
|------------|---|---------|----------|---------|
| EXAM 2     | 8 | 84.6250 | 7.8182   | 2.7642  |
| EXAM 1     | 8 | 82.5000 | 13.3095  | 4.7056  |
| Difference | 8 | 2.12500 | 10.78938 | 3.81462 |

**90% CI for mean difference: (-5.10210, 9.35210)**
**T-Test of mean difference = 0 (vs not = 0): T-Value = 0.56  P-Value = 0.595**

Since each variable has a missing value, this t interval is computed using only the eight valid pairs. You are 90% confident that the interval from -5.10 to 9.35 contains the difference of mean exam score for all students taking Exam 2 minus the mean exam score for all students taking Exam 1. From the result of this confidence interval there is no reason to believe that any real difference exists between the average scores on the two exams for all students in the large statistics class.

Example 6.7: Caffeine supplements are often used by drivers to help them "keep alert." While caffeine likely helped the drivers stay awake, a researcher questioned the alertness of drivers using this supplement. In a controlled experiment, she kept 25 drivers awake for 18½ hours and tested their reaction time. One week later (after these 15 drivers had their normal rest), she kept the same 25 drivers up for 18 hours and then gave them a caffeine supplement. One-half hour later she used the same test of their reaction times. The mean difference in these reaction times was 1.34 seconds, the standard deviation of the differences was 1.2863 seconds and these difference times are normally distributed. Compute a 95% confidence interval for the mean difference in reaction times of all sleep deprived drivers not using caffeine versus all sleep deprived drivers using the caffeine supplement.

(continued on the next page)

Population 1 is all sleep deprived drivers who do not use caffeine.

Population 2 is all sleep deprived drivers who do use a caffeine supplement.

Since the difference scores are normally distributed, but the population standard deviation is unknown; the formula **(v)** $\bar{d} \mp t\dfrac{s_d}{\sqrt{n}}$ is used to compute the confidence interval.

Click on *Stat* , *Basic Statistics* , *Paired t ...*

In the Paired t (Test and Confidence Interval) dialog box: click on the circle to the left of *Summarized data (differences).* Next click in the box to the right of *Sample size:*. If a previous value is shown, erase this number; or you may press the $\boxed{\text{F3}}$ key to clear the contents of this dialog box and reset all options and erase any previous variables. Now type in the common sample size of 15. Next click in the next box down that is to the right of *Mean:* and type in the value of the sample mean of differences which is 1.34 . Next click inside of the box to the right of *Standard deviation:,* erase any current incorrect value, and type in the given value of the sample standard deviation of the differences which is 1.2863 . And then click on the $\boxed{\text{Options...}}$ button.

In the Paired t - Options dialog box: if the value in the *confidence level:* box is not 95, erase this value and type in the correct confidence level of 95. Leave the 0.0 in the box to the right of *Test mean:*. Then make sure that the box to the right of *Alternative:* contains *not equal*. If not, click on the down triangle ( $\boxed{\blacktriangledown}$ ), and click on the *not equal* choice. Then click on the $\boxed{\text{OK}}$ button.

Back in the Paired t (Test and Confidence Interval) dialog box, click on $\boxed{\text{OK}}$ .

The following results will appear in the Session Window.

## *Paired T-Test and CI*

| | N | Mean | StDev | SE Mean |
|---|---|---|---|---|
| **Difference** | **15** | **1.34000** | **1.28630** | **0.33212** |

**95% CI for mean difference: (0.62767, 2.05233)**
**T-Test of mean difference = 0 (vs not = 0): T-Value = 4.03  P-Value = 0.001**

You are 95% confident that the interval from 0.63 to 2.05 contains the difference of mean reaction times for all sleep deprived drivers who do not use caffeine minus the mean exam reaction times for all sleep deprived drivers who do use a caffeine supplement. From the result of this confidence interval the researcher has good reasdon to believe that caffeine does slow down a sleep deprived driver's reaction time.

When formula (vi) is used with **raw data**, the computation of the confidence interval is more involved. Minitab does not have a Paired Z procedure, and so you must compute the "difference" scores first and then use the equivalent *1-Sample Z* procedure. To create this new "difference" variable, choose a column number that is different than any of the existing column numbers in the current worksheet and name it **difference**.

Click on *Calc , Calculator...*

In the Calculator dialog box: click inside the box to the right of *Store result in variable:*; highlight the difference variable and click on the | **Select** | button (or type in a **new, unused** column number). Next click inside of the box under *Expression:* click on the variable containing the **first** sample's data, click on the button with the minus sign (-) on it (or press the minus sign key), and click on the variable containing the **second** sample's data. Then click on the | **OK** | button.

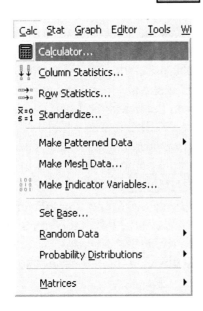

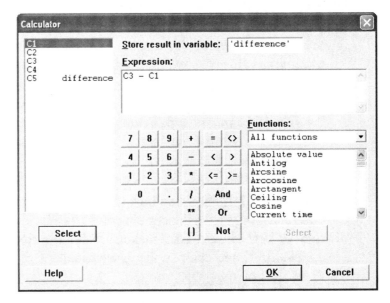

This performs the calculation in the *Expression:* box for <u>every</u> row with a <u>valid</u> pair of scores and store the results into the corresponding rows in the new variable. If either of the variables in the *Expression:* box contains a missing value in a particular row, that row in the new variable will also contain a missing value. These missing values are displayed as an asterisk (*). The dialog box above illustrates the case when there are four variables, C1, C2, C3 and C4, and you want to calculate the difference between the third and first variables. The usual statistical notation for this difference variable is D; however this new variable may be explicitly named to clearly identify its interpretation.

Once this "difference" variable has been computed, a confidence interval using the formula

$$\bar{d} \mp Z \frac{s_d}{\sqrt{n}}$$ is computed using the *1-Sample Z* procedure as described in Chapter 5, Section 1.

Example 6.8: A random sample of professional baseball players was taken, and each player was asked to run from home plate to first base when batting right handed. Then the same players were asked to run from home plate to first base when batting left handed. This data is saved in the Proball.mtw worksheet on your data disc. Compute a 98% confidence interval for the difference in mean times to run from home plate to first base when batting left handed versus right handed.

(continued on the next page)

Use the *File , Open Worksheet...* to open the worksheet Proball.mtw that is saved on your data disc.

Click in the name row of the C3 column and type in difference to name this column.

Population 1 is all professional baseball players batting **left handed**.

Population 2 is all professional baseball players batting **right handed**.

Since the data in the two samples is measured on the same players, but batting from different sides, this is paired data.

Click on *Calc , Calculator...*

In the Calculator dialog box: click inside the box to the right of *Store result in variable:*, highlight the difference (C3) variable and click on the $\boxed{\text{Select}}$ button. Next click inside of the box under *Expression:* click on Left H (C2) which contains the **first** sample's data, click on the button with the minus sign (-) on it, and click on Right H (C1) containing the **second** sample's data. Then click on $\boxed{\text{OK}}$.

Click in the Session Window to the right of the *MTB >* prompt, type info and press the $\boxed{\text{Enter}}$ key.

Nothing is known about the distribution of these difference scores; but since the common sample size is 40, the confidence interval is computed using formula (vi) $\bar{d} \mp Z\dfrac{s_d}{\sqrt{n}}$ .

From the work shown in Chapter 5 or from the Reference Guide in the **One Sample Confidence Intervals for the Population Mean** section, compute a *1-Sample Z* confidence interval (with unknown population standard deviation) for the difference (C3) variable.

Click on *Calc , Column Statistics...*

In the Column Statistics dialog box: click on the circle to the left of *Standard deviation*, click inside of the *Input variable:* box, click on the difference (C3) variable, and click on the $\boxed{\text{Select}}$ button. Next click in the box to the **right** of *Store results in:*, and type in k1 as the constant name. Then click on the $\boxed{\text{OK}}$ button.

The resulting output below will appear in the Session Window.

## Standard Deviation of difference

### Standard deviation of difference = 0.224408

The next step is to compute the 98% confidence interval.

Click on *Stat, Basic Statistics, 1-Sample Z ...*

In the 1-Sample Z (Test and Confidence Interval) dialog box: make sure the button to the left of *Samples in columns* is selected, and then click inside of the box below. Now the variables (columns) will appear in the large box on the left side of this dialog box, highlight the difference (C3) variable, and click on the $\boxed{\text{Select}}$ button. Next click inside of the box to the right of *Standard deviation:*, and the constant K1 will appear in the large box on the left side of this dialog box. Click on this K1 and click on the $\boxed{\text{Select}}$ button (or just type k1 into this box). Make sure that the box to the right of *Test mean:* is empty, and then click on the $\boxed{\text{Options...}}$ button.

(continued on the next page)

In the 1-Sample Z - Options dialog box: if the value in the *confidence level:* box is not 98, erase this value and type in the correct confidence level of 98. Then make sure that the box to the right of *Alternative:* contains *not equal*. If not, click on the down triangle ( ▾ ), and click on the *not equal* choice. Then click on ▢ **OK** ▢ .

Back in the 1-Sample Z (Test and Confidence Interval) dialog box, click on ▢ **OK** ▢ .

The 98% confidence interval shown below will appear in the Session Window.

### One-Sample Z: difference

**The assumed standard deviation = 0.224408**

| Variable | N | Mean | StDev | SE Mean | 98.0 % C.I. |
|---|---|---|---|---|---|
| difference | 40 | -0.170000 | 0.224408 | 0.035482 | ( -0.252544, -0.087456) |

You are 98% confident that the interval from -0.25 to -0.09 seconds contains the difference of mean time to run from home plate to first base by all professional baseball players batting left handed versus batting right handed. From the result of this confidence interval, you could conclude that the mean time to run from home plate to first base by all professional baseball players is faster (less time) when they bat left handed.

If the data in a problem is in the form of **summary statistics**, then the confidence interval using the formula $\overline{d} \mp Z\dfrac{s_d}{\sqrt{n}}$ is computed using the *1-Sample Z* procedure for summary statistics data as described in Chapter 5, Section 1.

Click on *Stat*, *Basic Statistics*, *1-Sample Z...*

In the 1-Sample Z (Test and Confidence Interval) dialog box: make sure the button to the left of *Summarized data* is selected, and then click inside of the box to the right of *Sample size:*. If a previous value is shown, erase this number; or you may press the ▢ **F3** ▢ key to clear the contents of this dialog box and reset all options and erase any previous variables. Now type in the value of the sample size. Next click in the next box down that is to the right of *Mean:* and type in the value of the sample mean. Next click inside of the box to the right of *Standard deviation:*, erase any current incorrect value, and type in the known value of the sample standard deviation (s). Make sure that the box to the right of *Test mean:* is empty, and then click on ▢ **Options...** ▢ .

In the 1-Sample Z - Options dialog box: if the value in the *confidence level:* box is not the level you want, erase this value and type in the correct confidence level. Then make sure that the box to the right of *Alternative:* contains *not equal*. If not, click on the down triangle ( ▾ ), and click on the *not equal* choice. Then click on ▢ **OK** ▢ .

Back in the 1-Sample Z (Test and Confidence Interval) dialog box, click on ▢ **OK** ▢ .

# Lab Assignment 6.2

**Name:**                                                **Date:**

**Course:**              **Section:**              **Data CD Number:**

1.  Start a Minitab session.  If you are unable to complete this lab assignment in one Minitab session, save the project as Lab 6-2 . **Never** use a period as part of the project  name; since Minitab uses the period to attach the file type to the file name.  Then at your next Minitab session, you may open this Lab 6-2.MPJ project and continue to work where you left off previously.

2.  Thirty-six people were randomly chosen from all overweight persons attending the Burn-Off clinic.  Each was weighed before the start of a two week program and weighed again at the end of the two week program.   The results are given in the following table.

| Person | Weight Before Program | Weight After Program | Person | Weight Before Program | Weight After Program |
|--------|-----------------------|----------------------|--------|-----------------------|----------------------|
| 1 | 129 | 114 | 19 | 187 | 180 |
| 2 | 134 | 122 | 20 | 138 | 143 |
| 3 | 188 | 179 | 21 | 198 | 173 |
| 4 | 201 | 200 | 22 | 265 | 253 |
| 5 | 287 | 234 | 23 | 227 | 219 |
| 6 | 175 | 178 | 24 | 175 | 182 |
| 7 | 166 | 156 | 25 | 123 | 120 |
| 8 | 121 | 119 | 26 | 187 | 179 |
| 9 | 145 | 140 | 27 | 151 | 138 |
| 10 | 188 | 186 | 28 | 183 | 178 |
| 11 | 245 | 203 | 29 | 193 | 175 |
| 12 | 176 | 183 | 30 | 245 | 213 |
| 13 | 154 | 138 | 31 | 183 | 156 |
| 14 | 198 | 189 | 32 | 203 | 186 |
| 15 | 137 | 134 | 33 | 185 | 168 |
| 16 | 164 | 157 | 34 | 191 | 182 |
| 17 | 254 | 248 | 35 | 263 | 248 |
| 18 | 221 | 213 | 36 | 214 | 184 |

Compute a 98% confidence interval for the difference of the mean weight before the program minus the mean weight after the program for all overweight people attending the Burn-Off clinic.   Would you recommend the Burn-Off clinic to a friend who wants to lose weight?

(lab assignment is continued on the second side of this page)

157

3. Open the worksheet Tasktime.mtw that is on your data disc. Copying from the description of this worksheet given in Lab Assignment 5.1.1 or 5.1.2; twenty-three workers from the Method A assembly line were randomly selected, and their production times (in minutes) were measured. Then these **same** workers were moved to the Method B assembly line, and their production times (in minutes) were measured. It is known that production times by either of these two methods are normally distributed. The order of which method was done first was randomly assigned to these workers so that any learning effect would be accounted for. Using the data in these two paired samples, compute a 95% confidence interval for the mean production time of all workers from the Method A assembly line minus the mean production time of all workers from the Method B assembly line. Does one of these methods seem preferable to (faster than) the other?

4. Open another worksheet using Cespud.mtw from your data disc. As described in Lab Assignment 5.1.2; this worksheet contains a sample from the 1972 U.S. Consumer Expenditure Survey. Several variables were measured on each household including the total household spending on food and clothing and the total household spending on shelter. Compute a 90% confidence interval for the mean difference in the amount spent on these two categories by all households in the United States in 1972.

5. Print your Session Window to the printer.

6. Attach both your Minitab output and your complete answers to this sheet and submit all three to your instructor.

**Section 3:** **Confidence Intervals For The Ratio of Two Variances and The Ratio of Two Standard Deviations of Two Normal Populations Using Two <u>Independent</u> Samples**

To compare the relative internal consistency (or homogeneity) of values between two populations, the ratio of variances or standard deviations of the two populations is examined. If this ratio is less than one, then the first population is more homogeneous than the second. If this ratio is greater than one, then the first population is more spread out than the second. If this ratio equals one, then the two populations have the same amount of dispersion. When the variable is a continuous type measurement and has a normal distribution, a confidence interval for the ratio of two populations's variances, $\dfrac{\sigma_1^2}{\sigma_2^2}$, is computed using the formula

$$(vii) \qquad \frac{\left(\dfrac{s_1^2}{s_2^2}\right)}{F_U} \quad to \quad \frac{\left(\dfrac{s_1^2}{s_2^2}\right)}{F_L}$$

where $F_U$ and $F_L$ are the upper and lower percentiles, respectively, of the F distribution with $(n_1-1)$ and $(n_2-1)$ degrees of freedom. For example; if the desired confidence level is 90%, then $F_U$ is the 95$^{th}$ (.95) percentile and $F_L$ is the 5$^{th}$ (.05) percentile of the F distribution with $(n_1-1)$ and $(n_2-1)$ degrees of freedom. When the problem contains **raw data**, this confidence interval may be computed using the macro **Ci-2v.mtb** (Confidence interval for **2** variances) which is saved on your data disc. And when the problem has only **summary statistics data**, the confidence interval is computed using the macro **Sumci2v.mtb**.

A confidence interval for the ratio of standard deviations of two normally distributed populations is computed by taking the square root of each term in formula (vii) above to get

$$(viii) \qquad \sqrt{\frac{\left(\dfrac{s_1^2}{s_2^2}\right)}{F_U}} \quad to \quad \sqrt{\frac{\left(\dfrac{s_1^2}{s_2^2}\right)}{F_L}}$$

For **raw data** problems, the macro that computes this confidence interval is called **Ci-2sd.mtb** (Confidence interval for **2** standard deviations). And for **summary statistics data**, the macro is **Sumci2sd.mtb**.

Both of these macros will prompt you for the specific numbers of the columns that contain the data in the two samples. You must be very careful to enter the number that represents population 1 first, and the number that represents population 2 second. These two column numbers should be separated with a comma. Then these macros will prompt you to enter the desired confidence level. As shown earlier, use *File , Other Files , Run an Exec* on the Minitab menu bar to execute a macro.

Example 6.9   Open the worksheet Majorage.mtw that is on your data disc.  This worksheet contains the ages of four independent samples of art, economics, mathematics and psychology majors at Bowling Green University.  The ages of college students are known to be normally distributed.  Compute a 90% confidence interval for the ratio of the standard deviation of age of all psychology majors over the standard deviation of age of all mathematics majors.

Use the *File , Open Worksheet...* to open the Majorage.mtw worksheet from your data disc. Now click in the Session window to the right of the **MTB >** prompt and enter the info command (type info and press the ⃞ **Enter** ⃞ key) to display the basic information about the variables stored in this worksheet.  The information shown below will appear in the Session Window.

## *Results for: Majorage.mtw*

**MTB >** info ⃞ **Enter** ⃞

### *Information on the Worksheet*

| Column | Count | Name |
|--------|-------|------|
| C1 | 33 | ART |
| C2 | 39 | ECON |
| C3 | 39 | MATH |
| C4 | 62 | PSYC |

Population 1 is all psychology majors, and so column C4 contains the data in the corresponding sample.

Population 2 is all mathematics majors, and so column C3 contains the data in the corresponding sample.

The appropriate confidence interval is computed using

$$\sqrt{\frac{\left(\dfrac{s_1^2}{s_2^2}\right)}{F_U}} \text{ to } \sqrt{\frac{\left(\dfrac{s_1^2}{s_2^2}\right)}{F_L}} \ ,$$

and since you have the raw data for this example in the worksheet, the macro to be executed is Ci-2sd.mtb.

Click on *File , Other Files , Run an Exec ...*

In the Run an Exec dialog box:  make sure the *Number of times to execute:* box contains the number 1, and then click on the ⃞ **Select File** ⃞ button.

In the Run an Exec dialog box:  make sure the *Data Disc* is active (if not already done so), click on ci-2sd.mtb, and click on the ⃞ **Open** ⃞ button.

(continued on the next page)

The steps for this macro and resulting confidence interval shown below will appear in the Session Window.

***After the DATA> prompt, enter the column numbers that contain the data of the first and second samples. Enter ONLY the numbers, but NOT the C's !***

**DATA>** 4, 3 | Enter |          (since <u>C4</u> contains the sample data from population 1
                                             and <u>C3</u> contains the sample data from population 2)

***After the DATA> prompt, enter the confidence level.***

**DATA>** 90 | Enter |

## Data Display

***90.0 percent confidence interval for***
***population 1 st.deviation of C 4  divided by  population 2 st.deviation of C 3:***

***1.0463  to    1.7008***

and so you are 90% confident that the interval from 1.05 to 1.70 contains the ratio of standard deviations of ages of all psychology majors to all mathematics majors at Bowling Green University.   Since this interval is completely above the value of 1, you are at least 90% sure that the ages of all psychology majors is more spread out than the ages of all mathematics majors at Bowling Green University.

Example 6.10:   The Becker Bottling Company wanted to know if there was any difference in the consistency of its assembly line that fills bottles versus its assembly line that fills cans. Two independent random samples of 60 bottles and 80 cans were taken and the amount of liquid was measured. The amount of liquid filled by both assembly lines is normally distributed. The standard deviations for the bottles and cans are 0.23 and 0.67 respectively. Compute a 95% confidence interval for the ratio of the two population variances.

The information in this example indicates that the appropriate confidence interval is

$$\frac{\left(\dfrac{s_1^2}{s_2^2}\right)}{F_U} \quad \text{to} \quad \frac{\left(\dfrac{s_1^2}{s_2^2}\right)}{F_L}$$

This example contains only the summary statistics data, and so from the Reference Guide in the table with the heading **Two Sample Confidence Intervals For The Ratio of Two Population Variances and Standard Deviations Using Two Independent Samples**, and in the Summary Statistics Technique column; the macro to be executed is **Sumci2v.mtb** .

(continued on the next page)

Click on *File , Other Files , Run an Exec ...*

In the Run an Exec dialog box: make sure the *Number of times to execute:* box contains the number 1, and then click on the | **Select File** | button.

In the Run an Exec dialog box: the *Data Disc* should be selected. Next click on Sumci2v.mtp to highlight this macro, and click on the | **Open** | button.

The steps for this macro and resulting confidence interval shown below will appear in the Session Window.

**After the DATA> prompt, enter the respective values of the two Samples' variances (NOT standard deviations).**

*DATA>* 0.0529 , 0.4489 | **Enter** |     (since $0.23^2 = 0.0529$ and $0.67^2 = 0.4489$)

**After the DATA> prompt, enter the respective sizes of the two Samples.**

*DATA>* 60 , 80 | **Enter** |

**After the DATA> prompt, enter the confidence level.**

*DATA>* 95 | **Enter** |

## Data Display

**95.0 percent confidence interval for**
**population 1 variance divided by population 2 variance:**

**0.0735   to   0.1923**

and so you are 95% confident that the interval from 0.07 to 0.19 contains the ratio of variances of liquid in all bottles over all cans filled on their respective assembly lines. Since this interval is completely below the value of 1, you are at least 95% sure that the assembly line that fills bottles is more consistent than the line that fills cans.

Notice that in this example, the summary statistics given were the two sample standard deviations, but that the macro prompted you to enter the two sample variances. Therefore you needed to use a calculator to square these two standard deviations and get $0.23^2 = 0.0529$ and $0.67^2 = 0.4489$ before entering these numbers into the macro in the Session Window.

# Lab Assignment 6.3

**Name:**                                                              **Date:**

**Course:**                    **Section:**                      **Data CD Number:**


1.    Start a Minitab session.  If you are unable to complete this lab assignment in one Minitab session, save the project as Lab 6-3.  **Never** use a period as part of the project name; since Minitab uses the period to attach the file type to the file name.  Then at your next Minitab session, you may open this Lab 6-3.MPJ project and continue to work where you left off previously.


2.    Calls for help to the fire and police departments of Beckman County are made directly to these departments and not through a centralized 911 telephone number.   A sample of response times (in minutes) during 1993 was taken from each department with the following results:

Fire department:        6.3, 2.0, 2.3, 5.5, 7.9, 3.2, 4.1, 4.0, 6.1, 3.5, 8.3, 5.7, 4.5, 6.3 and  6.2


Police department:     13.7, 20.6, 15.9, 28.4, 19.3, 18.4, 11.6, 7.5, 16.2  and  13.0


Compute a 98% confidence interval for the ratio of the standard deviations (fire to police) of response times to all calls for help to these two Beckman County departments.


3.    Open the worksheet Run400.mtw that is on your data disc.    As described in Lab Assignment 6.1.1; the track officials sampled boys and girls in both the eight and twelve year old age groups and measured their times (in seconds) in a 400 meter race.   These times are normally distributed for all four populations.   Compute a 95% confidence interval for the ratio of variances of race times of all eight year old boys to all eight year old girls.

4.    Open another worksheet using Cityidx.mtw from your data disc.   As described in Lab Assignment 6.1.2; five variables were measured on a sample of cities in each of East, Central and West geographical regions of the United States, and the four index variables are normally distributed in each geographical region.

   a.   Compute a 90% confidence interval for the ratio of standard deviations of the urban unemployment index in all U.S. Central cities to all U.S. Western cities.

   b.   Compute a 95% confidence interval for the ratio of variances of the rural unemployment index in all U.S. Central cities to all U.S. Eastern cities.

(lab assignment is continued on the second side of this page)

5. Expansion and contraction in sealing rings can cause major problems with unwanted leakage. Two type of sealing rings are under consideration; rubber and soft plastic. The expansion of these two types of rings is known to be normally distributed. Samples of 35 rubber and 30 soft plastic sealing rings were tested by measuring how much each ring expanded when raised from 30 to 60 degrees. The standard deviations of the two samples are 0.023 and 0.018 respectively. Compute a 98% confidence interval for the ratio of standard deviations of the expansion of sealing rings in the two populations. Can you conclude that one type of sealing ring is more stable than the other?

6. In some audiological testing tuning forks are used. Two of the metals used to make these tuning forks are stainless steel and titanium. The tone produced must be very consistent if the test results are to be accurate. Samples of each type of tuning forks were taken and the tones produced by were measured with a precision audio instrument. The chart below summarizes the results. The tones produced are normally distributed for both types of metals.

| Metal Used | Sample Size | $\bar{x}$ | $s^2$ |
|---|---|---|---|
| Stainless Steel | 23 | 300.01 | 1.45 |
| Titanium | 16 | 300.02 | 1.03 |

Compute a 90% confidence interval for the ratio of variances of tone produced by the stainless steel tuning forks versus the titanium tuning forks. Does this data indicate that one type of metal is preferable for producing consistent tones?

7. Print your Session Window to the printer.

8. Attach both your Minitab output and your complete answers to this sheet and submit all three to your instructor.

## Section 4: Confidence Interval For The Difference of Two Population Proportions of "Successes"

The variables in the previous three sections were a continuous type of measurement. This section will describe how to compute a confidence interval for the difference between the proportion of "successes" in two populations when the variable is a Bernoulli type of measurement. If the sample sizes are sufficiently large (often interpreted as requiring all four of: $n_1\hat{p}_1$, $n_1(1 - \hat{p}_1)$, $n_2\hat{p}_2$ and $n_2(1 - \hat{p}_2)$ to be greater than or equal to 5 ), a confidence interval for this difference in population proportions ($p_1 - p_2$) is computed using the formula

$$
(ix) \qquad (\hat{p}_1 - \hat{p}_2) \mp Z \sqrt{\frac{\hat{p}_1(1 - \hat{p}_1)}{n_1} + \frac{\hat{p}_2(1 - \hat{p}_2)}{n_2}}
$$

where $\hat{p}_1$ is the proportion of "successes" in sample 1, and $\hat{p}_2$ is the proportion of "successes" in sample 2. As described in Section 3 of Chapter 5; the data for a Bernoulli type variables **must** be entered in the Worksheet Window into two variables (columns) such that the **exact same** coding is used for each "success" and the **exact same** coding is used for each "failure" for both variables. If you are entering alphabetic symbols or words, then you must use the exact same upper case and lower case letters each time for each "success" and for each "failure." As an alternative you may code each "success" outcome an one (1) and each "failure" outcome as a zero (0). If the variables contain data in alphabetic (text) form, as shown in Chapter 5 Section 3 , you may use *Data, Code , Text to Numeric ...* to code the alphabetic data into zeros and ones. Otherwise, you may use any of the coding (*Numeric to Text... , Numeric to Numeric..., or Text to Text...*) to make "Success"the larger number or word. Furthermore, if you enter alphabetic symbols or words, Minitab **always** assigns "failure" to the one that comes first in alphabetical order, and assigns "success" to the one that comes last in alphabetical order. So if you enter M for male and F for female: (1) you must use all of the same case for the Ms and all of the same case for the Fs, and (2) Minitab will assign "success" to the M (male) outcome.

For problems that contain **raw data**, the first thing to do is be certain that the "Success" outcome is number or word that is "larger." If this is not the case then you must code the data as described above. Once the **raw data** data is in the correct format, the confidence interval is computed from formula (ix) using the *2 Proportions* procedure as follows.

Click on *Stat , Basic Statistics , 2 Proportions ...*

In the 2 Proportions (Test and Confidence Interval) dialog box: make sure the button to the left of *Samples in different columns* is selected, click inside of the box to the right of *First:*, erase any previous variable, click on the variable that contains the data from the **first** sample, and click on Select . The cursor will move into the box to the right of *Second:*, click on the variable that contains the data from the **second** sample, and click on Select . Then click on Options... .

In the 2 Proportions - Options dialog box: if the value in the *confidence level:* box is not the level you want, erase this value and type in the correct confidence level. Leave the 0.0 in the box to the right of *Test difference:*. Then make sure that the box to the right of *Alternative:* contains *not equal*. If not, click on the down triangle ( ▾ ), and click on the *not equal* choice. Then click on the OK button.

Back in the 2 Proportions (Test and Confidence Interval) dialog box, click on OK .

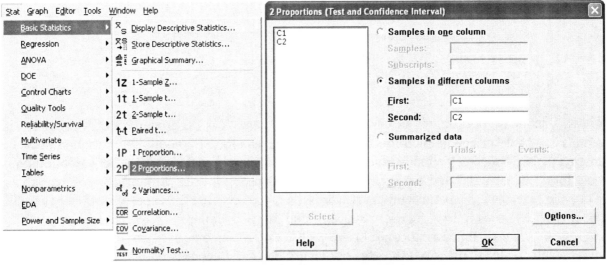

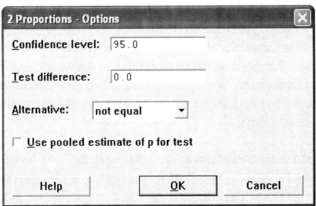

Problems that contain only **summary statistic data** instead of raw data also can be done using the *2 Proportions* procedure. The only change is in the 2 Proportions dialog box where you indicate you are using summary statistics (*Summarized data:*) instead of raw data.

Click on *Stat , Basic Statistics , 2 Proportions ...*

In the 2 Proportions (Test and Confidence Interval) dialog box: you may want to press the ⬚ F3 ⬚ key to erase all previous contents from the dialog boxes. Then make sure the button to the left of *Summarized data* is selected, and then click inside of the box to the right of *First:* and under *Trials:*. In this box erase any previous value and type in the first sample size. Next click inside of the box to the right under *Events:*, erase any previous value, and type in the number of "successes" in the first sample. Now repeat this for the second sample size and the number of "successes" in the second sample. Then click on the ⬚ **Options...** ⬚ button.

In the 2 Proportions - Options dialog box: if the value in the *confidence level:* box is not the level you want, erase this value and type in the correct confidence level. Leave the 0.0 in the box to the right of *Test difference:*. Then make sure that the box to the right of *Alternative:* contains *not equal*. If not, click on the down triangle ( ⬚▼⬚ ), and click on the *not equal* choice. Then click on the ⬚ **OK** ⬚ button.

Back in the 2 Proportions (Test and Confidence Interval) dialog box, click on ⬚ **OK** ⬚ .

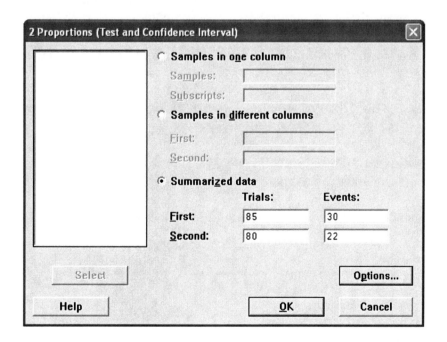

167

The output of the *2 Proportions* procedure contains:

(1) the outcome Minitab assigns as "success" written as *Event = outcome* (only for raw data),

(2) the variable names or column numbers (for raw data) or the sample number - usually 1 and 2 - (for summarized data), number of "successes" for each variable (Minitab uses a heading of X), sample sizes, and each sample's proportion of "successes" - $\hat{p}$,

(3) the value of the point estimate of the difference of $p_1 - p_2$,

(4) the specified confidence interval for $p_1 - p_2$,

(5) the value of the Z test statistic and p-value (explained in Chapter 8), and

(6) a warning if the criteria for using formula (ix) are not met.

Example 6.11   An independent agency randomly sampled "1040" tax forms prepared in 2005 by the IRS staff and randomly sampled forms prepared in 2005 by Bart & Land, CPA. Each form was examined and judged to be correct (C) or to be in error (E). The results of these two samples are:

IRS staff:   C, E, C, C, E, E, C, E, E, C, C, E, E, C, C, C, E, C, E, C, C, E, C, C, E, C, C, E, E, C, E, E and E

Bart & Land, CPA:   C, C, C, E, C, E, C, C, E, E, C, C, E, C, C, C, E, C, C, E, C, C, C, C, C, E, C, C, C, C, E, C, E, C, C and C

Compute a 90% confidence interval for the difference between the proportion of all "1040" tax forms that were incorrectly prepared in 2005 by the IRS staff and the proportion of all "1040" tax forms that were incorrectly prepared in 2005 by Bart & Land, CPA.

Enter the data into columns 1 and 2 and in the Worksheet Window, and then name these two variables B & L and IRS.

Population 1 is all "1040" forms prepared in 2005 by the IRS staff, and so column C1 contains the data in the corresponding sample.

Population 2 is all "1040" forms prepared in 2005 by Bart and Land, and so column C2 contains the data in the corresponding sample.

The confidence interval is computed using formula (ix)

$$(\hat{p}_1 - \hat{p}_2) \mp Z \sqrt{\frac{\hat{p}_1(1 - \hat{p}_1)}{n_1} + \frac{\hat{p}_2(1 - \hat{p}_2)}{n_2}}$$

and is computed using the *2 Proportions* procedure.

(continued on the next page)

Click on *Stat , Basic Statistics , 2 Proportions ...*

In the 2 Proportions (Test and Confidence Interval) dialog box: make sure the button to the left of *Samples in different columns* is selected, click inside of the box to the right of *First:*, erase any previous variable, click IRS (C1), and click on $\boxed{\text{Select}}$ . The cursor will move into the box to the right of *Second:*, click on B & L (C2), and click on $\boxed{\text{Select}}$ . Then click on $\boxed{\text{Options...}}$ .

In the 2 Proportions - Options dialog box: if the value in the *confidence level:* box is not the level you want, erase this value and type in the correct confidence level. Leave the 0.0 in the box to the right of *Test difference:*. Then make sure that the box to the right of *Alternative:* contains *not equal*. If not, click on the down triangle ( $\boxed{\blacktriangledown}$ ), and click on the *not equal* choice. Then click on the $\boxed{\text{OK}}$ button.

Back in the 2 Proportions (Test and Confidence Interval) dialog box, click on $\boxed{\text{OK}}$ .

The resulting output shown below will appear in the Session Window.

## *Test CI for Two Proportions: IRS, B & L*

### *Event = E*

| Variable | X | N | Sample p |
|----------|-----|-----|----------|
| IRS | 16 | 33 | 0.484848 |
| B & L | 10 | 36 | 0.277778 |

*Difference = p (IRS) - p (B & L)*
*Estimate for difference: 0.207071*
*90% CI for difference: (0.0185106, 0.395631)*
*Test for difference = 0 (vs not = 0): Z = 1.77 P-Value = 0.076*

and so you are 90% confident that the interval from 0.019 to 0.40 contains the difference between the proportion of all 2005 "1040" forms prepared incorrectly by the IRS staff and the proportion of all 2005 "1040" forms incorrectly prepared by Bart & Land, CPA. Since this interval contains only positive values (and thus does <u>not</u> contain 0), you may be reasonably confident (90%) that the IRS has a higher proportion of prepared forms with errors than Bart & Land. Therefore Bart & Land, CPA did a "better" job than the IRS staff of preparing 2005 "1040" forms.

Example 6.12: A random sample of 85 men and 80 women were shown a movie that contained a subliminal message to buy popcorn. Thirty of the men and 22 of the women subsequently bought popcorn. Find a 95% confidence interval for the difference in the proportion of all men and all women who are influenced by subliminal messages.

From the information in this example, the confidence interval is

$$(ix) \quad (\hat{p}_1 - \hat{p}_2) \mp Z \sqrt{\frac{\hat{p}_1(1 - \hat{p}_1)}{n_1} + \frac{\hat{p}_2(1 - \hat{p}_2)}{n_2}} ,$$

and since this example has summary statistic data, this formula is computed as follows.

(continued on the next page)

Click on *Stat*, *Basic Statistics*, *2 Proportions* ...

In the 2 Proportions (Test and Confidence Interval) dialog box: you may want to press the | **F3** | key to erase all previous contents from the dialog boxes. Then make sure the button to the left of *Summarized data* is selected, and then click inside of the box to the right of *First:* and under *Trials:*. In this box erase any previous value and type in the first sample size of 85. Next click inside of the box to the right under *Events:*, erase any previous value, and type in 30 which is the number of "successes" in the first sample. Now repeat this for the second sample size of 80 and the number of "successes" in the second sample which is 22. Then click on the | **Options...** | button.

In the 2 Proportions - Options dialog box: if the value in the *confidence level:* box is 95, erase this value and type in the correct confidence level of 95. Leave the 0.0 in the box to the right of *Test difference:*. Then make sure that the box to the right of *Alternative:* contains *not equal*. If not, click on the down triangle ( ▾ ), and click on the *not equal* choice. Then click on the | **OK** | button.

Back in the 2 Proportions (Test and Confidence Interval) dialog box, click on | **OK** |.

The results shown below will appear in the Session Window.

## Test and CI for Two Proportions

| Sample | X | N | Sample p |
|--------|-----|-----|----------|
| 1 | 30 | 85 | 0.352941 |
| 2 | 22 | 80 | 0.275000 |

**Difference = p (1) - p (2)**
**Estimate for difference: 0.0779412**
**95% CI for difference: (-0.0631073, 0.218990)**
**Test for difference = 0 (vs not = 0): Z = 1.08  P-Value = 0.279**

and so you are 95% confident that the interval from -0.06 to 0.22 contains the difference between the proportion of all men who were subliminally affected and the proportion of all women who were subliminally affected. Since this interval contains zero, you have no reason to believe that there is a real difference in how men and women are affected by these subliminal messages.

# Lab Assignment 6.4

**Name:**                                                   **Date:**

**Course:**                    **Section:**                         **Data CD Number:**

1. Start a Minitab session. If you are unable to complete this lab assignment in one Minitab session, save the project as Lab 6-4 . **Never** use a period as part of the project name; since Minitab uses the period to attach the file type to the file name. Then at your next Minitab session, you may open this Lab 6-4.MPJ project and continue to work where you left off previously.

2. In a research project on gender academic differences in the United States, a random sample of spelling bee winners and a random sample of science fair winners were taken. The gender of each winner was recorded as "M" for male and "F" for female with the following results:

    Science fair winners: F, M, M, F, M, M, M, F, F, M, M, M, M, M, F, M, M, M, F, F, M, F M, M, F and F

    Spelling bee winners: F, F, M, M, F, F, F, M, M, F, F, M, F, M, F, F, M, M, F, F, F, M, M F, M, M, M, F, F, M, F and F

    Enter the data into the current Worksheet Window in columns 1 and 2 using the alphabetic symbols M and F. Compute a 95% confidence interval for the difference between the proportions of all U.S. spelling bee and all U.S. science fair winners who are female. What conclusion, if any, is reasonable?

3. From a random sample of 40 adult males that were mailed a long questionnaire, ten responded. A second sample of 46 adult males were called on the telephone and asked if they would answer the long questionnaire. Sixteen of the 46 agreed to answer. Compute a 99% confidence interval for the difference between the proportion of all adult males who would respond to a mailed survey and the proportion who would respond to a telephone survey. Do the two survey techniques seem to elicit the same degree of cooperation?

4. Open the worksheet Cityidx.mtw that is on your data disc. As described in Lab Assignment 6.1.2; five variables were measured on a sample of cities in each of East, Central and West geographical regions of the United States. One of the variables measured in each region was the municipal bond rating; where a "good" rating of A or better was recorded as a 1, and a rating of below A was recorded as a 0.

    a. Compute a 90% confidence interval for the difference between the proportions of all U.S. Eastern cities and all U.S. Western cities that have a "good" municipal bond rating.

    b. Compute a 99% confidence interval for difference between the proportions of all U.S. Western cities and all U.S. Central cities that have a "good" bond rating.

(lab assignment is continued on the second side of this page)

5.   A marketing firm wanted to compare audio-only with audio-visual advertisements. Two random samples of 1000 people were chosen. Everyone in the first sample listened to an audio-only advertisement for Santos Spring Water, while the second sample saw an audio-visual advertisement for the same product. After the presentation of the advertisement; 175 people in the audio-only group said they would buy Santos Spring Water, and 240 people from the audio-visual group said they would buy the product. Compute a 95% confidence interval for the difference in the proportion of people influenced by the two types of advertisements.

6.   A random sample of 94 people infected with streptococcus were given an oral antibiotic, and 14 of them exhibited an undesirable reaction to the treatment. A second random sample of 76 people infected with streptococcus were given the antibiotic as an injection, and 10 of them exhibited the same undesirable reaction. Compute a 90% confidence interval for the difference in the proportion of all people receiving the two types of antibiotic delivery who have the undesired reaction.

7.   First print your **Worksheet 1** Window, but **not** the Cityidx.mtw Worksheet Window to the printer, and then print your Session Window on the printer.

8.   Attach both your Minitab output and <u>your complete answers</u> to this paper and submit all three to your instructor.

# CHAPTER 7:    One Sample Hypothesis Tests

**Section 1:    Hypothesis Tests For The Population Mean**

Constructing and testing hypotheses about population parameters is another of the primary objectives of statistical inference.  Hypothesis testing is the most common method used to evaluate the results of research projects.   The organization and procedures in this chapter closely parallel those given in Chapter 5.   This section will focus on data from a continuous type of measurement where the parameter of interest is the population mean ($\mu$).

The "one sample" hypothesis test of the mean from a single population may take one of the following three forms:

(a)  $H_0: \mu = \mu_0$
     $H_a: \mu \neq \mu_0$

(b)  $H_0: \mu \geq \mu_0$
     $H_a: \mu < \mu_0$

(c)  $H_0: \mu \leq \mu_0$
     $H_a: \mu > \mu_0$

The alternative hypothesis ($H_a$) in test (a) is called "two-sided", and the entire test procedure is called a "two tail" test; while the alternative hypotheses in tests (b) and (c) are called "one-sided", and the entire test procedures are called "one tail" tests.  In particular, form (b) is called a "left tail" test and form (c) is called a "right tail" test.   Depending upon the distribution type and which parameters are known, the test statistic for these tests is computed using one of the following three formulas:

(i)  $Z = \dfrac{\bar{x} - \mu_0}{\dfrac{\sigma}{\sqrt{n}}}$

(ii)  $Z = \dfrac{\bar{x} - \mu_0}{\dfrac{s}{\sqrt{n}}}$

(iii)  $t = \dfrac{\bar{x} - \mu_0}{\dfrac{s}{\sqrt{n}}}$

These three test statistic formulas parallel the three formulas for confidence intervals given in Chapter 5.   Minitab computes the test statistics given in formulas (i) and (ii) using *Stat , Basic Statistics , 1-Sample Z* and the test statistic given in formula (iii) is computed using *Stat , Basic Statistics , 1-Sample t*. Their formats are very similar to the confidence interval procedures in Chapter 5.

For a problem with **raw data** where formula (i) has been chosen as the appropriate test statistic; the value of the population standard deviation ($\sigma$) will be known, and the *1-Sample Z* test statistic is computed.

Click on *Stat*, *Basic Statistics*, *1-Sample Z...*

In the 1-Sample Z (Test and Confidence Interval) dialog box: you may press the F3 key to clear the contents of this dialog box and reset all options and erase any previous variables. Make sure the button to the left of *Samples in columns* is selected, and then click inside of the box below. The variables (columns) will appear in the large box on the left side of this dialog box. If a previous variable is shown, erase the variable, click on the variable you want to analyze, and click on the Select button. Next click inside of the box to the right of *Standard deviation:*, erase any current incorrect value, and type in the known value of the population standard deviation ($\sigma$). Check the box to the left of *Perform hypothesis test*, click inside of the box to the right of *Hypothesized mean:*, delete any current value, and type in the specified value of $\mu_0$ in the null hypothesis ($H_0$:), and then click on the Options... button. Remember, do **not** press the Enter key after you have typed in anything, but use the mouse to move to another place in the dialog box.

In the 1-Sample Z - Options dialog box: ignore the value in the *Confidence level:* box, and then make sure that the box to the right of *Alternative:* contains the correct inequality for your problem (*not equal* or *less than* or *greater than*). If not, click on the down triangle ( ▼ ), and click on the correct choice. Then click on OK .

Back in the 1-Sample Z (Test and Confidence Interval) dialog box, click on OK .

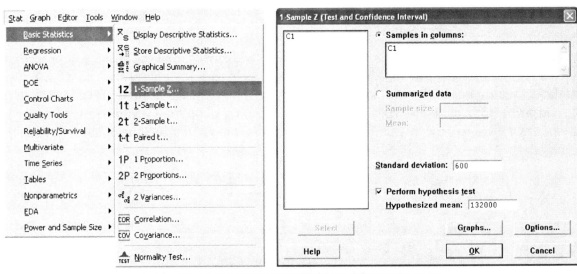

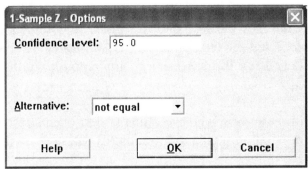

174

However, when the problem has **summary statistics** data, this formula (i) is computed by

Click on *Stat , Basic Statistics , 1-Sample Z...*

In the 1-Sample Z (Test and Confidence Interval) dialog box: you may press the F3 key to clear the contents of this dialog box and reset all options and erase any previous variables. Make sure the button to the left of *Summarized data* is selected, and then click inside of the box to the right of *Sample size:*. Now type in the value of the sample size. Next click in the next box down that is to the right of *Mean:* and type in the value of the sample mean. Next click inside of the box to the right of *Standard deviation:*, erase any current incorrect value, and type in the known value of the population standard deviation ($\sigma$). Check the box to the left of *Perform hypothesis test*, click inside of the box to the right of *Hypothesized mean:*, delete any current value, and type in the specified value of $\mu_0$ in the null hypothesis ($H_0$:), and then click on the Options... button.

In the 1-Sample Z - Options dialog box: ignore the value in the *Confidence level:* box , and then make sure that the box to the right of *Alternative:* contains the correct inequality for your problem (*not equal* or *less than* or *greater than*). If not, click on the down triangle ( ▼ ), and click on the correct choice. Then click on OK .

Back in the 1-Sample Z (Test and Confidence Interval) dialog box, click on OK .

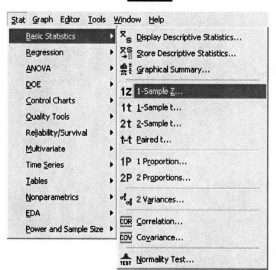

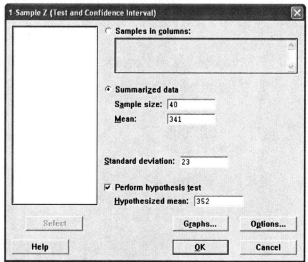

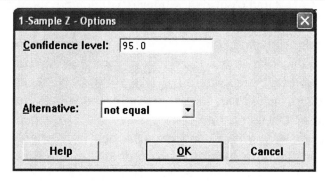

The output of *1-Sample Z* contains:

(1)    The null and alternative hypotheses,
(2)    the value you specified for σ; printed as **The assumed standard deviation = xx**,
(3)    the variable column label or name (only when problem has raw data),
(4)    the number of valid observations, the mean, standard deviation (only for raw data problem) and standard error of the variable,
(5)    the upper or lower bound of a one sided confidence interval when the alternative is *less than* or *greater than* respectively, or a regular two sided confidence interval (when the alternative is *not equal* (ignore this information when doing hypothesis testing),
(6)    the value of the Z test statistic and
(7)    the p-value for the test.

The p-value may be interpreted as "based upon the data of this sample, if you decide to reject the null hypothesis then the probability of this decision being an error is equal to the p-value."

Even though the *1-Sample Z* procedure may compute the sample standard deviation, this is for information purposes only. The standard error of the mean and the Z test statistic are calculated using the entered value of sigma; that is, **the assumed standard deviation** value.

Example 7.1:    A random sample of five typewriter carbon film ribbon cartridges was taken, and the number of characters that could be typed from each cartridge was measured. The results were: 132,841 , 131,347 , 132,756 , 131,720 and 132,706. For all such cartridges, this measurement is normally distributed with a population standard deviation of 600 characters. At the 0.05 level of significance, test the hypothesis that the mean number of characters that can be typed from all such cartridges is equal to 132,000.

Enter these five raw data scores into column 1 of the Worksheet Window.

The hypothesis testing problem is

$H_0$: $\mu = 132000$
$H_a$: $\mu \neq 132000$
$\alpha = 0.05$

and the test statistic is $Z = \dfrac{\bar{x} - \mu_0}{\dfrac{\sigma}{\sqrt{n}}}$ given in formula (i).

Click on *Stat , Basic Statistics , 1-Sample Z...*

In the 1-Sample Z (Test and Confidence Interval) dialog box: you may press the [ **F3** ] key to clear the contents of this dialog box and reset all options and erase any previous variables. Make sure the button to the left of *Samples in columns* is selected, and then click inside of the box below. If a previous variable is shown, erase the variable, click on the C1 variable and click on the [ **Select** ] button. Next click inside of the box to the right of *Standard deviation:*, erase any current incorrect value, and type in 600, the known value of the population standard deviation (σ).Check the box to the left of *Perform hypothesis test*, click inside of the box to the right of *Hypothesized mean:*, delete any current value, and type in 132000, the specified value of $\mu_0$ in the null hypothesis ($H_0$:), and then click on the [ **Options...** ] button.

(continued on the next page)

In the 1-Sample Z - Options dialog box: ignore the value in the *Confidence level:* box and then make sure that the box to the right of *Alternative:* contains the correct inequality of *not equal.* If not, click on the down triangle ( ▾ ), and click on the correct choice. Then click on ⬛ **OK** .

Back in the 1-Sample Z (Test and Confidence Interval) dialog box, click on ⬛ **OK** .

The resulting output which includes the null and alternative hypotheses, the value of the Z test statistic and the p-value will appear in the Session Window.

### One-Sample Z: C1

**Test of mu = 132000 vs not = 132000**

**The assumed standard deviation = 600**

| Variable | N | Mean | StDev | SE Mean | 95% CI | Z | P |
|----------|---|------|-------|---------|--------|---|---|
| C1 | 5 | 132274 | 690 | 268 | (131748, 132800) | 1.02 | 0.307 |

Since the p-value of 0.307 is greater than 0.05 ($\alpha$), you may not reject the null hypothesis. Also note that the value of the Z test statistic is 1.02, and that this value is not in the rejection region ( $Z \leq -1.96$ or $Z \geq 1.96$ ).

Note that the first line of the Minitab output contains the correct alternative hypothesis as **... vs not = 132000** . You should always look at this part of the output to double check that you entered the correct alternative for your specific problem.

Example 7.2:   A researcher in anatomy and physiology is studying the heights of U.S. males over the last century. In 1902 the mean height of all U.S. males was known to have been 67.5 inches. This year the researcher took a sample of 50 U.S. males and found that the mean height is 69.2 inches. Also much current research shows that the standard deviation of height of current U.S. males is 4.25 inches. Using a significance level of 0.01, did the researcher conclude that the current mean height has not increased?

This example contains summary statistic data, and the the hypothesis testing problem is

$H_0: \mu \leq 67.5$
$H_a: \mu > 67.5$
$\alpha = 0.01$

and the test statistic is $Z = \dfrac{\overline{x} - \mu_0}{\dfrac{\sigma}{\sqrt{n}}}$ given in formula (i).

(continued on the next page)

Click on *Stat* , *Basic Statistics* , *1-Sample Z...*

In the 1-Sample Z (Test and Confidence Interval) dialog box: make sure the button to the left of *Summarized data* is selected, and then click inside of the box to the right of *Sample size:* and type in100, the value of the sample size. Next click in the next box down that is to the right of *Mean:* and type in 69.2, the value of the sample mean. Next click inside of the box to the right of *Standard deviation:* and type in 3.95, the known value of the population standard deviation ($\sigma$). Check the box to the left of *Perform hypothesis test*, click inside of the box to the right of *Hypothesized mean:*, delete any current value, and type in 67.5, the specified value of $\mu_0$ in the null hypothesis ($H_0$:), and then click on the Options... button.

In the 1-Sample Z - Options dialog box: ignore the value in the *Confidence level:* box , and then make sure that the box to the right of *Alternative:* contains the correct inequality of *greater than*. If not, click on the down triangle ( ▼ ), and click on the correct choice. Then click on OK .

Back in the 1-Sample Z (Test and Confidence Interval) dialog box, click on OK .

The results shown below of this one sample t test, which includes the null and alternative hypotheses, the value of the t test statistic and the p-value, will appear in the Session Window.

## One-Sample Z

**Test of mu = 67.5 vs > 67.5**
**The assumed standard deviation = 4.25**

| N | Mean | SE Mean | 95% Lower Bound | Z | P |
|---|------|---------|-----------------|---|---|
| 50 | 69.2000 | 0.6010 | 68.2114 | 2.83 | 0.002 |

Since the p-value of 0.002 is less than 0.01 ($\alpha$), the researcher may reject the null hypothesis and conclude that the mean height of all current U.S. males has increased over the past century. Also note that the value of the Z test statistic is 2.83, and that this value is in the rejection region ( $Z \geq 2.326$ ).

When the problem has **raw data** and the test statistic is given by formula (ii) $Z = \dfrac{\bar{x} - \mu_0}{\dfrac{s}{\sqrt{n}}}$,

the population variance is unknown and the sample standard deviation (s) must be calculated first and stored in the constant k1. As described in Chapter 5, this is done by

Click on *Calc* , *Column Statistics...*
In the Column Statistics dialog box: click on the circle to the left of *Standard deviation*, click inside of the *Input variable:* box, click on the variable that contains the sample data, and click on the Select button. Next click in the box to the **right** of *Store results in:*, and type in k1 as the constant name. Then click on the OK button.

(See graphic on the next page.)

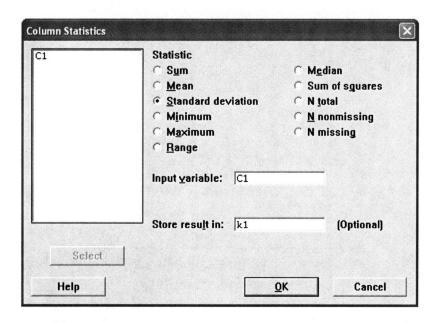

Then the Z test statistic itself is computed again using the *1-Sample Z* procedure, but this time inserting the computed standard deviation in place of sigma.

Click on *Stat , Basic Statistics , 1-Sample Z...*

In the 1-Sample Z (Test and Confidence Interval) dialog box: you may press the F3 key to clear the contents of this dialog box and reset all options and erase any previous variables. Make sure the button to the left of *Samples in columns* is selected, and then click inside of the box below. Now the variables (columns) will appear in the large box on the left side of this dialog box. If a previous variable is shown, erase the variable, click on the variable you want to analyze, and click on the Select button. Next click inside of the box to the right of *Standard deviation:,* erase any current incorrect value, highlight the K1 constant and click on the Select button (or just type in k1). Check the box to the left of *Perform hypothesis test*, click inside of the box to the right of *Hypothesized mean:*, delete any current value, and type in the specified value of $\mu_0$ in the null hypothesis (H$_0$:), and then click on the Options... button. Remember, do **not** press the Enter key after you have typed in anything, but use the mouse to move to another place in the dialog box.

In the 1-Sample Z - Options dialog box: ignore the value in the *Confidence level:* box, and then make sure that the box to the right of *Alternative:* contains the correct inequality for your problem (*not equal* or *less than* or *greater than*). If not, click on the down triangle ( ▼ ), and click on the correct choice. Then click on OK . (graphic shown on page 162)

Back in the 1-Sample Z (Test and Confidence Interval) dialog box, click on OK .

(Only the graphic for the second step is shown on the next page.)

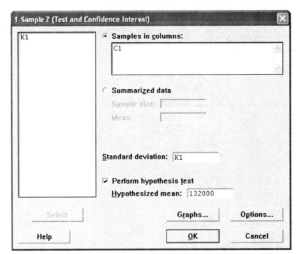

However, when the problem has **summary statistics** data, this formula (ii) is computed by

Click on *Stat , Basic Statistics , 1-Sample Z...*

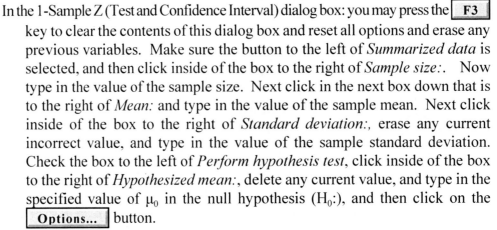

In the 1-Sample Z (Test and Confidence Interval) dialog box: you may press the 【 F3 】 key to clear the contents of this dialog box and reset all options and erase any previous variables. Make sure the button to the left of *Summarized data* is selected, and then click inside of the box to the right of *Sample size:*. Now type in the value of the sample size. Next click in the next box down that is to the right of *Mean:* and type in the value of the sample mean. Next click inside of the box to the right of *Standard deviation:*, erase any current incorrect value, and type in the value of the sample standard deviation. Check the box to the left of *Perform hypothesis test*, click inside of the box to the right of *Hypothesized mean:*, delete any current value, and type in the specified value of $\mu_0$ in the null hypothesis ($H_0$:), and then click on the 【 Options... 】 button.

In the 1-Sample Z - Options dialog box: ignore the value in the *Confidence level:* box , and then make sure that the box to the right of *Alternative:* contains the correct inequality for your problem (*not equal* or *less than* or *greater than*). If not, click on the down triangle ( ▾ ), and click on the correct choice. Then click on 【 OK 】.

Back in the 1-Sample Z (Test and Confidence Interval) dialog box, click on 【 OK 】.

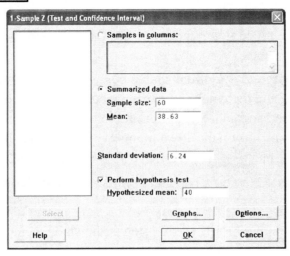

180

Example 7.3:   A random sample of size 73 was taken from all first grade students in Tampa, Florida.   The students' heights (in inches) and weights (in pounds) were measured, and the results are in the Fstgrade.mtw worksheet saved on your data disk.   Previous research has determined that the distribution of heights of all first grade students in Tampa is non-normal.   The average height of all first graders in the United States is 43½ inches.   At the 0.10 level of significance test to see if Tampa's first grade students are taller than the U.S. average.

Use *File , Open Worksheet...* to open the worksheet Fstgrade.mtw from your data disk.

Note that while the example says "... if Tampa's first grade students are taller ...", this does <u>not</u> imply that each and every Tampa first grade student is taller than the U.S. average. When a measurement of an entire group is referred to, what is meant is the **mean** of that group and <u>not</u> each of the individuals in the group.   So this example is asking you to test if the mean height of all first graders in Tampa is greater than (taller) the U.S. average of 43½ inches.

The distribution of heights of all first grade students in Tampa is non-normal, and the population standard deviation is not given in the example.   But the sample size is greater than 30; so the Z test statistic given in formula (ii) is appropriate, and the sample standard deviation needs to be computed.

This example contains raw data, and the hypothesis testing problem is

$H_0$: $\mu \le 43.5$
$H_a$: $\mu > 43.5$
$\alpha = 0.10$

and the test statistic is $Z = \dfrac{\bar{x} - \mu_0}{\dfrac{s}{\sqrt{n}}}$ given in formula (ii).

Click on *Calc , Column Statistics...*

In the Column Statistics dialog box: press the $\boxed{\text{F3}}$ to clear previous contents; click on the circle to the left of *Standard deviation*, click inside of the *Input variable:* box, click on the  the Height (C1) variable, and click on the $\boxed{\text{Select}}$ button. Next click in the box to the **right** of *Store results in:*, and type in k1 as the constant name. Then click on $\boxed{\textbf{OK}}$ .

Click on *Stat , Basic Statistics , 1-Sample Z...*

In the 1-Sample Z (Test and Confidence Interval) dialog box: you may press the $\boxed{\text{F3}}$ key to clear the contents of this dialog box and reset all options and erase any previous variables.  Make sure the button to the left of *Samples in columns* is selected, and then click inside of the box below.  Click on the Height (C1) variable, and click on the $\boxed{\text{Select}}$ button. Next click inside of the box to the right of *Standard deviation:*, erase any current incorrect value, highlight the K1 constant and click on the $\boxed{\text{Select}}$ button (or just type in k1).  Check the box to the left of *Perform hypothesis test*, click inside of the box to the right of *Hypothesized mean:*, delete any current value, and type in 43.5, the specified value of $\mu_0$ in the null hypothesis ($H_0$:), and then click on the $\boxed{\textbf{Options...}}$ button.

(continued on the next page)

In the 1-Sample Z - Options dialog box: ignore the value in the *Confidence level:* box, and then make sure that the box to the right of *Alternative:* contains the correct inequality of *greater than*. If not, click on the down triangle ( ▾ ), and click on the correct choice. Then click on ⬛ OK ⬛.

Back in the 1-Sample Z (Test and Confidence Interval) dialog box, click on ⬛ OK ⬛.

The resulting output shown below which includes the null and alternative hypotheses, the value of the Z test statistic and the p-value will appear in the Session Window.

## One-Sample Z: Height

***Test of mu = 43.5 vs > 43.5***
***The assumed standard deviation = 8.55416***

| Variable | N | Mean | StDev | SE Mean | 95%<br>Lower<br>Bound | Z | P |
|----------|----|---------|--------|---------|-------------|------|-------|
| Height | 73 | 45.1130 | 8.5542 | 1.0012 | 43.4662 | 1.61 | 0.054 |

Notice that the first line of the output now contains the correct alternative hypothesis as ***... vs > 43.50*** . Since the p-value of 0.054 is less than 0.10 (α), you may reject the null hypothesis, and conclude that the mean height of all first grade students in Tampa, Florida is greater than (taller) the U.S. average of 43½ inches. Also note that the value of the Z test statistic is 1.61, and this is in the rejection region ( $Z \geq 1.282$ ).

You should notice that even though the null hypothesis is stated as less than or equal to ($H_0: \mu \leq \mu_0$), Minitab **always** displays it results in the form of ***Test of mu = $\mu_0$ vs > $\mu_0$*** and when $H_0: \mu \geq \mu_0$ , as ***Test of mu = $\mu_0$ vs < $\mu_0$*** ; that is Minitab always shows the null hypothesis as equal to (**=**).

When the test statistic is $Z = \dfrac{\overline{x} - \mu_0}{\dfrac{s}{\sqrt{n}}}$ given in formula (ii), and the problem that contains

**summary statistic** data, the procedure is the same as described previous for formula (i); except that the sample standard deviation is type in instead of the population standard deviation. So that this formula (ii) is computed by

Click on *Stat , Basic Statistics , 1-Sample Z...*

In the 1-Sample Z (Test and Confidence Interval) dialog box: you may press the ⬛ F3 ⬛ key to clear the contents of this dialog box and reset all options and erase any previous variables. Make sure the button to the left of *Summarized data* is selected, and then click inside of the box to the right of *Sample size:*. Now type in the value of the sample size. Next click in the next box down that is to the right of *Mean:* and type in the value of the sample mean. Next click inside of the box to the right of *Standard deviation:*, erase any current incorrect value, and type in the value of the sample standard deviation (s). Check the box to the left of *Perform hypothesis test*, click inside of the box to the right of *Hypothesized mean:*, delete any current value, and type in the specified value of $\mu_0$ in the null hypothesis ($H_0$:), and then click on the ⬛ Options... ⬛ button.

(continued on the next page)

In the 1-Sample Z - Options dialog box: ignore the value in the *Confidence level:* box , and then make sure that the box to the right of *Alternative:* contains the correct inequality for your problem (*not equal* or *less than* or *greater than*). If not, click on the down triangle ( ▾ ), and click on the correct choice. Then click on [ **OK** ] .

Back in the 1-Sample Z (Test and Confidence Interval) dialog box, click on [ **OK** ] .

For samples that are taken from normally distributed populations; hypothesis tests for the population mean employ a test statistic having the Student's t distribution, and the test statistic given in formula (iii) is used. Since this procedure always uses the sample standard deviation, you do not have to compute the sample value of s separately. For problems that have **raw data**, the test statistic $t = \dfrac{\overline{x} - \mu_0}{\dfrac{s}{\sqrt{n}}}$ given in formula (iii) is computed by

Click on *Stat , Basic Statistics , 1-Sample t...*

In the 1-Sample t (Test and Confidence Interval) dialog box: you may press the [ **F3** ] key to clear the contents of this dialog box and reset all options and erase any previous variables. Make sure the button to the left of *Samples in columns* is selected, and then click inside of the box below. Now the variables (columns) will appear in the large box on the left side of this dialog box. If a previous variable is shown, erase the variable, click on the variable you want to analyze, and click on the [ **Select** ] button. Next check the box to the left of *Perform hypothesis test*, click inside of the box to the right of *Hypothesized mean:*, delete any current value, and type in the specified value of $\mu_0$ in the null hypothesis (H$_0$:), and then click on the [ **Options...** ] button. Remember, do **not** press the [ **Enter** ] key after you have typed in anything, but use the mouse to move to another place in the dialog box.

In the 1-Sample t - Options dialog box: ignore the value in the *Confidence level:* box, and then make sure that the box to the right of *Alternative:* contains the correct inequality for your problem (*not equal* or *less than* or *greater than*). If not, click on the down triangle ( ▾ ), and click on the correct choice. Then click on [ **OK** ] .

Back in the 1-Sample t (Test and Confidence Interval) dialog box, click on [ **OK** ] .

(See graphics on the next page.)

183

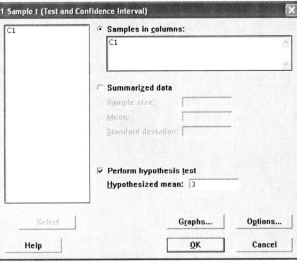
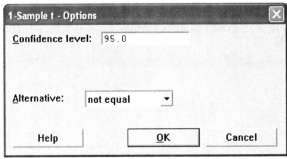

However, when the problem has **summary statistics** data, this formula (ii) is computed by

Click on *Stat , Basic Statistics , 1 Sample t ...*

In the 1-Sample t (Test and Confidence Interval) dialog box: you may press the F3 key to clear the contents of this dialog box and reset all options and erase any previous variables. Make sure the button to the left of *Summarized data* is selected, and then click inside of the box to the right of *Sample size:*. Now type in the value of the sample size. Next click in the next box down that is to the right of *Mean:* and type in the value of the sample mean. Next click in the next box down that is to the right of *Standard deviation:*, erase any current incorrect value, and type in the value of the sample standard deviation. Check the box to the left of *Perform hypothesis test*, click inside of the box to the right of *Hypothesized mean:*, delete any current value, and type in the specified value of $\mu_0$ in the null hypothesis ($H_0$:), and then click on the Options... button.

In the 1-Sample t - Options dialog box: ignore the value in the *Confidence level:* box, and then make sure that the box to the right of *Alternative:* contains the correct inequality for your problem (*not equal* or *less than* or *greater than*). If not, click on the down triangle ( ▾ ), and click on the correct choice. Then click on OK .

Back in the 1-Sample t (Test and Confidence Interval) dialog box, click on OK .

(See graphics on the next page.)

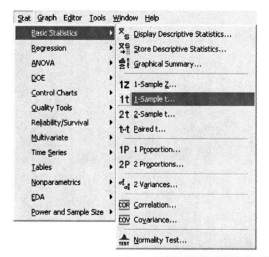
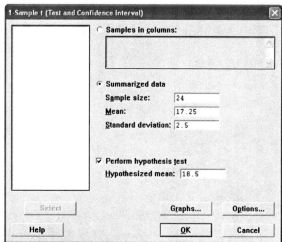
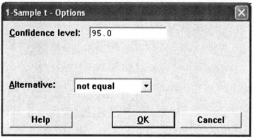

The output of *1-Sample t* contains:

(1)     The null and alternative hypotheses,
(2)     the variable column label or name (only when problem has raw data),
(3)     the number of valid observations, the mean, standard deviation (only for raw data problem) and standard error of the variable,
(4)     the upper or lower bound of a one sided confidence interval when the alternative is *less than* or *greater than* respectively, or a regular two sided confidence interval(when the alternative is *not equal* (ignore this information when doing hypothesis testing),
(5)     the value of the **t** test statistic and
(6)     the p-value for the test.

Example 7.4:   Open Study4.mtw from your data disk as another worksheet.  As described in Example 5.4, G.P.A. is normally distributed in the population.   Test the hypothesis that the mean G.P.A. of all students in the population is less than 3.00 .  Let α = 0.05 .   Then finish this Minitab session.

Use the *File , Open Worksheet...* to open another worksheet Study4.mtw that is saved on your data disk.

When the problem says "Test the hypothesis that ...", you must carefully examine this statement because it does <u>not</u> say which hypothesis this is.  If the statement contains an equality ( = or ≤ or ≥ ) then this is the null hypothesis ($H_0$:), but if the statement contains a strict inequality ( ≠ or > or < ) then this is the alternative hypothesis ($H_a$:).

(continued on the next page)

This example has raw data, and the hypothesis testing problem is

$H_0$: $\mu \geq 3.00$
$H_a$: $\mu < 3.00$
$\alpha = 0.05$

and the test statistic is $t = \dfrac{\bar{x} - \mu_0}{\dfrac{s}{\sqrt{n}}}$ given in formula (iii).

Click on *Stat*, *Basic Statistics*, *1-Sample t...*

In the 1-Sample t (Test and Confidence Interval) dialog box: make sure the button to the left of *Samples in columns* is selected, and then click inside of the box below. Now the variables (columns) will appear in the large box on the left side of this dialog box. Click on the G.P.A. (C2) variable and click on the [ **Select** ] button. Next check the box to the left of *Perform hypothesis test*, click inside of the box to the right of *Hypothesized mean:*, delete any current value, and type in 3.00 which is the specified value of $\mu_0$ in the null hypothesis ($H_0$:). Now click on the [ **Options...** ] button. Remember, do **not** press the [ **Enter** ] key after you have typed in anything, but use the mouse to move to another place in the dialog box.

In the 1-Sample t - Options dialog box: ignore the value in the *Confidence level:* box, and then make sure that the box to the right of *Alternative:* contains the correct inequality of *less than*. If not, click on the down triangle ( [▼] ), and click on the correct choice. Then click on [ **OK** ].

Back in the 1-Sample t (Test and Confidence Interval) dialog box, click on [ **OK** ].

The results shown below of this one sample t test, which includes the null and alternative hypotheses, the value of the t test statistic and the p-value, will appear in the Session Window.

## One-Sample T: G.P.A.

### Test of mu = 3 vs < 3

| Variable | N | Mean | StDev | SE Mean | 95% Upper Bound | T | P |
|---|---|---|---|---|---|---|---|
| G.P.A. | 29 | 2.65897 | 0.80617 | 0.14970 | 2.91363 | -2.28 | 0.015 |

The first line of output contains the correct alternative hypothesis *... vs < 3* . Since the p-value of 0.015 is less than 0.05 ($\alpha$), you may reject the null hypothesis and conclude that the mean G.P.A. of all students in the population is less than 3.00 . Also note that the value of the t test statistic, with 28 degrees of freedom, is -2.28, and this value is in the rejection region ( $t \leq -1.701$ ).

Example 7.5: The hourly wages in the Steel industry are normally distributed. The steel industry has set $18.50 as the standard hourly wage. The hourly wages of a random sample of 24 steel workers for the Krypton Steel Company has a mean of $17.25 and a standard deviation of $2.50 . At the 0.02 level of significance, can the Krypton Steel Company be accused of under paying all of its workers?

For this example the data is summary statistics, and the hypothesis testing problem is

$H_0$: $\mu \geq 18.50$
$H_a$: $\mu < 18.50$
$\alpha = 0.02$

and the test statistic is $t = \dfrac{\overline{x} - \mu_0}{\dfrac{s}{\sqrt{n}}}$ given in formula (iii).

Click on *Stat*, *Basic Statistics*, *1 Sample t ...*

In the 1-Sample t (Test and Confidence Interval) dialog box: press the ⬚**F3** key to clear the contents of this dialog box and reset all options and erase any previous variables. Make sure the button to the left of *Summarized data* is selected, and then click inside of the box to the right of *Sample size:*.   Now type in 24 which is the value of the sample size. Next click in the next box down that is to the right of *Mean:* and type in 17.25 which is the value of the sample mean. Next click in the next box down that is to the right of *Standard deviation:* and type in 2.50 which is the value of the sample standard deviation. Check  the box to the left of *Perform hypothesis test*, click inside of the box to the right of *Hypothesized mean:*, delete any current value, and type in 18.50 which is the specified value of $\mu_0$ in the null hypothesis ($H_0$:), and then click on the **Options...** button.

In the 1-Sample t - Options dialog box: ignore the value in the *Confidence level:* box, and then make sure that the box to the right of *Alternative:* contains the correct of *less than*. If not, click on the down triangle ( ▾ ), and click on the correct choice. Then click on **OK** .

Back in the 1-Sample t (Test and Confidence Interval) dialog box, click on **OK** .

The results shown below of this one sample t test, which includes the null and alternative hypotheses, the value of the t test statistic and the p-value, will appear in the Session Window.

## One-Sample T
**Test of mu = 18.5 vs < 18.5**

| N | Mean | StDev | SE Mean | 95%<br>Upper<br>Bound | T | P |
|---|------|-------|---------|-----------------------|---|---|
| 24 | 17.2500 | 2.5000 | 0.5103 | 18.1246 | -2.45 | 0.011 |

(continued on the next page)

The output contains the correct alternative hypothesis *... vs < 18.500*. Since the p-value of 0.011 is less than 0.02 (α), you may reject the null hypothesis and conclude that the mean hourly wage of all Krypton Steel Company workers is less than $18.50, and so the company does seem to be under paying its workers. Also note that the value of the t test statistic, with 23 degrees of freedom, is -2.45, and this value is in the rejection region ( $t \leq -2.177$ ).

# Lab Assignment 7.1.1

**Name:**                                                    **Date:**

**Course:**                    **Section:**                    **Data CD Number:**

1.  Start a Minitab session. If you are unable to complete this lab assignment in one Minitab session, save the project as Lab 7-1-1 . **Never** use a period as part of the project name; since Minitab uses the period to attach the file type to the file name. Then at your next Minitab session, you may open this Lab 7-1-1.MPJ project and continue to work where you left off previously.

2.  After receiving the state tax assessment of $87,500 for his house, John decided to appeal this assessment. He was told that his assessment was made as the average of all houses in his neighborhood. John hired a consulting company to randomly sample and assess eight houses in the neighborhood. The results are: $85,200 ; $86,400 ; $84,250 ; $85,300 ; $87,600 ; $84,750 ; $90,100 and $85,800 . The consultant verified that house values in John's neighborhood are normally distributed. Use a 0.05 level of significance and test the hypothesis that the average assessed value of all houses in John's neighborhood is less than the $87,500 he was originally assessed. Did John get the state to lower its tax assessment of his house?

3.  Open the worksheet Tasktime.mtw that is on your data disc. As described in Lab Assignment 5.1.1; a random sample of "cleaning" workers was taken and the time (in minutes) required to clean the production machine was recorded. Then twenty-three workers from the Method A assembly line were randomly selected, and their production times (in minutes) were measured. Then these **same** workers were moved to the Method B assembly line, and their production times (in minutes) were measured. It is known that production times for both of these two methods are normally distributed.

    a.  Test the hypothesis that the mean cleaning time for all "cleaning" workers is less than 24 minutes. Use a 0.05 level of significance.

    b.  Test to see if the mean production time of all workers from the Method A assembly line is equal to 33 minutes. Use a 0.01 level of significance.

(lab assignment is continued on the second side of this page)

4. Open another worksheet using Homesale.mtw from your data disc. This worksheet contains information about one-family housing sales in Raleigh, North Carolina. The mean selling price for all one-family houses in the nearby city of Durham, North Carolina is $ 52,500. At the 0.10 level of significance, test to see if the selling price of one-family houses in Raleigh is more than the Durham price.

5. The Banner Drug Company claims that its headache remedy stops headache pain in the average patient in at most 14 minutes. A random sample of 50 headache patients was selected. Each was given the Banner Drug remedy and the time until the pain stopped was recorded. The results were a mean of 17 minutes and a standard deviation of 8 minutes. Do these results support or deny the Banner Drug Company's claim for their product? Use $\alpha = 0.05$ .

6. The average daily yield of a chemical manufactured by the usual process is 850 tons. A new process is being tested to see if it will produce a higher daily yield. This new process is known to have a population variance of 441 tons$^2$. A random sample of production from 36 days from the new process yielded a mean and standard deviation of 890 and 23 tons respectively. With a 0.025 level of significance, test to see if the new process produces a higher average daily yield than the usual process.

7. Print your Session Window to the printer.

8. Attach both your Minitab output and your complete answers to this paper and submit all three to your instructor.

# Lab Assignment 7.1.2

**Name:**                                                         **Date:**

**Course:**                    **Section:**                    **Data CD Number:**


1.  Start a Minitab session. If you are unable to complete this lab assignment in one Minitab session, save the project as Lab 7-1-2 . **Never** use a period as part of the project name; since Minitab uses the period to attach the file type to the file name. Then at your next Minitab session, you may open this Lab 7-1-2.MPJ project and continue to work where you left off previously.

2.  Georgio's Pizza claims that it will deliver pizza to your home in less than 25 minutes. The distribution of pizza delivery times is approximately normally distributed. A competitor, knowing that this fast of a delivery time was unusual, challenged Georgio's to prove this claim. An independent survey company was contracted, and it randomly sampled twenty of Georgio's pizza delivery times with the following results: 23, 26, 16, 5, 31, 23, 19, 32, 23, 22, 35, 18, 21, 9, 24, 12, 22, 36, 20 and 23 minutes. At the 0.05 level of significance, test to see if Georgio's claim is substantiated. After testing the hypothesis, say if Georgio's Pizza is allowed to continue advertising a speedy delivery of less than 25 minutes.

3.  Open the worksheet Cespud.mtw that is on your data disc. As described in Lab Assignment 5.1.2; this worksheet contains a sample of five variables from the 1972 Consumer Expenditure Survey. Two of these variables are age of the head of the household and total income of the household.

    a.  Test the hypothesis that the mean age of all head of households in 1972 was equal to 45 years old. Use a 0.10 level of significance.

    b.  Test the hypothesis that the average income of all households in 1972 was greater than $9,000 . Use a 0.05 level of significance.

4.  Open another worksheet using Tasktime.mtw from your data disc. As described in Lab Assignment 5.1.1; a random sample of "loading" workers was taken and the time (in minutes) to load the raw materials into the machine was recorded. The distribution of load times among all workers is normal. Use a 0.05 level of significance and test the hypothesis that the mean loading time for all workers is less than 42 minutes.

(lab assignment is continued on the second side of this page)

5. The Ranger Tire Corporation claims that on average its Green Streak tires last at least 30,000 miles. A consumer testing agency randomly sampled 20 Green Streak tires and measured how many miles each tire lasted. The results were a mean of 28,450 miles and a standard deviation of 3612 miles. Tire wear is known to be normally distributed. Do these results support the Ranger Tire Corporation's claim? Use $\alpha = 0.10$.

6. The owner of a large office building charges all tenants the same rent, based on his claim that the mean area of the offices is at least 1250 square feet. One of the suspicious tenants randomly selected 60 of the offices and found their mean area was 1215 square feet and the standard deviation was 170 square feet. At the 0.10 level of significance, should the owner be accused of overcharging the tenants?

7. Print your Session Window to the printer.

8. Attach both your Minitab output and your complete answers to this paper and submit all three to your instructor.

# Section 2: Hypothesis Tests For The Variance and The Standard Deviation of a Normal Population

The variance ($\sigma^2$) and standard deviation ($\sigma$) measure the spread of the scores in a population. These parameters are often tested to determine if a population exhibits a desired amount of homogeneity. The "one sample" hypothesis test for the variance of a population may be in one of the following three forms:

(a) $H_0$: $\sigma^2 = \sigma_0^2$       (b) $H_0$: $\sigma^2 \geq \sigma_0^2$       (c) $H_0$: $\sigma^2 \leq \sigma_0^2$

      $H_a$: $\sigma^2 \neq \sigma_0^2$          $H_a$: $\sigma^2 < \sigma_0^2$          $H_a$: $\sigma^2 > \sigma_0^2$

Very often the hypothesis test will be in terms of the population standard deviation instead of the population variance, and will be in one of the following three forms:

(a) $H_0$: $\sigma = \sigma_0$       (b) $H_0$: $\sigma \geq \sigma_0$       (c) $H_0$: $\sigma \leq \sigma_0$

      $H_a$: $\sigma \neq \sigma_0$          $H_a$: $\sigma < \sigma_0$          $H_a$: $\sigma > \sigma_0$

The tests are equivalent, whether given in terms of the population variance ($\sigma^2$) or in terms of the population standard deviation ($\sigma$). The choice, $\sigma^2$ versus $\sigma$, is usually determined by the statement of the problem. Test (a) is called a "two tail" test, and tests (b) and (c) are called "one tail" tests.

If the population is normally distributed, then the test statistic for all of these tests is based upon the Chi-Square distribution with (n-1) degrees of freedom and has the formula:

$$\text{(iv)} \qquad \chi^2 = \frac{(n-1)s^2}{\sigma_0^2}$$

This same test statistic is used for hypothesis tests concerning both the population variance ($\sigma^2$) and the population standard deviation ($\sigma$).

For problems with **raw data**, hypothesis tests for the population variance ($\sigma^2$) may be computed using the macro **Ht-1v.mtb** (**H**ypothesis **t**est for **1** **v**ariance) that is saved on your data disc.

A more explicit description of executing a macro is given in Section 2 of Chapter 5, so what is shown next is an abbreviated description.

Click on *File* , *Other Files* , *Run an Exec...*

In the Run an Exec dialog box: the *Number of times to execute:* box should be 1, then click on the *Select File* button.

In the Run an Exec dialog box: make sure that *Data Disc* is in the *Look in:* or *Address* box. Then in the box highlight the Ht-1v.mtb macro file name (you may need to scroll through the list box), and click on the | **Open** | button.

This macro will prompt you for the number of the column being analyzed; **do <u>not</u> enter the letter C, but enter only the column <u>number</u>**. Next this macro will prompt you for the value of $\sigma_0^2$ specified in the null hypothesis of the particular problem. Last, this macro will prompt you for the type of test; enter 0 for a two tail test (a), enter -1 for a left tail test (b), and enter +1 for a right tail test (c).

The macro **Ht-1sd.mtb** (**H**ypothesis **t**est for **1** **s**tandard **d**eviation) is used to compute hypothesis tests about the population standard deviation ($\sigma$), and similarly to the previous macro, you will be prompted for the number of the column being analyzed; **do <u>not</u> enter the letter C, but enter only the column <u>number</u>**. Next this macro will prompt you for the value of $\sigma_0$ specified in the null hypothesis of the particular problem. Be certain to enter the specified value of the $\sigma_0$ and <u>not</u> the squared value of $\sigma_0^2$. Last, this macro will prompt you for the type of test; enter 0 for a two tail test (a), enter -1 for a left tail test (b), and enter +1 for a right tail test (c).

Potential careless mistakes when entering information into a macro and solutions for these errors are described at the end of Section 2 in Chapter 5.

Example 7.6: Open the worksheet Majorage.mtw from your data disk. This worksheet contains the ages of four independent samples of different majors at Bowling Green University. Each population of age is normally distributed. At the 0.05 level of significance, test to see if the variance of age of all psychology majors at Bowling Green is greater than 13.

Use *File , Open Worksheet...* to open the Majorage.mtw Worksheet from your data disc.

This example contains raw data and the hypothesis testing problem is

$H_0$: $\sigma^2 \le 13$
$H_a$: $\sigma^2 > 13$
$\alpha = 0.05$ .

Since the ages are normally distributed, the test statistic is $\chi^2 = \dfrac{(n-1)s^2}{\sigma_0^2}$ given in

formula (iv). From the Reference Guide in the table with the heading **One Sample Hypothesis Test for the Population Variance**, the **raw data** instructions say to execute the Ht-1v.mtb macro. From the Majorage.mtw Worksheet Window you see that the psychology data is in column 4.

Click on *File , Other Files , Run an Exec ...*
In the Run an Exec dialog box: make sure the *Number of times to execute:* box contains the number 1, and then click on the $\boxed{\text{Select File}}$ button.

In the Run an Exec dialog box: make sure that *Data Disc* is in the *Look in:* or *Address* box. Next highlight the Ht-1v.mtb macro file name (you may need to scroll through the list box), and click on the $\boxed{\text{Open}}$ button.

The steps for this macro are shown below. The ***bold italicized*** words are displayed by Minitab in the Session Window, and the numbers you are to enter in the Session Window are shown in regular print.

(continued on the next page)

**After the DATA> prompt, enter the column number that contains the data. Enter ONLY the number, but NOT the C !**

DATA> 4 [ Enter ]  (since the age of psychology majors is in column 4; i.e., C4)

**After the DATA> prompt, enter the value of SIGMA-squared given in the Null Hypothesis.**

DATA> 13 [ Enter ]

**After the DATA> prompt, enter the direction of the test:**
**-1 for a left tail test**
**0 for a two tail test**
**+1 for a right tail test**

DATA> +1 [ Enter ]

## Data Display

| | | |
|---|---|---|
| **Null Hyp: Variance of C 4 = 13.0000** | | |
| **Alt. Hyp: Variance of C 4 > 13.0000** | | |

| **Chi-square test statistic** | **d.f.** | **p-value** |
|---|---|---|
| 75.8821 | 61 | 0.0950 |

Since the p-value of this test is .0950 which is greater than the given value of $\alpha = 0.05$, you may not conclude that the variance of the ages of all psychology majors at Bowling Green University is greater than 13 years[2]. Note that the value of the Chi-Square test statistic is 75.8821, and this is not in the rejection region ($\chi^2 \geq 80.2318$).

Example 7.7: Use the data in the current worksheet. At the 0.10 level of significance, test to see if the standard deviation of ages of all mathematics majors at Bowling Green is different from 3.75 .

The hypothesis testing problem is

$H_0: \sigma = 3.75$
$H_a: \sigma \neq 3.75$
$\alpha = 0.10$

and the test statistic is $\chi^2 = \dfrac{(n-1)s^2}{\sigma_o^2}$ given in formula (iv).

(continued on the next page)

From the Reference Guide in the table with the heading **One Sample Hypothesis Test for the Population Standard Deviation**, the **raw data** instructions say to execute the Ht-1sd.mtb macro. The information about this current worksheet tells you that the ages of mathematics majors at Bowling Green are stored in column 3.

Click on *File*, *Other Files*, *Run an Exec* ...

In the Run an Exec dialog box: make sure the *Number of times to execute:* box contains the number 1, and then click on the | **Select File** | button.

In the Run an Exec dialog box: *Data Disc* should be in the *Look in:* or *Address* box. Next highlight the Ht-1sd.mtb macro file name, and click on the | **Open** | button.

The steps for this macro, the value of the Chi-square test statistic and the p-value for this test are shown next and appear in the Session Window.

**After the DATA> prompt, enter the column number that contains the data. Enter ONLY the number and NOT the C !**

**DATA>** 3 | **Enter** |  (since the age of mathematics majors is in column 3; i.e., <u>C3</u>)

**After the DATA> prompt, enter the value of SIGMA given in the Null Hypothesis.**

**DATA>** 3.75 | **Enter** |

**After the DATA> prompt, enter the direction of the test:**
            **-1  for a left tail test**
             **0  for a two tail test**
            **+1  for a right tail test**

**DATA>** 0 | **Enter** |

## Data Display

            **Null Hyp: Sigma of C 3   =       3.7500**
            **Alt. Hyp: Sigma of C 3  not =    3.7500**

            **Chi-square test statistic   d.f.     p-value**
                  **24.1705              38      0.0793**

Since the p-value of 0.0793 is less than the given value of $\alpha = 0.10$, you may conclude that the standard deviation of age of all mathematics majors at Bowling Green is different from 3.75 years. Note that the value of the Chi-Square test statistic is 24.1705, and this is in the rejection region ( $\chi^2 \leq 24.884$ or $\chi^2 \geq 53.384$ ).

196

The next example presents the data as summary statistics and uses the Summary Statistics macros stored on your data disk.

Example 7.8: The manufacturer of gasoline pumps claims that all of the pumps have meters which measure the amount of gasoline pumped with a standard deviation of at most 0.08 gallons. The measurements made by these meters are known to be normally distributed. A random sample of 15 of this manufacturer's gasoline pumps was taken, and 10 gallons as read by the meter were pumped. Then the actual amount of gasoline was precisely measured with a known accurate device, and yielded a mean of 12.001 and a standard deviation of 0.094 gallons. At the 0.01 level of significance, test the manufacture's claim about the standard deviation of the pumps.

This example has summary statistic data, the hypothesis testing problem is

$H_0: \sigma \le 0.08$
$H_a: \sigma > 0.08$
$\alpha = 0.01$

and the test statistic is $\chi^2 = \dfrac{(n-1)s^2}{\sigma_o^2}$ given in formula (iv). From the Reference Guide in the table with the heading **One Sample Hypothesis Test for the Population Standard Deviation**, and in the Summary Statistics Technique column; the macro to be executed is Sumht1sd.mtb .

Click on *File , Other Files , Run an Exec ...*

In the Run an Exec dialog box: make sure the *Number of times to execute:* box contains the number 1, and then click on the ⬚ **Select File** ⬚ button.

In the Run an Exec dialog box: *Data Disc* should be in the *Look in:* or *Address* box. Next highlight the Sumht1sd.mtb macro file name (you may need to scroll through the list box), and click on the ⬚ **Open** ⬚ button.

The macro begins by prompting you for the specific value of $\sigma_o$ given in the null hypothesis. Next you are prompted to enter the type of test, and you will enter +1 for a "right tail" test for this example. Then the macro prompts you to enter the sample standard deviation and then the sample size. The steps for this macro and resulting hypothesis test results shown below will appear in the Session Window.

***After the DATA> prompt, enter the value of SIGMA
given in the Null Hypothesis.***

***DATA>*** 0.08 ⬚ **Enter**

(continued on the next page)

*After the DATA> prompt, enter the direction of the test:*
   *-1 for a left tail test*
   *0 for a two tail test*
   *+1 for a right tail test*

*DATA>* +1 [ **Enter** ]

*After the DATA> prompt, enter the Sample standard deviation.*

*DATA>* 0.094 [ **Enter** ]

*After the DATA> prompt, enter the Sample size.*

*DATA>* 15 [ **Enter** ]

## Data Display

| Null Hyp: Sigma | = | 0.0800 |
|---|---|---|
| Alt. Hyp: Sigma | > | 0.0800 |

| Chi-square test statistic | d.f. | p-value |
|---|---|---|
| 19.3288 | 14 | 0.1528 |

The output contains the correct alternative hypothesis ... **Sigma > 0.0800.** Since the p-value of 0.1527 is greater than the given value of $\alpha = 0.01$, you may **not** conclude that the standard deviation amount of gasoline actually pumped by all of this manufacturer's gasoline pumps is greater than 0.08 gallons. And so the manufacturer's claim is upheld. Note that the value of the Chi-Square test statistic is 19.3288, and this is **not** in the rejection region ($\chi^2 \geq 29.141$ ).

# Lab Assignment 7.2.1

**Name:**                                                              **Date:**

**Course:**                    **Section:**                    **Data CD Number:**

1. Start a Minitab session. If you are unable to complete this lab assignment in one Minitab session, save the project as Lab 7-2-1 . **Never** use a period as part of the project name; since Minitab uses the period to attach the file type to the file name. Then at your next Minitab session, you may open this Lab 7-2-1.MPJ project and continue to work where you left off previously.

2. Open the worksheet Tasktime.mtw that is on your data disc. As described in Lab Assignment 5.1.1; a random sample of "cleaning" workers was taken and the time (in minutes) required to clean the production machine was recorded. Another sample of "loading" workers was taken and the time (in minutes) to load the raw materials into the machine was recorded. The distribution of load times among all workers is normal. Then twenty-three workers from the Method A assembly line were randomly selected, and their production times (in minutes) were measured. Then these **same** workers were moved to the Method B assembly line, and their production times (in minutes) were measured. It is known that production times by either of these two methods are normally distributed.

   a. Test the hypothesis that the standard deviation of load times of all "loading" workers is equal to 12 minutes. Use a 0.05 significance level.

   b. Test the hypothesis that the variance of production times of all workers from the Method A assembly line is less than 100 minutes$^2$. Use a 0.05 level of significance.

   c. At the 0.025 level of significance, test to see if the standard deviation of production times of all workers from the Method B assembly line is greater than 5 minutes.

3. The amount of area (in square yards) that can be spray painted with a gallon of Top Ram paint is normally distributed. The Top Ram company claims that the standard deviation of coverage when its product is spray painted is 10 square yards or less. A random sample of 12 gallon cans of Top Ram paint were spray painted on test surfaces. The results of this test were an average coverage of 65.3 and a standard deviation of 13.8 square yards. Use a significance level of 0.05 and test to see if Top Ram's claim about the consistency of its product (standard deviation) is correct.

(lab assignment is continued on the second side of this page)

4.  MemTech manufactures high quality computer memory chips. The company claims the variance of access time for its 60 ns memory chips is 2 ns$^2$. A random sample of 25 chips was taken and their access times were tested. The results of this were a mean access time of 59.34 and a standard deviation of 1.76 ns. Assuming that the access times are normally distributed and with $\alpha = 0.05$, test to see if the advertised variance of all MemTech 60 ns chips is correct.

5.  Print your Session Window to the printer.

6.  Attach both your Minitab output and <u>your complete answers</u> to this paper and submit all three to your instructor.

# Lab Assignment 7.2.2

**Name:**                                                                    **Date:**

**Course:**                     **Section:**                    **Data CD Number:**


1.   Start a Minitab session. If you are unable to complete this lab assignment in one Minitab session, save the project as Lab 7-2-2 . **Never** use a period as part of the project name; since Minitab uses the period to attach the file type to the file name. Then at your next Minitab session, you may open this Lab 7-2-2.MPJ project and continue to work where you left off previously.


2.   Summarizing question 2 of Lab Assignment 7.1.1; John was appealing his tax assessment. John hired a consulting company to randomly sample and assess eight houses in the neighborhood. The results are: $85,200 ; $86,400 ; $84,250 ; $85,300 ; $87,600 ; $84,750 ; $90,100 and $85,800 . The consultant verified that house values in John's neighborhood are normally distributed. Since all of the houses in John's neighborhood are of the same type and were constructed by the same contractor, the state tax agency knows that the standard deviation of assessment in John's neighborhood is less than or equal to $1,500. The tax agency challenged the ability of the consulting firm, and based this challenge on the apparent wide range of assessments. The appeals judge agreed that the sample standard deviation did seem somewhat large, but she was not convinced. Since the burden of proof now rested with the state, the judge required the tax agency to perform an hypothesis test to see if the population of houses from which the consulting company sampled does have a standard deviation greater than $1,500 , and she set the level of significance at 0.10 . Test the hypothesis, and then say whether or not the tax agency's challenge of the consulting firm was upheld.


3.   Open the worksheet Cityidx.mtw that is on your data disc. As described in Lab Assignment 6.1.2; five variables were measured on a sample of cities in each of East (in C1 - C5), Central (in C6 - C10) and West (in C11 - C15) geographical regions of the United States, and the four index variables are normally distributed in each geographical region.

   a.   Test the hypothesis that the variance of the construction index for all cities in the Eastern region is different than 60 . Use a 0.10 level of significance.

   b.   At the 0.05 level of significance, test to see if the standard deviation of the retail sales index for all cities in the Western region is greater than 4.2 .


(lab assignment is continued on the second side of this page)

4.	The lengths of Sammy's foot-long hot dogs are normally distributed. Sammy claims that the variance of the length of all of his foot-long hot dogs is no more than 1.2 inches. A random sample of 35 of these hot dogs was measured, and yielded a mean length of 11.98 inches and a variance of 1.53 inches$^2$. Use a 0.10 significance level to test Sammy's claim about the variance of lengths of all of his foot-long hot dogs.

5.	SimEd company writes educational computer simulation games for economics. The company claims that the beginning balance of its simulations has a standard deviation of $800. Anything larger would introduce too much variability to the simulation and thus loose its educational value. A smaller standard deviation would cause the simulation to become to predictable, and thus not of much value after several uses. These beginning balances are known to be normally distributed. A random sample of 15 SimEd computer simulations produced a mean beginning balance of $45,796.75 and a standard deviation of $745.15 . With $\alpha = 0.01$ test to see if the SimEd Company's claim is verified.

6.	Print your Session Window to the printer.

7.	Attach both your Minitab output and your complete answers to this paper and submit all three to your instructor.

# Section 3: Hypothesis Test For The Population Proportion of "Successes"

The previous two sections considered variables which were a continuous type of measurement. This section will describe how to compute a hypothesis test for the proportion of "successes" of a population when the variable is a Bernoulli type of measurement. The one sample hypothesis test about the proportion of "successes" of a population (p) may take on one of the following three forms:

(a)  $H_0: p = p_0$            (b)  $H_0: p \geq p_0$            (c)  $H_0: p \leq p_0$
     $H_a: p \neq p_0$               $H_a: p < p_0$                 $H_a: p > p_0$

If the sample size is sufficiently large, the test statistic is based upon the Standard Normal distribution and has the formula:

$$(v) \qquad Z = \frac{\hat{p} - p_0}{\sqrt{\dfrac{p_0(1 - p_0)}{n}}}$$

where $\hat{p} = \dfrac{Y}{n}$ is the proportion of the sample that is "success", and Y is the number of "successes" in the sample.

The data for a Bernoulli type variable **must** be entered in the Worksheet Window into a variable (column) such that the **exact same** coding is used for each "success" and the **exact same** coding is used for each "failure." If you are entering alphabetic symbols or words, then you must use the exact same upper case and lower case letters each time for each "success" and for each "failure." As an alternative you may code each "success" outcome as an one (1) and each "failure" outcome as a zero (0). Furthermore, if you enter alphabetic symbols or words, Minitab **always** assigns "failure" to the one that comes first in alphabetical order, and assigns "success" to the one that comes last in alphabetical order. So if you enter M for male and F for female: (1) you must use all of the same case for the Ms and all of the same case for the Fs, and (2) Minitab will assign "success" to the M (male) outcome.

If you want female to be the "success" outcome, you have two options. One is to code male and female so that the female code comes alphabetically after the male code; for example, code male as X-Male and code female as Y-Female. You may use Minitab to recode these using the *Data, Code , Text to Text* procedure. A second option is to have Minitab recode the Ms to 0s and the Fs to 1s. This is done using the *Data, Code, Text to Numeric* item from the menu bar. Whenever you are going to compute or code values into a new variable (column) in Minitab, you should name that column **beforehand**.

In the Worksheet Window, click in the name box (between the column number and the first data row) and type in a descriptive name.

Click on *Data, Code , Text to Numeric ...*

In the Code - Text to Numeric dialog box only the columns with alphabetic (text) will be displayed in the box on the left. The cursor should be in the *Code data from columns:* box, then click on the variable (column) that contains the text you want to code to 0s and 1s and click on the ┌ **Select** ┐ button. Next click in the *Into columns:* box, highlight the new variable that you just named and click on the ┌ **Select** ┐ button (or type in a **new** column number C#. Then click in the first box under the *Original values* heading and type in the alphabetic symbol or word that was used for the "failure" outcome. Next click in the first box under the *New:* heading and type in the number 0. Similarly on the second row enter the symbol or word that was used for the "success" outcome and the number 1. Then click on ┌ **OK** ┐ .

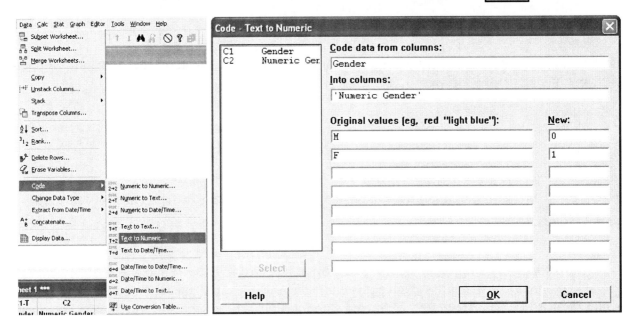

So that before you code the Gender (C1) variable, the Worksheet Window might look like the graphic below on the left; and after you use *Data, Code, Text to Numeric*, the Worksheet Window might look like the graphic below on the right.

To code *Text to Text*, you will get the same dialog box (it will be labeled Code - Text to Text), and you enter the new text in the boxes under the *New:* heading.

204

Once the **raw data** is in the correct format, the test statistic $Z = \dfrac{\hat{p} - p_0}{\sqrt{\dfrac{p_0(1 - p_0)}{n}}}$ is computed using the *1 Proportion* procedure as follows.

Click on *Stat , Basic Statistics , 1 Proportion ...*

In the 1 Proportion (Test and Confidence Interval) dialog box: make sure the button to the left of *Samples in columns* is selected, click inside of the box below *Samples in columns* and erase any previous variables. The variables (columns) will appear in the large box on the left side of this dialog box, click on the variable you want to analyze, and click on the $\boxed{\text{Select}}$ button. Then click on the $\boxed{\text{Options...}}$ button.

In the 1 Proportion - Options dialog box: ignore the value in the *Confidence level:* box, and then click inside of the box to the right of *Test proportion:*. Delete any current value, and type in the specified value of $p_0$ in the null hypothesis ($H_0$:). Next make sure that the box to the right of *Alternative:* contains the correct inequality for your problem (*not equal* or *less than* or *greater than*). If not, click on the down triangle ( $\boxed{\blacktriangledown}$ ), and click on the correct choice. Next make sure that the box to the left of *Use test and interval based on normal distribution* is checked. Then click on $\boxed{\text{OK}}$ .

Back in the 1 Proportion dialog box, click on $\boxed{\text{OK}}$ .

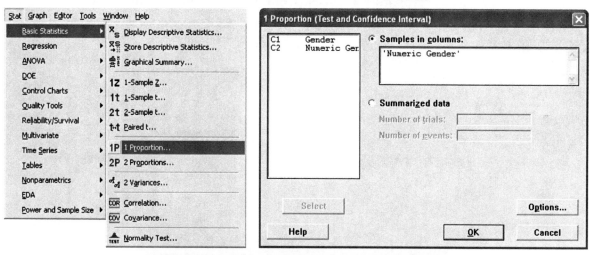

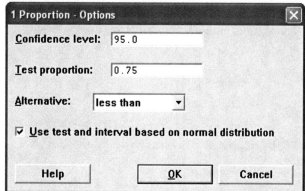

However when the problem contains **summary statistic** data, the test statistic $Z = \dfrac{\hat{p} - p_0}{\sqrt{\dfrac{p_0(1 - p_0)}{n}}}$ is computed using the *1 Proportion* procedure as follows.

Click on *Stat* , *Basic Statistics* , *1 Proportion ...*

In the 1 Proportion (Test and Confidence Interval) dialog box: you may press the F3 key to clear the contents of this dialog box and reset all options and erase any previous variables. Make sure the button to the left of *Summarized data* is selected, and then click inside of the box to the right of *Number of trials:*. Now type in the value of the sample size. Next click in the next box down that is to the right of *Number of events:* and type in the value of the number of "successes" in the sample. Then click on the Options... button.

In the 1 Proportion - Options dialog box: ignore the value in the *Confidence level:* box, and then click inside of the box to the right of *Test proportion:*. Delete any current value, and type in the specified value of $p_0$ in the null hypothesis ($H_0$:). Next make sure that the box to the right of *Alternative:* contains the correct inequality for your problem (*not equal* or *less than* or *greater than*). If not, click on the down triangle ( ▾ ), and click on the correct choice. Next make sure that the box to the left of *Use test and interval based on normal distribution* is checked. Then click on OK .

Back in the 1 Proportion (Test and Confidence Interval) dialog box, click on OK .

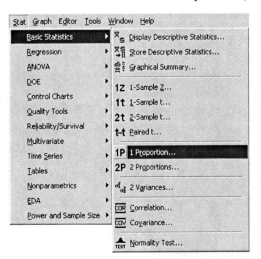

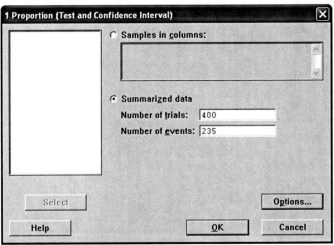

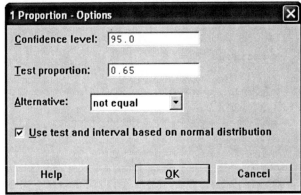

This *1 Proportion* procedure computes both a confidence interval and a hypothesis test (discussed in Chapter 7) for the population proportion of "successes" - p. The output of the *1 Proportion* procedure contains:

(1) the statement of the null and alternative hypotheses,
(2) the outcome Minitab assigns as "success" written as **Event = outcome** (only for raw data),
(3) the variable name or column number (for raw data) or the sample number - usually 1 - (for summarized data)
(4) the number of "successes" (which is labeled **X**),
(5) the sample size,
(6) the value of the sample proportion of "successes" - $\hat{p}$ (which is labeled **Sample p**),
(7) the upper or lower bound of a one sided confidence interval when the alternative is *less than* or *greater than* respectively, or a regular two sided confidence interval (when the alternative is *not equal* (ignore this information when doing hypothesis testing),
(8) the value of the Z test statistic,
(9) the p-value, and
(10) a warning if the criteria for using formula (vi) are not met.

Example 7.9:   A random sample of 24 people who purchased a new automobile in 2004 was taken. Each person was asked if he/she would buy the same make and model of car again, and the answers were:

No, Yes, No, Yes, No, Yes, No, Yes, Yes, No, Yes, Yes, Yes, No, Yes, Yes, No, Yes, Yes, No, No, Yes, No and Yes

At the 0.05 level of significance, test the hypothesis that less than 75% of all 2004 new car buyers would purchase the same make and model car again.

Enter the raw data into column 1 in the Worksheet Window (if your current worksheet has data in this column, first open a new worksheet with *File , Open Worksheet*). Here the "success" outcome is a Yes answer; and since Yes comes after No alphabetically, there is no need to recode this data.

This example has raw data,  the hypothesis testing problem is

$H_0$: p $\geq$ 0.75
$H_a$: p $<$ 0.75
$\alpha$ = 0.05

and the test statistic is  $Z = \dfrac{\hat{p} - p_0}{\sqrt{\dfrac{p_0(1 - p_0)}{n}}}$  given in formula (v).

(continued on the next page)

Click on *Stat* , *Basic Statistics* , *1 Proportion* ...

In the 1 Proportion (Test and Confidence Interval) dialog box: make sure the button to the left of *Samples in columns* is selected, click inside of the box below *Samples in columns* and erase any previous variables. The variables (columns) will appear in the large box on the left side of this dialog box, click on the C1 variable, and click on the | **Select** | button. Then click on the | **Options...** | button.

In the 1 Proportion - Options dialog box: ignore the value in the *Confidence level:* box, and then click inside of the box to the right of *Test proportion:*. Delete any current value, and type in 0.75 which is the specified value of $p_0$ in the null hypothesis ($H_0$:). Next make sure that the box to the right of *Alternative:* contains the correct inequality of *less than*. If not, click on the down triangle ( ▾ ), and click on the correct choice. Next make sure that the box to the left of *Use test and interval based on normal distribution* is checked. Then click on | **OK** | .

Back in the 1 Proportion dialog box, click on | **OK** | .

The resulting output shown below will appear in the Session Window.


### Test and CI for One Proportion: C1


### Test of p = 0.75 vs p < 0.75


### Event = Yes


| Variable | X | N | Sample p | 95% Upper Bound | Z-Value | P-Value |
|----------|---|---|----------|-----------------|---------|---------|
| C1 | 14 | 24 | 0.583333 | 0.748862 | -1.89 | 0.030 |


The value of the Z test statistic is -1.89, and the p-value of this test is 0.030 which is less than the given value of $\alpha = 0.05$. Therefore you may conclude that the proportion of all 1998 new car buyers who would purchase the same make and model car again is less than 75%. Note that the value of the Z test statistic is -1.89 and this is in the rejection region ($Z \leq -1.645$).

The next example presents the data as summary statistics and also can be done using the *1 Proportion* procedure.

Example 7.10:   Before voting on an important issue a congresswoman wants to know if her constituency has changed its opinion from the last time this issue was debated. At that previous time 65% of her constituency was in favor of the issue. She now takes a random sample of 400 voters in her district and finds that 235 are in favor. At the 0.01 level of significance, does this data indicate a change in opinion of all voters in her district?

This example has summary statistic data, the hypothesis testing problem is

$H_0$: p = 0.65
$H_a$: p ≠ 0.65
α = 0.01

and the test statistic is $Z = \dfrac{\hat{p} - p_0}{\sqrt{\dfrac{p_0(1 - p_0)}{n}}}$ given in formula (v).

Click on *Stat*, *Basic Statistics*, *1 Proportion* ...

In the 1 Proportion (Test and Confidence Interval) dialog box: press the ⎡ **F3** ⎤ key to clear the contents of this dialog box and reset all options and erase any previous variables. Make sure the button to the left of *Summarized data* is selected, and then click inside of the box to the right of *Number of trials:*. Now type in 400 which is the number of people in the sample. Next click in the next box down that is to the right of *Number of events:* and type in 235 which is the number of people in the sample who are in favor of the issue (i.e., the number of "successes" in the sample). Then click on the ⎡ **Options...** ⎤ button.

In the 1 Proportion - Options dialog box: ignore the value in the *Confidence level:* box, and then click inside of the box to the right of *Test proportion:*. Delete any current value, and type in 0.65 which is the specified value of $p_0$ in the null hypothesis ($H_0$:). Next make sure that the box to the right of *Alternative:* contains the correct inequality of *not equal*. If not, click on the down triangle ( ▾ ), and click on the correct choice. Next make sure that the box to the left of *Use test and interval based on normal distribution* is checked. Then click on ⎡ **OK** ⎤.

Back in the 1 Proportion dialog box, click on ⎡ **OK** ⎤.

The resulting output shown below will appear in the Session Window.

## *Test and CI for One Proportion*

**Test of p = 0.65 vs p not = 0.65**

| Sample | X | N | Sample p | 95% CI | Z-Value | P-Value |
|--------|-----|-----|----------|----------------------|---------|---------|
| 1 | 235 | 400 | 0.587500 | (0.539257, 0.635743) | -2.62 | 0.009 |

(continued on the next page)

The value of the Z test statistic is -2.62, and the p-value of this test is 0.009 which is less than the given value of $\alpha = 0.01$. Therefore you may conclude that the proportion of all voters in the congresswoman's district who are in favor of the issue is different than 65% (0.65). Note that the value of the Z test statistic is -2.62 and this is in the rejection region ($Z \leq -2.326$).

When the problem involves raw data; sometimes it may be easier to count the number of "successes" and the total number in the sample, and then compute the test statistic and p-value using the summary statistics method (instead of entering the raw data into the Worksheet Window).

# Lab Assignment 7.3.1

**Name:**                                                    **Date:**

**Course:**              **Section:**                **Data CD Number:**

1.  Start a Minitab session. If you are unable to complete this lab assignment in one Minitab session, save the project as Lab 7-3-2 . Never use a period as part of the project name; since Minitab uses the period to attach the file type to the file name. Then at your next Minitab session, you may open this Lab 7-3-2.MPJ project and continue to work where you left off previously.

2.  Twenty-five (25) people who had taken a student loan in 1990 were randomly selected. Each person's loan record was examined to determine if the loan had been paid or if the loan was still open, and the results were:

    paid, paid, open, paid, paid, open, paid, open, open, open, paid, paid, open, paid, open, paid, paid, open, paid, paid, paid, open, open, paid and paid

    Enter the data into the current Worksheet Window in column 1 using the alphabetic words paid and open. Since paid is the "success" outcome, there is no need to do any coding of this data. At the 0.05 level of significance, test the hypothesis that more than one-half of all 1980 student loans have been paid.

3.  Open the worksheet Homesale.mtw that is on your data disc. This worksheet contains information about one-family housing sales in Raleigh, North Carolina. If the house was sold by an agent, a 1 (one) was entered for the Sold By variable; but if the sale was made by the owner, a 0 (zero) was entered for the Sold By variable. Test the hypothesis that 80% of all one-family housing sales in Raleigh are made by agents. Use a 0.10 level of significance.

4.  Open the worksheet Sociology.mtw that is on your data disc. This worksheet contains data about different colleges as well as the midterm and final exam letter grades for a random sample of students taking the Sociology 102 course at Canton State University. The department Curriculum Committee has set a policy that the proportion of all students in Sociology 101 classes who earn a grade of A or B on the Final Exam should never be more that 50%. Name an unused column as Soc 101, and then code the A and B scores as Top andcode the rest of the grades at Bottom. Use a 0.05 level of significance, and test to see if theCurriculum Committee's policy is being followed in all Sociology 101 classes at Canton State University.

    (lab assignment is continued on the second side of this page)

5.  In 2002 the proportion of all male college students who planned to enter the same profession as their fathers was 0.20 . A new 2008 survey of a random sample of 500 male college students showed that 81 planned to enter their fathers' profession. Using $\alpha = 0.05$, does this data indicate that the proportion of all male college students in 2008 who plan to enter the same profession as their fathers has decreased from 2002?

6.  Print your Session Window to the printer.

7.  Attach both your Minitab output and your complete answers to this paper and submit all three to your instructor.

# Lab Assignment 7.3.2

**Name:**                                                              **Date:**

**Course:**                    **Section:**                    **Data CD Number:**

1.  Start a Minitab session. If you are unable to complete this lab assignment in one Minitab session, save the project as Lab 7-3-2 . Never use a period as part of the project name; since Minitab uses the period to attach the file type to the file name. Then at your next Minitab session, you may open this Lab 7-3-2.MPJ project and continue to work where you left off previously.

2.  Whenever rain is in the forecast, the local weather lady WMTU give the prediction as a percent chance of rain. Over the past several years, students at a local middle school have been collecting data on these forecasts. In particular; for a random sample of days on which the forecast was 80% chance of rain, the students recorded whether or not it actually rained that day. The results were:

    rain, sun, rain, rain, rain, sun, rain, rain, rain, rain, rain, sun, rain, rain, sun, sun, rain, rain, rain, rain, rain, rain, rain, sun, rain, sun, rain, sun, rain, sun, rain, rain, sun, sun, rain, rain, rain, sun, rain, rain and rain.

    To check the accuracy of the WMTU weather lady, test the hypothesis that the proportion of all 80% rain forecasted days on which it actually rains is equal to 80%. Use a 0.10 level of significance.

3.  Open the worksheet Sociology.mtw that is on your data disc. This worksheet contains data about different colleges as well as the midterm and final exam letter grades for a random sample of students taking the Sociology 102 course at Canton State University. The department Curriculum Committee has set a policy that the proportion of all students in Sociology 101 classes who earn a grade of A or B on the Final Exam should never be more that 50%. Name an unused column as Soc 101, and then code the A and B scores as Top and code the rest of the grades at Bottom. Use a 0.05 level of significance, and test to see if the Curriculum Committee's policy is being followed in all Sociology 101 classes at Canton State University.

(lab assignment is continued on the second side of this page)

4.	Open the worksheet Clinic.mtw that is on your data disc. This worksheet contains data taken from random samples at the Orange County's Clinic for Advanced Research. Among the data in this worksheet are Hamilton change in depression scores from a random sample of patients originally diagnosed as clinically depressed. These scores measure the change in the depression score after the patients had been on an experimental anti-depressant for five weeks, and the data has an underlying continuous distribution. A negative change indicates that the patient has become more depressed, while a positive score indicates an improvement in the patient's state of mind. At the 0.05 significance level, test to see if more than half of all clinically depressed patients at the Orange County Clinic have Hamilton change scores above 1.3 .

5.	In 2007 it was estimated that three out of every five personal computers have at least one computer virus somewhere in their system. A research company holds the optimistic view that in 2009 more people have finally learned the lesson of keeping their anti-virus software up to date. The company surveyed 500 randomly selected personal computers and found that 274 were infected with at least one virus. Test the hypothesis that the proportion of all personal computers in 2008 which have at least one virus somewhere in their system has actually decreased from the 2007 proportion. Use a 0.01 level of significance

6.	Print your Session Window to the printer.

7.	Attach both your Minitab output and your complete answers to this paper and submit all three to your instructor.

**Section 4:     The Power of a Test**

Until this point; we have always concentrated on the significance level (α) of an hypothesis test, and comparing the p-value to α in order to make the appropriate "Reject the null hypotheses" or "Do not reject the null hypothesis" decision.  Depending whether or not the null hypothesis is actually true or false, there are four possible scenarios which are summarized in the table below.

| **Table 1:** | | **The Null Hypothesis is Actually** | |
|---|---|---|---|
| | | **True** | **False** |
| **Decision Based on Sample Data** | **Reject $H_o$:** | Type I error | Correct decision |
| | **Do Not Reject $H_o$:** | Correct decision | Type II error |

The significance level of a test is equal to the probability of making a Type I error; that is, $\alpha = P(\text{Type I error})$.  Since this type of error is often expensive in terms of money, prestige and otherwise, we usually set the value of α low - often at 0.05 .

The usual notation for the probability of a Type II error is β, where a Type II error is the probability of not rejecting $H_0$ when $H_0$ is actually false.  That is, β is the probability of failing to detect a true alternative hypothesis.  For any specific test, the values of α and β are inversely related; i.e.; as one decreases the other increases.  Consider the following example.

$H_0: \mu \leq 50$
$H_a: \mu > 50$
$\alpha = 0.05$
and the test statistic is $Z = \dfrac{\overline{x} - \mu_0}{\dfrac{\sigma}{\sqrt{n}}}$ .

For this example, we will let the population standard deviation $\sigma = 40$ and the sample size be n = 16 .  The rejection region is $z \geq 1.645$ , and $\alpha = 0.05$ is the area under the curve above the rejection region.  When this is transformed to the $\overline{x}$ axis (instead of the z axis), the rejection region becomes $\overline{x} \geq 66.45$ (66.45 is the critical point of the rejection region).  This is pictured as shown on the next page.

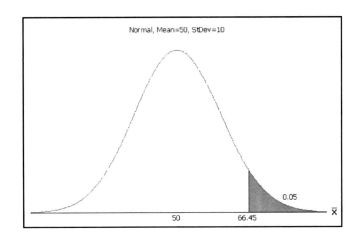

Now suppose that the null hypothesis is actually false and the value of the population mean is really $\mu = 75$. The do not rejection region is $z < 1.645$, and $\beta = P(\text{Type II error})$ is the area under the curve above this do not reject region. When this is transformed to the $\overline{x}$ axis (instead of the z axis), the do not rejection region is $\overline{x} < 66.45$, $\beta = 0.196$ and this is pictured as

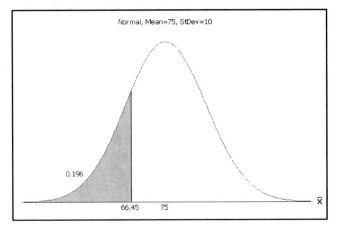

Next we plot these two graphs on the same axis to get the following picture.

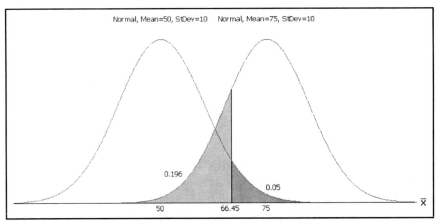

It is easy to see from this graph that when α increases, the critical point will move to the left, the rejection region will become larger, and the do not rejection region will become smaller. So the value of β will decrease. Suppose we increase the value of α to 0.10 . Then the critical value becomes 1.282 on the z axis, this transforms to 62.82 on the $\bar{x}$ axis, and β decreases to 0.112. This situation is pictured as

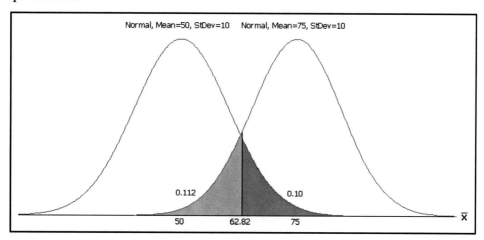

And if we decrease the value of α; then we see that the critical point moves to the right, and that the value of β will increase.

Also notice that if the sample size is increased from 16 to 25, then the standard deviation of the sample mean $\bar{x}$ becomes $\dfrac{\sigma}{\sqrt{n}} = \dfrac{40}{5} = 8$, and the spread of the both curves is smaller. For the same value of α, the critical point moves to the left, the left tail of the alternative curve moves to the right, and thus the value of β will decrease. For example if we set α = 0.10 and let n = 64, then the critical point on the z axis is still 1.282. But when this is transformed to the $\bar{x}$ axis, the critical point becomes 60.26 instead of the previous value of 62.82. The rejection region is $\bar{x} \geq 60.26$, the do not reject region is $\bar{x} < 60.26$, and the P( Type II error ) decreases from 0.112 to β = 0.0327. This is pictured below.

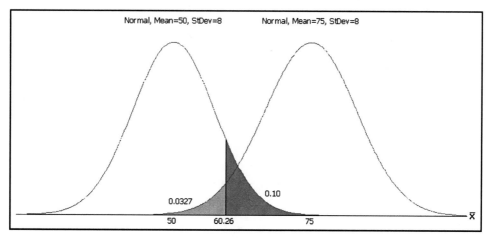

As in most situations when doing statistical analysis, taking a larger sample size makes the overall analysis better!

With this as preparatory material, the concept of the power of a test is easily understood. First the definition of the power of a test is the probability of rejecting $H_0$: when $H_a$: is really true; that is, power of a test is the probability of correctly detecting a true alternative hypothesis. From Table 1: we see that the probability of rejecting $H_0$: when $H_a$: is really true is the complement of the probability of Type II error. And so

power of a test = P( rejecting $H_0$: when $H_a$: is really true ) = 1 - P (Type II error ) = 1 - $\beta$.

In our example when $H_a$: $\mu = 75$ is actually true and n = 8, then $\beta$ was 0.196, and so the power the test is 1 - 0.196 = 0.804 as is pictured below.

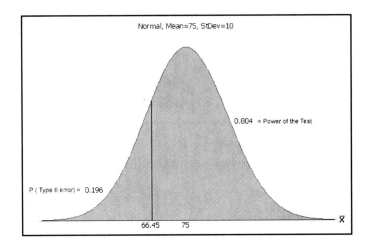

From this definition we also have several relationships. One is that as the significance level $\alpha$ increases, then the power of the test also increases; since as $\alpha$ increases then the critical point moves to the left and $\beta$ decreases, and so the power of a test = 1 - $\beta$ increases. A second relationship easy to see is that as the difference between the value of $H_a$: and $H_0$: increases, the above curve will move further to away from the null value curve. And since the critical point remains at 66.45, the power of the test also will increase. In our example suppose that $H_a$: $\mu = 80$ is actually true and n = 8, then the power of the test = 0.912 as is pictured below

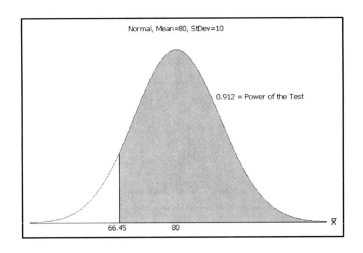

218

Our example used a right-tail test as we had $H_a$: $\mu > 50$; but the same relationships and similar pictures occur for left-tail and two-tail tests.

Instead of computing the power of the test for individual specific values of the alternative hypothesis, Minitab computes the power for all possible values in $H_a$: and graphs the results as a power curve. Given a fixed value of $\alpha$ there are three quantities that are inter-related: (1) the sample size, (2) the difference between the $H_0$: and $H_a$: values, and (3) the value of the power of the test is equal to $1 - \beta$. Once any two of these values are entered, Minitab will compute and graph the corresponding power curve. In applications, the power of a test tells us the chance of rejecting the null hypothesis and thus the chance of concluding the alternative hypothesis **when a specific value of $H_a$: is actually true**.

A common scenario is knowing the sample size and the specific value of the alternative hypothesis, and wanting to compute the power of this test. That is, with a given sample size, we want to know the chance of being able to detect a specific $H_a$: value when it is actually true.

However when the data is in a worksheet, and you do not already know the sample size, an easy method for obtaining that number is to use the Calc , *Column Statistics* procedure to compute the number of non-missing scores in the variable (column) as explained in Section 1 of Chapter 5. This is done as

Click on *Calc , Column Statistics...*

In the Column Statistics dialog box: click on the circle to the left of *N nonmissing*, click inside of the *Input variable:* box, click on the variable that contains the sample data, and click on the | Select | button. Next click in the box to the **right** of *Store results in:*, and type in k1 as the constant name. (Minitab accepts lowercase k1 or uppercase K1 as the same constant.) Then click on the | OK | button.

When using a 1-sample Z test, a power curve is computed and graphed as follows.

Click on *Stat , Power and Sample Size, 1-Sample Z...*

In the Power and Sample Size for 1-Sample Z dialog box you may press the | F3 | key to clear the contents of this dialog box and reset all options. Click in the box to the right of *Sample sizes:* and type the given sample size or K1 if you needed to calculate the sample size. Then click in the box to the right of *Differences:* and type the difference between the $H_a$: and $H_0$: values. **Note that the difference must be <u>positive</u> for a right-tail test (greater than), and the difference must be <u>negative</u> for a left-tail test (less than). The difference may be either positive or negative for a two-tail test (not equal to).** Next click in the box to the right of *Standard deviation:* type the value of $\sigma$, and then click on the | Options... | button.

(continued on the next page)

In the Power and Sample Size for 1-Sample Z - Options dialog box under the *Alternative Hypothesis* heading, click on the circle that corresponds to the type of alternative for this case. In the box to the right of *Significance level:* will be the default value of 0.05 . If this is nor correct for your problem, erase this value and type in the correct value of α. Optionally you could store the values of the sample size, difference and computed power in three separate columns. If you decide to do this optional storage, you should name the empty columns as "n", "Difference" and "Power" ahead of time. Then click on OK .

Back in the Power and Sample Size for 1-Sample Z dialog box, click on OK .

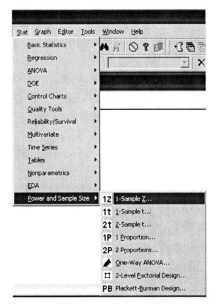
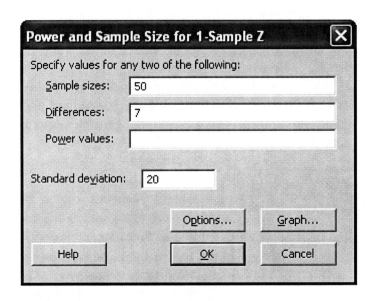

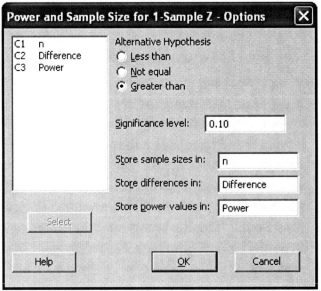

The output of the *Power and Sample Size* procedure contains:

(1)   The direction of the test ( $<$ , $>$ or not $=$ ),

(2)   the values entered for the significance level - $\alpha$, and the assumed standard deviation - $\sigma$,

(3)   the values entered for the difference and the sample size,

(4)   the computed value of the power of the test given in decimal form,

(5)   a graphic window of the power curve with a dot marking the entered difference, and

(6)   if you selected columns to store any of: sample size, difference and/or power, these will be in the Worksheet Window.

If you let the cursor rest on the dot, the values of the difference and power will display in a few seconds.  If you let the cursor rest on any other part of the curve, a table with about 20 different differences and corresponding powers will display in a few seconds.

Example 7.11:   For the example discussed at the beginning of this section we have

$$H_0: \mu \le 50$$
$$H_a: \mu > 50$$
$$\alpha = 0.05 \quad n = 16$$

and the test statistic is $Z = \dfrac{\overline{x} - \mu_0}{\dfrac{\sigma}{\sqrt{n}}}$ .

The value of the population standard deviation is $\sigma = 40$.  Compute the power of the test when the alternative is $\mu = 75$.

First note that the sample size is 16, and the difference between $H_a$: and $H_0$: is $75 - 50 = 25$. Click on *Stat , Power and Sample Size, 1-Sample Z...*

In the Power and Sample Size for 1-Sample Z dialog box you may press the $\boxed{\textbf{F3}}$ key to clear the contents of this dialog box and reset all options.   Click in the box to the right of *Sample sizes:* and type in 16.   Then click in the box to the right of *Differences:* and type in 25, the difference between the $H_a$: and $H_0$:.  Next click in the box to the right of *Standard deviation:* type in 40, the value $\sigma$; and then click on $\boxed{\textbf{Options...}}$ .

In the Power and Sample Size for 1-Sample Z - Options dialog box under the *Alternative Hypothesis* heading, click on the circle that corresponds to the *Greater than* alternative. In the box to the right of *Significance level:* will be the default value of 0.05 , and this is fine as is.  Then click on $\boxed{\textbf{OK}}$ .

Back in the Power and Sample Size for 1-Sample Z dialog box, click on $\boxed{\textbf{OK}}$ .

(continued on the next page)

The results of the power computation shown below will appear in the Session Window.

## Power and Sample Size

### 1-Sample Z Test

**Testing mean = null (versus > null)**
**Calculating power for mean = null + difference**
**Alpha = 0.05  Assumed standard deviation = 40**

| Difference | Sample Size | Power |
|---|---|---|
| 25 | 16 | 0.803765 |

The output contains the correct direction of the test - **versus > null** - (right tail test), the correct value of the significance level - **Alpha = 0.05** -, the given value of the population standard deviation - **40**, the correct difference of 75 - 50 = 25, the given sample size, and the computed power of this test is 0.803765. This agrees with the rounded value of 0.804 shown at the beginning of this section. And so we are about 80 % sure that this test will result in a reject the null decision when the population mean is actually equal to 75. That is, we are 80% sure that this test will detect a population mean that is actually 75.

The graph in the Power Curve for 1-Sample Z Test Graphics Window is shown below.

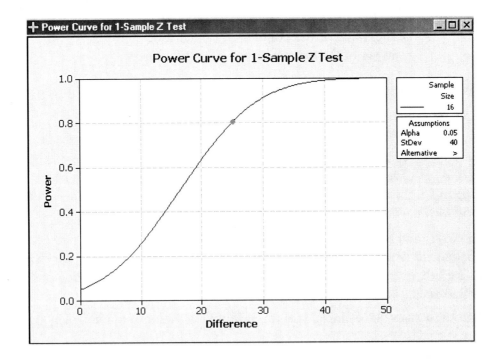

(continued on the next page)

If you let the cursor rest on the dot, after a few seconds the difference and the power will display as

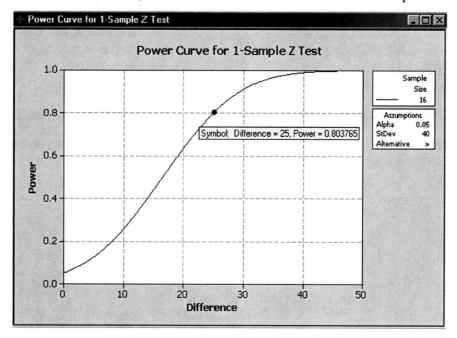

And if you let the cursor rest on any other part of the curve, after a few seconds a table with about 20 different differences and corresponding powers will display as shown on the next page.

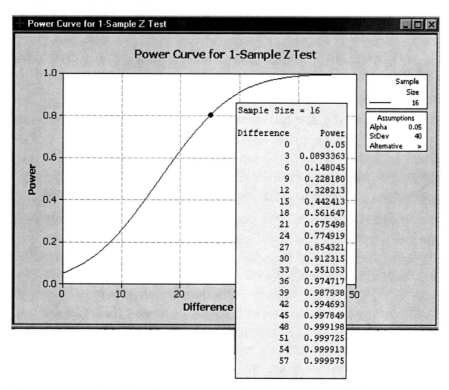

From this you see that the chances are only about 15% of detecting a true alternative hypothesis when the actual value is $\mu = 56$; i.e., difference is 56 - 50 = 6. On the othe hand, the chances are an excellent 99.5 % of detecting a true alternative hypothesis when the actual value is $\mu = 92$; i.e., difference is 92 - 50 = 42.

If you want to compute the power for a series of alternative values, you type in the list of specific differences in the box to the right of *Differences:* in the dialog box for Power and Sample Size for 1-Sample Z. You may type each difference separated by a space; or for a patterend list, you may use the shortcut of a:b / c where a is the first difference, b is the last difference, and c is the increment in the pattern. For example; 5:30 / 5 is the shortcut for 5  10  15  20  25  30. Note that you may not use zero as a difference, as this will produce an error message of

**\* ERROR \* Cannot solve for the sample size under the null hypothesis.**

(When the difference = 0, the power is equivalent to the probability of a Type I error and thus equals the value of $\alpha$.)  For left tail tests, you will need to enter negative differences.

Example 7.12:  $H_0$: $\mu \geq 18$
$H_a$: $\mu < 18$
$\alpha = 0.10$    $n = 45$
and the test statistic is $Z = \dfrac{\bar{x} - \mu_0}{\dfrac{\sigma}{\sqrt{n}}}$ .

The value of the population standard deviation is $\sigma = 8.5$.  Compute the power of the test when the alternative are $\mu = 15.0, 15.5, 16.0, 16.5, 17.0$ and 17.5 .  Also store these results in the Worksheet.

First note that the differences between $H_a$: and $H_0$: are 15 - 18 = -3, 15.5 - 18 = -2.5, and so on to 17.5 - 18 = -0.5.

Since the sample size is 45 for each of these differences, we only need to name two unused columns (C1and C2) in the Worksheet as "Difference" and "Power."

Click on *Stat , Power and Sample Size, 1-Sample Z...*

In the Power and Sample Size for 1-Sample Z dialog box you may press the  F3  key to clear the contents of this dialog box and reset all options.    Click  in the box to the right of *Sample sizes:* and type in the sample size of 45.  Then click in the box to the right of *Differences:* and type in either -3 -2.5 -2 -1.5 -1 -0.5 or -3:-0.5 / 0.5 .   Next click in the box to the right of *Standard deviation:* type in 8.5; and then click on  **Options...** .

In the Power and Sample Size for 1-Sample Z - Options dialog box under the *Alternative Hypothesis* heading, click on the circle that corresponds to the *Less than* alternative.  In the box to the right of *Significance level:* erase the default value of 0.05 , and type in 0.10 .  Now click inside of the box to the right of *Store differences in:* and select the Difference (C1) variable.  The cursor will automatically move inside of the box to the right of *Store power values in:* and select the Power (C2) variable.  (If you have not named unused columns ahead of time, you will need to click into each box and type in an unused column number.)  Then click on  **OK** .

Back in the Power and Sample Size for 1-Sample Z dialog box, click on  **OK**  .

The results of the power computation shown on the next page will appear in the Session Window.

(continued on the next page)

## Power and Sample Size

### 1-Sample Z Test

**Testing mean = null (versus < null)**
**Calculating power for mean = null + difference**
**Alpha = 0.1  Assumed standard deviation = 8.5**

| Difference | Sample Size | Power |
|---|---|---|
| -3.0 | 45 | 0.861272 |
| -2.5 | 45 | 0.755358 |
| -2.0 | 45 | 0.616709 |
| -1.5 | 45 | 0.461065 |
| -1.0 | 45 | 0.311236 |
| -0.5 | 45 | 0.187553 |

The Worksheet Window will contain the differences and respective powers as shown below.

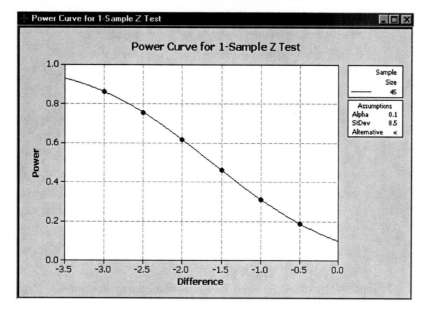

The graph in the Power Curve for 1-Sample Z Test Graphics Window is shown below, and the dots are located at each of the six listed differences.

As with any Graphics Window and described in Chapter 3; you may edit the title, axis labels, scaling of the axes, and even the shape and color of the dots.

225

If the test statistic is $Z = \dfrac{\bar{x} - \mu_0}{\dfrac{s}{\sqrt{n}}}$, then you will need to know or compute the sample

standard deviation before computing the power of the test. When you have summary statistic data, the sample is given to you, but otherwise you will need to compute the value of s and store it into a constant. As explained in Section 1 of Chapter 5, this is done using *Column Statistics*

Click on *Calc , Column Statistics...*

In the Column Statistics dialog box: click on the circle to the left of *Standard deviation*, click inside of the *Input variable:* box, click on the variable that contains the sample data, and click on the | Select | button. Next click in the box to the **right** of *Store results in:*, and type in k2 as the constant name. (Minitab accepts lowercase k2 or uppercase K2 as the same constant.) Then click on the | OK | button.

Then the power of the test is computed exactly as described previously in this section with the exception that you will select the constant k2 instead of typing in the known value of the standard deviation. The exact steps are

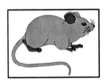

Click on *Stat , Power and Sample Size, 1-Sample Z...*

In the Power and Sample Size for 1-Sample Z dialog box you may press the | F3 | key to clear the contents of this dialog box and reset all options. Click in the box to the right of *Sample sizes:* and type the given sample size or K1 if you needed to calculate the sample size. Then click in the box to the right of *Differences:* and type the difference between the H$_a$: and H$_0$: values. Next click in the box to the right of *Standard deviation:* and type the value of the sample standard deviation (s) or K2 into this box, and then click on the | Options... | button.

In the Power and Sample Size for 1-Sample Z - Options dialog box under the *Alternative Hypothesis* heading, click on the circle that corresponds to the type of alternative for this case. In the box to the right of *Significance level:* will be the default value of 0.05 . If this is nor correct for your problem, erase this value and type in the correct value of α. Optionally you may store the values of the sample size, difference and computed power in three separate columns. If you decide to do this, you should name the empty columns as "n", "difference" and "power" ahead of time. Then click on | OK | .

Back in the Power and Sample Size for 1-Sample Z dialog box, click on | OK | .

226

Example 7.13:   Open the Study4.mtw worksheet that is on your data disc. A researcher believes that the mean number of hours per week studied by the students is considerably greater than the claimed value of 12. By considerably, he means 15 hours per week. Compute the power of this test for the researcher's belief using a significance level of 0.10.

Use the *File, Open Worksheet...* to open the Study4.mtw worksheet from your data disc into a second worksheet. First the sample standard deviation must be computed and stored into the K2 constant.

Click on *Calc, Column Statistics...*

In the Column Statistics dialog box: click on the circle to the left of *N nonmissing*, click inside of the *Input variable:* box, click on the StudyHrs variable, and click on the *Select* button. Next click inside of the *Store result in:* box and type K1. Then click on $\boxed{\textbf{OK}}$ .

From the output in the Session window, we see that the sample size is 35.
This hypothesis testing problem sets up as

$$H_0: \mu \le 12$$
$$H_a: \mu > 12$$
$$\alpha = 0.10 \quad n = 35$$
$$\text{and the test statistic is } Z = \frac{\bar{x} - \mu_0}{\dfrac{s}{\sqrt{n}}} .$$

Next note that since the researcher is interested in a difference of at least three hours, the difference between $H_a$: and $H_0$: is 15 - 12 = 3.

Before you can compute the power of this test, the sample standard deviation must be computed and stored in the K2 constant.

Click on *Calc, Column Statistics...*

In the Column Statistics dialog box: click on the circle to the left of *Standard deviation*, the StudyHrs variable should still be in the box to the right of the *Input variable:* label. Next click in the box to the **right** of *Store results in:*, and type in k2 as the constant name. Then click on $\boxed{\textbf{OK}}$ .

Now the power of the test may be computed.

Click on *Stat, Power and Sample Size, 1-Sample Z...*

In the Power and Sample Size for 1-Sample Z dialog box press the $\boxed{\textbf{F3}}$ key to clear the contents of this dialog box and reset all options. Click in the box to the right of *Sample sizes:* and type in k1 or 35, the computed sample size. Then click in the box to the right of *Differences:* and type in 3, the difference between the $H_a$: and $H_0$: values. Next click into the box to the right of *Standard deviation:* and type k2 into this box, and then click on the $\boxed{\textbf{Options...}}$ button.

(continued on the next page)

In the Power and Sample Size for 1-Sample Z - Options dialog box under the *Alternative Hypothesis* heading, click on the circle that corresponds to the *Greater than* alternative. In the box to the right of *Significance level:* erase the current value and type in the correct value of 0.10 . Then click on **OK** .

Back in the Power and Sample Size for 1-Sample Z dialog box, click on **OK** .

The results of the power computation shown below will appear in the Session Window.

## Power and Sample Size

### 1-Sample Z Test

**Testing mean = null (versus > null)**
**Calculating power for mean = null + difference**
**Alpha = 0.1  Assumed standard deviation = 6.47205**

| Difference | Sample Size | Power |
|---|---|---|
| 3 | 35 | 0.927957 |

And so the researcher knows that if the mean number of hours per week studied by the students is actually 15, he is about 93% sure this test will correctly detect such a difference.

The Power Curve Graphic Window for this example is not shown.

If the test statistic is $t = \dfrac{\bar{x} - \mu_0}{\dfrac{s}{\sqrt{n}}}$ instead of the Z test statistic, then you will need to know the sample standard deviation. If you have already taken the sample, use *Calc, Column Statistics...* to compute and store the sample standard deviation into a constant, say k2. Otherwise you will need to have a good estimate of the population standard deviation from a similar, previous study; or from a small, pilot sample, or from making a good educated guess. Then after clicking on *Stat, Power and Sample Size*, you will choose *1-Sample t...* instead of *1-Sample Z...* You will get a Power and Sample Size for 1-Sample t dialog box, and may continue exactly as described earlier in this chapter for the 1-Sample Z case.

Example 7.14:   In today's society it seems that many people have stopped working at a younger age than in the past with the goal of throughly enjoying their retirement. On the other hand, with the economic climate and Social Security rules, other people seem to be retiring later than in the past. A sociologist wishes to determine if the average age at retirement has changed from the previous known value of 65 years old. A sample of 26 people who retired this year was taken, and its standard deviation was computed to be 1.28 . The age at retirement is known to be normally distributed. A change of less than 9 months is considered casual. The sociologist will be using a 0.10 significance level. What is the power of this test for detecting a change of 9 months when such a change actually exists?

(continued on the next page)

This hypothesis testing problem sets up as

$H_0: \mu = 65$
$H_a: \mu \neq 65$
$\alpha = 0.10 \quad n = 26$

and the test statistic is $t = \dfrac{\overline{x} - \mu_0}{\dfrac{s}{\sqrt{n}}}$.

Since the sociologists want to be able to detect a change of 9 months - which is 0.75 years, the difference between $H_a$: and $H_0$: is either 64.25 - 65 = -0.75 or 65.75 - 65 = 0.75 .

Click on *Stat , Power and Sample Size, 1-Sample t...*

In the Power and Sample Size for 1-Sample t dialog box you may press the ⎢ **F3** ⎢ key to clear the contents of this dialog box and reset all options. Then type the 26 into the box to the right of *Sample sizes:* and type -0.75 0.75 into the box to the right of *Differences:* . Next type the 1.28 into the box to the right of *Standard deviation:* , and then click on ⎢ **Options...** ⎢ .

In the Power and Sample Size for 1-Sample t - Options dialog box under the *Alternative Hypothesis* heading, click on the circle that corresponds to the *Not equal* alternative. In the box to the right of *Significance level:*, erase the default value of 0.05 and type in this example's significance value of 0.10 . Then click on ⎢ **OK** ⎢.

Back in the Power and Sample Size for 1-Sample t dialog box, click on ⎢ **OK** ⎢ .

The results of the power computation shown below will appear in the Session Window.

## *Power and Sample Size*

### *1-Sample t Test*

**Testing mean = null (versus not = null)**
**Calculating power for mean = null + difference**
**Alpha = 0.1   Assumed standard deviation = 1.28**

| Difference | Sample Size | Power |
|---|---|---|
| -0.75 | 26 | 0.896254 |
| 0.75 | 26 | 0.896254 |

Notice that the power is the same for the negative and the positive differences as the alternatives are same distance away, on either side, from the null value of $\mu = 65$ .

The graph in the Power Curve for 1-Sample t Test Graphics Window is shown on the next page, and the dots are located at the two differences of -0.75 and 0.75 .

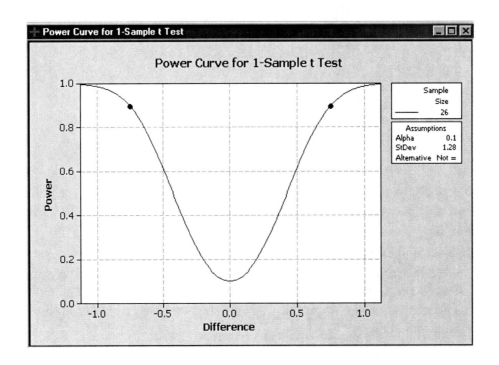

And so the sociologist is almost 90% sure that if there actually has been a change of 9 months in the average retirement age, he will be able to detect this change using the given one-sample t test.

In Example 7.14 the rejection region is $t \leq -1.71$ and $t \geq 1.71$, and the graph below on the Student t axis shows the power of the test when the alternative of $\mu = 65.75$ is actually true.

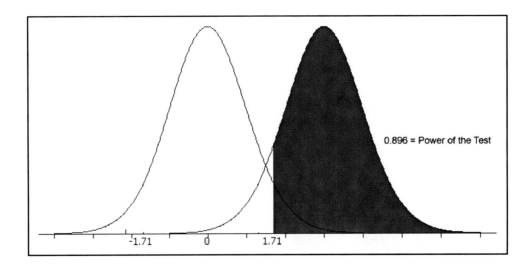

If the sociologist was only interested in determining whether or not the average age had increased, then he would have use a one-tail test instead of the two-tail test used in Example 7-12. In this case the right-tail rejection region would be $t \geq 1.316$, and the new critical point of 1.316 would be to the left of 1.71. From the picture above we see that the power would increase, as the area under the right curve would increase down to 1.316.

Example 7.15: For the data given in Example 7.14, repeat the computation of the power of the test when the sociologist only wants to determine if the average age at retirement is 9 months older than it was before.

Now this hypothesis testing problem sets up as

$$H_0: \mu \leq 65$$
$$H_a: \mu > 65$$
$$\alpha = 0.10 \quad n = 26$$

and the test statistic is $t = \dfrac{\bar{x} - \mu_0}{\dfrac{s}{\sqrt{n}}}$.

Since the sociologists want to be able to detect an increase of 9 months - which is 0.75 years, the difference between $H_a$: and $H_0$: is 65.75 - 65 = 0.75 .

Click on *Stat , Power and Sample Size, 1-Sample t...*

In the Power and Sample Size for 1-Sample t dialog box you will only need to make a few changes, so do not press the | **F3** | key. Now erase the -0.75 from the box to the right of *Differences:* leaving only 0.75 . Next click on | **Options...** | .

In the Power and Sample Size for 1-Sample t - Options dialog box under the *Alternative Hypothesis* heading, click on the circle that corresponds to the *Greater than* alternative. leave the 0.10 in the box to the right of *Significance level:*. Then click on | **OK** |.

Back in the Power and Sample Size for 1-Sample t dialog box, click on | **OK** | .

The results of the power computation shown below will appear in the Session Window.

## *Power and Sample Size*

### *1-Sample t Test*

*Testing mean = null (versus not > null)*
*Calculating power for mean = null + difference*
*Alpha = 0.1   Assumed standard deviation = 1.28*

| Difference | Sample Size | Power |
|------------|-------------|----------|
| 0.75 | 26 | 0.951143 |

Now the sociologist is 95% sure that if there has been an increase of 9 months in the average retirement age, he will be able to detect this change using the given one-sample t test.

The conclusion to be made from this exercise is that **when you are primarily interested in a one sided alternative, always perform a one-tail test; as it will be more powerful than the corresponding two-tail test.**

When the variable is a Bernoulli type of measurement and you are testing hypotheses about the proportion of "successes" of a population, the power of the test is computed very similarly. The only difference is that now for the population proportions, you will enter the null hypothesized value and the specific alternative values separately. When using a 1-sample test for the proportion of "successes" in a population, a power curve is computed and graphed as follows.

Click on *Stat , Power and Sample Size, 1 Proportion...*

In the Power and Sample Size for 1 Proportion dialog box you may press the [ F3 ] key to clear the contents of this dialog box and reset all options. Then type the given sample size into the box to the right of *Sample sizes:* and type the specific Hₐ: value of the proportion into the box to the right of *Alternative values of p:* . Next type the null hypothesized value of the proportion into the box to the right of *Hypothesized p:*, and then click on the [ Options... ] button.

In the Power and Sample Size for 1 Proportion - Options dialog box under the *Alternative Hypothesis* heading, click on the circle that corresponds to the type of alternative for this case. In the box to the right of *Significance level:* will be the default value of 0.05 . If this is nor correct for your problem, erase this value and type in the correct value of α. Optionally you may store the values of the sample size, difference and computed power in three separate columns. If you decide to do this, you should name the empty columns as "n", "difference" and "power" ahead of time. Then click on [ OK ] .

Back in the Power and Sample Size for 1 proportion dialog box, click on [ OK ] .

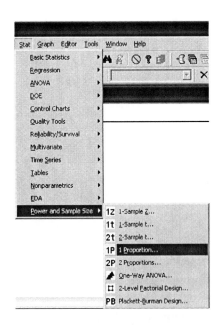

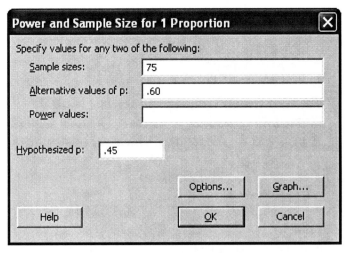

Only the first two graphics are shown, as the Options graphic is exactly the same as for the 1-Sample Z and 1-Sample t.

Example 7.16: A local electronics industry buys components and then assembles the finished product. The quality control engineer is responsible to testing the incoming shipments of components. The acceptable proportion of defective items in any one shipment is 3%. The engineer conducts the inspection by sampling 50 components, checking each one to see if it is good or defective, and then testing the hypothesis that the proportion of defective components is greater than 0.03 using a 0.10 significance level. If the engineer believes that a shipment contains more than 3% defective items, he sends the entire shipment back to the supplier for a replacement. However this delays the assembly process and may be costly to his company, and so it is often more economical to accept shipments that contain marginally more than 3% defective components. For this reason the engineer is only really interested in returning shipments that contains at least 8% defective items. Compute the power of the test when the alternative hypothesis is $H_a$: $p = 0.08$ and graph the power curve. The management of this local electronics industry would like the power to be at least 85%

This hypothesis testing problem sets up as

$H_0$: $p \leq 0.03$
$H_a$: $p > 0.03$
$\alpha = 0.10$     $n = 50$
and the test statistic $Z = \dfrac{\hat{p} - p_0}{\sqrt{\dfrac{p_0(1 - p_0)}{n}}}$ .

Click on *Stat , Power and Sample Size, 1 Proportion...*

In the Power and Sample Size for 1 Proportion dialog box you may press the $\boxed{\text{F3}}$ key to clear the contents of this dialog box and reset all options. Then type 50 into the box to the right of *Sample sizes:* and type the specific $H_a$: value of 0.08 into the box to the right of *Alternative values of p:* . Next type the null hypothesized value of 0.03 into the box to the right of *Hypothesized p:*, and then click on the $\boxed{\text{Options...}}$ button.

In the Power and Sample Size for 1 Proportion - Options dialog box under the *Alternative Hypothesis* heading, click on the circle to the left of *Greater than*. In the box to the right of *Significance level:*, erase the default value of 0.05 and type in 0.10 . Then click on the $\boxed{\text{OK}}$ button.

Back in the Power and Sample Size for 1 proportion dialog box, click on $\boxed{\text{OK}}$ .

The results of the power computation shown on the next page will appear in the Session Window.

(continued on the next page)

## Power and Sample Size

### Test for One Proportion

**Testing proportion = 0.03 (versus > 0.03)**
**Alpha = 0.1**

| Alternative Proportion | Sample Size | Power |
|---|---|---|
| 0.08 | 50 | 0.690541 |

And so the quality control engineer is 69% sure that he will be able to detect a shipment that actually contains 8% defective components. Since this power is not up to management's expectations, a change in the quality control procedure is needed. A larger sample size is the simplest change to make to the procedure, and the next section of this chapter will discuss how to determine the needed sample size.

And the Graphics window containing the power curve with the dot at p = 0.08 is shown below.

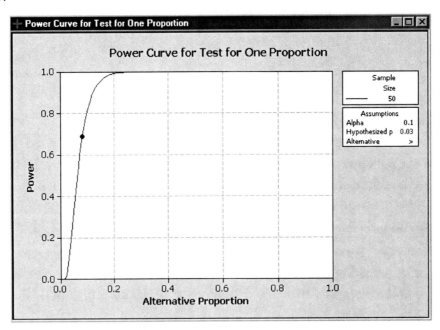

If you let the cursor rest on the dot for a few seconds, the specific value of $H_a$: and the computed value of the power of the test are displayed as shown on the next page.

(continued on the next page)

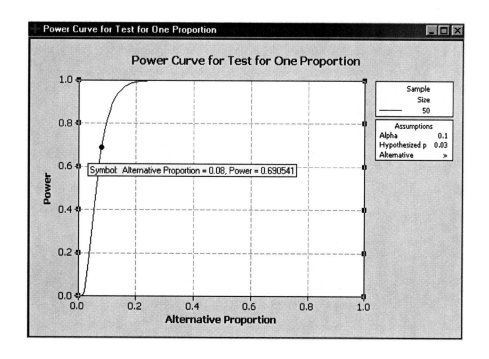

And as before, if you let the cursor rest anywhere on the curve other than the dot, after a few seconds a table with about 18 different specific alternative values of p and corresponding powers will display as shown below.

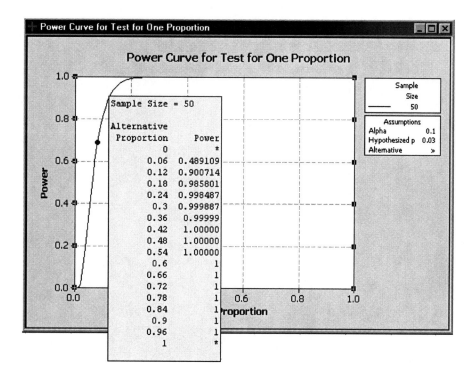

# Lab Assignment 7.4

Name:                                                            Date:

Course:                       Section:                       Data CD Number:

1.  Start a Minitab session. If you are unable to complete this lab assignment in one Minitab session, save the project as Lab 7-4 . **Never** use a period as part of the project name; since Minitab uses the period to attach the file type to the file name. Then at your next Minitab session, you may open this Lab 7-4.MPJ project and continue to work where you left off previously.

2.  A major food company is developing a new milk substitute for lactose intolerant people. The similar products already on the market are tolerated by 70% of the lactose intolerant population. The company plans to test this new substitute on 160 people, and it wants to see if the new product can be tolerated by at least 75% of this population. Using a significance level of 0.10 , what is the power of the test?

3.  Open the worksheet Homesale.mtw that is on your data disc. This worksheet contains information about one-family housing sales in Raleigh, North Carolina. The mean selling price for all one-family houses in the nearby city of Durham, North Carolina is $ 52,500. At the 0.10 level of significance, the realtor want test to see if the mean selling price of one-family houses in Raleigh is different than the known Durham mean selling price. What is the power of this test if the realtor needs to detect a difference of $5500 ?

4.  The average person who undergoes knee replacement surgery requires 32 day of physical therapy rehabilitation. A medical researcher believes that the amount of physical therapy can be reduced if the patient is in good physical condition before the surgery is performed. The researcher plans to take a random sample of 16 knee replacement patients who were in good physical condition before the surgery, and measure how many days are required for physical therapy. Previous studies of this population have shown that the data is normally distributed with a standard deviation of 5.41 days. The researcher believes that the reduction in physical therapy time will be at 4 days. Using a significance level of 0.05 , what is the power of the test in this case?

(lab assignment is continued on the second side of this page)

5.      Print your Session Window and all Graphics Windows to the printer.


6.      Attach both your Minitab output and your complete answers to this sheet and submit all three to your instructor.

**Section 5:     Choosing a Sample Size**

Similar to the situation described in Section 4 of Chapter 5, all of the examples and lab assignment problems up to here in this chapter have the sample size given as one of the known pieces of information for the problem. However, when one begins a "real world" hypothesis testing problem, often the sample does not exist. One of the first tasks is to choose an appropriate sample size. There are several ways to approach such problems. One is to take as large of a sample as possible, constrained only by the time and money allocated to the specific problem. This approach has the advantage that for any given value of $\alpha$, it will produce the smallest probability of Type II Error and thus the greatest power of the test for any alternative hypothesis. However similarly to the situation for confidence intervals, this approach may result in a sample size considerably larger than needed, and thus wasteful of resources.

A second approach is to choose an optimal size sample satisfying two predetermined needs. Before collecting sample data, one must decide upon (1) a specific value of the difference between $H_a$: - $H_0$: that is of interest and (2) the desired power of the test for this specific difference. This section will show how to compute such optimal sample sizes in two situations. One where the data is continuous and the population mean is to be tested after the sample size is determined, and the second situation is for Bernoulli data where the population proportion of "successes" is to be tested after the sample size has been determined. In either case, once the optimal sample size has been computed, you would need to determine if you have enough time and money allocated to take a sample of this size.

In the situation where the data is continuous and the population mean is to be tested, you also will need to determine whether you will be using a Z test statistic or a t test statistic. Once you know the appropriate test statistic, the specific difference(s) between $H_a$: - $H_0$: that is of interest, and the desired power(s) of the test for this specific difference; the procedure to compute the optimal sample size is very similar to that of finding the power of the test described in the previous section. Note that the sample sizes for a variety of differences and/or powers may be computed in just one application of the Minitab procedure.

When using the 1- sample $Z = \dfrac{\overline{x} - \mu_0}{\dfrac{\sigma}{\sqrt{n}}}$ test statistic, the computation of the optimal sample

size is done as shown on the next page.

Click on *Stat , Power and Sample Size, 1-Sample Z...*

In the Power and Sample Size for 1-Sample Z dialog box you may press the F3 key to clear the contents of this dialog box and reset all options. Click in the box to the right of *Differences:* and type the difference between the $H_a$: - $H_0$: values. You may type in a list of values here using either the explicit listing or the shortcut format of a:b / c as described in Section 4. Then click in the box to the right of *Power values:* and type the value of power of the test desired. **This must be in decimal form and not as a percent!** You may type in a list of explicit values here, but Minitab **does not accept the shortcut method in this box**. Next click in the box to the right of *Standard deviation:* type the value of σ, and then click on the Options... button.

In the Power and Sample Size for 1-Sample Z - Options dialog box under the *Alternative Hypothesis* heading, click on the circle that corresponds to the type of alternative for this case. In the box to the right of *Significance level:* will be the default value of 0.05 . If this is not correct for your problem, erase this value and type in the correct value of α. Optionally you may store the values of the sample size, difference and computed power in three separate columns. If you decide to do this, you should name the empty columns as "n", "Difference" and "Power" ahead of time. Then click on OK .

Back in the Power and Sample Size for 1-Sample Z dialog box, click on OK .

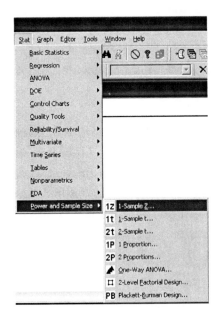

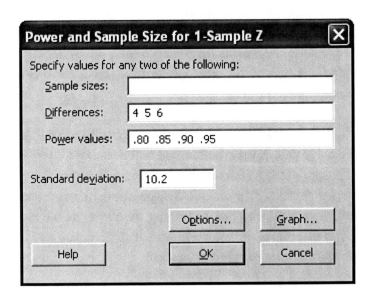

(See the third graphic on the next page.)

The output of the *Power and Sample Size for 1-Sample Z* procedure contains:

(1)    The direction of the test ( $<$ , $>$ or not $=$ ),

(2)    the values entered for the significance level - $\alpha$, and the assumed standard deviation - $\sigma$,

(3)    the values entered for the difference and the power; if a list of differences and or powers were entered, then every combination of the values in these lists is displayed

(4)    the computed value of the sample size(s) and the actual power(s) of the test; since it usually is not possible to achieve the exact power(s) entered,

(5)    a graphic window of the power curve with a dot marking the entered difference, and

(6)    if you selected columns to store any of: sample size, difference and/or power, these will be in the Worksheet Window.


If the population standard deviation $\sigma$ is unknown, and you are using the 1- sample $Z = \dfrac{\bar{x} - \mu_0}{\dfrac{s}{\sqrt{n}}}$ test statistic, you must have an estimated value of s; i.e., an estimate of the population

standard deviation, before the computation of the optimal sample size can be done. This estimated value may come from a previous study or from a pilot sample. Once you have this estimated value of s, you type this value in the box to the right of *Standard deviation:* in the Power and Sample Size for 1-Sample Z dialog box (since the value of $\sigma$ is unknown). All other steps just shown are the same, and the output is the same as just described.

Example 7.17:    ToolTech Company is a wholesale tool maker which sell its products throughout the Southwest region of the United States.    One of its specialties is a line of metric sized wrenches.  A batch of wrenches will work fine as long as its mean size is not more than 0.02 mm larger than the stated size. (The process of making the wrenches guarantees that none of them will ever be smaller than the stated size.)  For the 25 mm wrench production line, historical data  has shown the wrench sizes are normally distributed with a standard deviation of 0.018 mm.  The ToolTech quality control engineer samples wrenches from each production run and performs a hypothesis test before the company sells any of those wrenches. While ToolTech and its customers would like the mean size to be exactly 25 mm, they realize that this is almost impossible, and they understand that very slightly larger wrenches still will work perfectly well.  With this in mind, a significance level of 0.01 is used so as not to stop the production unnecessarily.  When the quality control engineer tests the hypothesis, he is not that concerned with minor variations in the mean size. But it is very important that he be able to detect when the mean size of the wrenches from a particular production run is 25.02 mm, since these wrenches will not work, and ToolTech will incur the cost of replacing them in addition to the loss of customer confidence.  How many wrenches must the quality control engineer sample if he wants to the power of the test be 0.98 ?

This hypothesis testing problem sets up as

$$H_0: \mu \leq 25$$
$$H_a: \mu > 25$$
$$\alpha = 0.01 , \quad \text{power} = 1 - \beta = 0.90 , \quad n = ?$$

and the test statistic is $Z = \dfrac{\overline{x} - \mu_0}{\dfrac{s}{\sqrt{n}}}$ .

Computation of the sample size needed in order to achieve the desired level of significance and power of the test is done as

Click on *Stat* , *Power and Sample Size*, *1-Sample Z...*

In the Power and Sample Size for 1-Sample Z dialog box you may press the $\boxed{\text{F3}}$ key to clear the contents of this dialog box and reset all options.  Click  in the box to the right of *Differences:* and type in 0.02, the required difference between the $H_a$: - $H_0$: values. Then click in the box to the right of *Power values:* and type 0.98, the value of power of the test desired.  Next click in the box to the right of *Standard deviation:* type in 0.018, the estimated value of $\sigma$, and then click on the $\boxed{\text{Options...}}$ button.

In the Power and Sample Size for 1-Sample Z - Options dialog box under the *Alternative Hypothesis* heading, click on the circle to the left of *Greater than*. Erase the 0.05 in the box to the right of *Significance level:* and type in 0.01, the correct value of $\alpha$. Then click on $\boxed{\text{OK}}$ .

(continued on the next page)

Back in the Power and Sample Size for 1-Sample Z dialog box, click on OK .

The results of the sample size computation shown below will appear in the Session Window.

## Power and Sample Size

### 1-Sample Z Test

**Testing mean = null (versus > null)**
**Calculating power for mean = null + difference**
**Alpha = 0.01  Assumed standard deviation = 0.018**

| Difference | Sample Size | Target Power | Actual Power |
|------------|-------------|--------------|--------------|
| 0.02 | 16 | 0.98 | 0.982917 |

The graph in the Power Curve for 1-Sample Z Test Graphics Window is shown below, and the dot is located at desired difference of 0.02.

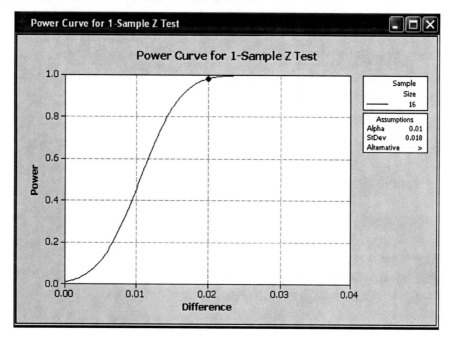

The computed sample size of 16 is shown both in the Session window and in a legend box to the right of the power curve in the Graphics Window. And so the ToolTech quality control engineer will randomly sample 16 wrenches from the each production run on the 25 mm line, and then perform the hypothesis test shown at the beginning of this example.

Example 7.18:   Use the information in Example 7.17 and compute the optimal sample sizes if the quality control engineer needs to be able to detect when the mean size of the wrenches are 25.010, 25.012, 25.014, 25.016, 25.018 and 25.020.

(continued on the next page)

Whenever several different sample sizes are going to be computed, you should name empty columns before doing the computation. In this example you will be computing sample sizes for different values of the difference between $H_a$: - $H_0$:, and so name two empty columns with "Difference" and "n". Since the power is the same for all differences, there is no need to name a power column).

Name the C1 column as "Difference" and the C2 column as "n".

Click on *Stat , Power and Sample Size, 1-Sample Z...*

In the Power and Sample Size for 1-Sample Z dialog box Minitab has remembered all of the values you entered in Example 17.7, so you will only need to make a few changes. Click in the box to the right of *Differences:*, erase the 0.02, and enter 0.01:0.02 /0.002 which is the shortcut for the required difference between the $H_a$: - $H_0$: values. Then click in the box to the right of *Power values:* will still have 0.98 in it, and the box to the right of *Standard deviation:* will still have 0.018 in it. Then click on the ⬚ **Options...** ⬚ button.

In the Power and Sample Size for 1-Sample Z - Options dialog box under the *Alternative Hypothesis* heading, the circle to the left of *Greater than* will be selected and 0.01 will be in the box to the right of *Significance level:*. Click inside the box to the right of *Store sample sizes in:*, highlight the n (C2) variable in the larger box to the left, and click on the ⬚ **Select** ⬚ button. Next click inside the box to the right of *Store differences in:*, highlight the Difference (C1) variable in the larger box to the left, and click on the ⬚ **Select** ⬚ button. Then click on ⬚ **OK** ⬚ .

Back in the Power and Sample Size for 1-Sample Z dialog box, click on ⬚ **OK** ⬚ .

The results of the sample size computation shown below will appear in the Session Window.

## Power and Sample Size

### 1-Sample Z Test

**Testing mean = null (versus > null)**
**Calculating power for mean = null + difference**
**Alpha = 0.01  Assumed standard deviation = 0.018**

| Difference | Sample Size | Target Power | Actual Power |
|---|---|---|---|
| 0.010 | 63 | 0.98 | 0.981385 |
| 0.012 | 44 | 0.98 | 0.981951 |
| 0.014 | 32 | 0.98 | 0.980934 |
| 0.016 | 25 | 0.98 | 0.982917 |
| 0.018 | 20 | 0.98 | 0.984055 |
| 0.020 | 16 | 0.98 | 0.982917 |

Notice that the last line in the output is the same as the result in Example 7.17 .

(continued on the next page)

The resulting sample sizes for each of the differences have also been stored in the two named columns in the worksheet as shown below.

| ↓ | C1 | C2 |
|---|---|---|
| | Difference | n |
| 1 | 0.010 | 63 |
| 2 | 0.012 | 44 |
| 3 | 0.014 | 32 |
| 4 | 0.016 | 25 |
| 5 | 0.018 | 20 |
| 6 | 0.020 | 16 |

Worksheet 1 ***

In most problems it will not be necessary to store these results in the worksheet, as they are always clearly displayed in the Session Window.

The graph in the Power Curve for 1-Sample Z Test Graphics Window shown below contains power curves for the six different sample sizes, and each has a dot corresponding to the actual power of the test.

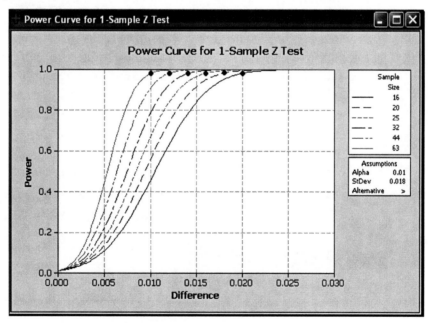

And so if the quality control engineer needs to detect a mean wrench size of 25.010 mm (a difference of 0.010) with a power of 0.98, the optimal sample size would be 63. The optimal sample sizes for detecting mean wrench sizes of 25.012, 25.014, 25.016, 25.018 and 25.020 are 44, 32, 25, 20 and 16 respectively.

When the appropriate test statistic is $t = \dfrac{\overline{x} - \mu_0}{\dfrac{s}{\sqrt{n}}}$, you will need a value for the sample

standard deviation - s. But since the sample has not been taken yet, you will have to estimate this standard deviation from a similar, previous study; or from a small, pilot sample, or from making a good educated guess. Then the computation of the optimal sample size is done using *Stat*, *Power and Sample Size*, *1-Sample t...* The rest of the steps are equivalent to those shown for the Z test statistic except that the dialog boxes are titled *Stat*, *Power and Sample Size*, *1-Sample t...* instead of *Stat*, *Power and Sample Size*, *1-Sample Z....*

Click on *Stat*, *Power and Sample Size*, *1-Sample t...*

In the Power and Sample Size for 1-Sample t dialog box you may press the ⬛ **F3** key to clear the contents of this dialog box and reset all options. Click in the box to the right of *Differences:* and type the difference between the $H_a$: - $H_0$: values. You may type in a list of values here using either the explicit listing or the shortcut format of a:b / c as described in Section 4. Then click in the box to the right of *Power values:* and type the value of power of the test desired. **This must be in decimal format!** You may type in a list of explicit values here, but Minitab **does not accept the shortcut method in this box**. Next click in the box to the right of *Standard deviation:* type the value of the estimated standard deviation, and then click on the ⬛ **Options...** button.

In the Power and Sample Size for 1-Sample t - Options dialog box under the *Alternative Hypothesis* heading, click on the circle that corresponds to the type of alternative for this case. In the box to the right of *Significance level:* will be the default value of 0.05 . If this is not correct for your problem, erase this value and type in the correct value of α. Optionally you may store the values of the sample size, difference and computed power in three separate columns. If you decide to do this, you should name the empty columns as "n", "Difference" and "Power" ahead of time. Then click on ⬛ **OK** .

Back in the Power and Sample Size for 1-Sample t dialog box, click on ⬛ **OK** .

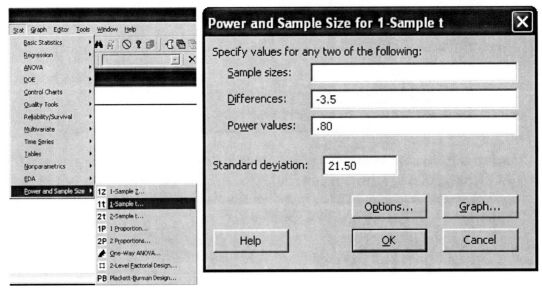

(See the third graphic on the next page.)

**Power and Sample Size for 1-Sample t - Options**

Alternative Hypothesis
- ● Less than
- ○ Not equal
- ○ Greater than

Significance level: 0.025

Store sample sizes in:

Store differences in:

Store power values in:

Select    Help    OK    Cancel

The output of the *Power and Sample Size for 1-Sample t* procedure contains:

(1)    The direction of the test ( < , > or not = ),

(2)    the values entered for the significance level - $\alpha$, and the assumed sample standard deviation,

(3)    the values entered for the difference and the power; if a list of differences and or powers were entered, then every combination of the values in these lists is displayed

(4)    the computed value of the sample size(s) and the actual power(s) of the test; since it usually is not possible to achieve the exact power(s) entered,

(5)    a graphic window of the power curve with a dot marking the entered difference, and

(6)    if you selected columns to store any of: sample size, difference and/or power, these will be in the Worksheet Window.

Example 7.19:    A university admissions officer is examining the entering freshman class of 2008. If this class's mean grade point average (G.P.A.) is substantially below the previous year's value of 3.20, then the admissions office will need to examine their policies for the future. Since a drop in the mean G.P.A. will have a negative impact on the university's regional reputation and ability to attract better students and faculty, the admissions officer must be able to detect a drop of 0.25 in the mean G.P.A. so that corrective action may be taken. The G.P.A scores are known to be normally distributed. Using a significance level of 0.02, how large of a sample does the admissions officer need to take if she wants the power of the test to be 0.85. In order to estimate the sample standard deviation, the data in the Study4.mtw worksheet saved on your data disc may be used as a previous, similar study.

(continued on the next page)

This hypothesis testing problem sets up as

$$H_0: \mu \geq 3.20$$
$$H_a: \mu < 3.20$$
$$\alpha = 0.02, \quad \text{power} = 1 - \beta = 0.80, \quad n = ?$$

and the test statistic is $t = \dfrac{\overline{x} - \mu_0}{\dfrac{s}{\sqrt{n}}}$ .

First the estimated sample standard deviation must be computed and stored into the K1 constant.

Use the *File , Open Worksheet ...* to open the Study4.mtw worksheet from your data disc. Click on *Calc , Column Statistics...*

In the Column Statistics dialog box: click on the circle to the left of *Standard deviation*, click inside of the *Input variable:* box, click on the G.P.A. variable, and click on the *Select* button. Next click inside of the *Store result in:* box and type k1 as the constant name. Then click on $\boxed{\textbf{OK}}$ .

Now the optimal sample size is computed.

Click on *Stat , Power and Sample Size, 1-Sample t...*

In the Power and Sample Size for 1-Sample t dialog box you may press the $\boxed{\textbf{F3}}$ key to clear the contents of this dialog box and reset all options. Click in the box to the right of *Differences:* and type in -0.25, the required difference between the $H_a$: - $H_0$: values. Then click in the box to the right of *Power values:* and type 0.80, the value of power of the test desired. Next click in the box to the right of *Standard deviation:* type in k1, the estimated value of s, and then click on the $\boxed{\textbf{Options...}}$ button.

In the Power and Sample Size for 1-Sample t - Options dialog box under the *Alternative Hypothesis* heading, click on the circle to the left of *Less than*. Erase the 0.05 in the box to the right of *Significance level:* and type in 0.02, the correct value of $\alpha$. Then click on $\boxed{\textbf{OK}}$ .

Back in the Power and Sample Size for 1-Sample Z dialog box, click on $\boxed{\textbf{OK}}$ .

The results of the sample size computation shown below will appear in the Session Window.

## Power and Sample Size

### 1-Sample t Test

**Testing mean = null (versus < null)**
**Calculating power for mean = null + difference**
**Alpha = 0.02  Assumed standard deviation = 0.806165**

| Difference | Sample Size | Target Power | Actual Power |
|---|---|---|---|
| -0.25 | 90 | 0.80 | 0.803230 |

(continued on the next page)

The graph in the Power Curve for 1-Sample t Test Graphics Window is shown below, and the dot is located at desired difference of -0.25 .

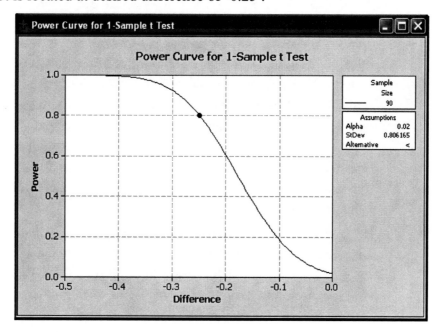

The computed sample size of 90 is shown both in the Session Window and in a legend box to the right of the power curve in the Graphics Window. And so the university admissions officer will randomly sample 90 students from the incoming freshman class of 2009, and then perform the hypothesis test shown at the beginning of this example.

In the situation where the variable is a Bernoulli type of measurement and the population proportion is to be tested, the determination of the sample size is based upon the assumption that the you will be using the Z test statistic. Since this is an approximation, the use of the Z test statistic requires a large enough sample to satisfy the certain requirements; a commonly used set of conditions is that $np_0 \geq 5$ and $n(1-p_0) \geq 5$. If the result of the sample size computation is less than the value of n needed to satisfy these conditions, you will need to increase the optimal sample size to the minimum value of n that will satisfy the conditions.

When using the 1 proportion test statistic $Z = \dfrac{\hat{p} - p_0}{\sqrt{\dfrac{p_0(1 - p_0)}{n}}}$ , the computation of the

optimal sample size is very similar to the methods shown earlier in this section (when testing for the population mean with continuous data). One difference is that the dialog box asks you to type in the specific value(s) of the alternative hypothesis $H_a$: in one place, and then type in and the given value of the null hypothesis $H_0$: in another place (instead of typing in the difference(s) of $H_a$: - $H_0$: as done for continuous data). The computation of the optimal sample size is done as shown on the next page.

Click on *Stat , Power and Sample Size, 1 Proportion...*

In the Power and Sample Size for 1 Proportion dialog box you may press the  F3 key to clear the contents of this dialog box and reset all options. Click in the box to the right of *Alternative values of p:* and type the specific value of $H_a$: . You may type in a list of values here using either the explicit listing or the shortcut format of a:b / c as described in Section 4. **This must be in decimal form!** Then click in the box to the right of *Power values:* and type the value of power of the test desired. You may type in a list of explicit values here, but Minitab **does not accept the shortcut method in this box**. Next click in the box to the right of *Hypothesized p:* type the value of $p_0$ given in the null hypothesis **in decimal form**, and then click on the Options... button.

In the Power and Sample Size for 1 Proportion - Options dialog box under the *Alternative Hypothesis* heading, click on the circle that corresponds to the type of alternative for this case. In the box to the right of *Significance level:* will be the default value of 0.05 . If this is not correct for your problem, erase this value and type in the correct value of α. Optionally you may store the values of the sample size, difference and computed power in three separate columns. If you decide to do this, you should name the empty columns as "n", "Alternative" and "Power" ahead of time. Then click on OK .

Back in the Power and Sample Size for 1 Proportion dialog box, click on OK .

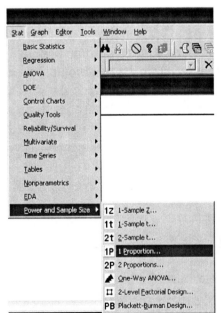

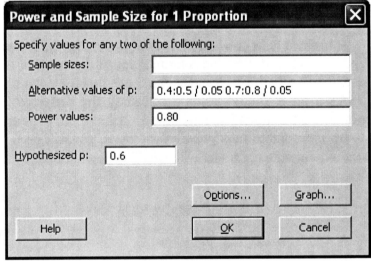

(See the third graphic on the next page.)

**Power and Sample Size for 1 Proportion - Options**

Alternative Hypothesis
- ○ Less than
- ⦿ Not equal
- ○ Greater than

Significance level: `0.05`

Store sample sizes in: `n`

Store alternatives in: `Alternative`

Store power values in: `_____`

[Select]   [Help]   [OK]   [Cancel]

The output of the *Power and Sample Size for 1 Proportion* procedure contains:

(1) The value entered for the null hypothesis $H_0$: direction of the test ( $<$, $>$ or not $=$ ),

(2) the value entered for the significance level - $\alpha$,

(3) the values entered for the alternative hypothesis $H_a$: and the power; if a list of alternatives and or powers were entered, then every combination of the values in these lists is displayed

(4) the computed value of the sample size(s) and the actual power(s) of the test; since it usually is not possible to achieve the exact power(s) entered,

(5) a graphic window of the power curve with a dot marking the entered difference, and

(6) if you selected columns to store any of: sample size, difference and/or power, these will be in the Worksheet Window.

> Example 7.20: Refer back to Example 7.16 in Section 4 of this chapter. A local electronics industry buys components and then assembles the finished product. The quality control engineer is responsible to testing the incoming shipments of components. The acceptable proportion of defective items in any one shipment is 3%. The engineer conducts the inspection by sampling components, checking each one to see if it is good or defective, and then testing the hypothesis that the proportion of defective components is greater than 0.03 using a 0.10 significance level. If the engineer believes that a shipment contains more than 3% defective items, he sends the entire shipment back to the supplier for a replacement. However this delays the assembly process and may be costly to his company, and so it is often more economical to accept shipments that contain marginally more than 3% defective components. For this reason the engineer is only really interested in returning shipments that contains at least 8% defective items. How large of a sample must be taken if the engineer needs to detect an increase to 8% detectives with the power of at least 85%.

(continued on the next page)

This hypothesis testing problem sets up as

$$H_0: p \leq 0.03$$
$$H_a: p > 0.03$$
$$\alpha = 0.10 \text{ , power} = 1 - \beta = 0.85 \text{ , } n = ?$$

and the test statistic $Z = \dfrac{\hat{p} - p_0}{\sqrt{\dfrac{p_0(1 - p_0)}{n}}}$.

The optimal sample size is computed by

Click on *Stat , Power and Sample Size, 1 Proportion...*

In the Power and Sample Size for 1 Proportion dialog box you may press the $\boxed{\textbf{F3}}$ key to clear the contents of this dialog box and reset all options. Click in the box to the right of *Alternative values of p:* and type in 0.08 - the specific value of $H_a$: . Then click in the box to the right of *Power values:* and type in 0.80 - the value of power of the test desired. Next click in the box to the right of *Hypothesized p:* type in 0.03 - the value of $p_0$ given in the null hypothesis, and then click on the $\boxed{\textbf{Options...}}$ button.

In the Power and Sample Size for 1 Proportion - Options dialog box under the *Alternative Hypothesis* heading, click on the circle to the left of *Greater than*. Erase the 0.05 in the box to the right of *Significance level:* and type in 0.10 - the correct value of $\alpha$. Then click on $\boxed{\textbf{OK}}$ .

Back in the Power and Sample Size for 1 Proportion dialog box, click on $\boxed{\textbf{OK}}$ .

The results of the sample size computation shown below will appear in the Session Window.

## Power and Sample Size

### Test for One Proportion

**Testing proportion = 0.03 (versus > 0.03)**
**Alpha = 0.1**

| Alternative Proportion | Sample Size | Target Power | Actual Power |
|---|---|---|---|
| 0.08 | 100 | 0.85 | 0.850177 |

The computed sample size of 100 is shown both in the Session Window and in a legend box to the right of the power curve in the Graphics Window on the next page. And so electronics industry's quality control engineer needs to randomly sample 100 components from the entire shipment, and then perform the hypothesis test shown at the beginning of this example.

(continued on the next page)

And the graph in the Power Curve for test for One Proportion Graphics Window is shown below, and the dot is located at desired alternative of $H_a$: $p = 0.08$ .

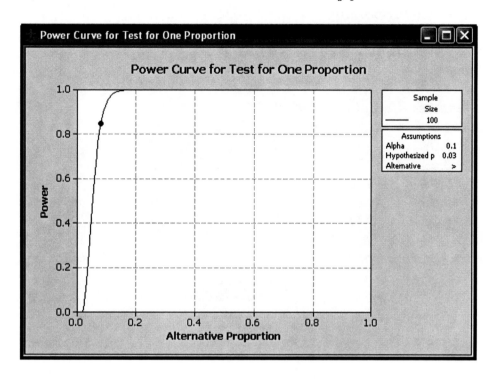

Example 7.21:   Refer back to Example 7.20, and compute the optimal sample sizes need when the power of the test is to be 0.75 , 0.80 , 0.85 , 0.90 and 0.95 .

First open a new, blank worksheet by File, New... , Minitab Worksheet and then name two unused columns (C1 and C2) as "Power" and "n".

Click on *Stat , Power and Sample Size, 1 Proportion...*

In the Power and Sample Size for 1 Proportion dialog box most of the entries will stay the same so do not press ▮ **F3** ▮ key to clear the contents.  Click in the box to the right of *Power values:*, erase the 0.80 and type in 0.75 : 0.95 / 0.05 - the values of power of the test desired.  Then click on the ▮ **Options...** ▮ button.

In the Power and Sample Size for 1 Proportion - Options dialog box click in the box to the right of *Store sample sizes in:*, highlight the n (C2) variable and click on ▮ **Select** ▮. Then click in the box to the right of *Store power values in:*, highlight the Power (C1) variable and  click on ▮ **Select** ▮.  Then click on ▮ **OK** ▮ .

Back in the Power and Sample Size for 1 Proportion dialog box, click on ▮ **OK** ▮ .

The results of the sample size computation shown will appear in the Session Window shown on the next page.

(continued on the next page)

253

## Power and Sample Size

### Test for One Proportion

*Testing proportion = 0.03 (versus > 0.03)*
*Alpha = 0.1*

| Alternative Proportion | Sample Size | Target Power | Actual Power |
|---|---|---|---|
| 0.08 | 65 | 0.75 | 0.751768 |
| 0.08 | 80 | 0.80 | 0.800280 |
| 0.08 | 100 | 0.85 | 0.850177 |
| 0.08 | 129 | 0.90 | 0.901030 |
| 0.08 | 177 | 0.95 | 0.950134 |

Also, these results appear in the new Worksheet window as shown below.

| Worksheet 2 *** | C1 | C2 |
|---|---|---|
| ↓ | Power | n |
| 1 | 65 | 0.751768 |
| 2 | 80 | 0.800280 |
| 3 | 100 | 0.850177 |
| 4 | 129 | 0.901030 |
| 5 | 177 | 0.950134 |

And so to achieve powers of the test of 0.75 , 0.80 , 0.85 , 0.90 and 0.95 ; the electronics industry's quality control engineer needs to randomly respectively ample 65, 80, 100, 129 and 177 components from the entire shipment, and then perform the hypothesis test shown at the beginning of Example 7.20 .

# Lab Assignment 7.5

**Name:**                                                            **Date:**

**Course:**                    **Section:**                    **Data CD Number:**

1.      Start a Minitab session. If you are unable to complete this lab assignment in one Minitab session, save the project as Lab 7-5 . **Never** use a period as part of the project name; since Minitab uses the period to attach the file type to the file name. Then at your next Minitab session, you may open this Lab 7-5.MPJ project and continue to work where you left off previously.

2.      The State Comptroller audits the sales tax payments by large corporations that do business in her state. For each fiscal quarter corporations submit the sales tax collected and the number of invoices from which the tax was computed. From this information, the state computes the corporation's mean sales tax per invoice for the quarter. The state's statistician take a sample of sales invoices from that same quarter and measure the amount of sales tax collected and compute the sample average. The next step is to compare this sample mean to mean reported by the corporation. If it appears that the corporation may have underpaid on the sales tax, the comptroller has to decide whether or not to perform a complete audit, which is a costly and time consuming task for both the state and the corporation. With a significance level of 0.05, the statistician uses a Z-test to see if the mean sales tax of collected for all invoices is greater than the mean submitted to the comptroller's office. If so, then a full audit is done. However because of the expense, a full audit is only cost-effective when the sample mean implies that the corporation's submitted mean was $10 too little. And so the comptroller needs to detect a difference of at least $10 per invoice, since a full audit will now be worthwhile to the state. How many invoices need to be sampled if the state wants to be 90% sure it will be able to detect the $10 difference. From a small pilot sample the statistician computed a sample standard deviation of $46.27 .

3.      For the past three years 30% of waste runoff emitted by the Glencord Iron Works has been composed of non-biodegradable material. The government will give Glencord tax incentives if it can lower this proportion by 5%. An independent consultant is used to take samples of waste runoff and perform the appropriate statistical test. Using $\alpha = 0.02$ , how large of a sample needs to be taken to detect a reduction to 25% , when the power of the test is to be 0.75 , 0.80 , 0.85 or 0.90 .

(lab assignment is continued on the second side of this page)

4.  Canton State College is planning a study to try to determine if the mean basic math skills, based on a standardized test, of its Freshman class has changed from the last known value of 65. For various political reasons, the college administration needs to be able to detect a change of 2 points in either direction. However for educational purposes the college also wants to be able to detect changes of 5 and 8 points in either direction. In any case, the administration will do a hypothesis test with the power of the test being 0.95 and will use a 0.025 significance level. The company that produces the standardized test has assured the administration that the basic math skills score are normally distributed. How large of a sample must be taken in each case? Use the Freshman scores from Trenton State University (in the Trenton.mtw worksheet that is on your data disc) as a previous similar study in order to calculate an estimate of the standard deviation of basic math skills scores at Canton State College.

5.  Print your Session Window and all Graphics Windows to the printer.

6.  Attach both your Minitab output and <u>your complete answers</u> to this sheet and submit all three to your instructor.

# CHAPTER 8:    Two Sample Hypothesis Tests

**Section 1:    Hypothesis Tests For Two Population Means Using Two _Independent_ Samples**

Testing an hypothesis about the equality or inequality of two population means is one of the most often used statistical procedures.  This chapter explains how to perform these tests, and the organization of this chapter parallels that of Chapter 6.

The "two sample" hypothesis test comparing the means of two populations may take on one of the following three forms:

(a)  $H_0$: $\mu_1 = \mu_2$        (b)  $H_0$: $\mu_1 \geq \mu_2$        (c)  $H_0$: $\mu_1 \leq \mu_2$
     $H_a$: $\mu_1 \neq \mu_2$          $H_a$: $\mu_1 < \mu_2$           $H_a$: $\mu_1 > \mu_2$

Form (a) is called a "two tail" test, form (b) is a "left tail" test, and form (c) is a "right tail" test.

When the data represent two independent samples from normally distributed populations with unknown variances, Minitab can compute a test statistic based upon the Student's t distribution. If the population variances are different (i.e., $\sigma_1^2 \neq \sigma_2^2$), the "separate variance" t test is used to compare $\mu_1$ and $\mu_2$.  The formula for the "separate variance" t test statistic is

(i)    $t = \dfrac{\bar{x}_1 - \bar{x}_2}{\sqrt{\dfrac{s_1^2}{n_1} + \dfrac{s_2^2}{n_2}}}$    ("separate variance" formula).

As described at the beginning of Chapter 6, there are two methods of entering data for two samples. The simplest and most straight forward is to enter each sample into a separate column. However, a second method is to enter all of the data into one column and to use a second column to indicate which sample, 1 or 2, each corresponding score came from.  This second method has some advantages when doing Analysis of Variance (see Chapter 9), but for all hypothesis tests in this chapter the first, simplest method will be used. The "separate variance" t hypothesis test for $\mu_1 = \mu_2$ is computed using the Minitab _2-Sample t_ procedure.  For problems with **raw data**, the procedure is the same  as used for computing two sample confidence intervals, but the dialog box is filled in somewhat differently.

Click on *Stat*, *Basic Statistics*, *2-Sample t* ...

In the 2-Sample t (Test and Confidence Interval) dialog box: click on the circle to the left of *Samples in different columns*, click in the box to the right of *First:*, click on the variable that contains the data from sample 1, and click on the   Select   button.  The cursor now will be in the box to the right of *Second:*, click on the variable that contains the data from sample 2, and click on the   Select   button.  Make sure that the *Assume equal variances* box is **not** checked; if it is checked, click on that box to un-check this option.  Then click on the   Options...   button.  Remember, do **not** press the   Enter   key after you have typed in anything, but use the mouse to move to another place in the dialog box.

In the 2-Sample t - Options dialog box: ignore the value in the *confidence level:* box and then click inside of the box to the right of *Test difference:*.  If the current value is not 0.0, delete this value and type in 0.0 .  Next make sure that the box to the right of *Alternative:* contains the correct inequality for your problem (*not equal* or *less than* or *greater than*).  If not, click on the down triangle ( ▼ ), and click on the correct choice.  Then click on   OK   .

Back in the 2-Sample t (Test and Confidence Interval) dialog box, click on   OK   .

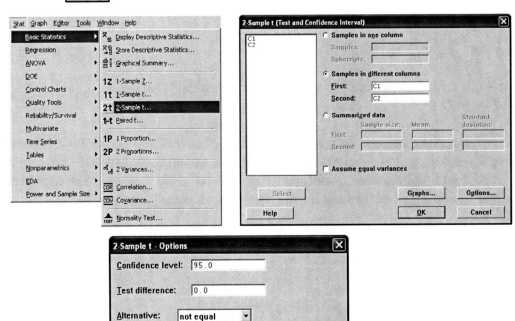

However, when the problem has **summary statistics data**, this formula

(i)   $t = \dfrac{\bar{x}_1 - \bar{x}_2}{\sqrt{\dfrac{s_1^2}{n_1} + \dfrac{s_2^2}{n_2}}}$   is computed by

Click on *Stat*, *Basic Statistics*, *2-Sample t* ...

In the 2-Sample t (Test and Confidence Interval) dialog box: you may press the [ F3 ] key to clear the contents of this dialog box and reset all options and erase any previous information. Click on the circle to the left of *Summarized data*, and then click inside of the box on the *First:* row and underneath of *Sample size:*. If a previous value is shown, erase this number and type in the value of the first sample size. Click in the next box to the right that is underneath of *Mean:* and type in the value of the first sample mean. Next click inside of the next box to the right that is underneath of *Standard deviation:* and type in the given value of the first sample standard deviation. Then repeat this on the *Second:* row for sample 2. Make sure that the *Assume equal variances* box is **not** checked, if it is checked, click on that box to un-check this option, and then click on the [ **Options...** ] button.

In the 2-Sample t - Options dialog box: ignore the value in the *confidence level:* box and then click inside of the box to the right of *Test difference:*. If the current value is not 0.0, delete this value and type in 0.0 . Next make sure that the box to the right of *Alternative:* contains the correct inequality for your problem (*not equal* or *less than* or *greater than*). If not, click on the down triangle ( ▼ ), and click on the correct choice. Then click on [ **OK** ].

Back in the 2-Sample t (Test and Confidence Interval) dialog box, click on [ **OK** ].

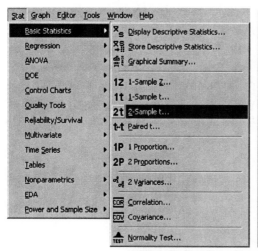

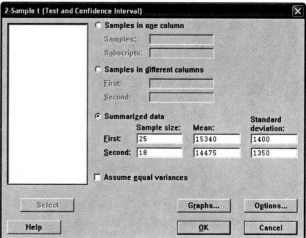

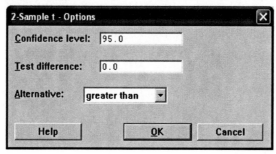

The output of this *2-Sample t* "separate variance" procedure contains:

(1) the column label or name of each variable
(2) the number of valid observations, the mean, standard deviation and standard error (which is the standard deviation divided by the square root of n) of each variable,
(3) the difference of the specific variables (columns),
(4) the point estimate for the difference $\mu_1 - \mu_2$,
(5) a confidence interval or confidence bound for $\mu_1 - \mu_2$ (explained in Chapter 6),
(4) the null hypothesis, always written as an equality,
(5) the alternative hypothesis,
(6) the value of the appropriate t test statistic,
(7) the p-value and
(8) the corresponding degrees of freedom for the t test statistic.

You should notice that even when the null hypothesis is stated as $H_0$: $\mu_1 \leq \mu_2$ , Minitab **always** displays it results in the form of **T-Test of difference = 0 (vs >)** and when $H_0$: $\mu_1 \geq \mu_2$ , as **T-Test of difference = 0 (vs <)**; that is Minitab <u>always</u> shows the null hypothesis as **=** .

Example 8.1:  Open the worksheet Callback.mtw that is on your data disc.   When the person, for whom an incoming telephone call is intended, is not available; a message is taken and the time of the call is recorded.   When this call is returned, the time is also recorded.   The difference between these two times is called the callback time.  A random sample of callback times (recorded in minutes) was taken from all Illinois sales industries, and a second independent sample was taken from all Illinois service industries. These callback times are known to be normally distributed, and the population standard deviations are known to be different.   Test the hypothesis that the mean callback time for all Illinois sales and service industries are equal.  Let $\alpha = 0.10$ .

Use the *File , Open Worksheet...* to open the Callback.mtw worksheet.

Population 1 is all Illinois sales industries, and so column C1 contains the data in the corresponding sample.

Population 2 is all Illinois service industries, and so column C2 contains the data in the corresponding sample.

This example contains raw data, hypothesis testing problem is

$H_0$: $\mu_1 = \mu_2$
$H_a$: $\mu_1 \neq \mu_2$
$\alpha = 0.10$

(continued on the next page)

and the test statistic is $t = \dfrac{\bar{x}_1 - \bar{x}_2}{\sqrt{\dfrac{s_1^2}{n_1} + \dfrac{s_2^2}{n_2}}}$ .

Click on *Stat , Basic Statistics , 2-Sample t ...*

In the 2-Sample t (Test and Confidence Interval) dialog box: click on the circle to the left of *Samples in different columns*, click in the box to the right of *First:*, click on the Sales (C1) variable that contains the data from sample 1, and click on the | Select | button. The cursor now will be in the box to the right of *Second:*, click on the Service (C2) variable that contains the data from sample 2, and click on the | Select | button. Make sure that the *Assume equal variances* box is **not** checked; if it is checked, click on that box to un-check this option. Then click on the | Options... | button.

In the 2-Sample t - Options dialog box: ignore the value in the *confidence level:* box and then click inside of the box to the right of *Test difference:*. If the current value is not 0.0, delete this value and type in 0.0 . Next make sure that the box to the right of *Alternative:* contains the correct inequality of *not equal*. If not, click on the down triangle ( |▼| ), and click on the correct choice. Then click on | OK | .

Back in the 2-Sample t (Test and Confidence Interval) dialog box, click on | OK | .

The resulting output shown below - which includes the null and alternative hypotheses, the value of the t test statistic and the p-value - will appear in the Session Window.

## Two-Sample T-Test and CI: Sales, Service

### Two-sample T for Sales vs Service

| | N | Mean | StDev | SE Mean |
|---|---|---|---|---|
| Sales | 18 | 47.8 | 24.7 | 5.8 |
| Service | 23 | 34.1 | 32.4 | 6.8 |

**Difference = mu (Sales) - mu (Service)**
**Estimate for difference: 13.7029**
**95% CI for difference: (-4.3322, 31.7380)**
**T-Test of difference = 0 (vs not =): T-Value = 1.54  P-Value = 0.132  DF = 38**

Since the p-value of 0.132 is greater than 0.10 ($\alpha$), you may not reject the null hypothesis; and therefore you may not conclude that the mean callback times are different between these two Illinois industries. Note that the value of the t test statistic, with 38 degrees of freedom, is 1.54; and this is not in the rejection region ( $t \leq -1.686$ or $t \geq 1.686$ ). Note that the correct alternative hypothesis of **not =** is listed. Also Minitab automatically produces a confidence interval, even if you do not want one.

Example 8.2:  Food-for Less supermarkets has stores in many shopping malls.  Sometimes their store is the only food store in the mall; while in other cases, they have at least one other competing supermarket in the mall.  The Fair Pricing Agency picked a set number of specific items, and then they purchased this shopping basket at randomly selected Food-for-Less supermarkets with the following results.

| Situation in Mall | Number of Stores in the Sample | Average Cost of Shopping Basket | Standard Deviation |
|---|---|---|---|
| Only Store | 23 | $ 64.57 | $ 6.15 |
| 2 or More  Stores | 18 | $ 61.73 | $ 3.65 |

The agency knows that the cost of the shopping baskets is normally distributed in both types of locations, and that the standard deviations are different in these two locations.  At the 0.05 level of significance, test to see if the average cost of the shopping basket in all Food-for-Less stores is higher when the stores have no other competing supermarket in the mall.

Population 1 is all Food-for-Less supermarkets where they are the only food store in the mall.

Population 2 is all Food-for-Less supermarkets where they have at leaset one other competing supermarket in the mall.

This example contains summary statistics, hypothesis testing problem is

$H_0$: $\mu_1 \le \mu_2$
$H_a$: $\mu_1 > \mu_2$
$\alpha = 0.05$

and the test statistic is  $t = \dfrac{\overline{x}_1 - \overline{x}_2}{\sqrt{\dfrac{s_1^2}{n_1} + \dfrac{s_2^2}{n_2}}}$ .

Click on  *Stat , Basic Statistics , 2-Sample t ...*

In the 2-Sample t (Test and Confidence Interval) dialog box:  press the $\boxed{\textbf{F3}}$ key to clear the contents of this dialog box and reset all options and erase any previous information. Click on the circle to the left of *Summarized data,* and then click inside of the box on the *First:* row and underneath of *Sample size:* and type in 23, which is the value of the first sample size.  Click in the next box to the right that is underneath of *Mean:* and type in 64.57, which  the value of the first sample mean.  Next click inside of the next box to the right that is underneath of *Standard deviation:* and type in 6.15 which is the given value of the first sample standard deviation.  Then repeat this for sample 2 by typing 18, 61.73 and 3.65 into the respective boxes on the *Second:* row.  Make sure that the *Assume equal variances* box is **not** checked, if it is checked, click on that box to un-check this option, and then click on the $\boxed{\textbf{Options...}}$ button.

(continued on the next page)

In the 2-Sample t - Options dialog box: ignore the value in the *confidence level:* box and then click inside of the box to the right of *Test difference:*. If the current value is not 0.0, delete this value and type in 0.0 . Next make sure that the box to the right of *Alternative:* contains the correct inequality of *greater than*. If not, click on the down triangle ( ▼ ), and click on the correct choice. Then click on OK .

Back in the 2-Sample t (Test and Confidence Interval) dialog box, click on OK .

The resulting output shown below - which includes the null and alternative hypotheses, the value of the t test statistic and the p-value - will appear in the Session Window.

## Two-Sample T-Test and CI

| Sample | N | Mean | StDev | SE Mean |
|--------|------|-------|-------|---------|
| 1 | 23 | 64.57 | 6.15 | 1.3 |
| 2 | 18 | 61.73 | 3.65 | 0.86 |

*Difference = mu (1) - mu (2)*
*Estimate for difference:  2.84000*
*95% lower bound for difference:  0.23291*
*T-Test of difference = 0 (vs >): T-Value = 1.84  P-Value = 0.037  DF = 36*

Since the p-value of 0.0372 is less than 0.05 ($\alpha$), you may reject the null hypothesis; and therefore you may conclude that the average cost of the shopping basket in all Food-for-Less stores where they are the only store in the mall is higher than the average cost of the shopping basket in all Food-for-Less stores where they have at least one competing store in the mall.  Note that the value of the t test statistic, with 36 degrees of freedom, is 1.84; and this is in the rejection region ( $t \geq 1.688$ ).  Also note that the correct alternative hypothesis of **>** is listed.  Minitab automatically produces a confidence lower bound, even if you do not want one.

If the two unknown population variances are equal (i.e., $\sigma_1^2 = \sigma_2^2$ ), the "pooled variance" t test is used to compare $\mu_1$ and $\mu_2$.  The formula for the "pooled variance" t test statistic is

(ii)     $t = \dfrac{\overline{x}_1 - \overline{x}_2}{\sqrt{s_p^2\left(\dfrac{1}{n_1} + \dfrac{1}{n_2}\right)}}$     ("pooled variance" formula)

$$s_p^2 = \frac{(n_1 - 1)s_1^2 + (n_2 - 1)s_2^2}{n_1 + n_2 - 2}$$

where

and is computed using the Minitab *2-Sample t* procedure again, but now you will check the box to the left of *Assume equal variances*.  If you do not know whether or not the two population standard deviations are equal, an "F test" for $\sigma_1 = \sigma_2$ is given in Section 3 of this chapter.  For problems that contain **raw data** this formula (ii) is computed by

Click on *Stat , Basic Statistics , 2-Sample t ...*

In the 2-Sample t (Test and Confidence Interval) dialog box: you may press the $\boxed{\text{F3}}$ key to clear the contents of this dialog box and reset all options and erase any previous information.  Click on the circle to the left of *Samples in different columns*, click in the box to the right of *First:*, click on the variable that contains the data from sample 1, and click on the $\boxed{\text{Select}}$ button.  The cursor now will be in the box to the right of *Second:*, click on the variable that contains the data from sample 2, and click on the $\boxed{\text{Select}}$ button.  Make sure that the *Assume equal variances* box **is** checked; if it is checked, click on that box to un-check this option.  Then click on the $\boxed{\text{Options...}}$ button.

In the 2-Sample t - Options dialog box: ignore the value in the *confidence level:* box and then click inside of the box to the right of *Test difference:*.  If the current value is not 0.0, delete this value and type in 0.0 .  Next make sure that the box to the right of *Alternative:* contains the correct inequality for your problem (*not equal* or *less than* or *greater than*).  If not, click on the down triangle ( $\boxed{\blacktriangledown}$ ), and click on the correct choice.  Then click on $\boxed{\text{OK}}$ .

Back in the 2-Sample t (Test and Confidence Interval) dialog box, click on $\boxed{\text{OK}}$ .

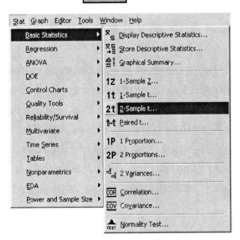

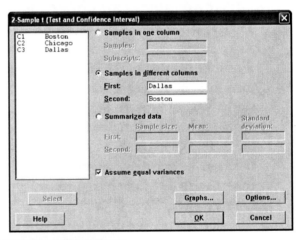

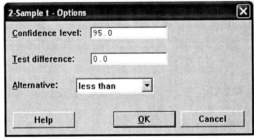

However, when the problem has **summary statistics data**, this formula

(ii)    $t = \dfrac{\overline{x}_1 - \overline{x}_2}{\sqrt{s_p^2\left(\dfrac{1}{n_1} + \dfrac{1}{n_2}\right)}}$    is computed by

264

Click on *Stat , Basic Statistics , 2-Sample t ...*

In the 2-Sample t (Test and Confidence Interval) dialog box: you may press the **F3** key to clear the contents of this dialog box and reset all options and erase any previous information. Click on the circle to the left of *Summarized data*, and then click inside of the box on the *First:* row and underneath of *Sample size:*. If a previous value is shown, erase this number and type in the value of the first sample size. Click in the next box to the right that is underneath of *Mean:* and type in the value of the first sample mean. Next click inside of the next box to the right that is underneath of *Standard deviation:* and type in the given value of the first sample standard deviation. Then repeat this on the *Second:* row for sample 2. Make sure that the *Assume equal variances* box **is** checked, if it is checked, click on that box to un-check this option, and then click on the **Options...** button.

In the 2-Sample t - Options dialog box: ignore the value in the *confidence level:* box and then click inside of the box to the right of *Test difference:*. If the current value is not 0.0, delete this value and type in 0.0 . Next make sure that the box to the right of *Alternative:* contains the correct inequality for your problem (*not equal* or *less than* or *greater than*). If not, click on the down triangle ( ▼ ), and click on the correct choice. Then click on **OK** .

Back in the 2-Sample t (Test and Confidence Interval) dialog box, click on **OK** .

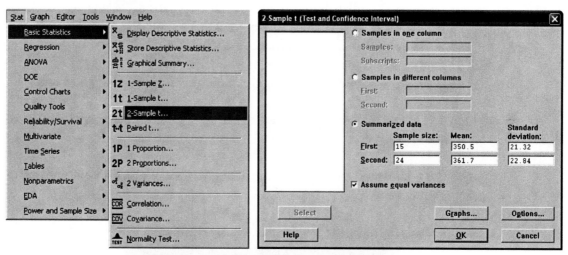

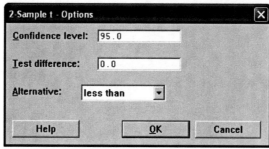

The output of this *2-Sample t* "pooled variance" procedure contains:

(1)    the column label or name of each variable

(2)    the number of valid observations, the mean, standard deviation and standard error (which is the standard deviation divided by the square root of n) of each variable,

(3)    the difference of the specific variables (columns),

(4)    the point estimate for the difference $\mu_1 - \mu_2$,

(5)    a confidence interval or confidence bound for $\mu_1 - \mu_2$ (explained in Chapter 6),

(4)    the null hypothesis, always written as an equality,

(5)    the alternative hypothesis,

(6)    the value of the appropriate t test statistic,

(7)    the p-value,

(8)    the corresponding degrees of freedom for the t test statistic. and

(9)    The value of the pooled standard deviation computed from the two samples.


Example 8.3:  Open another worksheet using Hospital.mtw from your data disc. As described in Example 6.2, these data are samples of daily room rates in hospitals in St. Louis, Richmond and Seattle. The three populations are normally distributed with equal population variances. At the 0.05 significance level, test to see if the mean room rate for all hospitals in Seattle is more than the mean room rate in St. Louis.

Use the *File , Open Worksheet...* to open Hospital.mtw in another worksheet.

Population 1 is all hospital rooms in Seattle, and so the column C3 contains the data in the corresponding sample.

Population 2 is all hospital rooms in St. Louis, and so the column C1 contains the data in the corresponding sample.

This example has raw data, the hypothesis testing problem is

$H_0$: $\mu_1 \leq \mu_2$
$H_a$: $\mu_1 > \mu_2$
$\alpha = 0.05$

and the test statistic is $\quad t = \dfrac{\overline{x}_1 - \overline{x}_2}{\sqrt{s_p^2\left(\dfrac{1}{n_1} + \dfrac{1}{n_2}\right)}} \quad$ given in formula (ii).

(continued on the next page)

Click on *Stat*, *Basic Statistics*, *2-Sample t ...*

In the 2-Sample t (Test and Confidence Interval) dialog box: press the $\boxed{\text{F3}}$ key to clear the contents of this dialog box and reset all options and erase any previous information. Click on the circle to the left of *Samples in different columns*, click in the box to the right of *First:*, click on the Seattle (C3) variable that contains the data from sample 1, and click on the $\boxed{\text{Select}}$ button. The cursor now will be in the box to the right of *Second:*, click on the St.Louis (C1) variable that contains the data from sample 2, and click on the $\boxed{\text{Select}}$ button. Make sure that the *Assume equal variances* box **is** checked; if it is checked, click on that box to un-check this option. Then click on the $\boxed{\text{Options...}}$ button.

In the 2-Sample t - Options dialog box: ignore the value in the *confidence level:* box and then click inside of the box to the right of *Test difference:*. If the current value is not 0.0, delete this value and type in 0.0 . Next make sure that the box to the right of *Alternative:* contains the correct inequality of *greater than*. If not, click on the down triangle ( $\boxed{\blacktriangledown}$ ), and click on the correct choice. Then click on $\boxed{\text{OK}}$ .

The resulting output shown below - which includes the null and alternative hypotheses, the value of the t test statistic and the p-value - will appear in the Session Window.

## Two-Sample T-Test and CI: Seattle, St.Louis

### Two sample T for Seattle vs St.Louis

|          | N  | Mean  | StDev | SE Mean |
|----------|----|-------|-------|---------|
| Seattle  | 16 | 130.0 | 21.3  | 5.3     |
| St.Louis | 15 | 117.2 | 16.6  | 4.3     |

**Difference = mu (Seattle) - mu (St.Louis)**
**Estimate for difference:  12.8000**
**95% lower bound for difference:  1.0907**
**T-Test of difference = 0 (vs >): T-Value = 1.86  P-Value = 0.037  DF = 29**
**Both use Pooled StDev = 19.1747**

Since the p-value of 0.037 is less than 0.05 ($\alpha$), you may reject the null hypothesis and conclude that the mean daily room rate of all hospitals in Seattle is more than the mean daily room rate of all hospitals in St. Louis. Note that the value of the t test statistic, with 29 degrees of freedom, is 1.86; and this is in the rejection region ( $t \geq 1.699$ ).

If the information concerning the original populations' parameters and types of distribution indicate that a test statistic based upon the Z distribution is needed, this test statistic is one of the following two formulas:

$$\text{(iii)} \qquad Z = \frac{\overline{x}_1 - \overline{x}_2}{\sqrt{\dfrac{\sigma_1^2}{n_1} + \dfrac{\sigma_2^2}{n_2}}} \qquad\qquad \text{(iv)} \qquad Z = \frac{\overline{x}_1 - \overline{x}_2}{\sqrt{\dfrac{s_1^2}{n_1} + \dfrac{s_2^2}{n_2}}}$$

If the values of $\sigma_1^2$ and $\sigma_2^2$ are known, formula (iii) is used; otherwise $s_1^2$ and $s_2^2$ must be computed and formula (iv) is used.

These two test statistics may be computed using two macros saved on your data disc. For problems that have **raw data**; the macro that computes the test statistic given in formula (iii) is **Ht-2mk.mtb** (Hypothesis test for **2 m**eans with **k**nown population variances), and the macro that computes the test statistic given in formula (iv) is called **Ht-2mun.mtb** (Hypothesis test for **2 m**eans with **un**known population variances).

A more explicit description of executing a macro is given in Chapter 5, so what is shown next is an abbreviated description.

Click on *File , Other Files , Run an Exec...*

In the Run an Exec dialog box: *Number of times to execute:* is 1 and click on the Select File button.

In the next Run an Exec dialog box: make sure the *Data Disc* is active (if not already done so), click on the specific macro, and click on the Open button.

These macros will prompt you for the specific numbers of the columns that contain the data in the two samples. You must be very careful to enter the number that represents population 1 first, and the number that represents population 2 second. These two column numbers should be separated with a comma. **Do not enter the letter C, but enter only the column numbers**. The Ht-2mk.mtb macro uses the test statistic given in formula (iii), and so the Ht-2mk.mtb macro will prompt you to enter the values of the two populations' standard deviations (i.e. $\sigma_1$ and $\sigma_2$). Even though formula (iii) uses the population variances, you must enter the values of the populations' standard deviations and **not** the variances. The Ht-2mun.mtb macro uses the test statistic given in formula (iv). This macro will compute the needed values of $s_1^2$ and $s_2^2$. Next these macros will prompt you to enter the type of test; enter 0 for a two tail test, enter -1 for a left tail test, and enter +1 for a right tail test. The potential careless mistakes when entering information into a macro and their solutions are discussed at the end of Section 2 in Chapter 5.

When applying any two-sample technique, you must clearly describe population 1 and population 2. The variable (column) numbers that correspond to the data from these samples must be carefully identified.

Example 8.4: Open another worksheet using Majorage.mtw from your data disc. This worksheet contains the ages of four independent samples of art, economics, mathematics and psychology majors at Bowling Green University. The population standard deviations of ages for all art and all economics majors are 6.5 and 3.9 respectively. At the 0.05 significance level, test the hypothesis that the mean age of all art majors is greater than the mean age of all economics majors.

Use the *File , Open Worksheet...* to open Majorage.mtw in another Worksheet Window.

(continued on the next page)

268

Population 1 is all art majors, and so column C1 contains the data in the corresponding sample.

Population 2 is all economics majors, and so column C2 contains the data in the corresponding sample.

This example has raw data and the hypothesis testing problem is

$H_0$: $\mu_1 \leq \mu_2$
$H_a$: $\mu_1 > \mu_2$
$\alpha = 0.05$

Since $\sigma_1$ and $\sigma_2$ are known, the test statistic is $Z = \dfrac{\bar{x}_1 - \bar{x}_2}{\sqrt{\dfrac{\sigma_1^2}{n_1} + \dfrac{\sigma_2^2}{n_2}}}$ given in formula (iii).

From the Reference Guide in the table with the heading **Two Sample Hypothesis Test for Two Population Means Using Two Independent Samples**, the **raw data** instructions say to execute the Ht-2mk.mtb macro.

Click on *File , Other Files , Run an Exec...*
In the Run an Exec dialog box: *Number of times to execute:* is 1 and click on the [ **Select File** ] button.
In the next Run an Exec dialog box: make sure the *Data Disc* is active (if not already done so), click on the Ht-2mk.mtb macro filename, and click on [ **Open** ] .

The steps for this macro are shown below and on the next page. The ***bold italicized*** words are displayed by Minitab in the Session Window, and the numbers you are to enter in the Session Window are shown in regular print. And then the value of the Z test statistic and the p-value for this test that will appear in the Session Window.

***After the DATA> prompt, enter the column numbers that contain the data of the first and second samples. Enter ONLY the numbers, but NOT the C's !***

***DATA>*** 1, 2 [ **Enter** ]           (since <u>C1</u> contains the sample data from population 1
                                                       and <u>C2</u> contains the sample data from population 2)

***After the DATA> prompt, enter the respective values of
the two populations' standard deviations (NOT variances).***

***DATA>*** 6.5, 3.9 [ **Enter** ]

(continued on the next page)

**After the DATA> prompt, enter the direction of the test:**
   *-1 for a left tail test*
   *0 for a two tail test*
   *+1 for a right tail test*

**DATA>** +1  | Enter |

## Data Display

**Null Hyp: Mu of C 1  =  Mu of C 2**
**Alt. Hyp: Mu of C 1  >  Mu of C 2**

| **Z test statistic** | **p-value** |
|:---:|:---:|
| **2.5918** | **0.0048** |

Since the p-value of 0.0048 is less than the value of $\alpha = 0.05$, you may reject the null hypothesis and conclude that the mean age of all art majors at Bowling Green University is greater than the mean age of all economics majors. Note that the value of the Z test statistic is 2.5918, and this is in the rejection region ( $Z \geq 1.645$ ).

Example 8.5:  Use the same Majorage.mtw worksheet data from the previous example. This worksheet contains the ages of four independent samples of art, economics, mathematics and psychology majors at Bowling Green University. At the 0.01 significance level, test the hypothesis that the mean age of all mathematics majors is less than the mean age of all psychology majors.

Population 1 is all psychology majors, and so column C4 contains the data in the corresponding sample.

Population 2 is all math majors, and so column C3 contains the data in the corresponding sample.

This example has raw data and the hypothesis testing problem is

$H_0: \mu_1 \geq \mu_2$
$H_a: \mu_1 < \mu_2$
$\alpha = 0.01$

Since $\sigma_1$ and $\sigma_2$ are unknown, the test statistic is $Z = \dfrac{\bar{x}_1 - \bar{x}_2}{\sqrt{\dfrac{s_1^2}{n_1} + \dfrac{s_2^2}{n_2}}}$ given in formula (iv).

(continued on the next page)

(continued on the next page)

(continued on the next page)

From the Reference Guide in the table with the heading **Two Sample Hypothesis Test for Two Population Means Using Two Independent Samples**, the **raw data** instructions say to execute the Ht-2mun.mtb macro.

Click on *File , Other Files , Run an Exec...*

In the Run an Exec dialog box: *Number of times to execute:* is 1 and click on the **Select File** button.

In the next Run an Exec dialog box: make sure the *Data Disc* is active (if not already done so), click on the Ht-2mun.mtb macro filename, and click on **Open** .

The steps for this macro are shown below and on the next page. The ***bold italicized*** words are displayed by Minitab in the Session Window, and the numbers you are to enter in the Session Window are shown in regular print. And then the value of the Z test statistic and the p-value for this test that will appear in the Session Window.

***After the DATA> prompt, enter the column numbers that contain the data of the first and second samples. Enter ONLY the numbers, but NOT the C's !***

***DATA>*** 3, 4 **Enter**  (since <u>C3</u> contains the sample data from population 1
and <u>C4</u> contains the sample data from population 2)

***After the DATA> prompt, enter the direction of the test:***
 ***-1  for a left tail test***
 ***0  for a two tail test***
 ***+1  for a right tail test***

***DATA>*** -1 **Enter**

## Data Display

 ***Null Hyp: Mu of C 3  =  Mu of C 4***
 ***Alt. Hyp: Mu of C 3  <  Mu of C 4***

 | ***Z test statistic*** | ***p-value*** |
 |---|---|
 | ***-1.9239*** | ***0.0272*** |

Since the p-value of 0.0272 is greater than the value of $\alpha = 0.01$, you may not reject the null hypothesis and may not conclude that the mean age of all mathematics majors at Bowling Green University is less than the mean age of all psychology majors. Note that the value of the Z test statistic is -1.9239, and this is not in the rejection region ( $Z \leq -2.326$ ).

For problems that have **summary statistic** data; the macro that computes the test statistic given in formula (iii) is **Sumht2mk.mtb**, and the macro that computes the test statistic given in formula (iv) is called **Sumht2mu.mtb**. The next example presents the data as summary statistics and uses a Summary Statistics macro stored on your data disk.

Example 8.6: In an experiment to compare a chemical fertilizer with an organic fertilizer, 35 seeds were fertilized with the chemical brand and 42 seeds from the same seed batch were treated with the organic fertilizer. After 21 days the growths of the seeds were measured on each plant. The results are given in the table on the next page.

| Fertilizer Type | Sample Size | Sample Mean | Sample Standard Deviation |
|---|---|---|---|
| Chemical | 35 | 27.3 cm | 3.2 cm |
| Organic | 42 | 25.8 cm | 2.6 cm |

Let $\alpha = 0.01$ , and test to see if there is a significant difference between the mean growth of all plants treated with the two different types of fertilizer.

Population 1 is all seeds treated with the chemical fertilizer.

Population 2 is all seeds treated with the organic fertilizer.

The hypothesis testing problem is

$H_0: \mu_1 = \mu_2$
$H_a: \mu_1 \neq \mu_2$
$\alpha = 0.01$

and the test statistic is $Z = \dfrac{\bar{x}_1 - \bar{x}_2}{\sqrt{\dfrac{s_1^2}{n_1} + \dfrac{s_2^2}{n_2}}}$ given in formula (iv).

From the Reference Guide in the table with the heading **Two Sample Hypothesis Test for Two Population Means Using Two Independent Samples**, and in the Summary Statistics Technique column; the macro to be executed is Sumht2mu.mtb .

Click on *File , Other Files , Run an Exec...*

In the Run an Exec dialog box: *Number of times to execute:* is 1 and click on the ⬛ **Select File** button.

In the next Run an Exec dialog box: make sure the *Data Disc* is active (if not already done so), click on the Sumht2mu.mtb macro filename (you may need to scroll through the box), and click on the ⬛ **Open** button.

(continued on the next page

272

The macro begins by prompting you for type of test, and you will enter 0 for the "two tail" in this example. Next the macro prompts for the two samples' means, and then for the two samples' standard deviations. Then the macro prompts you to enter the sample sizes for the two samples. The steps for this macro and resulting hypothesis test results shown on the next page will appear in the Session Window.

**After the DATA> prompt, enter the direction of the test:**
- **-1 for a left tail test**
- **0 for a two tail test**
- **+1 for a right tail test**

**DATA>** 0  `Enter`

**After the DATA> prompt, enter the mean of Sample 1, a comma, and then the mean of Sample 2.**

**DATA>** 27.3 , 25.8  `Enter`

**After the DATA> prompt, enter the respective values of the two Samples' standard deviations (NOT variances).**

**DATA>** 3.2 , 2.6  `Enter`

**After the DATA> prompt, enter the respective sizes of the two Samples.**

**DATA>** 35 , 42  `Enter`

## Data Display

**Null Hyp: Mu of Pop. 1   =   Mu of Pop. 2**
**Alt. Hyp: Mu of Pop. 1 not = Mu of Pop. 2**

| Z test statistic | p-value |
|:---:|:---:|
| 2.2274 | 0.0259 |

Since the p-value of 0.0259 is greater than the value of $\alpha = 0.01$, you may not reject the null hypothesis. So do not conclude that the mean growth of all seeds treated with the chemical fertilizer is different than the mean growth of all seeds treated with the organic fertilizer. Note that the value of the Z test statistic is 2.2274, and this is not in the rejection region ( $Z \leq -2.576$ or $Z \geq 2.576$ ).

# Lab Assignment 8.1.1

**Name:**                                                                    **Date:**

**Course:**                      **Section:**                      **Data CD Number:**

1.    Start a Minitab session. If you are unable to complete this lab assignment in one Minitab session, save the project as Lab 8-1-1 . **Never** use a period as part of the project name; since Minitab uses the period to attach the file type to the file name. Then at your next Minitab session, you may open this Lab 8-1-1.MPJ project and continue to work where you left off previously.

2.    Stress and level of exercise are well known factors that affect a person's lifespan. In an interesting longitudinal experiment, a team of doctors took a random sample from a population of people with low stress and low exercise level jobs and a second independent random sample from a population of people with high stress and high exercise level jobs. The lifespans were measured as age (in years) at death. The standard deviation of lifespan in the "low level" population was known to be 10 years, and the standard deviation of lifespan in the "high level" population was known to be 9 years. The following are the lifespans of the two samples:

"low level"     67.2 , 70.3 , 66.7 , 59.2 , 55.7 , 80.8 , 74.0 , 63.6 , 67.4 , 61.6 , 74.5 , 81.3
                83.7 , 67.3 , 58.6 , 64.9 , 42.5 , 61.4 , 74.6 , 83.6 , 62.5 , 76.3 , 69.2 , 62.6
                74.2 , 78.5 , 84.6 , 58.9 , 72.1 , 85.2 , 71.7 , 93.5 , 72.5 , 68.3 , 55.7 , 68.1
                77.0 . 72.9 , 65.7  and  70.3

"high level"    73.2 , 57.2 , 59.6 , 82.3 , 66.0 , 59.6 , 76.2 , 71.3 , 69.7 , 70.2 , 82.4 , 61.4
                62.7 , 52.9 , 72.7 , 63.9 , 64.0 , 70.2 , 58.2 , 67.1 , 64.0 , 71.3 , 62.8 , 51.7
                39.4 , 60.7 , 58.3 , 77.8 , 63.8 , 69.3 , 75.3 , 78.9 , 73.1 , 60.2  and  65.0

At the 0.05 level of significance, was the team of doctors able to conclude that there is any difference in mean lifespan of people between the two populations of job categories?

3.    Open the worksheet Run400.mtw that is on your data disc. As described in Lab Assignment 6.1.1; the track officials sampled boys and girls in both the eight and twelve year old age groups and measured their times (in seconds) in a 400 meter race. These times are normally distributed for all four populations. It is known that the population standard deviation of 400 meter race times are different for eight year old boys and girls, but that the standard deviations of the 400 meter race times are the same for the twelve year old boys and girls.

a.    Test the hypothesis that the mean 400 meter race times of the populations of all twelve year old boys and of all twelve year old girls are the same. Use a 0.05 level of significance.

(lab assignment is continued on the second side of this page)

275

b. At the 0.10 level of significance, test to see if eight year old boys are faster than eight year old girls in the 400 meter race.

When discussing eight year old boys as a group, the group is treated as if it were represented by **one** "typical" boy. And so any statements made about the speed of this group are done using the value attached to the "typical" eight year old boy, and this value is the average (mean) 400 meter race time of the population of all eight year old boys. Therefore the question if eight year old boys are faster than eight year old girls in the 400 meter race is equivalent to asking if the "typical" eight year old boy is faster than the "typical" eight year old girl. Since <u>faster</u> means less time to run the race, this question becomes is the mean of the population of all eight year old boys less than the mean of the population of all eight year old girls.

4. Open another worksheet using Econ2.mtw from your data disc. This worksheet contains three independent samples of hourly wages (in dollars) from the populations of all Private Sector, all Non-Profit Sector and all Public Sector employees. The population distributions are unknown. This worksheet also contains a sample of price and demand data.

Test the hypothesis that the mean hourly wage of all Private Sector Employees is greater than the mean hourly wage of all Non-Profit Sector employees. Use a 0.05 significance level.

5. A random sample of 50 union workers in the retail sales field was taken and their hourly wages was measured. An independent sample of 40 non union workers was taken and their hourly wages were measured. In both cases the wages did not include any benefits. The population standard deviations of hourly wages of the two groups are known to be $3.40 and $3.85 respectively. The sample results are means of $14.75 and $16.30 respectively. At the 0.10 level of significance, do these data indicate that the mean hourly wages, not including benefits, of non union workers is higher than the union workers.

6. The local police claim that the average speed **above** the legal speed limit is greater on highways with a 65 mph limit than on those highways with a 55 mph limit. Previous studies have verified that the excess speed is normally distributed with equal variances on all highways of the two speed limits. Random samples of 14 and 17 were taken from all cars traveling on highways with speed limits of 65 mph and 55 mph respectively, and the results are mean excess speeds of 9.12 mph and 7.83 mph. The samples' standard deviations are 2.63 mph and 2.44 mph. Do these data support the local police claim, use $\alpha = 0.05$ .

7. Print your Session Window to the printer.

8. Attach both your Minitab output and <u>your complete answers</u> to this paper and submit all three to your instructor.

# Lab Assignment 8.1.2

**Name:**                                                    **Date:**

**Course:**                    **Section:**                    **Data CD Number:**

1.  Start a Minitab session. If you are unable to complete this lab assignment in one Minitab session, save the project as Lab 8-1-2 . **Never** use a period as part of the project name; since Minitab uses the period to attach the file type to the file name. Then at your next Minitab session, you may open this Lab 8-1-2.MPJ project and continue to work where you left off previously.

2.  Public utility stocks have always been popular among certain investors. A stock broker was interested in knowing if the average earnings per dollar invested is higher for electric only utilities than for gas only utilities. These earnings are known to be normally distributed; and since these are regulated companies, the standard deviation of each population is known. For all electric only utilities, $\sigma = 0.10$ , and for all gas only utilities, $\sigma = 0.05$ . Independent random samples were taken from each population with the following results:

    Electric only:   0.12 , 0.05 , -0.04 , 0.11 , 0.15 , 0.21 , 0.07 , 0.31 , 0.03 , 0.13 , 0.04 , 0.09
                     0.31 , 0.04 , 0.05 , 0.11 , 0.24 and 0.08 .

    Gas only:        0.04 , 0.06 , 0.13 , 0.07 , 0.11 , 0.01 , 0.04 , 0.09 , 0.15 , 0.12 , 0.06 , 0.12
                     0.01 , 0.04 , 0.02 , 0.16 , 0.06 , 0.03 , 0.08 , 0.06 , 0.00 , 0.14 , 0.03 , 0.07
                     0.10 and 0.09 .

    Use a 0.05 level of significance, and test to see if the average earnings per dollar invested is higher for all electric only utilities than for all gas only utilities.

3.  Trenton State University took independent random samples of 40 students from each of its Freshmen, Sophomore, Junior and Senior classes. Each student was given a basic math skills test. The distribution of these test scores in unknown. This data is saved in the Trenton.mtw worksheet on your data disk.

    a.  Open the worksheet Trenton.mtw that is on your data disc. Test the hypothesis that the mean basic math skills test scores of all Trenton Seniors is higher than the mean basic math skills test scores of all Trenton Freshmen. Use a 0.01 level of significance.

    b.  At the 0.05 level of significance, test to determine if there is any difference between the mean basic math skills test scores of all Trenton Freshmen and all Trenton Sophomores.

(lab assignment is continued on the second side of this page)

4. Open another worksheet using Cityidx.mtw from your data disc. As described in Lab Assignment 6.1.2; this worksheet contains data about five variables where each was measured on cities in three different geographical regions: C1 - C5 in the East, C6 - C10 in the Central, and C11 - C15 in the West. The municipal bond measurement is a Bernoulli variable where 1 = A or better rating and 0 = below an A rating. The other four are indices and are known to be normally distributed in each of the three regions. At the 0.05 level of significance, test to see if the mean urban unemployment index (U-Unpl) is the same for all cities in the East as for all cities in the West. It is known that the standard deviation of the urban unemployment index is the same in both of these regions.

5. A random sample of 37 women who exercised exactly twice a week was taken. Their resting heart rates were measured and yielded a mean of 66.4 bpm (beats per minute) and a standard deviation of 3.8 bpm. An independent sample of 34 women who exercised more than twice a week was taken, and the mean and standard deviation of their heart rates were 64.1 and 7.2 bpm. Previous research has shown that the two corresponding populations have standard deviations of 3.4 bpm and 7.2 bpm respectively. With $\alpha = 0.01$, test the hypothesis that the heart rate of all women who exercise twice per week is higher than the mean heart rate all of those women who exercise more than twice a week.

6. While the Thanksgiving weekend is the busiest travel time of the year, an airline wanted to know if people traveled shorter distances than during the New Year's holiday. The flight distances of travelers during these two time periods are normally distributed, but the population standard deviations are known to be different. A random sample of 24 airline travelers was taken during the Thanksgiving weekend, and their mean and standard deviation of the flight distances were 448.5 and 66.3 miles. Another random sample of 17 travelers was taken during the New Year's holiday, and the results were 507.6 and 98.7 miles for the mean and standard deviation of their flight distances. At the 0.05 level of significance, test to see if the mean flight distance for all Thanksgiving weekend travelers is less than that of all New Year's holiday travelers.

7. Print your Session Window to the printer.

8. Attach both your Minitab output and your complete answers to this paper and submit all three to your instructor.

## Section 2:    Hypothesis Tests For Two Population Means Using Two Paired Samples

When paired samples are taken from the two populations, hypothesis tests comparing two populations' means $\mu_1$ to $\mu_2$ are easily done.

Depending upon whether the test procedure is (a) "two tailed", (b) "left tailed" or (c) "right tailed" the hypotheses may be written as:

(a)  $H_0: \mu_1 = \mu_2$            (b)  $H_0: \mu_1 \geq \mu_2$            (c)  $H_0: \mu_1 \leq \mu_2$
     $H_a: \mu_1 \neq \mu_2$                  $H_a: \mu_1 < \mu_2$                  $H_a: \mu_1 > \mu_2$

If $\mu_2$ is subtracted from both sides of each hypothesis above, the test procedure may be written as:

(a)  $H_0: \mu_1 - \mu_2 = 0$       (b)  $H_0: \mu_1 - \mu_2 \geq 0$       (c)  $H_0: \mu_1 - \mu_2 \leq 0$
     $H_a: \mu_1 - \mu_2 \neq 0$           $H_a: \mu_1 - \mu_2 < 0$           $H_a: \mu_1 - \mu_2 > 0$

And since the computations are done using the "difference" variable ($d = x_1 - x_2$), these three forms of the hypotheses may written as the following equivalent forms:

(a)  $H_0: \mu_d = 0$               (b)  $H_0: \mu_d \geq 0$               (c)  $H_0: \mu_d \leq 0$
     $H_a: \mu_d \neq 0$                  $H_a: \mu_d < 0$                  $H_a: \mu_d > 0$

The correct test statistic depends upon what you know about the populations' parameters, the distribution types and the sample sizes; and may be based upon either the Z or Student's t distribution.  The test statistic is one of the following two formulas:

$$(v) \qquad t = \frac{\overline{d}}{\left[\dfrac{s_d}{\sqrt{n}}\right]} \qquad\qquad (vi) \qquad Z = \frac{\overline{d}}{\left[\dfrac{s_d}{\sqrt{n}}\right]}$$

In both of these formulas, d  represents the "difference" variable between each pair of scores in the two samples; that is, $d = x_1 - x_2$.  To compute the test statistic given in formula (v) and p-value, the *Paired t* procedure is used.  When the problems have **raw data**, it is very important to correctly identify which variable contains the data from sample **one** and which variable contains the data from sample **two**. These variables often are **not in columns C1 and C2** respectively.  For problems with **raw data** this test statistic  $t = \dfrac{\overline{d}}{\left[\dfrac{s_d}{\sqrt{n}}\right]}$  given in formula (v) is computed by

Click on *Stat , Basic Statistics , Paired t ...*

In the Paired t (Test and Confidence Intervals): click on the circle to the left of *Samples in columns*, click in the box to the right of *First sample:*, click on the variable that contains the data from sample 1, and click on the | Select | button. The cursor now will be in the box to the right of *Second:*, click on the variable that contains the data from sample 2, and click on the | Select | button. Then click on the | Options... | button.

In the Paired t - Options dialog box: ignore the value in the *confidence level:* box and then click inside of the box to the right of *Test difference:*. If the current value is not 0.0, delete this value and type in 0.0 . Next make sure that the box to the right of *Alternative:* contains the correct inequality for your problem (*not equal* or *less than* or *greater than*). If not, click on the down triangle ( ▼ ), and click on the correct choice. Then click on | OK | .

Back in the Paired t (Test and Confidence Interval) dialog box, click on | OK | .

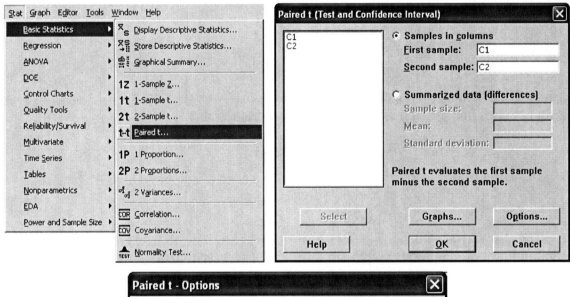

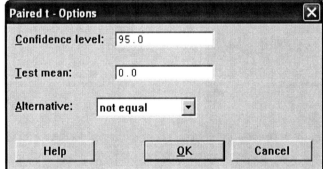

However, when the problem has **summary statistics data**, the difference (d) scores of the two samples have been computed and only the sample mean and standard deviation of these difference (d) scores are presented in the problem. Then this formula (v) is computed by

Click on *Stat , Basic Statistics , Paired t ...*

In the Paired t (Test and Confidence Intervals): you may press the [ F3 ] key to clear the contents of this dialog box and reset all options and erase any previous variables. Make sure the button to the left of *Summarized data (differences)* is selected, and then click inside of the box to the right of *Sample size:*. Now type in the value of the common sample size. Next click in the next box down that is to the right of *Mean:*, erase any current incorrect value, and type in the value of the difference sample mean. Next click inside of the box to the right of *Standard deviation:*, erase any current incorrect value, and type in the value of the difference sample standard deviation ($s_d$). Then click on the [ **Options...** ] button.

In the Paired t - Options dialog box: ignore the value in the *confidence level:* box and then click inside of the box to the right of *Test difference:*. If the current value is not 0.0, delete this value and type in 0.0 . Next make sure that the box to the right of *Alternative:* contains the correct inequality for your problem (*not equal* or *less than* or *greater than*). If not, click on the down triangle ( [▼] ), and click on the correct choice. Then click on [ **OK** ] .

Back in the Paired t (Test and Confidence Interval) dialog box, click on [ **OK** ] .

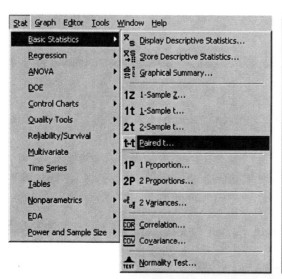

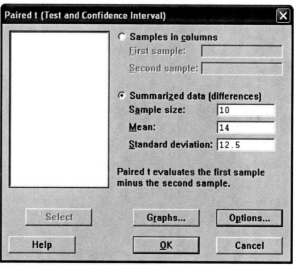

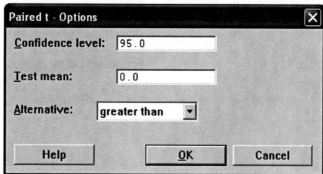

The output of the *Paired t* procedure contains:

(1) the sample size, mean, standard deviation, and standard error of the mean for each sample (for raw data only),

(2) the sample size, mean, standard deviation, and standard error of the mean for the sample of "difference" scores,

(3) the confidence interval or confidence lower/upper bound (for greater than / less than alternatives) for the population mean of the "difference" scores (which is explained in Chapter 6),

(4) the null hypothesis, always written as an equality and the alternative hypothesis,

(5) the value of the paired t test statistic and

(6) the p-value.

Example 8.7:  Open the worksheet Exam.mtw that is on your data disk.  This contains the results of exam 1 and exam 2 for ten students taken randomly from a large statistics class.  Since the same students took each exam, these two samples are paired.  Use a 0.10 significance level, and test the hypothesis that the mean of exam 1 is equal to the mean of exam 2 for all students in the statistics class.  The difference scores in these populations are known to be normally distributed, but nothing is known about the population standard deviation.

Use the *File , Open Worksheet...* to open the worksheet Exam.mtw that is saved on your data disk.

Population 1 is all students in the class who took **exam 1**, and so EXAM 1 (C1) contains the data in the corresponding sample.

Population 2 is all students in the class who took **exam 2**, and so EXAM 2 (C2) contains the data in the corresponding sample.

This problem contains raw data and the hypothesis testing problem is:

$H_0: \mu_1 = \mu_2$      or      $H_0: \mu_d = 0$
$H_a: \mu_1 \neq \mu_2$      equivalently      $H_a: \mu_d \neq 0$
$\alpha = 0.10$                         $\alpha = 0.10$

Since the difference scores are normally distributed, but the population standard deviation is unknown; the test statistic is $t = \dfrac{\bar{d}}{\left[\dfrac{s_d}{\sqrt{n}}\right]}$ given in formula (v).

(continued on the next page)

282

Click on *Stat , Basic Statistics , Paired t ...*

In the Paired t (Test and Confidence Intervals): click on the circle to the left of *Samples in columns*, click in the box to the right of *First sample:*, click on the EXAM 1 (C1) variable that contains the data from the **first** sample, and click on the | **Select** | button. The cursor now will be in the box to the right of *Second:*, click on the EXAM 2 (C2) variable that contains the data from **second** sample, and click on the | **Select** | button. Then click on the | **Options...** | button.

In the Paired t - Options dialog box: ignore the value in the *confidence level:* box and then click inside of the box to the right of *Test difference:*. If the current value is not 0.0, delete this value and type in 0.0 . Next make sure that the box to the right of *Alternative:* contains the correct inequality of *not equal*. If not, click on the down triangle ( ▾ ), and click on the correct choice. Then click on | **OK** | .

Back in the Paired t (Test and Confidence Interval) dialog box, click on | **OK** | .

The results shown on the next page will appear in the Session Window.

## Paired T-Test and CI: EXAM 1, EXAM 2

### Paired T for EXAM 1 - EXAM 2

|  | N | Mean | StDev | SE Mean |
|---|---|---|---|---|
| EXAM 1 | 8 | 82.5000 | 13.3095 | 4.7056 |
| EXAM 2 | 8 | 84.6250 | 7.8182 | 2.7642 |
| Difference | 8 | -2.12500 | 10.78938 | 3.81462 |

**95% CI for mean difference: (-11.14515, 6.89515)**
**T-Test of mean difference= 0 (vs not = 0): T-Value = -0.56  P-Value = 0.595**

Since the p-value of 0.595 is greater than 0.10 ($\alpha$), you may not reject the null hypothesis, and so you may **not conclude** that the mean of exam 1 is different than the mean of exam 2 for all students in the statistics class.  Note that the value of the t test statistic is 0.56; and this is **not** in the rejection region ( $t \leq -1.895$ or $t \geq 1.895$ ).

Example 8.8:   While most researchers agree that consumption of alcohol slows a person's reaction time, this slowing is usually attributed to the reduced mental ability to process information.  A recent study was conducted to determine if alcohol slows a person's pure physical reflex time.  A random sample of 20 sober men were tested for knee reflex times.  Then each man consumed alcohol until his blood level reached 0.08, his knee reflex time was measured again, and the difference in times was computed.  The sample results of these differences were a mean of -31 milliseconds and a standard deviation of 67 milliseconds.  These differences of times are known to be normally distributed.  At the 0.05 significance level, do these results indicate that the mean knee reflex times of all sober men is less than that of all men who are legally drunk?

(continued on the next page)

Population 1 is all sober men.

Population 2 is all men with a blood alcohol level of 0.10 (legally drunk).

This example uses summary statistics, the hypothesis testing problem is

$H_0: \mu_1 \geq \mu_2$      or      $H_0: \mu_d \geq 0$
$H_a: \mu_1 < \mu_2$    equivalently    $H_a: \mu_d < 0$
$\alpha = 0.05$                               $\alpha = 0.05$

and the test statistic is $t = \dfrac{\overline{d}}{\left[\dfrac{s_d}{\sqrt{n}}\right]}$ given in formula (v).

Click on *Stat , Basic Statistics , Paired t ...*

In the Paired t (Test and Confidence Intervals): press the $\boxed{\textbf{F3}}$ key to clear the contents of this dialog box and reset all options and erase any previous variables. Make sure the button to the left of *Summarized data (differences)* is selected, and then click inside of the box to the right of *Sample size:*. Now type in 20, the value of the sample size. Next click in the next box down that is to the right of *Mean:* and type in -31, the value of the sample difference mean. Next click inside of the box to the right of *Standard deviation:* and type in 67, the value of the sample difference standard deviation. Then click on the $\boxed{\textbf{Options...}}$ button.

In the Paired t - Options dialog box: ignore the value in the *confidence level:* box and then click inside of the box to the right of *Test difference:*. If the current value is not 0.0, delete this value and type in 0.0 . Next make sure that the box to the right of *Alternative:* contains the correct inequality of *less than*. If not, click on the down triangle ( $\boxed{\blacktriangledown}$ ), and click on the correct choice. Then click on $\boxed{\textbf{OK}}$ .

Back in the Paired t (Test and Confidence Interval) dialog box, click on $\boxed{\textbf{OK}}$ .

The results shown on the next page will appear in the Session Window.

## *Paired T-Test and CI*

|  | N | Mean | StDev | SE Mean |
|---|---|---|---|---|
| Difference | 20 | -31.0000 | 67.0000 | 14.9817 |

*95% upper bound for mean difference: -5.0947*
*T-Test of mean difference = 0 (vs < 0): T-Value = -2.07  P-Value = 0.026*

Since the p-value of 0.026 is less than 0.05 ($\alpha$), you may reject the null hypothesis and conclude that the mean knee reflex time for all sober men is less than the mean knee reflex time for all legally "drunk" men. Note that the value of the t test statistic is -2.07; and this is in the rejection region ( $t \leq -1.729$ ).

When the problem has **raw data**, and the test statistic given in formula (vi) is used; the computation of the test statistic and p-value is more involved. Minitab does not have a Paired Z procedure, and so you must compute the "difference" scores first and then use the equivalent *1-Sample Z* procedure. To create this new "difference" variable, choose a column number that is different than any of the existing column numbers in the current worksheet, click in the name box for this column and type in the letter d for the name of this column. The values for this d variable are calculated and stored in this new d variable by

Click on *Calc , Calculator...*

In the Calculator dialog box the cursor will be inside the box to the right of *Store result in variable:*. Highlight the new d variable and click on the  Select  button. Next click inside of the box under *Expression:*, click on the variable containing the **first** sample's data, click on the  Select  button, click on the button with the minus sign (-) on it, click on the variable containing the **second** sample's data, and click on the  Select  button. (Optionally you may just type in the first sample's column number, followed by a minus sign, and then the second sample's column number.) Then click on  OK  .

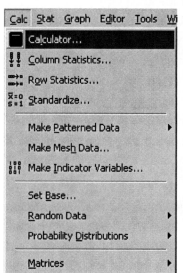
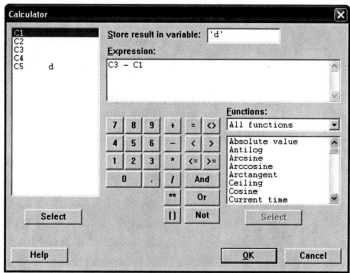

This performs the calculation in the *Expression:* box for every row with a valid pair of scores and stores the results into the corresponding rows in the new variable. If either of the variables in the *Expression:* box contains a missing value in a particular row, that row in the new variable will also contain a missing value. These missing values are displayed as an asterisk (*). The dialog box above illustrates the case when there are four variables, C1, C2, C3 and C4, and you want to calculate the difference between the third and first variable.

Once this "difference" variable has been computed, the test statistic $Z = \dfrac{\overline{d}}{\left[\dfrac{s_d}{\sqrt{n}}\right]}$ given in

formula (vi) is computed using the *1-Sample Z* procedure as described in Chapter 7, Section 1.

Since the test statistic in formula (vi) is based upon the Z distribution and uses the <u>sample</u> standard deviation ($s_d$) of the "difference" variable, the value of $s_d$ first must be computed and stored into the k1 constant using *Calc, Column Statistics* from the Minitab menu.

Click on *Calc, Column Statistics...*

In the Column Statistics dialog box: click on the circle to the left of *Standard deviation*, click inside of the *Input variable:* box, click on the new difference variable d, and click on the ⬚ **Select** ⬚ button. Next click in the box to the right of *Store results in:*, and type in k1 as the constant name. Then click on the ⬚ **OK** ⬚ button.

Then the Z test statistic and p-value are computed using *Stat, Basic Statistics, 1-Sample Z*.

Click on *Stat, Basic Statistics, 1-Sample Z...*

In the 1-Sample Z (Test and Confidence Interval) dialog box: you may press the ⬚ **F3** ⬚ key to clear the contents of this dialog box and reset all options and erase any previous variables. Make sure the button to the left of *Samples in columns* is selected, and then click inside of the box below. Now the variables (columns) will appear in the large box on the left side of this dialog box. If a previous variable is shown, erase the variable, click on the new difference variable d, and click on the ⬚ **Select** ⬚ button. Next click inside of the box to the right of *Standard deviation:*, erase any current incorrect value, highlight the K1 constant and click on the ⬚ **Select** ⬚ button (or just type in k1). Check the box to the left of *Perform hypothesis test*, click inside of the box to the right of *Hypothesized mean:*, delete any current value, and type in 0 (zero) as specified in the null hypothesis ($H_0$:), and then click on the ⬚ **Options...** ⬚ button.

In the 1-Sample Z - Options dialog box: ignore the value in the *Confidence level:* box, and then make sure that the box to the right of *Alternative:* contains the correct inequality for your problem (*not equal* or *less than* or *greater than*. If not, click on the down triangle ( ⬚▾⬚ ), and click on the correct choice. Then click on ⬚ **OK** ⬚ .

Back in the 1-Sample Z (Test and Confidence Interval) dialog box, click on ⬚ **OK** ⬚ .

Example 8.9: Open a second worksheet using Ispaint.mtw that is on your data disk. This worksheet contains data for different brands of highway paint. In particular, parallel (paired) strips of the BriLite and DayGlo brands were painted on the highway at various test locations. By using parallel lines; different weather, road and traffic conditions are equalized. The time at which each paint strip was no longer viable was measured, and this score is called the wear time. At the 0.025 significance level, test the hypothesis that the mean wear time of all DayGlo painted lines is greater than the mean wear time of all BriLite painted lines.

(continued on the next page)

Use the *File , Open Worksheet...* to open a second worksheet Ispaint.mtw from your data disk.

Population 1 is all highway lines painted with DayGlo, and so column C3 contains the data in the corresponding sample.

Population 2 is all highway lines painted with BriLite, and so column C2 contains the data in the corresponding sample.

Since this problem uses raw data, first compute the new "difference" variable $d = x_1 - x_2$. Here $x_1$ represents the DayGlo data in column 3 and $x_2$ represents the BriLite data in column 2.

Click in the name block of column C5 and type in **d** and press the | **Enter** | key to name this column.

Click on *Calc , Calculator...*

In the Calculator dialog box the cursor will be inside the box to the right of *Store result in variable:*. Highlight the new d variable and click on the | **Select** | button. Next click inside of the box under *Expression:*, click on the DayGlo (C3) variable containing the **first** sample's data, click on the | **Select** | button, click on the button with the minus sign (-) on it, click on the BriLite (C2) variable containing the **second** sample's data, and click on the | **Select** | button. (Optionally you may just type in the expression **C3 - C2**.) Then click on | **OK** | . Now the **d** variable has been calculated in the Worksheet Window.

The hypothesis testing problem is:

| | | |
|---|---|---|
| $H_0: \mu_1 \leq \mu_2$ | or | $H_0: \mu_d \leq 0$ |
| $H_a: \mu_1 > \mu_2$ | equivalently | $H_a: \mu_d > 0$ |
| $\alpha = 0.025$ | | $\alpha = 0.025$ |

Since the distribution of the difference scores is unknown, but the common sample size (n = 38) is greater than 30, and the test statistic $Z = \dfrac{\overline{d}}{\left[\dfrac{s_d}{\sqrt{n}}\right]}$ given in formula (vi).

Next the <u>sample</u> standard deviation ($s_d$) of the "difference" variable must be computed and stored into the k1.

Click on *Calc , Column Statistics...*

In the Column Statistics dialog box: click on the circle to the left of *Standard deviation*, click inside of the *Input variable:* box, click on the new difference variable **d**, and click on the | **Select** | button. Next click in the box to the right of *Store results in:*, and type in k1 as the constant name. Then click on the | **OK** | button.

(continued on the next page)

And **Standard deviation of d = 2.00553** will appear in the Session Window.

Then compute the value of the Z test statistic and the p-value.

Click on *Stat* , *Basic Statistics* , *1-Sample Z...*

In the 1-Sample Z (Test and Confidence Interval) dialog box: press the | **F3** | key to clear the contents of this dialog box and reset all options and erase any previous variables. Make sure the button to the left of *Samples in columns* is selected, and then click inside of the box below. Now the variables (columns) will appear in the large box on the left side of this dialog box. Click on the new difference variable **d**, and click on the | **Select** | button. Next click inside of the box to the right of *Standard deviation:*, highlight the K1 constant and click on the | **Select** | button (or just type in k1). Check the box to the left of *Perform hypothesis test*, click inside of the box to the right of *Hypothesized mean:*, delete any current value, and type in 0 (zero) as specified in the null hypothesis ($H_0$:), and then click on the | **Options...** | button.

In the 1-Sample Z - Options dialog box: ignore the value in the *Confidence level:* box, and then make sure that the box to the right of *Alternative:* contains the correct inequality of *greater than*. If not, click on the down triangle ( | ▼ | ), and click on the correct choice. Then click on | **OK** | .

Back in the 1-Sample Z (Test and Confidence Interval) dialog box, click on | **OK** | .

The resulting output below which includes the null and alternative hypotheses, the value of the Z test statistic and the p-value will appear in the Session Window.

## One-Sample Z: d

**Test of mu = 0 vs > 0**
**The assumed standard deviation = 2.00553**

| Variable | N | Mean | StDev | SE Mean | 95%<br>Lower<br>Bound | Z | P |
|---|---|---|---|---|---|---|---|
| d | 38 | 0.800000 | 2.005533 | 0.325340 | 0.264863 | 2.46 | 0.007 |

Since the p-value of 0.007 is less than 0.025 ($\alpha$), you may reject the null hypothesis and conclude that the mean wear time for all highway lines painted with DayGlo paint is greater than the mean wear time for all highway lines painted with BriLite paint. Note that the value of the Z test statistic is 2.46; and this is in the rejection region ( $Z \geq 1.96$ ).

However, when the problem has **summary statistics data**, the difference (d) scores of the two samples have been computed and only the sample mean and standard deviation of these difference (d) scores are presented in the problem. Then this formula (vi) $Z = \dfrac{\overline{d}}{\left[\dfrac{s_d}{\sqrt{n}}\right]}$ is computed by using the *1-Sample Z* procedure as described in Chapter 7, Section 1.

Click on *Stat , Basic Statistics , 1-Sample Z...*

In the 1-Sample Z (Test and Confidence Interval) dialog box: you may press the F3 key to clear the contents of this dialog box and reset all options and erase any previous variables. Make sure the button to the left of *Summarized data* is selected, and then click inside of the box to the right of *Sample size:*. Now type in the value of the common sample size. Next click in the next box down that is to the right of *Mean:* and type in the value of the difference sample mean. Next click inside of the box to the right of *Standard deviation:*, erase any current incorrect value, and type in the value of the difference sample standard deviation ($s_d$). Check the box to the left of *Perform hypothesis test*, click inside of the box to the right of *Hypothesized mean:*, delete any current value, and type in 0 (zero) as specified in the null hypothesis ($H_0$:), and then click on the Options... button.

In the 1-Sample Z - Options dialog box: ignore the value in the *Confidence level:* box , and then make sure that the box to the right of *Alternative:* contains the correct inequality for your problem (*not equal* or *less than* or *greater than*. If not, click on the down triangle ( ▼ ), and click on the correct choice. Then click on OK .

Back in the 1-Sample Z (Test and Confidence Interval) dialog box, click on OK .

Example 8.10:  The Fast-Line web site claims that its interactive program can increase your typing speed. They offer this program for a fee of $25 per person. Before paying this fee to train all of their secretaries, the Greengage Corporation randomly selected 40 secretaries and paid for them to take this interactive program. These 40 secretaries were tested for typing speed and accuracy the day before they participated in the program and again the day after they completed the program. For each secretary the difference between the after and before program scores was computed, and the results were a difference mean of 2.43 and a difference standard deviation of 9.89 . Using a significance level of 0.05, can the Greengage Corporation conclude that this interactive program will increase the mean typing skills of all of its secretaries?

Population 1 is all Greengage secretaries <u>after</u> they have participated in the Fast-Line interactive program.

Population 2 is all Greengage secretaries <u>before</u> they have participated in the Fast-Line interactive program.

This example uses summary statistics, the hypothesis testing problem is:

$H_0$: $\mu_1 \leq \mu_2$          or          $H_0$: $\mu_d \leq 0$
$H_a$: $\mu_1 > \mu_2$     equivalently     $H_a$: $\mu_d > 0$
$\alpha = 0.05$                              $\alpha = 0.05$ .

(continued on the next page)

Since the distribution of the difference scores is unknown, but the common sample size of 40 is greater than 30, and the test statistic $Z = \dfrac{\overline{d}}{\left[\dfrac{s_d}{\sqrt{n}}\right]}$ given in formula (vi).

Click on *Stat*, *Basic Statistics*, *1-Sample Z...*

In the 1-Sample Z (Test and Confidence Interval) dialog box: you may press the | **F3** | key to clear the contents of this dialog box and reset all options and erase any previous variables. Make sure the button to the left of *Summarized data* is selected, and then click inside of the box to the right of *Sample size:*. Now type in 40, the common sample size. Next click in the next box down that is to the right of *Mean:* and type in 2.43, the difference sample mean. Next click inside of the box to the right of *Standard deviation:* and type in 9.89, the difference sample standard deviation ($s_d$). Check the box to the left of *Perform hypothesis test*, click inside of the box to the right of *Hypothesized mean:*, delete any current value, and type in 0 (zero) as specified in the null hypothesis ($H_0$:), and then click on the | **Options...** | button.

In the 1-Sample Z - Options dialog box: ignore the value in the *Confidence level:* box , and then make sure that the box to the right of *Alternative:* contains the correct inequality of *greater than*. If not, click on the down triangle ( ▾ ), and click on the correct choice. Then click on | **OK** |.

Back in the 1-Sample Z (Test and Confidence Interval) dialog box, click on | **OK** |.

The resulting output below which includes the null and alternative hypotheses, the value of the Z test statistic and the p-value will appear in the Session Window.

## One-Sample Z

**Test of mu = 0 vs > 0**
**The assumed standard deviation = 9.89**

| N | Mean | SE Mean | 95% Lower Bound | Z | P |
|----|---------|---------|---------|------|-------|
| 40 | 2.43000 | 1.56375 | -0.14213 | 1.55 | 0.060 |

Since the p-value of 0.060 is greater than 0.05 ($\alpha$), you may not reject the null hypothesis. So the Greengage Corporation did not conclude that the mean typing skills of all of its secretaries after they have participated in the Fast-Line interactive program is greater than the mean typing skills of all of its secretaries before they have participated in the interactive program. Note that the value of the Z test statistic is 2.46; and this is not in the rejection region ( $Z \geq 1.645$ ). And so the Greengage Corporation did not pay to have all of its secretaries participate in this interactive program.

# Lab Assignment 8.2.1

**Name:**                                                        **Date:**

**Course:**                    **Section:**                **Data CD Number:**

1.  Start a Minitab session. If you are unable to complete this lab assignment in one Minitab session, save the project as Lab 8-2-1 . **Never** use a period as part of the project name; since Minitab uses the period to attach the file type to the file name. Then at your next Minitab session, you may open this Lab 8-2-1.MPJ project and continue to work where you left off previously.

2.  The Vermont Cancer Society conducted a study to investigate the effect of smoking on lung capacity. The Society randomly sampled 36 pairs of identical twins where one twin is a "heavy" smoker and the other twin is a non-smoker. The lung capacities (in cc's) of each pair of twins are:

| Smoker | Non-Smoker | | Smoker | Non-Smoker | | Smoker | Non-Smoker |
|--------|------------|---|--------|------------|---|--------|------------|
| 234 | 238 | | 274 | 267 | | 213 | 220 |
| 276 | 280 | | 244 | 231 | | 274 | 279 |
| 294 | 301 | | 209 | 214 | | 208 | 204 |
| 260 | 263 | | 201 | 204 | | 227 | 236 |
| 304 | 313 | | 274 | 274 | | 198 | 201 |
| 238 | 236 | | 286 | 288 | | 290 | 296 |
| 282 | 290 | | 232 | 222 | | 240 | 242 |
| 267 | 271 | | 289 | 300 | | 212 | 213 |
| 248 | 252 | | 211 | 215 | | 236 | 230 |
| 270 | 265 | | 327 | 328 | | 274 | 281 |
| 193 | 196 | | 227 | 230 | | 265 | 269 |
| 254 | 260 | | 259 | 251 | | 205 | 206 |

At the 0.05 level of significance, test the hypothesis that the mean lung capacity of all smokers is less than the mean lung capacity of all non-smokers.

3.  Open the worksheet Tasktime.mtw that is on your data disc. As described in Lab Assignment 5.1.1; twenty-three workers from the Method A assembly line were randomly selected, and their production times (in minutes) were measured. Then these **same** workers were moved to the Method B assembly line, and their production times (in minutes) were measured. It is known that production times by either of these two methods are normally distributed. Test the hypothesis that the mean production time for all workers from the Method A assembly line is less than the mean production time for all workers from the Method B assembly line. Use a 0.025 level of significance.

(lab assignment is continued on the second side of this page)

4.  The Chem-Rad Corporation claims that its Screen Guard reduces the radiation emitted by video display terminals. The UL Laboratory measured the amount of radiation produced by 15 video display terminals without the Screen Guard device. Then 15 of the Screen Guards were randomly sampled and placed on the these same terminals. The radiation levels were measured again with these Screen Guards in place. The results of this test were:

| Terminal Number | Without Screen Guard | With Screen Guard |
|---|---|---|
| 1 | 23 | 20 |
| 2 | 14 | 12 |
| 3 | 30 | 32 |
| 4 | 25 | 21 |
| 5 | 20 | 17 |
| 6 | 32 | 29 |
| 7 | 18 | 17 |
| 8 | 24 | 23 |
| 9 | 39 | 38 |
| 10 | 21 | 22 |
| 11 | 33 | 31 |
| 12 | 8 | 6 |
| 13 | 13 | 10 |
| 14 | 5 | 8 |
| 15 | 20 | 18 |

In other experiments, the difference in radiation levels has been shown to be normally distributed. Start a new Minitab worksheet and enter these data into columns 1 and 2 in that new worksheet. Use a 0.01 level of significance and test to see if the claim that, on the average, the amount of radiation is reduced by using Chem-Rad's Screen Guards.

5.  A university administrator wanted to know if there was any difference in the academic performance between dorm students and students who lived at home. A random sample of 60 pairs of beginning juniors were matched so that each pair had the same (1) grade point average, (2) major area of study, (3) extra curricular activities, (4) motivation and (5) other personality factors. At the end of the junior year the grade point average of each pair of students was measured and the difference of dorm minus at home student's grade point average was calculated. The results were a mean difference of 0.17 and a standard deviation of 0.62 . Let $\alpha = 0.01$ , and test to see if there is a significant difference in the mean grade point average between all of these two types of students.

6.  Print your Session Window and the first Worksheet Window to the printer.

7.  Attach both your Minitab output and <u>your complete answers</u> to this paper and submit all three to your instructor.

# Lab Assignment 8.2.2

**Name:**                                                          **Date:**

**Course:**                    **Section:**                    **Data CD Number:**

1.   Start a Minitab session. If you are unable to complete this lab assignment in one Minitab session, save the project as Lab 8-2-2 . **Never** use a period as part of the project name; since Minitab uses the period to attach the file type to the file name. Then at your next Minitab session, you may open this Lab 8-2-2.MPJ project and continue to work where you left off previously.

2.   In the sport of track, the 200 meter race is very competitive. Currently the two best male runners in this race are Usain Bolt and Wallace Spearman, but there is no consensus opinion about which is the faster runner. Since track, weather and wind condition all affect race times, comparing their times in different races is difficult due to different conditions at these races. So a random sample of all 200 meter races in which both men were entered was taken, and their race times (in seconds) were recorded with the following results.

| Race | 1 | 2 | 3 | 4 | 5 | 6 | 7 | 8 | 9 | 10 |
|------|------|------|------|------|------|------|------|------|------|------|
| Bolt's Time | 19.4 | 19.7 | 20.1 | 19.7 | 19.9 | 19.6 | 20.0 | 19.4 | 19.9 | 19.7 |
| Spearman's Time | 19.5 | 19.6 | 20.1 | 19.8 | 20.0 | 19.8 | 19.9 | 20.2 | 20.3 | 19.9 |

Previous research has shown that the difference of their race times is normally distributed. At the 0.05 level of significance test the hypothesis that over all 200 meter races both men race in, Usain Bolt is the faster runner ; that is, the mean of Bolt's race times is less than Wallace's mean time.

3.   Open the worksheet Homesale.mtw that is on your data disc. As described in Lab Assignment 7.1.1; this worksheet contains information about one-family housing sales in Raleigh, North Carolina. Each asking and selling price is for the same home. In this example you are asked to do something that was not illustrated previously in this section of the workbook. Test the hypothesis that the mean asking price is more than \$3,500 higher than the mean selling price. This asks if $\mu_{asking} > \mu_{selling} + 3500$. If $\mu_{selling}$ is subtracted from both sides, the the question may be written as $\mu_{asking} - \mu_{selling} > 3500$. And since the computations are done using the "difference" variable ($d = x_{asking} - x_{selling}$), this may written as the following equivalent form of $\mu_d > 3500$. The only difference in this problem and those shown previously in the this section is that this can be setup as $H_a: \mu_d > 3500$ ( instead of $H_a: \mu_d > 0$ ). And so in the Paired t Options dialog box, you will need to specify the value in the *Test mean:* box as 3500 instead of 0.0 . Use a 0.05 level of significance.

(lab assignment is continued on the second side of this page)

293

4.  The term "white coat syndrome" refers to the notion that a person's blood pressure is usually higher when taken in the doctors office that when taken anyplace else. In a small controlled study, 12 people were randomly selected during the week in a doctors office. First a medical technician wearing fashionable, informal clothing took the patients into a pleasant interview room and recorded their blood pressure. Within a few minutes, these same patients were led into an examination room and the doctor in a typical medial white coat took their blood pressure again. The results of this test were:

| Patient | BP by Tech | BP by Doctor |
|---------|-----------|--------------|
| 1 | 123 | 129 |
| 2 | 114 | 118 |
| 3 | 130 | 132 |
| 4 | 125 | 131 |
| 5 | 120 | 117 |
| 6 | 132 | 144 |
| 7 | 118 | 123 |
| 8 | 124 | 125 |
| 9 | 109 | 110 |
| 10 | 111 | 118 |
| 11 | 123 | 123 |
| 12 | 108 | 111 |

In other experiments, the difference in blood pressure levels has been shown to be normally distributed. Start a new Minitab worksheet and enter these data into columns 1 and 2 in that new worksheet. Use a 0.01 level of significance and test to see if the claim that, on the average, blood pressure taken under the "white coat" situation is higher than when taken in a less formal setting .

5.  The Environmental Protection Agency (EPA) conducted an experiment to determine the effect of adding ethanol to gasoline. First 40 automobiles had their gas tanks completely drained and then filled with exactly 15 gallons of gasoline without ethanol. Then these autos were driven on a closed course for 200 miles. Next their gas tanks were drained and the amount of gasoline used by each auto was thus determined. The second phase of the experiment was to fill these same automobiles with 15 gallons of gasoline with ethanol, drive them on the same closed course for 200 miles, and then drain their gas tanks to determine the amount of fuel used by each auto. The differences between the gasoline without and with ethanol were computed for each automobile, and the EPA computed the mean of these differences as 0.31 gallons and a standard deviation of 0.74 . Let $\alpha = 0.01$ , and test to see if there is a significant difference in the mean number of gallons used between the two types of gasoline.

6.  Print your Session Window and the first Worksheet Window to the printer.

7.  Attach both your Minitab output and your complete answers to this paper and submit all three to your instructor.

**Section 3: Hypothesis Tests for the Variances and the Standard Deviations of Two Normal Populations Using Two Independent Samples**

If two competing brands of a product both have the same mean value, the decision of which brand to purchase often is based upon which brand exhibits a greater degree of internal consistence (or homogeneity). To make this decision, a hypothesis test about the relative sizes of the variances (or standard deviations) of the two populations may be done. Also, as discussed in Section 1 of Chapter 7 and Section 1 of this chapter, the hypothesis test of $\sigma_1^2 = \sigma_2^2$ may need to be completed before determining whether to use the "separate variance" or a "pooled variance" technique. The "two sample" hypothesis test comparing the variances of two populations may be in one of the following three forms:

(a) $H_0: \sigma_1^2 = \sigma_2^2$
    $H_a: \sigma_1^2 \neq \sigma_2^2$

(b) $H_0: \sigma_1^2 \geq \sigma_2^2$
    $H_a: \sigma_1^2 < \sigma_2^2$

(c) $H_0: \sigma_1^2 \leq \sigma_2^2$
    $H_a: \sigma_1^2 > \sigma_2^2$

Very often the hypothesis test will be in terms of the population standard deviations instead of the variances, and may be in one of the following three forms:

(a) $H_0: \sigma_1 = \sigma_2$
    $H_a: \sigma_1 \neq \sigma_2$

(b) $H_0: \sigma_1 \geq \sigma_2$
    $H_a: \sigma_1 < \sigma_2$

(c) $H_0: \sigma_1 \leq \sigma_2$
    $H_a: \sigma_1 > \sigma_2$

The tests are equivalent, whether given in terms of the population variance ($\sigma^2$) or in terms of the population standard deviation ($\sigma$). The choice, $\sigma^2$ versus $\sigma$, is usually determined by the statement of the problem. If both of the populations are normally distributed and the two samples are taken independently of each other, the test statistic is based upon the F distribution with ($n_1 - 1$) and ($n_2 - 1$) degrees of freedom. The formula for this F test statistic is

$$\text{(vii)} \qquad F = \frac{s_1^2}{s_2^2}$$

where $s_1^2$ and $s_2^2$ are the variances of sample 1 and sample 2 respectively.

The same test statistic is used for both hypothesis tests comparing population variances or population standard deviations. For problems that have **raw data**, the macro that computes this test statistic for either case is called **Ht-2vsd.mtb** (**H**ypothesis **t**est for **2** **v**ariances or **s**tandard **d**eviations).

Click on *File , Other Files , Run an Exec...*

In the Run an Exec dialog box: make sure the *Number of times to execute:* box contains the number 1, and then click on the [ **Select File** ] button.

In the Run an Exec dialog box: the *Data Disc* should be selected. Next click on Ht-2vsd.mtb to highlight this macro (you may need to scroll through the box), and click on the [ **Open** ] button.

This macro will prompt you to enter the specific numbers of the columns that contain the data in the two samples. You must be very careful to enter the number that represents population 1 first, and the number that represents population 2 second. These two column numbers should be separated with a comma. **Do not enter the letter C, but enter only the column numbers**. Next the macro will prompt you to enter the type of test; enter 0 for a two tail test, enter -1 for a left tail test, and enter +1 for a right tail test.

Example 8.11: Open the worksheet Majorage.mtw from your data disk. This worksheet contains the ages of four independent samples of art, economics, mathematics and psychology majors at Bowling Green University. The age of college students is known to be normally distributed. At the 0.05 level of significance, test to determine if the variance of ages of all psychology majors is greater than the variance of ages of all mathematics majors at Bowling Green University.

Use the *File, Open Worksheet...* to open the worksheet Majorage.mtw that is on your data disk.

Population 1 is all psychology majors, and so column C4 contains the data in the corresponding sample.

Population 2 is all mathematics majors, and so column C3 contains the data in the corresponding sample.

This example contains raw data, the hypothesis testing problem is

$H_0: \sigma_1^2 \leq \sigma_2^2$

$H_a: \sigma_1^2 > \sigma_2^2$

$\alpha = 0.05$

and the test statistic is $F = \dfrac{s_1^2}{s_2^2}$ given in formula (vii).

From the Reference Guide in the table with the heading **Two Sample Hypothesis Test for the Ratio of Two Population Variances and Two Population Standard Deviations Using Two Independent Samples**, the **raw data** instructions say to execute the Ht-2vsd.mtb macro.

Click on *File, Other Files, Run an Exec...*

In the Run an Exec dialog box: make sure the *Number of times to execute:* box contains the number 1, and then click on the ⬚ Select File ⬚ button.

In the Run an Exec dialog box: the *Data Disc* should be selected. Next click on Ht-2vsd.mtb to highlight this macro (you may need to scroll through the box), and click on the ⬚ Open ⬚ button.

(continued on the next page)

The steps for this macro are shown below. The **bold italicized** words are displayed by Minitab in the Session Window, and the numbers you are to enter in the Session Window are shown in regular print. And then the value of the F test statistic and the p-value for this test that will appear in the Session Window are shown next

***After the DATA> prompt, enter the column numbers that contain the data of the first and second samples. Enter ONLY the numbers, but NOT the C's !***

***DATA>*** 4, 3 Enter          (since C4 contains the sample data from population 1

                                                    and C3 contains the sample data from population 2)

***After the DATA> prompt, enter the direction of the test:***
             ***-1 for a left tail test***
              ***0 for a two tail test***
             ***+1 for a right tail test***

***DATA>*** +1 Enter

## Data Display

***Null Hyp: Variance / St.Dev. of C 4  =  Variance / St.Dev. of C 3***
***Alt. Hyp: Variance / St.Dev. of C 4  >  Variance / St.Dev. of C 3***

| F test statistic | d.f. | p-value |
|---|---|---|
| 1.8080 | 61, 38 | 0.0265 |

Since the p-value of 0.0265 is less than the value of $\alpha = 0.05$, you may reject the null hypothesis and conclude that the variance of ages of all psychology majors is greater than the variance of ages of all mathematics majors at Bowling Green University. Note that the value of the F test statistic is 1.8080, and this is in the rejection region ($F \geq 1.652$).

For problems that have **summary statistics** data, the macro that computes this test statistic

for formula (vii)  $F = \dfrac{s_1^2}{s_2^2}$  is called **Sumht2vsd.mtb**.

The next example presents the data as summary statistics and uses a Summary Statistics macro stored on your data disk.

Example 8.12:  Cola is bottled in both 12 ounce bottles and in 12 ounce cans. Since the amount of cola can be seen in the bottles but not in the cans, a study was conducted to determine if there is a greater degree of consistency in the amount of cola in bottles. The filling process for both bottles and cans has a normal distribution. A random sample of 24 bottles was measured, and the mean and standard deviation were 12.0 and 0.14 ounces respectively. An independent random sample of 24 cans produced a mean and standard deviation of 12.0 and 0.19 ounces respectively.  Let $\alpha = 0.05$ and test to see if the standard deviation of amount of cola in all bottles is less than the standard deviation of amount of cola in all cans.

Population 1 is all 12 ounce bottles of cola.

Population 2 is all 12 ounce cans of cola.

This example has summary statistics data, the hypothesis testing problem is

$H_0: \sigma_1 \geq \sigma_2$

$H_a: \sigma_1 < \sigma_2$

$\alpha = 0.05$

and the test statistic is $F = \dfrac{s_1^2}{s_2^2}$ given in formula (vii).

From the Reference Guide in the table with the heading **Two Sample Hypothesis Test for the Ratio of Two Population Variances and Two Population Standard Deviations Using Two <u>Independent</u> Samples,** the **summary statistics** instructions say to execute the **Sumht2vs.mtb** macro.

Click on  *File , Other Files , Run an Exec...*

In the Run an Exec dialog box:  make sure the *Number of times to execute:* box contains the number 1, and then click on the $\boxed{\textbf{Select File}}$ button.

In the Run an Exec dialog box: the *Data Disc* should be selected.  Next click on Sumht2vs.mtb to highlight this macro (you may need to scroll through the box), and click on the $\boxed{\textbf{Open}}$ button.

The macro begins by prompting you for type of test, and you will enter -1 for the "left tail" in this example.  Next the macro prompts for the two samples' standard deviations.  Then the macro prompts you to enter the sample sizes for the two samples.  The steps for this macro and resulting hypothesis test results shown below will appear in the Session Window.

**After the DATA> prompt, enter the direction of the test:**
**-1  for a left tail test**
**0  for a two tail test**
**+1  for a right tail test**

**DATA>** -1 $\boxed{\textbf{Enter}}$

(continued on the next page)

**After the DATA> prompt, enter the standard deviation of Sample 1,
a comma, and then the standard deviation of Sample 2.
Enter the standard deviations and NOT the variances of the samples.**

**DATA>** 0.14 , 0.19 ┃ **Enter** ┃

**After the DATA> prompt, enter the respective sizes of the two Samples.**

**DATA>** 24 , 24 ┃ **Enter** ┃

**The two-sample test of the population variances/standard deviations
is now executing.**

## Data Display

**Null Hyp: Variance / St.Dev. of Pop. 1  =  Variance / St.Dev. of Pop. 2
Alt.  Hyp: Variance / St.Dev. of Pop. 1  <  Variance / St.Dev. of Pop. 2**

| F test statistic | d.f. | p-value |
|---|---|---|
| 0.5429 | 23, 23 | 0.0752 |

Since the p-value of 0.0752 is greater than the value of $\alpha = 0.05$, you may **not** reject the null hypothesis and  so may **not** conclude that the standard deviation of amount of cola in all 12 ounce bottles is less than the standard deviation of amount of cola in all 12 ounce cans. Therefore you may **not** conclude that there is a greater degree of consistency in the filling of bottles of cola versus filling of cans.  Note that the value of the F test statistic is 0.5429, and this is **not** in the rejection region ($F \leq 0.4964$).

The macros just described work for all three forms of the hypothesis testing scenario:

(a)  $H_0: \sigma_1^2 = \sigma_2^2$
     $H_a: \sigma_1^2 \neq \sigma_2^2$

(b)  $H_0: \sigma_1^2 \geq \sigma_2^2$
     $H_a: \sigma_1^2 < \sigma_2^2$

(c)  $H_0: \sigma_1^2 \leq \sigma_2^2$
     $H_a: \sigma_1^2 > \sigma_2^2$

However when the problem involves a two-sided alternative and calls for the two-tailed test of:

$$H_0: \sigma_1^2 = \sigma_2^2$$
$$H_a: \sigma_1^2 \neq \sigma_2^2,$$

Minitab can also compute the test statistic  $F = \dfrac{s_1^2}{s_2^2}$  given in formula (vii) by using the menu command *Stat, Basic Statistics, 2 Variances*.  When the problem contain **raw data**, this test statistic is computed by

Click on *Stat , Basic Statistics , 2 Variances...*

In the 2 Variances dialog box: you may press the F3 key to clear the contents of this dialog box and reset all options and erase any previous variables. Click on the circle to the left of *Samples in different columns*, click in the box to the right of *First:*, click on the variable that contains the data from sample 1, and click on the Select button. The cursor now will be in the box to the right of *Second:*, click on the variable that contains the data from sample 2, and click on the Select button. Then click on OK . (There is no need to click on Options... button, since this always computes a **not equal** alternative.)

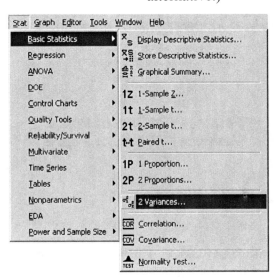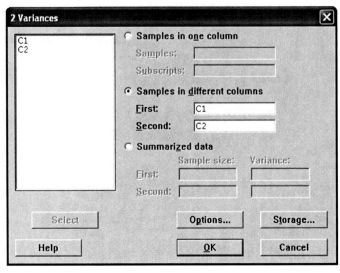

However, when the problem has **summary statistics data**, this formula $F = \dfrac{s_1^2}{s_2^2}$ is computed by

Click on *Stat , Basic Statistics , 2 Variances...*

In the 2 Variances dialog box: you may press the F3 key to clear the contents of this dialog box and reset all options and erase any previous information. Click on the circle to the left of *Summarized data*, and then click inside of the box on the *First:* row and underneath of *Sample size:*. If a previous value is shown, erase this number and type in the value of the first sample size. Click in the next box to the right that is underneath of *Variance:* and type in the value of the first sample's variance. Next click inside of the box on the *Second:* row and underneath of *Sample size:* and type in the second sample size. Click in the next box to the right that is underneath of *Variance:* and type in the value of the second sample's variance. Then click on OK . (There is no need to click on Options... button, since this always computes a **not equal** alternative.)

(See graphics on the next page.)

300

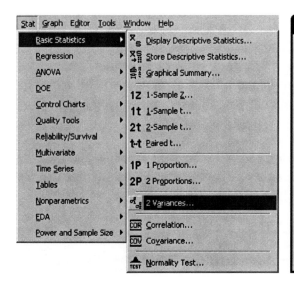
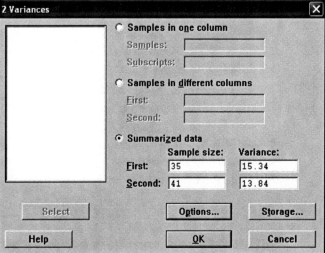

The output of *2 Variances* contains the following information in the Session Window:

(a)     a 95% Bonferroni confidence intervals for standard deviations,

(b)     the value of the F test statistic and the p-value for the test, assuming that the data in both populations is normally distributed, and

(c)     the value of Levene's test statistic and the p-value for the test, for any continuous population distribution (only for raw data).

The *2 Variances* procedure also produces a separate Graphics Window which contains the same information as in the Session Window plus two box plots when the problem has raw data.

Example 8.13:   Use the data in the Majorage.mtw worksheet. This worksheet contains the ages of four independent samples of art, economics, mathematics and psychology majors at Bowling Green University. The age of college students is known to be normally distributed. At the 0.05 level of significance, test to determine if the variance of ages of all art majors is different than the variance of ages of all economics majors at Bowling Green University.

Population 1 is all art majors, and so column C1 contains the data in the corresponding sample.

Population 2 is all economics majors, and so column C2 contains the data in the corresponding sample.

This example contains raw data which is normally distributed , the hypothesis testing problem is

$H_0: \sigma_1^2 = \sigma_2^2$
$H_a: \sigma_1^2 \neq \sigma_2^2$
$\alpha = 0.05$

and the test statistic is   $F = \dfrac{s_1^2}{s_2^2}$   given in formula (vii).

(continued on the next page)

Click on *Stat , Basic Statistics , 2 Variances...*

In the 2 Variances dialog box: click on the circle to the left of *Samples in different columns*, click in the box to the right of *First:*, click on the ART (C1) variable that contains the data from sample 1, and click on the ⬚ Select ⬚ button. The cursor now will be in the box to the right of *Second:*, click on the ECON (C2) variable that contains the data from sample 2, and click on the ⬚ Select ⬚ button. Then click on ⬚ **OK** ⬚ .

The resulting output below contains what will appear in the Session Window and then the separate Graphics Window. The null and alternative hypotheses are **not** included in the output since this is **always** a **not equal** alternative.

## Test for Equal Variances: ART, ECON

### 95% Bonferroni confidence intervals for standard deviations

|      | N  | Lower    | StDev   | Upper   |
|------|----|----------|---------|---------|
| ART  | 33 | 4.94076  | 6.33084 | 8.73844 |
| ECON | 39 | 3.19683  | 4.02221 | 5.38695 |

**F-Test (normal distribution)**
**Test statistic = 2.48, p-value = 0.008**

**Levene's Test (any continuous distribution)**
**Test statistic = 4.00, p-value = 0.049**

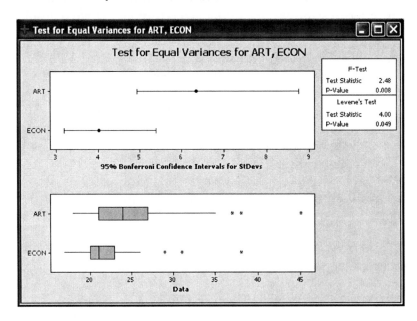

Since the p-value of 0.008 is less than the value of α = 0.05, you may reject the null hypothesis and conclude that the variance of ages of all art majors is different than the variance of ages of all economics majors at Bowling Green University. Note that the value of the F test statistic is 2.48, and this is in the rejection region ( F ≤ 0.504 or F ≥ 1.947 ).

When testing the means of two populations using two independent samples, this procedure is often used to test the homogeneity of variance condition.

302

# Lab Assignment 8.3.1

**Name:**                                                                 **Date:**

**Course:**               **Section:**                      **Data CD Number:**

1.  Start a Minitab session. If you are unable to complete this lab assignment in one Minitab session, save the project as Lab 8-3-1 . **Never** use a period as part of the project name; since Minitab uses the period to attach the file type to the file name. Then at your next Minitab session, you may open this Lab 8-3-1.MPJ project and continue to work where you left off previously.

2.  Independent random samples of closing stock prices for the Hi-Tech Corporation and for the Foodway Corporation were taken. Closing stock prices for both corporations are normally distributed. At the 0.05 level of significance, test the hypothesis that Hi-Tech's stock is more volatile (variable) than the Foodway Corporation's stock.

    High-Tech:    17.500 , 18.250 , 16.625 , 19.125 , 17.750 , 21.250 , 20.625
                          16.125 , 18.750 , 22.250 , 21.000 , 16.500 , 23.500 , 15.750
                          18.375 , 19.000 , 18.500 , 18.675 , 17.875 , 18.000

    Foodway:        8.250 ,   9.500 ,   7.750 , 10.125 ,   8.875 ,   9.000 ,   7.875
                          9.250 , 10.000 ,   7.500 ,   9.250 ,   8.625 ,   7.875 ,   9.500
                        10.250 ,   8.125 ,   7.000 ,   8.125 , 11.250 , 11.000 ,   9.875
                          6.500 ,   7.125 , 10.875

3.  Open the worksheet Run400.mtw that is on your data disc. As described in Lab Assignment 6.1.1; the track officials sampled boys and girls in both the eight and twelve year old age groups and measured their times (in seconds) in a 400 meter race. These times are normally distributed for all four populations. It was claimed that the standard deviations of the 400 meter race times are the same for the twelve year old boys and girls. Test this claim using a 0.10 level of significance.

4.  Open another worksheet using Callback.mtw from your data disc. As described in Example 8.1, a random sample of callback times (in seconds) was taken from all Illinois sales industries, and a second independent sample was taken from all Illinois service industries. These callback times are known to be normally distributed, and the population variances are claimed to be different. At the 0.01 level of significance, test the hypothesis that the variance of callback times for all Illinois sales industries is less than the variance of callback times for all Illinois service industries.

(lab assignment is continued on the second side of this page)

303

5. A random sample of 15 aluminum bicycle tubes was taken, the wall thickness was measured, and the results were a mean of 3.2 mm and a variance of 0.85 mm². An independent sample of 23 steel bicycle tubes was taken, the wall thickness was measured, and the results were a mean of 3.0 mm and a variance of 0.48 mm². The manufacturing process produces bicycle tubes whose wall thickness is normally distributed. At the 0.10 level of significance, can you conclude that the variance of all aluminum bicycle tubes is greater than the variance of all steel bicycle tubes?

6. A random sample of 20 quality made quartz crystal wrist watches was taken and a second independent sample of 25 high quality spring driven wrist watches was taken. Each watch was used to measure the time of the same event. The mean and standard deviation of the first sample was 243.4 minutes and 1.46 minutes respectively. The mean and standard deviation of the second sample was 242.8 minutes and 2.18 minutes respectively. These times are known to have a normal distribution. Do these data support the claim that the standard deviation of all quality made quartz crystal wrist watches is less than for all high quality spring driven wrist watches? Let $\alpha = 0.05$ .

7. Print your Session Window to the printer.

8. Attach both your Minitab output and your complete answers to this paper and submit all three to your instructor.

# Lab Assignment 8.3.2

**Name:**                                                    **Date:**

**Course:**                    **Section:**                    **Data CD Number:**

1.  Start a Minitab session. If you are unable to complete this lab assignment in one Minitab session, save the project as Lab 8-3-2 . **Never** use a period as part of the project name; since Minitab uses the period to attach the file type to the file name. Then at your next Minitab session, you may open this Lab 8-3-2.MPJ project and continue to work where you left off previously.

2.  In a union contract negotiating session, management wanted to reduce the number of union assemblers and replace them with robots. The union argued that although the robots could assemble the parts more quickly than human workers, the human workers produced a more uniform product. The union argued that the experienced workers could see small imperfections and correct these problems, but the robots were unable to do this. Management agreed to test this claim before purchasing the robots. Nine randomly selected products made by the union workers were measured for their smoothness and the results were:

    23.1 , 24.2 , 22.9 , 23.6 , 23.5 , 24.0 , 23.7 , 23.6 and 23.2 .

    At a test site where robots were already in use, 12 products made by robots were randomly selected and their smoothness was measured with the following results:

    22.8 , 23.7 , 24.1 , 23.8 , 23.1 , 24.1 , 22.9 23.1 , 23.7 , 22.9 , 23.6 and 23.5 .

    Past experience has shown that for products made both by union members and by robots, the smoothness scores of these products are normally distributed. Test the hypothesis that the standard deviation of all products assembled by union workers is less than the standard deviation of all products assembled by robots. Did the union save the jobs of some of its members? Use a 0.05 level of significance.

3.  Brand name producers of aspirin claim that one advantage of their aspirin over generic aspirin is that brand name aspirin is much more consistent in the amount of active ingredient used. This in turn means that users can expect the same results each time they use the brand name aspirin, while the effects of the generic aspirin can be a lot more variable. A random sample of 200 brand name aspirin tablets had a mean and standard deviation of active ingredient of 325.01 and 10.12 mg. A second independent sample of 180 generic aspirin tablets was measured for the amount of active ingredient, and the mean and standard deviation were 323.47 and 11.43 mg. Given that the amount of active ingredient is normally distributed for both the brand name and the generic aspirin, do these data support the brand name producers claim? Let $\alpha = 0.025$ .

    (lab assignment is continued on the second side of this page)

4.	Open the worksheet Cityidx.mtw that is on your data disc. As described in Lab Assignment 6.1.2; this worksheet contains data about five variables where each was measured on cities in three different geographical regions: C1 - C5 in the East, C6 - C10 in the Central, and C11 - C15 in the West. The municipal bond measurement is a Bernoulli variable where 1 = A or better rating and 0 = below an A rating. The other four are indices and are known to be normally distributed in each of the three regions. In problem 4 of Lab Assignment 8.1.2, you are asked to see if the urban unemployment index (U-Unpl) is the same for all cities in the East as in the West regions. Also in that problem, there is the statement "It is known that the standard deviation of the urban unemployment index is the same in both of these regions". As indicated above, the urban unemployment index is normally distributed in both of these regions. Use a 0.05 level of significance and test the hypothesis to determine if these two population standard deviations are the same.

5.	In the manufacturing of an internal combustion engine, piston rings are used. If these piston rings are not of the correct size, the engine will break down before the warranty period is completed. For this reason, it is very important to the auto makers that these piston rings all be the same size. In deciding whether to buy QuickSeal or Titan piston rings, the purchasing agent took two independent random samples and measured the diameter of these rings in inches. The distribution of ring diameters is known to be normal for both companies. The results are given in the table below.

| Brand | Sample Size | Mean | Standard Deviation |
|---|---|---|---|
| Titan | 80 | 5 | 0.043 |
| QuickSeal | 80 | 5 | 0.035 |

The purchasing agent will buy the higher quality brand; that is, the brand with the smaller standard deviation for all of that brand's piston rings. However, the Titan piston rings are slightly cheaper. And so unless the standard deviation of the Titan piston rings is more than that of the QuickSeal Company, the purchasing agent will buy Titan piston rings. Use a 0.05 significance level to determine if the purchasing agent will buy Titan or QuickSeal piston rings.

6.	Print your Session Window to the printer.

7.	Attach both your Minitab output and your complete answers to this paper and submit all three to your instructor.

# Section 4: Hypothesis Test For Two Population Proportions of "Successes"

The variables in the previous three sections were a continuous type of measurement. This section will consider a Bernoulli type of variable and how to compute a test of hypothesis about the equality or inequality for the proportion of "successes" of two populations. The "two sample" hypotheses comparing the proportion of "successes" of two populations may take on one of the following three forms:

(a) $H_0$: $p_1 = p_2$       (b) $H_0$: $p_1 \geq p_2$       (c) $H_0$: $p_1 \leq p_2$
    $H_a$: $p_1 \neq p_2$           $H_a$: $p_1 < p_2$           $H_a$: $p_1 > p_2$

Form (a) is the "two tail" test, form (b) is the "left tail" test, and form (c) is the "right tail" test.

When the two independent sample sizes are sufficiently large, the test statistic has an approximate Standard Normal distribution and is given by the formula

$$\text{(viii)} \qquad Z = \frac{\hat{p}_1 - \hat{p}_2}{\sqrt{p^*(1 - p^*)\left(\dfrac{n_1 + n_2}{n_1 n_2}\right)}}$$

$$\text{where } p^* = \frac{Y_1 + Y_2}{n_1 + n_2} .$$

In this formula $\hat{p}_1$ and $\hat{p}_2$ are the proportions of "successes" in sample 1 and sample 2, and $Y_1$ and $Y_2$ are the numbers of "successes" in sample 1 and sample 2 respectively. Since the null hypothesis states that the two populations have the same proportion of "successes", the formula uses $p^*$ which is the "pooled" estimate of this common population proportion. As described in Chapter 5, Section 3; the data for a Bernoulli type variable **must** be entered in the Worksheet Window into a variable (column) such that the <u>exact same</u> coding is used for each "success" and the <u>exact same</u> coding is used for each "failure" for both variables. If you are entering alphabetic symbols or words, then you must use the exact same upper case and lower case letters each time for each "success" and for each "failure." As an alternative you may code each "success" outcome an one (1) and each "failure" outcome as a zero (0). If the variables contain alphabetic (text) data, you may use the *Data, Code, Text to Numeric* procedure to code the alphabetic data into zeros and ones as was also shown in Chapter 5, Section 3. Or you may use *Data , Code , Text to Text* to recode the alphabetic data. Furthermore, if you enter alphabetic symbols or words, Minitab <u>always</u> assigns "failure" to the one that comes first in alphabetical order, and assigns "success" to the one that comes last in alphabetical order. So if you enter M for male and F for female: (1) you must use all of the same case for the Ms and all of the same case for the Fs, and (2) Minitab will assign "success" to the M (male) outcome.

Once the **raw data** is in the correct format, the test statistic in formula (viii) and p-value are computed using the *2 Proportions* procedure as follows.

Click on *Stat* , *Basic Statistics* , *2 Proportions* ...

In the 2 Proportions (Test and Confidence Interval) dialog box: you may press the F3 key to clear the contents of this dialog box and reset all options and erase any previous information. Make sure the button to the left of *Samples in different columns* is selected, click inside of the box to the right of *First:*, delete any previous variable, click on the variable that contains the data from the **first** sample, and click on Select . The cursor will move into the box to the right of *Second:*, delete any previous variable, click on the variable that contains the data from the **second** sample, and click on Select . Then click on Options... .

In the 2 Proportions - Options dialog box: ignore the value in the *confidence level:* box and then click inside of the box to the right of *Test difference:*. If the current value is not 0.0, delete this value and type in 0.0 . Next make sure that the box to the right of *Alternative:* contains the correct inequality for your problem (*not equal* or *less than* or *greater than*). If not, click on the down triangle ( ▼ ), and click on the correct choice. Next click in the square to the left of *Use pooled estimate of p for test:* to check this box, if it is not already checked. Then click on OK .

Back in the 2 Proportions (Test and Confidence Interval) dialog box: click on OK .

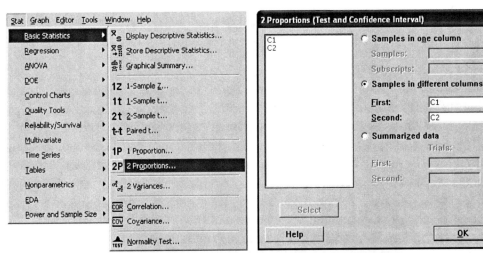

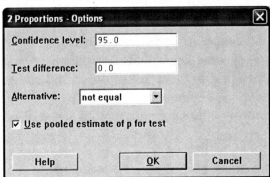

However, for problems that contain **summary statistics** data, this formula (viii)

$$Z = \frac{\hat{p}_1 - \hat{p}_2}{\sqrt{p^*(1 - p^*)\left(\dfrac{n_1 + n_2}{n_1 n_2}\right)}}$$ is computed by

Click on *Stat , Basic Statistics , 2 Proportions ...*

In the 2 Proportions (Test and Confidence Interval) dialog box: you may want to press the ⬚ F3 ⬚ key to erase all previous contents from the dialog boxes. Then make sure the button to the left of *Summarized data* is selected, and then click inside of the box to the right of *First:* and under *Trials:*. In this box erase any previous value and type in the first sample size. Next click inside of the box to the right under *Events:*, erase any previous value, and type in the number of "successes" in the first sample. Now repeat this for the second sample size and the number of "successes" in the second sample. Then click on the ⬚ **Options...** ⬚ button.

In the 2 Proportions - Options dialog box: ignore the value in the *confidence level:* box and then click inside of the box to the right of *Test difference:*. If the current value is not 0.0, delete this value and type in 0.0 . Next make sure that the box to the right of *Alternative:* contains the correct inequality for your problem (*not equal* or *less than* or *greater than*). If not, click on the down triangle ( ⬚▾⬚ ), and click on the correct choice. Next click in the square to the left of *Use pooled estimate of p for test:* to check this box, if it is not already checked. Then click on ⬚ **OK** ⬚ .

Back in the 2 Proportions (Test and Confidence Interval) dialog box: click on ⬚ **OK** ⬚ .

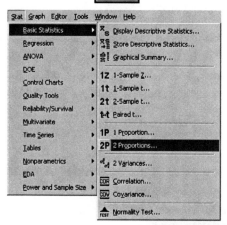

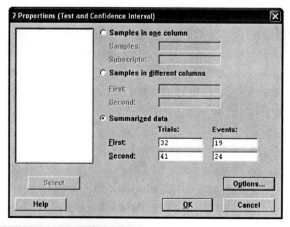

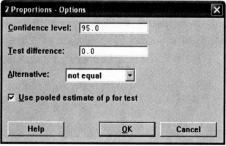

The output of the *2 Proportions* procedure contains:

(1) the outcome Minitab assigns as "success" written as *Event = outcome* (only for raw data),

(2) the variable names or column numbers (for raw data) or the sample number - usually 1 and 2 - (for summarized data), number of "successes" for each variable (Minitab uses a heading of X), sample sizes, and each sample's proportion of "successes" - $\hat{p}$ ,

(3) the value of the point estimate of the difference of $p_1 - p_2$ ,

(4) a confidence interval or confidence bound for $p_1 - p_2$ (explained in Chapter 6),

(5) the value of the Z test statistic and p-value, and

(6) a warning if the criteria for using formula (viii) are not met.

Example 8.14:   A sample of NewMark tires and an independent sample of Camden tires were tested. Each tire was judged to be good (G) or defective (D) with the following results:

NewMark:   G, G, D, G, G, G, G, G, G, G, D, G, G, G, G, D, G, G, G, D
G, G, G, D, G, D, D, G, D, G, G, G, D, G and D

Camden:   D, G, G, G, D, D, G, D, G, G, D, G, G, D, G, G, G, D, D, G
G, D, G, D, G, G, D, G, G, D, D, D, G, D, D and G

At the 0.05 level of significance, test the claim that the proportion of all NewMark tires that are defective is smaller than the proportion of all Camden tires that are defective.

Enter the data as G or D into two separate columns of the current Worksheet Window. Since defective (D) is the outcome of interest ("success"), you must recode this data so that the defective ("success") code comes <u>after</u> the good ("failure") code. Name the next two unused columns as "NewMark" and "Camden. Use the *Data, Code, Text to Text* procedure to recode the data in the two columns so that G becomes Accept ("success") and D becomes Defect ("failure").

Click on the *Data, Code, Text to Text*

In the Code - Text to Text dialog box: the cursor will be in the box under *Code data from columns:*. Drag the mouse over the two columns to highlight **both** variables and click on ⬛ **Select** . Next click inside of the box under *Into columns:*, drag the mouse over the NewMark and Camden columns and click on ⬛ **Select** . Now click inside the first box under the *Original values* heading and type in G. Next click inside of the first box under the *New* heading and type in Accept (to recode as "success"). Similarly on the second row, type in D and Defect (to recode as "failure"). Then click on ⬛ **OK** .

The first few rows of your Worksheet Window should look similar to that shown on the next page.

(continued on the next page)

| ↓ | C1-T | C2-T | C3-T | C4-T |
|---|------|------|------|------|
|   |      |      | NewMark | Camden |
| 1 | G | D | Accept | Defect |
| 2 | G | G | Accept | Accept |
| 3 | D | G | Defect | Accept |
| 4 | G | G | Accept | Accept |
| 5 | G | D | Accept | Defect |
| 6 | G | D | Accept | Defect |
| 7 | G | G | Accept | Accept |
| 8 | G | D | Accept | Defect |

**Worksheet 1 \*\*\***

Population 1 is all NewMark tires, and so column C3-T contains the coded data in the corresponding sample.

Population 2 is all Camden tires, and so column C4-T contains the coded data in the corresponding sample.

This example contains raw data, the hypothesis testing problem is

$H_0$: $p_1 \geq p_2$
$H_a$: $p_1 < p_2$
$\alpha = 0.05$

and the test statistic is $Z = \dfrac{\hat{p}_1 - \hat{p}_2}{\sqrt{p^*(1 - p^*)\left(\dfrac{n_1 + n_2}{n_1 n_2}\right)}}$ given in formula (viii).

Click on *Stat , Basic Statistics , 2 Proportions ...*

In the 2 Proportions (Test and Confidence Interval) dialog box: make sure the button to the left of *Samples in different columns* is selected, click inside of the box to the right of *First:*, click on the New Mark (C3-T) variable that contains the data from the **first** sample, and click on [ Select ] . The cursor will move into the box to the right of *Second:*, click on the Camden (C4-T) variable that contains the data from the **second** sample, and click on [ Select ] . Then click on [ Options... ] .

In the 2 Proportions - Options dialog box: ignore the value in the *confidence level:* box and then click inside of the box to the right of *Test difference:*. If the current value is not 0.0, delete this value and type in 0.0 . Next make sure that the box to the right of *Alternative:* contains the correct inequality of *less than*). If not, click on the down triangle ( ▼ ), and click on the correct choice. Next click in the square to the left of *Use pooled estimate of p for test:* to check this box, if it is not already checked. Then click on [ **OK** ] .

Back in the 2 Proportions (Test and Confidence Interval) dialog box: click on [ **OK** ] .

The results shown on the next page will appear in the Session Window.

(continued on the next page)

## *Test and CI for Two Proportions: NewMark, Camden*

*Event = Defect*

| Variable | X | N | Sample p |
|----------|-----|-----|----------|
| *NewMark* | *10* | *35* | *0.285714* |
| *Camden* | *16* | *36* | *0.444444* |

*Difference = p (NewMark) - p (Camden)*
*Estimate for difference: -0.158730*
*95% upper bound for difference: 0.0265596*
*Test for difference = 0 (vs < 0):  Z = -1.39  P-Value = 0.083*

Since the p-value of 0.083 is greater than the given value of $\alpha = 0.05$, you may **not** reject the null hypothesis, and so you may **not** conclude that the proportion of all NewMark tires that are defective is smaller than the proportion of all Camden tires that are defective. Note that the value of the Z test statistic is -1.39, and this is not in the rejection region ( $Z \leq -1.645$ ).

Example 8.15:  A random sample of 150 people who never used Morgan Tissues was shown a television advertisement, and then each person was asked if he/she would switch to Morgan Tissues.  Twenty-six (26) said yes.  Another random sample of 120 people who never used Morgan Tissues listened to a radio advertisement, and then each person was asked if he/she would switch to Morgan Tissues. Twelve (12) people in this second sample said yes.  At the 0.10 level of significance, test to see if there is any difference in the effectiveness of the two type of advertisements.

Population 1 is all people who never used Morgan Tissues and saw the television advertisement.

Population 2 is all people who never used Morgan Tissues and listened to the radio advertisement.

This example contains summary statistics data, the hypothesis testing problem is

$H_0$: $p_1 = p_2$
$H_a$: $p_1 \neq p_2$
$\alpha = 0.10$

and the test statistic is  $Z = \dfrac{\hat{p}_1 - \hat{p}_2}{\sqrt{p^*(1 - p^*)\left(\dfrac{n_1 + n_2}{n_1 n_2}\right)}}$  given in formula (viii).

(continued on the next page)

Click on *Stat , Basic Statistics , 2 Proportions ...*

In the 2 Proportions (Test and Confidence Interval) dialog box: press the ▐ **F3** ▌ key to erase all previous contents from the dialog boxes. Then make sure the button to the left of *Summarized data* is selected, and then click inside of the box to the right of *First:* and under *Trials:*. In this box type in 150, the first sample size. Next click inside of the box to the right under *Events:*, and type in 21, the number of "successes" in the first sample. Now click inside of the box to the right of *Second:* and under *Trials:*, and type in 120, the second sample size. Next click inside of the box to the right under *Events:*, and type in 10, the number of "successes" in the second sample. Then click on the ▐ **Options...** ▌ button.

In the 2 Proportions - Options dialog box: ignore the value in the *confidence level:* box and then click inside of the box to the right of *Test difference:*. If the current value is not 0.0, delete this value and type in 0.0 . Next make sure that the box to the right of *Alternative:* contains the correct inequality of *not equal*). If not, click on the down triangle ( ▐▼▌ ), and click on the correct choice. Next click in the square to the left of *Use pooled estimate of p for test:* to check this box, if it is not already checked. Then click on ▐ **OK** ▌ .

Back in the 2 Proportions (Test and Confidence Interval) dialog box: click on ▐ **OK** ▌ .

The results shown below will appear in the Session Window.

## *Test and CI for Two Proportions*

| *Sample* | *X* | *N* | *Sample p* |
|----------|-----|-----|------------|
| *1* | *26* | *150* | *0.173333* |
| *2* | *12* | *120* | *0.100000* |

*Difference = p (1) - p (2)*
*Estimate for difference:  0.0733333*
*95% CI for difference:  (-0.00760296, 0.154270)*
*Test for difference = 0 (vs not = 0):  Z = 1.72  P-Value = 0.085*

Since the p-value of 0.085 is less than the given value of $\alpha = 0.10$, you **may** reject the null hypothesis, and so you **may** conclude that the proportion of all people who never used Morgan Tissues and saw the television advertisement who would switch to Morgan Tissues is different than the proportion of all people who never used Morgan Tissues and listened to the radio advertisement and then would switch. In other words, there **is** a significant difference in the effectiveness of these two types of advertisements. Note that the value of the Z test statistic is 1.45, and this is not in the rejection region ( $Z \leq -1.645$ or $Z \geq 1.645$).

# Lab Assignment 8.4.1

**Name:**                                                                                    **Date:**

**Course:**                          **Section:**                          **Data CD Number:**

1.  Start a Minitab session. If you are unable to complete this lab assignment in one Minitab session, save the project as Lab 8-4-1 . **Never** use a period as part of the project name; since Minitab uses the period to attach the file type to the file name. Then at your next Minitab session, you may open this Lab 8-4-1.MPJ project and continue to work where you left off previously.

2.  The Career Office at Palmer College conducted a study to determine the relative marketability of its 1998 Science graduates compared to its 1998 Liberal Arts graduates. A sample of the 1998 Science graduates and a independent sample of 1998 Liberal Arts graduates were asked if they had found a job by August 1. The results of these surveys are (Yes=Y and No=N):

    Science graduates:     Y, N, Y, Y, N, Y, Y, Y, N, Y, Y, Y, N, Y, Y, N, N, Y, Y, Y, N
                           N, Y, Y, Y, Y, N, Y, N, Y, Y, Y, N, Y, Y, Y and Y

    Liberal Arts graduates:   N, Y, Y, N, Y, N, Y, Y, Y, N, Y, N, Y, Y, Y, N, N, Y, N, N, Y
                              N, N, Y, N, N, Y, N, Y, Y, N, Y, N, N, Y and N

    Use the symbols Y and N to enter the data into columns C1 and C2 of the current Worksheet Window. Name the columns Science and LibArts. Let $\alpha = 0.10$, and test the hypothesis that the Palmer College 1998 Science graduates are more marketable than the College's 1998 Liberal Arts graduates (i.e., that the proportion of all Palmer College 1998 Science graduates who found a job by August 1 is greater than the proportion of all 1998 Liberal Arts graduates who found a job by August 1).

3.  A random sample of 52 first grade students were taught to read by the Phonics method. At the end of the year, 40 of them passed a standard reading test. Another sample of 48 first grade students were taught to read using the Recognition method. At the end of the year, 30 in this sample passed the same standard reading test. At the 0.05 level of significance test to see if the proportion of all first grade Phonics readers who can pass the standard test is different than the proportion of all first grade Recognition readers who can pass the standard reading test.

4.  Open the worksheet Homesale.mtw that is on your data disc. This worksheet contains information about one-family housing sales in Raleigh, North Carolina. A sample of houses five years old or older and another independent sample of newer houses were taken. If a house was sold within 3 months, a 1 was recorded; but if the house took longer than 3 months to sell, a 0 was entered. At the 0.05 level of significance, test the hypothesis that the proportion of all older one-family houses in Raleigh that were sold within 3 months is less than the same proportion of all newer one-family houses in Raleigh.

(lab assignment is continued on the second side of this page)

315

5.  Open another worksheet using Cityidx.mtw from your data disc. As described in Lab Assignment 6.1.2; this worksheet contains data about five variables where each was measured on cities in three different geographical regions: C1 - C5 in the East, C6 - C10 in the Central, and C11 - C15 in the West. The municipal bond measurement is a Bernoulli variable where 1 = A or better rating and 0 = below an A rating. At the 0.10 level of significance test the hypothesis that the proportion of all cities with a good (A or better) municipal bond rating is the same in both the Eastern and the Western regions of the United States.

6.  An audiologist wants to test her theory that rock band musicians are more prone to have some hearing loss than symphony orchestra musicians. She takes a random sample of 45 rock band musicians and a second sample of 60 symphony orchestra musicians and measures whether they have either normal hearing or some hearing loss. Among the rock band sample, 19 have some hearing loss; and of the symphony orchestra sample, 11 have some hearing loss. The audiologist wants to use a 0.01 level of significance. Test her hypothesis.

7.  Some software companies have their technical support done by company trained employees, while other software companies completely out source their technical support. There is a common perception that in house technical support is favored by end users, however many companies find it easier and less expensive to out source this support. In a recent survey; a random sample of 200 end users of in house support was taken, and 168 said they were satisfied with the quality of support they received. Another sample of 250 end users of out source support was taken, and 193 said they were satisfied with the quality of support they received. Test to see if there is any difference in the proportion of satisfied end users receiving in house technical support versus the proportion of satisfied end users receiving out source technical support. Let $\alpha = 0.05$ .

8.  Print your Session Window to the printer.

9.  Attach both your Minitab output and your complete answers to this paper and submit all three to your instructor.

# Lab Assignment 8.4.2

**Name:**                                                                 **Date:**

**Course:**                          **Section:**                          **Data CD Number:**

1.  Start a Minitab session. If you are unable to complete this lab assignment in one Minitab session, save the project as Lab 8-4-2 . **Never** use a period as part of the project name; since Minitab uses the period to attach the file type to the file name. Then at your next Minitab session, you may open this Lab 8-4-2.MPJ project and continue to work where you left off previously.

2.  The Camera.dat raw data file is stored on your data disc and contains data for two text variables - PhotoHouse and MegaCam - as described next. A popular consumer advocacy group collects data about consumer satisfaction with major companies. One study was conducted to compare follow-up customer service at large "brick and mortar" stores with the same service from "on line only" sellers. A random sample of people who purchased digital cameras from the PhotoHouse Superstore (a brick and mortar store) was taken, and three months after the purchase date, they were asked if they were satisfied with the costumer service. An independent random sample of people who purchased digital camera over the internet from the MegaCam (an on line only operation) was taken, and three months after the purchase date, they were asked if they were satisfied with the costumer service. Name two columns PhotoHouse and MegaCam, and then import the two columns of data from the Camera.dat raw data file into these two columns. At the 0.05 significance level, test to see if there is any difference in the proportions of consumers who are satisfied with follow up customer service at these two types of companies.

3.  A market consultant wants to know if consumers loyalty to a specific brand name is different for food products than it is for non-food products. As an example the consultant used margarine versus paper towels. A random sample of 40 consumers of margarine were asked if they always buy the same brand, or whether they buy whichever brand is available and or cheapest. An independent random sample of 37 consumers of paper towels were asked the same question. Consumers who answered always buy the same brand were coded as "L" for loyalty, while those who answered any brand were coded as "X." The results are shown below.

    Margarine :  L, L, L, L, X, L, L, L, X, L, L, L, X, L, L, X, X, L, L, L, X, L, L, L, L, L, X, L, X, L, L, L, X, L, L, L, X, L, X and L

    Paper Towels:  X, X, L, X, L, X, L, L, X, L, L, L, X, L, X, X, L, X, L, L, X, X, X, L, L, X, L, X, L, L, X, L, L, X, X, L and X

    Use a 0.05 level of significance to test if the consumers of margarine are more loyal to their specific brand than are the consumers of paper towels.

(lab assignment is continued on the second side of this page)

317

4. Open a worksheet using the Cespud.mtw from your data disc. As described in Lab Assignment 5.1.2, the Cespud.mtw worksheet contains data from the U.S. Department of Labor conducts Consumer Expenditure Surveys about U.S. households. A sample from the 1972 survey was taken and the following five variables were recorded: (i) age of head of household, (ii) marital status of head of household, (iii) total household income after taxes, (iv) spending on food and clothing, and (v) spending on shelter (rent, utilities, mortgages, etc.). Compute the means of the total household income and the spending on shelter variables. With $\alpha = 0.05$, test to see if there is a difference between the proportion all household in 1972 whose total income is above average and the proportion of all households in 1972 who spend more than average on shelter. Name two new columns as "T>Avg" and "S>Avg" and use the Code menu item appropriately.

5. It is commonly believed that women are more conscious of their physical appearance than are men, and thus a small proportion of America women seem to be obese. Conway and Barth believed that this was driven by the social climate of Twentieth Century, and were curious to find out if the same social force was at work in the Twenty-first century. In June of 2008, they took a random sample of 2000 American men and found 219 of them were obese. In an independent sample of 2300 American women, they found 224 were obese. At the 0.10 level of significance, is the proportion of 21st Century American women who are obese still smaller than the corresponding proportion of American men?

6. For people married for a long time, the death of a spouse is devastating. A local mental health agency was interested in determining if this effected men and women differently, and two independent random samples were taken from widows and widowers who were married for at least 40 years before the death of their spouses. The first sample consisted of 125 widow (women) and the second sample consisted of 85 widowers (men). In all cases the surviving spouses were in good physical health at the time of their spouse's death. The agency kept track of each person in the two samples for a period of three years or until the person died. Of the 125 women, 97 were still living after three years; and of the 85 men, 56 were still alive after three years. The mental health agency hypothesized that women are better prepared for life without their spouses, and therefore are more like to continue living for at least 3 years, than are men. Do these data support that theory? Use a 0.05 level of significance.

7. Print your Session Window to the printer.

8. Attach both your Minitab output and your complete answers to this paper and submit all three to your instructor.

# CHAPTER 9: Analysis of Variance (ANOVA)

**Section 1:    One-Way Analysis of Variance - The Completely Randomized Design**

When the variable is a continuous type of measurement, testing the hypothesis about the equality of two population means is described in Section 1 of Chapter 8. Analysis of variance is the statistical technique that generalizes this procedure to testing the hypothesis about the equality of two or more population means. The populations are identified by different values (often called levels) of a single factor (often called the "treatment variable"). Each of the multiple populations is considered a level of the factor (or treatment). For example, a researcher wants to test if there are any differences in the average production from workers under three different types of management expectation: none, moderate, and high. Here the factor is management expectation. The "none", "moderate", "high" are the different levels of this factor indicating that there are three different populations being analyzed: (1) all workers with no management expectation, (2) all workers with a moderate expectation from management, and (3) all workers with a high expectation from management.

A "Completely Randomized Design" occurs when independent samples are taken from each of the multiple populations, and the means of these populations are compared using the statistical technique of **one-way analysis of variance**, usually referred to as **ANOVA**.

The analysis of variance hypothesis test for comparing the means of **c** different populations may be written as

$$H_0: \mu_1 = \mu_2 = \mu_3 = ... = \mu_c$$
$$H_a: \text{At least two of the } \mu_i\text{s are different}$$

The average of the **c** population means is called the "grand mean" and is symbolized by $\mu$. Each population mean may be considered as a deviation from this grand mean and represented as

$$\mu_i = \mu + \tau_i \qquad \text{for i = 1, 2, 3, ... , c}$$

where the $\tau_i$s are called the treatment effects. If all of the population means are equal, then all of the $\tau_i$s must be equal to zero (0). And so an alternative form of the hypothesis test is

$$H_0: \tau_1 = \tau_2 = \tau_3 = ... = \tau_c = 0$$
$$H_a: \text{At least one } \tau_i \text{ not equal to 0}$$

A random sample is taken from each population. The statistical techniques and conclusions of one-way analysis of variance depend upon the validity of the following two assumptions:

(1)    each population is normally distributed and

(2)    the variances of all populations are equal; that is $\sigma_1^2 = \sigma_2^2 = \sigma_3^2 = \ldots = \sigma_c^2$; this property is called "homogeneity of variance."

Many textbooks differentiate between the "Fixed Effects" model where the different populations sampled are the <u>only</u> populations of interest, and the "Random Effects" model where the different populations sampled were themselves randomly selected from a larger entire set of populations. For the "Fixed Effects" model; if large sample sizes are used, the results of one-way analysis of variance are relatively unaffected by violations of assumption (1), and when all of the samples are of the same size, the results of one-way analysis of variance are relatively unaffected by violations of assumption (2).

In the "Random Effects" model the null hypothesis of equal means, given on the previous page, must be augmented with the statement that the population standard deviation of the treatment effects equals zero ($\sigma_\tau = 0$); that is, there are no differences among the treatment effects of the entire set of populations of interest. Since the hypotheses are more general for this model, violations of either or both of these assumptions may seriously affect the correctness of any inferences. Therefore, it is always advisable to check both assumptions (1) and (2), especially when small and/or unequal sample sizes are used. The computations are the same for both models when the design is a one-way analysis of variance. All of the examples used in this section are "Fixed Effects" models.

Example 9.1:   Three random samples of four workers each were subjected to different levels of management expectation: none, moderate, and high. The production of each worker is given in the following table:

| None | Moderate | High |
|------|----------|------|
| 1    | 3        | 6    |
| 2    | 5        | 10   |
| 1    | 4        | 7    |
| 4    | 6        | 7    |

Enter these data directly into the Worksheet Window and name these three variables: None, Moderate and High.

Your Worksheet Window should like the graphic below.

| ↓ | C1 | C2 | C3 |
|---|------|----------|------|
|   | None | Moderate | High |
| 1 | 1 | 3 | 6 |
| 2 | 2 | 5 | 10 |
| 3 | 1 | 4 | 7 |
| 4 | 4 | 6 | 7 |

Worksheet 1 ***

Once the data have been entered **into separate columns** and **if the two required assumptions are known to be valid**, Minitab is able to perform a simple, unstacked one-way analysis of variance. However; since these assumptions are rarely known to be valid ahead of time, and since post-hoc multiple comparisons (which are explained later in this section) can not be performed on the data that is stored in separate columns, this workbook will present only the more general method of performing the analysis of variance computations.

In order to use the more general method and to compute the multiple comparison procedures, Minitab expects: (a) all samples' data to be in just one (new) column, and (b) the corresponding sample identification or levels of the factor to be in a second (new) column. The levels will be the column names. But if the columns have not been named, the levels will be consecutive whole numbers (1, 2, 3, ...) corresponding to the order of how the variables are entered in the stacking box. This is called stacking the data and is done as follows. In general you should name columns before you use them, so name the C4 column as AllData as a reminder that this new variable contains all of the data stacked into one column. The C5 column should be named Factor since this represents the different levels of the factor (or "treatment variable").

Click on *Data , Stack , Columns ...*

In the Stack Columns dialog box: the cursor will be in the box under the *Stack the following columns:*. Block the columns that contain the data for each of the samples (hold the ⬛ **Ctrl** ⬛ key and click on each variable or drag the mouse over the variables, if consecutive) and click on the ⬛ **Select** ⬛ button. Next click on the button to the left of *Column of current worksheet:* and then click inside of the box to its right. Highlight the AllData variable and click on ⬛ **Select** ⬛ . Then cursor will be inside the box to the right of *Store subscripts in:*, highlight the Factor variable and click on ⬛ **Select** ⬛ . **If** the columns with the original data have been named, make sure the box to the left of *Use variable names in subscript column* is checked. But if the columns with the original data have **not** been named, click on this box to **un**check it. Click on ⬛ **OK** ⬛ .

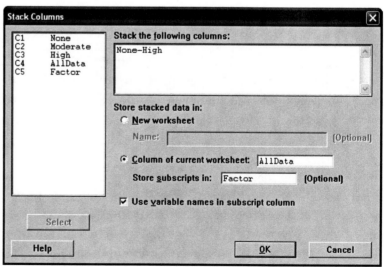

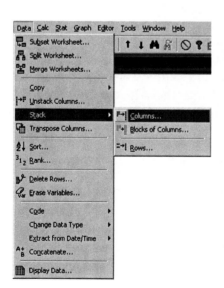

Example 9.2: Use the data in the current worksheet. Name the new variables AllData and Factor, and combine the three samples' data so that all of the data are in the AllData variable and the sample identification numbers (levels) are in the Factor variable. Then display all of the variables on the screen.

Click on *Data , Stack , Columns ...*

In the Stack Columns dialog box: the cursor will be in the box under the *Stack the following columns:*. Block the None (C1), Moderate (C2) and High (C3) columns that contain the data for each of the samples (hold the ⊡ **Ctrl** key and click on each variable or drag the mouse over the variables, if consecutive) and click on the ⊡ **Select** button. Next click on the button to the left of *Column of current worksheet:* and then click inside of the box to its right. Highlight the AllData variable and click on ⊡ **Select** . Then cursor will be inside the box to the right of *Store subscripts in:*, highlight the Factor variable and click on ⊡ **Select** . Since the columns with the original data have been named, make sure the box to the left of *Use variable names in subscript column* is checked. Click on ⊡ **OK** .

Then use the *Data , Display Data ...* menu item, block all five variables and click on the *Select* button. The data will be displayed in the Session Window as shown below.

| ROW | None | Moderate | High | AllData | Factor |
|-----|------|----------|------|---------|----------|
| 1 | 1 | 3 | 6 | 1 | None |
| 2 | 2 | 5 | 10 | 2 | None |
| 3 | 1 | 4 | 7 | 1 | None |
| 4 | 4 | 6 | 7 | 4 | None |
| 5 | | | | 3 | Moderate |
| 6 | | | | 5 | Moderate |
| 7 | | | | 4 | Moderate |
| 8 | | | | 6 | Moderate |
| 9 | | | | 6 | High |
| 10 | | | | 10 | High |
| 11 | | | | 7 | High |
| 12 | | | | 7 | High |

The data in sample 1 (None C1), sample 2 (Moderate C2) and sample 3 (High C3) have been stacked upon each other in the listed order and stored into the AllData column. The corresponding factor levels (None, Moderate and High) have been stored in the Factor column.

Once the data have been combined into one new variable, you are ready to begin the Analysis of Variance process. The two assumptions given at the top of page 260 upon which analysis of variance depends must be verified. Assumption (1) is that each population is normally distributed. In order to verify this first assumption, you first must compute the residual variable. This is the difference of each score in a sample and the respective sample mean. The residuals are computed in the following way.

Click on *Stat , ANOVA , One-way ...*

In the One-way Analysis of Variance dialog box: the cursor will be in the *Response:* box; click on the variable that contains the stacked data (AllData) and click on ⬚ **Select** . The cursor will move to the *Factor:* box; click on the variable (Factor) that contains the levels of the factor (where the subscripts are stored) and click on ⬚ **Select** . If the square to the left of *Store residuals* is **not checked, click on the square to check this option.** A **new** column to the right of the last column in your worksheet will **automatically** be created **and** be named RESI1. These residual values will be used to check the validity of the assumption that the populations are normally distributed. You may ignore the value in the box to the right of *Confidence level:*. Then click on ⬚ **OK** .

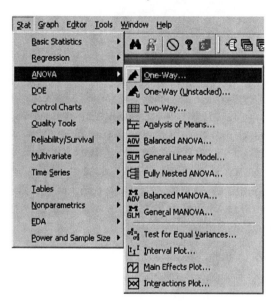

For now we will ignore the output in the Session Window and just concentrate on the resulting residuals. In the current Worksheet Window, column C6 will be named RESI1 and contains the residuals for each score.

Example 9.3: Use the data in the current worksheet and do the analysis of variance procedure to compute the residuals.

Click on *Stat , ANOVA , One-way ...*

In the One-way Analysis of Variance dialog box: the cursor will be in the *Response:* box; click on the C4 (AllData) variable and click on ⬚ **Select** . The cursor will move to the *Factor:* box; click on the C5 (Factor) variable that contains the levels of the factor and click on ⬚ **Select** . If the square to the left of *Store residuals* is **not checked, click on the square to check this option.** A new column numbered C6 will **automatically** be created **and** be named RESI1. Then click on the ⬚ **OK** button.

(continued on the next page)

Ignore the output in the Session Window. In the current Worksheet Window, column C6 will be named RESI1 and contains the residuals for each score. Your Worksheet Window should look like the graphic below.

| ↓ | C1 None | C2 Moderate | C3 High | C4 AllData | C5-T Factor | C6 RESI1 |
|---|---|---|---|---|---|---|
| 1 | 1 | 3 | 6 | 1 | None | -1.0 |
| 2 | 2 | 5 | 10 | 2 | None | 0.0 |
| 3 | 1 | 4 | 7 | 1 | None | -1.0 |
| 4 | 4 | 6 | 7 | 4 | None | 2.0 |
| 5 | | | | 3 | Moderate | -1.5 |
| 6 | | | | 5 | Moderate | 0.5 |
| 7 | | | | 4 | Moderate | -0.5 |
| 8 | | | | 6 | Moderate | 1.5 |
| 9 | | | | 6 | High | -1.5 |
| 10 | | | | 10 | High | 2.5 |
| 11 | | | | 7 | High | -0.5 |
| 12 | | | | 7 | High | -0.5 |

Assumption (1), that each population is normally distributed, may be verified by graphing a **Q-Q plot**. This graph uses the residual values (computed by the one-way analysis of variance) on the horizontal axis and the standard normalized values of these residuals on the y axis. After the residuals are sorted into increasing order; for each individual residual, the percentage of all of the residuals that are less than this residual is computed. This percentage is sometimes called the quantile. The standard normalized scores are values of Z that have the same quantile as the corresponding residual. This is why the graph is called a **Q-Q plot**. If each residual quantile is equal (or almost equal) to each corresponding standard normal quantile, the graph will be approximately a straight line. The Q-Q plot is graphed as follows.

Click on *Stat , Basic Statistics , Normality Test...*

In the Normality Test dialog box: the cursor will be in the box to the right of *Variable:* click on the RESI1 variable (the automatically named column that contains the residual values) and click on the | Select | button. Under the heading of *Percentile lines*, the button to the left of *None* should be chosen. Make sure that under the *Tests for Normality* that the *Anderson-Darling* choice is marked. Next click inside of the *Title:* box and type Q-Q Plot, but remember do **not** press the | Enter | key. Then click on the | OK | button.

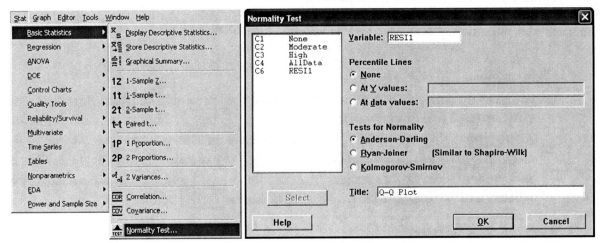

324

The resulting graph will appear in a separate Graphic Window titled Q-Q Plot. In addition to the actual Q-Q plot, the results of the Anderson-Darling test for normality will be given. This test essentially is

> $H_0$: the population of scores **is** normally distributed
> $H_a$: the population of scores is **not** normally distributed
> $\alpha = 0.10$.

The AD test statistic and corresponding p-value are given in this Graphic Window. If the p-value is greater than 0.10, we usually do **not** reject the null hypothesis, so we have no reason to doubt the validity of assumption (1). However; if this p-value is less than or equal to 0.10, the null hypothesis **is** rejected, and assumption (1) is **not** validated.

> Example 9.4 Use the data in the current worksheet and check the validity of assumption (1) by graphing the Q-Q plot and testing for normality. Use a 0.10 significance level.

The hypothesis testing problem is

$H_0$: the population of scores **is** normally distributed
$H_a$: the population of scores is **not** normally distributed
$\alpha = 0.10$

and the test statistic is labeled AD.

Click on *Stat* , *Basic Statistics* , *Normality Test...*

In the Normality Test dialog box: the cursor will be in the box to the right of *Variable:* click on the RESI1 variable and click on the | Select | button. Under the heading of *Percentile lines*, the button to the left of *None* should be chosen. Make sure that under the *Tests for Normality* that the *Anderson-Darling* choice is marked. Next click inside of the *Title:* box and type Q-Q Plot, but remember do **not** press the | Enter | key. Then click on | OK | .

You may need to "maximize" the Graphic Window in order to clearly read the AD test statistic and p-value. The resulting Graphic Window Q-Q Plot is shown below.

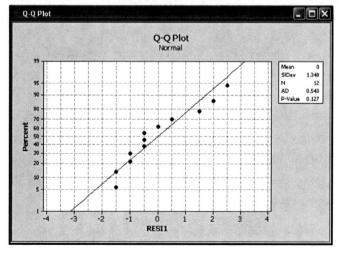

(continued on the next page)

325

Since the p-value of 0.127 is greater than 0.10, you may not reject the null hypothesis of normality, and so you may conclude that assumption (1) **is** valid. Also notice that the points in the graph are close to the superimposed straight line that Minitab draws for comparison.

Analysis of variance also assumes that although different samples may come from populations with different means, they have the same variance. This is Assumption 2 shown at the top of page 260. The effect of unequal variances upon inferences depends in part upon whether your model includes fixed or random effects, disparities in sample sizes, and the choice of multiple comparison procedure. The ANOVA F-test is only slightly affected by inequality of variance if the model contains fixed factors only and has equal sample sizes. F-tests involving random effects may be substantially affected, however. So it is advisable to test the validity of the equal variance assumption. Depending upon the results of the test for normally distributed populations; i.e.; assumption (1), the equal variance assumption (2) may be verified by the either **Bartlett's** or the modified **Levene's** test for homogeneity of variance. When assumption (1) of normality **is** verified, Bartlett's test should be used. But if assumption (1) of normality is **not** verified, Levene's test should be used. In either case the hypotheses for testing homogeneity of variance, assumption (2), may be setup as

$$H_0: \sigma_1^2 = \sigma_2^2 = \sigma_3^2 = ... = \sigma_c^2$$
$$H_a: \text{at least two } \sigma_i^2 \text{ are different}$$
$$\alpha = 0.10 \quad (\text{usually}).$$

If the p-value for this test is greater than the pre-selected level of significance, usually 0.10; the null hypothesis of equal variances (homogeneity) may not be rejected, and thus assumption (2) is verified. But if the p-value is less than or equal to $\alpha$; then the null hypothesis is rejected, assumption (2) is **not** valid. If either or both of the assumptions are not valid then analysis of variance must be used with caution, if at all. A nonparametric approach using the Kruskal-Wallis test may be the appropriate technique for analyzing the data.

Both the Bartlett's and Levene's test statistics and corresponding p-values are computed using the *Test for Equal Variances* procedure. These are computed as follows.

Click on *Stat , ANOVA , Test for Equal Variances...*

In the Test for Equal Variances dialog box: the cursor will be in the box to the right of *Response:*. Click on the AllData variable (that contains the stacked data) and click on the Select button. The cursor will move to the large box to the right of *Factors:*, click on the Factor variable (that contains the corresponding levels of the stacked data in AllData) and then click on the Select button. You may ignore the boxes to the right of *Confidence level:* and *Title:*. Then click on the OK button.

(See graphics on the next page.)

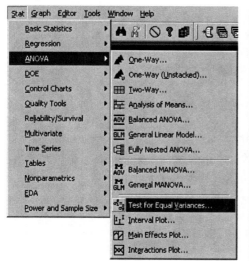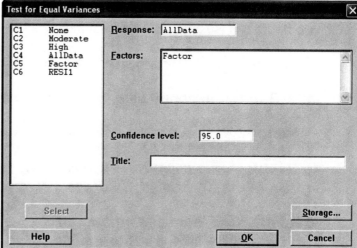

The output of the *Test for Equal Variances* (or *Homogeneity of Variance*) procedure contains:

(1) Simultaneous Bonferroni confidence intervals for the population standard deviations,
(2) the Bartlett's (for normal distributions) F test statistic and p-value,
(3) the Levene's (for any continuous distribution) test statistic and p-value, and
(4) a Graphic Window, labeled *Test for Equal Variances: AllData versus Factor* containing the same information.

Even though the test results are most easily read from the Graphic Window, since it is active and appears on top after the *Test of Equal Variances* is completed; there is no need to print this Graphic Window since the same information appears in the Session Window and will be printed when you print the Session Window.

Example 9.5: For the data in the current worksheet the assumption (1) of normality was verified in Example 9.4, so use Bartlett's test to check the validity of assumption (2), that the variances of the three populations are all equal. Use a 0.10 level of significance.

The hypothesis testing problem is

$H_0$: $\sigma_1^2 = \sigma_2^2 = \sigma_3^2$
$H_a$: at least two $\sigma_i^2$ are different
$\alpha = 0.10$ .

Click on *Stat , ANOVA , Test for Equal Variances...*

In the Test for Equal Variances dialog box: the cursor will be in the box to the right of *Response:*. Click on the AllData variable and click on the ⬛ **Select** button. The cursor will move to the large box to the right of *Factors:*, click on the Factor variable and then click on the ⬛ **Select** button. Then click on the ⬛ **OK** button.

(continued on the next page)

The results shown below will appear in the Session Window and the Test for Equal Variances: AllData versus Factor Graphic Window is shown after this below.

## Test for Equal Variances: AllData versus Factor

### 95% Bonferroni confidence intervals for standard deviations

| Factor | N | Lower | StDev | Upper |
|---|---|---|---|---|
| High | 4 | 0.875604 | 1.73205 | 9.42026 |
| Moderate | 4 | 0.652637 | 1.29099 | 7.02145 |
| None | 4 | 0.714928 | 1.41421 | 7.69161 |

**Bartlett's Test (normal distribution)**
**Test statistic = 0.24, p-value = 0.886**

**Levene's Test (any continuous distribution)**
**Test statistic = 0.00, p-value = 1.000**

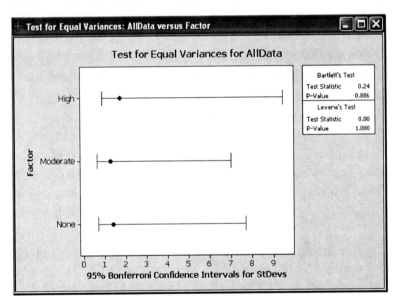

Since the p-value for the Bartlett's test of 0.886 is greater than $\alpha = 0.10$; you may not reject the null hypothesis of homogeneity of variance, and thus assumption (2) is verified.

Once the two assumptions have been verified, you may analyze and interpret the results of the one-way analysis of variance. However, statisticians have shown that analysis of variance is a fairly robust testing procedure. That is; even if the assumptions are not verified, the results still may be approximately correct under certain conditions. If assumption (1) of normality is **not** verified, but each sample size is greater than or equal to 30; ANOVA is robust, and you may proceed as if assumption (1) was verified. In this latter case, assumption (2) of homogenity of variance would be tested using Levene's test instead of Bartlett's test. If assumption (2) of homogeneity of variance is **not** verified, but each sample is the exact same size; ANOVA with Fixed Effects is robust, and you may proceed to use the Analysis of Variance results. The Analysis of Variance computations are done by

Click on *Stat , ANOVA , One-way ...*

In the One-way Analysis of Variance dialog box: the cursor will be in the *Response:* box; click on the variable that contains the stacked data (AllData) and click on Select . The cursor will move to the *Factor:* box; click on the variable (Factor) that contains the level numbers of the factor (where the subscripts are stored) and click on Select . If the square to the left of *Store residuals* **is checked**, click on the square to **uncheck this option.** If you forget to uncheck this box, a new column to the right of the last column (RESI1) in your worksheet will **automatically** be created **and** be named RESI2. This will not effect any of the computations, but an extra column, that is identical to the RESI1 column, will be created in your worksheet. You may ignore the value in the box to the right of *Confidence level:*. Then click on **OK** . **Note** that since Minitab remembers the previous entries used in a dialog box, the only thing you will actually need to do is to uncheck the *Store residuals* option.

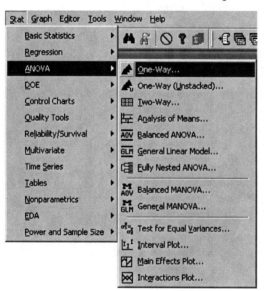
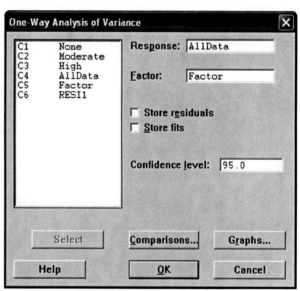

The output of the One-way Analysis of Variance computation contains:

(1) the ANOVA table with the following headings:
    (a) Source = source of variation (Factor, Error, Total),
    (b) DF = degrees of freedom for each source,
    (c) SS = sum of squares for each source,
    (d) MS = mean square for the factor and error sources of variation,
    (e) F = value of the F test statistic and
    (f) p = the p-value of the test,

(2) the pooled sample standard deviation (an estimate of the common population standard deviation), R-sq and R-sq (adj) - you may ignore these last two values,

(3) the sample size, mean and standard deviation for each sample (level),

(4) the graph of 95% confidence intervals for each level population mean $\mu_i$ or a different percent if you changed the *Confidence level:* in the One Way Analysis of Variance dialog box, and

(5) the pooled standard deviation is repeated at the bottom of the output.

The sources of variation are always labeled Factor (assuming that you have named the column containing the factor levels that way), Error and Total. The levels for each confidence interval are labeled with the different values in the Factor column of the worksheet in alphabetical order. These will be the original data column names (if you named those columns and checked the box to the left of *Use variable names in subscript column* in the *Data , Stack , Columns* procedure. If you did not check that box, the levels under the Factor1 heading will be 1 , 2 , 3 , etc.

Example 9.6:  For the data in the current worksheet, test the hypothesis that the mean production is the same for all workers under each of the three management expectation styles.  Use a 0.05 level of significance.

Population 1 is all workers with no management expectation, and is level None of the Factor.

Population 2 is all workers with a moderate expectation from management, and is level Moderate of the Factor.

Population 3 is all workers with a high expectation from management, and is level High of the Factor.

The hypothesis testing problem is

$H_0$: $\mu_1 = \mu_2 = \mu_3$
$H_a$: At least two of the $\mu_i$s are different
$\alpha = 0.05$ .

Click on *Stat , ANOVA , One-way ...*

In the One-way Analysis of Variance dialog box: the cursor will be in the *Response:* box; click on the variable that contains the stacked data (AllData) and click on $\boxed{\textbf{Select}}$ . The cursor will move to the *Factor:* box; click on the variable (Factor) that contains the level numbers of the factor (where the subscripts are stored) and click on $\boxed{\textbf{Select}}$ . If the square to the left of *Store residuals* **is checked**, click on the square to **un**check this option. If you forget to uncheck this box, a new column to the right of the last column (RESI1) in your worksheet will **automatically** be created **and** be named RESI2. This will not effect any of the computations, but an extra column, that is identical to the RESI1 column, will be created in your worksheet. You may ignore the value in the box to the right of *Confidence level:*.  Then click on $\boxed{\textbf{OK}}$ .  **Note** that since Minitab remembers the previous entries used in a dialog box, the only thing you will actually need to do is to uncheck the *Store residuals* option.

The results shown on the next page will appear in the Session Window.

(continued on the next page)

## One-way ANOVA: AllData versus Factor

| Source | DF | SS | MS | F | p |
|--------|----|----|----|----|----|
| Factor | 2 | 60.67 | 30.33 | 13.65 | 0.002 |
| Error | 9 | 20.00 | 2.22 | | |
| Total | 11 | 80.67 | | | |

**S = 1.491   R-Sq = 75.21%   R-Sq(adj) = 69.70%**

Individual 95% CIs For Mean Based On
Pooled StDev

| Level | N | Mean | StDev | |
|-------|---|------|-------|---|
| High | 4 | 7.500 | 1.732 | (------*------) |
| Moderate | 4 | 4.500 | 1.291 | (------*------) |
| None | 4 | 2.000 | 1.414 | (------*------) |

```
                                    ---------+---------+---------+---------+
                                            2.5       5.0       7.5      10.0
```

**Pooled StDev = 1.491**

Since the p-value of 0.002 is less than $\alpha = 0.05$, you may reject the null hypothesis and conclude that at least two of the $\mu_i$s are different. Note that the value of the F test statistic, with 2 and 9 degrees of freedom, is 13.65; and this is in the rejection region ($F \geq 4.26$).

When the analysis of variance test indicates that you are to reject the null hypothesis, as in the previous example, the question of which population means are different from each other naturally arises. One method is to examine the 95% confidence intervals shown above that are produced by the *Stat, ANOVA, One-way...* computations. In Example 9.6 just done; since the 95% confidence intervals for $\mu_1$ (none) and $\mu_3$ (High) do not overlap, you may conclude that $\mu_1$ is different from $\mu_3$. However, since the 95% confidence interval for $\mu_2$ (Moderate) overlaps the intervals for both $\mu_1$ and $\mu_3$, you would need to further investigate whether or not $\mu_2$ is different from either $\mu_1$ or $\mu_3$. Techniques called multiple comparisons attempt to answer this question. While statisticians have developed many different numerical procedures for making these comparisons, this chapter will discuss three methods that may be computed using Minitab: Fisher's LSD (least significant difference) method, Tukey's HSD (honestly significant difference) method, and Dunnett's method.

Briefly, once you know that at least two of the $\mu_i$s are different, multiple comparisons involve comparing many different combinations of two (or more) population means. For example, if there were three populations, we could test to see if $\mu_1 = \mu_2$, $\mu_1 = \mu_3$ and $\mu_2 = \mu_3$. A separate test can be done for each comparison with its *individual error rate*, which sets the *critical point* (rejection region) with this level of significance for the specific comparison. But since the different comparisons overlap and utilize some of the same data, the complete set of comparisons has a *family error rate*, often called the *experimentwise error rate*. This family error rate sets the critical point with this level of significance for the complete set of comparisons. The family error rate is always larger than the individual error rate; but since we are usually interested in examining all of the different comparisons and not just an individual specific comparison, the family error rate is usually the one we use.

Fisher's LSD method compares all possible pairs of population means, it lets **you control the individual error rate**, and it computes the family error rate appropriately. Use Fisher's LSD method when you are interested in making just one specific comparison, or in a screening situation where you do not want to miss rejecting a true alternative hyposthesis due to a possible Type II error.. Tukey's HSD method also compares all possible pairs of population means, it lets **you control the family error rate**, and it computes the individual error rate appropriately. Thus use Tukey's HSD multiple comparisons when you are interested in examining the complete set of pairwise comparisons among the population means, or in a situation where it is important that you minimize the possibility of any Type I errors in the group of decisions. Dunnett's method compares a specific *control* population mean with the mean of each of the other populations, it lets **you control the family error rate**, and it computes the individual error rate appropriately. Use Dunnett's multiple comparisons when you are interested in comparing the mean of the *control* population with the mean of each of the other populations.

In those problems where you **have rejected the null hypotheses** that all of the $\mu_i$s are equal, you may compute the multiple comparisons by using the *Comparisons* feature of the *one-way...* analysis of variance. Once the analysis of variance has been done once and the residuals have been computed, it is not necessary to repeat the residual computations. So you should click on the box to the left of *Store residuals* to uncheck this option whenever doing the multiple comparisons. If you forget, no harm is done, but you will get additional columns automatically computed and named RESI2, RESI3 etc. These will be equivalent to the RESI1 column.

When computing the Dunnett's multiple comparisons, you also must enter the both the **family error rate** and the factor's level that corresponds to the *control* population. If the levels of the Factor variable are words (text data), you must enclose the level within quotation marks, but if the levels are simply numbers, than type in the number without quotation marks.

Click on *Stat , ANOVA , One-way ...*

In the One-way Analysis of Variance dialog box: *Select* AllData as the *Response:* and Factor as the *Factor:* (these probably will already be selected from the first time you did the analysis). If the square to the left of *Store residuals* is **checked, click on the square to <u>uncheck</u> this option.** Then click on the | Comparisons... | button.

In the One-way Multiple Comparisons dialog box: click on the square to the left of *Dunnett's, family error rate:* to check this option. Make sure that all other options are **unchecked.** Click inside of the box to the right of *Dunnett's, family error rate:*, delete any value currently in this box and type in the desired family error rate. Next click inside the box to the right of *Control group level:* and type in the level of the "control group" - remember to enclose text data with quotations marks). Then click on the | OK | button.

In the One-way Analysis of Variance dialog box: click on the | OK | button.

(See graphics on the next page.)

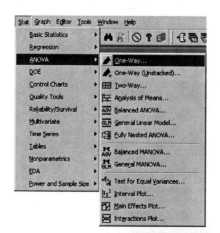
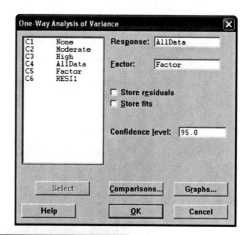
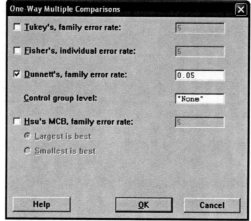

The output for Dunnett's multiple comparison procedure contains:

(1) the Family error rate,
(2) the Individual error rate,
(3) a Critical value, and
(4) Confidence Intervals for the difference of every **non**-*control* population mean minus the *control* population mean.

When computing the Fisher's LSD multiple comparisons, you must enter the **individual error rate**. But since there is no control group, you do not need to enter a control group level. The procedure is as follows.

Click on *Stat , ANOVA , One-way ...*

In the One-way Analysis of Variance dialog box: *Select* AllData as the *Response:* and Factor as the *Factor:* (these probably will already be selected from the first time you did the analysis). If the square to the left of *Store residuals* is **checked, click on the square to uncheck this option.** Then click on the Comparisons... button.

In the One-way Multiple Comparisons dialog box: click on the square to the left of *Fisher's, individual error rate:* to check this option. Make sure that all other options are **unchecked.** Click inside of the box to the right of *Fisher's, individual error rate:* , delete any value currently in this box, type in the desired **individual error rate**, and click on the OK button.

In the One-way Analysis of Variance dialog box: click on the OK button.

(See graphic on the next page).

333

Since the first two graphics are exactly the same for all three multiple comparison computations, only the actual One-Way Multiple Comparisons dialog box graphic will be shown below.

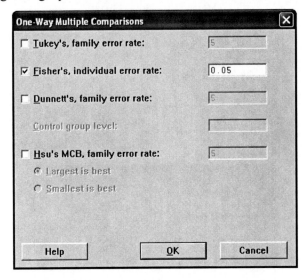

The output for Fisher's multiple comparison procedure contains:

(1) the Individual Confidence Interval level - **you must subtract this from 1.00 to get the Individual Error Rate**,

(2) the Simultaneous confidence level (this is the same as the Family confidence level) - **you must subtract this from 1.00 to get the Family Error Rate** and

(3) Confidence Intervals for the difference of **every possible pair** of population means - these are given in groups by taking each other Factor level minus the Factor level for that specific group (note that redundant pairs are not given).

When computing the Tukey's HSD multiple comparisons, you must enter the **family error rate**. The procedure is almost identical to the Fisher's procedure, except that you will check the box to the left of Tukey's and enter the family error rate.

Click on *Stat , ANOVA , One-way ...*   (graphic shown above)

In the One-way Analysis of Variance dialog box: *Select* AllData as the *Response:* and Factor as the *Factor:* (these probably will already be selected from the first time you did the analysis). If the square to the left of *Store residuals* is **checked, click on the square to uncheck this option.** Then click on the | **Comparisons...** | button.   (graphic shown above)

In the One-way Multiple Comparisons dialog box: click on the square to the left of *Tukey's, family error rate:* to check this option. Make sure that all other options are **unchecked**. Click inside of the box to the right of *Tukey's, family error rate:* , delete any value currently in this box, type in the desired family error rate, and click on the | **OK** | button.

In the One-way Analysis of Variance dialog box: click on the | **OK** | button.

(See graphic on the next page.)

Since the first two graphics are exactly the same for all three multiple comparison computations, only the actual One-Way Multiple Comparisons dialog box graphic will be shown below.

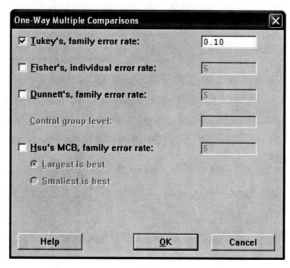

The output for Tukeys's multiple comparison procedure contains:

(1) the Simultaneous Confidence Interval level (this is the same as the Family confidence level) - **and so you must subtract this from 1.00 to get the Family Error Rate**,

(2) the Individual confidence level- **and so you must subtract this from 1.00 to get the Individual Error Rate** and

(3) Confidence Intervals for the difference of **every possible pair** of population means - these are given in groups by taking each other Factor level minus the Factor level for that specific group (note that redundant pairs are not given).

**Note that for all three of these methods, the error rate must be between 0.001 and 0.5 .** Otherwise Minitab will display an error message.

For all three multiple comparison methods the interpretation of the confidence interval and it relationship to the corresponding hypothesis test are the same. When the confidence interval **does contain zero**; then the difference of the two population means being compared may be equal to zero, and so the two population means are **not** significantly different. But when the confidence interval **does not contain zero**; then the difference of the two population means being compared are different than zero, and so the two population means being compared **are** significantly different.

Example 9.7: Use the data in the current worksheet. In examples 9.4 and 9.5, the two assumptions for analysis of variance have been verified. In example 9.6 , the analysis of variance has been done and the null hypothesis was rejected. In order to determine which population means are different, compute all pairwise multiple comparisons using Tukey's HSD method with a family error rate of 0.05 .

(continued on the next page)

Click on *Stat* , *ANOVA* , *One-way* ...

In the One-way Analysis of Variance dialog box: *Select* AllData as the *Response:* and Factor as the *Factor:* (these probably will already be selected from the first time you did the analysis). If the square to the left of *Store residuals* is **checked, click on the square to <u>un</u>check this option.** Then click on the | **Comparisons...** | button.

In the One-way Multiple Comparisons dialog box: click on the square to the left of *Tukey's, family error rate:* to check this option. Make sure that all other options are **unchecked.** Click inside of the box to the right of *Tukey's, family error rate:* , delete any value currently in this box, type in 0.05, the desired family error rate, and click on | **OK** | .

In the One-way Analysis of Variance dialog box: click on the | **OK** | button

The resulting output shown below will appear in the Session Window.


## One-way ANOVA: AllData versus Factor

| Source | DF | SS | MS | F | p |
|--------|----|----|----|----|----|
| Factor | 2 | 60.67 | 30.33 | 13.65 | 0.002 |
| Error | 9 | 20.00 | 2.22 | | |
| Total | 11 | 80.67 | | | |

S = 1.491  R-Sq = 75.21%  R-Sq(adj) = 69.70%

Individual 95% CIs For Mean Based On Pooled StDev

| Level | N | Mean | StDev | |
|-------|---|------|-------|---|
| | | | | ---------+---------+---------+---------+ |
| High | 4 | 7.500 | 1.732 | (------*------) |
| Moderate | 4 | 4.500 | 1.291 | (------*------) |
| None | 4 | 2.000 | 1.414 | (------*------) |
| | | | | ---------+---------+---------+---------+ |
| Pooled StDev = | | 1.491 | | 2.5       5.0       7.5       10.0 |

Tukey 95% Simultaneous Confidence Intervals
All Pairwise Comparisons among Levels of Factor

Individual confidence level = 97.91%

Factor = High subtracted from:

| Factor | Lower | Center | Upper | |
|--------|-------|--------|-------|---|
| | | | | ----+---------+---------+---------+------ |
| Moderate | -5.944 | -3.000 | -0.056 | (-------*--------) |
| None | -8.444 | -5.500 | -2.556 | (-------*--------) |
| | | | | ----+---------+---------+---------+------ |
| | | | | -7.0      -3.5       0.0       3.5 |

Factor = Moderate subtracted from:

| Factor | Lower | Center | Upper | |
|--------|-------|--------|-------|---|
| | | | | ----+---------+---------+---------+------ |
| None | -5.444 | -2.500 | 0.444 | (--------*-------) |
| | | | | ----+---------+---------+---------+------ |
| | | | | -7.0      -3.5       0.0       3.5 |

(continued on the next page)

The Simultaneous Confidence Interval level is shown as 95%. Subtracting 0.95 from 1.00 gives $1.00 - 0.95 = 0.05$, and this is the **given family error rate**. The Individual confidence level is shown as 97.91%. Subtracting 0.9791 from 1.00 gives $1.00 - 0.9791 = 0.0209$, and this is the **individual error rate**. Before interpreting the confidence intervals, remember that population 1 is the None level, population 2 is the Moderate level, and population 3 is the High level. The first group of confidence intervals is for the other levels minus the High level; and represent confidence intervals for $\mu_2 - \mu_3$ and $\mu_1 - \mu_3$; which in turn correspond to testing $H_0: \mu_2 = \mu_3$ and $H_0: \mu_1 = \mu_3$. The second group of confidence intervals is for the other levels minus the Moderate level; and represents the confidence interval for $\mu_1 - \mu_2$; which in turn correspond to testing $H_0: \mu_1 = \mu_2$. Note that the High - Moderate interval is redundant with the Moderate - High interval in the first group, and so is not computed in the second group.

The interval for $\mu_2 - \mu_3$ is from -5.944 to -0.056; and since this **does not** contain zero, you **do** reject $H_0: \mu_2 = \mu_3$. And so there **is** a significant difference between the mean production of the population of all workers with moderate expectation from management ($\mu_2$) and the mean production of all workers with high expectation from management ($\mu_3$).

The interval for $\mu_1 - \mu_3$ is from -8.444 to -2.556; and since this **does not** contain zero, you **do** reject $H_0: \mu_1 = \mu_3$. And so there **is** a significant difference between the mean production of the population of all workers with no management expectation ($\mu_1$) and the mean production of all workers with high expectation from management ($\mu_3$).

The interval for $\mu_1 - \mu_2$ is from -5.444 to 0.444, and since this **does** contain zero, you do **not** reject $H_0: \mu_1 = \mu_2$. And so there is **not** a significant difference between the mean production of the population of all workers with no management expectation ($\mu_1$) and the mean production of all workers with moderate expectation from management ($\mu_2$).

Note that even though the 95% confidence intervals for $\mu_2$ and $\mu_3$ overlap somewhat, Tukey's HSD method leads us to reject the comparison that $\mu_2 = \mu_3$. This illustrates the need for doing multiple comparisons when the analysis of variance leads to a rejection of the null hypothesis that all $\mu_i$s are equal and not rely solely on the graphs of the individual confidence interval shown in the first part of the Analysis of Variance output.

Example 9.8:  Use the data in the current worksheet. In examples 9.4 and 9.5, the two assumptions for analysis of variance have been verified. In example 9.6, the analysis of variance has been done and the null hypothesis was rejected. Consider the population of workers with no management expectation as the *control* group, and use Dunnett's method to compare the two different management expectation population means to the mean of the **control** population. Use a family error rate of 0.05.

The control group of no management expectation is level None.

(continued on the next page)

Click on *Stat* , *ANOVA* , *One-way* ...

In the One-way Analysis of Variance dialog box: *Select* AllData as the *Response:* and Factor as the *Factor:* (these probably will already be selected from the first time you did the analysis). If the square to the left of *Store residuals* is **checked, click on the square to <u>un</u>check this option.** Then click on the | **Comparisons...** | button.

In the One-way Multiple Comparisons dialog box: click on the square to the left of *Dunnett's, family error rate:* to check this option. Make sure that all other options are **unchecked.** Click inside of the box to the right of *Dunnett's, family error rate:* , delete any value currently in this box and type in 0.05, the desired family error rate. Next click inside the box to the right of *Control group subscript:* and type in "none" (don't forget the quotes) the level of the "control group." Then click on the | **OK** | button.

In the One-way Analysis of Variance dialog box: click on the | **OK** | button.

The results shown below will appear in the Session Window.


## One-way ANOVA: AllData versus Factor

| Source | DF | SS | MS | F | p |
|--------|----|----|----|----|----|
| Factor | 2 | 60.67 | 30.33 | 13.65 | 0.002 |
| Error | 9 | 20.00 | 2.22 | | |
| Total | 11 | 80.67 | | | |

S = 1.491    R-Sq = 75.21%    R-Sq(adj) = 69.70%

Individual 95% CIs For Mean Based On Pooled StDev

| Level | N | Mean | StDev | | | | |
|-------|---|------|-------|---|---|---|---|
| | | | | --------+---------+---------+---------+ | | | |
| High | 4 | 7.500 | 1.732 | | | (------*------) | |
| Moderate | 4 | 4.500 | 1.291 | | (------*------) | | |
| None | 4 | 2.000 | 1.414 | (------*------) | | | |
| | | | | --------+---------+---------+---------+ | | | |
| | | | | 2.5 | 5.0 | 7.5 | 10.0 |

Pooled StDev =    1.491

*Dunnett's comparisons with a control*

Family error rate = 0.0500
Individual error rate = 0.0281

Critical value = 2.61

Control = level (None) of Factor

| Level | Lower | Center | Upper | | | | |
|-------|-------|--------|-------|---|---|---|---|
| | | | | -+---------+---------+---------+--------- | | | |
| High | 2.745 | 5.500 | 8.255 | | (----------*----------) | | |
| Moderate | -0.255 | 2.500 | 5.255 | (----------*----------) | | | |
| | | | | -+---------+---------+---------+--------- | | | |
| | | | | 0.0 | 2.5 | 5.0 | 7.5 |

(continued on the next page)

The family error rate is given as 0.05 and the individual error rate is computed by Minitab as 0.0281. Fewer comparisons are done in Dunnett's method than in Tukey's HSD method; and so for the same family error rate, the individual error rate is larger when using Dunnett's method to compute multiple comparisons. Thus Dunnett's method is more sensitive (powerful) than Tukey's HSD method in finding actual differences between the control population mean and the other population means. Since Dunnett's method tests the comparisons of each **non**-control population mean against the control population mean, the Lower and Upper values give the endpoints of the confidence interval for testing $\mu_3 = \mu_1$ and $\mu_2 = \mu_1$ . These confidence intervals are shown graphically to the right of each numerical description.

The interval for $\mu_3 - \mu_1$ is from 2.745 to 8.255; and since this **does not** contain zero, you **do** reject $H_0$: $\mu_3 = \mu_1$ . And so there **is** a significance difference between the mean production of the population of all workers with high expectation from management ($\mu_3$) and the mean production of the (control) population of all workers with no management expectation ($\mu_1$).

The interval for $\mu_2 - \mu_1$ is from -0.255 to 5.255; and since this **does** contain zero, you do **not** reject $H_0$: $\mu_2 = \mu_1$ . And so there is **not** a significance difference between the mean production of the population of all workers with moderate expectation from management ($\mu_2$) and the mean production of the (control) population of all workers with no management expectation ($\mu_1$).

This section ends with a complete example that puts all of the steps together in one example.

Example 9.9: Open the worksheet Wellmar.mtw that is saved on your data disk. The Wellmar company sells its product throughout North America. Wellmar uses four modes of transportation: railroad, bus line, shipping, and airline. The company has derived an index that combines cost, damage and customer satisfaction for each mode of transportation. Larger index scores are more desirable. Two hundred orders were randomly assigned among these four methods of transportation; however, for this study the shipping method is to be excluded. At the 0.05 level of significance, test to see if there are any differences in the mean index values among any of the other three methods of transportation. **If the null hypothesis is rejected**, use Fisher's LSD method with a 0.025 individual error rate for doing multiple comparisons.

Use the *File , Open Worksheet...* to open the worksheet Wellmar.mtw from your data disk.

Population 1 is all orders sent by railroad, and so column C1 contains the data in the corresponding sample.

Population 2 is all orders sent by bus line, and so column C2 contains the data in the corresponding sample.

Population 3 is all orders sent by airline, and so column C4 contains the data in the corresponding sample.

(continued on the next page)

The hypothesis testing problem is

$H_0$: $\mu_1 = \mu_2 = \mu_3$
$H_a$: At least two of the $\mu_i$s are different
$\alpha = 0.05$ .

Erase the column names so that this example will show what happens when the original data is in columns that have not been named.

The first step is to name two new columns and stack the appropriate data. So in the name column C5 as AllData and name column C6 as Factor. While there are four columns of unstacked data, you will only be using columns 1, 2 and 4.

Click on *Data , Stack , Columns ...*
In the Stack Columns dialog box: press the [ **F3** ] key to clear all previous information. Now the cursor will be in the box under the *Stack the following columns:* block the Railroad (C1), Busline (C2) and Airline (C4) variables (hold the [ **Ctrl** ] key and click on each of the three variables) and then click on the [ **Select** ] button. Next click on the button to the left of *Column of current worksheet:* and then click inside of the box to its right. Highlight the AllData variable and click on [ **Select** ]. Then cursor will be inside the box to the right of *Store subscripts in:*, highlight the Factor variable and click on [ **Select** ]. Since the columns with the original data have **not** been named, make sure the box to the left of *Use variable names in subscript column* is **un**checked. Click on [ **OK** ].

For this example where the original data is are in **unnamed** columns, the Factor column in the worksheet contains 1's 2's and 3's. The 1 corresponds to the data from sample 1 which is in column C1, the 2 corresponds to the data from sample 2 which is in column C2, and the 3 corresponds to the data from sample 3 which is in column **C4**. Below is an excerpt of the worksheet showing rows 98 to 103.

**Wellmar.mtw** ***

| ↓ | C1 | C2 | C3 | C4 | C5 AllData | C6 Factor |
|---|---|---|---|---|---|---|
| 98 | | | | | 121.375 | 2 |
| 99 | | | | | 123.615 | 2 |
| 100 | | | | | 181.081 | 2 |
| 101 | | | | | 109.517 | 3 |
| 102 | | | | | 125.670 | 3 |
| 103 | | | | | 118.622 | 3 |

The second step is to check assumption (1) of normality. This is done by: (a) computing the residuals in the analysis of variance, but ignoring for now any output that appears in the Session Window; and (b) plotting the Q-Q plot and testing the null hypothesis $H_0$: the population is normally distributed by examining the Anderson-Darling p-value.

(continued on the next page)

Click on *Stat*, *ANOVA*, *One-way* ...

In the One-way Analysis of Variance dialog box: press the $\boxed{\textbf{F3}}$ key to clear all previous information. The cursor will be in the *Response:* box; click on the variable that contains the stacked data (AllData) and click on $\boxed{\textbf{Select}}$. The cursor will move to the *Factor:* box; click on the variable (Factor) that contains the level numbers of the factor (where the subscripts are stored) and click on $\boxed{\textbf{Select}}$. If the square to the left of *Store residuals* is **not checked, click on the square to check this option.** A **new** column to the right of the last column in your worksheet (C6) will **automatically** be created **and** be named RESI1. These residual values will be used to check the validity of the assumption that the populations are normally distributed. You may ignore the value in the box to the right of *Confidence level:*. Then click on $\boxed{\textbf{OK}}$.

The hypothesis testing problem is

$H_0$: the population of scores **is** normally distributed
$H_a$: the population of scores is **not** normally distributed
$\alpha = 0.10$.

Click on *Stat*, *Basic Statistics*, *Normality Test...*

In the Normality Test dialog box: press the $\boxed{\textbf{F3}}$ key to clear all previous information. The cursor will be in the box to the right of *Variable:* click on the RESI1 variable and click on the $\boxed{\textbf{Select}}$ button. Under the heading of *Percentile lines*, the button to the left of *None* should be chosen. Make sure that under the *Tests for Normality* that the *Anderson-Darling* choice is marked. Next click inside of the *Title:* box and type Q-Q Plot, but remember do **not** press the $\boxed{\textbf{Enter}}$ key. Then click on $\boxed{\textbf{OK}}$.

You may need to "maximize" the Graphic Window in order to clearly read the AD test statistic and the p-value. The Q-Q plot Graphic Window is shown below.

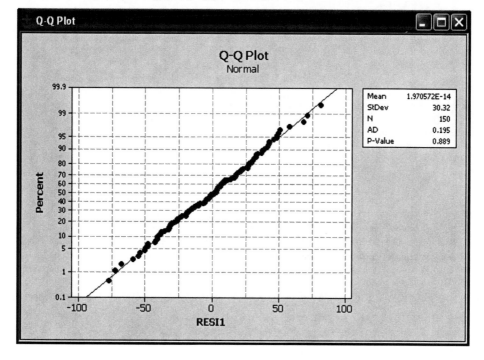

(continued on the next page)

Since the p-value of 0.889 is greater than 0.10, you may not reject the null hypothesis of normality, and so you may conclude that assumption 1 **is** valid. Also notice that the points in the graph are close to the superimposed straight line that Minitab draws for comparison.

Now minimize this Graphic Window.

The third step is to check assumption (2) of homogeneity of variance. This is done by testing the null hypothesis $H_0$: $\sigma_1^2 = \sigma_2^2 = \sigma_3^2$. Since the normality assumption has been verified, the homogeneity of variance hypothesis is tested using Bartlett's test.

The hypothesis testing problem is

$H_0$: $\sigma_1^2 = \sigma_2^2 = \sigma_3^2$
$H_a$: at least two $\sigma_i^2$ are different
$\alpha = 0.10$.

Click on *Stat*, *ANOVA*, *Test of Equal Variances...*

In the Test for Equal Variances dialog box: the cursor will be in the box to the right of *Response:*. Click on the AllData variable and click on the │ **Select** │ button. The cursor will move to the large box to the right of *Factors:*, click on the Factor variable and then click on the │ **Select** │ button. Then click on the │ **OK** │ button.

Only the results appearing in the resulting Test for Equal Variances: AllData versus Factor Graphic Window are shown below.

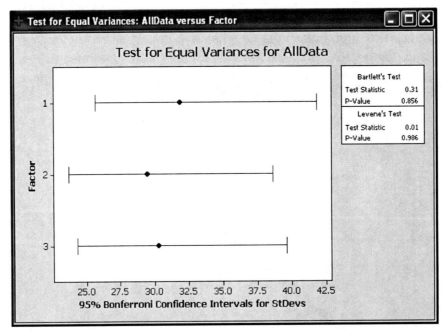

Since the Bartlett's test p-value of 0.856 is greater than the 0.10 significance level; you may **not** reject the null hypothesis, and thus assumption (2) of homogeneity of variance **is** verified.

(continued on the next page)

Now that both of the required assumptions for analysis of variance have been verified, the one way analysis of variance procedure is used to test the hypothesis testing problem of

$H_0$: $\mu_1 = \mu_2 = \mu_3$
$H_a$: At least two of the $\mu_i$s are different
$\alpha = 0.05$ .

Click on *Stat* , *ANOVA* , *One-way* ...

In the One-way Analysis of Variance dialog box: *Select* AllData as the *Response:* and Factor as the *Factor:* (these probably will already be selected from the first time you did the analysis). The square to the left of *Store residuals* should be **checked** from the last time, **so click on the square to <u>uncheck</u> this option.** You may ignore the value in the box to the right of *Confidence level:*. Then click on the | **OK** | button.

The results shown below will appear in the Session Window.

## *One-way ANOVA: AllData versus Factor*

**Analysis of Variance ON AllData**

| Source | DF | SS | MS | F | p |
|--------|-----|--------|------|------|-------|
| Factor | 2 | 7005 | 3503 | 3.76 | 0.026 |
| Error | 147 | 136963 | 932 | | |
| Total | 149 | 143968 | | | |

$S = 30.52$     $R\text{-}Sq = 4.87\%$     $R\text{-}Sq(adj) = 3.57\%$

**Individual 95% CIs For Mean Based On Pooled StDev**

| Level | N | Mean | StDev | |
|-------|----|--------|-------|---|
| | | | | ---------+---------+---------+---------+ |
| 1 | 50 | 166.46 | 31.85 | (-------*--------) |
| 2 | 50 | 149.76 | 29.46 | (--------*--------) |
| 3 | 50 | 157.14 | 30.22 | (--------*--------) |
| | | | | ---------+---------+---------+---------+ |
| Pooled StDev = | | 30.52 | | 150     160     170     180 |

In the analysis of variance table the p-value is 0.026, and this is less than 0.05, the given value of $\alpha$ in this hypothesis testing problem. So you may reject the null hypothesis of $H_0$: $\mu_1 = \mu_2 = \mu_3$ and conclude that at least two of the $\mu_i$s are different. Note that the value of the F test statistic, with 2 and 147 degrees of freedom, is 3.76; and this is in the rejection region ( $F \geq 3.07$ ).

Since the null hypothesis **has been rejected**, you may now perform all possible pairwise multiple comparisons using Fisher's LSD method.

(continued on the next page)

343

Click on *Stat , ANOVA , One-way ...*

In the One-way Analysis of Variance dialog box: *Select* AllData as the *Response:* and Factor as the *Factor:* (these probably will already be selected from the first time you did the analysis). If the square to the left of *Store residuals* is **checked, click on the square to <u>uncheck</u> this option.** Then click on the $\boxed{\textbf{Comparisons...}}$ button.

In the One-way Multiple Comparisons dialog box: click on the square to the left of *Fisher's, individual error rate:* to check this option. Make sure that all other options are **unchecked.** Click inside of the box to the right of *Fisher's, individual error rate:* , delete any value currently in this box, type in 0.025, the desired **individual error rate,** and click on the $\boxed{\textbf{OK}}$ button.

In the One-way Analysis of Variance dialog box: click on the $\boxed{\textbf{OK}}$ button.

In addition to the analysis of variance output shown above, the results of Fisher's multiple comparisons shown on the below also will appear in the Session Window.

### Fisher 97.5% Individual Confidence Intervals
### All Pairwise Comparisons among Levels of Factor

### Simultaneous confidence level = 93.59%

### Factor = 1 subtracted from:

```
Factor   Lower   Center   Upper   +---------+---------+---------+---------
2        -30.53  -16.70   -2.88   (--------*--------)
3        -23.14  -9.31    4.51            (--------*--------)
                                  +---------+---------+---------+---------
                                  -30       -15       0        15
```

### Factor = 2 subtracted from:

```
Factor   Lower   Center   Upper   +---------+---------+---------+---------
3        -6.44   7.39     21.21                     (--------*--------)
                                  +---------+---------+---------+---------
                                  -30       -15       0        15
```

In the first line of the above output, the 97.5% in ***Fisher 97.5% Individual Confidence Intervals*** corresponds to the inputted <u>individual error rate</u> of 0.025 since $1.00 - .975 = 0.025$. On the third line the 93.59% in ***Simultaneous confidence level = 93.59%*** corresponds to the Fisher <u>family error rate</u> of 0.641 since $1.00 - .9359 = 0.0641$.

The Fisher's confidence interval of from -30.53 to -2.88 for $\mu_2 - \mu_1$ does **not** contain zero; and so we may reject the comparison of $\mu_1 = \mu_2$ and thus conclude that there **is** a significant difference between the mean transportation index of all orders sent by railroad and the mean index of all orders sent by bus line. Furthermore, since this interval is completely negative, we may conclude that $\mu_1$ is greater than $\mu_2$; that is, the mean index for all orders sent by railroad is greater than the mean index for all orders sent by the bus line. The Fisher's confidence intervals of from -23.14 to 4.51 for $\mu_3 - \mu_1$ and from -6.44 to 21.21 for $\mu_3 - \mu_2$ both contain zero, and so we may not conclude that there are any other significant differences between population means.

# Lab Assignment 9.1.1

**Name:**                                                 **Date:**

**Course:**                 **Section:**                            **Data CD Number:**

1.     Start a Minitab session. If you are unable to complete this lab assignment in one Minitab session, save the project as Lab 9-1-1 . **Never** use a period as part of the project name; since Minitab uses the period to attach the file type to the file name. Then at your next Minitab session, you may open this Lab 9-1-1.MPJ project and continue to work where you left off previously.

2.     The cost of medical care varies in different parts of the United States. A sociologist wanted to conduct a unique study of these medical costs. She randomly sampled doctors in the New England area and asked each doctor where he/she had gone to medical school. She then asked each doctor what he/she charged for the same procedure, a routine well-care physical exam. The following table gives the charges by four independent samples of doctors who went to medical schools in the four geographical areas of the United States.

Went to Medical School In:

| Northeast | Northwest | Southeast | Southwest |
|-----------|-----------|-----------|-----------|
| $ 95.00 | $ 96.00 | $ 90.00 | $ 118.00 |
| 105.00 | 117.00 | 85.00 | 130.00 |
| 123.00 | 110.00 | 105.00 | 120.00 |
| 115.00 | 90.00 | 70.00 | 125.00 |
| 120.00 | 95.00 | 80.00 | 100.00 |
| 117.00 | | | 121.00 |
| 109.00 | | | |

At the 0.05 level of significance, test to determine if there are any differences in the average charge for a routine well-care physical exam among doctors trained at medical schools in the four geographical areas of the United States. Check the validity of both assumptions required for analysis of variance. **If** the null hypothesis of equal population means **is rejected**, use Tukey's HSD method, with a 0.10 family error rate, to perform all pairwise comparisons.

(lab assignment is continued on the second side of this page)

3.  Trenton State University randomly chose 40 students from each of its Freshmen, Sophomore, Junior and Senior classes. Each student was given a basic math skills test that contained material expected of all high school seniors. The data collected is in the Trenton.mtw worksheet saved on your data disk. Open the worksheet Trenton.mtw that is on your data disc. The University wanted to know if the mean basic math skill is the same for each of its four classes. However, due to a large number of junior college transfers, Trenton State decided not to include the Juniors in this particular study. At the 0.05 level of significance, test the hypothesis that the mean basic math skill is the same for all Trenton State University Freshmen, Sophomores and Seniors. Check the validity of both assumptions required for analysis of variance. **If** the null hypothesis of equal population means **is rejected**, use Dunnett's method, with a 0.05 family error rate, to compare the means of all Sophomores and Seniors to the mean of the **control** population of all Freshmen.

4.  Print your Session Window and all Graphic Windows to the printer.

5.  Attach both your Minitab output and <u>your complete answers</u> to this paper and submit all three to your instructor.

# Lab Assignment 9.1.2

**Name:**                                                    **Date:**

**Course:**            **Section:**                  **Data CD Number:**

1.  Start a Minitab session. If you are unable to complete this lab assignment in one Minitab session, save the project as Lab 9-1-2. **Never** use a period as part of the project name; since Minitab uses the period to attach the file type to the file name. Then at your next Minitab session, you may open this Lab 9-1-2.MPJ project and continue to work where you left off previously.

2.  An experiment to determine if physical fitness has any effect on a person's alertness was conducted. People were classified as being in one of five possible physical fitness populations: (1) non-fit, (2) minimal, (3) average, (4) above average and (5) excellent. Random samples from each population were taken and an alertness test was given to each person. The results are shown below.

## Level of Physical Fitness

| Non-Fit | Minimal | Average | Above Average | Excellent |
|---------|---------|---------|---------------|-----------|
| 6.7     | 7.2     | 4.7     | 6.1           | 5.6       |
| 3.7     | 4.5     | 6.2     | 5.0           | 6.3       |
| 4.8     | 3.6     | 8.3     | 7.1           | 7.9       |
| 3.0     | 3.5     | 5.5     | 7.8           | 6.4       |
| 4.8     | 8.2     | 6.1     | 4.4           | 8.6       |
| 1.9     | 5.0     | 3.1     | 6.0           | 9.3       |
| 4.7     |         | 7.2     | 9.0           | 8.6       |
| 5.9     |         | 6.3     | 5.9           |           |
| 3.7     |         | 4.0     |               |           |
|         |         | 7.2     |               |           |

At the 0.01 level of significance, test to see if there are any differences between the mean alertness score among the different levels of physical fitness populations. Check the validity of both assumptions required for analysis of variance. **If** the null hypothesis of equal population means **is rejected**, use Dunnett's method, with a 0.10 family error rate, to compare the mean alertness of the **control** population of Non-Fit people with the means of each of the other populations.

(lab assignment is continued on the second side of this page)

347

3. Open the worksheet Cityidx.mtw that is on your data disc. As described in Lab Assignment 6.1.2; this worksheet contains data about five variables where each was measured in cities in three different geographical regions: C1 – C5 in the East, C6 – C10 in the Central, and C11 – C15 in the West. The municipal bond measurement is a Bernoulli variable where 1 represents an "A or better" rating and 0 represents a "below A" rating. The other four are indices and are known to be normally distributed in each of the three regions.

   a. Test to see if there are any differences in the average retail sales index (Retail) among the cities in the three geographical regions of the United States. Use a 0.10 level of significance. Since the populations are known to be normally distributed, only check the assumption (2) of equal population variances in the three regions (therefore you do not need to compute the residuals). Check the second assumption of homogeneity of variance using the appropriate test. **If the null hypothesis of equal population means is rejected**, use Tukey's HSD method, with a 0.15 family error rate, to make all possible pairwise comparisons.

   b. At the 0.025 level of significance, test to see if there are any differences in the mean rural unemployment index (R-Unpl) among the cities in the three geographical regions of the United States. Since the populations are known to be normally distributed, only check the assumption (2) of equal population variances in the three regions (therefore you do not need to compute the residuals). Check the second assumption of homogeneity of variance using the appropriate test. **If the null hypothesis of equal population means is rejected**, use Fisher's LSD method, with a 0.025 individual error rate, to make all possible pairwise comparisons.

4. Print your Session Window and all Graphic Windows to the printer.

5. Attach both your Minitab output and <u>your complete answers</u> to this paper and submit all three to your instructor.

## Section 2:    The Randomized Complete Block Design

When testing two population means; using two paired samples reduces some of the variation (noise), and so the paired sample test is more sensitive (powerful) in being able to identify real differences between the population means. The process in paired samples is to have homogeneous pairs of objects in the two samples. A similar approach is taken when designing a one-way analysis of variance experiment. Blocks (instead of pairs) of homogeneous objects are chosen; and then within each block, the objects are randomly assigned to the different treatment samples.

Strictly speaking, this "Randomized Complete Block Design" falls under the category of two-way analysis of variance since there are now two factors: the different treatment populations and the different blocks. These are often called the *main effects*, however we are usually only interested in the differences between the treatment means.

In such a design there is a possible interaction between these two factors; that is, one block of objects may have a higher mean in one of the treatments but a lower mean in another treatment. If there is an interaction then the interpretation of any decision about this hypothesis is problematic. In fact, many statisticians recommend against even performing the analysis of variance when there is an interaction present.

If there are c different treatments and r different blocks, there are a total of c times r observations; one in each of the cxr different treatment-block combinations, often called *cells*. Each object in these combinations may be thought of as a random sample of size one from cxr separate populations, and each population has its own mean $\mu_{i,j}$ and variance $\sigma_{i,j}^2$ for i = 1,2,...,r and j = 1,2,...,c. Here each $\mu_{i,j} = \mu + \tau_j + \beta_i + (\tau\beta)_{ij}$ , where $\mu$ is the grand mean, $\tau_j$ is the treatment effect, $\beta_i$ is the block effect, and $(\tau\beta)_{ij}$ is the treatment-block interaction effect. The statistical techniques and conclusions of two-way analysis of variance for this situation depend upon the following assumptions:

(1)    each population is normally distributed,

(2)    the variances of all populations are equal; ("homogeneity of variance"), and

(3)    the treatment and block effects are additive; that is, there are **no** interaction effects (all $(\tau\beta)_{ij} = 0$).

The analysis of variance hypothesis test for comparing the c different treatment means may be written as

$$H_0: \tau_1 = \tau_2 = \tau_3 = ... = \tau_c = 0$$
$$H_a: \text{At least one } \tau_j \text{ not equal to } 0$$

where the $\tau_j$s again are the treatment effects.

349

Before computing a two-way analysis of variance, Minitab expects to have: (a) all data in one column, (b) the treatment level numbers in a second column and (c) the block level numbers in a third column. Consider the example of a market research company that is studying automobile sales when three different modes of compensation are used; commission only, salary only, and combined salary and commission. The research company could take a random sample of salespersons from each type of compensation mode. But since whether or not the prices of the automobiles are negotiable is believed to be a related factor, the research company decides to "block" on that factor. And so three randomly selected salespersons from negotiable price dealerships are randomly assigned to the three different compensation modes, and three randomly selected salespersons from non-negotiable price dealerships are randomly assigned to the three different compensation modes. The following table gives the yearly sales figures for each combination of compensation mode (treatment) and pricing policy (block).

|  | Commission | Salary | Combined |
|---|---|---|---|
| **Negotiable** | 210 | 140 | 220 |
| **Non-negotiable** | 180 | 100 | 200 |

Then Minitab expects three columns as:

| Compensation | Treatment Level | Block Level |
|---|---|---|
| 210 | 1 | 1 |
| 180 | 1 | 2 |
| 140 | 2 | 1 |
| 100 | 2 | 2 |
| 220 | 3 | 1 |
| 200 | 3 | 2 |

The data column may be named anything you like (this workbook uses AllData as was done in section 1), but the second and third columns should be named Treatment and Block respectively. You may enter the data from the above table and name the three variables directly in the Worksheet Window as illustrated below.

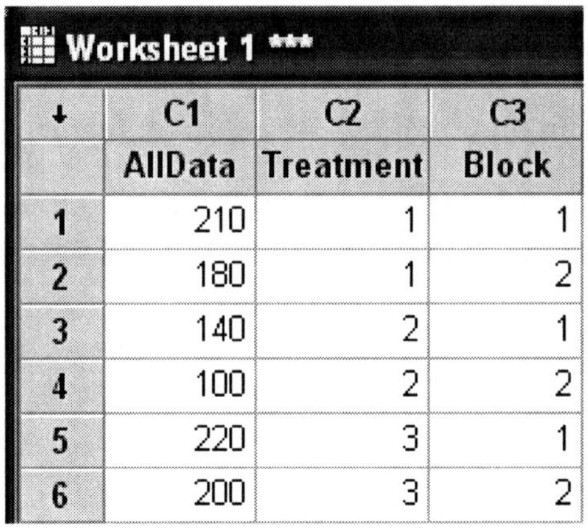

| ↓ | C1 | C2 | C3 |
|---|---|---|---|
| | AllData | Treatment | Block |
| 1 | 210 | 1 | 1 |
| 2 | 180 | 1 | 2 |
| 3 | 140 | 2 | 1 |
| 4 | 100 | 2 | 2 |
| 5 | 220 | 3 | 1 |
| 6 | 200 | 3 | 2 |

**Worksheet 1 ***

350

However it is more natural to enter the data just as it appears in the table above. That is, to enter the data so that each column contains the data for a treatment, and thus there will be as many columns as there are treatment levels. When doing this it is **very important** to keep the data for each block together and entered in the same row positions for each column. When the data are stored in columns in this more natural manner and there is exactly <u>one measurement per cell</u>, the macro **Stak-b1.mtb** may be executed to create the necessary three columns of stacked data that Minitab expects. This macro will prompt you for the number of treatment levels and the number of block levels. Next you will be prompted to enter the column numbers that contain the original, unstacked data for the c different treatments; **enter only the numbers and <u>not</u> the letter C**. The macro will store the measurements in column 26 (C26) and name this column "AllData"; the treatment levels will be stored in C27 and named "Treatment", and the block levels will be stored in C28 and named "Block."

Example 9.10: If Minitab has been started and you have data in the current worksheet, start a new Minitab project. Enter the compensation data described on the previous page (and repeated in the table below) into three separate columns, stack the data so that Minitab is able to compute the two-way analysis of variance, and then display in the Session Window **all** data that is in the current worksheet.

|  | Commission | Salary | Combined |
|---|---|---|---|
| **Negotiable** | 210 | 140 | 220 |
| **Non-negotiable** | 180 | 100 | 200 |

Enter the data from the table above directly into three columns and the Worksheet Window should look as shown next.

| ↓ | C1 | C2 | C3 |
|---|---|---|---|
|  | Commission | Salary | Combined |
| 1 | 210 | 140 | 220 |
| 2 | 180 | 100 | 200 |

Worksheet 1 ***

Click on *File , Other Files , Run an Exec...*

In the Run an Exec dialog box: the *Number of times to execute:* box should be 1, then click on the | **Select File** | button.

In the next Run an Exec dialog box: select the *Data Disc* in the *Look in:* box. Next find and highlight the Stak-b1.mtb macro file name, and then click on the | **Open** | button.

(continued on the next page)

**After the DATA> prompt, enter the number of "Treatments",
a comma and the number of "Blocks".**

DATA> 3, 2   | Enter |

## Data Display

**After the DATA> prompt, enter the  3 column numbers that contain
the data for the  3 different "Treatment" samples.
Enter ONLY the numbers, but NOT the Cs !**

DATA> 1, 2, 3   | Enter |

**The "Stacked" data are in column number 26.
The "Treatment" levels are in column number 27 (sequential numbering).
The "Block" levels are in column number 28.**

Click on the *Data , Display Data ...* menu bar item, block all six variables, click on the | Select | button and then click on | OK |. The data will be displayed in the Session Window as shown below.

| Row | Commission | Salary | Combined | AllData | Treatment | Block |
|-----|------------|--------|----------|---------|-----------|-------|
| 1 | 210 | 140 | 220 | 210 | 1 | 1 |
| 2 | 180 | 100 | 200 | 180 | 1 | 2 |
| 3 | | | | 140 | 2 | 1 |
| 4 | | | | 100 | 2 | 2 |
| 5 | | | | 220 | 3 | 1 |
| 6 | | | | 200 | 3 | 2 |

Once the data have been stacked into the three new columns, the three assumptions given at the beginning of this section should be verified.  As done in Section 1 of this chapter, the normality assumption (1) will be checked using a Q-Q plot of the residual values and the Anderson-Darling test's corresponding p-value. The residuals are computed in the following way.

Click on *Stat , ANOVA , General Linear Model ...*

In the General Linear Mopdel dialog box: the cursor will be in the *Responses:* box; click on the AllData (C26) variable that contains the stacked data and click on the | Select | button.  Next click inside of the box under the *Model:* heading, hold the | Ctrl | key while clicking on the Treatment (C27) and Block (C28) variables and click on the | Select | button.  Next click on the | Storage... | button.

In the General Linear Model - Storage dialog box; if the square to the left of *Residuals* is **not checked, click on this square to check this option**. A new column to the right of the last column  in your worksheet will **automatically** be created (usually C29) **and** will be named RESI1. Then click on | OK |.

Back in the General Linear Model dialog box: click on | OK |.

(See graphics on the next page.)

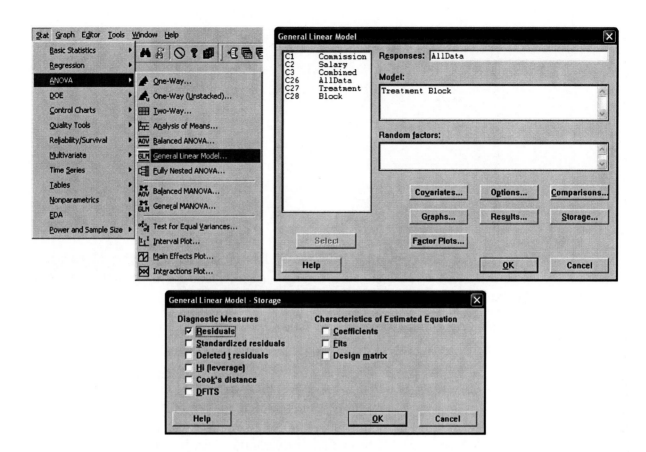

For now we will ignore the output in the Session Window and just concentrate on the resulting residuals.  In the current worksheet, column C29 will be named RESI1 and contain the residuals for each score.


Example 9.11:    Use the data in the current worksheet and do the General Linear Model procedure to compute the residuals.

Click on *Stat , ANOVA , General Linear Model ...*

In the General Linear Model dialog box: the cursor will be in the *Responses:* box; click on the AllData (C26) variable and click on  Select  .  Next click inside of the box under the *Model:* heading, hold the  Ctrl  key while clicking on the Treatment (C27) and Block (C28) variables and click on  Select  .  Click on the  Storage...  button.

In the General Linear Model - Storage dialog box; click on the square to the left of *Residuals* to check this option.  A new column numbered C29 will **automatically** be created **and** be named RESI1.  Then click on  OK  .

Back in the General Linear Model dialog box: click on  OK  .


Ignore the output in the Session Window.  In the current worksheet, column C29 will be named RESI1 and contain the residuals for each score.  After scrolling to the right of the Worksheet Window in order to view columns C26 through C29, your Worksheet Window should look like the graphic shown on the next page.

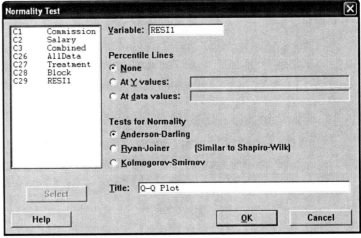

| ↓ | C25 | C26 | C27 | C28 | C29 |
|---|-----|-----|-----|-----|-----|
| | | **AllData** | **Treatment** | **Block** | **RESI1** |
| **1** | | 210 | 1 | 1 | 0 |
| **2** | | 180 | 1 | 2 | 0 |
| **3** | | 140 | 2 | 1 | 5 |
| **4** | | 100 | 2 | 2 | -5 |
| **5** | | 220 | 3 | 1 | -5 |
| **6** | | 200 | 3 | 2 | 5 |

Assumption (1), that each population is normally distributed, may be verified by graphing a **Q-Q plot**. This graph uses the residual values on the horizontal axis and the percentages on the y axis, as is explained in Section 1.

Click on *Stat* , *Basic Statistics* , *Normality Test...*

In the Normality Test dialog box: the cursor will be in the box to the right of *Variable:* click on the RESI1 variable (the automatically named column that contains the residual values) and click on the ⏹ Select button. Under the heading of *Percentile lines*, the button to the left of *None* should be chosen. Make sure that under the *Tests for Normality* that the *Anderson-Darling* choice is marked. Next click inside of the *Title:* box and type Q-Q Plot, but remember do **not** press the ⏹ Enter key. Then click on the ⏹ OK button.

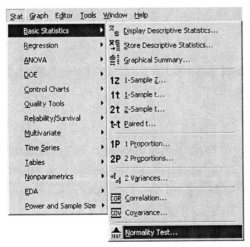

The resulting graph will appear in a separate Graphic Window titled Q-Q Plot. In addition to the actual Q-Q plot, the results of the Anderson-Darling test for normality will be given. This test essentially is

$H_0$: the population of scores **is** normally distributed
$H_a$: the population of scores is **not** normally distributed
$\alpha = 0.10$.

The AD test statistic and corresponding p-value are given in this Graphic Window. If the p-value is greater than 0.10, we usually do **not** reject the null hypothesis, so we have no reason to doubt the validity of assumption (1). However; if this p-value is less than or equal to 0.10, the null hypothesis **is** rejected, and assumption (1) is **not** validated.

Example 9.12: Use the data in the current worksheet and check the validity of assumption (1) by graphing the Q-Q plot and testing for normality.

The hypothesis testing problem is

$H_0$: the population of scores **is** normally distributed
$H_a$: the population of scores is **not** normally distributed
$\alpha = 0.10$

and the test statistic is labeled AD.

Click on *Stat , Basic Statistics , Normality Test...*
In the Normality Test dialog box: the cursor will be in the box to the right of *Variable:* click on the RESI1 (C29) variable and click on the ⎡ **Select** ⎤ button. Under the heading of *Percentile lines*, the button to the left of *None* should be chosen. Make sure that under the *Tests for Normality* that the *Anderson-Darling* choice is marked. Next click inside of the *Title:* box and type Q-Q Plot, but remember do **not** press the ⎡ **Enter** ⎤ key. Then click on ⎡ **OK** ⎤ .

You may need to "maximize" the Graphic Window in order to clearly read the AD test statistic and p-value. The resulting Graphic Window Q-Q Plot is shown below.

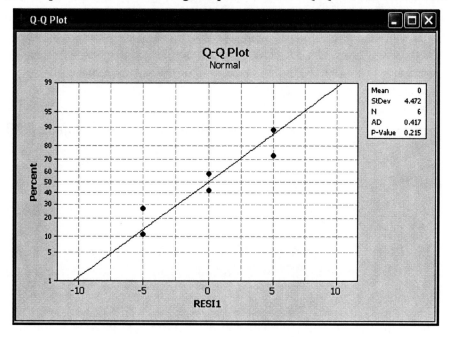

(continued on the next page)

Since the p-value of 0.215 is greater than 0.10, you may not reject the null hypothesis of normality, and so you may conclude that the normality assumption (1) **is** valid. Also notice that the points in the graph are close to the superimposed straight line that Minitab draws for comparison.

When there is only one observation in each cell, verifying assumption (2) of homogeneity of variance is more difficult in a Randomized Complete Block Design and is beyond the scope of this level workbook; and so it will not be discussed in this workbook.

Assumption (3), that the treatment and block effects are additive, should be verified. In the situation where there is **exactly one score for each treatment-block combination** this additivity assumption may be tested using a procedure developed by J. Tukey. The null and alternative hypotheses are

$H_0$: treatment and block effects **are** additive
$H_a$: treatment and block effects are **not** additive
$\alpha = 0.10$

The test statistic has a F distribution with r and (rc-r-c) degrees of freedom, and is computed by executing the **Ht-add.mtb** macro. This macro expects the data to be in three columns: data as described above, treatment levels and block levels. The Ht-add.mtb macro will prompt you for number of treatment levels and the number of block levels. Next you will be prompted for the column numbers that contain the data, treatment levels and block levels; **enter only the numbers and not the letter C.** If you used the Stak-b1.mtb macro to create these three stacked column, then these column numbers will always be 26, 27 and 28. The output will contain: the F test statistic, the degrees of freedom and the p-value for the test. If the p-value is greater than the value of α that you choose (usually 0.10), then the null hypothesis is **not** rejected, and the additivity assumption **is** verified. But if the p-value is less than or equal to α, then $H_0$ is rejected, and the additivity assumption is **not** verified. If the treatment and block effects are **not** additive, then an interaction is present and the two-way analysis of variance should not be computed for this case with one score per treatment-block combination. (It may be possible to perform a data-stabilizing transformation, but that is beyond the scope of this workbook.)

Example 9.13:    Use the data in the current worksheet, and compute the Tukey test for additivity to check assumption (3).

Click on *File , Other Files , Run an Exec...*

In the Run an Exec dialog box: the *Number of times to execute:* box should be 1, then click on the | **Select File** | button.

In the next Run an Exec dialog box: Make sure that the *Data Disc* is in the *Look in:* box. Next find and highlight the Ht-add.mtb macro file name, and then click on the | **Open** | button.

The steps for this macro and the results shown on the next page will appear in the Session Window.

(continued on the next page)

**After the DATA> prompt, enter the number of "Treatments",**
**a comma and the number of "Blocks".**

**DATA>** 3, 2 [ **Enter** ]

**After the DATA> prompt, enter the column numbers of the Measurements,**
**Treatment Levels and Block Levels in this order.**

**DATA>** 26, 27, 28 [ **Enter** ]        (these will always be 26, 27 and 28 if you used Stak-b1.mtb)

## Data Display

### The Tukey Test for Additivity

| F test statistic | d.f. | p-value |
|:---:|:---:|:---:|
| 6.7500 | 1, 1 | 0.7661 |

Since the p-value of 0.7661 is greater than 0.10, you may not reject the null hypothesis, and thus you may conclude that assumption (3) of additivity is valid.

Once the assumptions have been verified, you may analyze and interpret the results of the Analysis of Variance. When there is just one (1) score in each Treatment-Block cell, the two-way analysis of variance computations are done in the following way.

Click on *Stat , ANOVA , General Linear Model ...*

In the General Linear Model dialog box: the cursor will be in the *Responses:* box; click on the AllData (C26) variable and click on [ **Select** ]. Next click inside of the box under the *Model:* heading, hold the [ **Ctrl** ] key while clicking on the Treatment (C27) and Block (C28) variables and click on [ **Select** ]. Click on the [ **Storage...** ] button.

In the General Linear Model - Storage dialog box: if the square to the left of *Residuals* **is** checked, click on this square to **uncheck this option.** If you forget to uncheck this box, a new column to the right of the last column (RESI1) in your worksheet will **automatically** be created **and** be named RESI2. This will not effect any of the computations, but an extra column, that is identical to the RESI1 column, will be created in your worksheet. Then click on [ **OK** ]. **Note** that since Minitab remembers the previous entries used in a dialog box, the only thing you will actually need to do is to uncheck the *Store residuals* option.

Back in the General Linear Model dialog box: click on [ **OK** ].

(See graphics on the next page.)

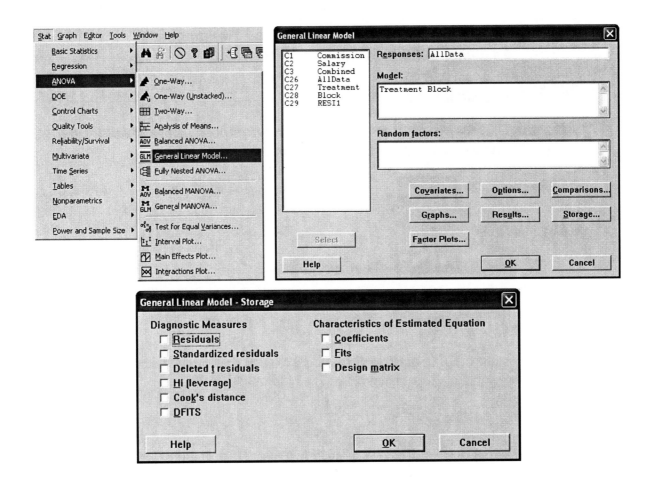

The output of the General Linear Model procedure contains:

(1)    information about the two factors including:
- (a)    the column numbers or names for the treatment and block levels,
- (b)    if each factor is a "fixed" or "random" effect ("fixed" is the default),
- (c)    how many levels there are for each factor,
- (d)    the level numbers for each factor,

(2)    the Analysis of Variance table with the following headings:
- (a)    Source  =  source of variation (Treatment, Block, Error, Total),
- (b)    DF   =  degrees of freedom for each source,
- (c)    SS   =  sum of squares for each source,
- (d)    MS   =  mean square for the factor and error sources of variation,
- (e)    F     =  value of the F test statistics for Treatment and Block,
- (f)    P     =  the p-value of the tests, and

(3)    the pooled sample standard deviation (an estimate of the common population standard deviation), R-sq and R-sq (adj) - you may ignore these last two values

Although the General Linear Model procedure produces a F test statistic and p-value for the block effect, these are usually ignored when analyzing a Randomized Complete Block Design.

Example 9.14: Use the compensation data in the current worksheet. In Example 9.12 you have verified assumption (1) of normality. In Example 9.13 you have verified assumption (3) of additivity. And, for this example, you may assume that assumption (2) of homogeneity of variance is valid. Now test the hypothesis that the mean sales figures are the same for the three different levels of compensation. Use $\alpha = 0.05$.

Population 1 is all automobile salespersons who are compensated by commission.

Population 2 is all automobile salespersons who are compensated by salary.

Population 3 is all automobile salespersons who are compensated by a combination of both commission and salary.

The hypothesis testing problem is

$H_0$: $\tau_1 = \tau_2 = \tau_3 = 0$
$H_a$: At least one $\tau_j$ not equal to 0
$\alpha = 0.05$.

Note that: (1) Compensation is the Treatment variable and Price Negotiable Status is the Block variable, and (2) the hypothesis that the means of the three different levels of Compensation (Treatment levels) are the same is equivalent to the hypothesis that Treatment effects the three different levels of Compensation ( $\tau_1$ , $\tau_2$ and $\tau_3$ ) are all equal to zero.

Click on *Stat , ANOVA , General Linear Model ...*

In the General Linear Model dialog box: the cursor will be in the *Responses:* box; click on the AllData (C26) variable that contains the stacked data and click on the ‖ **Select** ‖ button. Next click inside of the box under the *Model:* heading, hold the ‖ **Ctrl** ‖ key while clicking on the Treatment (C27) and Block (C28) variables and click on the ‖ **Select** ‖ button. Next click on the ‖ **Storage...** ‖ button.

In the General Linear Model - Storage dialog box:if the square to the left of *Residuals* **is** checked, click on this square to **uncheck this option.** If you forget to uncheck this box, a new column to the right of the last column (RESI1) in your worksheet will **automatically** be created **and** be named RESI2. This will not effect any of the computations, but an extra column, that is identical to the RESI1 column, will be created in your worksheet. Then click on ‖ **OK** ‖ . **Note** that since Minitab remembers the previous entries used in a dialog box, the only thing you will actually need to do is to uncheck the *Store residuals* option.

Back in the General Linear Model dialog box: click on ‖ **OK** ‖ .

The results shown on the next page will appear in the Session Window.

(continued on the next page)

# General Linear Model: AllData versus Treatment, Block

| Factor | Type | Levels | Values |
|---|---|---|---|
| Treatment | fixed | 3 | 1, 2, 3 |
| Block | fixed | 2 | 1, 2 |

### Analysis of Variance for AllData, , using Adjusted SS for Tests

| Source | DF | Seq SS | Adj SS | Adj MS | F | P |
|---|---|---|---|---|---|---|
| Treatment | 2 | 9300.0 | 9300.0 | 4650.0 | 93.00 | 0.011 |
| Block | 1 | 1350.0 | 1350.0 | 1350.0 | 27.00 | 0.035 |
| Error | 2 | 100.0 | 100.0 | 50.0 | | |
| Total | 5 | 10750.0 | | | | |

$S = 7.07107$     $R\text{-}Sq = 99.07\%$     $R\text{-}Sq(adj) = 97.67\%$

Since the p-value of 0.011 for the Treatment effect is less than $\alpha = 0.05$, you may reject the null hypothesis and conclude that at least one of the treatment effects is different from zero; that is, at least one $\tau_j \neq 0$. Or equivalently, at least two of the $\mu_j$s are different from each other.

When the analysis of variance test indicates that you are to reject the null hypothesis of all treatment effects being equal to zero, the question of which levels of the treatment are different from each other arises; that is, which treatment means are different from each other. J. Tukey developed a procedure for doing multiple comparisons for a Randomized Complete Block Design (in addition to his HSD procedure for a Completely Randomized Design as discussed in Section 1). These Tukey multiple comparison procedure is computed by

Click on *Stat*, *ANOVA*, *General Linear Model* ...

In the General Linear Model dialog box: the cursor will be in the *Responses:* box; click on the AllData (C26) variable and click on Select . Next click inside of the box under the *Model:* heading, hold the Ctrl key while clicking on the Treatment (C27) and Block (C28) variables and click on Select . Click on the Comparisons... button. **Note** that since Minitab remembers the previous entries used in a dialog box, the only thing you will actually need to do is click on the Comparisons... button.

In the General Linear Model - Comparisons dialog box: click on the circle to the left of *Pairwise comparisons*, and then click in the box under the heading *Terms:*. Now click on the Treatment (C27) variable and click on Select . Under the heading *Method* if the box to the left of *Tukey* is **not** checked, click on this box to **check** this option. Next click in the box to the left of *Confidence interval, with confidence level:* to **uncheck** this option. Now click on the OK button.

Back in the General Linear Model dialog box: click on OK .

(See graphics on the next page.)

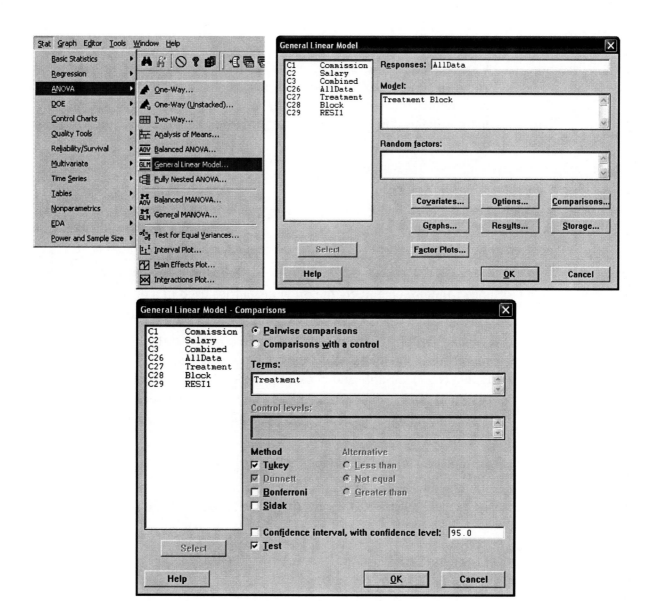

The output for Tukeys's multiple comparison procedure contains hypothesis tests for the difference of **every possible pair** of population means - these are given in groups by taking each other Factor level minus the Factor level for that specific group (note that redundant pairs are not given). For each pair being compared the output displays:

(1)  the treatment level from which the group treatment level is being subtracted; so that this give the specific comparison,

(2)  the difference of the two treatment means,

(3)  the standard error of the difference of the two treatment means,

(4)  the value of the t test statistic, and

(5)  the (adjusted) individual p-value for this test.

Example 9.15: Use the data in the current worksheet. Since the two-way analysis of variance done in Example 9.14 resulted in rejecting the null hypothesis that all treatment means are equal, use the Tukey multiple comparison procedure to try to determine which compensation means are different from each other. Let $\alpha = 0.05$.

Click on *Stat*, *ANOVA*, *General Linear Model* ...

In the General Linear Model dialog box: the cursor will be in the *Responses:* box; click on the AllData (C26) variable and click on | **Select** | . Next click inside of the box under the *Model:* heading, hold the | **Ctrl** | key while clicking on the Treatment (C27) and Block (C28) variables and click on | **Select** | . Click on the | **Comparisons...** | button. **Note** that since Minitab remembers the previous entries used in a dialog box, the only thing you will actually need to do is click on the | **Comparisons...** | button.

In the General Linear Model - Comparisons dialog box: click on the circle to the left of *Pairwise comparisons*, and then click in the box under the heading *Terms:*. Now click on the Treatment (C27) variable and click on | **Select** | . Under the heading *Method* if the box to the left of *Tukey* is **not** checked, click on this box to **check** this option. Next click in the box to the left of *Confidence interval, with confidence level:* to **uncheck** this option. Now click on the | **OK** | button.

Back in the General Linear Model dialog box: click on | **OK** | .

The resulting output in the Session Window. Since the first part of the output is exactly the same as shown at the top of page 300, only the output pertaining to the multiple comparisons is shown below.

### Tukey Simultaneous Tests
### Response Variable AllData
### All Pairwise Comparisons among Levels of Treatment

**Treatment = 1  subtracted from:**

| Treatment | Difference of Means | SE of Difference | T-Value | Adjusted P-Value |
|-----------|---------------------|------------------|---------|------------------|
| 2 | -75.00 | 7.071 | -10.61 | 0.0160 |
| 3 | 15.00 | 7.071 | 2.12 | 0.2884 |

**Treatment = 2  subtracted from:**

| Treatment | Difference of Means | SE of Difference | T-Value | Adjusted P-Value |
|-----------|---------------------|------------------|---------|------------------|
| 3 | 90.00 | 7.071 | 12.73 | 0.0112 |

(continued on the next page)

For the test on $H_0$: $\mu_2 = \mu_1$ , the value of the t test statistic is -10.61 and the p-value for this test is 0.0160 . Since this p-value of 0.0160 is less than the given value of $\alpha = 0.05$, you **do** reject $H_0$: $\mu_2 = \mu_1$ , and you **may** conclude that there **is** a significant difference between the mean salary of all automobile salespersons who are compensated by salary only ($\mu_2$) and the mean salary of all automobile salespersons who are compensated by commission only ($\mu_1$). Also since you have **rejected** the hypothesis $H_0$: $\mu_2 = \mu_1$ , and the difference of sample means is **negative**; this indicates that $\mu_2 - \mu_1$ is negative and thus $\mu_2 < \mu_1$ . So you may also conclude that the mean sales figure for all salary only salespersons is less than the mean sales figure for all commission only salespersons.

For the test on $H_0$: $\mu_3 = \mu_1$ , the value of the t test statistic is 2.12 and the p-value for this test is 0.2284 . Since this p-value of 0.2284 is greater than the given value of $\alpha = 0.05$, you do **not** reject $H_0$: $\mu_3 = \mu_1$ , and you may **not** conclude that there is a significant difference between the mean salary of all automobile salespersons who are compensated by a combination of both commission and salary ($\mu_3$) and the mean salary of all automobile salespersons who are compensated by commission only ($\mu_1$).

For the test on $H_0$: $\mu_3 = \mu_2$ , the value of the t test statistic is 12.73 and the p-value for this test is 0.0112 . Since this p-value of 0.0112 is less than the given value of $\alpha = 0.05$, you **do** reject $H_0$: $\mu_3 = \mu_2$ , and you **may** conclude that there **is** a significant difference between the mean salary of all automobile salespersons who are compensated by a combination of both commission and salary ($\mu_3$) and the mean salary of all automobile salespersons who are compensated by salary only ($\mu_2$). Also since you have **rejected** the hypothesis $H_0$: $\mu_3 = \mu_2$ , and the difference of sample means is **positive**; this indicates that $\mu_3 - \mu_2$ is positive and thus $\mu_3 > \mu_2$ . So you may also conclude that the mean sales figure for all combined commission and salary salespersons is greater than the mean sales figure for all salary only salespersons.

The previous example of a Randomized Complete Block Design had **one** measurement per cell. In such cases, the additivity assumption is tested with the Ht-add.mtb macro. Also, the two-way analysis of variance computations are the same whether or not the treatment and/or block effects are "fixed" or "random". However if there is more than one observation per cell, these methods change. The full version of Minitab has provisions for both the "fixed effects" and "random effects" models; however the Student Edition of Minitab only computes the two-way analysis of variance for the **"fixed effects"** model.

Reconsider the example in section 1 of determining if there is a difference in worker production for three management expectations. Believing that workers on the day shift are similar and workers on the night shift are similar, but that day shift workers are different from night shift workers; the researcher randomly selected six workers from the day shift and six workers from the night shift. Then the two workers from each shift are randomly assigned to each of the three orientation sessions where each session is given either no, moderate or high management expectation talks. In this case there are three treatment levels (None, Moderate and High) and two block levels (Day Shift and Night Shift). [Note: if you could argue that the management expectations are three of what could be many different expectation levels, the management expectation treatment would be treated as a random effect. However in this case, these were the only three levels of management expectation, and so this is a "fixed effects" model.] The following table contains the data.

| | None | Moderate | High |
|---|---|---|---|
| **Day Shift** | 4<br>2 | 4<br>5 | 8<br>11 |
| **Night Shift** | 1<br>2 | 2<br>4 | 9<br>8 |

The Minitab General Linear Model procedure expects the current worksheet to contain three columns as:

| Production | Treatment Level | Block Level |
|---|---|---|
| 4 | 1 | 1 |
| 2 | 1 | 1 |
| 1 | 1 | 2 |
| 2 | 1 | 2 |
| 4 | 2 | 1 |
| 5 | 2 | 1 |
| 2 | 2 | 2 |
| 4 | 2 | 2 |
| 8 | 3 | 1 |
| 11 | 3 | 1 |
| 9 | 3 | 2 |
| 8 | 3 | 2 |

You could enter the data from the above table and name the three variables directly in the Worksheet Window; however, as before, it is more natural to enter the data just as it appears in the table above. That is, to enter the data so that each column contains the data for a treatment, and thus there will be as many columns as there are treatment levels. When doing this it is **very important** to keep the data for each block together and entered in the same row numbers for each column. When the data are stored in columns in this more natural manner, there is <u>more than one observation per cell</u>, and <u>there are the **same number** of observations in each cell</u>, then the macro **Stak-bk.mtb** may be executed to create the necessary three columns. This macro (just as the Stak-b1.mtb macro) will prompt you for number of treatment levels, the number of block levels <u>and</u> the number of observations per cell. Next you will be prompted to enter the column numbers that contain the data for the c different treatments; **enter only the numbers and <u>not</u> the letter C**. The macro will store the measurements in C26 and name this column "AllData"; the treatment levels will be stored in C27 and named "Treatment", and the block levels will be stored in C28 and named "Block." However, if the number of observations in each cell are not all the same, then **you must enter the data** into three columns that **you have labeled** AllData, Treatment and Block

Example 9.16:   Open a new Minitab worksheet and enter the production data described on the previous page (and repeated in the table below) into three separate columns. Then stack the data so that Minitab is able to compute the analysis of variance and display the data in columns 27, 28 and 29 in the Session Window.

|  | **None** | **Moderate** | **High** |
|---|---|---|---|
| **Day Shift** | 4<br>2 | 4<br>5 | 8<br>11 |
| **Night Shift** | 1<br>2 | 2<br>4 | 9<br>8 |

Click on *File , New , Minitab Worksheet* and the $\boxed{\textbf{OK}}$ button to open a new Worksheet Window. Enter the data from the table directly into three columns in this new Worksheet Window and name these columns None, Moderate and High. The Worksheet Window should look as shown below.

| ↓ | C1<br>None | C2<br>Moderate | C3<br>High |
|---|---|---|---|
| **1** | 4 | 4 | 8 |
| **2** | 2 | 5 | 11 |
| **3** | 1 | 2 | 9 |
| **4** | 2 | 4 | 8 |

Click on *File , Other Files , Run an Exec...*

In the Run an Exec dialog box: the *Number of times to execute:* box should be 1, then click on the $\boxed{\textbf{Select File}}$ button.

In the next Run an Exec dialog box: Make sure that the *Data Disc* is in the *Look in:* box. Next find and highlight the Stak-bk.mtb macro file name, and click on $\boxed{\textbf{Open}}$ .

The steps for this macro and the results shown on the next page will appear in the Session Window.

(continued on the next page)

**After the DATA> prompt, enter the number of "Treatments",
the number of "Blocks", and the number of observations per cell.**

*DATA>* 3, 2, 2

## Data Display

**After the DATA> prompt, enter the  3 column numbers that contain
the data for the  3 different "Treatment" samples.
Enter ONLY the numbers, but NOT the Cs !**

*DATA>* 1, 2, 3  | Enter |

**The "Stacked" data are in column number 26.
The "Treatment" levels are in column number 27 (sequential numbering).
The "Block" levels are in column number 28.**

Click on the *Data , Display Data ...* menu bar item and press the | **F3** | key to clear any previous variables in the right side box. Block all six variables, click on the | **Select** | button and then click on | **OK** | . The data will be displayed in the Session Window as shown below.

| ROW | None | Moderate | High | AllData | Treatment | Block |
|-----|------|----------|------|---------|-----------|-------|
| 1 | 4 | 4 | 8 | 4 | 1 | 1 |
| 2 | 2 | 5 | 11 | 2 | 1 | 1 |
| 3 | 1 | 2 | 9 | 1 | 1 | 2 |
| 4 | 2 | 4 | 8 | 2 | 1 | 2 |
| 5 | | | | 4 | 2 | 1 |
| 6 | | | | 5 | 2 | 1 |
| 7 | | | | 2 | 2 | 2 |
| 8 | | | | 4 | 2 | 2 |
| 9 | | | | 8 | 3 | 1 |
| 10 | | | | 11 | 3 | 1 |
| 11 | | | | 9 | 3 | 2 |
| 12 | | | | 8 | 3 | 2 |

Once the data have been stacked into one column, and the treatment and block levels stored into two other columns, the two-way analysis of variance on the Randomized Complete Block design can be done. When there are two or more scores in each treatment-block combination (often called a "cell"), the analysis of variance model legitimately may contain an interaction term. The *Model:* in the General Linear Model dialog box is modified to include the interaction effect in the model. Assuming that the data have been stacked into a column named AllData (C26 if you used Stak-bk.mtb), the treatment levels into a column named Treatment (C27 if you used Stak-bk.mtb), and the block levels into a column named Block (C28 if you used Stak-bk.mtb); the additional treatment-block interaction effect is specified in the *Model:* as Treatment*Block.

Click on *Stat , ANOVA , General Linear Model ...*

In the General Linear Mopdel dialog box: the cursor will be in the *Responses:* box; click on the AllData (C26) variable that contains the stacked data and click on the | Select | button. Next click inside of the box under the *Model:* heading, hold the | Ctrl | key while clicking on the Treatment (C27) and Block (C28) variables and click on the | Select | button. Next highlight **only** the Treatment (C27) variable and click on the | Select | button. Then (using the keyboard) type in an asterisk. Now highlight **only** the Block (C28) variable and click on the | Select | button. Now click on the | Storage... | button.

In the General Linear Model - Storage dialog box; if the square to the left of *Residuals* is **not checked, click on this square to check this option.** A new column to the right of the last column in your worksheet will **automatically** be created (usually C29) **and** will be named RESI1. Then click on | OK |.

Back in the General Linear Model dialog box: click on | OK |.

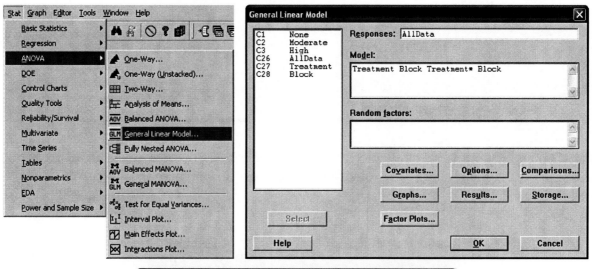

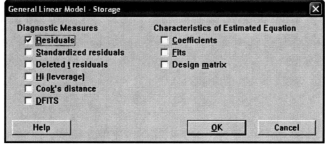

The output of the General Linear Model procedure is described earlier on page 298. For now we will ignore the output in the Session Window and just concentrate on the resulting residuals. In the current worksheet, column C29 will be named RESI1 and contain the residuals for each score.

Assumption (1), that each population is normally distributed, may be verified by graphing a **Q-Q plot**., as is explained earlier in this section.

Click on *Stat*, *Basic Statistics*, *Normality Test...*

In the Normality Test dialog box: the cursor will be in the box to the right of *Variable:* click on the RESI1 variable (the automatically named column that contains the residual values) and click on the ⬚ Select ⬚ button. Under the heading of *Percentile lines*, the button to the left of *None* should be chosen. Make sure that under the *Tests for Normality* that the *Anderson-Darling* choice is marked. Next click inside of the *Title:* box and type Q-Q Plot, but remember do **not** press the ⬚ Enter ⬚ key. Then click on the ⬚ OK ⬚ button.

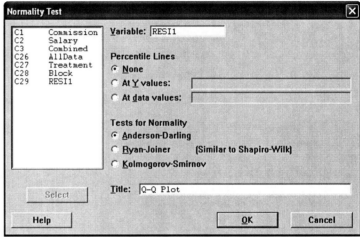

The resulting graph will appear in a separate Graphic Window titled Q-Q Plot. In addition to the actual Q-Q plot, the results of the Anderson-Darling test for normality will be given. This test essentially is

$H_0$: the population of scores **is** normally distributed
$H_a$: the population of scores is **not** normally distributed
$\alpha = 0.10$.

The AD test statistic and corresponding p-value are given in this Graphic Window. If the p-value is greater than 0.10, we usually do **not** reject the null hypothesis, so we have no reason to doubt the validity of assumption (1). However; if this p-value is less than or equal to 0.10, the null hypothesis **is** rejected, and assumption (1) is **not** validated.

When there are two observations per cell, verifying assumption (2) of homogeneity of variance is done using **Bartlett's** test. When there are three or more observations per cell, verifying assumption (2) of homogeneity of variance is done using **Bartlett's** test or the modified **Levene's** test for homogeneity of variance. When assumption (1) of normality **is** verified, Bartlett's test should be used. But if assumption (1) of normality is **not** verified, Levene's test should be used. In either case the hypotheses for testing homogeneity of variance, assumption (2), may be setup as

$H_0$: the variances in all (Treatment by Block) populations are equal
$H_a$: at least two variances are different
$\alpha = 0.10$ .


Both the Bartlett's and Levene's test statistics and corresponding p-values are computed using the *Test for Equal Variances* procedure. These are computed as follows.

Click on *Stat , ANOVA , Test for Equal Variances...*

In the Test for Equal Variances dialog box: the cursor will be in the box to the right of *Response:*. Click on the AllData (C26) variable (that contains the stacked data) and click on the Select button. The cursor will move to the large box to the right of *Factors:*, while holding the Ctrl key, click on the Treatment (C27) and Block (C28) variables (that contain the corresponding levels of the stacked data in AllData) and then click on the Select button. You may ignore the boxes to the right of *Confidence level:* and *Title:*. Then click on the OK button.

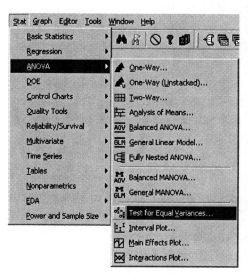
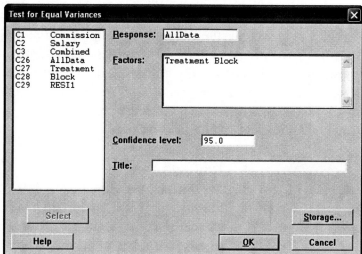

The output of the *Test for Equal Variances* (or *Homogeneity of Variance*) procedure contains:

(1) Simultaneous Bonferroni confidence intervals for the population standard deviations,
(2) the Bartlett's (for normal distributions) test statistic and p-value,
(3) the Levene's (for any continuous distribution) test statistic and p-value, and
(4) a Graphic Window, labeled *Test for Equal Variances: AllData versus Factor* containing the same information.


Even though the test results are most easily read from the Graphic Window, since it is active and appears on top after the *Test of Equal Variances* is completed; there is no need to print this Graphic Window since the same information appears in the Session Window and will be printed when you print the Session Window.

If the p-value for this test is greater than the pre-selected level of significance, usually 0.10; the null hypothesis of equal variances (homogeneity) may not be rejected, and thus assumption (2) is verified. But if the p-value is less than or equal to $\alpha$; then the null hypothesis is rejected, assumption (2) is **not** valid. If either or both of these two assumptions are not valid then analysis of variance must be used with caution, if at all. A nonparametric approach using the Kruskal-Wallis test may be the appropriate technique for analyzing the data.

Assumption (3), that the treatment and block effects are additive, should be verified. In the situation where there is **more than one score for each treatment-block combination** this additivity assumption may be tested using the F test statistic and p-value for the Treatment*Block interaction effect that are computed and displayed in the Analysis of Variance table. This table is contained in the Session Window output thatr results from the General Linear Model procedure done earlier for computing the Residuals. You will need to **slowly** scroll upward in the Session Window until you come to this output. Again the hypotheses are

$H_0$: treatment and block effects **are** additive
$H_a$: treatment and block effects are **not** additive
$\alpha = 0.10$ .

If the p-value is greater than the value of $\alpha$ that you choose (usually 0.10), then the null hypothesis is **not** rejected, and the additivity assumption **is** verified. But if the p-value is less than or equal to $\alpha$, then $H_0$ is rejected, and the additivity assumption is **not** verified. If the treatment and block effects are **not** additive, then an interaction is present and interpretation of the two-way analysis of variance is problematic. In such cases you should examine the interaction plot. This graph has the treatment levels on the x-axis, the means of each treatment for each block are plotted above the treatment levels, and the points for each block are connected across the treatment levels. The procedure for graphing an interaction plot is as follows.

Click on *Stat* , *ANOVA* , *Interactions Plot* ...

In the Interactions Plot dialog box, the cursor will be in the box under *Responses:*. Click on the AllData (C26) variable to highlight and then click on the ⬚ Select ⬚ button. Next click inside the box under the *Factors:* heading. While holding the ⬚ Ctrl ⬚ key, click on the Treatment (C27) and Block (C28) variables to highlight them both, and then click on the ⬚ Select ⬚ button. Then click on the ⬚ OK ⬚ button.

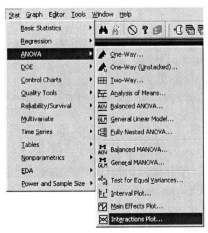

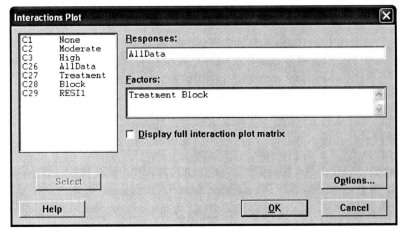

If all three assumptions are verified, the overall test of the hypothesis that all treatment means are equal is done using the values of the F test statistic and p-value computed for the **Treatment** and displayed in the General Linear Model Analysis of Variance for AllData table.

Example 9.17:   Use the data in the current worksheet and use the General Linear Model procedure with the Treatment*Block interaction term included in the model to compute the residuals. Graph the Q-Q plot and test to see if normality, assumption (1) is valid. Test to see if homogeneity of variance, assumption (2), is valid. Use the F statistic and p-value of the Treatment*Block interaction to see if the assumption (3) of additivity is valid. If all three of these assumptions are valid, then test the hypothesis that the mean production values are the same for the three different levels of management expectation. Use $\alpha = 0.05$.

Population 1 is all workers with no management expectation, and is level 1 of the Treatment.

Population 2 is all workers with a moderate expectation from management, and is level 2 of the Treatment.

Population 3 is all workers with a high expectation from management, and is level 3 of the Treatment.

The hypothesis testing problem is

$H_0$: $\tau_1 = \tau_2 = \tau_3 = 0$
$H_a$: At least one $\tau_j$ not equal to 0
$\alpha = 0.05$ .

The first step of stacking the data into three columns named AllData, Treatment and Block has already been done in Example 0.16.

The second step is to check assumption (1) of normality. This is done by: (a) computing the residuals in the analysis of variance, but ignoring for now any output that appears in the Session Window; and (b) plotting the Q-Q plot and testing the null hypothesis $H_0$: the population is normally distributed by examining the Anderson-Darling p-value.

Click on *Stat , ANOVA , General Linear Model ...*

In the General Linear Mopdel dialog box: the cursor will be in the *Responses:* box; click on the AllData (C26) variable that contains the stacked data and click on the | Select | button. Next click inside of the box under the *Model:* heading, hold the | Ctrl | key while clicking on the Treatment (C27) and Block (C28) variables and click on the | Select | button. Next highlight **only** the Treatment (C27) variable and click on the | Select | button. Then (using the keyboard) type in an asterisk. Now highlight **only** the Block (C28) variable and click on the | Select | button. Now click on the | Storage... | button.

(continued on the next page)

In the General Linear Model - Storage dialog box; if the square to the left of *Residuals* is **not checked, click on this square to check this option.** A new column to the right of the last column in your worksheet will **automatically** be created (C29) **and** will be named RESI1. Then click on OK .

Back in the General Linear Model dialog box: click on OK .

For now ignore the output in the Session Window. Verify assumption (1) of normality by graphing the Q-Q Plot and testing for normality. The hypothesis testing problem is

$H_0$: the population of scores is normally distributed
$H_a$: the population of scores is **not** normally distributed.
$\alpha = 0.10$

Click on *Stat , Basic Statistics , Normality Test...*

In the Normality Test dialog box: the cursor will be in the box to the right of *Variable:* click on the RESI1 variable (the automatically named column that contains the residual values) and click on the Select button. Under the heading of *Percentile lines*, the button to the left of *None* should be chosen. Make sure that under the *Tests for Normality* that the *Anderson-Darling* choice is marked. Next click inside of the *Title:* box and type Q-Q Plot, but remember do **not** press the Enter key. Then click on the OK button.

You may need to "maximize" the Graphic Window in order to clearly read the AD test statistic and the p-value. The Q-Q plot Graphic Window is shown below.

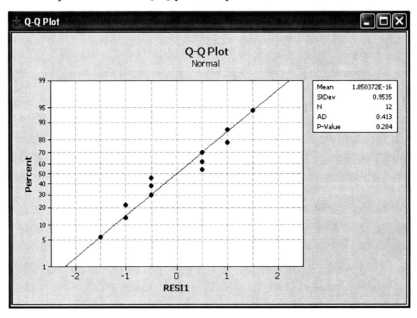

Since the p-value of 0.284 is greater than 0.10, you may not reject the null hypothesis of normality, and so you may conclude that assumption (1) **is** valid. Also notice that the points in the graph are close to the superimposed straight line that Minitab draws for comparison.

(continued on the next page)

Since the normality assumption is valid, verifying assumption (2) of homogeneity of variance is done using Bartlett's test.

The hypotheses for testing homogeneity of variance is

$H_0$: the variances in all (Treatment by Block) populations are equal
$H_a$: at least two variances are different
$\alpha = 0.10$ .

Click on *Stat* , *ANOVA* , *Test for Equal Variances...*

In the Test for Equal Variances dialog box: the cursor will be in the box to the right of *Response:*. Click on the AllData (C26) variable (that contains the stacked data) and click on the Select button. The cursor will move to the large box to the right of *Factors:*, while holding the Ctrl key, click on the Treatment (C27) and Block (C28) variables (that contain the corresponding levels of the stacked data in AllData) and then click on the Select button. You may ignore the boxes to the right of *Confidence level:* and *Title:*. Then click on the OK button.

The computations and results of this test will appear in the Session Window, but only the resulting Graphic Window is shown below.

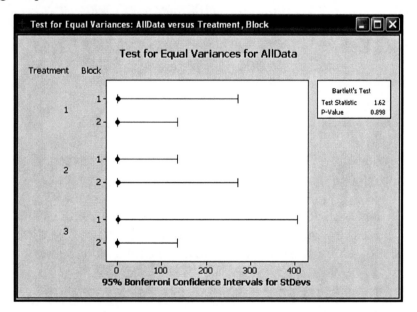

Since the p-value of 0.898 is greater than 0.10, you may not reject the null hypothesis of homogeneity. So you may conclude that homogeneity of variance, assumption (2), **is** valid. Also notice that since there are only two observations per cell, Levene's test and its p-value were **not** computed.

You now proceed to check assumption (3), that the treatment and block effects are additive. This is setup as

$H_0$: treatment and block effects **are** additive
$H_a$: treatment and block effects are **not** additive
$\alpha = 0.10$ ,

(continued on the next page)

or this assumption (3) also may be setup as

$H_0$: all $(\tau\beta)_{ij} = 0$
$H_a$: at least one $(\tau\beta)_{ij}$ is not 0
$\alpha = 0.10$ .

This is tested using the values of the F test statistic and p-value for the Treatmnt*Block interaction effect in the Analysis of Variance. Click on *Window*, *Session* to activate the Session Window. Then **slowly** scroll up to the output from the **General Linear Model: AllData versus Treatment, Block**; which is repeated below.

## General Linear Model: AllData versus Treatment, Block

| Factor | Type | Levels | Values |
|--------|------|--------|--------|
| Treatmnt | fixed | 3 | 1, 2, 3 |
| Block | fixed | 2 | 1, 2 |

### Analysis of Variance for AllData, , using Adjusted SS for Tests

| Source | DF | Seq SS | Adj SS | Adj MS | F | P |
|--------|-----|--------|--------|--------|-----|-----|
| Treatment | 2 | 100.500 | 100.500 | 50.250 | 30.15 | 0.001 |
| Block | 1 | 5.333 | 5.333 | 5.333 | 3.20 | 0.124 |
| Treatment*Block | 2 | 0.167 | 0.167 | 0.083 | 0.05 | 0.952 |
| Error | 6 | 10.000 | 10.000 | 1.667 | | |
| Total | 11 | 116.000 | | | | |

**S = 1.29099    R-Sq = 91.38%    R-Sq(adj) = 84.20%**

Since the p-value of 0.952 for the Treatment*Block source is greater than 0.10, you may not reject the null hypothesis, and so you may conclude that assumption (3) of additivity **is** valid.

Now that all three assumptions have been verified, you may test the main hypothesis that all Treatment means are equal; that is, in the three populations of different management expectation styles, all workers have the same mean production scores.

The hypothesis testing problem as shown on page 311 is

$H_0$: $\tau_1 = \tau_2 = \tau_3 = 0$
$H_a$: At least one $\tau_j$ not equal to 0
$\alpha = 0.05$ .

Again look in the Session Window and examine the results for the Treatment effect in the Analysis of Variance table (shown above); the F test statistic is 30.15 and the p-value is 0.001 . Since this p-vaue is less than $\alpha = 0.05$ , you may reject the null hypothesis and conclude that at least one treatment effect is different from zero; that is, at least one $\tau_j \neq 0$. Or equivalently, at least two of the (treatment) management expectation populations have different means.

**Only** when you reject the null hypothesis and conclude that at least two of the treatment population means are different, does the question of which levels of the treatment are different from each other arises. That is, you want to make pairwise comparisons of $\mu_{.i}$ with $\mu_{.j}$ for each distinct pair of treatments, where $\mu_{.i}$ and $\mu_{.j}$ represent the means of the $i^{th}$ and $j^{th}$ treatments for all blocks combined. As done earlier in this section when there is only one observation per cell, these questions are answered using the Tukey multiple comparisons procedure.

Click on *Stat , ANOVA , General Linear Model ...*

In the General Linear Model dialog box: the cursor will be in the *Responses:* box; click on the AllData (C26) variable and click on [ **Select** ] . Next click inside of the box under the *Model:* heading, hold the [ **Ctrl** ] key while clicking on the Treatment (C27) and Block (C28) variables and click on [ **Select** ] . Next highlight **only** the Treatment (C27) variable and click on the [ **Select** ] button. Then (using the keyboard) type in an asterisk. Now highlight **only** the Block (C28) variable and click on the [ **Select** ] button. Next click on the [ **Storage...** ] button. **Note** that since Minitab remembers the previous entries used in a dialog box, the only thing you will actually need to do is click on the [ **Storage...** ] button.

In the General Linear Model - Storage dialog box: if the square to the left of *Residuals* **is** checked, click on this square to **uncheck this option**. If you forget to uncheck this box, a new column to the right of the last column (RESI1) in your worksheet will **automatically** be created **and** be named RESI2. This will not effect any of the computations, but an extra column, that is identical to the RESI1 column, will be created in your worksheet. Then click on [ **OK** ] .

Back in the General Linear Model dialog box: click on the [ **Comparisons...** ] button.

In the General Linear Model - Comparisons dialog box: click on the circle to the left of *Pairwise comparisons*, and then click in the box under the heading *Terms:*. Now click on the Treatment (C27) variable and click on [ **Select** ] . Under the heading *Method* if the box to the left of *Tukey* is **not** checked, click on this box to **check** this option. Next click in the box to the left of *Confidence interval, with confidence level:* to **uncheck** this option. Now click on the [ **OK** ] button.

Back in the General Linear Model dialog box: click on [ **OK** ] .

(See graphics on the next page.)

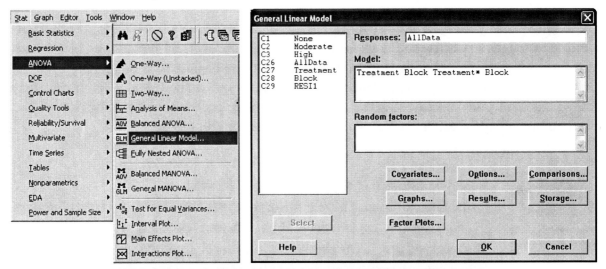

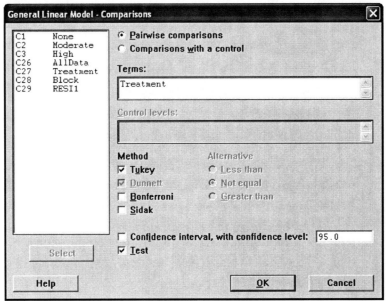

The output for Tukeys's multiple comparison procedure contains hypothesis tests for the difference of **every possible pair** of population means. As described earlier in this section on page 301, for each pair being compared the output displays:

(1)  the treatment level from which the group treatment level is being subtracted; so that this give the specific comparison,

(2)  the difference of the two treatment means,

(3)  the standard error of the difference of the two treatment means,

(4)  the value of the t test statistic, and

(5)  the (adjusted) individual p-value for this test.

Example 9.18:    In Example 9.17 you concluded that at least two of the management expectation groups' mean production values are different.    Use the Tukey method of multiple comparisons to test the three possible pairwise comparisons.  Use an individual α of 0.05 .

Click on *Stat , ANOVA , General Linear Model ...*

In the General Linear Model dialog box: the cursor will be in the *Responses:* box; click on the AllData (C26) variable and click on $\boxed{\text{Select}}$ .  Next click inside of the box under the *Model:* heading, hold the $\boxed{\text{Ctrl}}$ key while clicking on the Treatment (C27) and Block (C28) variables and click on $\boxed{\text{Select}}$ .  Next highlight **only** the Treatment (C27) variable and click on the $\boxed{\text{Select}}$ button.  Then (using the keyboard) type in an asterisk.  Now highlight **only** the Block (C28) variable and click on the $\boxed{\text{Select}}$ button. Next click on the $\boxed{\text{Storage...}}$ button. **Note** that since Minitab remembers the previous entries used in a dialog box, the only thing you will actually need to do is click on the $\boxed{\text{Storage...}}$ button.

In the General Linear Model - Storage dialog box:if the square to the left of *Residuals* **is** checked, click on this square to **uncheck this option**.  Then click on $\boxed{\text{OK}}$ .

Back in the General Linear Model dialog box: click on the $\boxed{\text{Comparisons...}}$ button.

In the General Linear Model - Comparisons dialog box: click on the circle to the left of *Pairwise comparisons*, and then click in the box under the heading *Terms:*.  Now click on the Treatment (C27) variable and click on $\boxed{\text{Select}}$ .  Under the heading *Method* if the box to the left of *Tukey* is **not** checked, click on this box to **check** this option.  Next click in the box to the left of *Confidence interval, with confidence level:* to **uncheck** this option.  Now click on the $\boxed{\text{OK}}$ button.

Back in the General Linear Model dialog box: click on $\boxed{\text{OK}}$ .

The resulting output in the Session Window.  Since the first part of the output is exactly the same as shown on page 314, only the output pertaining to the multiple comparisons is shown below.


### Tukey Simultaneous Tests
### Response Variable AllData
### All Pairwise Comparisons among Levels of Treatment

**Treatment = 1  subtracted from:**

| Treatment | Difference of Means | SE of Difference | T-Value | Adjusted P-Value |
|---|---|---|---|---|
| 2 | 1.500 | 0.9129 | 1.643 | 0.3000 |
| 3 | 6.750 | 0.9129 | 7.394 | 0.0008 |

**Treatment = 2  subtracted from:**

| Treatment | Difference of Means | SE of Difference | T-Value | Adjusted P-Value |
|---|---|---|---|---|
| 3 | 5.250 | 0.9129 | 5.751 | 0.0029 |

(continued on the next page)

For the test on $H_0$: $\mu_2 = \mu_1$, the value of the t test statistic is 1.643 and the p-value for this test is 0.3000. Since this p-value of 0.3000 is greater than the given value of $\alpha = 0.05$, you do **not** reject $H_0$: $\mu_2 = \mu_1$, and you may **not** conclude that there is a significant difference between the mean production of all workers with a moderate expectation from management ($\mu_2$) and the mean production of all workers with no management expectation ($\mu_1$).

For the test on $H_0$: $\mu_3 = \mu_1$, the value of the t test statistic is 7.394 and the p-value for this test is 0.0008. Since this p-value of 0.0008 is less than the given value of $\alpha = 0.05$, you **do** reject $H_0$: $\mu_3 = \mu_1$, and you **may** conclude that there **is** a significant difference between the mean production of all workers with a high expectation from management ($\mu_3$) and the mean production of all workers with no management expectation ($\mu_1$). Also since you have **rejected** the hypothesis $H_0$: $\mu_3 = \mu_1$, and the difference of sample means is **positive**; this indicates that $\mu_3 - \mu_1$ is positive and thus $\mu_3 > \mu_1$. So you may also conclude that the mean production of all workers with a high expectation from management is greater than the mean production of all workers with no management expectation.

For the test on $H_0$: $\mu_3 = \mu_2$, the value of the t test statistic is 5.7513 and the p-value for this test is 0.0029. Since this p-value of 0.0029 is less than the given value of $\alpha = 0.05$, you **do** reject $H_0$: $\mu_3 = \mu_2$, and you **may** conclude that there **is** a significant difference between the mean production of all workers with a high expectation from management ($\mu_3$) and the mean production of all workers with a moderate expectation from management ($\mu_2$). Also since you have **rejected** the hypothesis $H_0$: $\mu_3 = \mu_1$, and the difference of sample means is **positive**; this indicates that $\mu_3 - \mu_1$ is positive and thus $\mu_3 > \mu_1$. So you may also conclude that the mean production of all workers with a high expectation from management is greater than the mean production of all workers a moderate expectation from management.

In the next example, the p-value for the Treatment*Block interaction is less than $\alpha=0.05$. In such cases interpretation of the analysis of variance results for the main Treatment effect is problematic; regardless of whether the Treatment effect p-value indicates you are to reject or not to reject the null hypothesis of all Treatment means being equal. The interaction graph will be illustrated and interpreted. Also, since there are an unequal number of observations in the cells, the data will need to be entered directly into three AllData, Treatment and Block columns.

Example 9.19: A study was done to compare the manual dexterity of all right-handed people with that of all left-handed people. Previous research has shown that dexterity scores are often different for males as compared to females, and so a Completely Randomized Block Design was chosen where the block factor was sex. Use $\alpha = 0.05$ The table below contains the data.

| | Right-Handed | Left-Handed |
|---|---|---|
| **Male** | 14.6<br>10.1<br>12.3 | 4.7<br>8.3<br>5.3 |
| **Female** | 8.4<br>9.2<br>6.7<br>8.1 | 9.2<br>8.4<br>11.1 |

(continued on the next page)

Compute the two-way analysis of variance to test the hypothesis that the mean dexterity score of all right-handed people is different from the mean dexterity score of all left-handed people. Use a significance level of 0.05 for all tests.

Population 1 is all right-handed people.

Population 2 is all left-handed people.

The hypothesis testing problem is

$H_0: \tau_1 = \tau_2 = 0$
$H_a:$ At least one $\tau_j$ not equal to 0
$\alpha = 0.05$ .

Open a new Minitab worksheet. Name column C1 as AllData, name column C2 as Treatment, and name column C3 as Block. Now enter the data directly into these three columns. You may use the descriptive Treatment levels of "Right-Handed"and "Left-Handed", and the Block levels as "Male" and "Female". The Worksheet Window should look as shown below.

**Worksheet 4 \*\*\***

| ↓ | C1 | C2-T | C3-T |
|---|---|---|---|
| | AllData | Treatment | Block |
| 1 | 14.6 | Right-Handed | Male |
| 2 | 10.1 | Right-Handed | Male |
| 3 | 12.3 | Right-Handed | Male |
| 4 | 8.4 | Right-Handed | Female |
| 5 | 9.2 | Right-Handed | Female |
| 6 | 6.7 | Right-Handed | Female |
| 7 | 8.1 | Right-Handed | Female |
| 8 | 4.7 | Left-Handed | Male |
| 9 | 8.3 | Left-Handed | Male |
| 10 | 5.3 | Left-Handed | Male |
| 11 | 9.2 | Left-Handed | Female |
| 12 | 8.4 | Left-Handed | Female |
| 13 | 11.1 | Left-Handed | Female |

Note that you do **not** need to execute the Stak-bk.mtb macro since the data is already stacked into the three needed columns. The first step is to compute the residuals and then check the first assumption of normality.

Click on *Stat , ANOVA , General Linear Model ...*

In the General Linear Model dialog box: the cursor will be in the *Responses:* box; click on the AllData (C1) variable that contains the stacked data and click on the ⎡ **Select** ⎤ button. Next click inside of the box under the *Model:* heading, hold the ⎡ **Ctrl** ⎤ key while clicking on the Treatment (C2) and Block (C3) variables and click on the ⎡ **Select** ⎤ button. Next highlight **only** the Treatment (C2) variable and click on the ⎡ **Select** ⎤ button. Then (using the keyboard) type in an asterisk. Now highlight **only** the Block (C3) variable and click on the ⎡ **Select** ⎤ button. Now click on the ⎡ **Storage...** ⎤ button.

(continued on the next page)

In the General Linear Model - Storage dialog box; if the square to the left of *Residuals* is **not checked, click on this square to check this option**. A new column to the right of the last column in your worksheet will **automatically** be created (C4) in this example) **and** will be named RESI1. Then click on OK .

Back in the General Linear Model dialog box: click on OK .

Column C4 has been named RESI1 and contains the residuals. Your Worksheet Window should look as shown below.

| ↓ | C1 | C2-T | C3-T | C4 |
|---|---|---|---|---|
|  | AllData | Treatment | Block | RESI1 |
| 1 | 14.6 | Right-Handed | Male | 2.26667 |
| 2 | 10.1 | Right-Handed | Male | -2.23333 |
| 3 | 12.3 | Right-Handed | Male | -0.03333 |
| 4 | 8.4 | Right-Handed | Female | 0.30000 |
| 5 | 9.2 | Right-Handed | Female | 1.10000 |
| 6 | 6.7 | Right-Handed | Female | -1.40000 |
| 7 | 8.1 | Right-Handed | Female | -0.00000 |
| 8 | 4.7 | Left-Handed | Male | -1.40000 |
| 9 | 8.3 | Left-Handed | Male | 2.20000 |
| 10 | 5.3 | Left-Handed | Male | -0.80000 |
| 11 | 9.2 | Left-Handed | Female | -0.36667 |
| 12 | 8.4 | Left-Handed | Female | -1.16667 |
| 13 | 11.1 | Left-Handed | Female | 1.53333 |

Worksheet 4 ***

For now ignore the output in the Session Window. Verify assumption (1) of normality by graphing the Q-Q Plot and testing for normality. The hypothesis testing problem is

$H_0$: the population of scores is normally distributed
$H_a$: the population of scores is **not** normally distributed.
$\alpha = 0.10$

Click on *Stat* , *Basic Statistics* , *Normality Test...*

In the Normality Test dialog box: the cursor will be in the box to the right of *Variable:* click on the RESI1 variable and click on the Select button. Under the heading of *Percentile lines*, the button to the left of *None* should be chosen. Make sure that under the *Tests for Normality* that the *Anderson-Darling* choice is marked. Next click inside of the *Title:* box and type Q-Q Plot. Then click on the OK button.

(continued on the next page)

You may need to "maximize" the Graphic Window in order to clearly read the AD test statistic and the p-value. The Q-Q plot Graphic Window is shown below.

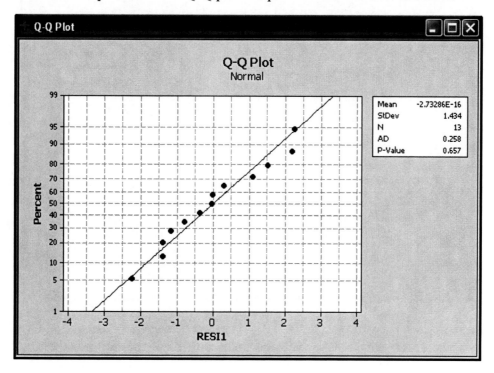

Since the p-value of 0.657 is greater than 0.10, you may not reject the null hypothesis of normality, and so you may conclude that assumption (1) **is** valid. Also notice that the points in the graph are close to the superimposed straight line that Minitab draws for comparison.

Since the normality assumption is valid, verifying assumption (2) of homogeneity of variance is done using Bartlett's test.

The hypotheses for testing homogeneity of variance is

$H_0$: the variances in all (Treatment by Block) populations are equal
$H_a$: at least two variances are different
$\alpha = 0.10$ .

Click on *Stat*, *ANOVA*, *Test for Equal Variances...*
In the Test for Equal Variances dialog box: the cursor will be in the box to the right of *Response:*. Click on the AllData (C1) variable (that contains the stacked data) and click on the ⟨ Select ⟩ button. The cursor will move to the large box to the right of *Factors:*, while holding the ⟨ Ctrl ⟩ key, click on the Treatment (C2) and Block (C3) variables and then click on the ⟨ Select ⟩ button. You may ignore the boxes to the right of *Confidence level:* and *Title:*. Then click on the ⟨ OK ⟩ button.

The computations and results of this test will appear in the Session Window, but only the resulting Graphic Window is shown on the next page.

(continued on the next page)

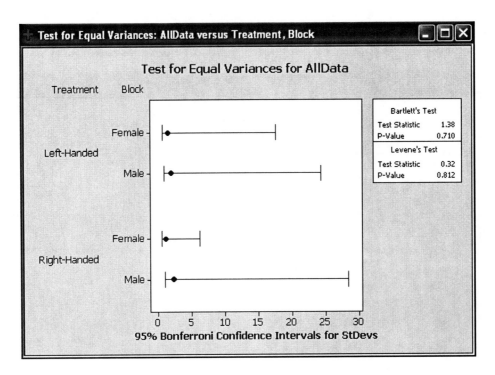

Since the Bartlett's Test p-value of 0.710 is greater than 0.10, you may not reject the null hypothesis of homogeneity. So you may conclude that homogeneity of variance, assumption (2), **is** valid.

You now proceed to check assumption (3), that the treatment and block effects are additive. This is setup as

$H_0$: treatment and block effects **are** additive
$H_a$: treatment and block effects are **not** additive
$\alpha = 0.10$ ,

or this assumption (3) also may be setup as

$H_0$: all $(\tau\beta)_{ij} = 0$
$H_a$: at least one $(\tau\beta)_{ij}$ is not 0
$\alpha = 0.10$ .

This is tested using the values of the F test statistic and p-value for the Treatmnt*Block interaction effect in the Analysis of Variance. Click on *Window* , *Session* to activate the Session Window. Then **slowly** scroll up to the output from the **General Linear Model: AllData versus Treatment, Block**; which is repeated below.

### General Linear Model: AllData versus Treatment, Block

| Factor | Type | Levels | Values |
|---|---|---|---|
| Treatment | fixed | 2 | Left-Handed, Right-Handed |
| Block | fixed | 2 | Female, Male |

(continued on the next page)

### Analysis of Variance for AllData, using Adjusted SS for Tests

| Source | DF | Seq SS | Adj SS | Adj MS | F | P |
|---|---|---|---|---|---|---|
| Treatment | 1 | 13.990 | 18.177 | 18.177 | 6.63 | 0.030 |
| Block | 1 | 1.317 | 0.470 | 0.470 | 0.17 | 0.688 |
| Treatment*Block | 1 | 47.432 | 47.432 | 47.432 | 17.30 | 0.002 |
| Error | 9 | 24.673 | 24.673 | 2.741 | | |
| Total | 12 | 87.412 | | | | |

**S = 1.65574    R-Sq = 71.77%    R-Sq(adj) = 62.36%**

The p-value for the Treatment*Block interaction effect of 0.002 is less than $\alpha$ = .10; and so you may conclude that there **is** a significant interaction effect, and the additivity assumption is **not** verified. Even though, in this example, the p-value for the main Treatment effect of 0.030 is less than $\alpha$ = .05; the interpretation of this poses potential problems. As described earlier in this section, an interaction graph should be plotted.

Click on *Stat , ANOVA , Interactions Plot ...*

In the Interactions Plot dialog box, the cursor will be in the box under *Responses:*. Click on the AllData (C1) variable to highlight and then click on the | **Select** | button. Next click inside the box under the *Factors:* heading. While holding the | **Ctrl** | key, click on the Treatment (C2) and Block (C3) variables to highlight them both, and then click on the | **Select** | button. Then click on the | **OK** | button.

The graph appears in a separate Interaction Plot (data means) for AllData Graphic Window and is shown below.

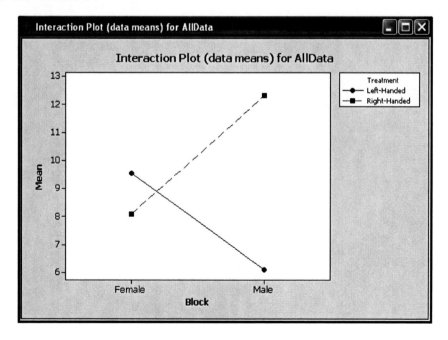

(continued on the next page)

The Treatment levels are Left-Handed and Right-Handed, and the Block levels are Female and Male. These are listed in the increasing alphabetical order.

From this graph you see that right-handed males have a considerably larger mean dexterity score than left-handed males. But for females the relationship is reversed; that is, right-handed females have a somewhat smaller mean dexterity score than left-handed females. So while the main effect p-value for Treatment (handedness) of 0.030 is less than $\alpha = 0.05$ ; with a significant interaction present, this does not necessarily imply that in general right-handed people have a higher dexterity score than left-handed people.

The interaction graph will have as many lines as the number of treatments, and as many reference points on the x-axis as the number of blocks. The interpretation of the graph becomes difficult if there are too many blocks, and the Treatment*Block interaction effect may need to be interpreted for pairs of Block values.

# Lab Assignment 9.2.1

**Name:**                                                        **Date:**

**Course:**                **Section:**                **Data CD Number:**

1.    Start a Minitab session. If you are unable to complete this lab assignment in one Minitab session, save the project as Lab 9-2-1 . **Never** use a period as part of the project name; since Minitab uses the period to attach the file type to the file name. Then at your next Minitab session, you may open this Lab 9-2-1.MPJ project and continue to work where you left off previously.

2.    The Dantor Taxi Company is evaluating four different brands of gasoline for use by its large fleet of taxis. Since the fleet has many different types of cars, a Randomized Complete Block Design is being used. Four cars were randomly selected from each make and model used by the Dantor Company, and then the cars in each block were randomly assigned to the different brands of gasoline. The makes and models of the taxis were designated by letters A, B, etc. The miles per gallon for each taxi in the evaluation are given in the table below.

| Make and Model | Brand of Gasoline | | | |
|---|---|---|---|---|
| | Shornell | Texas Plus | ArXtra | Delta |
| A | 12.4 | 13.1 | 10.4 | 8.6 |
| B | 11.3 | 15.2 | 9.3 | 9.7 |
| C | 10.1 | 13.6 | 11.2 | 10.7 |
| D | 14.3 | 18.7 | 13.5 | 13.1 |
| E | 9.2 | 10.5 | 8.9 | 8.3 |
| F | 9.6 | 8.9 | 8.1 | 8.2 |
| G | 18.7 | 22.4 | 15.4 | 16.2 |

It is known that the distributions of gas mileage have approximately equal standard deviations for all combinations in the table above. Use Tukey's test to verify the additivity assumption. If this assumption is valid, compute the two-way analysis of variance. Then verify the normality assumption. Use $\alpha = 0.05$ for all tests. If the normality assumption is valid, what recommendation would you give the Dantor Taxi Company about purchasing gasoline for its fleet of cars?

3.    Open the worksheet Trenton.mtw that is on your data disc. Trenton State University has two degree programs; one in liberal arts, and one in mathematics and sciences. For each of the classes (Freshmen, Sophomore, Junior and Senior), twenty students from each program were chosen and given the basic skills test. Using the two degree programs as blocks, test the hypothesis that the mean basic skills scores for all students in each class are equal. Verify assumptions (1), (2) and (3). If the null hypothesis is rejected, compute all pairwise multiple comparisons. Use a 0.10 level of significance.

(lab assignment is continued on the second side of this page)

4.  In a study conducted to see if calcium supplements taken by pregnant women have any effect on the bone density of newborn babies, three different levels of the calcium supplement were used: none, 50, and 100. Since these are but three of many different possibilities, this is a random effect. The researcher felt that maternal smoking could be related to the newborn's bone density, and so a Randomized Complete Block Design was used with two blocks: smoker and non-smoker. Random samples of pregnant smokers and non-smokers were taken and randomly assigned to the three different calcium supplement programs. The newborn bone density data are in the table below. Open a new Worksheet Window and enter the data. Then use $\alpha = 0.01$, and perform a complete two-way analysis of variance for this study (include verifying assumptions).

| Smoker | Calcium Supplement | | |
| --- | --- | --- | --- |
| | None | 50 | 100 |
| No | 4.2 | 7.5 | 5.7 |
| | 5.1 | 9.6 | 5.1 |
| | 6.3 | 7.1 | 8.2 |
| | 4.7 | 8.5 | 3.7 |
| | 6.9 | 11.7 | 7.0 |
| Yes | 3.2 | 5.5 | 4.7 |
| | 4.6 | 7.3 | 7.8 |
| | 2.8 | 4.0 | 1.9 |
| | 5.3 | 4.9 | 5.4 |
| | 4.9 | 6.0 | 3.9 |

5.  Open another worksheet using Wellmar.mtw from your data disc. As described in Example 9.9 of Section 1, the Wellmar company sells its product throughout North America. Wellmar uses four modes of transportation: railroad, bus line, shipping, and airline. The company has derived an index that combines cost, damage and customer satisfaction for each mode of transportation. Since the size of the order may be related to the transportation index, orders of the same size were randomly assigned to the four different methods of transportation. This produced a design with fifty blocks of one observation per cell. The standard deviations of all populations are known to be equal. Verify the normality and additivity assumptions. If the assumptions are verified, test the hypothesis that the mean transportation index is the same for all four methods. If this hypothesis is rejected, which method(s) are preferable? Use $\alpha = 0.05$ for all tests.

6.  Print your Session Window and all Graphic Windows to the printer.

7.  Attach both your Minitab output and your complete answers to this paper and submit all three to your instructor.

# Lab Assignment 9.2.2

**Name:**                                              **Date:**

**Course:**                  **Section:**                        **Data CD Number:**

1. Start a Minitab session. If you are unable to complete this lab assignment in one Minitab session, save the project as Lab 9-2-2 . **Never** use a period as part of the project name; since Minitab uses the period to attach the file type to the file name. Then at your next Minitab session, you may open this Lab 9-2-2.MPJ project and continue to work where you left off previously.

2. A long-term study was conducted to test if survival time is the same for four different types of post heart attack exercise programs. The four programs studied were: no exercise, easy walking, fast walking and recreational bicycling. Since there are many exercise programs, and these four were chosen at random, exercise is a random main effect. The study also considered the weight of the subjects as a possible effect, and grouped patients as being within ten pounds of average weight, underweight or overweight. Then patients in each weight group were randomly assigned an exercise program. The survival times (in years) of the patients in the study are shown in the table below. Test the hypothesis that the mean survival time is the same for all patients in the four different exercise programs. The three assumptions must be validated. If the hypothesis is rejected, which program(s) would be recommended for heart attack patients? Use a 0.01 significance level.

| Weight | Exercise Program | | | |
|---|---|---|---|---|
| | None | Easy Walking | Fast Walking | Bicycling |
| Underweight | 6.2<br>7.4 | 7.3<br>8.6 | 6.8<br>8.1 | 9.2<br>9.6 |
| Average | 7.9<br>9.1 | 10.0<br>8.9 | 8.7<br>9.7 | 9.5<br>10.2 |
| Overweight | 5.7<br>4.9 | 6.7<br>5.9 | 6.5<br>5.4 | 7.7<br>6.8 |

3. Open the worksheet Trenton.mtw that is on your data disc. Trenton State University randomly selected one student with the same SAT score from each of its Freshman, Sophomore, Junior and Senior classes. They repeated this process, using different SAT scores, until they had selected 40 blocks of similar students. Each student was given a basic mathematics skills test. Use a Randomized Complete Block Design with one observation per cell to test the hypothesis that the mean basic mathematics skills scores are the same for all four classes at Trenton State. The standard deviations of all populations are known to be equal, but the normality and additivity assumptions must be verified. If the hypothesis is rejected, try to determine any order (higher to lower) of the classes by using Tukey's multiple comparison procedure. Use a 0.05 level of significance for all tests. This may not produce a 1-2-3-4 order, but only that some class(es) is(are) better than some other class(es).

(lab assignment is continued on the second side of this page)

4.    Open another worksheet using Wellmar.mtw from your data disc.    As described in Example 9.9 in Section 1, the Wellmar company sells its product throughout North America. Wellmar uses four modes of transportation: railroad, bus line, shipping, and airline. Since these are the only modes of transportation available to the Wellmar company, transportation is a fixed treatment effect. The company has derived an index that combines cost, damage and customer satisfaction for each mode of transportation. The size of the order is related to the transportation index.   So the 100 small orders and 100 large orders were randomly selected to be in the current study. Then each set of 100 orders was randomly divided into four groups and transported by the four different methods. So that the first 25 rows in each column are for small orders and the next 25 rows contain scores for large orders.   The three assumptions must be verified. But if homogeneity of variance is not verified, you may continue since the sample sizes are all equal and Analysis of Variance is robust in this case. Test the hypothesis that the mean transportation index is the same for all four methods.   If this hypothesis is rejected, which method(s) are preferable?   Use $\alpha = 0.10$ for all tests.

5.    Value Home, a large hardware company with many stores, is concerned about theft and profitability of its sales of one inch bolts.   The company is investigating three packaging methods: loose in a bin, packed one to a 2" by 3" piece of cardboard, and packed five together on a 3" by 4" piece of cardboard.    Individual stores were grouped together according to their previous history of theft.   Then three stores from each group were chosen at random to use one of the three packaging methods.   After two months, the profit margin for the sale of the one inch bolts in each store for each packaging method was recorded, and the results are in the table below.   Open a new Worksheet Window and enter the data from the table below. The population standard deviations may be assumed to be equal, but the normality and additivity assumptions must be validated.   Test to see if any of the packaging methods is superior to the others.   Use a 0.05 level of significance.

| Theft History | Packaging Method | | |
| | Loose | One Pack | Five Pack |
| --- | --- | --- | --- |
| 1 | 1.13 | 1.22 | 1.08 |
| 2 | 1.08 | 1.42 | 1.10 |
| 3 | 0.96 | 1.19 | 0.92 |
| 4 | 1.02 | 1.11 | 1.35 |
| 5 | 1.52 | 1.91 | 0.99 |
| 6 | 1.05 | 1.42 | 1.41 |
| 7 | 1.19 | 1.37 | 1.21 |
| 8 | 1.27 | 1.63 | 1.19 |

6.    Print your Session Window and all Graphic Windows to the printer.

7.    Attach both your Minitab output and your complete answers to this paper and submit all three to your instructor.

# CHAPTER 10:    Nonparametric Techniques

In Chapters 5 through 9, methods for computing confidence intervals and hypothesis tests for the population mean from one, two or several populations were shown. Those methods required that the data be continuous, and either (1) that data be normally distributed or (2) that the sample size(s) be "large' (usually at least 30). However when (1) the data is ordinal (discrete) or (2) the sample(s) is "small" (usually less than 30) **and** the distribution of the data is unknown, then these (parametric) methods in Chapters 5 through 9 are inappropriate! Instead, the nonparametric (or often called distribution free) methods discussed in this chapter may be used to do the analysis. The different methods will be presented by first discussing the assumptions about the data for the specific method, and then showing how to do the computations with the Minitab software. The derivation and explanation of these methods is not included in this chapter, as they may differ depending upon which text is used. Only a few of the most common nonparametric techniques will be discussed, and only those that are supported by the Minitab software.

For most nonparametric confidence intervals, the exact desired confidence level cannot be achieved due to the discrete nature of these methods. And so Minitab computes an interval with achieved confidence levels that are close to the desired level. In some cases Mintab will compute intervals with the closest smaller and closest larger achieved confidence level, and then compute an exact confidence interval using interpolation. The confidence coefficients for confidence intervals, and the p-values for hypothesis test computed by Minitab may or may not exactly match your test answers. This is usually due to either round off error or, in some cases, slightly different computational formulas.

The population median will be symbolized with an upper case M throughout this chapter, and the sample median will be symbolized with a lower case m. The terminology of "one-sided" and "two-sided" alternative as well as "one-tail" and "two-tail" tests introduced in Chapter 7 also will be used in this chapter.

**Section 1:**     **One Sample Confidence Intervals and Hypothesis Tests for the Population Location Parameter (Median)**

The "one sample" hypothesis test of the median from a single population may take one of the following three forms:

(a) $H_0: M = M_0$          (b) $H_0: M \geq M_0$          (c) $H_0: M \leq M_0$
     $H_a: M \neq M_0$               $H_a: M < M_0$                 $H_a: M > M_0$

Two techniques will be presented; the Sign Test which is less restrictive, and the Wilcoxon Signed-Ranks Test which is more restrictive but also more powerful.

The **Sign Test** and corresponding confidence interval assume that the data in the random sample is inherently **ordinal** as well as being measured on an ordinal scale. This is the least restrictive assumption when dealing with the population median, and so this test is valid for almost any situation where parametric methods do not work. While different texts may give slightly different rules for the test statistic, one fairly common method is to subtract the value of $M_0$ from each score, and then use the number of these values that are positive; i.e., the number of $+$ signs or the number of original scores that are above the value of $M_0$. This test statistic and the corresponding p-value are computed by

Click on *Stat*, *Nonparametrics*, *1-Sample Sign...*

In the 1-Sample Sign dialog box: you may press the ⟨ **F3** ⟩ key to clear the contents of this dialog box and reset all options and erase any previous variables. The variables (columns) will appear in the large box on the left side of this dialog box, click on the variable you want to analyze, and click on the ⟨ **Select** ⟩ button. Next click inside of the circle to the left of *Test Median:*, erase any current incorrect value, and type in the given value of the population median ($M_0$). Then make sure that the box to the right of *Alternative:* contains the correct inequality for your problem (*not equal* or *less than* or *greater than*). If not, click on the down triangle ( ⟨▾⟩ ), and click on the correct choice. Then click on ⟨ **OK** ⟩ .

(See the graphics on the next page.)

.

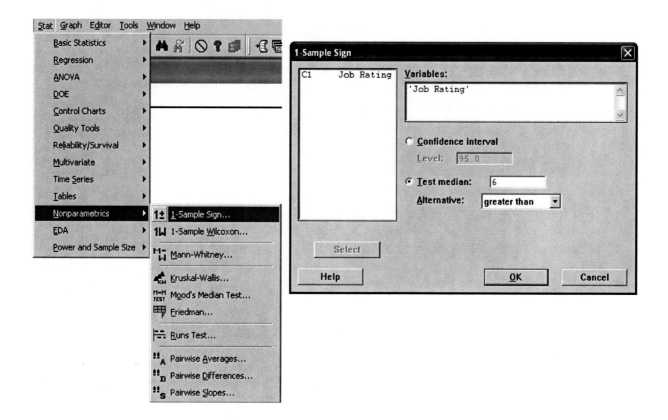

The output of *1-Sample Sign* Test contains:

    (1)    The null and alternative hypotheses,

    (2)    the variable column label or name,

    (3)    the number of valid observations, the number of differences below the hypothesized median $M_0$ (number of - signs), the number of differences equal to $M_0$ (number of ties or zeros), and the number of differences above $M_0$ (number of + signs),

    (4)    the p-value for the test and

    (5)    the value of the sample median.

The p-value may be interpreted as "based upon the data of this sample, if you decide to reject the null hypothesis then the probability of this decision being an error is equal to the p-value."

Example 10.1:    A random sample of 12 students at Lanston University was taken, and the class rank (Freshman, Sophomore, Junior, Senior or Graduate) was recorded. The results were: Fresh, Jr, Jr, Grad, Sr, Soph, Sr, Fresh, Grad, Jr, Grad and Sr. At the 0.05 level of significance, test the hypothesis that the median class rank of all students at Lanston University is greater than Sophomore.

Since the 1-Sample Sign test requires numerical data, these outcomes must be coded as Freshman = 1, Sophomore = 2, Junior = 3, Senior = 4 and Graduate = 5. Enter these ten scores into column 1 of the Worksheet Window and label the column Class Rank. Your Worksheet Window should look as shown on the next page.

(continued on the next page)

| | C1 |
|---|---|
| ↓ | **Class Rank** |
| 1 | 1 |
| 2 | 3 |
| 3 | 3 |
| 4 | 5 |
| 5 | 4 |
| 6 | 2 |
| 7 | 4 |
| 8 | 1 |
| 9 | 5 |
| 10 | 3 |
| 11 | 5 |
| 12 | 4 |

The hypothesis testing problem is

$H_0$: M ≤ 2
$H_a$: M > 2
$\alpha = 0.10$

and the test statistic is $T_+$ (number of + signs or number of differences above zero).

Click on *Stat* , *Nonparametrics* , *1-Sample Sign...*

In the 1-Sample Sign dialog box: press the ⬛ **F3** key to clear the contents of this dialog box and reset all options and erase any previous variables. The variables (columns) will appear in the large box on the left side of this dialog box, click on the Class Rank (C1) variable, and click on the ⬛ **Select** ⬛ button. Next click inside of the circle to the left of *Test Median:*, erase any current incorrect value, and type in 2 - the given value of the population median ($M_0$). Then make sure that the box to the right of *Alternative:* contains the correct inequality of *greater than*.

The resulting output which includes the null and alternative hypotheses, the value of the $T_+$ (**Above**) test statistic and the p-value will appear in the Session Window and is shown below.

## Sign Test for Median: Class Rank

**Sign test of median = 2.000 versus > 2.000**

| | N | Below | Equal | Above | P | Median |
|---|---|---|---|---|---|---|
| **Class Rank** | 12 | 2 | 1 | 9 | 0.0327 | 3.500 |

Since the p-value of 0.0327 is less than 0.05 ($\alpha$), you may reject the null hypothesis and conclude that the median class rank of all students at Lanston University is greater than Sophomore. Also note that the value of the $T_+$ test statistic is 9.

When the data is measured on the **ordinal** scale, the computation of a confidence interval for the population median $M_0$ is **based upon the Sign Test**. The procedures are calculated according to binomial probabilities and so only a limited number of exact confidence level are possible. Usually this procedure can not produce an interval with the exact confidence level that is desired. And so two exact confidence intervals are computed; one with a confidence level that is the closest exact smaller level, and the other with a confidence level that is the closest exact larger level. Then Minitab uses nonlinear interpolation to compute an approximate confidence interval with the desired confidence level. This is done by

Click on *Stat*, *Nonparametrics*, *1-Sample Sign...*

In the 1-Sample Sign dialog box: you may press the $\boxed{\text{F3}}$ key to clear the contents of this dialog box and reset all options and erase any previous variables. The variables (columns) will appear in the large box on the left side of this dialog box, click on the variable you want to analyze, and click on the $\boxed{\text{Select}}$ button. Next click inside of the circle to the left of *Confidence interval*, then click inside of the box to the right of *Level:*, erase any current incorrect value, and type in the correct confidence level. Then click on $\boxed{\text{OK}}$.

(Since the first graphic is the same as before, only the second graphic is shown below)

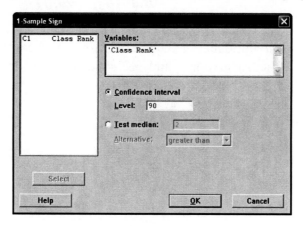

The output of *1-Sample Sign* confidence interval contains:
  (1) The variable column label or name,
  (2) the number of valid observations and the value of the sample median,
  (3) a confidence interval with the closest smaller exact achieved confidence level,
  (4) a confidence interval with the closest larger exact achieved confidence level,
  (5) an nonlinear interpolated confidence interval with the desired achieved confidence level and
  (6) for the two exact confidence intervals in (3) and (4) above, the *Position* number, say pn, indicates that the respective confidence interval goes from the pn[th] smallest score in the data to the pn[th] largest score in the data.

Example 10.2:  Using the same data from Example 10.1, compute a 90% confidence interval for the median class rank of all students at Lanston University.

Click on *Stat*, *Nonparametrics*, *1-Sample Sign...*

In the 1-Sample Sign dialog box: note that Class Rank is already in the *Variables:* box. Next click inside of the circle to the left of *Confidence interval*, click inside of the box to the right of *Level:*, erase any current incorrect value, and type in 90 - the correct confidence level. Then click on $\boxed{\text{OK}}$.

(continued on the next page)

The output containing the three confidence intervals will appear in the Session Window is shown below.

## Sign CI: Class Rank

### Sign confidence interval for median

| | N | Median | Achieved Confidence | Confidence Interval Lower | Upper | Position |
|---|---|---|---|---|---|---|
| Class Rank | 12 | 3.500 | 0.8540 | 3.000 | 4.000 | 4 |
| | | | 0.9000 | 2.800 | 4.200 | NLI |
| | | | 0.9614 | 2.000 | 5.000 | 3 |

And so you are 85.40% confident that the interval from 3 to 4 contains the median class rank of all students at Lanston University and 96.14% confident that the interval from 2 to 5 contains the median class rank of all students at Lanston University. Using nonlinear interpolation, you may say that a 90% confidence interval for the median class rank of all students at Lanston University is from 2.8 to 4.2 .

The **Wilcoxon Signed-Rank Test** and corresponding confidence interval assumes that the data in the random sample is inherently **continuous**, but may be measured on an ordinal scale. This assumption of an underlying continuous distribution is more restrictive than the assumption for the previous Sign Test; and as such is more powerful for continuous data, but should not be used when the data is purely ordinal. While different texts may give slightly different rules for the test statistic, one fairly common method is to subtract the value of $M_0$ from each score, rank the absolute values of these differences (eliminating and zero differences), and then compute the sum of these ranks only for the originally positive differences. This test statistic and the corresponding p-value are computed by

Click on *Stat , Nonparametrics , 1-Sample Wilcoxon...*

In the 1-Sample Wilcoxon dialog box: you may press the $\boxed{\text{F3}}$ key to clear the contents of this dialog box and reset all options and erase any previous variables. The variables (columns) will appear in the large box on the left side of this dialog box, click on the variable you want to analyze, and click on the $\boxed{\text{Select}}$ button. Next click inside of the circle to the left of *Test Median:*, erase any current incorrect value, and type in the given value of the population median ($M_0$). Then make sure that the box to the right of *Alternative:* contains the correct inequality for your problem (*not equal* or *less than* or *greater than*). If not, click on the down triangle ( $\boxed{\blacktriangledown}$ ), and click on the correct choice. Then click on $\boxed{\text{OK}}$ .

(See the graphics on the next page.)

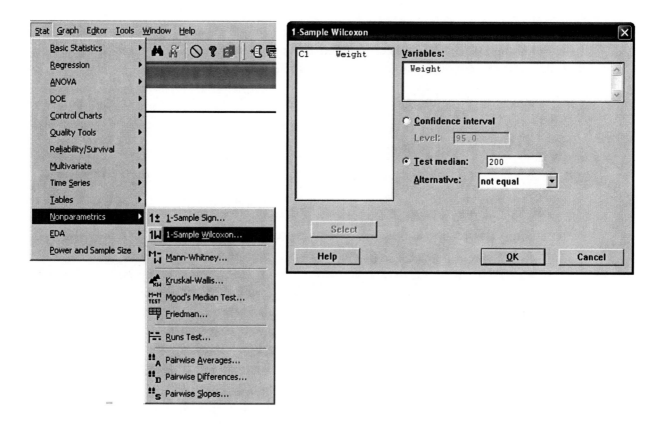

The output of *1-Sample Wilcoxon Signed-Rank* Test contains:
- (1)  The null and alternative hypotheses,
- (2)  the variable column label or name,
- (3)  the number of objects in the sample and the number of non-zero differences used in the computation,
- (4)  the value of the Wilcoxon (Signed-Rank) test statistic,
- (5)  the  p-value for the test and
- (6)  the value of the sample median.

The p-value may be interpreted as "based upon the data of this sample, if you decide to reject the null hypothesis then the probability of this decision being an error is equal to the p-value."

Example 10.3    The Department of Health is investigating the growing problem of obesity in the State of Maryland.  In particular the department is studying adult males who are not actively involved in any form of exercise.  A random sample of 14 such males was taken and their weights are: 210, 170, 210, 160, 220, 240, 180, 215, 220, 160, 225, 175, 210 and 200. The department believes that the typical weight is now above 180 pounds.  At the 0.01 significance level test  this belief.

Enter these 14 scores into column 3 of the Worksheet Window and label the column Weight.

(continued on the next page)

Since this data is continuous, but was measured to the closest 5 pounds (making the measurement ordinal), the Wilcoxon Signed-Rank Test is appropriate. And for this example we will use the population median as the typical score.

The hypothesis testing problem is
$H_0$: M ≤ 180
$H_a$: M > 180
α = 0.01
and the test statistic is the sum of the ranks of the differences that are originally positive.

Click on *Stat* , *Nonparametrics* , *1-Sample Wilcoxon...*

In the 1-Sample Wilcoxon dialog box: you may press the | **F3** | key to clear the contents of this dialog box and reset all options and erase any previous variables. The variables (columns) will appear in the large box on the left side of this dialog box, click on the Weight (C3) variable and click on the | **Select** | button. Next click inside of the circle to the left of *Test Median:*, erase any current incorrect value, and type in185 - the given value of the population median ($M_0$). Then make sure that the box to the right of *Alternative:* contains the correct inequality of *greater than*. If not, click on the down triangle ( | ▾ | ), and click on the correct choice. Then click on | **OK** | .

The resulting output which includes the null and alternative hypotheses, the value of the Wilcoxon (Signed-Rank) test statistic and the p-value will appear in the Session Window shown below.

## *Wilcoxon Signed Rank Test: Weight*

### *Test of median = 180.0 versus median > 180.0*

|  | N | N for Test | Wilcoxon Statistic | P | Estimated Median |
|---|---|---|---|---|---|
| *Weight* | *14* | *13* | *80.0* | *0.009* | *200.0* |

Since the p-value of 0.009 is less than 0.01 (α), the Department of Health may reject the null hypothesis and conclude that the median weight of all adult males who are not actively involved in any form of exercise is greater than 180 pounds. Also, the value of the Wilcoxon (Signed-Rank) test statistic (the sum of the ranks only for the originally positive differences) is 9.

When the data is inherently **continuous**, but may be measured on an ordinal scale , the computation of a confidence interval for the population median M is **based upon the Wilcoxon Signed-Rank Test**. The procedures are calculated according to discrete probabilities and so only a limited number of exact confidence level are possible. Usually this procedure can not produce an interval with the exact confidence level that is desired. Minitab computes the confidence interval with the achieved confidence level that is closest to the desired confidence level. This is done by

Click on *Stat*, *Nonparametrics*, *1-Sample Wilcoxon...*

In the 1-Sample Wilcoxon dialog box: you may press the F3 key to clear the contents of this dialog box and reset all options and erase any previous variables. The variables (columns) will appear in the large box on the left side of this dialog box, click on the variable you want to analyze, and click on the Select button. Next click inside of the circle to the left of *Confidence interval*, then click inside of the box to the right of *Level:*, erase any current incorrect value, and type in the correct confidence level. Then click on OK.

(Since the first graphic is the same as before, only the second graphic is shown below)

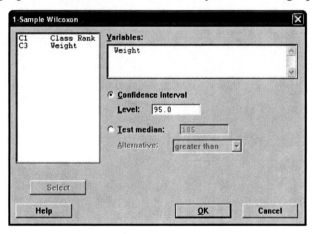

The output of *1-Sample Wilcoxon* confidence interval contains:

    (1)    The variable column label or name,

    (2)    the number of valid observations and the value of the sample median,

    (3)    the confidence level with the closest exact achieved confidence level,

    (4)    the corresponding confidence interval.

Example 10.4:    Using the same data from Example 10.3, compute a 90% confidence interval for the median weight of all adult males who are not actively involved in any form of exercise.

Click on *Stat*, *Nonparametrics*, *1-Sample Wilcoxon...*

In the 1-Sample Wilcoxon dialog box: note that Weight is already in the *Variables:* box. Next click inside of the circle to the left of *Confidence interval*, click inside of the box to the right of *Level:*, erase any current incorrect value, and type in 90 - the correct confidence level. Then click on OK.

The output containing the closest confidence interval will appear in the Session Window shown on the next page.

(continued on the next page)

## Wilcoxon Signed Rank CI: Weight

| | N | Estimated Median | Achieved Confidence | Confidence Interval | |
|---|---|---|---|---|---|
| | | | | Lower | Upper |
| Weight | 14 | 200.0 | 94.8 | 185.0 | 215.0 |

And so the Department of Health may be 94.8% confident that the interval from 185.0 to 215.0 contains the median weight of all adult males who are not actively involved in any form of exercise.

# Lab Assignment 10.1

**Name:**                                                            **Date:**

**Course:**                    **Section:**                    **Data CD Number:**

1.  Start a Minitab session. If you are unable to complete this lab assignment in one Minitab session, save the project as Lab 10-1 . **Never** use a period as part of the project name; since Minitab uses the period to attach the file type to the file name. Then at your next Minitab session, you may open this Lab 10-1.MPJ project and continue to work where you left off previously.

2.  A local state representative wanted to know how her constituents felt about raising the minimum wage, and so she asked a random sample of people in her district their opinion on the increase of the minimum wage law. The possible responses were strongly against (SA), against (A), neutral (N), in favor (F) and strongly in favor (SF). The sample results were:

    A, SA, SF, F, F, N, SF, F, SF,  F, A, N, SF and F

    Code the data as SA = 1, A = 2, N = 3, F = 4 and SF = 5.  Test the hypothesis that all of her constituents were in favor of increasing the minimum wage; i.e., that the median response is more positive than neutral.  Use a significance level of 0.10

3.  Open the worksheet Sociology.mtw that is on your data disc. This worksheet contains the midterm and final exam letter grades for a random sample of students taking the Sociology 102 course at Canton State University. Code the midterm letter grade with the usual grade point average equivalents of A=4, B=3, C=2, D=1 and F=0. Compute a 90% confidence interval for the median grade of all students taking the Sociology 102 course at Canton State University. Report all three intervals and interpret them in terms of letter grades.

4.  Open the worksheet Clinic.mtw that is on your data disc. This worksheet contains data taken from random samples at the Orange County's Clinic for Advanced Research. Among the data in this worksheet are Hamilton change in depression scores from a random sample of patients originally diagnosed as clinically depressed. These scores measure the change in the depression score after the patients had been on an experimental anti-depressant for five weeks, and the data has an underlying continuous distribution. A negative change indicates that the patient has become more depressed, while a positive score indicates an improvement in the patient's state of mind. At the 0.05 significance level, test to see if this experimental drug would bring about a median improvement of more than 1.5 points on the Hamilton scale.

    (lab assignment is continued on the second side of this page)

5.  Using the same data from problem 4, compute a 90% confidence interval for the median Hamilton change in depression scores of all patients diagnosed as clinically depressed.

6.  Since the detection of blood doping is not effective after four days, a few cyclists will try to get away with this illegal practice by blood doping 4 days before the event. Two new detection methods are being tested at the Orange County Clinic for Advanced Research. The manufacturers of both of these methods claim that they will detect blood doping for more than the current four day lapse in time. Two independent samples of blood injected with the doping agent were taken. Detection method Gamma was used on one sample and method Omega was used on the second sample. The number of days elapsed until the doping agent was no longer detectable was measured in each blood sample. Use $\alpha = 0.05$, and test to determine if the median Gamma method detection time of all cyclists who engage in blood doping is greater than four days.

7.  Print your Session Window to the printer.

8.  Attach both your Minitab output and your complete answers to this sheet and submit all three to your instructor.

**Section 2:     Two Independent Sample Confidence Intervals and Hypothesis Tests for the Difference of Population Location Parameters (Medians)**

Comparison of two separate populations is the goal in many research situations, and the methods used are usually called "two sample" techniques. When using the z or t confidence intervals and tests as presented in Chapters 6 and 8, the parameters of interest were the population means $\mu_1$ and $\mu_2$. However when the sample sizes are small and the population distributions are unknown, we use nonparametric techniques and analyze the population medians $M_1$ and $M_2$.

The "two sample" hypothesis test comparing the medians of two populations may take on one of the following three forms:

(a)  $H_0\colon M_1 = M_2$       (b)  $H_0\colon M_1 \geq M_2$       (c)  $H_0\colon M_1 \leq M_2$
  $H_a\colon M_1 \neq M_2$             $H_a\colon M_1 < M_2$              $H_a\colon M_1 > M_2$

The objects in two samples may be chosen independently of each other, or the objects may be paired or matched as they are selected for each sample. A technique for independent samples is presented in this section, and a technique for two paired samples is given in the next section.

The **Wilcoxon Rank-Sum Test** or the **Mann-Whitney Test** is the analog to the parametric t test. These two tests were developed independently and use somewhat different test statistics, but they are equivalent when testing the hypothesis of equal population medians. Since Minitab uses the Mann-Whitney test, this is what will be described in this workbook. The Mann-Whitney test corresponding confidence interval assumes that: (1) the two random samples are taken independently, (2) the data is inherently **continuous**, but may be measured on an ordinal scale and (3) the two population distributions are the same in all respects other than possible their medians.

The data for each sample need to be in two different variables (columns) of the Minitab worksheet. The procedure for the Mann-Whitney test is to combine the two samples and then rank the scores in this combined sample. Next the sum of the ranks for those scores that are in the first sample is computed, and this is the Mann-Whitney test statistic. This test statistic and the corresponding p-value are computed by

Click on *Stat , Nonparametrics , Mann-Whitney...*

In the Mann-Whitney dialog box: you may press the ⬚ **F3** ⬚ key to clear the contents of this dialog box and reset all options and erase any previous variables. The variables (columns) will appear in the large box on the left side of this dialog box and the cursor will be inside of the box to the right of *First Sample:*. Click on the variable that contains the data for the first sample, and click on the ⬚ **Select** ⬚ button. The cursor will now be inside of the box to the right of *Second Sample:*. Click on the variable that contains the data for the second sample, and click on the ⬚ **Select** ⬚ button. When doing hypothesis testing you may ignore the value inside of the box to the right of *Confidence level:*. Next make sure that the box to the right of *Alternative:* contains the correct inequality for your problem (*not equal* or *less than* or *greater than*). If not, click on the down triangle ( ▾ ), and click on the correct choice. Then click on ⬚ **OK** ⬚.

(See graphics on the next page.)

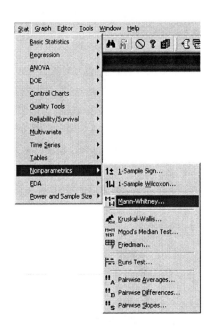
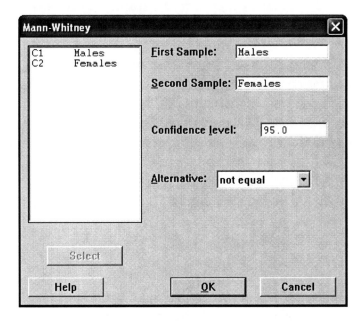

The output of *Mann-Whitney* Test contains:

(1) the variable column labels or names, the number of objects in each sample and the medians of each sample,.

(2) a point estimate for the difference of population medians,

(4) the closest achieved confidence interval for the difference on population medians,

(4) the value of the Mann-Whitney (W) test statistic,

(5) the null and alternative hypotheses, and the p-value for the test and

(6) if there are tied ranks, the p-value for the test after adjustments for tied rankings has been made.

Note that Minitab labels the medians as - note that Minitab labels this difference as *ETA1* and *ETA2* in its output.

Example 10.5:  Students in School District 6 take the functional reading test in both the ninth and eleventh grade. The superintendent of schools wants to determine if there is a gain in scores on the functional reading test over this time period. Two independent samples of ninth and eleventh grade scores gave the following results:

Ninth Grade:  6, 8, 13 and 10
Eleventh Grade:  9, 15 and 11.

At the 0.025 significance level, test the hypothesis that the scores on the functional reading test in the eleventh grade have increased over those scores in the ninth grade.

(continued on the next page)

Open a new worksheet (*File -> New -> Worksheet*), name Columns 1 and 2 as Grade 9 and Grade 11 respectively, and enter the above data into these columns. Your worksheet should look as shown below.

| C1 | C2 |
|---|---|
| Grade 9 | Grade 11 |
| 6 | 9 |
| 8 | 15 |
| 13 | 11 |
| 10 | |

Population 1 is all ninth grade students in School District 6, and so column C1 contains the data in the corresponding sample.

Population 2 is all eleventh grade students in School District 6, and so column C2 contains the data in the corresponding sample.

While this data was measured on an ordinal scale, the underlying distribution could be considered to be inherently continuous (by considering each instant in the grade as a fractional part of that grade). And so the the Mann-Whitney test is appropriate. And for this example we will use the population median as the representative score in each population.

The hypothesis testing problem is
$H_0: M_1 \geq M_2$
$H_a: M_1 < M_2$
$\alpha = 0.025$
and the test statistic is the sum of the ranks of the first (Grade 9) sample.

Click on *Stat , Nonparametrics , Mann-Whitney...*

In the Mann-Whitney dialog box: you may press the $\boxed{\text{F3}}$ key to clear the contents of this dialog box and reset all options and erase any previous variables. The variables (columns) will appear in the large box on the left side of this dialog box and the cursor will be inside of the box to the right of *First Sample:*. Click on the Grade 9 (C1) variable that contains the data for the first sample, and click on the $\boxed{\text{Select}}$ button. The cursor will now be inside of the box to the right of *Second Sample:*. Click on the Grade 11 (C2) variable that contains the data for the second sample, and click on the $\boxed{\text{Select}}$ button. Ignore the value inside of the box to the right of *Confidence level:*. Next make sure that the box to the right of *Alternative:* contains the correct inequality of *less than*. If not, click on the down triangle ( $\boxed{\blacktriangledown}$ ), and click on the correct choice. Then click on $\boxed{\text{OK}}$.

The resulting output which includes the null and alternative hypotheses, the value of the Mann-Whitney W test statistic and the p-value will appear in the Session Window as shown on the next page.

(continued on the next page.)

403

## Mann-Whitney Test and CI: Grade 9, Grade 11

|          | N | Median |
|----------|---|--------|
| Grade 9  | 4 | 9.000  |
| Grade 11 | 3 | 11.000 |

**Point estimate for ETA1-ETA2 is -2.500**
**94.8 Percent CI for ETA1-ETA2 is (-9.000,4.001)**
**W = 13.0**
**Test of ETA1 = ETA2 vs ETA1 < ETA2 is significant at 0.1884**

Since the p-value of 0.1884 is greater than 0.025 ($\alpha$), the Superintendent of School District 6 may not reject the null hypothesis and therefore may <u>not</u> conclude that the median functional reading scores of all ninth grade students in School District 6 is less than the functional reading scores of all eleventh grade students in School District 6. That is the superintendent may <u>not</u> conclude that the scores on the functional reading test in the eleventh grade have increased over those scores in the ninth grade. Also, the value of the Mann-Whitney W test statistic (the sum of the ranks for the first sample) is 13.

When the data is inherently **continuous**, but may be measured on an ordinal scale , the computation of a confidence interval for the difference of population medians $M_1$ - $M_2$ is **based upon the Mann-WhitneyTest**. The procedures are calculated according to discrete probabilities and so only a limited number of exact confidence levels are possible. Usually this procedure cannot produce an interval with the exact confidence level that is desired. Minitab computes the confidence interval with the achieved confidence level that is closest to the desired confidence level. This is done by

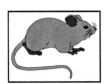

Click on *Stat , Nonparametrics , Mann-Whitney...*

In the Mann-Whitney dialog box: you may press the F3 key to clear the contents of this dialog box and reset all options and erase any previous variables. The variables (columns) will appear in the large box on the left side of this dialog box and the cursor will be inside of the box to the right of *First Sample:*. Click on the variable that contains the data for the first sample, and click on the Select button. The cursor will now be inside of the box to the right of *Second Sample:*. Click on the variable that contains the data for the second sample, and click on the Select button. Next Click inside the box to the right of *Confidence level:*, erase any current incorrect value, and type in the correct confidence level. When doing a confidence interval you may ignore box to the right of *Alternative:*. Then click on OK .

(See graphics on the next page.)

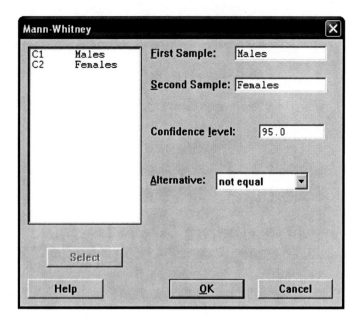

The output of *Mann-Whitney* confidence interval contains:

- (1) the variable column labels or names, the number of objects in each sample and the medians of each sample,
- (2) a point estimate for the difference of population medians,
- (4) the closest achieved confidence interval for the difference on population medians,
- (4) the value of the Mann-Whitney (W) test statistic (which may be ignored when doing confidence intervals),
- (5) the null and alternative hypotheses, and the p-value for the test (which may be ignored when doing confidence intervals) and
- (6) if there are tied ranks, the p-value for the test after adjustments for tied rankings has been made (which may be ignored when doing confidence intervals).

Note that Minitab labels the medians as - note that Minitab labels this difference as *ETA1* and *ETA2* in its output.

Example 10.6:  Using the same data from Example 10.5, compute a 85% confidence interval for the difference in median functional reading scores of all ninth grade students versus all eleventh grade students in School District 6.

Click on *Stat*, *Nonparametrics*, *Mann-Whitney...*

In the Mann-Whitney dialog box: you may press the **F3** key to clear the contents of this dialog box and reset all options and erase any previous variables. The variables (columns) will appear in the large box on the left side of this dialog box and the cursor will be inside of the box to the right of *First Sample:*. Click on the Grade 9 (C1) variable that contains the data for the first sample, and click on the **Select** button. The cursor will now be inside of the box to the right of *Second Sample:*. Click on the Grade 11 (C2) variable that contains the data for the second sample, and click on the **Select** button. Next Click inside the box to the right of *Confidence level:*, erase any current incorrect value, and type in 85 - the correct confidence level. Ignore box to the right of *Alternative:*. Then click on **OK**.

(continued on the next page)

The output containing the closest confidence interval shown below will appear in the Session Window.

### Mann-Whitney Test and CI: Grade 9, Grade 11

|          | N | Median |
|----------|---|--------|
| Grade 9  | 4 | 9.000  |
| Grade 11 | 3 | 11.000 |

Point estimate for ETA1-ETA2 is -2.500
88.8 Percent CI for ETA1-ETA2 is (-7.001,2.002)
W = 13.0
Test of ETA1 = ETA2 vs ETA1 not = ETA2 is significant at 0.3768

And so the Superintendent may be 88.8% confident that the interval from -7.001 to 2.002 contains the difference in median functional reading scores of all ninth grade students versus all eleventh grade students in School District 6.

# Lab Assignment 10.2

**Name:**                                                          **Date:**

**Course:**                    **Section:**                    **Data CD Number:**

1.  Start a Minitab session. If you are unable to complete this lab assignment in one Minitab session, save the project as Lab 10-2 . **Never** use a period as part of the project name; since Minitab uses the period to attach the file type to the file name. Then at your next Minitab session, you may open this Lab 10-2.MPJ project and continue to work where you left off previously.

2.  The Bass Corporation is planning to upgrade the computers for all of its employees. The current operation system is Windows 2000, and the Information Technology Office is considering upgrading to new PC computers with Widows Vista or new Macintosh computers. A major concern is the employee's learning curve time required for the upgrade. Two independent samples of current employees was taken; one sample was trained on the new PC with Windows Vista, and the other sample was trained on new Macintosh computers. The learning curve time (in hours) to become proficient was measured for each employee with the following results:

    PC with Windows Vista: 8, 12, 5, 9, 11, 15, 7, 21, 16, 13, 9, 10, 7 and 14

    Macintosh: 7, 17, 23, 15, 8, 10, 22, 18, 28, 12, 16, 27 and 18.

    Using $\alpha = 0.05$, test the hypothesis that for all employees in the Bass Corporation, the median learning curve time to upgrade the PC with Windows Vista is less than the median learning curve time to upgrade to the new Macintosh computers.

3.  Since the detection of blood doping is not effective after four days, a few cyclists will try to get away with this illegal practice by blood doping 4 days before the event. Two new detection methods are being tested at the Orange County Clinic for Advanced Research. The manufacturers of both of these methods claim that they will detect blood doping for more than the current four day lapse in time. Open the Clinic.mtw worksheet that is on your data disc. Two independent samples of blood injected with the doping agent were taken. Detection method Gamma was used on one sample and method Omega was used on the second sample. The number of days elapsed until the doping agent was no longer detectable was measured in each blood sample. Test to see if there is any difference in the median detection time of these two methods for all cyclists who engage in the practice of blood doping. Use a 0.10 level of significance.

(lab assignment is continued on the second side of this page)

4. Use the detection of blood doping data from problem 3, and compute an approximate 90% confidence interval for the difference in median detection times for the Gamma versus the Omega method.

5. Print your Session Window to the printer.

6. Attach both your Minitab output and <u>your complete answers</u> to this sheet and submit all three to your instructor.

**Section 3:** **Two Paired Sample Confidence Intervals and Hypothesis Tests for the Difference of Population Location Parameters (Medians)**

When the data is collected in two paired samples, most techniques first need to compute a difference variable. This is true for both parametric and nonparametric methods. This was demonstrated in Chapter 8 Section 2 when using the Paired-Z test. Then a 1-Sample Z method was used to analyze this difference variable. The same approach is used when nonparametric techniques are appropriate. To create this new difference variable, choose a column number that is different than any of the existing column numbers in the current worksheet, click in the name box for this column and type in the letter d for the name of this column. The values for this difference variable are calculated and stored in this new d variable by

Click on *Calc , Calculator...*

In the Calculator dialog box the cursor will be inside the box to the right of *Store result in variable:*. Highlight the new d variable and click on the ⬜ **Select** button. Next click inside of the box under *Expression:*, click on the variable containing the **first** sample's data, click on the ⬜ **Select** button, click on the button with the minus sign (-) on it, click on the variable containing the **second** sample's data, and click on the ⬜ **Select** button. (Optionally you may just type in the first sample's column number, followed by a minus sign, and then the second sample's column number.) Then click on ⬜ **OK** .

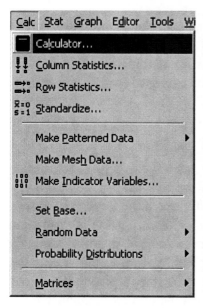
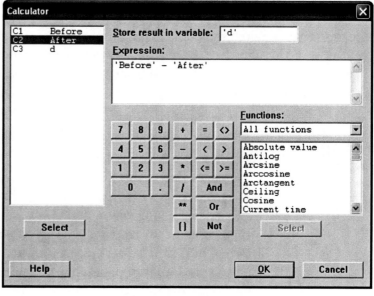

This performs the calculation in the *Expression:* box for <u>every</u> row with a <u>valid</u> pair of scores and stores the results into the corresponding rows in the new variable. If either of the variables in the *Expression:* box contains a missing value in a particular row, that row in the new variable will also contain a missing value. These missing values are displayed as an asterisk (*). The dialog box above illustrates the case when you want to calculate the difference between the Before and After variable and store the result in the d variable.

The "two sample" hypothesis test comparing the medians of two populations shown in Section 2 are:

(a) $H_0: M_1 = M_2$
    $H_a: M_1 \neq M_2$

(b) $H_0: M_1 \geq M_2$
    $H_a: M_1 < M_2$

(c) $H_0: M_1 \leq M_2$
    $H_a: M_1 > M_2$

but these may be rewritten as:

(a) $H_0: M_1 - M_2 = 0$
    $H_a: M_1 - M_2 \neq 0$

(b) $H_0: M_1 - M_2 \geq 0$
    $H_a: M_1 - M_2 > 0$

(c) $H_0: M_1 - M_2 \leq 0$
    $H_a: M_1 - M_2 > 0$.

Since we compute the difference variable as $d = x_1 - x_2$, the median of the differences ($M_d$) is the same as the difference of the medians; i.e., $M_d = M_1 - M_2$, and so these may again be rewritten as:

(a) $H_0: M_d = 0$
    $H_a: M_d \neq 0$

(b) $H_0: M_d \geq 0$
    $H_a: M_d > 0$

(c) $H_0: M_d \leq 0$
    $H_a: M_d > 0$.

And so the hypothesis tests for M1 versus M2 and confidence intervals for $M_1 - M_2$ may be computed as a 1 sample procedure on the median of the differences - $M_d$.

As discussed in Section 1, the **Sign Test** and corresponding confidence interval assume that the data in the two paired sample is inherently **ordinal** as well as being measured on an ordinal scale. This is the least restrictive assumption when dealing with the population median, and so this test is valid for almost any situation where parametric methods do not work. For hypothesis testing, the test statistic and the corresponding p-value are computed by

Click on *Stat , Nonparametrics , 1-Sample Sign...*

In the 1-Sample Sign dialog box: you may press the [ **F3** ] key to clear the contents of this dialog box and reset all options and erase any previous variables. The variables (columns) will appear in the large box on the left side of this dialog box, click on d - the difference variable you want to analyze, and click on the [ **Select** ] button. Next click inside of the circle to the left of *Test Median:*, erase any current incorrect value, and type in 0 - the given value of the population difference median ($M_d$). Then make sure that the box to the right of *Alternative:* contains the correct inequality for your problem (*not equal* or *less than* or *greater than*). If not, click on the down triangle ( [ ▾ ] ), and click on the correct choice. Then click on [ **OK** ].

(See graphics on the next page.)

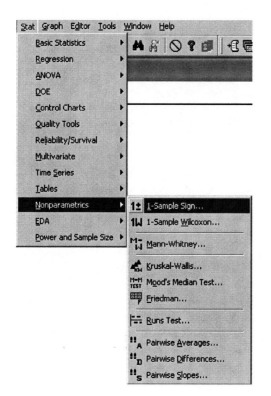

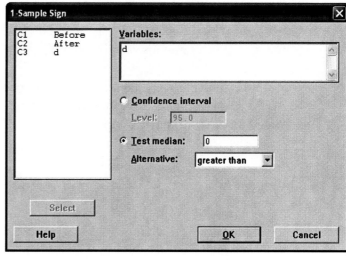

Similarly as shown in Section 1, the output of *1-Sample Sign* Test contains:

 (1) The null and alternative hypotheses,

 (2) the difference variable column label or name,

 (3) the common number of valid paired observations, the number of differences below the hypothesized median difference $M_d$, which is usually 0, (number of - signs), the number of differences equal to $M_d$ (number of ties or zeros), and the number of differences above $M_d$ (number of + signs),

 (4) the p-value for the test and

 (5) the value of the sample median difference.

Example 10.7: On a popular televison program where two critics judge movies, many people believe that Randy is an easier critic than Marty. To test this perception, a random sample of seven movies was chosen. A rating scale 1 to 10 was used with 1 being terrible and 10 being great. Randy and Marty judged each movie and the results are:

| Movie | Shilo | Beautiful Mind | Seabiscuit | Heat | JFK | Closer | English Patient |
|---|---|---|---|---|---|---|---|
| **Randy** | 5 | 10 | 6 | 4 | 8 | 9 | 10 |
| **Marty** | 3 | 9 | 8 | 4 | 6 | 5 | 7 |

With $\alpha = 0.10$, test the hypothesis that in general (median) Randy's ratings are higher than Marty's ratings.

(continued on the next page)

Population 1 is all movies seen by Randy.

Population 2 is all movies seen by Marty.

This data is inherently ordinal and paired on the same movie seen by each critic, and so the Sign test is appropriate. And for this example we will use the population median as the representative score in each population.

The hypothesis testing problem is

$H_0$: $M_1 \leq M_2$

$H_a$: $M_1 > M_2$

$\alpha = 0.10$

and the test statistic is number of differences above 0 (number of +s).

Open a new worksheet, name columns 1 and 2 as Marty and Randy respectively. Then enter the ratings given in the table on the previous page into these columns. Your worksheet should look as shown below.

**Worksheet 4 ***

| ↓ | C1 | C2 |
|---|---|---|
| | Randy | Marty |
| 1 | 5 | 3 |
| 2 | 10 | 9 |
| 3 | 6 | 8 |
| 4 | 4 | 4 |
| 5 | 8 | 6 |
| 6 | 9 | 5 |
| 7 | 10 | 7 |

Next name column 3 as d (for difference) and compute the differences of Randy's minus Marty's ratings.

Click on *Calc , Calculator...*

In the Calculator dialog box the cursor will be inside the box to the right of *Store result in variable:*. Highlight the new d variable and click on the $\boxed{\text{Select}}$ button. Next click inside of the box under *Expression:*, click on the Randy (C1) variable containing the **first** sample's data, click on the $\boxed{\text{Select}}$ button, click on the button with the minus sign (-) on it, click on the Marty (C2) variable containing the **second** sample's data, and click on the $\boxed{\text{Select}}$ button. Then click on $\boxed{\text{OK}}$ .

Now your worksheet should look like:

**Worksheet 4 ***

| ↓ | C1 | C2 | C3 |
|---|---|---|---|
| | Randy | Marty | d |
| 1 | 5 | 3 | 2 |
| 2 | 10 | 9 | 1 |
| 3 | 6 | 8 | -2 |
| 4 | 4 | 4 | 0 |
| 5 | 8 | 6 | 2 |
| 6 | 9 | 5 | 4 |
| 7 | 10 | 7 | 3 |

(continued on the next page)

Next compute the Sign test by

Click on *Stat , Nonparametrics , 1-Sample Sign...*

In the 1-Sample Sign dialog box: you may press the $\boxed{\text{F3}}$ key to clear the contents of this dialog box and reset all options and erase any previous variables. The variables (columns) will appear in the large box on the left side of this dialog box, click on d - the difference variable you want to analyze, and click on the $\boxed{\text{Select}}$ button. Next click inside of the circle to the left of *Test Median:*, erase any current incorrect value, and type in 0 - the given value of the population difference median ($M_d$). Then make sure that the box to the right of *Alternative:* contains the correct inequality of *greater than*. Then click on $\boxed{\text{OK}}$ .

The resulting output which includes the null and alternative hypotheses, the value of the $T_+$ (**Above**) test statistic and the p-value will appear in the Session Window is shown below.

## Sign Test for Median: d

### Sign test of median = 0.00000 versus > 0.00000

|   | N | Below | Equal | Above | P | Median |
|---|---|-------|-------|-------|---|--------|
| d | 7 | 1 | 1 | 5 | 0.1094 | 2.000 |

Since the p-value of 0.1094 is greater than 0.10 ($\alpha$), you may not reject the null hypothesis and therefore not conclude that the median of Marty's ratings of all movies is greater than the median of Randy's ratings of all movies; i.e., you may not conclude that Marty is an easier critic than Marty. Also note that the value of the $T_+$ test statistic is 5.

A confidence interval for the difference $M_1 - M_2 = M_d$ is computed the same way as described in Section 1 by using the difference variable, d, and the output also is similar to that as described in Section 1 (except now the use the difference variable).

Example 10.8:   Using the same data from Example 10.7, compute a 90% confidence interval for the difference in Marty's and Randy' median rating of all movies they have seen.

Click on *Stat , Nonparametrics , 1-Sample Sign...*

In the 1-Sample Sign dialog box: note that the d variable is already in the *Variables:* box. Next click inside of the circle to the left of *Confidence interval*, click inside of the box to the right of *Level:*, erase any current incorrect value, and type in 90 - the correct confidence level. Then click on $\boxed{\text{OK}}$.

The output containing the three confidence intervals will appear in the Session Window is shown on the next page.

(continued on the next page)

## Sign CI:  d

**Sign confidence interval for median**

| | N | Median | Achieved Confidence | Confidence Interval Lower | Upper | Position |
|---|---|---|---|---|---|---|
| Class Rank | 7 | 2.000 | 0.8750 | 0.000 | 3.000 | 2 |
| | | | 0.9000 | -0.094 | 3.047 | NLI |
| | | | 0.9444 | -2.000 | 4.000 | 1 |

And so you are 87.50% confident that the interval from 0 to34 contains the difference in Marty's and Randy' median rating of all movies they have seen and 94.44% confident that the interval from -2 to 4 contains the difference in Marty's and Randy' median rating of all movies they have seen. Using nonlinear interpolation, you may say that a 90% confidence interval for the difference in Marty's and Randy' median rating of all movies they have seen is from -0.094 to 3.047 .

As discussed in Section 1, the **Wilcoxon Signed-Rank Test** and corresponding confidence interval assumes that the data in the random sample is inherently **continuous**, but may be measured on an ordinal scale. This assumption of an underlying continuous distribution is more restrictive than the assumption for the previous Sign Test; and as such is more powerful for continuous data, but should not be used when the data is purely ordinal. This test statistic and the corresponding p-value are computed by

Click on *Stat , Nonparametrics , 1-Sample Wilcoxon...*

In the 1-Sample Wilcoxon dialog box: you may press the [ **F3** ] key to clear the contents of this dialog box and reset all options and erase any previous variables. The variables (columns) will appear in the large box on the left side of this dialog box, click on  d - the difference variable you want to analyze, and click on the [ **Select** ] button. Next click inside of the circle to the left of *Test Median:,* erase any current incorrect value, and type in 0 - the given value of the population difference median ($M_d$). Then make sure that the box to the right of *Alternative:* contains the correct inequality for your problem (*not equal* or *less than* or *greater than*). If not, click on the down triangle ( [▼] ), and click on the correct choice. Then click on [ **OK** ] .

(See graphics on the next page.)

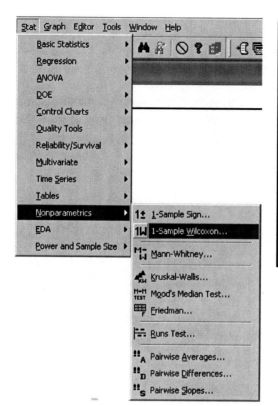

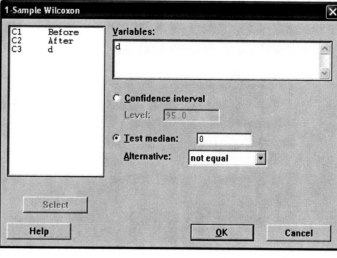

Similarly as shown in Section 1, the output of *1-Sample Wilcoxon Signed-Rank* Test contains:

  (1)   The null and alternative hypotheses,
  (2)   the difference variable column label or name,
  (3)   the common number of objects in each of the two paired samples and the number of non-zero differences used in the computation,
  (4)   the value of the Wilcoxon (Signed-Rank) test statistic,
  (5)   the p-value for the test and
  (6)   the value of the sample difference median.

Example 10.9:   Ten married couples were randomly selected and each husband and wife were asked how much money they spent of their spouse's birthday present this year. The results were:

| | Couple | | | | | | | | | |
|---|---|---|---|---|---|---|---|---|---|---|
| | 1 | 2 | 3 | 4 | 5 | 6 | 7 | 8 | 9 | 10 |
| Husband | 25 | 21 | 38 | 64 | 52 | 16 | 26 | 33 | 45 | 8 |
| Wife | 16 | 42 | 56 | 80 | 40 | 36 | 26 | 50 | 67 | 50 |

Test the hypothesis that in general wives spend more than their husbands on their spouse's birthday present. Use a 0.05 significance level.

(continued on the next page)

Population 1 is all husbands.

Population 2 is all wives.

This data the amount of money spent on spouse's birthday gift, is inherently continuous and paired on the same couple being measured. And so the Wilcoxon Signed-Sign test on the differences is appropriate. The population median as the representative score in each population.

The hypothesis testing problem is

$H_0: M_1 \geq M_2$

$H_a: M_1 < M_2$

$\alpha = 0.05$

and the test statistic is the sum of the ranks of the differences that are originally positive.

Open a new worksheet, name columns 1 and 2 as Husband and Wife respectively. Then enter the ratings given in the table on the previous page into these columns. Your worksheet should look as shown below.

| Worksheet 5 *** | | |
|---|---|---|
| ↓ | C1 | C2 |
| | Husband | Wife |
| 1 | 25 | 16 |
| 2 | 21 | 42 |
| 3 | 38 | 56 |
| 4 | 64 | 80 |
| 5 | 52 | 40 |
| 6 | 16 | 36 |
| 7 | 26 | 26 |
| 8 | 33 | 50 |
| 9 | 45 | 67 |
| 10 | 8 | 50 |

Next name column 3 as d (for difference) and compute the differences of husband's minus wife's amount of money spent on spouse's birthday gift.

Click on *Calc , Calculator...*
In the Calculator dialog box the cursor will be inside the box to the right of *Store result in variable:*. Highlight the new d variable and click on the | **Select** | button. Next click inside of the box under *Expression:*, click on the Husband (C1) variable containing the **first** sample's data, click on the | **Select** | button, click on the button with the minus sign (-) on it, click on the Wife (C2) variable containing the **second** sample's data, and click on the | **Select** | button. Then click on | **OK** | .

Now your worksheet should look as shown on the next page:

(continued on the next page)

| Worksheet 5 *** | | | |
|---|---|---|---|
| ↓ | C1 | C2 | C3 |
| | Husband | Wife | d |
| 1 | 25 | 16 | 9 |
| 2 | 21 | 42 | -21 |
| 3 | 38 | 56 | -18 |
| 4 | 64 | 80 | -16 |
| 5 | 52 | 40 | 12 |
| 6 | 16 | 36 | -20 |
| 7 | 26 | 26 | 0 |
| 8 | 33 | 50 | -17 |
| 9 | 45 | 67 | -22 |
| 10 | 8 | 50 | -42 |

Click on *Stat*, *Nonparametrics*, *1-Sample Wilcoxon...*

In the 1-Sample Wilcoxon dialog box: you may press the [ F3 ] key to clear the contents of this dialog box and reset all options and erase any previous variables. The variables (columns) will appear in the large box on the left side of this dialog box, click on the d (C3) variable and click on the [ Select ] button. Next click inside of the circle to the left of *Test Median:*, erase any current incorrect value, and type in 0 - the given value of the population difference median ($M_d$). Then make sure that the box to the right of *Alternative:* contains the correct inequality of *less than*. If not, click on the down triangle ( [▼] ), and click on the correct choice. Then click on [ OK ].

The resulting output which includes the null and alternative hypotheses, the value of the Wilcoxon (Signed-Rank) test statistic and the p-value will appear in the Session Window shown below.

## Wilcoxon Signed Rank Test:  d

*Test of median = 0.000000 versus median > 0.000000*

| | N | N for Test | Wilcoxon Statistic | P | Estimated Median |
|---|---|---|---|---|---|
| d | 10 | 9 | 3.0 | 0.012 | -16.5 |

Since the p-value of 0.012 is less than 0.05 ($\alpha$), you may reject the null hypothesis and conclude that the median amount of money spent on their spouses birthday gift by all husbands is less than the median amount of money spent on their spouse's birthday gift by all wives; i.e., you may conclude that in general wives do spend more than their husbands for their spouse's birthday gift. Also, the value of the Wilcoxon (Signed-Rank) test statistic (the sum of the ranks only for the originally positive differences) is 3.

For inherently continuous data, even when measured on an ordinal scale, a confidence interval for the difference $M_1 - M_2 = M_d$ based on the Wilcoxon Signed-Rank test is computed the same way as described in Section 1 by using the difference variable, d, and the output also is described in Section 1.

Example 10.10:  Using the same data from Example 10.9, compute a 95% confidence interval for the difference in husbands and wives median amount of money spent on their spouse's birthday gifts.

Click on *Stat*, *Nonparametrics*, *1-Sample Wilcoxon...*

In the 1-Sample Wilcoxon dialog box: note that d is already in the *Variables:* box. Next click inside of the circle to the left of *Confidence interval*, click inside of the box to the right of *Level:*, erase any current incorrect value, and type in 95 - the correct confidence level. Then click on  OK .

The output containing the closest confidence interval shown below will appear in the Session Window.

## Wilcoxon Signed Rank CI:  d

| | N | Estimated Median | Achieved Confidence | Confidence Interval Lower | Upper |
|---|---|---|---|---|---|
| d | 10 | -16.5 | 94.7 | -21.5 | -3.0 |

And so you may be 94.7% confident that the interval from -21.5 to -3.0 contains the difference in the median amount of money spent by husbands versus wives on their spouses birthday gifts.

# Lab Assignment 10.3

**Name:**                                                    **Date:**

**Course:**              **Section:**                **Data CD Number:**

1.    Start a Minitab session. If you are unable to complete this lab assignment in one Minitab session, save the project as Lab 10-3 . **Never** use a period as part of the project name; since Minitab uses the period to attach the file type to the file name. Then at your next Minitab session, you may open this Lab 10-3.MPJ project and continue to work where you left off previously.

2.    A new baseball manager wanted to determine if the idea that pitchers do better against hitters who bat from the same side of home plate as the pitcher throws; i.e. do right handed pitchers do better against right handed hitters than against left handed hitters, and similarly for left handed pitchers? The manager randomly selected 15 pitchers and researched their performance over the past two years. For each pitcher in the sample, he separated the hitters into same side and opposite side hitters. Then, for each pitcher, he computed the number of strikeouts per 27 same side batters, and the number of strikeouts per 27 opposite side batters. The results are shown in the following table.

| Pitcher | 1 | 2 | 3 | 4 | 5 | 6 | 7 | 8 | 9 | 10 | 11 | 12 | 13 | 14 | 15 |
|---|---|---|---|---|---|---|---|---|---|---|---|---|---|---|---|
| Strikeouts per 27 same side batters | 5 | 3 | 6 | 2 | 1 | 5 | 7 | 4 | 4 | 5 | 7 | 6 | 5 | 8 | 4 |
| Strikeouts per 27 opposite side batters | 3 | 4 | 2 | 0 | 3 | 6 | 3 | 1 | 2 | 4 | 7 | 4 | 2 | 2 | 1 |

Consider the data as being ordinal, and with $\alpha = 0.05$, test the hypothesis that pitchers strikeout more same side batters than opposite side batters.

3.    Open the worksheet Sociology.mtw that is on your data disc. This worksheet contains the midterm and final exam letter grades for a random sample of students taking the Sociology 102 course at Canton State University. Code both the midterm and final letter grades with the usual grade point average equivalents of A=4, B=3, C=2, D=1 and F=0. Compute the difference variable if final - midterm. Now compute a 95% confidence interval for the median change in grade of final compared to midterm, and interpret the result in terms of letter grades.

(lab assignment is continued on the second side of this page)

4. Open the Clinic.mtw worksheet that is on your data disc. A random sample of people was selected, and they were shown a green light. After a random amount of time, the light was changed to red. Each person was told to press a foot pedal as soon as they noticed the change, and the reaction (elapsed) time was measured for each person. Next each person was given one can of beer to drink and the experiment was repeated. Immediately after this repetition, each person was given two additional cans of beer to drink, and again the experiment was repeated. These three scores for each person are in the Clinic.mtw worksheet. Test the hypothesis that there is no difference in the median reaction time between all people who have had nothing to drink and the median reaction time of all people who have had one can of beer to drink. Use a 0.10 significance level, and treat this data as having an underlying continuous distribution.

5. Using the reaction time data in the Cinic.mtw worksheet as described in problem 4, compute an 80% confidence interval for the change (difference) in reaction time of all people who have had nothing to drink versus the reaaction time of all people who have had a total of three cans of beer to drink.

6. Print your Session Window to the printer.

7. Attach both your Minitab output and <u>your complete answers</u> to this sheet and submit all three to your instructor.

**Section 4: One-Way Analysis of Variance; Hypothesis Tests on Population Location Parameters (Medians) Using Multiple Independent Samples**

In Section 1 of Chapter 9, analysis of variance using multiple intendant samples was explained. The typical ANOVA procedure requires that:

1.  the data is continuous,
2.  each population is normally distributed and
3.  the variances of all populations are equal; that is $\sigma_1^2 = \sigma_2^2 = \sigma_3^2 = ... = \sigma_c^2$; this property is called "homogeneity of variance."

However when some or all of these requirements are not satisfied, a nonparametric approach may be used to do the analysis. This approach usually tests about the population medians as opposed to the population means shown in Chapter 9.

The analysis of variance hypothesis test for comparing the medians of **c** different populations may be written as

$$H_0: M_1 = M_2 = M_3 = ... = M_c$$
$$H_a: \text{At least two of the } M_i\text{s are different}$$

Two such methods are presented in this section: **Mood's Median Test** which requires only that the data be measured on an ordinal scale, and the **Kruskal-Wallis Test** which requires that the data be inherently continuous even if measure only on an ordinal scale.

The Median Test is less restrictive and is presented first. The Median Test assumes that (1) the samples are taken randomly and independently of each other and (2) the data is inherently **ordinal** as well as being measured on an ordinal scale. This is the least restrictive assumption when dealing with the population median, and so this test is valid for almost any situation where the parametric analysis of variance does not work. The test statistic has a Chi-square distribution and is computed by first calculating the overall median of all the data (of the combined samples). Then in each sample calculate the number of observations less or equal to and greater than the overall median. If there are k different samples, this generates a 2 by k table of counts. Lastly a Chi-square test for association is done on this table. Large values of Chi-square indicate that the null hypothesis is false

Before Minitab can do the computations for the Mood's Median test, the data from all of the samples must be stacked into just <u>one</u> (new) column, and the corresponding sample identification must be stored in a second (new) column. It is best to name the new columns <u>before</u> you use them. For example; you may name the first new column Data or Ranks or anything else that describes the measurement being made; and then you should name the second new column as Factor. If the original columns containing the different samples have not been named, the data will be identified by either the column numbers (C1, C2, etc.) or consecutive whole numbers (1, 2, 3, ...) corresponding to the order of how the variables are entered in the stacking box. This stacking of the data was shown in Chapter 9 and is done as follows.

Click on *Data , Stack , Columns ...*

In the Stack Columns dialog box: the cursor will be in the box under the *Stack the following columns:*. Block the columns that contain the data for each of the samples (hold the | **Ctrl** | key and click on each variable or drag the mouse over the variables, if consecutive) and click on the | **Select** | button. Next click on the button to the left of *Column of current worksheet:* and then click inside of the box to its right. Highlight the stacked data column (Data) and click on | **Select** | . Then cursor will be inside the box to the right of *Store subscripts in:*, highlight the column (Factor) that contains the sample identification and click on | **Select** | . **If** the columns with the original data have been named, make sure the box to the left of *Use variable names in subscript column* is checked. But if the columns with the original data have **not** been named, click on this box to **un**check it. Click on | **OK** | .

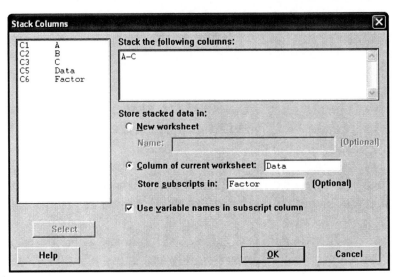

Once the data have been stacked into one new column and the sample identification stored into a second column, the Mood's Median test statistic and p-value are computed by

Click on *Stat , Nonparametrics , Mood's Median Test...*

In the Mood's Median Test dialog box: you may press the | **F3** | key to clear the contents of this dialog box and reset all options and erase any previous variables. The cursor will be in the box to the right of *Response:* and the variables (columns) will appear in the large box on the left side of this dialog box; click on the new column (Data) that contains the stacked data, and click on the | **Select** | button. The cursor will move to the *Factor:* box; click on the variable (Factor) that contains the sample identification information (where the subscripts are stored) and click on | **Select** | . Then click on | **OK** | .

(See graphics on the next page.)

422

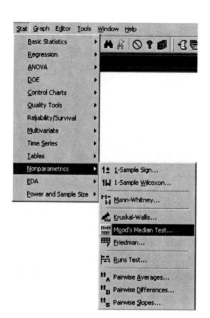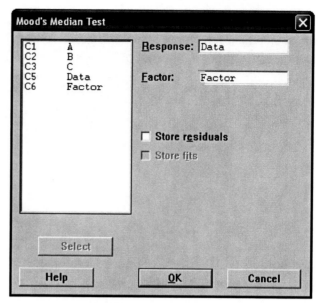

The output of the Median Test computation contains:

(1) the Chi-Square test statistic,
(2) the degrees of freedom,
(3) the p-value for this test,
(4) for each sample: the sample size, the number of scores less than or equal to and the number greater than the overall median
(5) the graph of 95% confidence intervals for each level population median $M_i$, and
(6) the value of the overall (combined samples) median.

If the samples have less than six observation, a warning note is also printed indicating that these intervals may have a confidence level less than 95%.

Example 10.11: The NCAA is concerned about the consistency in the way the 3 different groups – (1) AP Sportswriters, (2) Radio & TV Sportscasters and (3) College Coaches – rank college football teams, as the medians of these ranking are used to decide which teams will play for the "National Collegiate Championship." Half way through the season random samples from each group were chosen and asked to rank Ohio State University. The table below contains the results of these rankings. Using a 0.05 significance level, test to see if there is any difference in the median rankings of these three groups.

| Group | Ranking of Ohio State Football Team |
|-------|-------------------------------------|
| AP | 3, 3, 1, 2, 2, 1 |
| Radio & TV | 4, 1, 5, 6, 4, 3 |
| Coaches | 3, 8, 4, 8, 9, 7, 9 |

(continued on the next page)

Use the current worksheet, name columns 5, 6 and 7 as AP, Radio & TV and Coaches respectively. Then enter the rankings given in the table on the previous page into these columns. Your worksheet should look as shown below.

| C5 | C6 | C7 |
|----|----|----|
| AP | Radio & TV | Coaches |
| 3 | 4 | 3 |
| 3 | 1 | 8 |
| 1 | 5 | 4 |
| 2 | 6 | 8 |
| 2 | 4 | 9 |
| 1 | 3 | 7 |
|   |   | 9 |

Population 1 is all AP sportswriters, and so column C5 contains the data in the corresponding sample.

Population 2 is all Radio & TV sportscasters, and so column C6 contains the data in the corresponding sample.

Population 3 is all college coaches, and so column C7 contains the data in the corresponding sample.

This data is the ranking of the Ohio State football team halfway through the season. Since this data is inherently ordinal, the Median Test is appropriate.

The hypothesis testing problem is

$H_0$: $M_1 = M_2 = M_3$
$H_a$: At least two of the $M_i$s are different
$\alpha = 0.05$

and the test statistic is the Chi-square computation on table containing the sample counts of under and over the overall median.

First the data must be combined and stacked into a single column, and a sample identification column must be created. Name column 8 as Data and name column 9 as Factor.

Click on *Data*, *Stack*, *Columns* ...

In the Stack Columns dialog box: the cursor will be in the box under the *Stack the following columns:*. Block the AP (C5), Radio & TV (C6) and Coaches (C7) variables that contain the data for each of the samples (hold the ⎡ **Ctrl** ⎤ key and click on each variable or drag the mouse over the variables, if consecutive) and click on the ⎡ **Select** ⎤ button. Next click on the button to the left of *Column of current worksheet:* and then click inside of the box to its right. Highlight the Data (C8) variable and click on ⎡ **Select** ⎤. Then cursor will be inside the box to the right of *Store subscripts in:*, highlight the Factor (C9) variable and click on ⎡ **Select** ⎤. Make sure the box to the left of *Use variable names in subscript column* is checked. Click on ⎡ **OK** ⎤ .

Your worksheet should look as shown on the next page.

| C5 | C6 | C7 | C8 | C9-T |
|---|---|---|---|---|
| AP | Radio & TV | Coaches | Data | Factor |
| 3 | 4 | 3 | 3 | AP |
| 3 | 1 | 8 | 3 | AP |
| 1 | 5 | 4 | 1 | AP |
| 2 | 6 | 8 | 2 | AP |
| 2 | 4 | 9 | 2 | AP |
| 1 | 3 | 7 | 1 | AP |
|  |  | 9 | 4 | Radio & TV |
|  |  |  | 1 | Radio & TV |
|  |  |  | 5 | Radio & TV |
|  |  |  | 6 | Radio & TV |
|  |  |  | 4 | Radio & TV |
|  |  |  | 3 | Radio & TV |
|  |  |  | 3 | Coaches |
|  |  |  | 8 | Coaches |
|  |  |  | 4 | Coaches |
|  |  |  | 8 | Coaches |
|  |  |  | 9 | Coaches |
|  |  |  | 7 | Coaches |
|  |  |  | 9 | Coaches |

Now compute the Median test statistic and p-value.

**Note:** In order to have Minitab display the samples in the same order as shown in the work sheet you must do the following (otherwise Minitab will display the samples in alphabetical order).

Click on the Factor column number that contains sample identification information to highlight the entire column. Then right click and left click on *Column* in the resulting menu. Next left click on *Value order...* in the resulting menu. Now in the Value Order dialog box, click on the button to the left of *Order of occurrence in worksheet*, and finally click on the **OK** button.

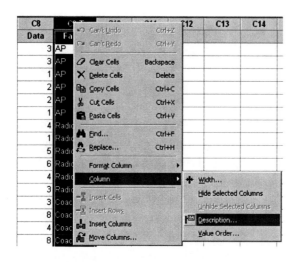

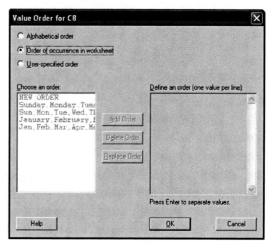

(continued on the next page)

Click on *Stat* , *Nonparametrics* , *Mood's Median Test...*

In the Mood's Median Test dialog box: you may press the [ **F3** ] key to clear the contents of this dialog box and reset all options and erase any previous variables. The cursor will be in the box to the right of *Response:* and the variables (columns) will appear in the large box on the left side of this dialog box; click on the Data (C8) column that contains the stacked data, and click on the [ **Select** ] button. The cursor will move to the *Factor:* box; click on the Factor (C9) variable that contains the sample identification information (where the subscripts are stored) and click on [ **Select** ] . Then click on [ **OK** ] .

The resulting output which includes the Chi-square test statistic and the p-value will appear in the Session Window and is shown below.

## Mood Median Test: Ranks versus Factor

**Mood median test for Ranks**
**Chi-Square = 7.13   DF = 2   P = 0.028**

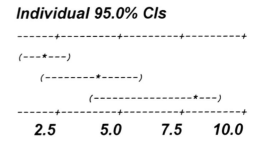

| Factor | N<= | N> | Median | Q3-Q1 |
|---|---|---|---|---|
| AP | 6 | 0 | 2.00 | 2.00 |
| Radio & TV | 4 | 2 | 4.00 | 2.75 |
| Coaches | 2 | 5 | 8.00 | 5.00 |

**Overall median = 4.00**

Since the p-value of 0.028 is less than 0.05 ($\alpha$), you may reject the null hypothesis and conclude that least two of median rankings of the Ohio State football team halfway through the season are different.  Also, the value of the Chi-square test statistic is 7.13 . From the graphs of the individual 95% confidence intervals, it appears that the median ranking of the AP sportswriters is less than the median ranking of the college coaches.

The **Kruskal-Wallis Test** assumes that the data in the random sample is inherently **continuous**, but may be measured on an ordinal scale. This assumption of an underlying continuous distribution is more restrictive than the assumption for the previous Mood's median Test; and as such is more powerful for continuous data, but should not be used when the data is purely ordinal. The data in the different samples are ranked as if they were combined into one group. Next the sum of these ranks for each sample is computed, and the expected sum of the ranks for that sample is computed under the assumption that the null hypothesis is true.  Then this expected value is subtracted from the actual sum, this difference is squared and the resulting values are added.  This sum is multiplied by 12 and then divided by $n_t*(n_t-1)$ where $n_t$ is the grand total of all of the samples sizes; and this is the typical Kruskal-Wallis test statistic.  When there are ties in the data, this test statistic is adjusted for ties.

426

As described earlier in this section, before Minitab can do the computations for the Kruskal-Wallis test, the data from all of the samples must be stacked into just <u>one</u> (new) column, and the corresponding sample identification must be stored in a second (new) column. It is best to name the new columns <u>before</u> you use them. For example; you may name the first new column Data or Ranks or anything else that describes the measurement being made; and then you should name the second new column as Factor. Then the Kruskal-Wallis test statistic and the corresponding p-value are computed by

Click on *Stat* , *Nonparametrics* , *Kruskal-Wallis...*

In the Kruskal-Wallis dialog box: you may press the $\boxed{\text{F3}}$ key to clear the contents of this dialog box and reset all options and erase any previous variables. The cursor will be in the box to the right of *Response:* and the variables (columns) will appear in the large box on the left side of this dialog box; click on the new column (Data) that contains the stacked data, and click on the $\boxed{\text{Select}}$ button. The cursor will move to the *Factor:* box; click on the variable (Factor) that contains the sample identification information (where the subscripts are stored) and click on $\boxed{\text{Select}}$ . Then click on $\boxed{\text{OK}}$ .

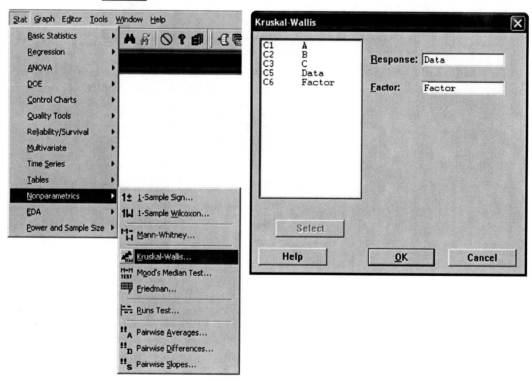

The output of the Kruskal-Wallis Test computation contains:

(1)  for each sample: the sample size, the median, the average rank and a z score showing how much that sample's average rank differs from the overall average rank

(2)  the overall sample size and average rank graph of 95% confidence intervals for each level population median $M_i$ , and

(3)  the Kruskal-Wallis H test statistic and p-value and

(4)  the Kruskal-Wallis H test statistic and p-value adjusted for any ties in the data.

Example 10.12:   In an experiment to test the effect of different pain remedies, four treatments were compared. A = no active ingredient (control group), B = aspirin, C = combination of aspirin and ibuprofen, and D = ibuprofen. Subjects suffering from arthritic pain were randomly assigned to one of these four treatments, and 15 minutes after administration of the pain remedy the subjects were asked to describe their pain level. The results are given in the table below. Do these data indicate that there is any differences among the four different remedies? Use a 0.02 level of significance.

| Remedy | | | |
|---|---|---|---|
| A | B | C | D |
| 1.6 | 1.9 | 1.5 | 0.5 |
| 2.6 | 1.6 | 1.9 | 1.2 |
| 2.0 | 2.1 | 2.4 | 0.3 |
| 2.5 | 0.6 | 1.0 | 0.2 |
| 1.7 | 1.3 | 1.9 | 0.4 |
| 2.0 | | | |

Start a new Minitab worksheet; name the first four columns as A, B, C and D; and enter the data into these columns. Your worksheet should look as shown below.

**Worksheet 7 ***

| ↓ | C1 | C2 | C3 | C4 |
|---|---|---|---|---|
| | A | B | C | D |
| 1 | 1.6 | 1.9 | 1.5 | 0.5 |
| 2 | 2.6 | 1.6 | 1.9 | 1.2 |
| 3 | 2.0 | 2.1 | 2.4 | 0.3 |
| 4 | 2.5 | 0.6 | 1.0 | 0.2 |
| 5 | 1.7 | 1.3 | 1.9 | 0.4 |
| 6 | 2.0 | | | |

Population 1 is all people with arthritic pain who receive Remedy A, and so column C1 contains the data in the corresponding sample.

Population 2 is all people with arthritic pain who receive Remedy B, and so column C2 contains the data in the corresponding sample.

Population 3 is all people with arthritic pain who receive Remedy C, and so column C3 contains the data in the corresponding sample.

Population 4 is all people with arthritic pain who receive Remedy D, and so column C4 contains the data in the corresponding sample.

This data is the perceived pain level of each person. This data is inherently continuous, but not normally distributed; and so the Kruskal-Wallis Test is appropriate.

(continued on the next page)

The hypothesis testing problem is

$H_0: M_1 = M_2 = M_3 = M_4$
$H_a$: At least two of the $M_i$s are different
$\alpha = 0.02$

and the test statistic is the Kruskal-Wallis H test statistic.

First the data must be combined and stacked into a single column, and a sample identification column must be created. Name column 6 as Data and name column 7 as Factor.

Click on *Data , Stack , Columns ...*

In the Stack Columns dialog box: the cursor will be in the box under the *Stack the following columns:*. Block the A (C1), B (C2), C (C3) and D (C4) variables that contain the data for each of the samples (hold the ⬜ **Ctrl** ⬜ key and click on each variable or drag the mouse over the variables, if consecutive) and click on the ⬜ **Select** ⬜ button. Next click on the button to the left of *Column of current worksheet:* and then click inside of the box to its right. Highlight the Data (C6) variable and click on ⬜ **Select** ⬜. The cursor will be inside the box to the right of *Store subscripts in:*, highlight the Factor (C7) variable and click on ⬜ **Select** ⬜. Make sure the box to the left of *Use variable names in subscript column* is checked. Click on ⬜ **OK** ⬜ .

Your worksheet should look as shown below.

| | C1 | C2 | C3 | C4 | C5 | C6 | C7-T |
|---|---|---|---|---|---|---|---|
| | **A** | **B** | **C** | **D** | | **Data** | **Factor** |
| **1** | 1.6 | 1.9 | 1.5 | 0.5 | | 1.6 | A |
| **2** | 2.6 | 1.6 | 1.9 | 1.2 | | 2.6 | A |
| **3** | 2.0 | 2.1 | 2.4 | 0.3 | | 2.0 | A |
| **4** | 2.5 | 0.6 | 1.0 | 0.2 | | 2.5 | A |
| **5** | 1.7 | 1.3 | 1.9 | 0.4 | | 1.7 | A |
| **6** | 2.0 | | | | | 2.0 | A |
| **7** | | | | | | 1.9 | B |
| **8** | | | | | | 1.6 | B |
| **9** | | | | | | 2.1 | B |
| **10** | | | | | | 0.6 | B |
| **11** | | | | | | 1.3 | B |
| **12** | | | | | | 1.5 | C |
| **13** | | | | | | 1.9 | C |
| **14** | | | | | | 2.4 | C |
| **15** | | | | | | 1.0 | C |
| **16** | | | | | | 1.9 | C |
| **17** | | | | | | 0.5 | D |
| **18** | | | | | | 1.2 | D |
| **19** | | | | | | 0.3 | D |
| **20** | | | | | | 0.2 | D |
| **21** | | | | | | 0.4 | D |

Worksheet 7 ***

(continued on the next page)

Now compute the Median test statistic and p-value.

**Note:** In order to have Minitab display the samples in the same order as shown in the work sheet you must do the following (otherwise Minitab will display the samples in alphabetical order).

Click on the Factor column number that contains sample identification information to highlight the entire column. Then right click and left click on *Column* in the resulting menu. Next left click on *Value order...* in the resulting menu. Now in the Value Order dialog box, click on the button to the left of *Order of occurrence in worksheet*, and finally click on the OK button.

In this example the sample identifications shown in the work sheet are in alphabetical order, and so this is not needed here.

Click on *Stat* , *Nonparametrics* , *Kruskal-Wallis...*

In the Kruskal-Wallis dialog box: you may press the F3 key to clear the contents of this dialog box and reset all options and erase any previous variables. The cursor will be in the box to the right of *Response:* and the variables (columns) will appear in the large box on the left side of this dialog box; click on the Data (C6) column that contains the stacked data, and click on the Select button. The cursor will move to the *Factor:* box; click on the Factor (C7) variable that contains the sample identification information (where the subscripts are stored) and click on Select . Then click on OK .

The resulting output which includes the Kruskal-Wallis H test statistic and the p-value will appear in the Session Window and is shown below.

## Kruskal-Wallis Test: Data versus Factor

### Kruskal-Wallis Test on Data

| Factor | N | Median | Ave Rank | Z |
|--------|----|--------|----------|-------|
| A | 6 | 2.0000 | 16.1 | 2.37 |
| B | 5 | 1.6000 | 11.1 | 0.04 |
| C | 5 | 1.9000 | 12.4 | 0.58 |
| D | 5 | 0.4000 | 3.4 | -3.14 |
| Overall | 21 | | 11.0 | |

$H = 11.78$   $DF = 3$   $P = 0.008$
$H = 11.83$   $DF = 3$   $P = 0.008$   *(adjusted for ties)*

After adjusting for ties in the data, the H test statistic has changed slightly, but in this case the p-values are the same. And since the p-value of 0.008 is less than 0.02 ($\alpha$), you may reject the null hypothesis and conclude that least two of median perceived pain level for people receiving the four drug remedies are different. From the Z values, it appears that the median perceived pain level of all people with arthritic pain who receive Remedy A (no active ingredient) is higher than the others, and the median perceived pain level of all people with arthritic pain who receive Remedy D (ibuprofen) is lower than the others.

# Lab Assignment 10.4

**Name:**                                          **Date:**

**Course:**              **Section:**              **Data CD Number:**

1. Start a Minitab session. If you are unable to complete this lab assignment in one Minitab session, save the project as Lab 10-4 . **Never** use a period as part of the project name; since Minitab uses the period to attach the file type to the file name. Then at your next Minitab session, you may open this Lab 10-4.MPJ project and continue to work where you left off previously.

2. A random sample of 15 adults who smoke at least two packs of cigarettes a day was randomly divided into 3 groups and each group received a different anti-smoking treatment daily for ten consecutive days. Group A was shown videos that demonstrated the harmful effects of smoking. Group B was given a stop-smoking chewing gum to chew each day. And Group C was given a stop-smoking patch to wear for the ten day period. At the end of the experiment, each participant was asked to rate their desire for a cigarette on a scale from "no desire" (0) to "uncontrollable desire" (5). The table below gives the results of these rankings. Test to see if there is any difference in the median effect of these three treatments on a persons desire to smoke cigarettes. Use a 0.05 significance level.

| Treatment Group | Ratings of Desire for a Cigarette | | | | | | |
|---|---|---|---|---|---|---|---|
| A | 5 | 3 | 5 | 3 | 2 | 4 | 5 |
| B | 3 | 1 | 4 | 2 | 0 | 3 | 2 |
| C | 0 | 3 | 1 | 0 | 1 | 1 | 0 |

3. Open the worksheet Sociology.mtw that is on your data disc. Random samples of students were taken from the five colleges at Canton State University. These colleges are: College of Business, College of Education, College of Fine Arts, College of Health Sciences and College of Mathematical and Physical Sciences. Each student was given the Survey of Study Habits and Attitudes (SSHA) test that measures study habits and attitudes towards learning. Scores on the SSHA test range from 0 to 200 and may be considered to form an inherently continuous distribution. The data for each sample is in the Sociology.mtw worksheet. Use a 0.05 significance level, and test to see if there are any differences in the median SSHA scores of all students in each these five colleges. Have the output listed in the order that the samples appear in the worksheet.

(lab assignment is continued on the second side of this page)

431

4.    Print your Session Window to the printer.


5.    Attach both your Minitab output and <u>your complete answers</u> to this paper and submit all three to your instructor.

**Section 5:** **Analysis of Variance - The Randomized Complete Block Design; Hypothesis Tests on Population Location Parameters (Medians) Using Multiple Related Samples**

As described in Section 2 of Chapter 9; when testing two population means; using two paired samples reduces some of the variation (noise), and so the paired sample test is more sensitive (powerful) in being able to identify real differences between the population means. The process in paired samples is to have homogeneous pairs of objects in the two samples. A similar approach is taken when designing a one-way analysis of variance experiment. Blocks (instead of pairs) of homogeneous objects are chosen; and then within each block, the objects are randomly assigned to the different treatment samples. Strictly speaking, this "Randomized Complete Block Design" falls under the category of two-way analysis of variance since there are now two factors: the different treatment populations and the different blocks. The Randomized Complete Block Design ANOVA procedure requires that:

(1)     each population is normally distributed,

(2)     the variances of all populations are equal; ("homogeneity of variance"), and

(3)     the treatment and block effects are additive; that is, there are **no** interaction effects (all $(\tau\beta)_{ij} = 0$).

However when some or all of these requirements are not satisfied, a nonparametric approach may be used to do the analysis. This approach usually tests about the population medians as opposed to the population means shown in Chapter 9.

The analysis of variance hypothesis test for comparing the medians of **c** different populations (or treatments) may be written as

$$H_0: M_1 = M_2 = M_3 = ... = M_c$$
$$H_a: \text{At least two of the } M_i s \text{ are different}$$

The **Friedman Two-Way Analysis of Variance by Ranks Test** is the nonparametric analog to the parametric ANOVA F test. The Friedman test assumes that:

(1)     there is exactly one observation in each block of each treatment (i.e.; one observation per cell),

(2)     the data is inherently **continuous**, but may be measured on an ordinal scale, and

(3)     there is no interaction between treatments and blocks.

The test statistic has a Chi-square distribution with (c - 1) degrees of freedom. Before computing the Friedman chi-square test statistic and corresponding p-valus, Minitab expects to have: (a) <u>all</u> data in one column, (b) the treatment level numbers in a second column and (c) the block level numbers in a third column.

Using Example 9.10 from Chapter 9, the following table gives the yearly sales figures for each combination of compensation mode (treatment) and pricing policy (block).

|  | Commission | Salary | Combined |
|---|---|---|---|
| **Negotiable** | 210 | 140 | 220 |
| **Non-negotiable** | 180 | 100 | 200 |

Then Minitab expects three columns as:

| Compensation | Treatment Level | Block Level |
|---|---|---|
| 210 | 1 | 1 |
| 180 | 1 | 2 |
| 140 | 2 | 1 |
| 100 | 2 | 2 |
| 220 | 3 | 1 |
| 200 | 3 | 2 |

The data column may be named anything you like (this workbook uses AllData), but the second and third columns should be named Treatment and Block respectively. You may enter the data from the above table and name the three variables directly in the Worksheet Window as illustrated below.

**Worksheet 1** ***

| ↓ | C1 AllData | C2 Treatment | C3 Block |
|---|---|---|---|
| 1 | 210 | 1 | 1 |
| 2 | 180 | 1 | 2 |
| 3 | 140 | 2 | 1 |
| 4 | 100 | 2 | 2 |
| 5 | 220 | 3 | 1 |
| 6 | 200 | 3 | 2 |

However it is more natural to enter the data just as it appears in the table above. That is, to enter the data so that each column contains the data for a treatment, and thus there will be as many columns as there are treatment levels. When doing this it is **very important** to keep the data for each block together and entered in the same row positions for each column. When the data are stored in columns in this more natural manner and there is exactly <u>one measurement per cell</u>, the macro **Stak-b1.mtb** may be executed to create the necessary three columns of stacked data that Minitab expects. This macro will prompt you for the number of treatment levels and the number of block levels. Next you will be prompted to enter the column numbers that contain the original, unstacked data for the c different treatments; **enter only the numbers and <u>not</u> the letter C**. The macro will store the measurements in column 26 (C26) and name this column "AllData"; the treatment levels will be stored in C27 and named "Treatment", and the block levels will be stored in C28 and named "Block."

434

Example 10.13: If Minitab has been started and you have data in the current worksheet, start a new Minitab project. Enter the compensation data described on the previous page (and repeated in the table below) into three separate columns, stack the data so that Minitab is able to compute the two-way analysis of variance, and then display in the Session Window **all** data that is in the current worksheet.

| | Commission | Salary | Combined |
|---|---|---|---|
| **Negotiable** | 210 | 140 | 220 |
| **Non-negotiable** | 180 | 100 | 200 |

Enter the data from the table above directly into three columns and the Worksheet Window should look as shown next.

| | C1 | C2 | C3 |
|---|---|---|---|
| | Commission | Salary | Combined |
| 1 | 210 | 140 | 220 |
| 2 | 180 | 100 | 200 |

Worksheet 1 ***

Click on *File*, *Other Files*, *Run an Exec...*

In the Run an Exec dialog box: the *Number of times to execute:* box should be 1, then click on the **Select File** button.

In the next Run an Exec dialog box: select the *Data Disc* in the *Look in:* box. Next find and highlight the Stak-b1.mtb macro file name, and then click on the **Open** button.

**After the DATA> prompt, enter the number of "Treatments", a comma and the number of "Blocks".**

**DATA>** 3, 2 **Enter**

## Data Display

**After the DATA> prompt, enter the 3 column numbers that contain the data for the 3 different "Treatment" samples.**
**Enter ONLY the numbers, but NOT the Cs !**

**DATA>** 1, 2, 3 **Enter**

**The "Stacked" data are in column number 26.**
**The "Treatment" levels are in column number 27 (sequential numbering).**
**The "Block" levels are in column number 28.**

Click on the *Data*, *Display Data ...* menu bar item, block all six variables, click on the **Select** button and then click on **OK**. The data will be displayed in the Session Window as shown on the next page.

(continued on the next page)

435

| Row | Commission | Salary | Combined | AllData | Treatment | Block |
|-----|-----------|--------|----------|---------|-----------|-------|
| 1 | 210 | 140 | 220 | 210 | 1 | 1 |
| 2 | 180 | 100 | 200 | 180 | 1 | 2 |
| 3 | | | | 140 | 2 | 1 |
| 4 | | | | 100 | 2 | 2 |
| 5 | | | | 220 | 3 | 1 |
| 6 | | | | 200 | 3 | 2 |

Once the data have been stacked into the three new columns, the Friedman Test's chi-Square test statistic and corresponding p-value are computed by

Click on *Stat , Nonparametrics , Friedman...*

In the Friedman dialog box: you may press the $\boxed{\textbf{F3}}$ key to clear the contents of this dialog box and reset all options and erase any previous variables. The cursor will be in the box to the right of *Response:* and the variables (columns) will appear in the large box on the left side of this dialog box; click the column that contains the stacked data - usually C26 (AllData), and click on the $\boxed{\textbf{Select}}$ button. The cursor will move to the *Treatment:* box; click on the column that contains the treatment numbers - usually C27 (Treatment), and click on the $\boxed{\textbf{Select}}$ button. The cursor will move to the *Blocks:* box; click on the column that contains the block numbers - usually C28 (Block), and click on $\boxed{\textbf{Select}}$ . Then click on $\boxed{\textbf{OK}}$ .

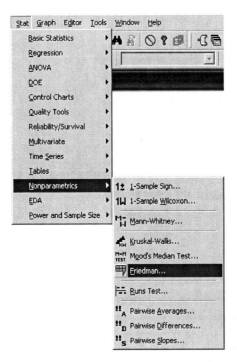

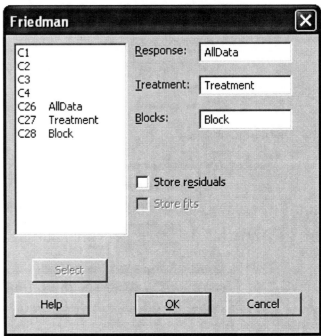

The output of the Friedman tests contains:

(1)   the Friedman chi-square S test statistic, the test's degrees of freedom and p-value computed **without** adjusting for ties in the rankings,

(2)   the Friedman chi-square S test statistic, the test's degrees of freedom and p-value computed **after** adjusting for ties in the rankings,

(3)   for each sample (treatment); the number of scores (blocks) in the treatment, the estimated treatment median, and the sum of the ranks for the treatment, and

(4)   the overall or Grand median.

Example 10.14:   An agronomist is researching the corn yield of three different types of hybrid corn stalks (OT, HT and HO). In order to control for other influences such as soil, fertilizer, etc., the agronomist randomly selected 5 different plots of land, and then planted one of each type of corn stalk in each different plot. The yield was measured as the weight of the kernels of corn produced by each hybrid stalk with the following results.

|  |  | Hybrid | | |
|---|---|---|---|---|
|  |  | OT | HT | HO |
| Plot Number | 1 | 254 | 325 | 234 |
|  | 2 | 263 | 314 | 260 |
|  | 3 | 290 | 287 | 214 |
|  | 4 | 277 | 258 | 227 |
|  | 5 | 267 | 309 | 277 |

Test the hypothesis that there is no difference in the median yield of the three different types of hybrid corn stalks. Use $\alpha = 0.05$ .

Start a new Minitab worksheet; name the first three columns as OT, HT and HO; and enter the data into these columns. Your worksheet should look as shown below.

**Worksheet 1 \*\*\***

| ↓ | C1 | C2 | C3 |
|---|---|---|---|
|  | OT | HT | HO |
| 1 | 25 | 32 | 23 |
| 2 | 26 | 31 | 26 |
| 3 | 29 | 28 | 21 |
| 4 | 27 | 29 | 22 |
| 5 | 26 | 30 | 26 |

(continued on the next page)

Population 1 is all OT type hybrid corn stalks, and so column C1 contains the data in the corresponding sample.

Population 2 is all HT type hybrid corn stalks, and so column C2 contains the data in the corresponding sample.

Population 3 is all HO type hybrid corn stalks, and so column C3 contains the data in the corresponding sample.

This data is the weight of kernels of corn produced by each hybrid stalk. This data is inherently continuous, but not normally distributed, and the samples are related where the blocking factor is the different plots of land; and so the Friedman Test is appropriate.

The hypothesis testing problem is

$H_0$: $M_1 = M_2 = M_3$
$H_a$: At least two of the $M_i$s are different
$\alpha = 0.05$

and the test statistic is the Friedman chi-square test statistic.

First the data must be combined and stacked into a single column, and two columns containing the treatment and a block sample identification must be created. To do this the macro stak-b1.mtb must be executed.

Click on *File*, *Other Files*, *Run an Exec...*

In the Run an Exec dialog box: the *Number of times to execute:* box should be 1, then click on the | **Select File** | button.

In the next Run an Exec dialog box: select the *Data Disc* in the *Look in:* box. Next find and highlight the Stak-b1.mtb macro file name, and then click on the | **Open** | button.

**After the DATA> prompt, enter the number of "Treatments",**
**a comma and the number of "Blocks".**

**DATA>** 3, 5 | Enter |

## Data Display

**After the DATA> prompt, enter the 3 column numbers that contain**
**the data for the 3 different "Treatment" samples.**
**Enter ONLY the numbers, but NOT the Cs !**

**DATA>** 1, 2, 3 | Enter |

**The "Stacked" data are in column number 26.**
**The "Treatment" levels are in column number 27 (sequential numbering).**
**The "Block" levels are in column number 28.**

(continued on the next page)

438

Next compute the Friedman chi-square test statistic and corresponding p-value.

Click on *Stat , Nonparametrics , Friedman...*
In the Friedman dialog box: you may press the F3 key to clear the contents of this dialog
box and reset all options and erase any previous variables. The cursor will be in the
box to the right of *Response:* and the variables (columns) will appear in the large box
on the left side of this dialog box; click the C26 (AllData) column that contains the
stacked data, and click on the Select button. The cursor will move to the
*Treatment:* box; click on the C27 (Treatment) column that contains the treatment
numbers, and click on the Select button. The cursor will move to the *Blocks:* box;
click on the C28 (Block) column that contains the block numbers), and click on
Select . Then click on OK .

The resulting output which includes the Friedman chi-square S test statistic and the p-value
will appear in the Session Window and is shown below.

## Friedman Test: AllData versus Treatment blocked by Block

S = 6.40   DF = 2   P = 0.041
S = 7.11   DF = 2   P = 0.029 (adjusted for ties)

| Treatment | N | Est Median | Sum of Ranks |
|-----------|---|------------|--------------|
| 1 | 5 | 25.333 | 10.0 |
| 2 | 5 | 29.667 | 14.0 |
| 3 | 5 | 23.000 | 6.0 |

**Grand median = 26.000**

After adjusting for ties in the data, the S test statistic has changed, but in this case the
p-values are of 0.041 and 0.029 (adjusted for ties) are both less than 0.05 ($\alpha$). So the
agronomist rejects the null hypothesis and concludes that least two of median corn kernal
yields are different. From the Estimated medians, it appears that the median yield of all HT
hybrid corn stalks is higher than the others, and the median yield of all HO hybrid corn
stalks is lower than the others.

# Lab Assignment 10.5

**Name:**                                                    **Date:**

**Course:**               **Section:**                **Data CD Number:**

1.    Start a Minitab session. If you are unable to complete this lab assignment in one Minitab session, save the project as Lab 10-5 . **Never** use a period as part of the project name; since Minitab uses the period to attach the file type to the file name. Then at your next Minitab session, you may open this Lab 10-5.MPJ project and continue to work where you left off previously.

2.    The manager of the Bears baseball team recently conducted a study in order to determine the best way to reach first base. The three methods studied were sliding head first, sliding feet first, and running without sliding. Six players were randomly selected to participate in the study. On three consecutive days at the beginning of practice, each used a different method and was timed to determine how fast he reached first base. The results are shown in the table below. Use a 0.10 significance level and test to see if any of the methods is superior to the others (i.e., is faster in reaching first base).

| Player | Head First Slide | Feet First Slide | No Slide |
|--------|------------------|------------------|----------|
| John   | 3.65             | 3.60             | 3.40     |
| Bob    | 3.90             | 3.85             | 3.70     |
| Tom    | 3.25             | 3.15             | 3.00     |
| Juan   | 3.85             | 3.80             | 3.70     |
| Fred   | 3.55             | 3.55             | 3.35     |
| Barry  | 3.40             | 3.50             | 3.55     |

3.    Open the Clinic.mtw worksheet that is on your data disc. A random sample of people was selected, and they were shown a green light. After a random amount of time, the light was changed to red. Each person was told to press a foot pedal as soon as they noticed the change, and the reaction (elapsed) time was measured for each person. Next each person was given one can of beer to drink and the experiment was repeated. Immediately after this repetition, each person was given two additional cans of beer to drink, and again the experiment was repeated. These three scores for each person are in the Clinic.mtw worksheet. Test the hypothesis that there is no difference in the median reaction time of all people after drinking no beer, versus after drinking one can of beer versus after drinking three cans of beer. Use $\alpha = 0.02$ .

(lab assignment is continued on the second side of this page)

4.    Print your Session Window to the printer.

5.    Attach both your Minitab output and <u>your complete answers</u> to this sheet and submit all three to your instructor.

# CHAPTER 11:     Chi-Square Analysis of Categorical Data

**Section 1:     Goodness of Fit Test**

A discrete variable may have two or more distinct outcomes.  For example; marital status may be measured as: (1) married, (2) single, (3) divorced and (4) widow/widower.  These distinct outcomes are often called categories, and the results of these variables are called categorical data.  A Bernoulli variable is a special case of categorical data and is usually analyzed using the techniques given in the previous chapters.  This chapter will consider categorical variables that have three or more outcomes.

The specific distribution of a categorical variable in the population is often of interest.  For example; a hospital may want to know if the four blood types (A, B, AB and O) are equally distributed in their service area.  Or a sociologist may believe that the proportions of all adults in her community who fit into the four marital status categories are: (1) 40% married, (2) 30% single, (3) 20% divorced and (4) 10% widow/widower.  A Goodness of Fit test is used to test hypotheses concerning the distribution of a categorical variable in the population, and the test statistic is based upon the Chi-square distribution.

The number of different categories (sometimes called cells) in which a variable may occur will be symbolized by the letter k.   The data of a categorical variable is usually collected and presented in a frequency table where the number of outcomes observed (frequency) in each category is given.  For example, the results of measuring the marital status of 200 people would be presented as

| marital status | frequency |
|---|---|
| married | 81 |
| single | 63 |
| divorced | 42 |
| widow/widower | 14 |

The frequency of the $i^{th}$ category is usually symbolized as $f_i$ or $O_i$.  The $O_i$ is popular as it stands for the **observed** number in the $i^{th}$ category.

The null hypothesis specifies a value for the population proportion in each of these k categories.  The symbol $p_i$ represents the proportion of the population which is in the $i^{th}$ category, where i can be 1, 2, 3, ..., k.  The symbol $p_{i,0}$ is use to represent the value specified for the parameter $p_i$ in the null hypothesis.  The null and alternative hypotheses for a Goodness of Fit test are in the form

$H_0$: $p_1 = p_{1,0}$ , $p_2 = p_{2,0}$ , $p_3 = p_{3,0}$ , ... , $p_k = p_{k,0}$
$H_a$: At least one of the specified proportions is wrong

Assuming the null hypothesis is true; the **expected** number in the sample that ideally would be in each category is symbolized by $E_i$ and is computed by multiplying the sample size by the hypothesized proportion for that category; i.e., $E_i = np_{i,0}$. If these $E_i$'s are sufficiently large, (often interpreted as requiring all of the $E_i$ to be greater than or equal to 1 <u>and</u> at least 80% of the $E_i$ to be greater than or equal to 5), the Goodness of Fit test statistic has an approximate Chi-square distribution with (k-1) degrees of freedom and is given by the formula

$$(i) \qquad \chi^2 = \sum_{i=1}^{k} \frac{(O_i - E_i)^2}{E_i} \ .$$

When the data has already been compiled in a frequency table, and you have the specified proportions given in the null hypothesis for each category; the Goodness of Fit test may be computed as follows. First the name of each category is entered into one column and the respective frequency or observed number in each category is entered into the next column. These two columns may be named Category and Observed. For the data given on the previous page, the worksheet would look like:

| | C1-T | C2 |
|---|---|---|
| | Category | Observed |
| 1 | married | 81 |
| 2 | single | 63 |
| 3 | divorced | 42 |
| 4 | widow/widower | 14 |

**Worksheet 1** \*\*\*

Once this information has been entered, the Goodness of Fit test is done by

Click on *Stat , Tables, Chi-Square Goodness-of-Fit Test (One Variable)...*

In the Chi-Square Goodness-of-Fit test dialog box: make sure the button to the left of *Observed Counts:* is selected and click inside the box to the right. Highlight the Observed variable in the large box on the left and click on Select . The cursor will move down to the next box below; highlight the Category variable and click on Select . Next make sure the button to the left of *Specific proportions* is selected. If the box under *Proportions specified by historical counts:* does **not** contain *Input constants*, click on the down triangle to its right and select *Input constants*. A box will open to the right that contains the *Category names* and a column named *Proportions*. Click in the box in the first row of the *Proportions* column and enter the specified proportion given in the null hypothesis for the respective category (must be in decimal form). Click in the next row down and enter its specified proportion given in the null hypothesis. Repeat this for each category. Now click on the Graphs... button.

In the Chi-Square Goodness-of-Fit Test - Graphs dialog box, click on the box to the left of *Bar chart of each category's contribution to the chi-square vale* to **un**select this graph. You may also **un**select the first graph if you wish. Then click on the OK button.

Back in the Chi-Square Goodness-of-Fit test dialog box, click on the OK button.

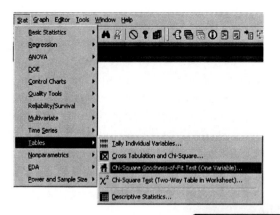
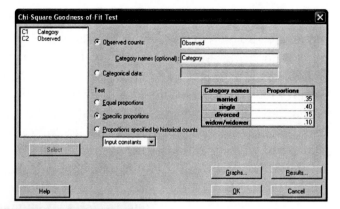
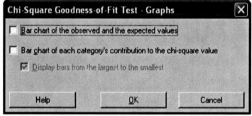

The output of the Chi-Square Goodness-of-Fit Test contains:

(1) the category names,

(2) the observed number in each category ($O_i$),

(3) the proportions specified in the null hypothesis for each category,

(4) the expected number in each category ($E_i$),

(5) the contribution to the chi-square test statistic for each category which we will call the *Cell CS*,

(4) the sample size,

(5) the degrees of freedom for the chi-square test statistic,

(6) the value of the chi-square test statistic and

(7) the p-value for the test.

If you left the first bar chart checked in the Chi-Square Goodness-of-Fit Test - Graphs dialog box, the output also will contain a graph comparing the observed and expected frequencies for each category.

If the p-value for the test is greater than the level of significance ($\alpha$), the null hypothesis may **not** be rejected, and "fit" of the population into the null hypothesized proportions is not contradicted. But if the p-value is less than or equal to the value of $\alpha$, you **do reject** the null hypothesis, and a further analysis may be done in order to determine which categories do not "fit" the null hypothesized values of $p_i$. The following is a suggested approach to this further analysis.

First the critical point of the rejection region for the given level of significance ($\alpha$) is computed. Then this number is divided by k (the number of cells), and the result is called the per cell critical value which we will call *Cell CV*. Next, each category's contribution to the chi-square test statistic (*Cell CS*) is compared to the per cell critical value (*Cell CV*). For any category whose *Cell CS* is greater than or equal to the *Cell CV* value, you may conclude that category's $p_i$ is different from the value specified in the null hypothesis. If the *Cell CS* value is less than the *Cell CV* value, you may not conclude that the category's null hypothesized value of $p_i$ is wrong. The motivation for this is that if all individual *Cell CS* values were less than the *Cell CV* value, then the sum of the *Cell CS* values (which is the value of the Chi-square test statistic) would be less than the critical point of the test's critical region; and you would **not** reject the null hypothesis. Therefore; those cells whose *Cell CS* is less than the *Cell CV* are not contributing towards the rejection decision, and only those cells whose *Cell CS* values are greater than or equal to the *Cell CV* have $p_i$ values that do **not** "fit" the null hypothesized values. After identifying the categories (cells) with $p_i$ values that do not "fit", a comparison of the $O_i$ and $E_i$ values will indicate the appropriate correction. If $O_i$ is greater than $E_i$, you would conclude that the $p_i$ is greater than $p_{i,0}$; but if $O_i$ is less than $E_i$, you would conclude that the $p_i$ is less than $p_{i,0}$.

The per cell critical value (*Cell CV*) is computed executing the **Goodfit.mtb** macro that is saved on your data disc.

Click on *File , Other Files , Run an Exec...*

In the Run an Exec dialog box: the *Number of times to execute:* box should be 1, then click on the $\boxed{\textbf{Select File}}$ button.

In the next Run an Exec dialog box: select the *Data Disc* in the *Look in::* box. Next find and highlight the Goodfit.mtb macro file name, and then click on the $\boxed{\textbf{Open}}$ button.

This macro will first prompt you for the degrees of freedom of the chi-square test statistic. Next you will be prompted for the level of significance of the test. The output of the Goodfit.mtb macro contains the per cell critical value (*Cell CV*) which is compared to each *Cell CS* shown in the output from the Goodness-of-Fit test.

Before going further, it is <u>very important</u> to point out that the post-hoc analysis described in the previous paragraph should be done **ONLY** if the null hypothesis **has been rejected!!** If the p-value $\leq \alpha$ and thus $H_0$ has been rejected; then at least one of the *Cell CS* <u>must</u> be greater than or equal to the *Cell CV* value, and the post-hoc analysis is logical (even if not based upon a known statistical theory). However; if the p-value $> \alpha$ and $H_0$ has <u>not</u> been rejected, even though it is still possible that a *Cell CS* <u>might</u> be greater than or equal to the *Cell CV* value, the post-hoc analysis should **not be done.** It is not logical to ask which category's $p_i$ is different from the value specified in the null hypothesis when the null hypothesis has <u>not</u> been rejected!

Example 11.1:    Adults in Iowa have four choices for medical care: (1) Private Doctor, (2) HMO, (3) Clinic or (4) No Health Care. The Iowa Secretary of Health believes that the proportions of all adults in his state who choose these options are 40%, 25%, 15% and 20% respectively. A random sample of adults in Iowa was taken and the number in this sample choosing each health care option are given on the next page.

| Medical Care | Frequency |
|---|---|
| Private Doctor | 278 |
| HMO | 130 |
| Clinic | 100 |
| No Health Care | 122 |

(continued on the next page)

Use a Goodness of Fit test to see if these hypothesized population proportions are correct. Use a 0.10 level of significance.

The hypothesis testing problem is

$H_0$: $p_1 = .40$  $p_2 = .25$  $p_3 = .15$  $p_4 = .20$
$H_a$: At least one of the specified proportions is wrong
$\alpha = 0.10$

and the test statistic is  $\chi^2 = \sum_{i=1}^{k} \frac{(O_i - E_i)^2}{E_i}$ .

Name the first column as Category and the second column as Observed, enter the four categories into column 1 and the respective frequencies into column 2. Then the Worksheet Window should look as shown below.

| | C1-T | C2 |
|---|---|---|
| | **Category** | **Observed** |
| 1 | Private Doctor | 278 |
| 2 | HMO | 130 |
| 3 | Clinic | 100 |
| 4 | No Health Care | 122 |

**Worksheet 1 ***

**Note:** In order to have Minitab display the categories in the same order as shown in the work sheet you must do the following (otherwise Minitab will display the categories in alphabetical order).

Click on the column number that contains the categories to highlight the entire column. Then right click and left click on *Column* in the resulting menu. Next left click on *Value order...* in the resulting menu. Now in the Value Order dialog box, click on the button to the left of *Order of occurrence in worksheet*, and finally click on the OK button.

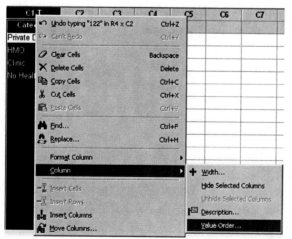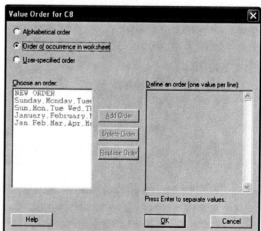

(continued on the next page)

Next you compute the chi-square test statistic by

Click on *Stat , Tables, Chi-Square Goodness-of-Fit Test (One Variable)...*

In the Chi-Square Goodness-of-Fit test dialog box: make sure the button to the left of *Observed Counts:* is selected and click inside the box to the right. Highlight the Observed variable in the large box on the left and click on | Select | . The cursor will move down to the next box below; highlight the Category variable and click on | Select | . Next make sure the button to the left of *Specific proportions* is selected. If the box under *Proportions specified by historical counts:* does **not** contain *Input constants*, click on the down triangle to its right and select *Input constants*. A box will open to the right that contains the *Category names* and a column named *Proportions*. Click in the box in the first row of the *Proportions* column (next to Private Doctor) and enter 0.40 (the specified proportion given in the null hypothesis for the Private Doctor category). Click in the next row down and enter 0.25 , the specified proportion given in the null hypothesis for HMO. Click in the next box down and enter 0.15 for the Clinic category proportion. Click in the next box down and enter 0.20 for the No Health Care category proportion. Now click on the | **Graphs...** | button.

In the Chi-Square Goodness-of-Fit Test - Graphs dialog box, click on the box to the left of *Bar chart of each category's contribution to the chi-square vale* to **un**select this graph. You may also **un**select the first graph if you wish. Then click on the | **OK** | button.

Back in the Chi-Square Goodness-of-Fit test dialog box, click on the | **OK** | button.

The resulting output which includes for each category; the names, observed frequencies, specified $p_{i,0}$ values, expected frequencies and contribution to chi-square test statistic (*Cell CS*) values. Also shown are the sample size, degrees of freedom, computed value of the chi-square test statistic and the p-value. This output appears in the Session Window as shown below.

### Chi-Square Goodness-of-Fit Test for Observed Counts in Variable: Observed

### Using category names in Category

| Category | Observed | Test Proportion | Expected | Contribution to Chi-Sq |
|---|---|---|---|---|
| Private Doctor | 278 | 0.40 | 252.0 | 2.68254 |
| HMO | 130 | 0.25 | 157.5 | 4.80159 |
| Clinic | 100 | 0.15 | 94.5 | 0.32011 |
| No Health Care | 122 | 0.20 | 126.0 | 0.12698 |

| N | DF | Chi-Sq | P-Value |
|---|---|---|---|
| 630 | 3 | 7.93122 | 0.047 |

Since the p-value of 0.0475 is less than $\alpha = 0.10$ , the null hypothesis is rejected, and the Secretary would now conclude that the proportion of all adults in Iowa choose the four different types of medical care differently than he first believed. Then the Secretary would continue with the further analysis.

(continued on the next page)

First the per cell critical value (*Cell CV*) is computed using the Goodfit.mtb macro.

Click on *File , Other Files , Run an Exec...*

In the Run an Exec dialog box: the *Number of times to execute:* box should be 1, then click on the Select File button.

In the next Run an Exec dialog box: select the *Data Disc* in the *Look in:* box. Next find and highlight the Goodfit.mtb macro file name, and then click on the Open button.

The macro will first prompt you for the degrees of freedom of the chi-square test statistic (3). Next you will be prompted for the level of significance of the test (0.10). The output of the Goodfit.mtb macro contains the per cell critical value (*Cell CV*). These prompts, your input, and the result of the computation shown below will appear in the Session Window.

**After the DATA> prompt, enter the degrees of freedom
for the Chi-Sq Test Statistic.**

**DATA>** 3 Enter

**After the DATA> prompt, enter the level of significance (alpha).**

**DATA>** 0.10 Enter

## Data Display

**Per Cell Critical Value (Cell CV) = 1.56285**

Comparing the values in the **Contribution to Chi-Sq** (*Cell CS*) column (shown on the previous page) to this *Cell CV* value of 1.56286; the Iowa Secretary of Health sees that for the categories of Private Doctor and HMO, the individual *Cell CS* values are greater than the *Cell CV* of 1.56286 . But for the categories of Clinic and No Health care, the individual *Cell CS* values are less than the *Cell CV* value. Therefore the Secretary may conclude that Private Doctor and HMO categories have population proportions which are different than those specified in the null hypothesis. The observed number in the Private Doctor category (278) is greater than the expected number (252.0) in this category, and this implies that $p_1 > .40$ ($p_{1,0}$). In the HMO category the observed number (130) is less than the expected number (157.5), and this implies that $p_2 < .25$ ($p_{2,0}$). Therefore the Secretary of Health would conclude that more than 40% of all adults in Iowa choose a Private Doctor for their health care, and that fewer than 25% of all adults in Iowa choose an HMO for their health care.

In Example 11.1 the number of individual scores in each category already had been tabulated, and the resulting $O_i$ values were given in the table. On some occasions the raw data for each individual object in the sample is recorded instead of the tabulated frequencies of those outcomes, as was done in Example 11.1. In these cases the Goodness-of-Fit test can be computed by

449

Click on *Stat*, *Tables*, *Chi-Square Goodness-of-Fit Test (One Variable)...*

In the Chi-Square Goodness-of-Fit test dialog box: make sure the button to the left of *Categorical Data:* is selected and click inside the box to the right. Highlight the Observed variable in the large box on the left and click on [ **Select** ]. The cursor will move down to the next box below; highlight the Categorical variable and click on [ **Select** ]. Next make sure the button to the left of *Specific proportions* is selected. If the box under *Proportions specified by historical counts:* does **not** contain *Input constants*, click on the down triangle to its right and select *Input constants*. A box will open to the right that contains the *Category names* and a column named *Proportions*. Click in the box in the first row of the *Proportions* column and enter the specified proportion given in the null hypothesis for the respective category (must be in decimal form). Click in the next row down and enter its specified proportion given in the null hypothesis. Repeat this for each category. Now click on the [ **Graphs...** ] button.

In the Chi-Square Goodness-of-Fit Test - Graphs dialog box, click on the box to the left of *Bar chart of each category's contribution to the chi-square vale* to **un**select this graph. You may also **un**select the first graph if you wish. Then click on the [ **OK** ] button.

Back in the Chi-Square Goodness-of-Fit test dialog box, click on the [ **OK** ] button.

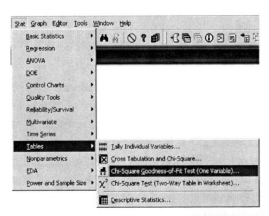

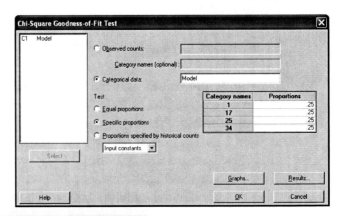

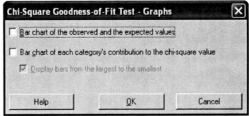

The output of the Chi-Square Goodness-of-Fit Test is exactly the same as shown before with the addition of a missing values (N*) heading. If you left the first bar chart checked in the Chi-Square Goodness-of-Fit Test - Graphs dialog box, the output also will contain a graph comparing the observed and expected frequencies for each category.

The next example uses a raw data file, so you may want to review in Chapter 2 how to *Import Special Text* from a raw data file into a current worksheet.

Example 11.2    A computer equipment distributer sells four models of hard disks labeled: 1, 17, 25 and 34. The distributer has been keeping equal proportions of each model in inventory, but the parts manager recently questioned this decision. A random sample of 185 invoices was taken from last quarter's sales records, and the model number of each sale is stored in the Hdisk.dat raw data file on your data disc. Open a new Worksheet Window and import this data from this raw data file into the new worksheet. Name the variable 'Model' and tally the scores in this variable. With $\alpha = 0.05$, test the hypothesis that for all of last quarter's sales, the computer equipment distributer sold 25% of each model hard disk.

Click on *File*, *New*, *Minitab Worksheet* from the menu bar to open a new Worksheet Window.

Name column 1 'Model' directly in the Worksheet Window.

Click on *File*, *Other Files*, *Import Special Text* ...

In the Import Special Text dialog box: highlight the Model (C1) variable and click on ⌷ Select ⌷.

In the Import Text From File dialog box: make sure that *Data Disc* is in the *Look in:* box, click on the Hdisk.dat raw data filename, and then click on ⌷ Open ⌷.

The first ten rows of this Worksheet Window should look as shown below.

| ⌷ Worksheet 2 | |
| --- | --- |
| ↓ | C1 |
| | Model |
| 1 | 17 |
| 2 | 25 |
| 3 | 1 |
| 4 | 34 |
| 5 | 1 |
| 6 | 1 |
| 7 | 17 |
| 8 | 25 |
| 9 | 17 |
| 10 | 1 |

(continued on the next page)

451

The hypothesis testing problem is

$H_0$: $p_1 = 0.25$  $p_2 = 0.25$  $p_3 = 0.25$  $p_4 = 0.25$
$H_a$: At least one of the specified proportions is wrong
$\alpha = 0.05$

and the test statistic is  $\chi^2 = \sum_{i=1}^{k} \frac{(O_i - E_i)^2}{E_i}$ .

Next you compute the chi-square test statistic by

Click on *Stat , Tables, Chi-Square Goodness-of-Fit Test (One Variable)...*

In the Chi-Square Goodness-of-Fit test dialog box: make sure the button to the left of *Categorical Data:* is selected and click inside the box to the right. Highlight the Observed variable in the large box on the left and click on ⬚ **Select** . The cursor will move down to the next box below; highlight the Model variable and click on ⬚ **Select** . Next make sure the button to the left of *Specific proportions* is selected. If the box under *Proportions specified by historical counts:* does **not** contain *Input constants*, click on the down triangle to its right and select *Input constants*. A box will open to the right that contains the *Category names* and a column named *Proportions*. Click in the box in the first row of the *Proportions* column (next to Category of 1) and enter 0.25 (the specified proportion given in the null hypothesis for the Model 1 category). Click in the next row down and enter 0.25 , the specified proportion given in the null hypothesis for Model 17. Click in the next box down and enter 0.25 for the Model 25 category proportion. Click in the next box down and enter 0.25 for the Model 34 category proportion. Now click on the ⬚ **Graphs...** button.

In the Chi-Square Goodness-of-Fit Test - Graphs dialog box, click on the box to the left of *Bar chart of each category's contribution to the chi-square vale* to **un**select this graph. You may also **un**select the first graph if you wish. Then click on the ⬚ **OK** button.

Back in the Chi-Square Goodness-of-Fit test dialog box, click on the ⬚ **OK** button.

The results of the computations shown below will appear in the Session Window.


## Chi-Square Goodness-of-Fit Test for Categorical Variable: Model

| Category | Observed | Test Proportion | Expected | Contribution to Chi-Sq |
|---|---|---|---|---|
| 1 | 50 | 0.25 | 46.25 | 0.30405 |
| 17 | 60 | 0.25 | 46.25 | 4.08784 |
| 25 | 33 | 0.25 | 46.25 | 3.79595 |
| 34 | 42 | 0.25 | 46.25 | 0.39054 |

| N | N* | DF | Chi-Sq | P-Value |
|---|---|---|---|---|
| 185 | 0 | 3 | 8.57838 | 0.035 |

(continued on the next page)

Since the p-value of 0.0355 is less than the given value of $\alpha = 0.05$; the null hypothesis is rejected, and the parts manager at the computer equipment distributing company would continue with the further analysis.

First the per cell critical value (*Cell CV*) is computed using the Goodfit.mtb macro.

Click on *File , Other Files , Run an Exec...*
In the Run an Exec dialog box: the *Number of times to execute:* box should be 1, then click on the | Select File | button.
In the next Run an Exec dialog box: select the *Data Disc* in the *Look in:* box. Next find and highlight the Goodfit.mtb macro file name, and then click on the | Open | button.

The macro will first prompt you for the degrees of freedom of the chi-square test statistic (3). Next you will be prompted for the level of significance of the test (0.05). The output of the Goodfit.mtb macro contains the per cell critical value (*Cell CV*). These prompts, your input, and the result of the computation shown below will appear in the Session Window.

**After the DATA> prompt, enter the degrees of freedom**
**for the Chi-Sq Test Statistic.**

**DATA>** 3 | Enter |

**After the DATA> prompt, enter the level of significance (alpha).**

**DATA>** 0.05 | Enter |

## Data Display

**Per Cell Critical Value (Cell CV) = 1.95368**

Comparing the values in the **Contribution to Chi-Sq** (*Cell CS*) column (shown on the previous page) to this *Cell CV* value; the parts manager sees that for the  categories of Model 17 and Model 25, the individual *Cell CS* values are greater than the *Cell CV* of 1.95368 . But for the categories of Model 1 and Model 34, the individual *Cell CS* values are less than the *Cell CV* value. Therefore the parts manger may conclude that Model 17 and Model 25 hard disks have population proportions which are different than those specified in the null hypothesis. The observed number in the Mode 1 category (60) is greater than the expected number (46.25) in this category, and this implies that $p_2 > .40$ ($p_{2,0}$).  In the Model 25 category the observed number (33) is less than the expected number (46.25), and this implies that $p_3 < .25$ ($p_{3,0}$). Therefore the parts manager would conclude that more than 25% of all hard disk sales in the last quarter were for model number 17, and that fewer than 25% of all hard disk sales by the computer equipment distributer were for model number 25.

In Examples 11.1 and 11.2; the p-values were less than the level of significance ($\alpha$), and further analyses of the data were completed.   However for problems where the p-value is greater than the level of significance, and thus the null hypothesis is <u>not</u> rejected; **no** further analysis should be done!

# Lab Assignment 11.1

**Name:**                                                      **Date:**

**Course:**                    **Section:**                    **Data CD Number:**

1.  Start a Minitab session. If you are unable to complete this lab assignment in one Minitab session, save the project as Lab 11-1 . **Never** use a period as part of the project name; since Minitab uses the period to attach the file type to the file name. Then at your next Minitab session, you may open this Lab 11-1.MPJ project and continue to work where you left off previously.

2.  A health insurance company is reviewing its rate schedule for Texas State employees. The company needs to know if the distribution of hospitalized days per person has changed from last year, which is given in the table below. A random sample of Texas State workers is taken, and the numbers of these workers within each category is also in the table below. At a 0.025 level of significance, should the insurance company change its rate schedule for this year; i.e., is the current distribution different from last year's proportions?

| Days in hospital | 0 | 1 | 2 | 3 | 4 or more |
|---|---|---|---|---|---|
| Last year's proportions | 0.10 | 0.25 | 0.35 | 0.20 | 0.10 |
| Sample observed frequency | 3 | 16 | 35 | 25 | 21 |

3.  A sports enthusiast kept random records of the post position (starting gate number) of the winning horse at the local race track, and these post positions are given below. Open a new Minitab Worksheet, enter this data into a variable directly in the new Worksheet Window, and then use the Tally procedure to tabulate this data. Test the hypothesis that a horse has an equal chance of winning from any of the five post positions. Let $\alpha = 0.05$. If the null hypothesis is rejected, what betting strategies might you adopt at this race track?

1, 2, 1, 3, 4, 1, 5, 2, 1, 4, 1, 2, 5, 3, 4, 1, 3, 2, 1, 3, 4, 1, 2, 4, 1, 1, 3, 2, 1, 4, 2
3, 2, 4, 1 ,5, 2, 3, 2, 4, 3, 1, 2, 1, 5, 4, 2, 1, 1, 2, 2, 3, 2, 4, 1, 5, 4, 2, 1, 1, 2, 5
2, 1, 1, 3, 4, 1, 5, 3, 1, 4, 1, 3, 1, 1, 2, 1, 3, 1, 4, 2, 5, 1, 2, 4, 1, 5, 2, 3, 1, 4, 5
2, 1, 4, 3, 1, 5, 3, 4, 1, 3, 1, 5, 4, 1, 2, 3, 1, 3, 4, 5, 4, 5, 2, 1, 3, 1, 3, 3, 4, 1, 3
3, 1, 5, 4, 3, 2, 3, 3, 1, 2, 1, 1, and 3

(lab assignment is continued on the second side of this page)

4.  When the machine that fills 20 ounce Top Cola bottles is working correctly, 68% of the bottles will contain a "middle fill", 16% of the bottles will contain a "low fill" and 16% of the bottles will contain a "high fill." Every four days the Quality Control Department takes a random sample of 20 ounce Top Cola bottles to determine if the filling machine is working correctly. The current random sample of 150 Top Cola bottles produced: 95 bottles containing a "middle fill", 20 bottles containing a "low fill", and 35 bottles containing a "high fill." Either open a new Minitab Worksheet, or use columns 5 and 6 of the current Worksheet Window to enter the observed counts and the null hypothesized proportions. At the 0.05 level of significance, do these data provide sufficient evidence to indicate that the filling machine is **not** functioning correctly? If the machine is found to be "out of control", where are the problems?

5.  Print your Session Window to the printer.

6.  Attach both your Minitab output and your complete answers to this paper and submit all three to your instructor.

## Section 2:    Test of Independence

In many situations two categorical variables are measured on each object, and whether these two variables are related or not is often of interest.   For example; suppose the two variables are gender (male and female) and job classification (low, middle and upper).   Most sex-bias cases are based upon the hypothesis that these two variables are not independent, but are related in such a way that females tend to occupy the lower classifications and males tend to occupy the higher classifications.   A Test of Independence is done in these situations, and has the form

$H_0$: the two variables are independent
$H_a$: the two variables are related .

In each particular situation, the context of the two variables would be used in the wording of these two hypotheses.

The data is collected and presented in a two-way contingency table, where one of the categorical variables is called the "row variable" and the other categorical variable is called the "column variable."   The number of categories for the "row variable" is symbolized with the letter "r", and the number of categories for the "column variable" is symbolized with the letter "c".   Thus a contingency table has **r** rows and **c** columns.   A cell is the combination of a row variable category and a column variable category.   For example, the combination of male gender and middle job classification is a cell, and anyone having both of these values for the two variables would be counted in that cell.   The observed frequencies in each cell of the contingency table are entered into the Minitab worksheet in the following manner:

(1)    use as many columns as there are categories of the "column variable" and
(2)    each row of the contingency table is entered on a separate row of the worksheet.

For example, if the contingency table were

| 12 | 19 | 25 |
|----|----|----|
| 16 | 13 | 21 |

r = 2 and c = 3, and you could enter these data into three columns directly in the Worksheet Window which would look as shown below.

| ↓ | C1 | C2 | C3 |
|---|----|----|----|
|   |    |    |    |
| 1 | 12 | 19 | 25 |
| 2 | 16 | 13 | 21 |

Worksheet 1 ***

Assuming the null hypothesis to be true, expected numbers in each cell may be computed. If these expected numbers are sufficiently large the test statistic has an approximate Chi-square distribution with (r-1)(c-1) degrees of freedom and is given by the formula

$$(ii) \qquad \chi^2 = \sum_{i=1}^{r} \sum_{j=1}^{c} \frac{\left(O_{i,j} - E_{i,j}\right)^2}{E_{i,j}} \; .$$

The double subscript of i,j indicates that the value is for the cell in the i$^{th}$ row and j$^{th}$ column. In the example on the previous page, $O_{2,3} = 21$ since this is the observed number for the cell in the second row and third column.

Once the values in the contingency table data have been entered into the current worksheet, the Chi-square test statistic is computed using *Stat*, *Tables*, *Chi-Square Test* from the menu bar.

Click on *Stat*, *Tables*, *Chi-Square Test* ...

In the Chi-Square Test (Table in Worksheet) dialog box: the cursor should be in the box under the heading *Columns containing the table:* , hold the ⎡Ctrl⎤ key and click on each of the columns that contain the data in the contingency table, click on the ⎡Select⎤ button, and then click on the ⎡OK⎤ button.

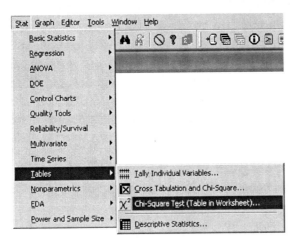 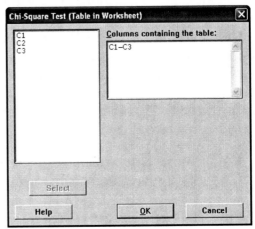

The output of the Chi-Square Test procedure contains:

   (1)   the observed number in each cell,

   (2)   the expected number in each cell,

   (3)   the individual cell Chi-square fractions for the test statistic ("CS$_{i,j}$"),

   (4)   the marginal total for each row variable,

   (5)   the marginal total for each column variable,

   (6)   the value of the Chi-square test statistic (the sum of the "CS$_{i,j}$"s),

   (7)   the degrees of freedom and the p-value, and

   (8)   if there are cells with $E_{i,j} < 5$, with $E_{i,j} < 1$, the number of such cells, and a warning in certain situations about the probable invalidness of the test.

Example 11.3 Enter the data in the contingency table shown on page 341 directly into the Worksheet Window. Then compute the Chi-Square analysis on this contingency table.

The Worksheet Window should look as shown the bottom of page 341. Next use the *Chi-Square Test* procedure from the menu bar to do the computations.

Click on *Stat , Tables , Chi-Square Test ...*

In the Chi-Square Test (Table in Worksheet) dialog box: the cursor should be in the box under the heading *Columns containing the table:* , hold the ⌐Ctrl⌐ key and click on each of the C1, C2 and C3 columns that contain the data in the contingency table, click on the ⌐Select⌐ button, and then click on the ⌐OK⌐ button.

The output shown below will appear in the Session Window.

## Chi-Square Test: C1, C2, C3

**Expected counts are printed below observed counts**
**Chi-Square contributions are printed below expected counts**

|   | C1 | C2 | C3 | Total |
|---|----|----|----|-------|
| 1 | 12 | 19 | 25 | 56 |
|   | 14.79 | 16.91 | 24.30 | |
|   | 0.527 | 0.259 | 0.020 | |
| 2 | 16 | 13 | 21 | 50 |
|   | 13.21 | 15.09 | 21.70 | |
|   | 0.590 | 0.291 | 0.02 | |
| Total | 28 | 32 | 46 | 106 |

**Chi-Sq = 1.710 , DF = 2 , P-Value = 0.425**

If the p-value is greater than the specified value of $\alpha$ (as it is in this example), you may **not** reject the null hypothesis. That is, you may not conclude that the two variables are related, and the hypothesis test is complete.

But if the p-value is less than or equal to the value of $\alpha$, you **do reject** the null hypothesis, and a further analysis may be done in order to determine how the two variables are related. The following is a suggested "logical" approach to this further analysis with the same rationale as used in Section 1 of this chapter.

Each individual cell Chi-Square fraction ($CS_{i,j}$) from the output of the *Chi-Square Test* procedure is compared to the per cell critical value ($CV_{i,j}$), and only those cells whose $CS_{i,j} \geq CV_{i,j}$ are examined. If the $O_{i,j}$ is greater than the $E_{i,j}$, the $i^{th}$ category of the "row variable" and the $j^{th}$ category of the "column variable" are said to go together. If the $O_{i,j}$ is less than the $E_{i,j}$, these two categories are said to avoid each other.

The per cell critical value ($CV_{i,j}$) is computed using the **Contapcv.mtb** (**Con**tingency **T**able **per c**ell **v**alue) macro. This macro will prompt you to enter the number of rows (value of r) and the number of columns (value of c) in the contingency table. Then this macro will prompt you to enter the level of significance of the test. Then this macro will display the corresponding cell critical value labeled as *Cell CV*.

Click on *File*, *Other Files*, *Run an Exec...*

In the Run an Exec dialog box: the *Number of times to execute:* box should be 1, then click on the | **Select File** | button.

In the next Run an Exec dialog box: select the *Data Disc* in the *Look in:* box. Next find and highlight the Contapcv.mtb macro file name, and then click on the | **Open** | button.

Example 11.4: Open a new Minitab Worksheet. In a study of heart disease of federal employees, a sample of 429 employees was examined and his/her cardiac condition was classified as being: poor, fair or good. Also, each employee's smoking habit was measured as being: heavy smoker, moderate smoker, or not a smoker. The results are given in the following table.

| **Smoking Habit** | **Cardiac Condition** | | |
| --- | --- | --- | --- |
| | Poor | Fair | Good |
| Heavy | 116 | 21 | 32 |
| Moderate | 82 | 31 | 30 |
| None | 63 | 16 | 38 |

At the 0.01 level of significance, test to see if cardiac condition and smoking habit are independent.

Smoking habit is the "row variable", and so r = 3. Cardiac condition is the "column variable", and so c = 3.

After entering the data into columns C1, C2 and C3, and naming these columns "Poor", "Fair" and "Good", the Worksheet Window should look as shown below.

| Worksheet 2 *** | | | |
| --- | --- | --- | --- |
| ↓ | C1 | C2 | C3 |
| | Poor | Fair | Good |
| 1 | 116 | 21 | 32 |
| 2 | 82 | 31 | 30 |
| 3 | 63 | 16 | 38 |

(continued on the next page)

The hypothesis testing problem is

$H_0$: Cardiac condition and smoking habit are independent
$H_a$: Cardiac condition and smoking habit are related
$\alpha = 0.01$

and the test statistic is $\chi^2 = \sum_{i=1}^{r} \sum_{j=1}^{c} \dfrac{\left(O_{i,j} - E_{i,j}\right)^2}{E_{i,j}}$ given in formula (ii) .

Now compute the *Chi-Square Test* computations on this contingency table.

Click on *Stat , Tables , Chi-Square Test ...*
In the Chi-Square Test (Table in Worksheet) dialog box: the cursor should be in the box under the heading *Columns containing the table:* , hold the ⬛ Ctrl ⬛ key and click on each of the Poor (C1) , Fair (C2) and Good (C3) variables in the contingency table, click on the ⬛ Select ⬛ button, and then click on the ⬛ OK ⬛ button.

The resulting computations shown below will appear in the Session Window.

## Chi-Square Test: Poor, Fair, Good

**Expected counts are printed below observed counts**
**Chi-Square contributions are printed below expected counts**

|       | Poor   | Fair  | Good  | Total |
|-------|--------|-------|-------|-------|
| 1     | 116    | 21    | 32    | 169   |
|       | 102.82 | 26.79 | 39.39 |       |
|       | 1.690  | 1.251 | 1.388 |       |
| 2     | 82     | 31    | 30    | 143   |
|       | 87.00  | 22.67 | 33.33 |       |
|       | 0.287  | 3.064 | 0.333 |       |
| 3     | 63     | 16    | 38    | 117   |
|       | 71.18  | 18.55 | 27.27 |       |
|       | 0.940  | 0.349 | 4.219 |       |
| Total | 261    | 68    | 100   | 429   |

**Chi-Sq = 13.522 , DF = 4 , P-Value = 0.009**

Since the p-value of 0.009 is less than the given value of $\alpha = 0.01$; the null hypothesis is rejected, and you may conclude that cardiac condition and smoking habit are related. Note that the test statistic is 13.522 and this is in the rejection region ( $\chi^2 \geq 13.277$ ).

As the null hypothesis was rejected, some further analysis may now be done. Next execute the Contapcv.mtb macro to determine the per cell critical value.

(continued on the next page)

Click on *File*, *Other Files*, *Run an Exec...*

In the Run an Exec dialog box: the *Number of times to execute:* box should be 1, then click on the | **Select File** | button.

In the next Run an Exec dialog box: select the *Data Disc* in the *Look in:* box. Next find and highlight the Contapcv.mtb macro file name, and then click on the | **Open** | button.

This macro will prompt you to enter the number of rows and columns in the contingency table. Then the significance level (value of $\alpha$) for the test will be asked for. These prompts, your inputs and the results shown below will appear in the Session Window.

**After the DATA> prompt, enter the number of rows, a comma and the number of columns in the contingency table.**

*DATA>* 3, 3 | **Enter** |

**After the DATA> prompt, enter the level of significance (alpha).**

*DATA>* 0.01 | **Enter** |

## Data Display

**For a contingency table with 3 rows and 3 columns**
**and where the level of significance is = 0.010**
**the per cell critical value  Cell CV = 1.4752**

Each cell chi-square fraction above (in decimal form) is compared to the per cell critical value **Cell CV** of 1.4752. Only the Heavy & Poor (1,1), the Moderate & Fair (2,2) and the None & Good (3,3) cells have individual cell Chi-square fractions ($CS_{i,j}$) greater than the **Cell CV** of 1.4752. In each one of these cells the observed number ($O_{i,j}$) is greater than the expected number ($E_{i,j}$). This implies that the smoking habit and cardiac condition combinations of: (1) heavy smoker and poor cardiac condition, (2) moderate smoker and fair cardiac condition, and (3) not a smoker and good cardiac condition seem to occur together. That is; for all employees, "better" (less) smoking habit and "better" cardiac condition go together. While this is **not** proof of a cause-and-effect relationship, you may say that employees who smoke less seem to have better cardiac conditions.

In Example 11.4 the number of observed outcomes in each cell already had been tabulated, and the resulting $O_{i,j}$ values were given in the table. On some occasions the values of the two categorical variables are recorded for **each** individual object in the sample. In this case you have **raw data** instead of the contingency table which would contain a summary of the raw data (as was done in Example 11.4). In such cases the raw data for the two categorical variables must be entered into two separate columns in the Minitab current worksheet. This may be done by directly entering the values in the Worksheet Window; however, the data is often in a "raw data" ASCII file that came from another program or source. Be careful to insure that the two values for each object being measured remain paired and in the same row of the Worksheet Window. The Minitab menu procedure **Stat, Tables, Cross Tabulation and Chi-Square** will tabulate this raw data into a contingency table, perform the Chi-Square Test of Independence, and display the results in the Session Window.

Click on *Stat , Tables , Cross Tabulation and Chi-Square ...*

In the Cross Tabulation and Chi-Square dialog box: the cursor should be in the box to the right of *For rows:*, highlight the row variable that contains the **raw data** and click on the Select button. Next click in the box to the right of *For columns:* , highlight the column variable that contains the **raw data** and click on the Select button. Make sure that the box to the left of *Counts* **is checked**. Now click on the Chi-Square... button.

In the Cross Tabulation - Chi-Square dialog box: click on the boxes to the left of *Chi-Square Analysis , Expected Cell Counts* , and *Each cell's contribution to the Chi-Square statistic* to select these statistics. Then click on OK .

Back in the Cross Tabulation and Chi-Square dialog box: click on the Options... button.

In the Cross Tabulation - Options dialog box: under the heading *Display marginal statistics for*, click on the circle to the left of *No variables*. This will suppress the marginal totals from printing since they are not needed and may cause one to think that there is an extra column and an extra row. Then click on the OK button.

Back in the Cross Tabulation and Chi-Square dialog box: click on OK .

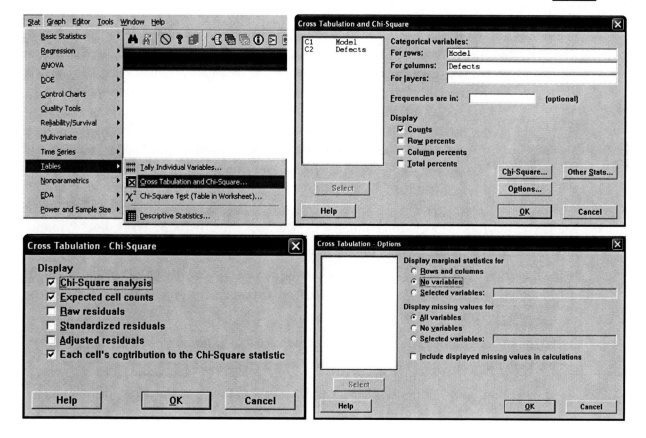

The output of this *Stat , Tables, Cross Tabulation and Chi-Square* procedure contains:

(1) the title **Rows:** followed by the corresponding variable or column number that contains the row raw data (the variable entered *For rows:* box)

(2) the title **Columns:** followed by the corresponding variable or column number that contains the column raw data (the variable entered *For columns:* box)

(3) a contingency table with:
   (a) the values of the different "row variable" outcomes on the left of the table,
   (b) the values of the different "column variable" outcomes on the top of the table,
   (c) the count (frequency), expected value, and individual cell Chi-square fractions for the test statistic ("$CS_{i,j}$") for each cell,
   (d) the value of the Pearson Chi-square test statistic (the sum of the "$_{Csi,j}$"s), its degrees of freedom and p-value,
   (e) the value of the Likelihood Ratio Chi-square test statistic, its degrees of freedom and p-value (we will ignore this line of output), and
   (f) if there are cells with $E_{i,j} < 5$, with $E_{i,j} < 1$, the number of such cells, and a warning in certain situations about the probable invalidness of the test.

Example 11.5: Open a new Minitab Worksheet. The Hdisk.dat raw data file described in Example 11.2 also contains the number of defects on each hard disk sold as a second variable. Import the raw data into columns 1 and 2 in the new worksheet, and since the first variable contains the Model number and the second variable contains the number of defects, name these two columns "Model" and "Defects" respectively. Use *Stat , Tables , Cross Tabulation and Chi-Square...* to test the hypothesis that the Model number and number of defects variables are independent at the 0.05 level of significance.

Name column 1 as 'Model' and column 2 as 'Defects' directly in the Worksheet Window
First click on *File , Other Files , Import Special Text ...*
In the Import Special Text dialog box: click in the *Store Data in Column(s)* box highlight the Model (C1) and Defects (C2) variables that are to contain the imported data, and click on `Select` . Then click on `OK` .
In the Import Text From File dialog box: make sure that *Data Disc* is in the *Look in:* box, click on the Hdisk.dat raw data filename, and then click on `Open` .

The first several rows of this Worksheet Window should look as shown on the next page.

(continued on the next page)

The hypothesis testing problem is

$H_0$: Hard disk Model number and number of defects are independent
$H_a$: Hard disk Model number and number of defects are related
$\alpha = 0.05$

and the test statistic is $\chi^2 = \displaystyle\sum_{i=1}^{r} \sum_{j=1}^{c} \frac{\left(O_{i,j} - E_{i,j}\right)^2}{E_{i,j}}$ given in formula (ii) .

Now do the Cross Tabulation and Chi-Square procedure to construct the corresponding contingency table and compute the Chi-Square test statistic.

Click on *Stat , Tables , Cross Tabulation and Chi-Square ...*

In the Cross Tabulation and Chi-Square dialog box: the cursor should be in the box to the right of *For rows:*, highlight the Model (C1) variable that contains the **raw data** and click on the $\boxed{\text{Select}}$ button. Next click in the box to the right of *For columns:* , highlight the Defects (C2) column variable that contains the **raw data** and click on the $\boxed{\text{Select}}$ button. Make sure that the box to the left of *Counts* **is checked**. Now click on the $\boxed{\text{Chi-Square...}}$ button.

In the Cross Tabulation - Chi-Square dialog box: click on the boxes to the left of *Chi-Square Analysis , Expected Cell Counts* , and *Each cell's contribution to the Chi-Square statistic* to select these statistics. Then click on $\boxed{\text{OK}}$ .

Back in the Cross Tabulation and Chi-Square dialog box: click on the $\boxed{\text{Options...}}$ button.

In the Cross Tabulation - Options dialog box: under the heading *Display marginal statistics for*, click on the circle to the left of *No variables*. This will suppress the marginal totals from printing since they are not needed and may cause one to think that there is an extra column and an extra row. Then click on the $\boxed{\text{OK}}$ button.

Back in the Cross Tabulation and Chi-Square dialog box: click on $\boxed{\text{OK}}$ .

The resulting contingency table shown on the next page will appear in the Session Window.

(continued on the next page)

## Tabulated statistics: Model, Defects

**Rows: Model   Columns: Defects**

|       | 0      | 1      | 2      | 3      |
|-------|--------|--------|--------|--------|
| **1** | 23     | 8      | 5      | 14     |
|       | 14.59  | 11.35  | 6.49   | 17.57  |
|       | 4.8409 | 0.9894 | 0.3407 | 0.7245 |
| **17**| 14     | 13     | 10     | 23     |
|       | 17.51  | 13.62  | 7.78   | 21.08  |
|       | 0.7049 | 0.0284 | 0.6310 | 0.1747 |
| **25**| 7      | 5      | 4      | 17     |
|       | 9.63   | 7.49   | 4.28   | 11.59  |
|       | 0.7194 | 0.8288 | 0.0185 | 2.5200 |
| **34**| 10     | 16     | 5      | 11     |
|       | 12.26  | 9.54   | 5.45   | 14.76  |
|       | 0.4164 | 4.3832 | 0.0369 | 0.9564 |

**Cell Contents:**   **Count**
**Expected count**
**Contribution to Chi-square**

**Pearson Chi-Square = 18.314 ,   DF = 9 ,   P-Value = 0.032**
**Likelihood Ratio Chi-Square = 17.021 ,   DF = 9 ,   P-Value = 0.048**

**\* NOTE \* 1 cells with expected counts less than 5**

We will use the Pearson Chi-Square as our standard Chi-Square test statistic and ignore the line with the Likelihood Ratio Chi-Square. Since the p-value for the Pearson Chi-Square of 0.032 is less than the given value of $\alpha = 0.05$; the null hypothesis is rejected, and you may conclude that the model number and the number of defects are related. Note, the test statistic is 18.314 and this is in the rejection region ( $\chi^2 \geq 16.919$ ).

As the null hypothesis is rejected, a further analysis may now be done.   Next execute the Contapcv.mtb macro to determine the per cell critical value.

Click on *File , Other Files , Run an Exec...*

In the Run an Exec dialog box: the *Number of times to execute:* box should  be 1, then click on the | **Select File** | button.

In the next Run an Exec dialog box: select the *Data Disc* in the *Look in:* box. Next find and highlight the Contapcv.mtb macro file name, and then click on the | **Open** | button.

(continued on the next page)

This macro will prompt you to enter the number of rows and columns in the contingency table. Then the significance level (value of α) for the test will be asked for. These prompts, your inputs and the results shown below will appear in the Session Window.

***After the DATA> prompt, enter the number of rows, a comma and the number of columns in the contingency table.***

***DATA>*** 4, 4 [ **Enter** ]

***After the DATA> prompt, enter the level of significance (alpha).***

***DATA>*** 0.05 [ **Enter** ]

## Data Display

***For a contingency table with 4 rows and 4 columns***
***and where the level of significance is = 0.050***
***the per cell critical value Cell CV = 1.0574***

Next, each cell chi-square fraction above (in decimal form) is compared to the per cell critical value ***Cell CV*** of 1.0574. Only the $(1,1)$, $(3,4)$ and $(4,2)$ cells have individual cell Chi-square fractions $(CS_{i,j})$, 4.8409, 2.5200 and 4.3832 respectively, which are greater than the ***Cell CV*** of 1.0574. In each one of these cells the observed number $(O_{i,j})$ is greater than the expected number $(E_{i,j})$. This implies that the model number and number of defects combinations of: (1) model 1 and 0 defects, (2) model 25 and 3 defects, and (3) model 34 and 1 defect seem to occur together. Thus it appears that among all four models of hard disks sold by the distributer: (1) model 1 tends to have the fewest number of defects, (2) model 34 tends to be the next best, and (3) model 25 tends to have the most defects. Model 17 does not seem to have any predominant number of defects.

# Lab Assignment 11.2

**Name:**                                                    **Date:**

**Course:**                    **Section:**                    **Data CD Number:**

1.  Start a Minitab session. If you are unable to complete this lab assignment in one Minitab session, save the project as Lab 11-2. **Never** use a period as part of the project name; since Minitab uses the period to attach the file type to the file name. Then at your next Minitab session, you may open this Lab 11-2.MPJ project and continue to work where you left off previously.

2.  A piece of equipment used in the manufacturing of automobiles can be set to run at three different speeds, which are 10, 12 or 15. The quality of each automobile made at this plant is examined, and the car is either redone, repaired or passed. These three ratings are coded 0, 1 and 2 respectively. The Mobile.dat raw data file saved on your data disc contains the values of these two variables. Import the data from this raw data file into two Minitab variables, C1 and C2, in the current worksheet. Tabulate this data into a contingency table, and test the hypothesis that the speed of the piece of equipment and the quality of the automobile are independent. Use a 0.01 level of significance.

3.  A Manfred County psychologist is researching a possible relationship between abuse received as a child and later adult drinking habits. She interviewed a random sample of County adults and asked each what level of parental abuse (none, infrequent or often) he/she received as a child and what his/her drinking habit is (none, light, moderate or heavy). The table below gives the results of her interviews. Open a new Minitab worksheet and enter these data into the first three rows of C1, C2, C3 and C4

| child abuse | drinking habit | | | |
|---|---|---|---|---|
|  | none | light | moderate | heavy |
| none | 51 | 38 | 37 | 14 |
| infrequent | 28 | 42 | 11 | 10 |
| often | 27 | 40 | 12 | 46 |

At the 0.01 level of significance, can the psychologist conclude that there is a relationship between abuse received as a child and later drinking habits for all adults in Manfred County?

(lab assignment is continued on the second side of this page)

469

4.  WMUS is a radio station that plays a wide variety of music including: Classical, Jazz, Hard Rock and Soft Rock. The station breaks up its on air time into three time slots labeled "Early", Mid Day" and "Late", and employs a different disk jockey for each of these three time slot. In the past, the type of music has been left up to the disk jockey. The programming director of a radio station is setting the schedule for the next month, and he is considering playing mostly a specific type of music each different time slot. Before he does this, he wants to know if the time a person listens to WMUS and the type of music preferred are related. The following table represents the results of a random sample of WMUS listeners taken recently. Open a third new Minitab Worksheet and enter these data into the C1, C2, C3 and C4.

| On Air Time Slot | Type of Music | | | |
|---|---|---|---|---|
| | Classical | Jazz | Hard Rock | Soft Rock |
| Early | 80 | 61 | 56 | 67 |
| Mid Day | 53 | 53 | 53 | 83 |
| Late | 39 | 58 | 44 | 45 |

Test to see if such a relationship does exist. Use a 0.025 level of significance. If the type of music and the on air time slots are independent, the program director will continue to let each disk jockey decide on the music selections for his/her on air time slot. But if a relationship does exist, how should the program director schedule the different types of music?

5.  Print your Session Window to the printer.

6.  Attach both your Minitab output and your complete answers to this paper and submit all three to your instructor.

# CHAPTER 12:    Simple Linear Regression and Correlation

**Section 1:    Simple Linear Regression Analysis**

Chapters 5 through 9 explain the Minitab procedures needed to perform statistical inference about one, two, and two or more populations when there is one continuous variable. When two or more continuous type measurements are made on each individual object, the relationship among these variables is of primary interest.

This chapter concentrates on the situation where there are simply two continuous variables which are linearly related, and thus the name Simple Linear Regression. And specifically, you will usually want to be able to predict the future value of one of the variables, called the "response" or "predicted" or dependent variable, based upon the present value of the other variable, called the "predictor" or independent variable. This prediction is done with both a point prediction and an interval prediction. The usual statistical notation is to label the "predictor" variable as X and label the "response" variable as Y. Additionally, the strength of the linear relationship between the two variables may be measured by either the Coefficient of Determination or the Coefficient of Correlation.

For each value of X there is a well defined subpopulation of Y values, each with a mean denoted $\mu_{y.x}$ and a standard deviation denoted $\sigma_{y.x}$. The statistical techniques discussed in this chapter depend upon the following assumptions about these subpopulations:

(1)    the means of the Y values in the subpopulations are linearly related to the X values which define the subpopulations and

(2)    the variances of all subpopulations ($\sigma_{y.x}^2$) are all equal and usually symbolized as just $\sigma^2$.

The technique for computing a prediction interval depends upon the additional assumption that

(3)    each subpopulation of Y values is normally distributed.

Assumption (1) of a linear relationship is expressed by the equation

(i)    $\mu_{y.x} = \beta_0 + \beta_1 x$

and the graph of this equation is called the Regression Line of Y on X. In this equation; $\beta_0$ represents the "y-intercept", and $\beta_1$ represents the "slope" of the line. The value of $\beta_1$ often is of particular interest as it describes how much the Y variable will change for a "unit" change in the X variable.

Point estimates of $\beta_0$ and $\beta_1$ are computed from the data in the baseline sample using the least squares criterion. These estimates are symbolized by $b_0$ and $b_1$ respectively. After these two estimates have been computed, the equation of the Estimated Regression Line of Y on X is written as

(ii)    $\hat{y} = b_0 + b_1 x$

where the $\hat{y}$ is a point estimate for $\mu_{y.x}$ and is used to predict unknown values of the Y variable. This $\hat{y}$ is called the "predicted value of Y" for a known value of the X variable.

At this point it is important to precisely define the word "linear" in linear regression. Linear refers to the functional form of the equation in terms of the parameters $\beta_i$. These parameters must appear as coefficients in the model. Equation (i) is the simplest case where $\beta_0$ is the constant coefficient, and $\beta_1$ is the coefficient of x. This case is called a **first-order** linear model, and is the subject of this chapter. In the first-order linear model, the X and Y variables are linearly related, and the corresponding y versus x graph displays a straight line pattern. However; for completeness, several other cases will be described.

The regression equation $\mu_{y.x} = \beta_0 + \beta_1 x + \beta_2 x^2$ is a linear model. Since the highest power of x in this model is 2, this is called a **second-order** linear model. In general, the highest power of x in the equation is the order of the model. Since the x-y graphs of these higher order models are not straight lines, these cases are often called **curvilinear** regression. The regression equation $\mu_{y.x} = \beta_0 + \beta_1 e^{\beta_2 x}$ is an example of a **nonlinear** model, since the $\beta_2$ parameter is used as an exponent instead of as a coefficient; and no transformation exists that will transform this into a linear model. Now back to our subject of this chapter where equation (i) is our model.

The baseline sample data is collected and entered into the Worksheet Window. It usually will be easier if the column containing the "predictor" variable is named X and the column containing the "response" variable is named Y. If these two columns have existing names, you still may want to rename these columns as X and Y. Before doing any numerical analysis, one should graph the (x,y) data in order to obtain a general picture. From this graph, one may usually see if the first-order linear model seems appropriate; or, if not, one may see what model pattern is described by the data. As described in Chapter 3, the *Graph , Plot...* menu item is used to graph the data.

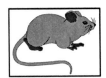

Click on *Graph , Scatterlot ...*

In the Scatterplots dialog box: the *Simple* graph should be highlighted. Next click on the | **OK** | button.

In the Scatterplot - Simple dialog box: the cursor will be in the box on the first line under the *Y variables* heading; click on the desired Y variable and click on the | **Select** | button. The cursor will move to the box in the first line under the *X variables* heading; click on the desired X variable and click on the | **Select** | button. Then click on the | **OK** | button.

(See graphics on the next page.)

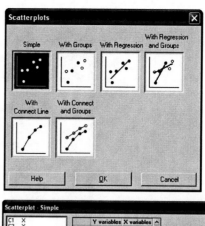
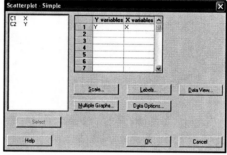

If the points display a linear pattern then assumption (1) appears to be valid. However the actual validity of this first assumption is numerically verified by the hypothesis testing of:

$H_0$: the X and Y variables are **not** linearly related
$H_a$: the X and Y variables **are** linearly related

How this test is done will be described several pages later in this section. If it is found that assumption (1) is not valid, then this graph will give an indication as to what type of model **is correct** for this data.

Example 12.1:   The shop manager wants to examine the linear relationship between a worker's job experience (months) and task completion time (minutes). In particular, he wants to be able to predict the task completion time for a worker with 65 months of experience. The baseline sample data are:

| job experience (X) | task completion time (Y) |
|---|---|
| 79 | 37 |
| 58 | 41 |
| 72 | 39 |
| 52 | 38 |
| 67 | 38 |
| 88 | 36 |
| 62 | 40 |
| 83 | 35 |
| 24 | 45 |

Plot the (x,y) graph for this baseline sample data and describe the pattern of these data.

(continued on the next page)

First enter these data into columns 1 and 2 in the Worksheet Window, and then name these two columns X and Y. Then the Worksheet Window will look as shown below.

| ↓ | C1 | C2 |
|---|----|----|
|   | X  | Y  |
| 1 | 79 | 37 |
| 2 | 58 | 41 |
| 3 | 72 | 39 |
| 4 | 52 | 38 |
| 5 | 67 | 38 |
| 6 | 88 | 36 |
| 7 | 62 | 40 |
| 8 | 83 | 35 |
| 9 | 24 | 45 |

Worksheet 1 ***

Click on *Graph*, *Scatterplot...* then in the Scatterplots dialog box: the *Simple* graph should be highlighted. Next click on the OK button.

In the Scatterplot - Simple dialog box: the cursor will be in the box on the first line under the *Y variables* heading; click on the Y variable and click on the Select button. The cursor will move to the box in the first line under the *X variables* heading; click on the X variable and click on the Select button. Then click on the OK button

The graph will appear in a separate Scatterplot of Y vs X Graphics Window as shown below.

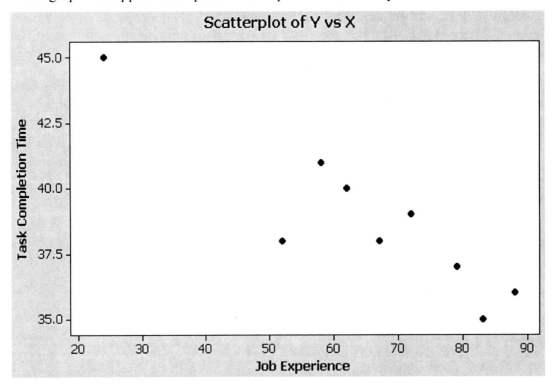

In general these points follow a straight line (first-order linear) pattern. However, the points (24,45) and (52,38) at the left seem to be out of place and need to be examined further.

474

Points on the graph that seem to be either relatively far away from the rest of the points or which do not appear to be in the linear pattern are potential outliers. Those points that are relatively far away (in the x direction) from the rest of the scores are labeled observations with unusual influence. Points which seem to relative far off of the linear pattern are labeled residual outliers, where the residual is the vertical distance from the actual point to the line that best describes the linear pattern. Minitab will identify these outliers, and then you must examine the data points for errors. This is done by using the Minitab *Stat, Regression, Regression* procedure from the menu bar.

Click on *Stat, Regression, Regression*...

In the Regression dialog box, if this is a **new** problem, press the | **F3** | key to clear any previous information from all Regression dialog boxes. The cursor should be in the box to the right of the *Response:* heading; click on the "response" (Y) variable and click on the | **Select** | button. The cursor will move down to the *Predictors:* box; click on the "predictor" (X) variable and click on the | **Select** | button. Then click on | **OK** |.

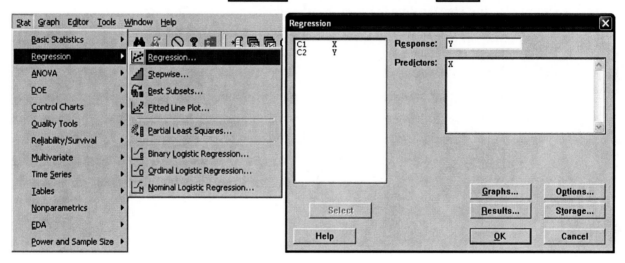

For now we will ignore most of the output in the Session Window. At the end of the output will be the heading **Analysis of Variance** and four lines of output under this heading. Then **if** there are any outliers, The output will contain the heading **Unusual Observations** followed by information on the outlier(s) listed. This information consists of the case number, and values of X, Y, the Fit, SE Fit, Residual and St Resid . Any unusual observations identified by the *Regression* procedure are classified as:

(a)    Cases with relative small or relative large X values, identified by an "X" next to the St Resid value. This type of unusual observation is called an **influential point**.

(b)    Cases with relative large Residual values, identified by an "R" next to the St Resid value.    This type of unusual observation is called a **residual outlier**.  Minitab identifies any observation whose St Resid value is either less than -2 or greater than 2 as a residual outlier.  Some statisticians disagree with this criterion and use less than -2.5 or greater than 2.5, while others use less than -3 and greater than 3.

The cases identified as unusual observations need to be examined. The values of the "predictor" and "response" variables are displayed for each unusual observation identified. If errors are found, make any necessary corrections directly in the Worksheet Window. If the data in the unusual observation is known to be incorrect, but the correct data is not available, this case should be deleted directly in the Worksheet Window by clicking on the row number at the left side corresponding to the case number being deleted and then press the | Del | key.

A third possibility is when the entered data is correct for a case identified as an unusual observation. This situation has troubled statisticians for many years, and there is no general consensus as to what course to follow. For example; while Minitab defines an outlier as a case with the St Resid > 2, other statisticians require the St Resid value to be greater than three in order to call this an outlier. When the data is correct; the decision of whether to retain or to delete an unusual observation is difficult and should not be taken lightly. In general, it is usually best to retain such cases.

Example 12.2: Use the data in the current worksheet and the *Stat*, *Regression*, *Regression* procedure to identify any outliers in this sample.

Click on *Stat*, *Regression*, *Regression* ...

In the Regression dialog box, since this is a **new** problem, press the | F3 | key to clear any previous information from all Regression dialog boxes. The cursor should be in the box to the right of the *Response:* heading; click on the "response" variable - Y (C2) and click on the | Select | button. The cursor will move down to the *Predictors:* box; click on the "predictor" variable - X (C1) and click on the | Select | button. Then click on the | OK | button.

Only the end of the output in the Session Window is shown below.

### Analysis of Variance

| Source | DF | SS | MS | F | P |
|---|---|---|---|---|---|
| Regression | 1 | 58.884 | 58.884 | 32.53 | 0.001 |
| Residual Error | 7 | 12.672 | 1.810 | | |
| Total | 8 | 71.556 | | | |

### Unusual Observations

| Obs | X | Y | Fit | SE Fit | Residual | St Resid |
|---|---|---|---|---|---|---|
| 4 | 52.0 | 38.000 | 40.596 | 0.550 | -2.596 | -2.11R |
| 9 | 24.0 | 45.000 | 44.512 | 1.101 | 0.488 | 0.63 X |

**R denotes an observation with a large standardized residual.**
**X denotes an observation whose X value gives it large influence.**

(continued on the next page)

The 4th and 9th observations have been identified as **Unusual Observations** or what we often call outliers. For the 4th observation, the **R** to the right of the -2.11 under the **St Resid** heading indicates that this point is relatively far away **vertically** from the pattern of the other points. That is, if a straight line were drawn to fit the pattern of the points, this (52,38) point would be relatively far below the line. Upon further examination of this outlier, the shop manager finds that the task completion time (Y) for case 4 was incorrectly copied as 38 minutes, and that the correct value is 40 minutes. For the 9th observation, the **X** to the right of 0.63 under the **St Resid** heading indicates that this point is relatively far away **in the x direction** from the rest of the data points. Upon further examination of this outlier, the shop manager finds that the job experience (X) for case 9 is impossible, but he does not have a record of which worker was assigned to this job. And so this outlier contains incorrect data that can not be corrected, and so case 9 needs to be removed from the sample.

When making changes to the data in a worksheet, **always** start with the largest case number and work back to the successively smaller case numbers. This is because if you need to delete a case, all of the observations with higher case numbers will have their case numbers reduced by 1, and this will make them no longer correspond to the case number in the Minitab output. But the observations with smaller case numbers will be unaffected, and their case numbers will still correspond to the Minitab output.

Example 12.3:   Correct and delete the outliers in the current worksheet.

Click on the 9 in the left margin of the worksheet to highlight the entire 9th row, and then press the Delete key to remove this observation from the sample.

To change the job completion time (Y) from the incorrect value of 38 to the correct value of 40; click on the cell in the 4th row of the Y (C2) column, and enter the correct value of 40 (which will replace the incorrect value of 38).

Then the Worksheet Window will look as shown below.

**Worksheet 1 \*\*\***

| ↓ | C1 | C2 |
|---|----|----|
|   | X  | Y  |
| 1 | 79 | 37 |
| 2 | 58 | 41 |
| 3 | 72 | 39 |
| 4 | 52 | 40 |
| 5 | 67 | 38 |
| 6 | 88 | 36 |
| 7 | 62 | 40 |
| 8 | 83 | 35 |
| 9 |    |    |

Once the outliers have been corrected and/or removed, the *Stat, Regression , Regression* procedure should be done again. This is because the definition of an outlier is that it is **relatively far away**, and once a set of outliers have been corrected and/or removed, other score may now be relatively far away and thus will be identified as outliers by Minitab. This process is repeated until either (1) there are no outliers listed by Minitab, or (2) all of the outliers listed by Minitab are known to be correct and thus are left in the sample data..

Example 12.4: Use the data in the current worksheet and the *Stat, Regression , Regression* procedure to identify any further outliers in this sample.

Click on *Stat , Regression , Regression ...*

In the Regression dialog box, the cursor should be in the box to the right of the *Response:* heading; click on the "response" variable - Y (C2) and click on the | **Select** | button. The cursor will move down to the *Predictors:* box; click on the "predictor" variable - X (C1) and click on the | **Select** | button. Then click on the | **OK** | button. Note that since Minitab remembers the information in the dialog boxes from the previous time, you will only need to click on the | **OK** | button.

Only the end of the output in the Session Window is shown below.

### Analysis of Variance

| Source | DF | SS | MS | F | P |
|---|---|---|---|---|---|
| Regression | 1 | 25.906 | 25.906 | 27.78 | 0.002 |
| Residual Error | 6 | 5.594 | 0.932 | | |
| Total | 7 | 31.500 | | | |

There are no Unusual Observations listed at the end of the output, so the sample data is "clean", and you are ready to check the validity of assumptions (1) and (2).

After all corrections and deletions have been made, the validity of assumptions (1) and (2) are checked. These two assumptions must be validated before any interpretation may be done for the regression results shown in the output!

Assumption (1) is that the means of the Y values in the subpopulations are linearly related to the X values which define the subpopulations. The validity of this first assumption is verified or in-validated by hypothesis testing of:

$H_0$: the X and Y variables are **not** linearly related
$H_a$: the X and Y variables **are** linearly related

The significance level for this test is usually set at $\alpha = 0.05$ , and the test statistic is

$$F = \frac{MS \ for \ Regression}{MS \ for \ Residual \ Error} .$$

478

The value of this F statistic and the corresponding p-value are computed and displayed in the **Analysis of Variance** table at the bottom of the output from the *Regression* procedure that appears in the Session Window. Assumption (1) is stated as the alternative hypothesis, $H_a$. And so if the p-value is less than or equal to $\alpha$ (usually 0.05), then the null hypothesis **is rejected**, and assumption (1) that the two variables **are** linearly related has been verified. However; if the p-value is greater than $\alpha$ (usually 0.05), then the null hypothesis is **not** rejected, assumption (1) is **not** verified, and the data should not be analyzed using the first-order linear regression and correlation techniques described in this chapter.

> Example 12.5:  Examine the results in the **Analysis of Variance** table in the re-computed Regression procedure that are in the Session Window, and determine if assumption (1) that job experience and task completion time are linearly related is or is not verified.

The hypothesis testing problem is:

$H_0$: Job Experience and Task Completion Time are **not** linearly related
$H_a$: Job Experience and Task Completion Time **are** linearly related
$\alpha = 0.05$,

and the test statistic is  $F = \dfrac{\text{MS for Regression}}{\text{MS for Residual Error}}$.

Look in the Session Window and you will see the **Analysis of Variance** table as shown below.

**Analysis of Variance**

| Source | DF | SS | MS | F | P |
|--------|----|------|------|------|------|
| Regression | 1 | 25.906 | 25.906 | 27.78 | 0.002 |
| Residual Error | 6 | 5.594 | 0.932 | | |
| Total | 7 | 31.500 | | | |

Since the p-value of 0.002 is less than the given value of $\alpha = 0.05$, the null hypothesis **is rejected** and you may conclude that assumption (1), that Job Experience and Task Completion Time are linearly related **is verified**.

A residual is the difference between the observed value of Y for a X value in the baseline sample and the predicted value of Y for the same X value. This is symbolized by $(y - \hat{y})$, where the lower case y represents the baseline sample value of the Y variable and the $\hat{y}$ represents the predicted value of the Y variable for the same X value. The residuals are the deviations of each y value from the estimated mean of its subpopulation, and are used to verify the second assumption that all subpopulations have equal variances. The residuals for each case in the baseline sample are computed and stored into a new column automatically named RESI1 by using the *Stat*, *Regression*, *Regression* in the following way.

Click on *Stat* , *Regression* , *Regression ...*

In the Regression dialog box, the cursor should be in the box to the right of the *Response:* heading; click on the "response" variable - Y (C2) and click on the Select button. The cursor will move down to the *Predictors:* box; click on the "predictor" variable - X (C1) and click on the Select button. Then click on the OK button. Next click on the Storage... button. Note that since Minitab remembers the information in the dialog boxes from the previous time, you will only need to click on the Storage... button

In the Regression - Storage dialog box, click in the square to the left of *Residuals* to check this option. No other options should be checked. Then click on OK . A new column automatically will be created and named RESI1. The column number will be one higher than the last column used in the current Worksheet Window.

Back in the Regression dialog box, click on OK .

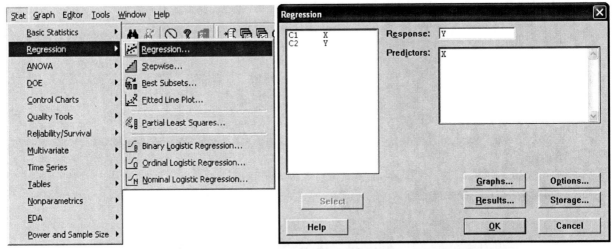

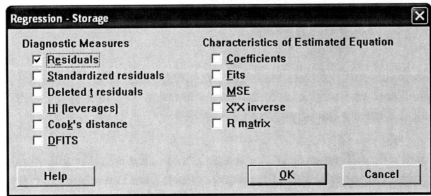

Example 12.6:   Use the corrected data in the current worksheet to compute the residuals.

Click on *Stat*, *Regression*, *Regression* ...

In the Regression dialog box, the Y variable should be in the box to the right of the *Response:* heading and the X variable should be in the *Predictors:*. Next click on the Storage... button.

In the Regression - Storage dialog box, click in the square to the left of *Residuals* to check this option. No other options should be checked. Then click on OK . A new column automatically will be created and named RESI1. The column number will be one higher than the last column used in the current Worksheet Window; i.e., C3.

Back in the Regression dialog box, click on OK .

The X, Y and RESI1 columns in the Worksheet Window are shown below.

| | C1 | C2 | C3 |
|---|---|---|---|
| | X | Y | RESI1 |
| 1 | 79 | 37 | 0.10044 |
| 2 | 58 | 41 | 0.90504 |
| 3 | 72 | 39 | 1.03530 |
| 4 | 52 | 40 | -1.00793 |
| 5 | 67 | 38 | -0.72551 |
| 6 | 88 | 36 | 0.46989 |
| 7 | 62 | 40 | 0.51369 |
| 8 | 83 | 35 | -1.29092 |
| 9 | | | |

Worksheet 1 ***

Assumption (2) is that the variances of all subpopulations ($\sigma^2_{y.x}$) are all equal and usually symbolized as just $\sigma^2$.  The validity of this second assumption may be  verified or in-validated **visually** checked by examining the graph of the x values in the baseline sample on the horizontal axis and the corresponding residuals on the vertical axis.

Click on *Graph*, *Scatterlot* ...

In the Scatterplots dialog box: the *Simple* graph should be highlighted.  Next click on the OK button.

In the Scatterplot - Simple dialog box: the cursor will be in the box on the first line under the *Y variables* heading; click on the RESI1 variable and click on the Select button.  The cursor will move to the box in the first line under the *X variables* heading; click on the desired X variable and click on the Select button.  Then click on the OK button.

It is desirable to label the X axis with the name of the predictor variable and to label the Y axis as  Residuals.


(See graphics on the next page.)

481

 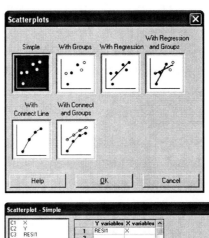

If the points on this graph look to be randomly and evenly spread within a general rectangular shape; this indicates that the variances ($\sigma_{y.x}^2$) of each subpopulation are all equal, and thus indicate that assumption (2) **is valid**. But if these points lie within a triangular or some other non-rectangular pattern; this implies that assumption (2) is **not** valid, and the techniques of first-order linear regression and correlation analysis shown in this chapter are **not** appropriate for describing the relationship between the X and Y variables nor for predicting new (future) Y values.

Example 12.7: Use the data in the current worksheet, and graph the residuals (y axis) versus the job experience (x axis). Name the axes appropriately. Does assumption (2) that the variances of all subpopulations are all equal seem to be verified?

Click on *Graph , Scatterlot ...*

In the Scatterplots dialog box: the *Simple* graph should be highlighted. Next click on the OK button.

In the Scatterplot - Simple dialog box: the cursor will be in the box on the first line under the *Y variables* heading; click on the RESI1 variable and click on the Select button. The cursor will move to the box in the first line under the *X variables* heading; click on the desired X variable and click on the Select button. Then click on the OK button.

It is desirable to label the X axis with the name of the predictor variable and to label the Y axis as Residuals.

(continued on the next page)

482

The graph below will appear in the Scatterplot of RESI1 vs X  Graphics Window.

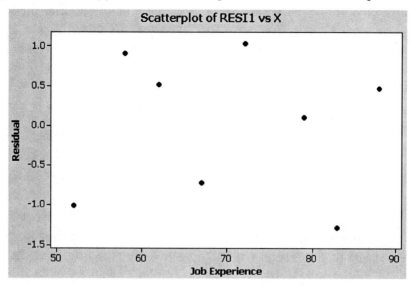

The points seem to be randomly and evenly scattered within a general rectangular shape, and this indicates that assumption (2), all subpopulation variances are equal, is verified.

However; this is a <u>subjective</u> decision, and it is often very difficult to determine the pattern with a small sample size.  This second assumption often may be numerically verified with a hypothesis test.  The test used is the modified **Levene's** for homogeneity of variance test that was introduced in Section 2 of Chapter 9.  This test only checks for a megaphone shape violation of assumption (2).  That is; if the population variances are consistently getting larger as the x values increase, or if the population variances are consistently getting smaller as the x values increase.  These produce a megaphone shape to the graph of the residuals versus the x values.  Other patterns that would invalidate assumption (2) are not detected with this test; for example, an hourglass pattern.  However, most of the situations in which assumption (2) is not valid turn out to be due to the megaphone pattern of the population variances.  Also, the graph of the residuals versus the x values, as done in Example 12.7, will indicate if Levene's test is appropriate.  Note that in order to use the Levene's test, there must be at least six objects in the baseline sample.

The alternative hypothesis for testing assumption (2) that all subpopulation variances are equal (i.e., homogeneity of variance) when using Levene's test slightly changes to

$H_0$:  all subpopulation variances are equal
$H_a$:  the subpopulation variances are in a megaphone shape
$\alpha = 0.10$ ,

and the test statistic is the Levene's test statistic.

Here assumption (2) is stated as the null hypothesis, $H_0$ .  And so if the p-value for this test is greater than the pre-selected level of significance, usually 0.10; the null hypothesis of equal subpopulation variances (homogeneity) may not be rejected.  And **as long as the graph of the residuals versus the x does not lead you to suspect an obvious non constant standard deviation pattern other than a megaphone shape**, assumption (2) **is** verified.  But if the p-value is less than or equal to $\alpha$; then the null hypothesis is rejected, and assumption (2) is **<u>not</u>** valid.

It is often more convenient to name columns **before** actually using them. So in the Worksheet Window, click in the name row of the first unused column after the Residual (RESI1) column and name the next three columns Sorted X, Corresp R and Factor. The procedure for computing Levene's test is as follows. First you must sort the x scores from smallest to largest and keep the corresponding residuals associated with the sorted x scores. This is done using the *Data , Sort...* procedure on the Minitab menu bar.

Click on *Data , Sort...*

In the Sort dialog box, the cursor will be in the box under the *Sort Column(s):* heading. Hold the ⃞ Ctrl ⃞ key and click on the X and RESI1 variables to highlight them both. Then click on ⃞ Select ⃞ . Next click inside the box to the right of the first *By column:* heading, click on the X variable, and click on ⃞ Select ⃞ . Next click on the circle to the left of *Column(s) of current worksheet:*, and then click inside of the box under this heading. inside of the box under the *Store sorted column(s) in:* heading, hold the ⃞ Ctrl ⃞ key and click on the Sorted X and Corresp R variables to highlight them both. Then click on ⃞ Select ⃞ . Now click on ⃞ **OK** ⃞ .

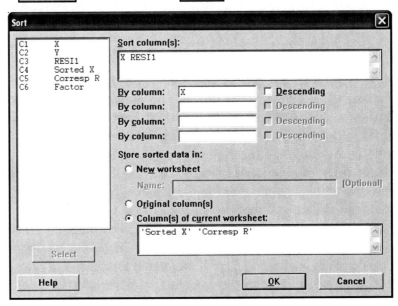

The results in the Worksheet Window are displayed in the graphic below. Notice that the Sorted X column contains the original X scores in sorted order, and that the RESI1 values that corresponded to each original X score are kept with that same value and placed in the Corresp R column.

**Worksheet 1 \*\*\***

| ↓ | C1 | C2 | C3 | C4 | C5 | C6 |
|---|---|---|---|---|---|---|
| | X | Y | RESI1 | Sorted X | Corresp R | Factor |
| 1 | 79 | 37 | 0.10044 | 52 | -1.00793 | |
| 2 | 58 | 41 | 0.90504 | 58 | 0.90504 | |
| 3 | 72 | 39 | 1.03530 | 62 | 0.51369 | |
| 4 | 52 | 40 | -1.00793 | 67 | -0.72551 | |
| 5 | 67 | 38 | -0.72551 | 72 | 1.03530 | |
| 6 | 88 | 36 | 0.46989 | 79 | 0.10044 | |
| 7 | 62 | 40 | 0.51369 | 83 | -1.29092 | |
| 8 | 83 | 35 | -1.29092 | 88 | 0.46989 | |

Next determine how many objects there are in the baseline sample. There are several ways to do this. You could scroll down the Worksheet Window until you come to the last data row, and then that row number is the number of objects in the baseline sample. You could enter the command info into the Session Window after the **MTB >** prompt, and the number of scores in the X column will be the number of observations in the baseline sample. A third and easiest option is to use the *Stat, Basic Statistics, Display Descriptive Statistics* procedure from the menu bar for the Sorted X variable. This will be demonstrated in the next example. You need to find the **middle** two scores of the Sorted X column. Now comes the part which may vary from problem to problem. If the number of objects, symbolized by n, is an even number then the two middle scores will be in the rows numbered $n/2$ and $(n/2 + 1)$. If n is an odd number then the two middle scores will be in either the rows numbered $(n-1)/2$ and $(n+1)/2$ or the rows numbered $(n+1)/2$ and $(n+3)/2$. In any of these three cases, you must use your best judgement as to which you want to call the middle two scores. For example; if the two Sorted X scores in these two rows are identical or very close in value, you will want to keep them together; and so you will need to choose the first different score (either smaller or larger) as the other middle score. This process is not governed by any formula. And it is not critical to get the exact correct two middle scores, as long as you choose two scores approximately in the middle. Next either use the *Stat, Basic Statistics, Display Descriptive Statistics* procedure or look in the first and last rows of the Worksheet Window to find the minimum and maximum of the Sorted X values.

Using the notation of: min for the smallest score, $m_1$ and $m_2$ for the **middle** two scores, and max for the largest score in the Sorted X column, proceed as follows. Use the *Data, Code, Numeric to Text...* procedure to put Lo in the first half of this new Factor column and to put Hi in the second half of the factor column. The *Data, Code* procedure was introduced in Section 3 of Chapter 5. In that section the coding explained was *Text to Numeric*. The *Numeric to Text* coding is similar and is done as follows.

Click on *Data, Code, Numeric to Text ...*

In the Code - Numeric to Text dialog box only the columns with numeric values will be displayed in the box on the left. The cursor should be in the box under the heading *Code data from columns:*, click on the Sorted X variable and click on the ⬛ **Select** button. Next click in the *Into columns:* box, click on the Factor variable, and click on the ⬛ **Select** button. Then click in the first box under the *Original values* heading and type in min : $m_1$ (the value of min, a colon and the value of $m_1$). Next click in the first box under the *New:* heading and type in the word Lo. Similarly click on the second row in the box under the *Original values* heading and type in $m_2$ : max (the value of $m_2$, a colon and the value of max). Next click in the box under the *New:* heading and type in the word Hi. Then click ⬛ **OK** .

(See graphics on the next page.)

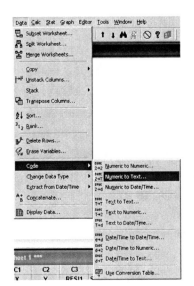
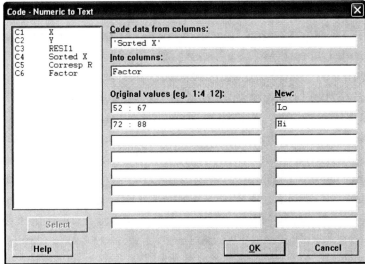

Now the Factor variable will have Lo in the first half of its rows and Hi in the second half of its rows.

Finally, assumption (2) is verified by the hypothesis testing of

$H_0$: all subpopulation variances are equal

$H_a$: the subpopulation variances are in a megaphone shape

$\alpha = 0.10$ .

The test statistic is the Levene's test statistic. The modified Levene's test statistic and corresponding p-value are calculated as follows.

Click on *Stat* , *ANOVA* , *Test for Equal Variances...*

In the Test for Equal Variances dialog box: the cursor will be in the box to the right of *Response:*. Click on the Corresp R variable and click on the Select button. The cursor will move to the large box to the right of *Factors:*, click on the Factor variable and then click on the Select button. You may ignore the boxes to the right of *Confidence level:* and *Title:*. Then click on the OK button.

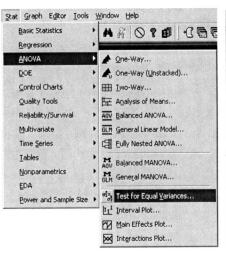
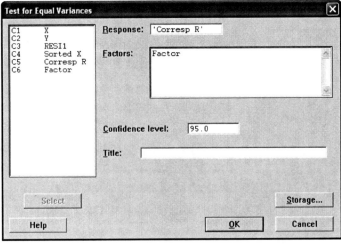

The output of the *Test for Equal Variances* (or *Homogeneity of Variance*) procedure contains:

(1) Simultaneous Bonferroni confidence intervals for the population standard deviations,
(2) the Bartlett's (for normal distributions) F test statistic and p-value,
(3) the Levene's (for any continuous distribution) test statistic and p-value, and
(4) a Graphic Window, labeled *Test for Equal Variances: AllData versus Factor* containing the same information.

Only the Levene's test statistic and p-value are used to test the hypothesis and check the validity of assumption (2).

Even though the test results are most easily read from the Graphic Window, since it is active and appears on top after the *Test of Equal Variances* is completed; there is no need to print this Graphic Window since the same information appears in the Session Window and will be printed when you print the Session Window.

Example 12.8: Use the data in the current worksheet, and perform the modified Levene's test to check the validity of assumption (2) that the variances of all subpopulations are all equal.

First name the three new columns (C4, C5 and C6) as Sorted X, Corresp R and Factor.

Click on *Data , Sort...*

In the Sort dialog box, the cursor will be in the box under the *Sort Column(s):* heading. Hold the ⎡ **Ctrl** ⎤ key and click on the X (C1) and RESI1 (C3) variables to highlight them both. Then click on ⎡ **Select** ⎤. Next click inside the box to the right of the first *By column:* heading, click on the X variable, and click on ⎡ **Select** ⎤. Next click on the circle to the left of *Column(s) of current worksheet:*, and then click inside of the box under this heading. inside of the box under the *Store sorted column(s) in:* heading, hold the ⎡ **Ctrl** ⎤ key and click on the Sorted X and Corresp R variables to highlight them both. Then click on ⎡ **Select** ⎤. Now click on ⎡ **OK** ⎤.

The Worksheet Window should look as shown below.

| | C1 | C2 | C3 | C4 | C5 | C6 |
|---|---|---|---|---|---|---|
| | X | Y | RESI1 | Sorted X | Corresp R | Factor |
| 1 | 79 | 37 | 0.10044 | 52 | -1.00793 | |
| 2 | 58 | 41 | 0.90504 | 58 | 0.90504 | |
| 3 | 72 | 39 | 1.03530 | 62 | 0.51369 | |
| 4 | 52 | 40 | -1.00793 | 67 | -0.72551 | |
| 5 | 67 | 38 | -0.72551 | 72 | 1.03530 | |
| 6 | 88 | 36 | 0.46989 | 79 | 0.10044 | |
| 7 | 62 | 40 | 0.51369 | 83 | -1.29092 | |
| 8 | 83 | 35 | -1.29092 | 88 | 0.46989 | |

Worksheet 1 ***

(continued on the next page)

Next the minimum, the middle two scores and the maximum need to be determined. The *Stat*, *Basic Statistics*, *Describe Statistics* menu procedure will find the minimum, the maximum and the number of scores for the Sorted X variable.

Click on *Stat*, *Basic Statistics*, *Describe Statistics*

In the Display Descriptive Statistics dialog box: highlight the Sorted X variable, click on the [ Select ] button, and then click on the [ Statistics... ] button.

In the Descriptive Statistics - Statistics dialog box: click to uncheck all boxes **except** for the *Minimum*, *Maximum* and *N nonmissing* statistics.

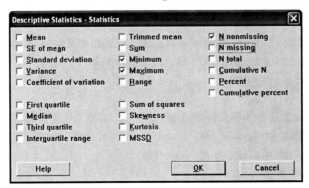

The results shown below will appear in the Session Window.

## Descriptive Statistics: Sorted X

| Variable | N | Minimum | Maximum |
|---|---|---|---|
| Sorted X | 8 | 52.00 | 88.00 |

There are 8 non-missing ( $N$ ) scores, and so that the number of objects is n = 8. Since n is even, the two middle rows are the $n/2 = 4^{th}$ and $(n/2 + 1) = 5^{th}$ rows. Look in the Worksheet Window and see that the scores in the Sorted X variable that are in these two rows, 67 and 72, are different; so let $m_1 = 67$ and $m_2 = 72$. The output in the Session Window shows the values of the minimum and maximum, and so min = 52 and max = 88.

Next put Lo in the first half of the Factor column and put Hi in the second half.

Click on *Data*, *Code*, *Numeric to Text ...*
In the Code - Numeric to Text dialog box, the cursor should be in the box under the heading *Code data from columns:*. Click on the Sorted X variable and click on the [ Select ] button. Next click in the *Into columns:* box, click on the Factor variable, and click on the [ Select ] button. Then click in the first box under the *Original values* heading and type in 52 : 67 (min : $m_1$). Next click in the first box under the *New:* heading and type in the word Lo. Similarly click on the second row in the box under the *Original values* heading and type in 72 : 88 ($m_2$ : max). Next click in the box under the *New:* heading and type in the word Hi. Then click on [ OK ].

(continued on the next page)

The Factor variable will be filled in and the Worksheet Window should look as shown below.

| ↓ | C1 | C2 | C3 | C4 | C5 | C6-T |
|---|---|---|---|---|---|---|
| | X | Y | RESI1 | Sorted X | Corresp R | Factor |
| 1 | 79 | 37 | 0.10044 | 52 | -1.00793 | Lo |
| 2 | 58 | 41 | 0.90504 | 58 | 0.90504 | Lo |
| 3 | 72 | 39 | 1.03530 | 62 | 0.51369 | Lo |
| 4 | 52 | 40 | -1.00793 | 67 | -0.72551 | Lo |
| 5 | 67 | 38 | -0.72551 | 72 | 1.03530 | Hi |
| 6 | 88 | 36 | 0.46989 | 79 | 0.10044 | Hi |
| 7 | 62 | 40 | 0.51369 | 83 | -1.29092 | Hi |
| 8 | 83 | 35 | -1.29092 | 88 | 0.46989 | Hi |

Finally, assumption (2) is verified by the hypothesis testing of

$H_0$: all subpopulation variances are equal
$H_a$: the subpopulation variances are in a megaphone shape
$\alpha = 0.10$,

and the test statistic is the Levene's test statistic.

Click on *Stat , ANOVA , Test for Equal Variances...*

In the Test for Equal Variances dialog box: the cursor will be in the box to the right of *Response:*. Click on the Corresp R (C5) variable and click on the $\boxed{\text{Select}}$ button. The cursor will move to the large box to the right of *Factors:*, click on the Factor (C6) variable and then click on the $\boxed{\text{Select}}$ button. Then click on the $\boxed{\text{OK}}$ button.

The results of the test will appear in the Graphics Window shown below.

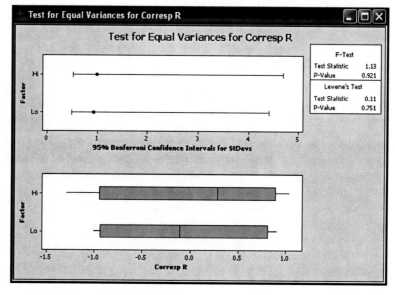

Since the Levene's test p-value of 0.751 is greater than $\alpha = 0.10$, the null hypothesis of equal subpopulation variances (homogeneity) may not be rejected. And since the graph of the residuals versus x in Example 12.7 is not suspicious, thus assumption (2) **is** verified.

Now that the baseline sample data has been checked for outliers and "cleaned", and assumption (1) and assumption (2) have been verified, you may use simple linear regression to analyze the data. The equation of the Estimated Regression Line of Y on X and other statistics are computed using the Minitab *Stat, Regression, Regression* procedure from the menu bar.

Click on *Stat, Regression, Regression ...*

In the Regression dialog box, the cursor should be in the box to the right of the *Response:* heading; click on the "response" variable - Y (C2) and click on the Select button. The cursor will move down to the *Predictors:* box; click on the "predictor" variable - X (C1) and click on the Select button. Then click on the OK button. Next click on the Storage... button. Note that since Minitab remembers the information in the dialog boxes from the previous time, you will only need to click on the Storage... button

In the Regression - Storage dialog box, click in the square to the left of *Residuals* to **uncheck** this option. If you forget to uncheck this box, a new column to the right of the last column (RESI1) in your worksheet will **automatically** be created **and** be named RESI2. This will not effect any of the computations, but an extra column, that is identical to the RESI1 column, will be created in your worksheet. No other options should be checked. Then click on OK .

Back in the Regression dialog box, click on OK .

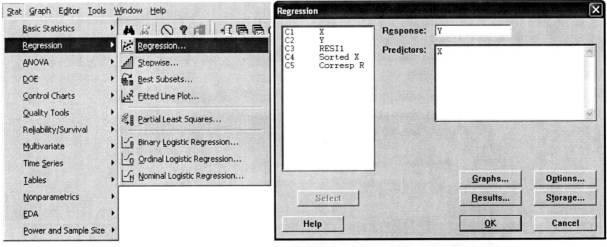

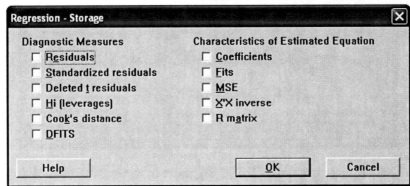

The output of the *Stat , Regression , Regression* procedure contains:

(1) the equation of the Estimated Regression Line of Y on X,

(2) the values of the coefficients $b_0$ and $b_1$ expressed with one or two more decimal places,

(3) the standard deviations of these two estimates,

(4) the values of the Student's t test statistic for testing the hypotheses

(a) $H_0: \beta_0 = 0$     and     (b) $H_0: \beta_1 = 0$
$H_a: \beta_0 \neq 0$             $H_a: \beta_1 \neq 0$ ,

(5) the p-value for these two tests,

(6) the value of $s_{y.x,}$ which is the point estimate of $\sigma$ (the common standard deviation of the Y values in each subpopulation),

(7) the value of the Coefficient of Determination $r^2$ and an adjusted $r^2$

(8) an analysis of variance table which contains several columns of numbers, the value of the F test statistic, and the p-value for hypothesis testing of assumption (1)

$H_0$: the X and Y variables are **not** linearly related

$H_a$: the X and Y variables **are** linearly related

When we say X and Y **are** linearly related in the alternative hypothesis, we are referring to the x-y graph; that is, we have a **first-order** linear model as described by equation (i) and

(9) a table of Unusual Observations (if such observations exist) with the case number, and values of X, Y, the Fit, SE Fit, Residual and St Resid .

Any unusual observations identified by the *Regression* procedure are classified as:

(a) Cases with relative small or relative large X values, identified by an "X" next to the St Resid value. This type of unusual observation is called an **influential point**.

(b) Cases with relative large St Resid values (less than -2 or greater than 2), identified by an "R" next to the St Resid value. This type of unusual observation is called an **residual outlier**.

Once the equation of the Estimated Regression Line of Y on X has been computed, this equation may be used to predict the unknown (future) value of Y when the value of X is known. Using the notation of $x_0$ for the **known** value of the X variable, the numerical value of $\hat{y}$ is found by substituting $x_0$ into equation (ii) and computing

$\hat{y} = b_0 + b_1 x_0$ .

The value of this point predictor ($\hat{y}$) is computed by clicking on the | **Options...** | button in the Regression dialog box. In most situations we combine the computation of the point predictor ($\hat{y}$) with the computation of the Estimated Regression Line of Y on X as follows.

Click on *Stat*, *Regression*, *Regression ...*

In the Regression dialog box, the cursor should be in the box to the right of the
*Response:* heading; click on the "response" variable - Y (C2) and click on the
 Select  button. The cursor will move down to the *Predictors:* box; click
on the "predictor" variable - X (C1) and click on the  Select  button. Then
click on the  OK  button.   Next click on the  Storage...  button. Note
that since Minitab remembers the information in the dialog boxes from the
previous time, you will only need to click on the  Storage...  button

In the Regression - Storage dialog box, click in the square to the left of *Residuals*
to **uncheck** this option. If you forget to uncheck this box, a new column to
the right of the last column (RESI1) in your worksheet will **automatically**
be created **and** be named RESI2.   This will not effect any of the
computations, but an extra column, that is identical to the RESI1 column,
will be created in your worksheet.  No other options should be checked.
Then click on  OK  ..

Back in the Regression dialog box, click on  the  Options...  button.

In the Regression-Options dialog box, click inside of the box below the
*Prediction intervals for new observations:* heading, type in the known value
of X for the new object (value of $x_0$).  For now you may ignore the number
in the box to the right of the *Confidence level:* heading.  Click on the  OK 
button.

Back in the Regression dialog box, click on  the  OK  button.

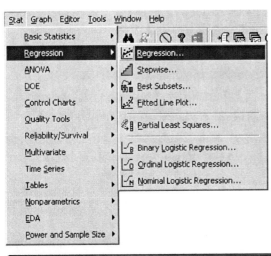

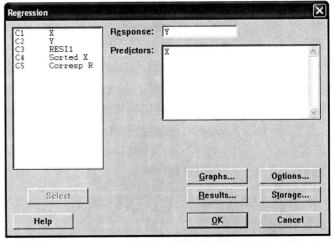

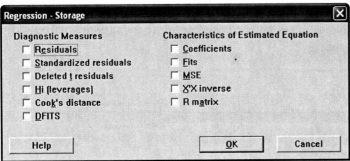

The additional output of the Prediction option contains:

(1) the heading **New Obs** and underneath this the sequential number of the new observation (you may predict Y for several new observations's $x_o$ values),

(2) the heading **Fit** and underneath this heading is the predicted value of the Y variable for the known $x_0$ value entered ($\hat{y} = b_0 + b_1 x_0$),

(3) the default heading **95% CI** and underneath this heading is a 95% confidence interval for the mean of the Y values ($\mu_{y.x}$) in the subpopulation defined by the each known $x_0$ entered,

(4) the default heading **95% PI** and underneath this heading is a 95% prediction interval for the unknown (future) value of Y for the new case(s) with the given $x_0$ value(s),

(5) a table listing the new observation sequential number(s) and the corresponding value(s) of the entered $x_o$ and

(6) a warning if any of the new cases have an X value that is an outlier for this baseline sample.

To predict Y for only **one** new case, you would enter the known value of X for the new object (value of $x_o$) directly in the box below the *Prediction intervals for new observations:* after clicking on the | **Options...** | button.

To predict Y for **more than one** new case you need to do the following:

(1) name a new column as Xo Values,

(2) enter the known values of X for each new case in a separate row of this column, **starting in row 1**, and

(3) in the Regression - Options dialog box of the *Stat, Regression, Regression* procedure; after clicking inside of the box below the *Prediction intervals for new observations:* heading, highlight the Xo Values column and click on the | **Select** | button.

Shown below is an example of what your worksheet would look like if you wanted to predict Y for three new cases where the given X values of these cases were 65, 58 and 71. Also shown below is the Regression - Options dialog box for this situation.

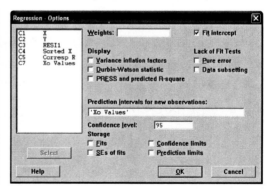

Example 12.9:  As originally stated in Example 12.1, the shop manager wants to predict the task completion time for a worker with 65 months job experience. Use the data in the current worksheet, and compute the desired point prediction.

(continued on the next page)

Click on *Stat* , *Regression* , *Regression ...*

In the Regression dialog box, the cursor should be in the box to the right of the *Response:* heading; click on the "response" variable - Y (C2) and click on the ⬛ Select ⬛ button. The cursor will move down to the *Predictors:* box; click on the "predictor" variable - X (C1) and click on the ⬛ Select ⬛ button. Then click on the ⬛ OK ⬛ button. Next click on the ⬛ Storage... ⬛ button. Note that since Minitab remembers the information in the dialog boxes from the previous time, you will only need to click on the ⬛ Storage... ⬛ button

In the Regression - Storage dialog box, click in the square to the left of *Residuals* to **uncheck** this option. No other options should be checked. Then click on ⬛ OK ⬛ .

Back in the Regression dialog box, click on the ⬛ Options... ⬛ button.

In the Regression-Options dialog box, click inside of the box below the *Prediction intervals for new observations:* heading, type in 65, the known value of X for the new object (value of $x_0$). For now you may ignore the number in the box to the right of the *Confidence level:* heading. Click on the ⬛ OK ⬛ button.

Back in the Regression dialog box, click on the ⬛ OK ⬛ button.

The output shown below will appear in the Session Window.

## Regression Analysis: Y versus X

**The regression equation is**
**Y = 48.9 - 0.152 X**

| Predictor | Coef | SE Coef | T | P |
|---|---|---|---|---|
| Constant | 48.920 | 2.053 | 23.83 | 0.000 |
| X | -0.15216 | 0.02887 | -5.27 | 0.002 |

S = 0.965614   R-Sq = 82.2%   R-Sq(adj) = 79.3%

**Analysis of Variance**

| Source | DF | SS | MS | F | P |
|---|---|---|---|---|---|
| Regression | 1 | 25.906 | 25.906 | 27.78 | 0.002 |
| Residual Error | 6 | 5.594 | 0.932 | | |
| Total | 7 | 31.500 | | | |

**Predicted Values for New Observations**

| New Obs | Fit | SE Fit | 95% CI | 95% PI |
|---|---|---|---|---|
| 1 | 39.030 | 0.372 | ( 38.119, 39.940) | ( 36.498, 41.562) |

**Values of Predictors for New Observations**

| New Obs | X |
|---|---|
| 1 | 65.0 |

(continued on the next page)

The first line of the output gives the equation of the Estimated Regression Line of Y on X as

$$\hat{y} = 48.9 - 0.152\ x.$$

Notice that Minitab omits the hat (^) from above the y in the actual output.

In the next part of the output, the values of $b_0$ and $b_1$ are displayed under the **Coef** column with more decimal places than in the equation above. The rest of this section of the output will be discussed in the next chapter. The next line of the output is the value of $s_{y.x}$, which is the point estimate of $\sigma$ (the common standard deviation of the Y values in each subpopulation), the value of the Coefficient of Determination $r^2$ and an adjusted $r^2$; and these will be discussed later in the next section of this chapter. The **Analysis of Variance** table is used to test the validity of assumption (1) that the two variables are linearly related, and has previously been discussed.

When $x_0 = 65$, the value entered for the predictor (job experience) in the Regression Options dialog box, the predicted value of y (task completion time) is $\hat{y} = 39.030$, which is displayed under the **Fit** heading near the end of the output.

The predicted task completion time for a worker with 65 months of experience could have been done using the Estimated Regression Equation given at the top of the output and a calculator. Substitute 65, the known value of the "predictor" (X) variable into the equation for the Estimated Regression Line and compute the predicted job completion time as

$$\hat{y} = 48.9 - 0.152(65)$$
$$\hat{y} = 39.02$$

However, Minitab computes this value using the values of $b_0$ and $b_1$ with more decimal places, and displays a somewhat more accurate result of 39.030 for $\hat{y}$ under the heading **Fit** in the output.

Once assumptions (1) and (2) have been verified, point estimates ($\hat{y}$) are legitimate; however prediction intervals may not be reported until the assumption (3) that each subpopulation of Y values is normally distributed has been verified. This assumption (3) can be verified using a Q-Q plot and the Anderson-Darling test which were introduced in Chapter 9.

Assumption (3), that each subpopulation of Y values is normally distributed, may be verified by graphing a **Q-Q plot**. This graph uses the residual values (computed by the storage option in the regression procedure) on the horizontal axis and the standard normalized values of these residuals on the y axis. After the residuals are sorted into increasing order; for each individual residual, the percentage of all of the residuals that are less than this residual is computed. This percentage is sometimes called the quantile. The standard normalized scores are values of Z that have the same quantile as the corresponding residual. This is why the graph is called a **Q-Q plot**. If each residual quantile is equal (or almost equal) to each corresponding standard normal quantile, the graph will be approximately a straight line. The Q-Q plot is graphed as follows.

Click on *Stat*, *Basic Statistics*, *Normality Test...*

In the Normality Test dialog box: the cursor will be in the box to the right of *Variable:* click on the RESI1 variable (the automatically named column that contains the residual values) and click on the [ Select ] button. Under the heading of *Percentile lines*, the button to the left of *None* should be chosen. Make sure that under the *Tests for Normality* that the *Anderson-Darling* choice is marked. Next click inside of the *Title:* box and type Q-Q Plot, but remember do **not** press the [ Enter ] key. Then click on the [ OK ] button.

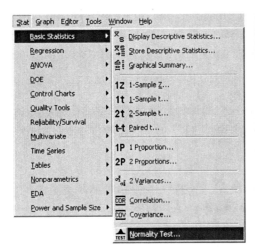
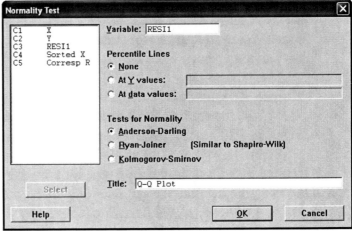

The resulting graph will appear in a separate Graphics Window. In addition to the actual Q-Q plot the results of the Anderson-Darling test for normality will be given. This test essentially is

$H_0$: the subpopulations of Y scores are all normally distributed
$H_a$: the subpopulations of Y scores are **not** all normally distributed
$\alpha = 0.10$ .

The AD test statistic and corresponding p-value are given in this Graphics Window. If the p-value is greater than 0.10, we usually do **not** reject the null hypothesis. And since we have no reason to doubt the validity of assumption (3), a prediction interval for the (future) actual value of Y corresponding to the given value of X may be used. However; if this p-value is less than or equal to 0.05, the null hypothesis **is** rejected, and assumption (3) is **not** validated. And so prediction intervals for the (future) actual values of Y **may not** be accurate and **should not** be reported.

Example 12.10:   Use the data in the current worksheet and check the validity of assumption (3) that the subpopulations of task completion times are all normally distributed by graphing the Q-Q plot and testing for normality.

(continued on the next page)

Click on *Stat , Basic Statistics , Normality Test...*

In the Normality Test dialog box: the cursor will be in the box to the right of *Variable:* click on the RESI1 variable (the automatically named column that contains the residual values) and click on the [Select] button. Under the heading of *Percentile lines*, the button to the left of *None* should be chosen. Make sure that under the *Tests for Normality* that the *Anderson-Darling* choice is marked. Next click inside of the *Title:* box and type Q-Q Plot, but remember do **not** press the [Enter] key. Then click on [OK] .

You will likely need to "maximize" the Graphics Window in order to clearly read the AD test statistic and p-value. The resulting Q-Q plot that appears in the Graphics Window is shown below.

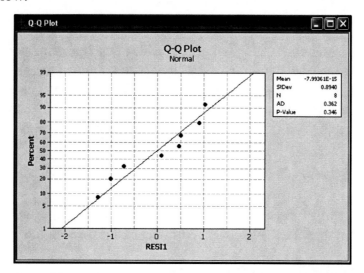

Since the p-value of 0.346 is greater than $\alpha = 0.10$, you may not reject the null hypothesis of normality; and so you may conclude that assumption (3) **is valid**. Also notice that the points in the graph are close to the superimposed straight line that Minitab draws for comparison.

Once assumption (3) that the subpopulations of Y scores are all normally distributed has been verified, prediction intervals for the unknown Y value corresponding to a given X value may be computed. While Minitab sets the default confidence level at 95%, for any specific problem the desired confidence level for the prediction interval is entered in box to the right of *Confidence level:* in the Regression-Options dialog box.

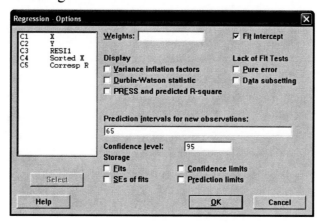

Example 12.11: Since assumption (3) of normality has been verified, use the data in the current worksheet and compute a 98% prediction interval for the task completion time of a worker with 65 months job experience.

Click on *Stat*, *Regression*, *Regression* ...

In the Regression dialog box, the cursor should be in the box to the right of the *Response:* heading; click on the "response" variable - Y (C2) and click on the | **Select** | button. The cursor will move down to the *Predictors:* box; click on the "predictor" variable - X (C1) and click on the | **Select** | button. Then click on the | **OK** | button. Next click on the | **Storage...** | button. Note that since Minitab remembers the information in the dialog boxes from the previous time, you will only need to click on | **Options...** | .

In the Regression-Options dialog box, click inside of the box below the *Prediction intervals for new observations:* heading, type in 65, the known value of X for the new object (value of $x_0$). (The 65 should be in this box from the previous example.) Now click inside of the box to the right of *Confidence level:*, erase the 95 that is currently in this box and type in 98, the desired confidence level for this example. Click on the | **OK** | button.

Back in the Regression dialog box, click on the | **OK** | button.

Since the first part of the output in the Session Window is the same as for the previous Example 12.9, only the last few lines pertaining to the prediction of Y are shown below.

**Predicted Values for New Observations**

| New Obs | Fit | SE Fit | 98% CI | 98% PI |
|---------|-----|--------|--------|--------|
| 1 | 39.030 | 0.372 | ( 37.861,  40.199 ) | ( 35.778,  42.282 ) |

**Values of Predictors for New Observations**

| New Obs | X |
|---------|-----|
| 1 | 65.0 |

The 39.030 under the *Fit* heading is the point predictor of the task completion time as illustrated in Example 12.9. Now that assumption (3) of normality has been verified, the 98% prediction interval under the **98% P.I.** heading may be reported. And so the shop manager is 98% certain that for a worker with 65 months job experience, that the interval from 35.78 to 42.28 minutes will contain that worker's task completion time.

The next example will combine all of the previous concepts and procedures into one unified example.

Example 12.12: Open another worksheet using Nrthelec.mtw from your data disc. The data represent a random baseline sample days in the area served by the Northen Electric Company. The maximum temperature and the amount of electricity used were measured on each of these days in the sample. The Northern Electric Company manager wants to predict, with 90% certainty, the electricity demand for days when the maximum temperature is 65 degrees and for days when the maximum temperature is 85 degrees.

Use the *File , Open Worksheet...* to open Nrthelec.mtw from your data disk into a second worksheet.

Next rename the Temp. (C1) variable as X and the Electric (C2) variable as Y. Then plot the x-y graph of the data; label the x-axis with Maximum Temperature for the Day and label the y-axis with Amount of Electricity Used.

Click on *Graph , Scatterplot...* then in the Scatterplots dialog box: the *Simple* graph should be highlighted. Next click on the ☐ **OK** ☐ button.

In the Scatterplot - Simple dialog box: press the ☐ **F3** ☐ key to clear the previous information. The cursor will be in the box on the first line under the *Y variables* heading; click on the Y variable and click on the ☐ **Select** ☐ button. The cursor will move to the box in the first line under the *X variables* heading; click on the X variable and click on the ☐ **Select** ☐ button. Then click on the ☐ **OK** ☐ button

Double click on the x axis label and rename it Maximum Temperature for the Day. Then double click on the y axis label and rename it Amount of Electricity Used.

The resulting x-y plot shown below will appear in a separate Graphics Window.

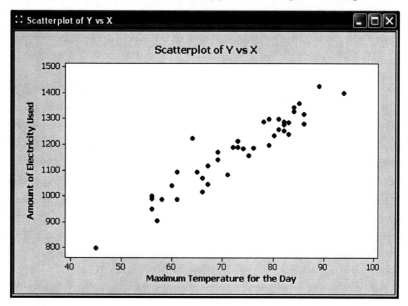

(continued on the next page)

This scatterplot indicates that the electricity demand is linearly related to the maximum daily temperature, and so linear regression analysis seems appropriate. Minimize this Graphics Window, and then use the *Stat , Regression , Regression...* procedure to check for any possible outliers.

Click on *Stat , Regression , Regression ...*

In the Regression dialog box, since this is a **new** problem, press the ☐ F3 ☐ key to clear any previous information from all Regression dialog boxes. The cursor should be in the box to the right of the *Response:* heading; click on the "response" variable - Y (C2) and click on the ☐ Select ☐ button. The cursor will move down to the *Predictors:* box; click on the "predictor" variable - X (C1) and click on the ☐ Select ☐ button. Then click on the ☐ OK ☐ button.

Only the end of the output in the Session Window is shown below.

### Unusual Observations

| Obs. | X | Y | Fit | SE Fit | Residual | St Resid | |
|------|------|--------|---------|--------|----------|----------|---|
| 11 | 45.0 | 797.60 | 834.71 | 19.52 | -37.11 | -0.88 | X |
| 20 | 64.0 | 1225.60 | 1065.74 | 9.20 | 159.86 | 3.49 | R |

**R denotes an observation with a large standardized residual.**
**X denotes an observation whose X value gives it large influence.**

The two cases 11 and 20 are identified as **Unusual Observations**. The maximum daily temperature recorded for observation 11 is determined to be in error; but the day of that reading is not available, and so the Northern Electric Company manager decides to delete this case from the baseline sample. Observation 20 is examined, and the manager discovers that the maximum daily temperature was 83 degrees that day, and not the 64 degrees recorded.

> **It is very important to make any corrections <u>before</u> deleting any observations. If you delete any observations <u>first</u>, then the positions of all of the observations after the deleted case become one less; and you could easily correct the <u>wrong</u> case. In this example, if you deleted observation 11 first, and <u>then</u> corrected observation 20, you would have mistakenly actually changed the original observation number 21. Also, if you are going to delete more than one observation; delete the largest observation number first, then delete the next largest, and continue until you have deleted the smallest number observation you want to delete.**

Directly in the Worksheet Window, correct the maximum daily temperature (X) to 83 for observation (row) 20 and delete the entire observation (row) 11. Then repeat the *Regression* procedure to check for any new outliers that may have arisen due to these changes.

(continued on the next page)

Click on *Stat*, *Regression*, *Regression ...*

In the Regression dialog box, the Y variable should be in the box to the right of the *Response:* heading and the X variable should be in the *Predictors:*. So just click on the OK button.

And now the output in the Session Window ends with the analysis of variance table shown below, but no additional outliers are identified.

### Analysis of Variance

| Source | DF | SS | MS | F | P |
|---|---|---|---|---|---|
| Regression | 1 | 631829 | 631829 | 382.83 | 0.000 |
| Residual Error | 39 | 64366 | 1650 | | |
| Total | 40 | 696195 | | | |

The next step is to check the validity of assumption (1) that X and Y are linearly related.

The hypothesis testing problem is:

$H_0$: Maximum Daily Temperature and Electricity Used are **not** linearly related
$H_a$: Maximum Daily Temperature and Electricity Used **are** linearly related
$\alpha = 0.05$,

and the test statistic is $F = \dfrac{MS \ for \ Regression}{MS \ for \ Residual \ Error}$.

At the bottom of the Session window as shown above, the p-value in the **Analysis of Variance** table is 0.000 which is less than the value of $\alpha = 0.05$, and so the Northern Electric Company manager may reject the null hypothesis. And so he concludes that maximum daily temperature and electric usage **are** linearly related, and thus assumption (1) is valid.

The next step is to verify the assumption (2) that the variances of Y in all of the subpopulations are equal. Compute the residuals and then plot the residual versus x graph to see if assumption (2) appears to be valid; and, if not, to see what the violating pattern looks like.

Click on *Stat*, *Regression*, *Regression ...*

In the Regression dialog box, the Y variable should be in the box to the right of the *Response:* heading and the X variable should be in the *Predictors:*. Next click on the Storage... button.

In the Regression - Storage dialog box, click in the square to the left of *Residuals* to check this option. No other options should be checked. Then click on OK. A new column automatically will be created and named RESI1. The column number will be one higher than the last column used in the current Worksheet Window; i.e., C3.

Back in the Regression dialog box, click on OK.

(continued on the next page)

The first five rows of the resulting Worksheet Window are shown below.

| ↓ | C1 | C2 | C3 |
|---|---|---|---|
| | X | Y | RESI1 |
| 1 | 56 | 1001.20 | 36.8750 |
| 2 | 79 | 1299.60 | 56.3576 |
| 3 | 84 | 1344.60 | 40.7234 |
| 4 | 85 | 1361.60 | 45.5966 |
| 5 | 89 | 1427.60 | 63.0892 |

Nrthelec.mtw ***

Click on *Graph , Scatterlot ...*

In the Scatterplots dialog box: the *Simple* graph should be highlighted. Next click on the [ **OK** ] button.

In the Scatterplot - Simple dialog box: the cursor will be in the box on the first line under the *Y variables* heading; click on the RESI1 variable and click on the [ **Select** ] button. The cursor will move to the box in the first line under the *X variables* heading; click on the desired X variable and click on the [ **Select** ] button. Then click on the [ **OK** ] button.

It is desirable to label the X axis as Maximum Temperature for the Day, the name of the predictor variable and to label the Y axis as Residuals.

The graph shown below will appear in a separate Graphics Window.

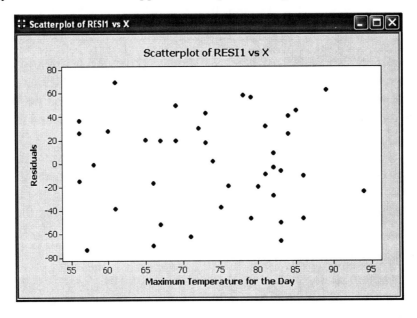

The points on the graph look to be randomly and evenly spread and within a general rectangular shape; and assumption (2) is probably valid. But the modified Levene's test is done next to numerically confirm that assumption (2) is valid. Minimize this Graphics Window.

Name the three new columns (C4, C5 and C6) as Sorted X, Corresp R and Factor, and then sort the X and RESI1 scores into the Sorted X and Corresp R columns.

(continued on the next page)

Click on *Data , Sort...*

In the Sort dialog box, press the [F3] key to clear any previous contents. The cursor will be in the box under the *Sort Column(s):* heading. Hold the [Ctrl] key and click on the X and RESI1 variables to highlight them both. Then click on [Select] . Next click inside the box to the right of the first *By column:* heading, click on the X variable, and click on [Select] . Next click on the circle to the left of *Column(s) of current worksheet:*, and then click inside of the box under this heading. inside of the box under the *Store sorted column(s) in:* heading, hold the [Ctrl] key and click on the Sorted X and Corresp R variables to highlight them both. Then click on [Select] . Now click on [OK] .

The first five rows of the resulting Worksheet Window are shown below.

| Nrthelec.mtw *** | C1 | C2 | C3 | C4 | C5 | C6 |
|---|---|---|---|---|---|---|
| ↓ | X | Y | RESI1 | Sorted X | Corresp R | Factor |
| 1 | 56 | 1001.20 | 36.8750 | 56 | 36.8750 | |
| 2 | 79 | 1299.60 | 56.3576 | 56 | 26.2750 | |
| 3 | 84 | 1344.60 | 40.7234 | 56 | -14.7250 | |
| 4 | 85 | 1361.60 | 45.5966 | 57 | -73.7519 | |
| 5 | 89 | 1427.60 | 63.0892 | 58 | -0.9786 | |

Next the minimum, the middle two scores and the maximum need to be determined. The *Stat , Basic Statistics , Describe Statistics* menu procedure will find the minimum, the maximum and the number of scores for the Sorted X variable.

Click on *Stat , Basic Statistics , Describe Statistics*

In the Display Descriptive Statistics dialog box: highlight the Sorted X variable, click on the [Select] button, and then click on the [Statistics...] button.

In the Descriptive Statistics - Statistics dialog box: click to uncheck all boxes **except** for the *Minimum* , *Maximum* and *N nonmissing* statistics.

The results shown below will appear in the Session Window.

### *Descriptive Statistics: Sorted X*

| *Variable* | *N* | *Minimum* | *Maximum* |
|---|---|---|---|
| *Sorted X* | *41* | *56.00* | *94.00* |

There are 41 non-missing ( *N* ) scores, and so that the number of objects is n = 41 Since n is odd, the two middle rows are the $(n - 1)/2 = 20^{th}$ and $(n + 1)/2 = 21^{st}$ rows. Look in the Worksheet Window and see that the scores in the Sorted X variable that are in these two rows, 74 and 75, and they are one unit apart. Notice that rows 22 and 23 are very close to the middle, and they contain the values of 76 and 78 which are two units apart. these two score give a bigger split between the Lo and Hi groups, and so let $m_1 = 76$ and $m_2 = 78$. The output in the Session Window shows the values of the minimum and maximum, and so min = 56 and max = 94

(continued on the next page)

503

Next put Lo in the first half of the Factor column and put Hi in the second half.

Click on *Data , Code , Numeric to Text ...*

In the Code - Numeric to Text dialog box, press the [ **F3** ] key to clear any previous contents. The cursor should be in the box under the heading *Code data from columns:*. Click on the Sorted X variable and click on [ **Select** ]. Next click in the *Into columns:* box, click on the Factor variable, and click on [ **Select** ]. Then click in the first box under the *Original values* heading and type in 56 : 76 (min : $m_1$). Next click in the first box under the *New:* heading and type in the word Lo. Similarly click on the second row in the box under the *Original values* heading and type in 78 : 94 ($m_2$ : max). Next click in the box under the *New:* heading and type in the word Hi. Then click on [ **OK** ].

This Factor (C6) column should now have Lo in the first 22 rows and Hi in the rows 23 through 41. Rows 20 through 24 of the Worksheet Window are shown in the graphic below.

| | C1 | C2 | C3 | C4 | C5 | C6-T |
|---|---|---|---|---|---|---|
| | X | Y | RESI1 | Sorted X | Corresp R | Factor |
| 18 | 84 | 1329.60 | 25.7234 | 73 | 43.1187 | Lo |
| 19 | 83 | 1225.60 | -66.1497 | 73 | 18.1187 | Lo |
| 20 | 61 | 986.50 | -38.4593 | 74 | 1.9919 | Lo |
| 21 | 86 | 1281.60 | -46.5303 | 75 | -37.1350 | Lo |
| 22 | 94 | 1401.60 | -23.5450 | 76 | -19.2618 | Lo |
| 23 | 82 | 1276.60 | -3.0229 | 78 | 58.4845 | Hi |
| 24 | 57 | 902.70 | -73.7519 | 79 | 56.3576 | Hi |
| 25 | 82 | 1252.60 | -27.0229 | 79 | -46.6424 | Hi |
| 26 | 80 | 1235.60 | -19.7692 | 80 | -19.7692 | Hi |
| 27 | 81 | 1299.60 | 32.1040 | 81 | 32.1040 | Hi |

Nrthelec.mtw ***

Finally, assumption (2) is verified by the hypothesis testing as:

$H_0$: all subpopulation variances are equal
$H_a$: the subpopulation variances are in a megaphone shape
$\alpha = 0.10$,

and the test statistic is the Levene's test statistic.

Click on *Stat , ANOVA , Test for Equal Variances...*

In the Test for Equal Variances dialog box, press the [ **F3** ] key to clear any previous contents. The cursor will be in the box to the right of *Response:*. Click on the Corresp R (C5) variable and click on the [ **Select** ] button. The cursor will move to the large box to the right of *Factors:*, click on the Factor (C6) variable and then click on the [ **Select** ] button. Then click on the [ **OK** ] button.

The results of the test will appear in a separate Graphics Window shown as on the next page.

(continued on the next page)

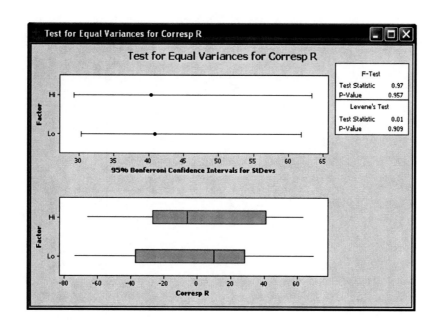

Since the Levene's test p-value of 0.909 is greater than $\alpha = 0.10$, the null hypothesis of equal subpopulation variances (homogeneity) may not be rejected. And since the graph of the residuals versus x shown at the bottom of page 386 is not suspicious, thus assumption (2) **is** verified. Now minimize this Graphics Window.

Now that assumptions (1) and (2) have been verified, a point estimate for the electricity demand on days when the maximum temperatures are 65 and 85 degrees may be computed. However, since the company manager wanted a 90% confidence interval, assumption (3) that the subpopulations of Y scores are all normally distributed needs to be checked.

The hypotheses are:

$H_0$: the subpopulations of Y scores are all normally distributed
$H_a$: the subpopulations of Y scores are **not** all normally distributed
$\alpha = 0.10$ ,

and the test statistic is AD.

Click on *Stat , Basic Statistics , Normality Test...*

In the Normality Test dialog box, press the F3 key to clear any previous contents. The cursor will be in the box to the right of *Variable:* click on the RESI1 variable (the automatically named column that contains the residual values) and click on the Select button. Under the heading of *Percentile lines*, the button to the left of *None* should be chosen. Make sure that under the *Tests for Normality* that the *Anderson-Darling* choice is marked. Next click inside of the *Title:* box and type Q-Q Plot, but remember do **not** press the Enter key. Then click on OK .

You will likely need to "maximize" the Graphics Window in order to clearly read the AD test statistic and p-value. The resulting Q-Q plot that appears in the Graphics Window is shown on the next page.

(continued on the next page)

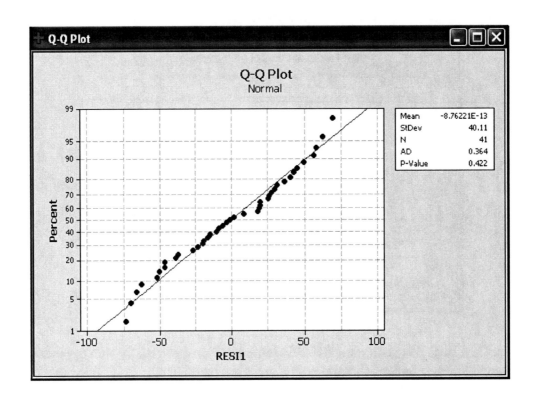

Since the p-value of 0.422 is greater than $\alpha = 0.10$, you may not reject the null hypothesis of normality. And so you may conclude that assumption (3) **is valid**, and prediction intervals using this baseline sample may be reported. Also notice that the points in the graph are close to the superimposed straight line that Minitab draws for comparison. Minimize this Graphics Window.

Since the manager wants to predict the electricity demand for **two** new cases, the next step is to name a new column as Xo Values and enter the two given X values of 65 and 85 in rows **1** and **2** of this column. The first eight rows of the Worksheet Window should now look as shown below.

**Nrthelec.mtw ***

| ↓ | C1 | C2 | C3 | C4 | C5 | C6-T | C7 |
|---|----|----|------|--------|---------|--------|----------|
|   | X | Y | RESI1 | Sorted X | Corresp R | Factor | Xo Values |
| 1 | 56 | 1001.20 | 36.8750 | 56 | 36.8750 | Lo | 65 |
| 2 | 79 | 1299.60 | 56.3576 | 56 | 26.2750 | Lo | 85 |
| 3 | 84 | 1344.60 | 40.7234 | 56 | -14.7250 | Lo | |
| 4 | 85 | 1361.60 | 45.5966 | 57 | -73.7519 | Lo | |
| 5 | 89 | 1427.60 | 63.0892 | 58 | -0.9786 | Lo | |
| 6 | 65 | 1093.60 | 20.1334 | 60 | 27.7677 | Lo | |
| 7 | 66 | 1068.70 | -16.8935 | 61 | 69.6408 | Lo | |
| 8 | 74 | 1184.60 | 1.9919 | 61 | -38.4593 | Lo | |

(continued on the next page)

The final step is to use the *Regression* procedure and the Regression - Options dialog box to compute the desired 90% prediction intervals.

Click on *Stat* , *Regression* , *Regression* ...

In the Regression dialog box, the cursor should be in the box to the right of the *Response:* heading; click on the "response" variable - Y (C2) and click on the **Select** button. The cursor will move down to the *Predictors:* box; click on the "predictor" variable - X (C1) and click on the **Select** button. Then click on the **OK** button. Next click on the **Storage...** button. Note that since Minitab remembers the information in the dialog boxes from the previous time, you will only need to click on the **Storage...** button

In the Regression - Storage dialog box, click in the square to the left of *Residuals* to **uncheck** this option. No other options should be checked. Then click on **OK** .

Back in the Regression dialog box, click on the **Options...** button.

In the Regression-Options dialog box, click inside of the box below the *Prediction intervals for new observations:* heading, highlight the Xo Values (C7) variable, and click on the **Storage...** button. Now click inside of the box to the right of *Confidence level:*, erase the current value in this box, and type in 90, the desired confidence level for this example. Click on the **OK** button.

Back in the Regression dialog box, click on the **OK** button.

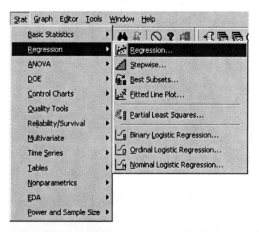

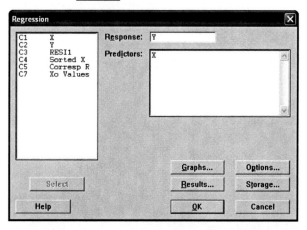

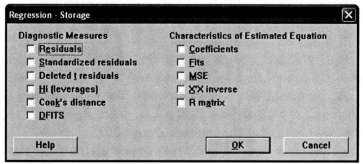

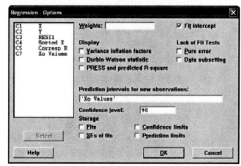

(continued on the next page)

507

The output shown below will appear in the Session Window.

## Regression Analysis: Y versus X

**The regression equation is**
**Y = 285 + 12.1 X**

| Predictor | Coef | SE Coef | T | P |
|---|---|---|---|---|
| Constant | 285.22 | 46.23 | 6.17 | 0.000 |
| X | 12.1268 | 0.6198 | 19.57 | 0.000 |

S = 40.6253      R-Sq = 90.8%      R-Sq(adj) = 90.5%

**Analysis of Variance**

| Source | DF | SS | MS | F | P |
|---|---|---|---|---|---|
| Regression | 1 | 631829 | 631829 | 382.83 | 0.000 |
| Residual Error | 39 | 64366 | 1650 | | |
| Total | 40 | 696195 | | | |

**Predicted Values for New Observations**

| New Obs | Fit | SE Fit | 90% CI | 90% PI |
|---|---|---|---|---|
| 1 | 1073.47 | 8.40 | (1059.32, 1087.62) | (1003.57, 1143.36) |
| 2 | 1316.00 | 9.37 | (1300.22, 1331.79) | (1245.76, 1386.25) |

**Values of Predictors for New Observations**

| New Obs | X |
|---|---|
| 1 | 65.0 |
| 2 | 85.0 |

The values of 1073.47 and 1316.00 underneath the **Fit** heading are the predicted value of the amount of electricity used ($\hat{y}$) for days when the maximum temperatures are 65 and 85 degrees respectively (these are the given values for the new cases 1 and 2 as listed in the last line of the output).

And so the Northern Electric Company manager reports that for days when the maximum temperatures are 65 and 85 degrees, the predicted demand for electricity will be 1073.47 and 1316.00 megawatts respectively. And since assumption (3) is valid, the 90% prediction interval may be reported. The manager reports that: (1) for a day when the maximum temperature is 65 degrees, he is 90% certain that the interval from 1003.57 to 1143.36 megawatts will contain the amount of electricity used, and (2) for a day when the maximum temperature is 85 degrees, he is 90% certain that the interval from 1245.76 to 1386.25 megawatts will contain the amount of electricity used.

Although not illustrated in the examples in this chapter, **it is important to note that** often the values displayed in the Worksheet Window are rounded off from their exact values. Because of this rounding, the min, $m_1$, $m_2$, and max values entered in the *Code: Numeric to Text* dialog box must be slightly changed. The range of these values must be slightly exaggerated on both the smaller and larger ends of the [min to $m_1$] and the [$m_2$ to max] intervals in order to accommodate the rounding of the Sorted Fit values. One might do as follows. At the two intervals' smaller (left) endpoints, subtract one from the **right most decimal place shown**. And at the two intervals' larger (right) endpoints, add one to **the right most decimal place shown**. If the minimum and first middle values shown were 3.16 and 8.34, then the min would become 3.15 and $m_1$ would become 8.35. And if the second middle and maximum values shown were 9.68 and 12.34, then the $m_2$ would become 9.67, and max would become 12.35. However in many cases, you may choose exaggerated values simply by picking values that are somewhat outside of the intervals. For [3.16 to 8.34] one could simply choose to use [3 to 8.5], and for [9.68 to 12.34] one could choose [9.5 to 13]. Just be careful that the value used for $m_1$ is less than the value used for $m_2$.

Example 12.13: Save the current Minitab project on your data disk with the file name Neupdate and then exit from Minitab.

Click on *File , Save Project As...*

In the Save Project As dialog box: delete the highlighted MINITAB.MPJ that is in the File name box, type in the specific filename Neupdate (this will replace the default MINITAB.MPJ), click on the *Save in:* drop down icon and select *Data Disc* (if it is not already selected); and click on ⌷ **Save** ⌷.

Minitab will display a message in the Session Window similar to that shown below.

```
MTB > Save "A:\Neupdate.MPJ";
SUBC>     Project;
SUBC>     Replace.
Saving file as: A:\Neupdate.MPJ
MTB >
```

Then use the *File , Exit* menu item to end this Minitab session.

**Section 2:     Simple Linear Correlation Analysis**

There are occasions when the value of the coefficient of correlation is desired, but a regression analysis is not needed.   The Minitab procedure *Stat , Basic Statistics , Correlation...* computes the Pearson Product Moment Coefficient of Correlation between two variables, or the correlation matrix among a set of three or more variables.   The correlation between two variables is computed by

Click on *Stat , Basic Statistics , Correlation ...*

In the Correlation dialog box, you may need to press the [ **F3** ] key to clear any previous information.  Hold the [ **Ctrl** ] key and click on the two variables. Now click on the [ **Select** ] button and then click on [ **OK** ] .

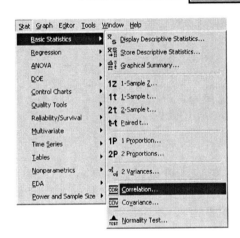 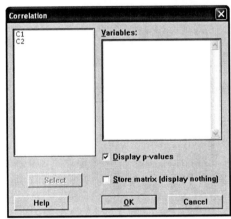

To compute the correlation matrix among three or more variables, you only need to select the desired set of variables in the Correlation dialog box.

Click on *Stat , Basic Statistics , Correlation ...*

In the Correlation dialog box, you may need to press the [ **F3** ] key to clear any previous information.  Hold the [ **Ctrl** ] key and click on each of the desired variables, and click on the [ **Select** ] button.  Next you will usually want to click on the square to the left of *Display p values* to **un**check this option. Then click on [ **OK** ] .

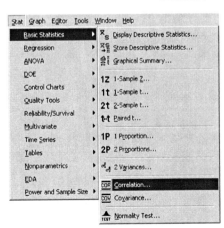 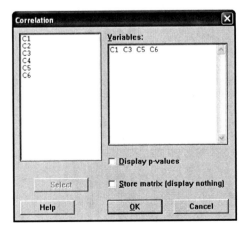

The output of the *Correlation* procedure between two variables contains:

(1) the sample Pearson coefficient of correlation between the two selected variables and
(2) the p-value for testing the hypothesis

$$H_0: \rho = 0$$
$$H_a: \rho \neq 0 .$$

The output of the *Correlation* procedure between more than two variables contains the sample Pearson coefficients of correlation between the selected variables in a truncated matrix form. If the square to the left of *Display p values* **is** checked, the p-value for testing the above hypothesis for each pair of variables is also displayed below the sample coefficients of correlation.

Example 12.14:  Open the Minitab project Neupdate.MPJ that is saved on your data disk. Compute the coefficient of correlation between the X and Y variables.

Use the *File , Open Project...* to retrieve the Neupdate.MPJ saved project from your data disk. Then use the *Correlation* procedure to compute the coefficient of correlation between the maximum daily temperature (X) and the electricity demand (Y) variables.

Click on *Stat , Basic Statistics , Correlation ...*

In the Correlation dialog box, you may need to press the | **F3** | key to clear any previous information. Hold the | **Ctrl** | key and click on X (C1) and Y (C2) variables. Now click on the | **Select** | button and then click on | **OK** | .

The correlation result shown below will appear in the Session Window.

## *Correlations: X, Y*

### *Pearson correlation of X and Y = 0.953*
### *P-Value = 0.000*

The common symbol for the coefficient of correlation is the letter r, and so in this example; $r = 0.953$. The *Regression* output has a line immediately above the **Analysis of Variance** table that contains three computations, one of which is **R-Sq**. This is simply the value of $r^2$ expressed as a percent instead of a decimal percentage. From the output of the *Regression* in Example 12.12 shown on page 392, $r^2 = 90.8\%$ (or $r^2 = 0.908$ in decimal format). If you compute the square root of 0.908, you will get the absolute value of r. In this example $|r| = \sqrt{0.908} = 0.953$ . Then the sign (+ or -) of r is determined by the sign of $b_1$, the slope of the regression line, which is positive in this example. So the coefficient of correlation in this example could have been computed from the *Regression* procedure as $r = 0.953$; however, the *Correlation* procedure is easier and more direct.

The Neupdate.MPJ project will not be used again with this workbook, and so you may delete this file from your data disk at any time.

Example 12.15: Open another worksheet using Study4.mtw from your data disc and compute the truncated correlation matrix among the Age, G.P.A., Study Hours and Work Hours variables.

Use the *File , Open Worksheet...* to open the saved worksheet Study4.mtw from your data disk. Then use the *Correlation* procedure to compute the coefficients of correlation among the Age, G.P.A., Study Hours and Work Hours variables.

Click on *Stat , Basic Statistics , Correlation ...*

In the Correlation dialog box, press the  F3  key to clear any previous information. Hold the  Ctrl  key and click on each of the Age (C1), G.P.A. (C2), Work Hrs (C3) and StudyHrs (C4) variables, and click on the  Select  button. Next click on the square to the left of *Display p values* to **un**check this option. Then click on  OK .

The resulting correlation matrix shown below will appear in the Session Window.

## Correlations: Age, G.P.A., Work Hrs, StudyHrs

|          | Age   | G.P.A. | Work Hrs |
|----------|-------|--------|----------|
| G.P.A.   | 0.028 |        |          |
| Work Hrs | 0.487 | -0.305 |          |
| StudyHrs | 0.103 | 0.440  | -0.297   |

The numbers in this matrix are interpreted as follows:

| | | | | |
|---|---|---|---|---|
| correlation between | G.P.A. | and | Age | = 0.028 |
| correlation between | Work Hrs | and | Age | = 0.487 |
| correlation between | Work Hrs | and | G.P.A. | = -0.305 |
| correlation between | StudyHrs | and | Age | = 0.103 |
| correlation between | StudyHrs | and | G.P.A. | = 0.440 |
| correlation between | StudyHrs | and | Work Hrs | = -0.297 |

There are many reports which contain the statement "the correlation was found to be significant at the 0.05 level of significance" or some very similar statement. This statement is equivalent to the following hypothesis test and <u>rejecting</u> the null hypothesis.

$$H_0: \rho = 0$$
$$H_a: \rho \neq 0$$

This test is done using the p-value in the output of the *Correlation* procedure when the square to the left of *Display p values* **is** checked. This test is for the population coefficient of correlation between a pair of variables.

Example 12.16: Use the data in the current worksheet, and test the hypothesis that the population coefficient of correlation between the student's grade point average and the number of hours worked per week is "significant"; i.e., that $\rho \neq 0$. Use a 0.025 level of significance.

The hypothesis testing problem is:

$H_0$: $\rho = 0$
$H_a$: $\rho \neq 0$
$\alpha = 0.025$ .

Click on *Stat , Basic Statistics , Correlation ...*

In the Correlation dialog box, press the $\boxed{\text{F3}}$ key to clear any previous information. Hold the $\boxed{\text{Ctrl}}$ key and click on the G.P.A. (C2) and Work Hrs (C3) variables, and click on the $\boxed{\text{Select}}$ button. If you pressed the $\boxed{\text{F3}}$ key, the square to the left of *Display p values* should now be checked. Then click on $\boxed{\text{OK}}$ .

The resulting output shown below will appear in the Session Window.

## *Correlations: G.P.A., Work Hrs*

### *Correlation of G.P.A. and Work Hrs = -0.305*
### *P-Value = 0.114*

Since the p-value of 0.114 is greater than the given value of $\alpha = 0.025$; you may not reject the null hypothesis, and thus the population coefficient of correlation between number of hours worked and grade point average is not found to be "significant." That is, the population coefficient of correlation has not been found to significantly differ from zero.

The next chapter describes the situation where there are two or more variables being used to predict the value of a Y variable. While the computations are much more involved, the concepts and procedures are very similar to those presented in this chapter.

**Section 3:     Cautions**


While simple linear regression and correlation is a very powerful analysis tool, one must exercise care and caution in using this tool. Listed below are some of the common cautions associated with simple linear regression and correlation.

1.     In general one should not use simple linear regression to predict the Y variable when the given value of X is **not** between the minimum and maximum of the baseline sample X values. This is because you have no baseline sample information on what type of relationship exists between X and Y out of this baseline range. Minitab will give you a warning if you try to predict Y for a new case when the given X value is so far out ot this range that it is considered an outlier.

2.     A strong (close to -1 or +1) value of the coefficient of correlation is **not** proof of a cause-and-effect relationship, but only an indicator of an association between the values of these two variable.

3,     $R^2$ is called the Coefficient of Determination, and measures the proportion of variation in the Y variable that is accounted for by its relationship with the X variable. In general it is a better measure of this relationship than the coefficient of correlation (r). The value of r is always larger (in absolute value) than $r^2$, and so r gives a somewhat inflated view of the strength of the relationship.

4.     Do not skip graphing the scatterplot when starting simple linear regression. There are situations where all three assumptions of simple linear regression may be verified, but clearly a linear equation is not the best way to describe the actual relationship. For example, the graph below shows a set of baseline data where Assumption (1) is verified with a p-value of 0.000, but that a cubic equation clearly would better describe the relationship between X and Y. If you did not see the scatterplot, you would "blindly" proceed with simple linear regression to make predictions and miss out on the far superior method of using a cubic equation.

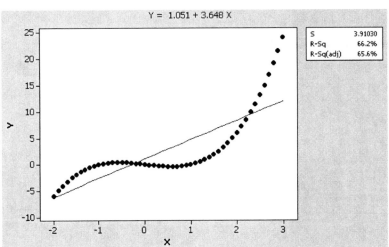

514

# Lab Assignment 12.1

**Name:**                                                                                  **Date:**

**Course:**                          **Section:**                          **Data CD Number:**

1.  Start a Minitab session. If you are unable to complete this lab assignment in one Minitab session, save the project as Lab 12-1 . **Never** use a period as part of the project name; since Minitab uses the period to attach the file type to the file name. Then at your next Minitab session, you may open this Lab 12-1.MPJ project and continue to work where you left off previously.

2.  Open the worksheet Econ2.mtw that is on your data disc. As described in Lab Assignment 8.1.1, this worksheet contains samples of hourly wages of three different sectors, and a sample of price and demand data. Let X be the price variable and Y be the demand variable. For this problem, you are to assume that any outlier (unusual observation) is correct and is not to be deleted.

    a.  Plot the x-y graph, and decide if a first-order linear regression model; i.e., assumption (1), is appropriate.

        YES ___ or NO ___

    b.  Use the *Regression* procedure and test the hypothesis to decide if assumption (1) is valid.

        YES ___ or NO ___

3.  Open another worksheet using Living.mtw from your data disc. These data represent weekly income and residential density of neighborhood. Let Y be the income variable and X be the density variable. For this problem, you are to assume that any outlier (unusual observation) is correct and is not to be deleted.

    a.  Check the two assumptions needed in order for a first-order linear regression model to be the correct technique to make point predictions.

        (i)  Assumption (1) p-value _____

            Is Y linearly related to X?    YES ___ or NO ___

        (ii)  Assumption (2) p-value _____

            Are all subpopulation variances equal?    YES ___ or NO ___

    b.  **If** your answers to both (i) and (ii) are YES, are each subpopulation's Y values normally distributed? Otherwise answer not applicable.

        YES ___     NO ___     Not Applicable ___

(lab assignment is continued on the second side of this page)

515

4. Open another worksheet using Babyarm.mtw from your data disc. These data are forearm length (in centimeters) at birth and adult height (in inches) from a baseline sample of people in Indiana. Do a complete linear regression analysis and find a 98% prediction interval for the adult heights of two Indiana newborns whose forearm lengths are 13.65 centimeters and 15.24 centimeters.

Since you do not have access to the actual people whose data is in this worksheet, you may not actually check the unusual observations for errors. So for this problem **only**; you are to assume that any "influential point" is correct, any "outlier" with a *St Resid* value between -2.5 and +2.5 is correct, but any "outlier" with a *St Resid* whose **absolute value** is greater than or equal to 2.5 is an error and is to be deleted.

a.  <u>forearm length</u>          <u>98 % prediction interval</u>

     13.65 cm          _____

     15.24 cm          _____

b. What is the coefficient of correlation between forearm length and adult height? _____

c. Test the hypothesis that the population coefficient of correlation between the forearm length and the adult height is "significantly" different from zero. Use a 0.05 level of significance. That is, test

$$H_0: \rho = 0$$
$$H_a: \rho \neq 0$$
$$\alpha = 0.05 .$$

5. Print your Session Window and all Graphics Windows to the printer.

6. Attach both your Minitab output and <u>your complete answers</u> to this sheet and submit all three to your instructor.

# Lab Assignment 12.2

**Name:**                                                         **Date:**

**Course:**                   **Section:**                               **Data CD Number:**

1. Start a Minitab session. If you are unable to complete this lab assignment in one Minitab session, save the project as Lab 12-2 . **Never** use a period as part of the project name; since Minitab uses the period to attach the file type to the file name. Then at your next Minitab session, you may open this Lab 12-2.MPJ project and continue to work where you left off previously.

2. Open the worksheet Fstgrade.mtw that is on your data disc. As described in Example 7.2 in Chapter 7, a random sample was taken from all first grade students in Tampa, Florida. Each student's height (in inches) and weight (in pounds) was measured. Let height be the "predictor" variable and weight be the "response" variable. For this problem, you are to assume that any outlier (unusual observation) is correct and is not to be deleted.

   a. Plot the x-y graph, and decide if a first-order linear regression model; i.e., assumption (1), is appropriate.

      YES ____ or NO ____

   b. Use the *Regression* procedure and test the hypothesis to decide if assumption (1) is valid.

      YES ____ or NO ____

3. Open another worksheet using Homesale.mtw from your data disc. As described in Lab Assignment 7.1.1, this worksheet contains data about the sales of one-family houses in Raleigh, North Carolina. Among the variables measured are the asking price and the selling price of each house in the sample. A local real estate agent is interested in determining the relationship between these two variables. In particular, he wants to be able to predict the selling price (Y) once the asking price (X) is known. For this problem, you are to assume that any outlier (unusual observation) is correct and is not to be deleted.

   a. Check the two assumptions needed in order for a first-order linear regression model to be the correct technique to make <u>point</u> predictions.

      (i) Assumption (1) p-value _____

                           Is Y linearly related to X?   YES ____ or NO ____

      (ii) Assumption (2) p-value _____

                           Are all subpopulation variances equal?   YES ____ or NO ____

   b. **If** your answers to both (i) and (ii) are YES, are each subpopulation's Y values normally distributed? Otherwise answer not applicable.

      YES ____     NO ____     Not Applicable ____

(lab assignment is continued on the second side of this page)

c.  Test the hypothesis that the population coefficient of correlation between the asking price and the selling price is "significantly" different from zero. Use a 0.05 level of significance. That is, test

$$H_0: \rho = 0$$
$$H_a: \rho \neq 0$$
$$\alpha = 0.05 .$$

d.  Explain how your answer to part (i) of part (a) of this question and your answer to part (c) above are related.

4.  Open another worksheet using Places.mtw from your data disc. This worksheet contains a sample of communities in the United States from 1975. The two variables in this worksheet are Health Care Cost per capita and Public School K-12 Education Expenditure per pupil. Do a complete linear regression analysis and, if appropriate, find (a) a point prediction and (b) a 90% prediction interval for the Health Care Cost per capita when a community spends $2630 per pupil on is Public School K-12 Education.

Since you do not have access to the actual communities whose data is in this worksheet, you may not actually check the unusual observations for errors. So for this problem **only**; you are to assume that any "influential point" is a data entry error and delete that community from the sample, any "outlier" with a **St.Resid.** value between -2.5 and +2.5 is correct, but any "outlier" with a **St.Resid.** whose **absolute value** is greater than 2.5 is an error and is to be deleted.

a.  Point Predictor: _____ (write "not applicable" if appropriate)

**If** you wrote "not applicable", in the space below explain why you made that choice.

b.  Prediction interval: _____ (write "not applicable" if appropriate)

**If** you checked not applicable, in the space below explain why you made that choice.

5.  Print your Session Window and all Graphics Windows to the printer.

6.  Attach both your Minitab output and your complete answers to this sheet and submit all three to your instructor.

# CHAPTER 13:    Multiple Linear Regression

In many situations where you need to predict the (future) value of a variable, there are several good predictor variables. Multiple linear regression is a statistical technique that allows you to make use of two or more predictor variables in the equation of the Estimated Regression Equation. The use of several good predictor variables increases the accuracy of the prediction over that obtained with simple linear regression (one predictor variable). The usual statistical notation is to label the "response" (predicted) variable as Y, the set of "predictor" variables $X_1, X_2, ... , X_k$, where the number of predictor variables is k.

For each different combination of values of $X_1, X_2, ... , X_k$ there is a well defined subpopulation of Y values, each with a mean denoted $\mu_{y.x}$ and a standard deviation denoted $\sigma_{y.x}$. The statistical technique of first-order multiple linear regression depends upon the following assumptions about these subpopulations:

(1)    the means of the Y values in the subpopulations are linearly related to the set of $X_1, X_2, ... , X_k$ values which define the subpopulations and

(2)    the variances of all subpopulations ($\sigma_{y.x}^2$) are all equal and usually symbolized as just $\sigma^2$.

The technique for computing a prediction interval depends upon the additional assumption that

(3)    each subpopulation of Y values is normally distributed.

Assumption (1) of a linear relationship is expressed by the equation

(i)    $\mu_{y.x} = \beta_0 + \beta_1 X_1 + \beta_2 X_2 + ... + \beta_k X_k$

and this is called the Multiple Linear Regression Equation of Y on $X_1, X_2, ... , X_k$. In this equation the value of each $\beta_i$ describes how much the Y variable will change for a "unit" change in the corresponding $X_i$ variable.

Point estimates of $\beta_0, \beta_1, \beta_2, ... , \beta_k$ are computed from the data in the baseline sample using the least squares criterion. These estimates are symbolized by $b_0, b_1, b_2, ... , b_k$ respectively. After these estimates have been computed, the Estimated Multiple Linear Regression Equation of Y on $(X_1, X_2, ... , X_k)$ is written as

(ii)    $\hat{y} = b_0 + b_1 X_1 + b_2 X_2 + ... + b_k X_k$

where the $\hat{y}$ is a point estimate for $\mu_{y.x}$ and is used to predict unknown (future) values of the Y variable. This $\hat{y}$ is called the "predicted value of Y" for known values of the set of $X_1, X_2, ... , X_k$ variables.

The procedures for doing point predictions and prediction intervals with multiple predictors are almost identical to those procedures with a single predictor and described in Chapter 11. There are a few minor differences that will be explained in this chapter. Perhaps one of the biggest differences is that graphing the scatterplot y versus the set of $x_1$, $x_2$, ... , $x_k$ is impossible when k is greater than 2. So instead one often graphs the scatterplot for y versus each of the $x_i$ variables. from these graphs, one gets an idea of which Xi variables are linearly related to the Y. When Minitab does this, it also graphs each $x_i$ versus $x_j$ scatterplot. These graphs may be used to examine interrelationships among the X variables, and in turn explain why some X variables may be unnecessary in the Estimated Multiple Linear Regression Equation. These graphs are done all at the same time and are called a matrix plot.

Click on *Graph , Matrix Plot...*

In the Matrix Plots dialog box: the *Matrix of plots Simple* graph should be highlighted. Next click on the $\boxed{\textbf{OK}}$ button.

In the Matrix Plots - Matrix of Plots Simple: you may need to press the $\boxed{\textbf{F3}}$ key to clear any previous information. The cursor will be in the box under the *Graph variables:* heading. Hold the $\boxed{\textbf{Ctrl}}$ key and click on each of the "predictor" (X) variables, and then click on the $\boxed{\textbf{Select}}$ button. Now highlight the "response" (Y) variable and click on the $\boxed{\textbf{Select}}$ button. Then click on the $\boxed{\textbf{Matrix Options...}}$ button.

In the Matrix Plot - Options dialog box: under the *Matrix Display* heading, click on the circle to the left of *Lower left*, and under the *Variable Label Placement* heading, click on the circle to the left of *Boundary*. Then click on the $\boxed{\textbf{OK}}$ button.

Back in Matrix Plots - Matrix of Plots Simple: click on the $\boxed{\textbf{OK}}$ button.

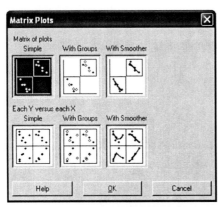

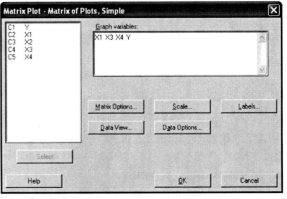

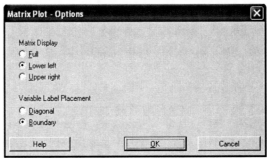

Example 13.1:   Open the worksheet Nurshome.mtw that is on your data disc. This worksheet contains data about the number of beds ($X_1$), annual total patient days ($X_2$), annual nursing salaries ($X_3$), and annual total patient care revenue in $100 (Y) for 38 licensed nursing facilities in New Mexico in 1988.   An industry financial advisor wants to predict, with 90% certainty, the annual total patient care revenue for a proposed new nursing facility that will have 75 beds and 160 annual total patient days. Plot the matrix plot for the number of beds ($X_1$), annual total patient days ($X_2$), and annual total patient care revenue in $100 (Y).  Note that the nursing salaries ($X_3$) will not be used in this example.

Use *File , Open Worksheet...* to open the worksheet Nurshome.mtw from your data disk. Since the financial advisor only wants to use the number of beds ($X_1$) and the annual total patient days ($X_2$) as predictors, the $X_3$ variable will not be used in this example.  The first step is to matrix scatterplots of Y on the set of ($X_1$, $X_2$), and check for any needed data corrections.

Click on *Graph , Matrix Plot...*

In the Matrix Plots dialog box: the *Matrix of plots Simple* graph should be highlighted. Next click on the ⬚ **OK** ⬚ button.

In the Matrix Plots - Matrix of Plots Simple: you may need to press the ⬚ **F3** ⬚ key to clear any previous information.  The cursor will be in the box under the *Graph variables:* heading.  Hold the ⬚ **Ctrl** ⬚ key and click on the X1 and X2 variables, and then click on the ⬚ **Select** ⬚ button.  Now highlight the Y variable and click on the ⬚ **Select** ⬚ button. Then click on the ⬚ **Matrix Options...** ⬚ button.

In the Matrix Plot - Options dialog box: under the *Matrix Display* heading, click on the circle to the left of *Lower left*, and under the *Variable Label Placement* heading, click on the circle to the left of *Boundary*.  Then click on the ⬚ **OK** ⬚ button.

Back in Matrix Plots - Matrix of Plots Simple: click on the ⬚ **OK** ⬚ button.

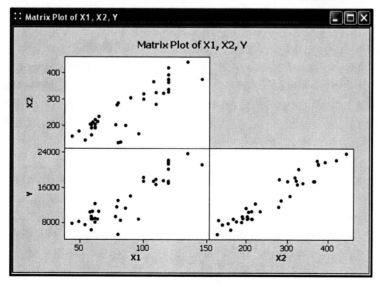

From these graphs, we see that the Y variable appears to be linearly related to both of the $X_1$ and $X_2$ variables.  Also there is some relationship between the two predictor ($X_1$ and $X_2$) variables.

The next step is to identify outliers and examine them for correctness as done in Chapter 11. In multiple regression, a case labeled as observations with unusual influence means that at least on of the $x_i$ values causes this set of $(x_1, x_2, \ldots, x_k)$ to be relatively far away from the rest of the baseline sample $(x_1, x_2, \ldots, x_k)$ sets. Cases that are relatively far off of the linear pattern are labeled residual outliers. Minitab will identify these outliers by

Click on *Stat*, *Regression*, *Regression ...*

In the Regression dialog box, if this is a **new** problem, press the [ **F3** ] key to clear any previous information from all Regression dialog boxes. The cursor should be in the box to the right of the *Response:* heading; click on the "response" (Y) variable and click on the [ **Select** ] button. The cursor will move down to the *Predictors:* box; hold the [ **Ctrl** ] key and click on each of the "predictor" (X) variables, and then click on the [ **Select** ] button. Then click on [ **OK** ] .

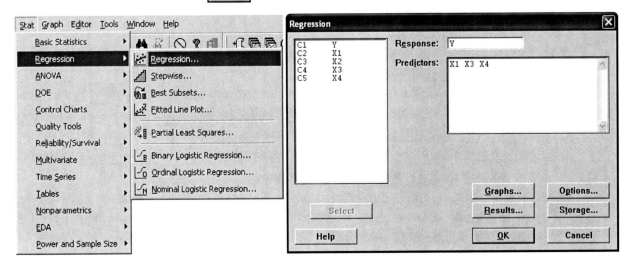

For now we will ignore most of the output in the Session Window. At the end of the output will be the heading **Analysis of Variance** and four lines of output under this heading. Then **if** there are any outliers, The output will contain the heading **Unusual Observations** followed by information on the outlier(s) listed. This information consists of the case number, and values of X, Y, the Fit, SE Fit, Residual and St Resid . Any unusual observations identified by the *Regression* procedure are classified as:

(a)   Cases with relative small or relative large X values, identified by an "X" next to the St Resid value. This type of unusual observation is called an **influential point**.

(b)   Cases with relative large Residual values, identified by an "R" next to the St Resid value.   This type of unusual observation is called a **residual outlier**.   Minitab identifies any observation whose St Resid value is either less than -2 or greater than 2 as a residual outlier.  Some statisticians disagree with this criterion and use less than -2.5 or greater than 2.5, while others use less than -3 and greater than 3.

The cases identified as unusual observations need to be examined. The data in the **ROW** that corresponds to the case number of each unusual observation (displayed underneath the **Obs.** heading) is examined; and if errors are found, necessary corrections are made directly in the Worksheet Window. If the entered data is in error for a case identified as an unusual observation and cannot be corrected, then you delete the case directly in the Worksheet Window by clicking on the row number at the left side corresponding to the case number being deleted and then press the Del key. As explained on page 384, the corrections must be done **before** any deletions are made.

A third possibility is when the entered data is correct for a case identified as an unusual observation. This situation has troubled statisticians for many years, and there is no general consensus as to what course to follow. For example; while Minitab defines an outlier as a case with the St Resid > 2, other statisticians require the St Resid value to be greater than three in order to call this an outlier. When the data is correct; the decision of whether to retain or to delete an unusual observation is difficult and should not be taken lightly. In general, it is usually best to retain such cases.

Example 13.2:    Use the data in the current worksheet and the *Stat, Regression, Regression* procedure to identify any outliers in this sample.

Click on *Stat, Regression, Regression ...*

In the Regression dialog box, since this is a **new** problem, press the F3 key to clear any previous information from all Regression dialog boxes. The cursor should be in the box to the right of the *Response:* heading; click on the "response" variable - Y (C4) and click on the Select button. The cursor will move down to the *Predictors:* box; hold the Ctrl key and click on the "predictor" variables - X1 (C1) and X2 (C2), and then click on the Select button. Then click on the OK button.

Only the end of the output in the Session Window is shown below.

**Source DF      Seq SS**
**X1        1      884665566**
**X2        1      174049878**

**Unusual Observations**

| Obs | X1 | Y | Fit | SE Fit | Residual | St Resid |
|-----|-----|-------|-------|--------|----------|----------|
| 15 | 110 | 11478 | 10242 | 827 | 1236 | 1.02 X |
| 23 | 62 | 5981 | 9326 | 327 | -3345 | -2.34 R |

**R denotes an observation with a large standardized residual.**
**X denotes an observation whose X value gives it large influence.**

Note that only the first predictor variable entered (X1) is listed in the output, but that does not indicate that it is this variable which is causing this case to be an outlier.

The industry financial advisor examines these two outliers and finds that observation 15 is incorrect, but cannot be corrected, and so this case needs to be deleted. Observation 23 has an incorrect Y value of 5981. The correct Y value is 8951 and this case needs to be corrected.

Example 13.3:   Use the data in the current worksheet, correct case 23 and delete case 15. Then redo the *Stat , Regression , Regression* procedure to identify any additional outliers in this sample.

To change the incorrect value of 5981 for the Y variable to the correct value of 8951; click on the cell in the 23$^{th}$ row of the Y (C4) column, and enter the correct value of 8951 (which will replace the incorrect value of 5981).

Click on the 15 in the left margin of the worksheet to highlight the entire 15$^{th}$ row, and then press the Delete key to remove this observation from the sample.

Click on *Stat , Regression , Regression ...*

In the Regression dialog box, the cursor should be in the box to the right of the *Response:* heading; click on the "response" variable - Y (C4) and click on the $\boxed{\text{Select}}$ button. The cursor will move down to the *Predictors:* box; hold the $\boxed{\text{Ctrl}}$ key and click on the "predictor" variables - X1 (C1) and X2 (C2), and then click on the $\boxed{\text{Select}}$ button. Then click on the $\boxed{\text{OK}}$ button. Note that since Minitab remembers the information in the dialog boxes from the previous time, you will only need to click on the $\boxed{\text{OK}}$ button.

Only the end of the output in the Session Window is shown below.

### Analysis of Variance

| Source | DF | SS | MS | F | P |
|---|---|---|---|---|---|
| Regression | 2 | 1033840731 | 516920365 | 283.27 | 0.000 |
| Residual Error | 35 | 63868332 | 1824809 | | |
| Total | 37 | 1097709063 | | | |

| Source | DF | Seq SS |
|---|---|---|
| X1 | 1 | 888442623 |
| X2 | 1 | 145398108 |

There are no Unusual Observations listed at the end of the output, so the sample data is "clean", and you are ready to check the validity of assumptions (1) and (2).

After all corrections and deletions have been made, the validity of assumptions (1) and (2) are checked. These two assumptions must be validated before any interpretation may be done for the regression results shown in the output!

The validity or non-validity of the first assumption is verified by the hypothesis testing:

$H_0$: the set of $X_1$, $X_2$, ... , $X_k$ and the Y variable are **not** linearly related
$H_a$: the set of $X_1$, $X_2$, ... , $X_k$ and the Y variable **are** linearly related

The significance level for this test is usually set at $\alpha = 0.05$ , and the test statistic is

$$F = \frac{MS \text{ for Regression}}{MS \text{ for Residual Error}} .$$

The value of this F statistic and the corresponding p-value are computed and displayed in the **Analysis of Variance** table at the bottom of the output from the *Regression* procedure that appears in the Session Window. If the p-value is less than or equal to $\alpha$ (usually 0.05); then the null hypothesis **is rejected**, and assumption (1) that the two variables **are** linearly related has been verified. However; if the p-value is greater than $\alpha$ (usually 0.05); then the null hypothesis is **not** rejected, assumption (1) is **not** verified, and the data should not be analyzed using the multiple linear regression techniques described in this chapter.

Note that this is exactly the same method described in Chapter 11 for checking the validity of the linear relationship between X and Y when there is only one predictor.

Example 13.4: Examine the results in the **Analysis of Variance** table in the re-computed Regression procedure that are in the Session Window, and determine if assumption (1) that the means of the Y in the subpopulations are linearly related to the set of $X_1$, $X_2$, ... , $X_k$ is or is not verified.

The hypothesis testing problem is:

$H_0$: the set of $X_1$, $X_2$ and the Y variable are **not** linearly related
$H_a$: the set of $X_1$, $X_2$ and the Y variable **are** linearly related
$\alpha = 0.05$

and the test statistic is $F = \dfrac{MS \text{ for Regression}}{MS \text{ for Residual Error}} .$

From the results in the **Analysis of Variance** table, the F test statistic is 283.27, and since the p-value of 0.000 is less than the given value of $\alpha = 0.05$, the null hypothesis **is rejected** and you may conclude that the annual total patient care revenue in hundreds is linearly related with the number of beds and the annual total patient days. And so assumption (1) **is verified**.

When there is only one predictor variable, the validity of assumption (2) is graphically verified by examining the x vs. residual graph. When there are two or more predictor variables, the graph of the set $X_1$, $X_2$, ... , $X_k$ with the Y variable is not possible. However; since the predicted value of Y (that is, $\hat{y}$) is a function the set of $X_1$, $X_2$, ... , $X_k$ , this assumption (2) may be verified by examining the residual vs $\hat{y}$ graph. The $\hat{y}$ values for each case in the baseline sample are computed and saved into a new Minitab column and named FITS1 by

Click on *Stat , Regression , Regression ...*

In the Regression dialog box, the cursor should be in the box to the right of the *Response:* heading; click on the "response" (Y) variable and click on the Select button. The cursor will move down to the *Predictors:* box; hold the Ctrl key and click on each of the "predictor" (X) variables, and then click on the Select button. Next click on the Storage... button. Note that since Minitab remembers the information in the dialog boxes from the previous time, you will only need to click on the Storage... button.

In the Regression - Storage dialog box, click in the squares to the left of *Residuals* and to the left of *Fits* to check these two options. No other options should be checked. Then click on OK . Two new columns automatically will be created and named FITS1 and RESI1. The column numbers will be one and two higher than the last column used in the current Worksheet Window.

Back in the Regression dialog box, click on OK .

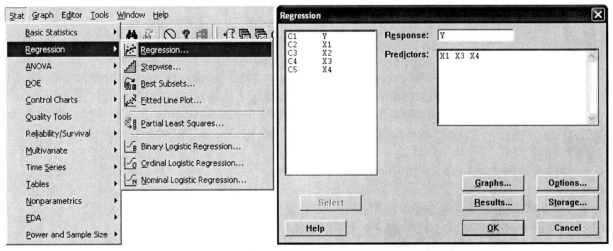

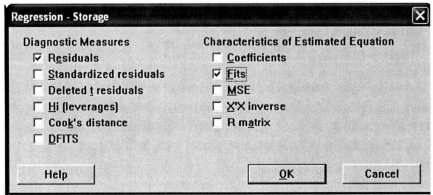

Once the Residuals and Fits ($\hat{y}$ values) are computer, the validity of assumption (2) may be **visually** check by plotting the residual vs $\hat{y}$ graph. This is done by

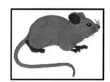

Click on *Graph , Scatterplot ...*

In the Scatterplots dialog box: the *Simple* graph should be highlighted. Next click on the [ OK ] button.

In the Scatterplot - Simple dialog box: the cursor will be in the box on the first line under the *Y variables* heading; click on the RESI1 variable and click on the [ Select ] button. The cursor will move to the box in the first line under the *X variables* heading; click on the FITS1 variable and click on the [ Select ] button. Then click on the [ OK ] button.

It is desirable to label the X axis with the name of "y hat"and to label the Y axis as "Residuals".

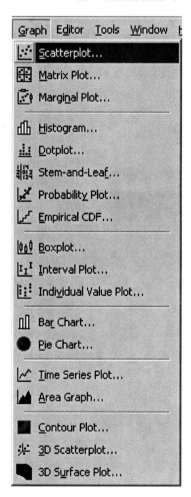

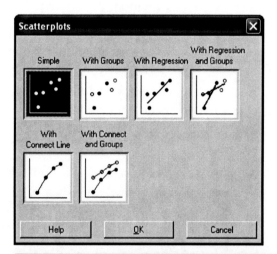

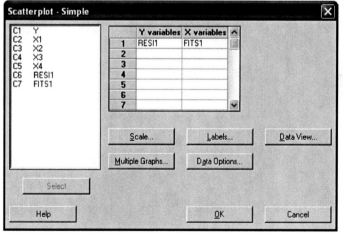

If the points on this graph look to be randomly and evenly spread within a general rectangular shape; this indicates that the variances ($\sigma^2_{y.x}$) of each subpopulation are all equal, and thus assumption (2) **is valid**. But if these points lie within a triangular or some other non-rectangular pattern; this implies that assumption (2) is **not** valid, and the techniques of multiple linear regression analysis shown in this chapter are **not** appropriate for describing the relationship between the set of $X_1$, $X_2$, ... , $X_k$ and Y variables nor for predicting new (future) Y values.

Example 13.5:  Use the data in the current worksheet, compute the residuals and fits, and graph the residuals (y axis) versus the fits (x axis). Name the axes appropriately. Does assumption (2) that the variances of all subpopulations are all equal seem to be verified?

Click on *Stat*, *Regression*, *Regression* ...

In the Regression dialog box, click on the "response" variable - Y (C4) and click on the ⎟ **Select** ⎟ button. The cursor will move down to the *Predictors:* box; hold the ⎟ **Ctrl** ⎟ key and click on the "predictor" variables - X1 (C1) and X2 (C2), and then click on the ⎟ **Select** ⎟ button. Then click on the ⎟ **OK** ⎟ button. Note that since Minitab remembers the information in the dialog boxes from the previous time, you will only need to click on the ⎟ **Storage...** ⎟ button.

In the Regression - Storage dialog box, click in the squares to the left of *Residuals* and to the left of *Fits* to check these two options. No other options should be checked. Then click on ⎟ **OK** ⎟. Two new columns automatically will be created and named FITS1 and RESI1. The column numbers will be one and two higher than the last column used in the current Worksheet Window.

Back in the Regression dialog box, click on ⎟ **OK** ⎟.

The first five rows of the Worksheet Window are shown below.

**▦ Nurshome.mtw ★★★**

| ↓ | C1 | C2 | C3 | C4 | C5 | C6 |
|---|------|------|------|-------|----------|---------|
|   | X1 | X2 | X3 | Y | RESI1 | FITS1 |
| 1 | 59 | 203 | 2459 | 8860 | -432.49 | 9292.5 |
| 2 | 120 | 392 | 6304 | 21900 | 819.49 | 21080.5 |
| 3 | 120 | 419 | 6590 | 22354 | 53.37 | 22300.6 |
| 4 | 120 | 363 | 5362 | 17421 | -2349.01 | 19770.0 |
| 5 | 65 | 234 | 3622 | 10531 | -481.76 | 11012.8 |

The next step is to examine the the residual vs $\hat{y}$ graph.

Click on *Graph*, *Scatterplot* ...

In the Scatterplots dialog box: the *Simple* graph should be highlighted. Next click on the ⎟ **OK** ⎟ button.

In the Scatterplot - Simple dialog box: the cursor will be in the box on the first line under the *Y variables* heading; click on the RESI1 variable and click on the ⎟ **Select** ⎟ button. The cursor will move to the box in the first line under the *X variables* heading; click on the FITS1 variable and click on the ⎟ **Select** ⎟ button. Then click on the ⎟ **OK** ⎟ button.

Double click on the X axis label of FITS1 and rename this axis as y hat. Double click on the Y axis label of RESI1 and rename this axis Residuals.

The graph shown on the next page will appear in the Scatterplot of RESI1 vs FITS1 Graphics Window.

(continued on the next page)

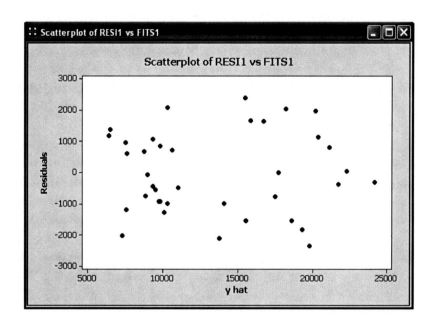

Since the points on this graph appear to be randomly and evenly spread within a general rectangular shape; this **visually** indicates that the variances ($\sigma_{y.x}^2$) of each subpopulation are all equal.

However, this is a <u>subjective</u> decision, and it is often very difficult to determine the pattern with a small sample size. This second assumption often may be numerically verified with a hypothesis test. The test used is the modified **Levene's** for homogeneity of variance test that was introduced in Section 2 of Chapter 9, and its use in the regression model was fully explained in Chapter 11. The only difference is that in Simple Linear Regression the residuals are graphed versus the one x variable, whereas in Multiple Linear Regression the residuals are graphed versus the group of $x_1$, $x_2$, ..., $x_k$ variables. This group is represented by $\hat{y}$, which is a linear function of the $x_1$, $x_2$, ..., $x_k$ variables. This test only checks for a megaphone shape violation of assumption (2). That is; if the population variances are consistently getting larger as the x values increase, or if the population variances are consistently getting smaller as the x values increase. These produce a megaphone shape to the graph of the residuals versus the $\hat{y}$ values. Other patterns that would invalidate assumption (2) are not detected with this test; for example, an hourglass pattern. However, most of the situations in which assumption (2) is not valid turn out to be due to the megaphone pattern of the population variances. The graph of the residuals versus the $\hat{y}$ values, as done in thr previous example, will indicate if Levene's test is appropriate. Also, in order to use the Levene's test, there must be at least six objects in the baseline sample.

The alternative hypothesis for testing assumption (2) that all subpopulation variances are equal (i.e., homogeneity of variance) when using Levene's test slightly changes to

$H_0$: all subpopulation variances are equal
$H_a$: the subpopulation variances are in a megaphone shape
$\alpha = 0.10$ ,

and the test statistic is the Levene's test statistic.

Here assumption (2) is stated as the null hypothesis, $H_0$. And so if the p-value for this test is greater than the pre-selected level of significance, usually 0.10; the null hypothesis of equal subpopulation variances (homogeneity) may not be rejected. And **as long as the graph of the residuals versus the $\hat{y}$ does not lead you to suspect an obvious non constant standard deviation pattern other than a megaphone shape**, assumption (2) **is** verified. But if the p-value is less than or equal to α; then the null hypothesis is rejected, and assumption (2) is **not** valid.

As done in Chapter 11, it is convenient to name columns **before** actually using them. So in the Worksheet Window, click in the name row of the first unused column after the FITS1 column and name the next three columns Sorted Fit, Corresp R and Factor. The procedure for computing Levene's test was shown in Chapter 11, and will be repeated here with the change that the $\hat{y}$ fitted values (FITS1) are used here instead of the X values that were used in Chapter 11. First you must sort the Fitted values (FITS1) from smallest to largest and keep the residuals associated with the corresponding $\hat{y}$ score. This is done using the *Data , Sort...* procedure on the Minitab menu bar.

Click on *Data , Sort...*

In the Sort dialog box, the cursor will be in the box under the *Sort Column(s):* heading. Highlight the FITS1 column only and click on Select. Then highlight the RESI1 column only and click on Select. **It is important that these two variables be entered in this order.** Next click inside the box to the right of the first *By column:* heading, click on the FITS1 variable, and click on Select. Next click on the circle to the left of *Column(s) of current worksheet:*, and then click inside of the box under this heading. inside of the box under the *Store sorted column(s) in:* heading, hold the Ctrl key and click on the Sorted Fit and Corresp R variables to highlight them both. **It is important that these two variables be entered in this order.** Then click on Select. Now click on OK.

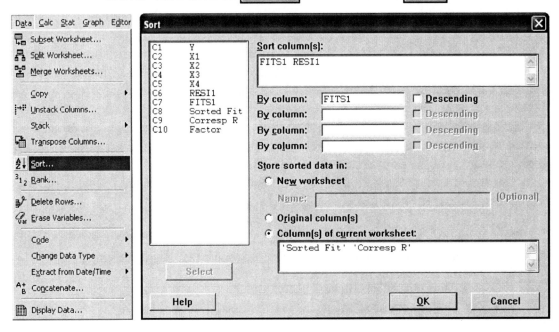

530

Next determine how many objects there are in the baseline sample. There are several ways to do this. You could scroll down the Worksheet Window until you come to the last data row, and then that row number is the number of objects in the baseline sample. You could enter the command info into the Session Window after the **MTB >** prompt, and the number of scores in the X column will be the number of observations in the baseline sample. A third and easiest option is to use the *Stat*, *Basic Statistics*, *Display Descriptive Statistics* procedure from the menu bar for the Sorted Fit variable. This will be demonstrated in the next example. You need to find the **middle** two scores of the Sorted Fit column. Now comes the part which may vary from problem to problem. If the number of objects, symbolized by n, is an even number then the two middle scores will be in the rows numbered n/2 and (n/2 + 1). If n is an odd number then the two middle scores will be in either the rows numbered (n-1)/2 and (n+1)/2 or the rows numbered (n+1)/2 and (n+3)/2. In any of these three cases, you must use your best judgement as to which you want to call the middle two scores. For example; if the two Sorted Fit scores in these two rows are identical, you will want to keep them together, and so you will need to choose the first different score (either smaller or larger) as the other middle score. This process is not governed by any formula. And it is not critical to get the exact correct two middle scores, as long as you choose two scores approximately in the middle. Next either use the *Stat, Basic Statistics, Display Descriptive Statistics* procedure or look in the first and last rows of the Worksheet Window to find the minimum and maximum of the Sorted Fit values.

Using the notation of min for the smallest score, $m_1$ and $m_2$ for the **middle** two scores, and max for the largest score in the Sorted Fit column, proceed as follows. Suppose there are 15 observations and the last three columns of the Worksheet Window were as shown below.

| | C8 | C9 | C10 |
|---|---|---|---|
| | Sorted Fit | Corresp R | Factor |
| 1 | 6.5376 | -0.53761 | |
| 2 | 9.3415 | 2.65853 | |
| 3 | 10.9221 | 1.07791 | |
| 4 | 21.6037 | -1.60367 | |
| 5 | 22.0083 | -0.00829 | |
| 6 | 23.9478 | -1.94780 | |
| 7 | 26.0398 | 6.96015 | |
| 8 | 29.9273 | -3.92732 | |
| 9 | 29.9578 | 0.04217 | |
| 10 | 30.9767 | -1.97668 | |
| 11 | 38.4281 | -4.42809 | |
| 12 | 47.6441 | -0.64409 | |
| 13 | 48.4076 | -4.40761 | |
| 14 | 50.1321 | 1.86793 | |
| 15 | 53.1255 | 6.87446 | |

**Worksheet 1** \*\*\*

The logical place to break the Sorted Fit values is between rows 7 and 8, since the difference between those two Sorted Fit scores is larger than the difference between the two Sorted Fit scores in rows 8 and 9. Now use the *Data*, *Code*, *Numeric to Text...* procedure to put Lo in the first half of this new Factor column and to put Hi in the second half of the factor column. This was shown in Chapter 11, but the Sorted X values were used instead of the Sorted Fit values. As described at the end of Section 1 in Chapter 11, here the Sorted Fit values displayed in the Worksheet Window are rounded off from their exact values. Because of this rounding, the min, $m_1$, $m_2$, and max values entered in the dialog box must be slightly changed. The range of the Sorted Fit values must be slightly exaggerated on both the smaller and larger ends of the [min to $m_1$] and the [$m_2$ to max] intervals in order to accommodate the rounding of the Sorted Fit values. One might do as follows. At the two intervals' smaller (left) endpoints, subtract one from the **right most decimal place shown**. And at the two intervals' larger (right) endpoints, add one to **the right most decimal place shown**. In the Worksheet Window shown on the previous page; min would become 6.5375 , and $m_1$ would become 26.0399 . In the Worksheet Window shown above; $m_2$ would become 29.9272, and max would become 53.1256 . This will slightly increase the range of the coded values on each end of the interval so as to include all exact values in the interval. Since $m_1$ and $m_2$ are not very close together, there is no need to be so precise in this case. So one could exaggerate more broadly; e.g.; use [3 to 27] for the Lo group and use [29 to 54] for the Hi group. The coding is done as follows.

 Click on *Data , Code , Numeric to Text ...*

In the Code - Numeric to Text dialog box only the columns with numeric values will be displayed in the box on the left. The cursor should be in the box under the heading *Code data from columns:*, click on the Sorted Fit variable and click on the [ **Select** ] button. Next click in the *Into columns:* box, click on the Factor variable, and click on the [ **Select** ] button. Then click in the first box under the *Original values* heading and type in min : $m_1$ (the value of min, a colon and the value of $m_1$). Next click in the first box under the *New:* heading and type in the word Lo. Similarly click on the second row in the box under the *Original values* heading and type in $m_2$ : max (the value of $m_2$, a colon and the value of max). Next click in the box under the *New:* heading and type in the word Hi. Then click [ **OK** ] .

 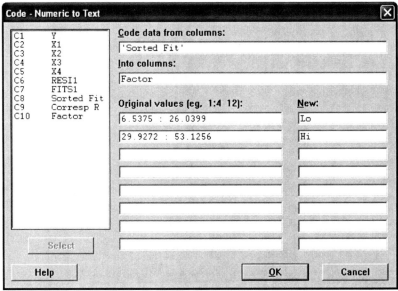

Now the Factor variable will have Lo in the first half of its rows and Hi in the second half of its rows.

Finally, assumption (2) is verified by the hypothesis testing of

$H_0$: all subpopulation variances are equal
$H_a$: the subpopulation variances are in a megaphone shape
$\alpha = 0.10$ .

The test statistic is the Levene's test statistic. The modified Levene's test statistic and corresponding p-value are calculated as follows.

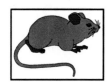

Click on *Stat* , *ANOVA* , *Test for Equal Variances...*

In the Test for Equal Variances dialog box: the cursor will be in the box to the right of *Response:*. Click on the Corresp R variable and click on the Select button. The cursor will move to the large box to the right of *Factors:*, click on the Factor variable and then click on the Select button. You may ignore the boxes to the right of *Confidence level:* and *Title:*. Then click on the OK button.

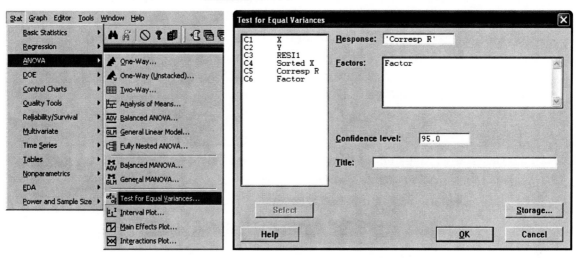

The output of the *Test for Equal Variances* (or *Homogeneity of Variance*) procedure contains:

(1) Simultaneous Bonferroni confidence intervals for the population standard deviations,
(2) the Bartlett's (for normal distributions) F test statistic and p-value,
(3) the Levene's (for any continuous distribution) test statistic and p-value, and
(4) a Graphic Window, labeled *Test for Equal Variances: AllData versus Factor* containing the same information.

Only the Levene's test statistic and p-value are used to test the hypothesis and check the validity of assumption (2).

Even though the test results are most easily read from the Graphic Window, since it is active and appears on top after the *Test of Equal Variances* is completed; there is no need to print this Graphic Window since the same information appears in the Session Window and will be printed when you print the Session Window.

533

Example 13.6: Use the data in the current worksheet, and perform the modified Levene's test to check the validity of assumption (2) that the variances of all subpopulations are all equal.

First name the three new columns

First name the three new columns (C7, C8 and C9) as Sorted Fit, Corresp R and Factor.

Click on *Data , Sort...*

In the Sort dialog box, the cursor will be in the box under the *Sort Column(s):* heading. Highlight the FITS1 column only and click on ☐ **Select** . Then highlight the RESI1 column only and click on ☐ **Select** . **It is important that these two variables be entered in this order.** Next click inside the box to the right of the first *By column:* heading, click on the FITS1 variable, and click on ☐ **Select** . Next click on the circle to the left of *Column(s) of current worksheet:*, and then click inside of the box under this heading. inside of the box under the *Store sorted column(s) in:* heading, hold the ☐ **Ctrl** key and click on the Sorted Fit and Corresp R variables to highlight them both. **It is important that these two variables be entered in this order.** Then click on ☐ **Select** . Now click on ☐ **OK** .

Next the minimum, the middle two scores and the maximum need to be determined. The *Stat , Basic Statistics , Describe Statistics* menu procedure will find the minimum, the maximum and the number of scores for the Sorted X variable.

Click on *Stat , Basic Statistics , Describe Statistics*

In the Display Descriptive Statistics dialog box: highlight the Sorted X variable, click on the ☐ **Select** button, and then click on the ☐ **Statistics...** button.

In the Descriptive Statistics - Statistics dialog box: click to uncheck all boxes **except** for the *Minimum* , *Maximum* and *N nonmissing* statistics. Then click on ☐ **OK** .

Back in the Display Descriptive Statistics dialog box, click on ☐ **OK** .

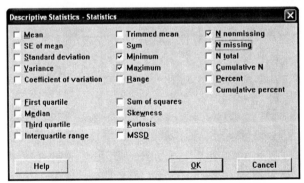

The results shown below will appear in the Session Window.

## *Descriptive Statistics: Sorted Fit*

| Variable | N | Minimum | Maximum |
|----------|-----|---------|---------|
| Sorted Fit | 38 | 6360 | 24138 |

There are 38 non-missing ( **N** ) scores, and so that the number of objects is n = 8. Since n is even, the two middle rows are the n/2 = 19th and (n/2 + 1)

(continued on the next page)

There are 38 non-missing ( **N** ) scores, and so that the number of objects is n = 8.  Since n is even, the two middle rows are the n/2 = 19$^{th}$ and (n/2 + 1) = 20$^{th}$ rows.  The middle eight rows of the Nurshome.mtw worksheet are displayed below.

| | C1 | C2 | C3 | C4 | C5 | C6 | C7 | C8 | C9 |
|---|---|---|---|---|---|---|---|---|---|
| | X1 | X2 | X3 | Y | RESI1 | FITS1 | Sorted Fit | Corresp R | Factor |
| 16 | 60 | 213 | 1914 | 8872 | -925.62 | 9797.6 | 10055.7 | -1273.74 | |
| 17 | 110 | 280 | 5173 | 17881 | 2394.06 | 15486.9 | 10303.9 | -976.90 | |
| 18 | 120 | 336 | 4630 | 17004 | -1545.88 | 18549.9 | 10310.8 | 2095.21 | |
| 19 | 135 | 442 | 7489 | 23829 | -309.48 | 24138.5 | 10594.2 | 717.81 | |
| 20 | 59 | 191 | 2051 | 9424 | 673.79 | 8750.2 | 11012.8 | -481.76 | |
| 21 | 64 | 214 | 4729 | 8782 | -1273.74 | 10055.7 | 13746.4 | -2097.36 | |
| 22 | 62 | 204 | 2367 | 8951 | -546.38 | 9497.4 | 14070.7 | -981.73 | |
| 23 | 108 | 366 | 5933 | 17446 | -1820.79 | 19266.8 | 15486.9 | 2394.06 | |

The 19$^{th}$ row of Sorted Fit contains 10594.2 , and the 20$^{th}$ row contains 11012.8 .  However notice that the 21$^{st}$ row of Sorted Fit contains 13746.4 , and that the difference between the 20$^{th}$ and 21$^{st}$ rows is much bigger that the difference between the 19$^{th}$ and 20$^{th}$ rows.  So we will break the scores into two groups between the 20$^{th}$ and 21$^{st}$ rows.  Since Minitab has rounded off these numbers, $m_1$ and $m_2$ must be slightly exaggerated. As described earlier in this chapter, one method is to add or subtract 1 in the **last place displayed**, which is the first decimal place for this problem.  So add 0.1 to 11012.8 to let $m_1$ = 11012.9 , and subtract 0.1 from 13746.4 to let $m_2$ = 13746.3 .  Next look in output shown above of the *Stat, Basic Statistics, Display Descriptive Statistics* procedure to find the minimum and maximum of the Sorted Fit values.  The Minitab rounded off values of the minimum and maximum values of the Sorted Fit variable are 6360 and 24138 respectively.  Adjust the min value by subtracting 1 from the 6360 , and adjust the max value by adding 1 to 24138.  In this example let min = 6359 and let max = 24139.

However, since the two middle scores of 11012.8 and 13746.4 are not very close together, the easy way is to exaggerate more broadly.  So for the Lo interval use the endpoints [6359 to 11013], and for the Hi interval use the endpoints [13746 to 24139].

Next put Lo in the first half of the Factor column and put Hi in the second half.

Click on *Data , Code , Numeric to Text* ...

In the Code - Numeric to Text dialog box, the cursor should be in the box under the heading *Code data from columns:*.  Click on the Sorted Fit variable and click on the  Select  button.  Next click in the *Into columns:* box, click on the Factor variable, and click on the  Select  button. Then click in the first box under the *Original values* heading and type in 6359 : 11013 (min : $m_1$).  Next click in the first box under the *New:* heading and type in the word Lo.  Similarly click on the second row in the box under the *Original values* heading and type in 13746 : 24139 ($m_2$ : max).  Next click in the box under the *New:* heading and type in the word Hi.  Then click on  OK  .

(continued on the next page)

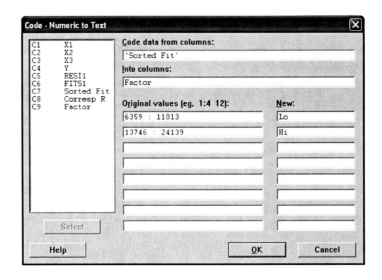

Now the Factor variable will have Lo in the first half of its rows and Hi in the second half of its rows. The middle eight rows of the Nurshome.mtw worksheet are displayed below.

**Nurshome.mtw ***

| ↓ | C1 | C2 | C3 | C4 | C5 | C6 | C7 | C8 | C9-T |
|---|----|----|----|----|-------|-------|-----------|----------|--------|
|   | X1 | X2 | X3 | Y | RESI1 | FITS1 | Sorted Fit | Corresp R | Factor |
| 16 | 60 | 213 | 1914 | 8872 | -925.62 | 9797.6 | 10055.7 | -1273.74 | Lo |
| 17 | 110 | 280 | 5173 | 17881 | 2394.06 | 15486.9 | 10303.9 | -976.90 | Lo |
| 18 | 120 | 336 | 4630 | 17004 | -1545.88 | 18549.9 | 10310.8 | 2095.21 | Lo |
| 19 | 135 | 442 | 7489 | 23829 | -309.48 | 24138.5 | 10594.2 | 717.81 | Lo |
| 20 | 59 | 191 | 2051 | 9424 | 673.79 | 8750.2 | 11012.8 | -481.76 | Lo |
| 21 | 64 | 214 | 4729 | 8782 | -1273.74 | 10055.7 | 13746.4 | -2097.36 | Hi |
| 22 | 62 | 204 | 2367 | 8951 | -546.38 | 9497.4 | 14070.7 | -981.73 | Hi |
| 23 | 108 | 366 | 5933 | 17446 | -1820.79 | 19266.8 | 15486.9 | 2394.06 | Hi |

Finally, assumption (2) is verified by the hypothesis testing of

$H_0$: all subpopulation variances are equal
$H_a$: the subpopulation variances are in a megaphone shape
$\alpha = 0.10$

and the test statistic is the Levene's test statistic.

Click on *Stat* , *ANOVA* , *Test for Equal Variances...*

In the Test for Equal Variances dialog box: the cursor will be in the box to the right of *Response:*. Click on the Corresp R variable and click on the ⟨ **Select** ⟩ button. The cursor will move to the large box to the right of *Factors:*, click on the Factor variable and then click on the ⟨ **Select** ⟩ button. You may ignore the boxes to the right of *Confidence level:* and *Title:*. Then click on the ⟨ **OK** ⟩ button.

The results shown on the next page will appear in a separate Graphics Window.

(continued on the next page)

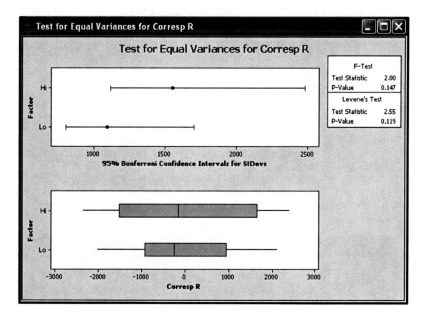

Test for Equal Variances for Corresp R

| F-Test | |
|---|---|
| Test Statistic | 2.00 |
| P-Value | 0.147 |
| Levene's Test | |
| Test Statistic | 2.55 |
| P-Value | 0.119 |

95% Bonferroni Confidence Intervals for StDevs

Since the Levene's test p-value of 0.119 is greater than $\alpha = 0.10$, the null hypothesis of equal subpopulation variances (homogeneity) may not be rejected. And since the graph of the Residuals versus the Fitted Values is not suspicious, thus assumption (2) is verified. Therefore **point predictions** may be made using multiple linear regression.

Now that the baseline sample data has been checked for outliers and "cleaned", and assumption (1) and assumption (2) have been verified, you may use multiple linear regression to analyze the data. The Estimated Multiple Linear Regression Equation of Y on $X_1$, $X_2$, ... , $X_k$ and other statistics are computed using the same Minitab *Stat*, *Regression*, *Regression* procedure as done in the previous chapter. Except that in the Regression dialog box, <u>multiple</u> "predictor" variables are entered into the *Predictors:* box.

Click on *Stat*, *Regression*, *Regression* ...

In the Regression dialog box, the cursor should be in the box to the right of the *Response:* heading; click on the "response" (Y) variable and click on the Select button. The cursor will move down to the *Predictors:* box; hold the Ctrl key and click on each of the "predictor" (X) variables, and then click on the Select button. Next click on the Storage... button. Note that since Minitab remembers the information in the dialog boxes from the previous time, you will only need to click on the Storage... button.

In the Regression - Storage dialog box, click in the squares to the left of *Residuals* and to the left of *Fits* to **uncheck** these two options. If you forget to uncheck this box, a new column to the right of the last column (RESI1) in your worksheet will **automatically** be created **and** be named RESI2. This will not effect any of the computations, but an extra column, that is identical to the RESI1 column, will be created in your worksheet. No other options should be checked. Then click on OK .

Back in the Regression dialog box, click on OK .

(See graphics on the next page.)

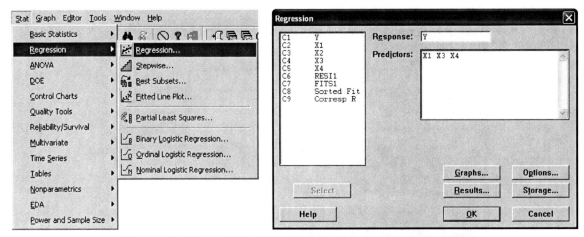

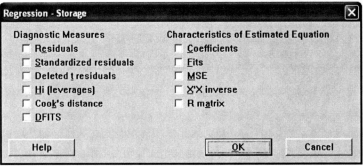

The output of the *Stat*, *Regression*, *Regression* procedure contains:

    (1) the equation of the Estimated Regression Line of Y on $X_1, X_2, \ldots, X_k$,

    (2) the values of the coefficients $b_0, b_1, b_2, \ldots b_k$,

    (3) the standard deviations of these (k + 1) estimates,

    (4) the values of the Student's t test statistic for testing the hypotheses

$$H_0: \beta_i = 0$$
$$H_a: \beta_i \neq 0 \qquad \text{for each } i = 0, 1, 2, \ldots, k,$$

    (5) the p-value for each of these (k + 1) tests,

    (6) the value of $s_{y.x}$, which is the point estimate of $\sigma$ (the common standard deviation of the Y values in each subpopulation),

    (7) the value of the Coefficient of Determination $r^2$ and an adjusted $r^2$

    (8) an analysis of variance table which contains several columns of numbers, the value of the F test statistic, and the p-value for testing the hypothesis

$H_0$: the set of $X_1, X_2, \ldots, X_k$ and the Y variable are **not** linearly related
$H_a$: the set of $X_1, X_2, \ldots, X_k$ and the Y variable **are** linearly related

    (9) possibly a table of Unusual Observations with the case number, and values of the first $X_1$ variable, Y, the Fit, SE Fit, Residual and St Resid.

Any unusual observations identified by the *Regression* procedure are classified as:

    (a) Cases with relative small or relative large $X_i$ values, identified by an "X" next to the St Resid value. This type of unusual observation is called an **influential point**.

    (b) Cases with relative large St Resid values (less than -2 or greater than 2), identified by an "R" next to the St Resid value. This type of unusual observation is called an **residual outlier**.

Once the equation of the Estimated Regression Line of Y on $X_1$, $X_2$, ... , $X_k$ has been computed, this equation may be used to predict the unknown (future) value of Y when the values of $X_1$, $X_2$, ... , $X_k$ are known. Using the notation of $x_{1o}$, $x_{2o}$, ... $x_{ko}$ for the **known** values of the $X_1$, $X_2$, ... , $X_k$ variables, the numerical value of $\hat{y}$ is found by substituting the $x_{1o}$, $x_{2o}$, ... $x_{ko}$ values into equation (ii) and computing

$$\hat{y} = b_0 + b_1 X_1 + b_2 X_2 + ... + b_k X_k.$$

The value of this point predictor ($\hat{y}$) is computed by clicking on the $\boxed{\text{Options...}}$ button in the Regression dialog box. In most situations we combine the computation of the point predictor ($\hat{y}$) with the computation of the Estimated Regression Line of Y on X as follows.

Click on *Stat*, *Regression*, *Regression*...

In the Regression dialog box, the cursor should be in the box to the right of the *Response:* heading; click on the "response" (Y) variable and click on the $\boxed{\text{Select}}$ button. The cursor will move down to the *Predictors:* box; hold the $\boxed{\text{Ctrl}}$ key and click on each of the "predictor" (X) variables, and then click on the $\boxed{\text{Select}}$ button. Next click on the $\boxed{\text{Storage...}}$ button. Note that since Minitab remembers the information in the dialog boxes from the previous time, you will only need to click on the $\boxed{\text{Storage...}}$ button.

In the Regression - Storage dialog box, click in the squares to the left of *Residuals* and to the left of *Fits* to **uncheck** these two options. If you forget to uncheck this box, a new column to the right of the last column (RESI1) in your worksheet will **automatically** be created **and** be named RESI2. This will not effect any of the computations, but an extra column, that is identical to the RESI1 column, will be created in your worksheet. No other options should be checked. Then click on $\boxed{\text{OK}}$.

Back in the Regression dialog box, click on the $\boxed{\text{Options...}}$ button.

In the Regression-Options dialog box, click inside of the box below the *Prediction intervals for new observations:* heading, type in the known values of $X_1$, $X_2$, ... , $X_k$ for the new object (values of $x_{1o}$, $x_{2o}$, ... $x_{ko}$ ). These values **must be typed in the exact order corresponding to the order of the** *Predictors:* **in the previous Regression dialog box; and separate these values with a space, but do NOT put a comma between these values.** For now you may ignore the number in the box to the right of the *Confidence level:* heading. Click on the $\boxed{\text{OK}}$ button.

Back in the Regression dialog box, click on the $\boxed{\text{OK}}$ button.

(See graphics on the next page.)

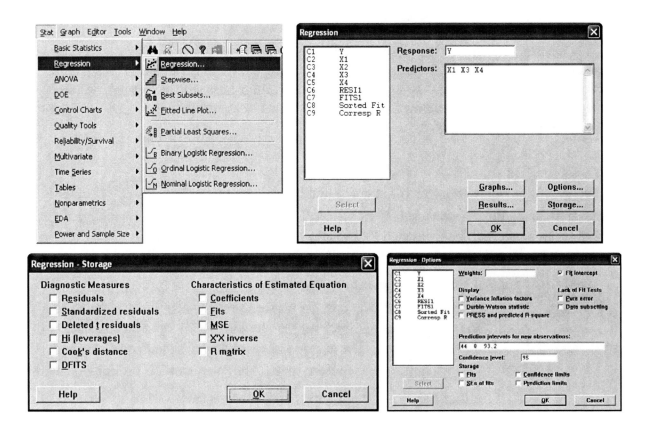

The additional output of the Prediction option contains:

(1)     the heading **New Obs** and underneath this the sequential number of the new observation (you may predict Y for several new observations's $x_{1o}$, $x_{2o}$, ... $x_{ko}$ values),

(2)     the heading **Fit** and underneath this heading is the predicted value of the Y variable for the known $x_0$ value entered $\hat{y} = b_0 + b_1 x_{1o} + b_2 x_{2o} + ... + b_k x_{ko}$),

(3)     the default heading **95% CI** and underneath this heading is a 95% confidence interval for the mean of the Y values ($\mu_{y.x}$) in the subpopulation defined by the each known $x_0$ entered,

(4)     the default heading **95% PI** and underneath this heading is a 95% prediction interval for the unknown (future) value of Y for the new case(s) with the given $x_{1o}$, $x_{2o}$, ... $x_{ko}$ values,

(5)     a table listing the new observation sequential number(s) and the corresponding values of the each entered $x_{1o}$, $x_{2o}$, ... $x_{ko}$ , and

(6)     a warning if any of the new cases have an X value that is an outlier for this baseline sample.

To predict Y for only **one** new case, you would enter the known value of $X_1$, $X_2$, ... , $X_k$ for the new object (values of $x_{1o}$, $x_{2o}$, ... $x_{ko}$) directly in the box below the *Prediction intervals for new observations:* after clicking on the ⎸ **Options...** ⎹ button.

To predict Y for **more than one** new case you need to do the following:

(1)    name k new columns as X1o Values, X2o Values, ... Xko Values

(2)    enter the known values of $X_1, X_2, ... , X_k$ for each new case in a separate row of this column, **starting in row 1**, and

(3)    in the Regression - Options dialog box of the *Stat , Regression , Regression* procedure; after clicking inside of the box below the *Prediction intervals for new observations:* heading, hold the [ **Ctrl** ] key and click on each of the X1o Values, X2o Values, ... Xko Values columns, and then click on the [ **Select** ] button.

Shown below is an example of what your worksheet would look like if you wanted to predict Y for three new cases where the given $x_{1o}$, $x_{3o}$ and $x_{4o}$ values of these cases were (50, 10, 98.4), (40, 11, 92.4) and (33, 8, 94.7).  Also shown below is the Regression - Options dialog box for this situation.

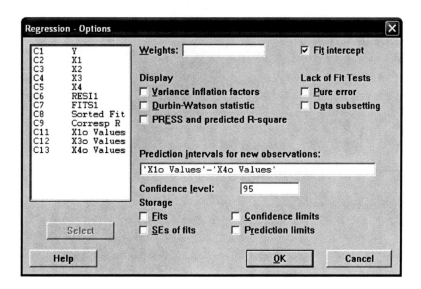

| | C1 | C2 | C3 | C4 | C5 | C6 | C7 | C8 | C9 | C10-T | C11 | C12 | C13 |
|---|---|---|---|---|---|---|---|---|---|---|---|---|---|
| | Y | X1 | X2 | X3 | X4 | RESI1 | FITS1 | Sorted Fit | Corresp R | Factor | X1o Values | X3o Values | X4o Values |
| 1 | 60 | 71 | 21 | 7 | 78.500 | 6.87446 | 53.1255 | 6.5376 | -0.53761 | Lo | 50 | 10 | 98.4 |
| 2 | 52 | 68 | 12 | 1 | 74.300 | 1.86793 | 50.1321 | 9.3415 | 2.65853 | Lo | 40 | 11 | 92.4 |
| 3 | 20 | 41 | 19 | 11 | 104.300 | -1.60367 | 21.6037 | 10.9221 | 1.07791 | Lo | 33 | 8 | 94.7 |
| 4 | 30 | 49 | 15 | 7 | 95.400 | 0.04217 | 29.9578 | 21.6037 | -1.60367 | Lo | | | |
| 5 | 47 | 66 | 19 | 11 | 87.600 | -0.64409 | 47.6441 | 22.0083 | -0.00829 | Lo | | | |
| 6 | 33 | 45 | 21 | 7 | 95.900 | 6.96015 | 26.0398 | 23.9478 | -1.94780 | Lo | | | |
| 7 | 22 | 42 | 18 | 11 | 109.200 | -0.00829 | 22.0083 | 26.0398 | 6.96015 | Lo | | | |
| 8 | 6 | 26 | 10 | 3 | 102.700 | -0.53761 | 6.5376 | 29.9273 | -3.92732 | Hi | | | |
| 9 | 44 | 66 | 5 | 1 | 72.500 | -4.40761 | 48.4076 | 29.9578 | 0.04217 | Hi | | | |
| 10 | 22 | 43 | 9 | 2 | 93.100 | -1.94780 | 23.9478 | 30.9767 | -1.97668 | Hi | | | |
| 11 | 26 | 50 | 23 | 21 | 115.900 | -3.92732 | 29.9273 | 38.4281 | -4.42809 | Hi | | | |
| 12 | 34 | 57 | 4 | 1 | 83.800 | -4.42809 | 38.4281 | 47.6441 | -0.64409 | Hi | | | |
| 13 | 12 | 31 | 18 | 11 | 113.300 | 1.07791 | 10.9221 | 48.4076 | -4.40761 | Hi | | | |
| 14 | 29 | 48 | 14 | 8 | 78.900 | -1.97668 | 30.9767 | 50.1321 | 1.86793 | Hi | | | |
| 15 | 12 | 29 | 19 | 10 | 109.400 | 2.65853 | 9.3415 | 53.1255 | 6.87446 | Hi | | | |

Example 13.7: As originally stated in Example 11.1, the industry financial advisor wants to predict the annual total patient care revenue for a proposed new nursing facility that will have 75 beds and 160 annual total patient days. Use the data in the current worksheet, and compute the desired point prediction.

Click on *Stat*, *Regression*, *Regression* ...

In the Regression dialog box, the cursor should be in the box to the right of the *Response:* heading; click on the "response" (Y) variable and click on the $\boxed{\text{Select}}$ button. The cursor will move down to the *Predictors:* box; hold the $\boxed{\text{Ctrl}}$ key and click on each of the "predictor" (X) variables, and then click on the $\boxed{\text{Select}}$ button. Next click on the $\boxed{\text{Storage...}}$ button. Note that since Minitab remembers the information in the dialog boxes from the previous time, you will only need to click on the $\boxed{\text{Storage...}}$ button.

In the Regression - Storage dialog box, click in the squares to the left of *Residuals* and to the left of *Fits* to **uncheck** these two options. Then click on $\boxed{\text{OK}}$.

Back in the Regression dialog box, click on the $\boxed{\text{Options...}}$ button.

In the Regression-Options dialog box, click inside of the box below the *Prediction intervals for new observations:* heading, type in 75  160, the known values of $X_1$ and $X_2$ for the new object. These values **must be typed in the exact order corresponding to the order of the *Predictors:* in the previous Regression dialog box; and separate these values with a space, but do NOT put a comma between these values.** For now you may ignore the number in the box to the right of the *Confidence level:* heading. Click on the $\boxed{\text{OK}}$ button.

Back in the Regression dialog box, click on the $\boxed{\text{OK}}$ button.

The output shown below will appear in the Session Window.

## Regression Analysis: Y versus X1, X2

**The regression equation is**
**Y = - 3022 + 53.2 X1 + 45.2 X2**

| Predictor | Coef | SE Coef | T | P |
|-----------|------|---------|------|-------|
| Constant | -3021.7 | 738.2 | -4.09 | 0.000 |
| X1 | 53.23 | 15.79 | 3.37 | 0.002 |
| X2 | 45.190 | 5.063 | 8.93 | 0.000 |

S = 1350.86     R-Sq = 94.2%     R-Sq(adj) = 93.8%

**Analysis of Variance**

| Source | DF | SS | MS | F | P |
|--------|-----|------------|-----------|--------|-------|
| Regression | 2 | 1033840731 | 516920365 | 283.27 | 0.000 |
| Residual Error | 35 | 63868332 | 1824809 | | |
| Total | 37 | 1097709063 | | | |

(continued on the next page)

| Source | DF | Seq SS |
|---|---|---|
| X1 | 1 | 888442623 |
| X2 | 1 | 145398108 |

**Predicted Values for New Observations**

| New Obs | Fit | SE Fit | 95% CI | 95% PI |
|---|---|---|---|---|
| 1 | 8201 | 422 | (7344, 9058) | (5328, 11074) |

**Values of Predictors for New Observations**

| New Obs | X1 | X2 |
|---|---|---|
| 1 | 75.0 | 160 |

The first line of the output gives the equation of the Estimated Regression Line of Y on $X_1$ and $X_2$ as

$$\hat{y} = -3022 + 53.2 \, x_1 + 45.2 \, x_2.$$

Notice that Minitab omits the hat (^) from above the y in the actual output.

In the next part of the output, the values of $b_0$, $b_1$ and $b_2$ are displayed under the **Coef** column with more decimal places than in the equation above. The rest of this section of the output will be discussed in the next chapter. The next line of the output is the value of $s_{y.x,}$ which is the point estimate of $\sigma$ (the common standard deviation of the Y values in each subpopulation), the value of the Coefficient of Determination $r^2$ and an adjusted $r^2$; and these will be discussed later in this chapter. The **Analysis of Variance** table is used to test the validity of assumption (1) that the two variables are linearly related, and has previously been discussed.

When $x_{1o} = 75$ and $x_{2o} = 160$, the values entered for the predictors (beds and annual total patient days) in the Regression Options dialog box, the predicted value of y (annual total patient care revenue) is $\hat{y} = \$820,100$ (remember that the values of Y were in $100 units, so you must multiple the $\hat{y}$ value of 8201 by 100), which is displayed under the **Fit** heading near the end of the output.

The predicted annual total patient care revenue in $100 for a proposed new nursing facility with 75 beds and 160 annual total patient days could have been done using the Estimated Regression Equation given at the top of the output and a calculator. Substitute 75, the known value of the "predictor" ($X_1$) and 160, the known value of the "predictor" ($X_2$) variables into the equation for the Estimated Regression Line and compute the predicted job completion time as

$$\hat{y} = [-3022 + 53.2(75) + 45.2(160)] \times 100$$
$$\hat{y} = 8200 \times 100$$
$$\hat{y} = \$820,000$$

However, Minitab computes this value using the values of $b_0$, $b_1$ and $b_2$ with more decimal places, and displays a somewhat more accurate result of 8201 for $\hat{y}$ under the heading **Fit** in the output.

Once assumptions (1) and (2) have been verified, point estimates ($\hat{y}$) are legitimate; however prediction intervals may not be reported until the assumption (3) that each subpopulation of Y values is normally distributed has been verified. This assumption (3) can be verified using a Q-Q plot and the Anderson-Darling test which were introduced in Chapter 9 and shown again in Chapter 11.

Assumption (3), that each subpopulation of Y values is normally distributed, may be verified by graphing a **Q-Q plot**. This graph uses the residual values (computed by the storage option in the regression procedure) on the horizontal axis and the standard normalized values of these residuals on the y axis. After the residuals are sorted into increasing order; for each individual residual, the percentage of all of the residuals that are less than this residual is computed. This percentage is sometimes called the quantile. The standard normalized scores are values of Z that have the same quantile as the corresponding residual. This is why the graph is called a **Q-Q plot**. If each residual quantile is equal (or almost equal) to each corresponding standard normal quantile, the graph will be approximately a straight line. The Q-Q plot is graphed as follows.

Click on *Stat*, *Basic Statistics*, *Normality Test...*

In the Normality Test dialog box: the cursor will be in the box to the right of *Variable:* click on the RESI1 variable (or Corresp R) and click on the Select button. Under the heading of *Percentile lines*, the button to the left of *None* should be chosen. Make sure that under the *Tests for Normality* that the *Anderson-Darling* choice is marked. Next click inside of the *Title:* box and type Q-Q Plot, but remember do **not** press the Enter key. Then click on the OK button.

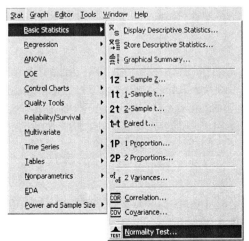

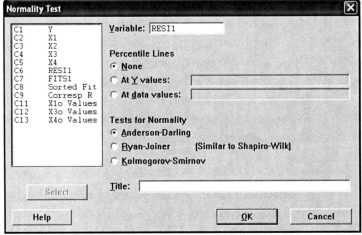

The resulting graph will appear in a separate Graphics Window. In addition to the actual Q-Q plot the results of the Anderson-Darling test for normality will be given. This test essentially is

H$_0$: the subpopulations of Y scores are all normally distributed
H$_a$: the subpopulations of Y scores are **not** all normally distributed
$\alpha = 0.10$ .

544

The AD test statistic and corresponding p-value are given in this Graphics Window. If the p-value is greater than 0.10, we usually do **not** reject the null hypothesis. And since we have no reason to doubt the validity of assumption (3), a prediction interval for the (future) actual value of Y corresponding to the given values of $X_1$, $X_2$, ... , $X_k$ may be used. However; if this p-value is less than or equal to 0.05, the null hypothesis **is** rejected, and assumption (3) is **not** validated. And so prediction intervals for the (future) actual values of Y **may not** be accurate and **should not** be reported.

> Example 13.8: Use the data in the current worksheet and check the validity of assumption (3) that the subpopulations of task completion times are all normally distributed by graphing the Q-Q plot and testing for normality.

Click on *Stat , Basic Statistics , Normality Test...*

In the Normality Test dialog box: the cursor will be in the box to the right of *Variable:* click on the RESI1 variable (you will get the exact same results if you click on the Corresp R variable instead of the RESI1 variable) and click on the | Select | button. Under the heading of *Percentile lines*, the button to the left of *None* should be chosen. Make sure that under the *Tests for Normality* that the *Anderson-Darling* choice is marked. Next click inside of the *Title:* box and type Q-Q Plot, but remember do **not** press the | Enter | key. Then click on | OK |.

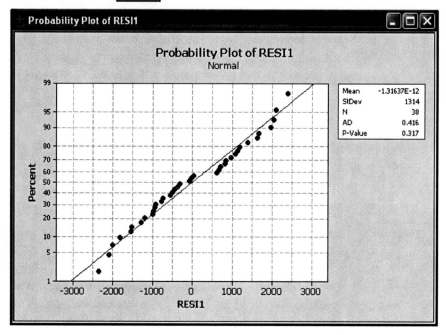

You will likely need to "maximize" the Graphics Window in order to clearly read the AD test statistic and p-value. The resulting Q-Q plot that appears in the Graphics Window is shown below.

Since the p-value of 0.317 is greater than $\alpha = 0.10$, you may not reject the null hypothesis of normality; and so you may conclude that assumption (3) **is valid**. Also notice that the points in the graph are close to the superimposed straight line that Minitab draws for comparison.

Once assumption (3) that the subpopulations of Y scores are all normally distributed has been verified, prediction intervals for the unknown Y value corresponding to a given $X_1, X_2, \ldots, X_k$ values may be computed. While Minitab sets the default confidence level at 95%, for any specific problem the desired confidence level for the prediction interval is entered in box to the right of *Confidence level:* in the Regression-Options dialog box.

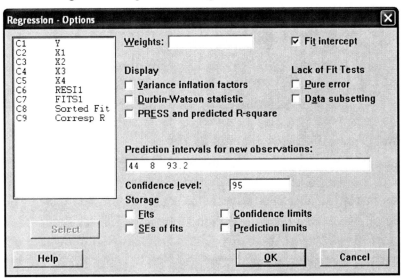

Example 13.9:   Since assumption (3) of normality has been verified, use the data in the current worksheet and complete the task in Example 13.1 by computing the 90% prediction interval for the annual total patient care revenue of a proposed new nursing facility that will have 75 beds and 160 annual total patient days.

Click on *Stat*, *Regression*, *Regression...*

In the Regression dialog box, the cursor should be in the box to the right of the *Response:* heading; click on the "response" (Y) variable and click on the Select button. The cursor will move down to the *Predictors:* box; hold the Ctrl key and click on each of the "predictor" (X) variables, and then click on the Select button. Next click on the Options... button. Note that since Minitab remembers the information in the dialog boxes from the previous time, you will only need to click on Options... .

In the Regression-Options dialog box, click inside of the box below the *Prediction intervals for new observations:* heading, type in 75  160, the known values of $X_1$ and $X_2$ for the new object. Now click inside of the box to the right of *Confidence level:*, erase the 95 that is currently in this box and type in 90, the desired confidence level for this example. Click on the OK button.

Back in the Regression dialog box, click on the OK button.

Since the first part of the output in the Session Window is the same as for the previous Example 13.7, only the last few lines pertaining to the prediction of Y are shown on the next page.

(continued on the next page)

**Predicted Values for New Observations**

**New**

| Obs | Fit | SE Fit | 90% CI | 90% PI |
|---|---|---|---|---|
| 1 | 8201 | 422 | (7488, 8914) | (5810, 10592) |

**Values of Predictors for New Observations**

**New**

| Obs | X1 | X2 |
|---|---|---|
| 1 | 75.0 | 160 |

The 8201 under the **Fit** heading is the point predictor of the task completion time as illustrated in Example 11.9. Now that assumption (3) of normality has been verified, the 90% prediction interval under the **90% P.I.** heading may be reported. And so the industry financial advisor is 90% certain that for a for a proposed new nursing facility with 75 beds and 160 annual total patient days, that the interval from $581,000 to $1,059,200 (5810 x 100 to 10592 x 100) will contain that proposed new nursing facility's annual total patient care revenue. This prediction interval is fairly wide; but this could have been anticipated since the estimated subpopulation standard deviation ($\sigma_{y.x}$) is s = $1,350.86, and this is relatively large.

The next example will combine all of the previous concepts and procedures into one unified example.

Example 13.10:  An official in the Department of Agriculture wants to be able to predict the grain yield per acre for the winter wheat crop. He decides that four potential "predictor" variables are: pounds per acre of fertilizer used, cost per pound of seed, previous summer crop grain yield per acre, and the soil quality index. The official wants to compute a 98% prediction interval for the winter wheat crop for the upcoming winter planting where the fertilizer used is 2.55, seed cost is 55, summer yield is 59 and soil index is 46. A baseline sample of plantings in ten previous years was taken with the following results:

| Fertilizer in Pounds | Cost of Seed | Summer Grain Yield | Soil Index | Winter Grain Yield |
|---|---|---|---|---|
| 2.40 | 38 | 67 | 65 | 49 |
| 2.25 | 47 | 64 | 54 | 58 |
| 2.35 | 45 | 63 | 59 | 52 |
| 2.50 | 49 | 161 | 52 | 59 |
| 2.50 | 57 | 60 | 40 | 70 |
| 2.30 | 46 | 72 | 57 | 56 |
| 2.75 | 57 | 66 | 43 | 64 |
| 3.00 | 46 | 65 | 65 | 50 |
| 3.25 | 50 | 60 | 55 | 61 |
| 2.80 | 49 | 64 | 42 | 92 |

(continued on the next page)

547

Click on *File, New, Minitab Project* to begin a fresh (new) Minitab Session. Enter these data into five variables directly in the Worksheet Window and name the Fertilizer in Pounds column as X1, the Cost of Seed column as X2, the Summer Grain Yield column as X3, the Soil Index column as X4, and the Winter GrainYield column as Y.

The first step is to matrix scatterplots of Y on the set of $(X_1, X_2)$, and check for any needed data corrections.

Click on *Graph , Matrix Plot...*

In the Matrix Plots dialog box: the *Matrix of plots Simple* graph should be highlighted. Next click on the | **OK** | button.

In the Matrix Plots - Matrix of Plots Simple: you may need to press the | **F3** | key to clear any previous information. The cursor will be in the box under the *Graph variables:* heading. Hold the | **Ctrl** | key and click on the X1 and X2 variables, and then click on the | **Select** | button. Now highlight the Y variable and click on the | **Select** | button. Then click on the | **Matrix Options...** | button.

In the Matrix Plot - Options dialog box: under the *Matrix Display* heading,click on the circle to the left of *Lower left*, and under the *Variable Label Placement* heading, click on the circle to the left of *Boundary*. Then click on the | **OK** | button.

Back in Matrix Plots - Matrix of Plots Simple: click on the | **OK** | button.

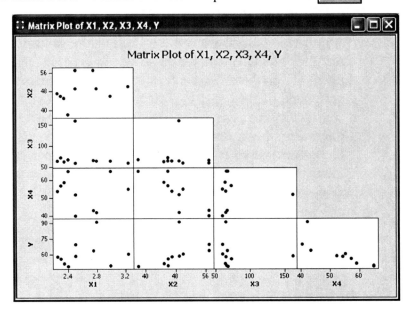

From these graphs, we see that Y appears to be linearly related to both $X_2$ and $X_4$, but marginally linearly related to $X_1$ and not related at all to $X_3$. We will see more about htis later in this Chapter. The interrelationships among the $X_i$ variables is left to a more advanced text.

The next step is to identify outliers and examine them for correctness.

(continued on the next page)

Click on *Stat*, *Regression*, *Regression* ...

In the Regression dialog box, since this is a **new** problem, press the | **F3** | key to clear any previous information from all Regression dialog boxes. The cursor should be in the box to the right of the *Response:* heading; click on the "response" variable - Y and click on the | **Select** | button. The cursor will move down to the *Predictors:* box; hold the | **Ctrl** | key and click on the "predictor" variables - X1, X2, X3 and X4, and then click on the | **Select** | button. Then click on the | **OK** | button.

Only the end of the output in the Session Window is shown below.

## Unusual Observations

| Obs | X1 | Y | Fit | SE Fit | Residual | St Resid |
|-----|------|-------|-------|--------|----------|----------|
| 4 | 2.50 | 59.00 | 59.18 | 4.17 | -0.18 | -0.47 X |
| 10 | 2.80 | 92.00 | 88.58 | 3.83 | 3.42 | 2.01 R |

**R denotes an observation with a large standardized residual.**
**X denotes an observation whose X value gives it large influence.**

After examining the data for cases (**ROW**s) 4 and 10, the official finds that:

(1)   Case 4 contains an incorrect value for the Summer Grain Yield (X3) variable; this value should have been 61 instead of 161; therefore this case will be corrected.

(2)   Case 10 contains no errors; and therefore, this case will be retained as is.

Click on the cell in the 4th row of the X3 column, and enter the correct value of 61.

Then redo the *Stat, Regression*, *Regression* procedure to identify any additional outliers in this sample.

Click on *Stat*, *Regression*, *Regression* ...

In the Regression dialog box, the cursor should be in the box to the right of the *Response:* heading; click on the "response" variable - Y and click on the | **Select** | button. The cursor will move down to the *Predictors:* box; hold the | **Ctrl** | key and click on the "predictor" variables - X1, X2, X3 and X4, and then click on the | **Select** | button. Then click on the | **OK** | button. Note that since Minitab remembers the information in the dialog boxes from the previous time, you will only need to click on the | **OK** | button.

Only the end of the output in the Session Window is shown below.

## Unusual Observations

| Obs | X1 | Y | Fit | SE Fit | Residual | St Resid |
|-----|------|-------|-------|--------|----------|----------|
| 10 | 2.80 | 92.00 | 88.81 | 3.81 | 3.19 | 2.01 R |

**R denotes an observation with a large standardized residual.**

Since this 10th observation is known to be correct, we leave it in the baseline sample and continue on to check assumption (1)

(continued on the next page)

The next step is to check the validity of assumption (1) that Y is linearly related to the set of $X_1, X_2, ... , X_k$.

The hypothesis testing problem is:

$H_0$: the set of $X_1$, $X_2$ and the Y variable are **not** linearly related
$H_a$: the set of $X_1$, $X_2$ and the Y variable **are** linearly related
$\alpha = 0.05$

and the test statistic is $F = \dfrac{\text{MS for Regression}}{\text{MS for Residual Error}}$.

Slowly scrow a few lines up in the Session Window until you see the following **Analysis of Variance** table.

### Analysis of Variance

| Source | DF | SS | MS | F | P |
|---|---|---|---|---|---|
| Regression | 4 | 1349.88 | 337.47 | 19.85 | 0.003 |
| Residual Error | 5 | 85.02 | 17.00 | | |
| Total | 9 | 1434.90 | | | |

From the results in the **Analysis of Variance** table, the F test statistic is 19.85, and since the p-value of 0.003 is less than the given value of $\alpha = 0.05$, the null hypothesis **is rejected** and you may conclude that the Y variable is linearly related to the set of $X_1, X_2, ... , X_k$ variables. And so assumption (1) **is verified**.

The next step is to verify the assumption (2) that the variances of Y in all of the subpopulations are equal. Compute the residuals and then plot the residual versus $\hat{y}$ graph to see if assumption (2) appears to be valid; and, if not, to see what the violating pattern looks like.

Click on *Stat , Regression , Regression ...*

In the Regression dialog box, the cursor should be in the box to the right of the *Response:* heading; click on the "response" variable - Y and click on the | **Select** | button. The cursor will move down to the *Predictors:* box; hold the | **Ctrl** | key and click on the "predictor" variables - X1, X2, X3 and X4, and then click on the | **Select** | button. Then click on the | **OK** | button. Next click on the | **Storage...** | button. Note that since Minitab remembers the information in the dialog boxes from the previous time, you will only need to click on the | **Storage...** | button.

In the Regression - Storage dialog box, click in the squares to the left of *Residuals* and to the left of *Fits* to check these two options. No other options should be checked. Then click on | **OK** | . Two new columns automatically will be created and named FITS1 and RESI1. The column numbers will be one and two higher than the last column used in the current Worksheet Window.

Back in the Regression dialog box, click on | **OK** | .

(continued on the next page)

The resulting Worksheet Window is shown below.

| | C1 | C2 | C3 | C4 | C5 | C6 | C7 |
|---|---|---|---|---|---|---|---|
| | X1 | X2 | X3 | X4 | Y | RESI1 | FITS1 |
| 1 | 2.40 | 38 | 67 | 65 | 49 | -5.25927 | 54.2593 |
| 2 | 2.25 | 47 | 64 | 54 | 58 | 1.69905 | 56.3010 |
| 3 | 2.35 | 45 | 63 | 59 | 52 | 1.36336 | 50.6366 |
| 4 | 2.50 | 49 | 61 | 52 | 59 | -0.89699 | 59.8970 |
| 5 | 2.50 | 57 | 60 | 40 | 70 | 0.49685 | 69.5032 |
| 6 | 2.30 | 46 | 72 | 57 | 56 | 1.58294 | 54.4171 |
| 7 | 2.75 | 57 | 66 | 43 | 64 | -4.23589 | 68.2359 |
| 8 | 3.00 | 46 | 65 | 65 | 50 | 4.10103 | 45.8990 |
| 9 | 3.25 | 50 | 60 | 55 | 61 | -2.03621 | 63.0362 |
| 10 | 2.80 | 49 | 64 | 42 | 92 | 3.18514 | 88.8149 |

Click on *Graph , Scatterplot ...*

In the Scatterplots dialog box: the *Simple* graph should be highlighted. Next click on the OK button.

In the Scatterplot - Simple dialog box: the cursor will be in the box on the first line under the *Y variables* heading; click on the RESI1 variable and click on the Select button. The cursor will move to the box in the first line under the *X variables* heading; click on the FITS1 variable and click on the Select button. Then click on the OK button.

Double click on the X axis label of FITS1 and rename this axis as y hat. Double click on the Y axis label of RESI1 and rename this axis Residuals.

The graph shown below will appear in the Scatterplot of FITS1 vs RESI1 Graphics Window.

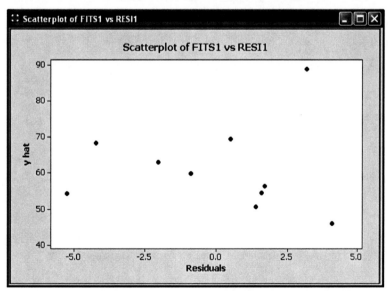

With only ten points it is difficult to determine any definite pattern, but since the points on this graph do not appear to have any well defined **non** rectangular shape, we will say that the points appear to be randomly and evenly spread within a general rectangular shape. Since the graph does not indicate any unusual pattern, the modified Levene's test is done next to confirm the validity of assumption (2).

(continued on the next page)

The hypotheses for testing assumption (2) that all subpopulation variances are equal (i.e., homogeneity of variance) when using Levene's test slightly change to

$H_0$: all subpopulation variances are equal
$H_a$: the subpopulation variances are in a megaphone shape
$\alpha = 0.10$

and the test statistic is the Levene's test statistic.

First name the three new columns (C8, C9 and C10) as Sorted Fit, Corresp R and Factor.

Click on *Data*, *Sort...*

In the Sort dialog box, the cursor will be in the box under the *Sort Column(s):* heading. Highlight the FITS1 column only and click on | Select | . Then highlight the RESI1 column only and click on | Select |. **It is important that these two variables be entered in this order.** Next click inside the box to the right of the first *By column:* heading, click on the FITS1 variable, and click on | Select | . Next click on the circle to the left of *Column(s) of current worksheet:*, and then click inside of the box under this heading. inside of the box under the *Store sorted column(s) in:* heading, hold the | Ctrl | key and click on the Sorted Fit and Corresp R variables to highlight them both. **It is important that these two variables be entered in this order.** Then click on | Select | . Now click on | OK | .

The resulting Worksheet Window is shown below.

| | C1 | C2 | C3 | C4 | C5 | C6 | C7 | C8 | C9 | C10 |
|---|------|-----|-----|-----|-----|---------|---------|------------|-----------|--------|
| | X1 | X2 | X3 | X4 | Y | RESI1 | FITS1 | Sorted Fit | Corresp R | Factor |
| 1 | 2.40 | 38 | 67 | 65 | 49 | -5.25927 | 54.2593 | 45.8990 | 4.10103 | |
| 2 | 2.25 | 47 | 64 | 54 | 58 | 1.69905 | 56.3010 | 50.6366 | 1.36336 | |
| 3 | 2.35 | 45 | 63 | 59 | 52 | 1.36336 | 50.6366 | 54.2593 | -5.25927 | |
| 4 | 2.50 | 49 | 61 | 52 | 59 | -0.89699 | 59.8970 | 54.4171 | 1.58294 | |
| 5 | 2.50 | 57 | 60 | 40 | 70 | 0.49685 | 69.5032 | 56.3010 | 1.69905 | |
| 6 | 2.30 | 46 | 72 | 57 | 56 | 1.58294 | 54.4171 | 59.8970 | -0.89699 | |
| 7 | 2.75 | 57 | 66 | 43 | 64 | -4.23589 | 68.2359 | 63.0362 | -2.03621 | |
| 8 | 3.00 | 46 | 65 | 65 | 50 | 4.10103 | 45.8990 | 68.2359 | -4.23589 | |
| 9 | 3.25 | 50 | 60 | 55 | 61 | -2.03621 | 63.0362 | 69.5032 | 0.49685 | |
| 10 | 2.80 | 49 | 64 | 42 | 92 | 3.18514 | 88.8149 | 88.8149 | 3.18514 | |

Next the minimum, the middle two scores and the maximum need to be determined. The *Stat*, *Basic Statistics*, *Describe Statistics* menu procedure will find the minimum, the maximum and the number of scores for the Sorted X variable.

Click on *Stat*, *Basic Statistics*, *Describe Statistics*

In the Display Descriptive Statistics dialog box: highlight the Sorted X variable, click on the | Select | button, and then click on the | Statistics... | button.

In the Descriptive Statistics - Statistics dialog box: click to uncheck all boxes **except** for the *Minimum*, *Maximum* and *N nonmissing* statistics. (See graphic on the next page).

(continued on the next page)

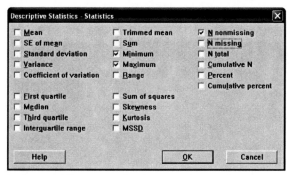

The results shown below will appear in the Session Window.

## Descriptive Statistics: Sorted Fit

| Variable | N | Minimum | Maximum |
|----------|-----|---------|---------|
| Sorted Fit | 10 | 45.90 | 88.81 |

Since the number of objects (n = 10) is an even number then the two middle scores will be in the rows numbered 5 (n/2) and 6 (n/2 + 1). Looking in the Worksheet window shown on the previous page, the $5^{th}$ row of Sorted Fit contains 56.3010, and the $6^{th}$ row contains 59.8970. Since Minitab has rounded off these numbers, $m_1$ and $m_2$ must be slightly exaggerated. As described earlier in this chapter let $m_1 = 56.3011$ and let $m_2 = 59.8969$. Next look in output shown above of the *Stat, Basic Statistics, Display Descriptive Statistics* procedure to find the minimum and maximum of the Sorted Fit values. The Minitab rounded off values of the minimum and maximum values of the Sorted Fit variable are 45.90 and 88.81 respectively. Adjust the min value by subtracting 0.01 from the 45.90, and adjust the max value by adding 0.01 to 88.81. In this example let min = 45.89 and let max = 88.82.

Next put Lo in the first half of the Factor column and put Hi in the second half.

Click on *Data, Code, Numeric to Text ...*

In the Code - Numeric to Text dialog box, the cursor should be in the box under the heading *Code data from columns:*. Click on the Sorted Fit variable and click on the | **Select** | button. Next click in the *Into columns:* box, click on the Factor variable, and click on the | **Select** | button. Then click in the first box under the *Original values* heading and type in 45.89 : 56.3011 (min : $m_1$). Next click in the first box under the *New:* heading and type in the word Lo. Similarly click on the second row in the box under the *Original values* heading and type in 59.8969 : 88.82 ($m_2$ : max). Next click in the box under the *New:* heading and type in the word Hi. Then click on | **OK** | .

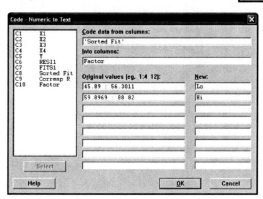

(continued on the next page)

The resulting Worksheet Window is shown below.

| ↓ | C1 | C2 | C3 | C4 | C5 | C6 | C7 | C8 | C9 | C10-T |
|---|------|------|------|------|------|---------|---------|------------|-----------|--------|
| | X1 | X2 | X3 | X4 | Y | RESI1 | FITS1 | Sorted Fit | Corresp R | Factor |
| 1 | 2.40 | 38 | 67 | 65 | 49 | -5.25927 | 54.2593 | 45.8990 | 4.10103 | Lo |
| 2 | 2.25 | 47 | 64 | 54 | 58 | 1.69905 | 56.3010 | 50.6366 | 1.36336 | Lo |
| 3 | 2.35 | 45 | 63 | 59 | 52 | 1.36336 | 50.6366 | 54.2593 | -5.25927 | Lo |
| 4 | 2.50 | 49 | 61 | 52 | 59 | -0.89699 | 59.8970 | 54.4171 | 1.58294 | Lo |
| 5 | 2.50 | 57 | 60 | 40 | 70 | 0.49685 | 69.5032 | 56.3010 | 1.69905 | Lo |
| 6 | 2.30 | 46 | 72 | 57 | 56 | 1.58294 | 54.4171 | 59.8970 | -0.89699 | Hi |
| 7 | 2.75 | 57 | 66 | 43 | 64 | -4.23589 | 68.2359 | 63.0362 | -2.03621 | Hi |
| 8 | 3.00 | 46 | 65 | 65 | 50 | 4.10103 | 45.8990 | 68.2359 | -4.23589 | Hi |
| 9 | 3.25 | 50 | 60 | 55 | 61 | -2.03621 | 63.0362 | 69.5032 | 0.49685 | Hi |
| 10 | 2.80 | 49 | 64 | 42 | 92 | 3.18514 | 88.8149 | 88.8149 | 3.18514 | Hi |

Finally, assumption (2) is verified by the hypothesis testing of

$H_0$: all subpopulation variances are equal
$H_a$: the subpopulation variances are in a megaphone shape
$\alpha = 0.10$

and the test statistic is the Levene's test statistic.

Click on *Stat* , *ANOVA* , *Test for Equal Variances...*

In the Test for Equal Variances dialog box: the cursor will be in the box to the right of *Response:*. Click on the Corresp R variable and click on the $\boxed{\text{Select}}$ button. The cursor will move to the large box to the right of *Factors:*, click on the Factor variable and then click on the $\boxed{\text{Select}}$ button. You may ignore the boxes to the right of *Confidence level:* and *Title:*. Then click on the $\boxed{\text{OK}}$ button.

The results shown on the next page will appear in a separate Graphics Window.

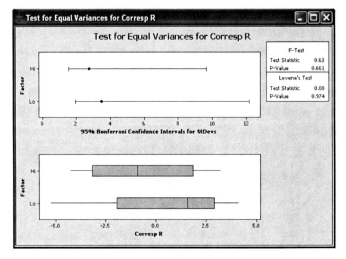

Since the Levene's test p-value of 0.974 is greater than $\alpha = 0.10$, the null hypothesis of equal subpopulation variances (homogeneity) may not be rejected. And since the graph of the Residuals versus the Fitted Values is not suspicious, thus assumption (2) is verified. Therefore **point predictions** may be made using multiple linear regression.

(continued on the next page)

Now that assumptions (1) and (2) have been verified, a point estimate may be computed. However, since the company manager wanted a 90% confidence interval, assumption (3) that the subpopulations of Y scores are all normally distributed needs to be checked.

The hypotheses are:

$H_0$: the subpopulations of Y scores are all normally distributed
$H_a$: the subpopulations of Y scores are **not** all normally distributed
$\alpha = 0.10$,

and the test statistic is AD.

Click on *Stat , Basic Statistics , Normality Test...*

In the Normality Test dialog box, press the $\boxed{\textbf{F3}}$ key to clear any previous contents. The cursor will be in the box to the right of *Variable:* click on the RESI1 variable (you will get the exact same results if you click on the Corresp R variable instead of the RESI1 variable) and click on the $\boxed{\textbf{Select}}$ button. Under the heading of *Percentile lines*, the button to the left of *None* should be chosen. Make sure that under the *Tests for Normality* that the *Anderson-Darling* choice is marked. Next click inside of the *Title:* box and type Q-Q Plot, but remember do **not** press the $\boxed{\textbf{Enter}}$ key. Then click on $\boxed{\textbf{OK}}$ .

You will likely need to "maximize" the Graphics Window in order to clearly read the AD test statistic and p-value. The resulting Q-Q plot that appears in the Graphics Window is shown below.

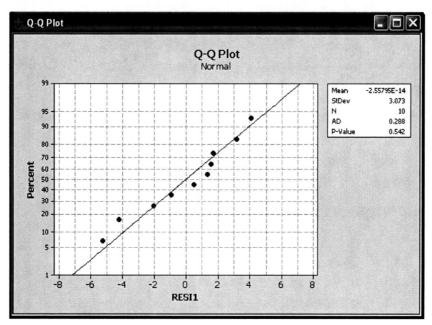

Since the p-value of 0.422 is greater than $\alpha = 0.10$, you may not reject the null hypothesis of normality. And so you may conclude that assumption (3) **is valid**, and prediction intervals using this baseline sample may be reported. Also notice that the points in the graph are close to the superimposed straight line that Minitab draws for comparison.

(continued on the next page)

Once assumption (3) that the subpopulations of Y scores are all normally distributed has been verified, the desired 98% prediction interval for the winter wheat crop for the upcoming winter planting where the fertilizer used is 2.55, seed cost is 55, summer yield is 59 and soil index is 46 may be computed.

Click on *Stat*, *Regression*, *Regression ...*

In the Regression dialog box, the cursor should be in the box to the right of the *Response:* heading; click on the "response" (Y) variable and click on the | **Select** | button. The cursor will move down to the *Predictors:* box; hold the | **Ctrl** | key and click on each of the four "predictor" (X) variables, and then click on the | **Select** | button. Next click on the | **Storage...** | button. Note that since Minitab remembers the information in the dialog boxes from the previous time, you will only need to click on the | **Storage...** | button.

In the Regression - Storage dialog box, click in the squares to the left of *Residuals* and to the left of *Fits* to **uncheck** these two options. Then click on | **OK** | .

Back in the Regression dialog box, click on the | **Options...** | button.

In the Regression-Options dialog box, click inside of the box below the *Prediction intervals for new observations:* heading, type in 2.55 55 59 46, the known values of $X_1$, $X_2$, $X_3$ and $X_4$ for the new planting. Now click inside of the box to the right of *Confidence level:*, erase the 95 that is currently in this box and type in 98, the desired confidence level for this example. Click on the | **OK** | button.

Back in the Regression dialog box, click on the | **OK** | button.

Only the last few lines pertaining to the prediction of Y of the output in the Session Window are shown below.

### Predicted Values for New Observations

| New Obs | Fit | SE Fit | 98% CI | 98% PI |
|---------|-------|--------|------------------|------------------|
| 1 | 60.69 | 2.96 | (50.73, 70.64) | (43.61, 77.76) |

### Values of Predictors for New Observations

| New Obs | X1 | X2 | X3 | X4 |
|---------|------|------|------|------|
| 1 | 2.55 | 55.0 | 59.0 | 46.0 |

And so the Department of Agriculture official is 98% certain that for a for a new planting when the fertilizer used is 2.55, seed cost is 55, summer yield is 59 and soil index is 46, that the interval from 43.61 to 77.76 will contain the winter grain yield per acre.

There are problems in which one can think of many potential "predictor" variables, but including all of these predictor variables may be cumbersome and expensive. Often, including some of the possible "predictor" variables does not make the predictions any better, and may be counter productive. This can be seen by examining the section of the *Regression* output that contains the values of the coefficients $b_0$, $b_1$, ... , $b_k$ to more decimal places than shown in the equation at the beginning of the output. In addition to these more accurate values, there are values of a t test statistic and p-value for testing the hypothesis of $H_0$: $\beta_i = 0$. If the p-value is small, then this indicates that $H_0$: should be rejected, that specific $\beta_i$ is different from 0, and so that the corresponding "predictor" variable belongs in the equation. However if the p-value is large, than this indicates that $H_0$: should not be rejected, that $\beta_i = 0$, and since 0 time $x_i$ equals 0, this specific "predictor" variable does not add anything to the prediction and should not be included in the equation. It is not as simple as the above makes it sound, since there are interrelationships that complicate the process, and so one must develop a strategy for deciding which "predictor" variables are to kept and which are not needed.

There are several different strategies for deciding which specific "predictor" variables should be included in the Estimated Multiple Linear Regression Equation. Stepwise regression is a common technique, easy to use, and usually an effective strategy. Stepwise regression finds the smallest subset of the "predictor" variables such that:

(1)     this subset of "predictor" variables are <u>linearly</u> related to the Y variable, and

(2)     the addition of any other "predictor" variable(s) will not add a statistically significant improvement to the prediction process.

The coefficient of determination ($r^2$) is computed between each potential "predictor" variable ($X_i$) and the "response" variable (Y), and these linear relationships are evaluated. If none of the $X_i$ variables have a significant linear relationship with Y, the process stops. But if at least one $r^2$ is statistically significant; the $X_i$ with the largest $r^2$ is chosen, and the Estimated Linear Regression Equation of Y on this one $X_i$ is computed. This is step 1.

After step 1, the amount of improvement to the prediction process that would be obtained by adding each of the remaining "predictor" variables is computed. If for all of the remaining variables this improvement is not statistically significant, the process stops; otherwise, the variable which adds the most improvement is added to the Estimated Multiple Linear Regression Equation, and this becomes step 2. Then each variable now in the Estimated Multiple Linear Regression Equation is re-evaluated. The amount of improvement provided by each "predictor" variable **now in** the equation over the **other** variable(s) <u>in</u> the equation is evaluated. If **any** variable's improvement is not statistically significant; that variable is removed from the equation, and the reduced Estimated Multiple Linear Regression Equation is computed as step 3. Sometimes a combination of variables added at later steps will cause an earlier added "predictor" variable to be superfluous. (When each "predictor" variable in the Estimated Multiple Linear Regression Equation at step 2 provides significant improvement to the prediction process, step 3 is not done.) Stepwise regression repeats the procedure just described in this paragraph until no new "predictor" variable is added and no included "predictor" variable is removed.

The Stepwise regression procedure is computed using the Minitab *Stat , Regression , Stepwise...* procedure.

Click on *Stat , Regression , Stepwise...*

In the Stepwise Regression dialog box: the cursor should be in the box to the right of the *Response:* heading; click on the "response" (Y) variable and click on the ☐ **Select** button. The cursor will move down to the *Predictors:* box. Hold the ☐ **Ctrl** key click and click on each of the potential "predictor" ($X_i$) variables, and then click on the ☐ **Select** button. Then click on the ☐ **OK** button.

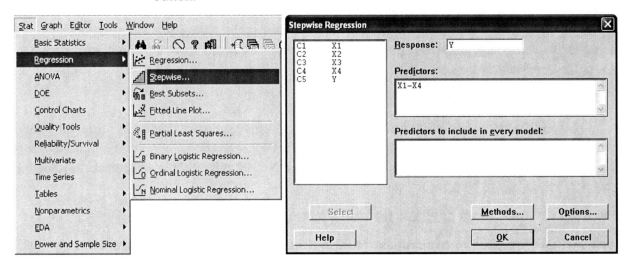

The output of the *Stepwise* regression procedure includes several pieces of information, but the main things of interest to us are the steps in the stepwise analysis. These steps are displayed as columns where each column contains:

(1)    the step number,

(2)    the value of the constant $b_0$ for that step,

(3)    the variable being added or subtracted from the Estimated Multiple Linear Regression Equation,

(4)    the value(s) of the coefficients $b_i$ for all "predictor" variables included for that step,

(5)    the value of the t test statistic and p-value used to decide if each included variable should remain or be removed, and

(6)    the values of s, $r^2$ and $r^2$ adjusted for that step.

The *Stepwise* procedure displays the following message at the bottom:

**MORE?  (Yes, No, Subcommand, or Help)**
**SUBC>**

If fewer than five (5) steps are shown; the stepwise regression is complete, and you are to enter **NO** in the Session Window to the right of the **SUBC>** prompt, and the *Stepwise* regression procedure is complete. But if five (5) steps are shown; then there <u>may</u> be more steps, and you are to enter **YES** in the Session Window to the right of the **SUBC>** prompt.

If there are exactly five steps, the following message is displayed

### *NO VARIABLES ENTERED OR REMOVED*
### *SUBC>*

and you are to enter **NO** in the Session Window to the right of the **SUBC>** prompt, and the *Stepwise* regression procedure is complete. But <u>if</u> there are more than five steps, the next screen will display the next series of five or fewer steps. If fewer than five steps are displayed; the stepwise regression process is complete, and you are to enter **NO** at the **SUBC>** prompt, but if a full five additional steps are shown; you are to enter **YES** at the **SUBC>** prompt and continue.


At this point a short description of $r^2$ adjusted, symbolized in Minitab as R-sq (adj), is needed. The Coefficient of Determination ($r^2$) measure the strength of the linear relationship between the Y variable and the set of $X_1$, $X_2$, ... , $X_k$ variables. However using multi-dimensional geometric concepts, it is easy to show that for a fixed number of observations, the value of $r^2$ automatically gets larger as you include more predictor variables into the equation. In fact if you have n observations in the baseline sample and (n-1) predictor variables in the equation, then the value of $r^2$ **must be equal to 1** regardless of whether or not there is any linear relationship. In other words, as you add additional "predictor" variables tpo the equation, the value of $r^2$ is inflated above its intended meaning. The formula used to compute $r^2$ adjusted attempts to adjust for this geometric inflation, and thus produces a reduced but usually more accurate value for the Coefficient of Determination. When using multiple regression, many people use the $r^2$ adjusted value to evaluate the strength of the linear relationship and to make comparisons with other sets of "predictor" variables.


Before the stepwise regression procedure is done, the standard Multiple Linear Regression analysis menu item *Stat , Regression, Regression* procedure should be computed and any "unusual observations" should be examined for errors. After any necessary corrections and/or deletions have been done, the *Stepwise* procedure is computed to find the smallest set of "predictor" variables needed for the particular problem. The *Stepwise* procedure will identify the significant "predictor" variables. Using those significant "predictor" variables, the standard Multiple Linear Regression process is performed. That is; these significant "predictor" variables are used in the Estimated Multiple Linear Regression Equation, the y-hat and residual values are computed, and the assumptions are checked. If assumptions (1) and (2) are verified, then a point prediction may be computed and reported. If assumption (3) is verified, the prediction interval may be reported. The following example incorporates all of these steps to compute the Estimated Multiple Linear Regression Equation.

Example 13.11: Open the worksheet Haldiec.mtw that is on your data disc. This worksheet contains data for one "response" variable Y and four "predictor" variables X1, X2, X3 and X4. Use the Stepwise Regression procedure to identify the best set of "predictor" variables.

Click on *File, New, Minitab Project* to begin a fresh (new) Minitab Session.

Use *File , Open Worksheet...* to open the worksheet Haldiec.mtw from your data disk.

First, in order to examine the data for outliers, use the *Regression* procedure using all four predictor variables.

Click on *Stat , Regression , Regression ...*

In the Regression dialog box, since this is a **new** problem, press the $\boxed{\text{F3}}$ key to clear any previous information from all Regression dialog boxes. The cursor should be in the box to the right of the *Response:* click on the Y variable and click on the $\boxed{\text{Select}}$ button. The cursor will move down to the *Predictors:* box; hold the $\boxed{\text{Ctrl}}$ key and click on each of the X1, X2, X3 and X4 variables, and then click on the $\boxed{\text{Select}}$ button. Then click on $\boxed{\text{OK}}$ .

The resulting output shown on the next page will appear in the Session Window.

## Regression Analysis: Y versus X1, X2, X3, X4

**The regression equation is**
**Y = 55.5 + 1.56 X1 + 0.602 X2 + 0.133 X3 - 0.069 X4**

| Predictor | Coef | SE Coef | T | P |
|-----------|--------|---------|-------|-------|
| Constant | 55.50 | 69.11 | 0.80 | 0.445 |
| X1 | 1.5606 | 0.7346 | 2.12 | 0.066 |
| X2 | 0.6018 | 0.7139 | 0.84 | 0.424 |
| X3 | 0.1329 | 0.7444 | 0.18 | 0.863 |
| X4 | -0.0688 | 0.6994 | -0.10 | 0.924 |

S = 2.41262   R-Sq = 98.3%   R-Sq(adj) = 97.4%

**Analysis of Variance**

| Source | DF | SS | MS | F | P |
|--------|-----|---------|--------|--------|-------|
| Regression | 4 | 2692.22 | 673.05 | 115.63 | 0.000 |
| Residual Error | 8 | 46.57 | 5.82 | | |
| Total | 12 | 2738.78 | | | |

| Source | DF | Seq SS |
|--------|-----|---------|
| X1 | 1 | 1426.25 |
| X2 | 1 | 1259.41 |
| X3 | 1 | 6.50 |
| X4 | 1 | 0.06 |

(continued on the next page)

First notice that there are no outliers identified by Minitab. Then notice that in the **Analysis of Variance** table; the p-value is 0.000, and this indicates that there is a linear relationship between Y and the set of $X_1$, $X_2$, $X_3$ and $X_4$. Also note the values of $s = 2.41262$, $r^2 = .983$ and $r^2$ adjusted $= .974$ which is reduced from the inflated value of $r^2$. Finally notice that the p-values in the coefficient table are all larger than 0.05, and some are very large. This indicates that some of these four "predictor" variables are not needed.

The next step is to use the *Stepwise* regression strategy to find the "best" subset of "predictor" variables.

Click on *Stat*, *Regression*, *Stepwise...*

In the Stepwise Regression dialog box: the cursor should be in the box to the right of the *Response:* heading; click on the Y variable and click on the ⬛ Select ⬛ button. The cursor will move down to the *Predictors:* box. Hold the ⬛ Ctrl ⬛ key click and click on each of the X!, X2, X3 and X4 variables, and then click on the ⬛ Select ⬛ button. Then click on the ⬛ OK ⬛ button.

The following output will appear in the Session Window.

## Stepwise Regression: Y versus X1, X2, X3, X4

**Alpha-to-Enter: 0.15  Alpha-to-Remove: 0.15**

**Response is Y on 4 predictors, with N = 13**

| Step | 1 | 2 | 3 | 4 |
|---|---|---|---|---|
| Constant | 118.01 | 103.77 | 67.55 | 52.28 |
| | | | | |
| X4 | -0.746 | -0.624 | -0.189 | |
| T-Value | -4.88 | -12.23 | -1.11 | |
| P-Value | 0.000 | 0.000 | 0.297 | |
| | | | | |
| X1 | | 1.42 | 1.43 | 1.44 |
| T-Value | | 9.76 | 12.39 | 12.43 |
| P-Value | | 0.000 | 0.000 | 0.000 |
| | | | | |
| X2 | | | 0.479 | 0.676 |
| T-Value | | | 2.62 | 15.40 |
| P-Value | | | 0.028 | 0.000 |
| | | | | |
| S | 8.87 | 2.87 | 2.28 | 2.30 |
| R-Sq | 68.37 | 97.00 | 98.29 | 98.06 |
| R-Sq(adj) | 65.49 | 96.40 | 97.72 | 97.67 |
| Mallows C-p | 139.8 | 7.1 | 3.0 | 2.1 |

**More? (Yes, No, Subcommand, or Help)**

**SUBC> NO**
**MTB >**

(continued on the next page)

Since there are only four (fewer than five) steps shown; the stepwise regression is complete, and you entered **NO** in the Session Window to the right of the **SUBC>** prompt.

This stepwise regression analysis has identified two statistically significant "predictor" variables: X1 and X2. These two are the "best" set of "predictor" variables and will be used in the Estimated Multiple Linear Regression Equation to predict values of the Y variable.

Example 13.12:  Use the data in the current worksheet, and compute a 90% prediction interval for the Y for two new observations: (a) $X_1 = 12$ and $X_2 = 31$, and (b) $X_1 = 16$ and $X_2 = 42$.

First graph the matrix scatterplots of Y on the set of $(X_1, X_2)$, and check for any needed data corrections.

Click on *Graph , Matrix Plot...*

In the Matrix Plots dialog box: the *Matrix of plots Simple* graph should be highlighted.  Next click on the ☐ **OK** ☐ button.

In the Matrix Plots - Matrix of Plots Simple: you may need to press the ☐ **F3** ☐ key to clear any previous information.  The cursor will be in the box under the *Graph variables:* heading.  Hold the ☐ **Ctrl** ☐ key and click on the X1 and X2 variables, and then click on the ☐ **Select** ☐ button.  Now highlight the Y variable and click on the ☐ **Select** ☐ button. Then click on the ☐ **Matrix Options...** ☐ button.

In the Matrix Plot - Options dialog box: under the *Matrix Display* heading, click on the circle to the left of *Lower left*, and under the *Variable Label Placement* heading, click on the circle to the left of *Boundary*.  Then click on the ☐ **OK** ☐ button.

Back in Matrix Plots - Matrix of Plots Simple: click on the ☐ **OK** ☐ button.

The following graph will appear in the separate Matrix Plot Graphics Window.

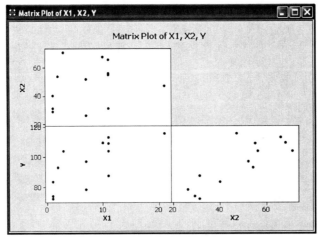

From these graphs, we see that y does seem to be linearly related to both $X_1$ and $X_2$, and that $X_1$ and $X_2$ are not related, which generally means that there is little overlap in the contribution these two variable make to the prediction process.

(continued on the next page)

562

The next step is to identify any outliers in this sample.

Click on *Stat , Regression , Regression ...*

In the Regression dialog box, since this is a **new** problem, press the | F3 | key to clear any previous information from all Regression dialog boxes. The cursor should be in the box to the right of the *Response:* heading; click on the "response" variable - Y and click on the | Select | button. The cursor will move down to the *Predictors:* box; hold the | Ctrl | key and click on the "predictor" variables - X1 and X2, and then click on the | Select | button. Then click on the | OK | button.

The output in the Session Window is shown below.

## Regression Analysis: Y versus X1, X2

### The regression equation is
### $Y = 52.3 + 1.44 X1 + 0.676 X2$

| Predictor | Coef | SE Coef | T | P |
|-----------|---------|---------|-------|-------|
| Constant | 52.281 | 2.190 | 23.88 | 0.000 |
| X1 | 1.4444 | 0.1162 | 12.43 | 0.000 |
| X2 | 0.67626 | 0.04392 | 15.40 | 0.000 |

$S = 2.30477$     $R\text{-}Sq = 98.1\%$     $R\text{-}Sq(adj) = 97.7\%$

### Analysis of Variance

| Source | DF | SS | MS | F | P |
|--------|----|--------|--------|--------|-------|
| Regression | 2 | 2685.7 | 1342.8 | 252.79 | 0.000 |
| Residual Error | 10 | 53.1 | 5.3 | | |
| Total | 12 | 2738.8 | | | |

| Source | DF | Seq SS |
|--------|----|--------|
| X1 | 1 | 1426.3 |
| X2 | 1 | 1259.4 |

Since there are no outliers identified by Minitab, the next step to check assumption (1)

The hypothesis testing problem is:

$H_0$: the set of $X_1$, $X_2$ and the Y variable are **not** linearly related
$H_a$: the set of $X_1$, $X_2$ and the Y variable **are** linearly related
$\alpha = 0.05$

and the test statistic is $F = \dfrac{MS \text{ for Regression}}{MS \text{ for Residual Error}}$ .

From the results in the **Analysis of Variance** table above, the F test statistic is 252.79, and since the p-value of 0.000 is less than the given value of $\alpha = 0.05$, the null hypothesis **is rejected** and you may conclude that the annual total patient care revenue in hundreds is linearly related with the number of beds and the annual total patient days. And so assumption (1) **is verified**.

(continued on the next page)

The next step is to verify the assumption (2) that the variances of Y in all of the subpopulations are equal. Compute the residuals and then plot the residual versus $\hat{y}$ graph to see if assumption (2) appears to be valid; and, if not, to see what the violating pattern looks like.

Click on *Stat , Regression , Regression ...*

In the Regression dialog box, the cursor should be in the box to the right of the *Response:* heading; click on the "response" variable - Y and click on the | Select | button. The cursor will move down to the *Predictors:* box; hold the | Ctrl | key and click on the "predictor" variables - X1 and X2, and then click on the | Select | button. Then click on the | OK | button. Next click on the | Storage... | button. Note that since Minitab remembers the information in the dialog boxes from the previous time, you will only need to click on the | Storage... | button.

In the Regression - Storage dialog box, click in the squares to the left of *Residuals* and to the left of *Fits* to check these two options. No other options should be checked. Then click on | OK | . Two new columns automatically will be created and named FITS1 and RESI1. The column numbers will be one and two higher than the last column used in the current Worksheet Window.

Back in the Regression dialog box, click on | OK | .

The first six lines of the resulting Worksheet Window is shown below.

| | C1 | C2 | C3 | C4 | C5 | C6 | C7 |
|---|---|---|---|---|---|---|---|
| | X1 | X2 | X3 | X4 | Y | RESI1 | FITS1 |
| 1 | 7 | 26 | 6 | 60 | 78.500 | -1.47475 | 79.975 |
| 2 | 1 | 29 | 15 | 52 | 74.300 | 0.96303 | 73.337 |
| 3 | 11 | 56 | 8 | 20 | 104.300 | -1.74012 | 106.040 |
| 4 | 11 | 31 | 8 | 47 | 87.600 | -1.53372 | 89.134 |
| 5 | 7 | 52 | 6 | 33 | 97.200 | -0.35741 | 97.557 |
| 6 | 11 | 55 | 9 | 22 | 109.200 | 3.83613 | 105.364 |

Haldiec.mtw ***

Click on *Graph , Scatterplot ...*

In the Scatterplots dialog box: the *Simple* graph should be highlighted. Next click on the | OK | button.

In the Scatterplot - Simple dialog box: the cursor will be in the box on the first line under the *Y variables* heading; click on the RESI1 variable and click on the | Select | button. The cursor will move to the box in the first line under the *X variables* heading; click on the FITS1 variable and click on the | Select | button. Then click on the | OK | button.

Double click on the X axis label of FITS1 and rename this axis as y hat. Double click on the Y axis label of RESI1 and rename this axis Residuals.

The graph shown on the next page will appear in the Scatterplot of FITS1 vs RESI1 Graphics Window.

(continued on the next page)

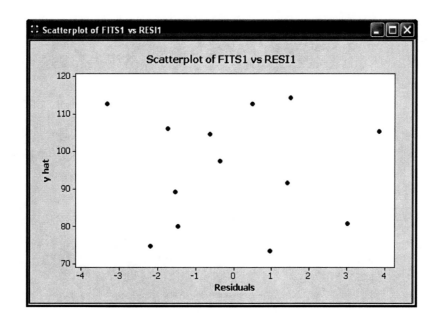

With only thirteen points it is difficult to determine any definite pattern, but since the points on this graph do not appear to have any well defined **non** rectangular shape, we will say that the points appear to be randomly and evenly spread within a general rectangular shape. Since the graph does not indicate any unusual pattern, the modified Levene's test is done next to confirm the validity of assumption (2).

The hypotheses for testing assumption (2) that all subpopulation variances are equal (i.e., homogeneity of variance) when using Levene's test slightly change to

$H_0$: all subpopulation variances are equal
$H_a$: the subpopulation variances are in a megaphone shape
$\alpha = 0.10$

and the test statistic is the Levene's test statistic.

First name the three new columns (C8, C9 and C10) as Sorted Fit, Corresp R and Factor.

Click on *Data , Sort...*

In the Sort dialog box, the cursor will be in the box under the *Sort Column(s):* heading. Highlight the FITS1 column only and click on $\boxed{\textbf{Select}}$ . Then highlight the RESI1 column only and click on $\boxed{\textbf{Select}}$ . **It is important that these two variables be entered in this order.** Next click inside the box to the right of the first *By column:* heading, click on the FITS1 variable, and click on $\boxed{\textbf{Select}}$ . Next click on the circle to the left of *Column(s) of current worksheet:*, and then click inside of the box under this heading. inside of the box under the *Store sorted column(s) in:* heading, hold the $\boxed{\textbf{Ctrl}}$ key and click on the Sorted Fit and Corresp R variables to highlight them both. **It is important that these two variables be entered in this order.** Then click on $\boxed{\textbf{Select}}$ . Now click on $\boxed{\textbf{OK}}$ .

The resulting Worksheet Window is shown on the next page.

(continued on the next page)

| ↓ | C1 | C2 | C3 | C4 | C5 | C6 | C7 | C8 | C9 | C10 |
|---|------|------|------|------|-------|----------|---------|-----------|----------|--------|
|   | X1 | X2 | X3 | X4 | Y | RESI1 | FITS1 | Sorted Fit | Corresp R | Factor |
| 1 | 7 | 26 | 6 | 60 | 78.500 | -1.47475 | 79.975 | 73.337 | 0.96303 | |
| 2 | 1 | 29 | 15 | 52 | 74.300 | 0.96303 | 73.337 | 74.689 | -2.18948 | |
| 3 | 11 | 56 | 8 | 20 | 104.300 | -1.74012 | 106.040 | 79.975 | -1.47475 | |
| 4 | 11 | 31 | 8 | 47 | 87.600 | -1.53372 | 89.134 | 80.776 | 3.02421 | |
| 5 | 7 | 52 | 6 | 33 | 97.200 | -0.35741 | 97.557 | 89.134 | -1.53372 | |
| 6 | 11 | 55 | 9 | 22 | 109.200 | 3.83613 | 105.364 | 91.688 | 1.41220 | |
| 7 | 3 | 71 | 17 | 6 | 104.000 | -0.62858 | 104.629 | 97.557 | -0.35741 | |
| 8 | 1 | 31 | 22 | 44 | 72.500 | -2.18948 | 74.689 | 104.629 | -0.62858 | |
| 9 | 2 | 54 | 18 | 22 | 93.100 | 1.41220 | 91.688 | 105.364 | 3.83613 | |
| 10 | 21 | 47 | 4 | 26 | 115.900 | 1.50194 | 114.398 | 106.040 | -1.74012 | |
| 11 | 1 | 40 | 23 | 34 | 83.800 | 3.02421 | 80.776 | 112.711 | -3.31077 | |
| 12 | 11 | 66 | 9 | 12 | 113.300 | 0.49732 | 112.803 | 112.803 | 0.49732 | |
| 13 | 10 | 68 | 8 | 12 | 109.400 | -3.31077 | 112.711 | 114.398 | 1.50194 | |

Next the minimum, the middle two scores and the maximum need to be determined. The *Stat , Basic Statistics , Describe Statistics* menu procedure will find the minimum, the maximum and the number of scores for the Sorted X variable.

Click on *Stat , Basic Statistics , Describe Statistics*

In the Display Descriptive Statistics dialog box: highlight the Sorted X variable, click on the ┌────────┐ **Select** button, and then click on the ┌──────────────┐ **Statistics...** button.

In the Descriptive Statistics - Statistics dialog box: click to uncheck all boxes **except** for the *Minimum , Maximum* and *N nonmissing* statistics.

The results shown below will appear in the Session Window.

### *Descriptive Statistics: Sorted Fit*

| Variable | N | Minimum | Maximum |
|----------|-----|---------|---------|
| Sorted Fit | 13 | 73.34 | 114.40 |

Since the number of objects (n = 13) is an odd number the then the two middle scores are in either the rows numbered 6 (n-1)/2 and 7 (n+1)/2 or the rows numbered 7 (n+1)/2 and 8 (n+3)/2. . Looking in the Worksheet window shown above, the difference between the Sorted Fit values in the 7th and 8th rows is slightly larger than the difference between the 6th and 7th rows, and so we will use $m_1$ = 97.557 and $m_2$ = 104.629 . Since Minitab has rounded off these numbers, $m_1$ and $m_2$ must be slightly exaggerated. As described earlier in this chapter let $m_1$ = 97.558 and let $m_2$ = 104.628 . Next look in output shown above of the *Stat, Basic Statistics, Display Descriptive Statistics* procedure to find the minimum and maximum of the Sorted Fit values. The Minitab rounded off values of the minimum and maximum values of the Sorted Fit variable are 73.34 and 114.40 respectively. Adjust the min value by subtracting 0.01 from the 73.34 , and adjust the max value by adding 0.01 to 114.40. In this example let min = 73.33 and let max = 114.41 .

Next put Lo in the first half of the Factor column and put Hi in the second half.

(continued on the next page)

Click on *Data , Code , Numeric to Text ...*

In the Code - Numeric to Text dialog box, the cursor should be in the box under the heading *Code data from columns:*. Click on the Sorted Fit variable and click on the [ **Select** ] button. Next click in the *Into columns:* box, click on the Factor variable, and click on the [ **Select** ] button. Then click in the first box under the *Original values* heading and type in 73.33 : 97.558 (min : $m_1$). Next click in the first box under the *New:* heading and type in the word Lo. Similarly click on the second row in the box under the *Original values* heading and type in 104.628 : 114.41 ($m_2$ : max). Next click in the box under the *New:* heading and type in the word Hi. Then click on [ **OK** ] .

The resulting Worksheet Window is shown below.

**Haldiec.mtw \*\*\***

| ↓ | C1 | C2 | C3 | C4 | C5 | C6 | C7 | C8 | C9 | C10-T |
|---|----|----|----|----|----|----|----|----|----|-------|
| | X1 | X2 | X3 | X4 | Y | RESI1 | FITS1 | Sorted Fit | Corresp R | Factor |
| 1 | 7 | 26 | 6 | 60 | 78.500 | -1.47475 | 79.975 | 73.337 | 0.96303 | Lo |
| 2 | 1 | 29 | 15 | 52 | 74.300 | 0.96303 | 73.337 | 74.689 | -2.18948 | Lo |
| 3 | 11 | 56 | 8 | 20 | 104.300 | -1.74012 | 106.040 | 79.975 | -1.47475 | Lo |
| 4 | 11 | 31 | 8 | 47 | 87.600 | -1.53372 | 89.134 | 80.776 | 3.02421 | Lo |
| 5 | 7 | 52 | 6 | 33 | 97.200 | -0.35741 | 97.557 | 89.134 | -1.53372 | Lo |
| 6 | 11 | 55 | 9 | 22 | 109.200 | 3.83613 | 105.364 | 91.688 | 1.41220 | Lo |
| 7 | 3 | 71 | 17 | 6 | 104.000 | -0.62858 | 104.629 | 97.557 | -0.35741 | Lo |
| 8 | 1 | 31 | 22 | 44 | 72.500 | -2.18948 | 74.689 | 104.629 | -0.62858 | Hi |
| 9 | 2 | 54 | 18 | 22 | 93.100 | 1.41220 | 91.688 | 105.364 | 3.83613 | Hi |
| 10 | 21 | 47 | 4 | 26 | 115.900 | 1.50194 | 114.398 | 106.040 | -1.74012 | Hi |
| 11 | 1 | 40 | 23 | 34 | 83.800 | 3.02421 | 80.776 | 112.711 | -3.31077 | Hi |
| 12 | 11 | 66 | 9 | 12 | 113.300 | 0.49732 | 112.803 | 112.803 | 0.49732 | Hi |
| 13 | 10 | 68 | 8 | 12 | 109.400 | -3.31077 | 112.711 | 114.398 | 1.50194 | Hi |

Finally, assumption (2) is verified by the hypothesis testing of

$H_0$: all subpopulation variances are equal
$H_a$: the subpopulation variances are in a megaphone shape
$\alpha = 0.10$

and the test statistic is the Levene's test statistic.

Click on *Stat , ANOVA , Test for Equal Variances...*

In the Test for Equal Variances dialog box: the cursor will be in the box to the right of *Response:*. Click on the Corresp R variable and click on the [ **Select** ] button. The cursor will move to the large box to the right of *Factors:*, click on the Factor variable and then click on the [ **Select** ] button. You may ignore the boxes to the right of *Confidence level:* and *Title:*. Then click on the [ **OK** ] button.

The results shown on the next page will appear in a separate Graphics Window.

(continued on the next page)

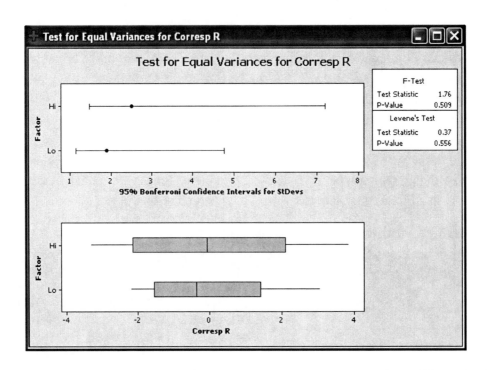

Since the Levene's test p-value of 0.556 is greater than $\alpha = 0.10$, the null hypothesis of equal subpopulation variances (homogeneity) may not be rejected. And since the graph of the Residuals versus the Fitted Values is not suspicious, thus assumption (2) is verified. Therefore **point predictions** may be made using multiple linear regression.

Now that assumptions (1) and (2) have been verified, a point estimate may be computed. However, since the company manager wanted a 90% confidence interval, assumption (3) that the subpopulations of Y scores are all normally distributed needs to be checked.

The hypotheses are:

$H_0$: the subpopulations of Y scores are all normally distributed
$H_a$: the subpopulations of Y scores are **not** all normally distributed
$\alpha = 0.10$ ,

and the test statistic is AD.

Click on *Stat* , *Basic Statistics* , *Normality Test...*

In the Normality Test dialog box, press the | **F3** | key to clear any previous contents. The cursor will be in the box to the right of *Variable:* click on the RESI1 variable (you will get the exact same results if you click on the Corresp R variable instead of the RESI1 variable) and click on the | **Select** | button. Under the heading of *Percentile lines*, the button to the left of *None* should be chosen. Make sure that under the *Tests for Normality* that the *Anderson-Darling* choice is marked. Next click inside of the *Title:* box and type Q-Q Plot, but remember do **not** press the | **Enter** | key. Then click on | **OK** | .

You will likely need to "maximize" the Graphics Window in order to clearly read the AD test statistic and p-value. The resulting Q-Q plot that appears in the Graphics Window is shown on the next page.

(continued on the next page)

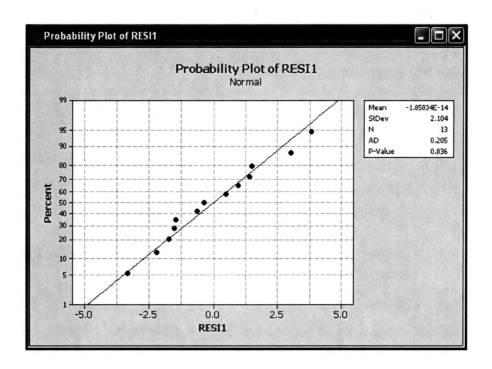

Since the p-value of 0.836 is greater than α = 0.10, you may not reject the null hypothesis of normality. And so you may conclude that assumption (3) **is valid**, and prediction intervals using this baseline sample may be reported. Also notice that the points in the graph are close to the superimposed straight line that Minitab draws for comparison.

Once assumption (3) that the subpopulations of Y scores are all normally distributed has been verified, the desired 90% prediction interval Y when (a) $X_1$ = 12 and $X_2$ = 31, and (b) $X_1$ = 16 and $X_2$ = 42 may be computed.

Since there are two new cases, the given values of $X_1$ and $X_2$ need to be entered into two new columns in the Worksheet. Name these new columns (C11 and C12) as X1o Values and X2o Values. Then enter the given values 12 and 16 into the first two rows ov X1o Values and enter the given values 31 and 42 into the first two rows of X2o Values. The resulting Worksheet window is shown below.

**Haldiec.mtw ***

| ↓ | C1 | C2 | C3 | C4 | C5 | C6 | C7 | C8 | C9 | C10-T | C11 | C12 |
|---|----|----|----|----|----|----|----|----|----|-------|-----|-----|
|   | X1 | X2 | X3 | X4 | Y | RESI1 | FITS1 | Sorted Fit | Corresp R | Factor | X1o Values | X2o Values |
| 1 | 7 | 26 | 6 | 60 | 78.500 | -1.47475 | 79.975 | 73.337 | 0.96303 | Lo | 12 | 31 |
| 2 | 1 | 29 | 15 | 52 | 74.300 | 0.96303 | 73.337 | 74.689 | -2.18948 | Lo | 16 | 42 |
| 3 | 11 | 56 | 8 | 20 | 104.300 | -1.74012 | 106.040 | 79.975 | -1.47475 | Lo | | |
| 4 | 11 | 31 | 8 | 47 | 87.600 | -1.53372 | 89.134 | 80.776 | 3.02421 | Lo | | |
| 5 | 7 | 52 | 6 | 33 | 97.200 | -0.35741 | 97.557 | 89.134 | -1.53372 | Lo | | |
| 6 | 11 | 55 | 9 | 22 | 109.200 | 3.83613 | 105.364 | 91.688 | 1.41220 | Lo | | |
| 7 | 3 | 71 | 17 | 6 | 104.000 | -0.62858 | 104.629 | 97.557 | -0.35741 | Lo | | |
| 8 | 1 | 31 | 22 | 44 | 72.500 | -2.18948 | 74.689 | 104.629 | -0.62858 | Hi | | |
| 9 | 2 | 54 | 18 | 22 | 93.100 | 1.41220 | 91.688 | 105.364 | 3.83613 | Hi | | |
| 10 | 21 | 47 | 4 | 26 | 115.900 | 1.50194 | 114.398 | 106.040 | -1.74012 | Hi | | |
| 11 | 1 | 40 | 23 | 34 | 83.800 | 3.02421 | 80.776 | 112.711 | -3.31077 | Hi | | |
| 12 | 11 | 66 | 9 | 12 | 113.300 | 0.49732 | 112.803 | 112.803 | 0.49732 | Hi | | |
| 13 | 10 | 68 | 8 | 12 | 109.400 | -3.31077 | 112.711 | 114.398 | 1.50194 | Hi | | |

(continued on the next page)

Next use the *Regression* procedure to compute the 90% prediction intervals.

Click on *Stat , Regression , Regression ...*

In the Regression dialog box, the cursor should be in the box to the right of the *Response:* heading; click on the "response" (Y) variable and click on the [ Select ] button. The cursor will move down to the *Predictors:* box; hold the [ Ctrl ] key and click on each of the four "predictor" (X) variables, and then click on the [ Select ] button. Next click on the [ Storage... ] button. Note that since Minitab remembers the information in the dialog boxes from the previous time, you will only need to click on the [ Storage... ] button.

In the Regression - Storage dialog box, click in the squares to the left of *Residuals* and to the left of *Fits* to **uncheck** these two options. Then click on [ OK ] .

Back in the Regression dialog box, click on the [ Options... ] button.

In the Regression-Options dialog box, click inside of the box below the *Prediction intervals for new observations:* heading, hold the [ Ctrl ] key and highlight the X1o Values and X2o Values columns, and then click on the [ Select ] button. Now click inside of the box to the right of *Confidence level:*, erase the current value in this box and type in 90, the desired confidence level for this example. Click on the [ OK ] button.

Back in the Regression dialog box, click on the [ OK ] button.

Only the last few lines pertaining to the prediction of Y of the output in the Session Window are shown below.

### Predicted Values for New Observations

| New Obs | Fit | SE Fit | 90% CI | 90% PI |
|---------|-----|--------|--------|--------|
| 1 | 90.578 | 1.198 | ( 88.406, 92.750) | (85.870, 95.286) |
| 2 | 103.795 | 1.260 | (101.510, 106.079) | (99.034, 108.556) |

### Values of Predictors for New Observations

| New Obs | X1 | X2 |
|---------|-----|-----|
| 1 | 12.0 | 31.0 |
| 2 | 16.0 | 42.0 |

And so you are 90% certain that: when (a) $X_1 = 12$ and $X_2 = 31$, interval from 85.870 to 95.286 will contain the value of Y; and (b) $X_1 = 16$ and $X_2 = 42$ , that the interval from 99.034 to 108.556 will contain the value of Y.

As a side note; if you would have used all four predictors and for the two new cases let the given values be (a) $X_1 = 12$, $X_2 = 31$, $X_3 = 9$ and $X_4 = 46$, and (a) $X_1 = 12$, $X_2 = 31$, $X_3 = 7$ and $X_4 = 31$, the two 90% prediction intervals would have been (a) 85.810 to 96.017 and (b) 98.913 to 110.171 . Both of these are larger and thus inferior to the results obtained above with the set of $X_1$ and $X_2$ chosen by the *stepwise* procedure. Also the $R^2$ adjusted in with all four predictors is 0.974 which is smaller than the $R^2$ adjusted of 0.977 when using only the set of $X_1$ and $X_2$ .

# Lab Assignment 13.1

**Name:**                                          **Date:**

**Course:**          **Section:**                 **Data CD Number:**

1.  Start a Minitab session. If you are unable to complete this lab assignment in one Minitab session, save the project as Lab 13-1 . **Never** use a period as part of the project name; since Minitab uses the period to attach the file type to the file name. Then at your next Minitab session, you may open this Lab 13-1.MPJ project and continue to work where you left off previously.

2.  Open the worksheet Draper.mtw that is on your data disc. This worksheet contains data for Culbertson County's Economic Productivity; and the three-month leading indicators of New Housing Starts, Prime Interest Rate, Retail Sales Index and Current Inventory Index.

    a.  How many cases are there in this worksheet; i.e., what is the sample size? _____

    b.  What are the variable names for:

        C1: _____

        C2: _____

        C3: _____

        C4: _____

        C5: _____

    c.  Rename the variables: . . . . . . . . .  as:

        New Housing Starts . . . . . . . . . X1

        Prime Interest Rate: . . . . . . . . . X2

        Retail Sales Index: . . . . . . . . . . X3

        Current Inventory Index: . . . . . X4

        Productivity . . . . . . . . . . . . . .  Y

    (lab assignment is continued on the second side of this page)

Since you do not have access to the original data in this worksheet, you may not actually check the unusual observations for errors. So for this problem **only**; you are to assume that any "influential point" is correct, any "outlier" with a **St Resid** whose absolute value is less than 2.8 is correct, but any "outlier" with a **St Resid** whose absolute value is greater than or equal to 2.8 is an error and is to be deleted.

d.  Given that this week's leading indicators are:

New Housing Starts:  . . . . . . . . 57

Prime Interest Rate:  . . . . . . . . . 6

Retail Sales Index:  . . . . . . . . . 10

Current Inventory Index:  . . . . . 27

Use the Stepwise procedure to do a **COMPLETE** multiple linear regression analysis; that is, determine:

(i)    if assumption (1) is valid or invalid,

(ii)   if assumption (2) is valid or invalid,

(iii)  if a point predictor is possible and describe why or why not,

(iv)  if assumption (3) is valid or invalid  and

(v)   if a 90% prediction interval is possible and describe why or why not.

If one or both of these predictions are possible, report the prediction(s).


3.    Print your Session Window and all Graphics Windows to the printer.


4.    Attach both your Minitab output and <u>your complete answers</u> to this sheet and submit all three to your instructor.

# Lab Assignment 13.2

**Name:**                                                           **Date:**

**Course:**                    **Section:**              **Data CD Number:**

1.   Start a Minitab session.  If you are unable to complete this lab assignment in one Minitab session, save the project as Lab 13-2 .  **Never** use a period as part of the project name; since Minitab uses the period to attach the file type to the file name.  Then at your next Minitab session, you may open this Lab 13-2.MPJ project and continue to work where you left off previously.

2.   Open the worksheet Cespud.mtw that is on your data disc.   This worksheet contains a sample of five variables from the 1972 Consumer Expenditure Study.   Four of these variables measure the: age of head of household, total household income after taxes, spending on food and clothing, and spending on shelter (rent, utilities, mortgages, etc.).

The following data is about two households that were not in the sample:

|                         | Sam's household | Sue's household |
|-------------------------|-----------------|-----------------|
| Age of Head             | 54              | 38              |
| Total household income  | $ 8,452.00      | $ 7,134.00      |
| Spending on shelter     | $ 3,055.00      | $ 2,550.00      |

You want to predict the amount of money spent on food and clothing by each household.

Since you do not have access to the original data in this worksheet, you may not actually check the unusual observations for errors.  So for this problem **only**; you are to assume that any "influential point" is correct, any "outlier" with a **St Resid** whose absolute value is less than 2.75 is correct, but any "outlier" with a **St Resid** whose absolute value is greater than or equal to 2.75 is an error and is to be deleted.

Use the Stepwise procedure to do a **<u>COMPLETE</u>** multiple linear regression analysis and determine for each household:
   (i)    if assumption (1) is valid or invalid,
   (ii)   if assumption (2) is valid or invalid,
   (iii)  if a point predictor is possible and describe why or why not,
   (iv)  if assumption (3) is valid or invalid and
   (v)   if a 90% prediction interval is possible and describe why or why not.

If one or both of these predictions are possible, report the prediction(s).

(lab assignment is continued on the second side of this page)

573

3.    Print your Session Window and all Graphics Windows to the printer.


4.    Attach both your Minitab output and <u>your complete answers</u> to this sheet and submit all three to your instructor.

# APPENDIX A:          Finite Population Corrections

All of the formulas given in Chapter 5, for computing one sample confidence intervals and for choosing an optimal sample size, are based upon the theory that the samples were being taken from populations which are infinitely large; or at least very large relative to the samples being used. However; when the population is relatively small compared to the sample, these formulas do **not** reflect the increased degree of representation the sample now possesses. In these cases where the populations are relatively small; the formulas given in Chapter 5 produce one sample confidence intervals that are too wide, and produce optimal sample sizes that are too large. This appendix contains the procedures for correcting the results given in Chapter 5. These procedures are called **finite population corrections** or **fpc** for short.

First one must decide when a population is relatively small, and thus, when the Chapter 5 formulas need to be corrected. A common criterion for using these finite population corrections is when the proportion of the sample size (n) over the population size (N) is greater than 0.05 ; that is, $\frac{n}{N} > 0.05$. Of course, one must know the size of the population to apply this criterion. If the population size is not given, we usually assume that the size is so large that the finite population correction is not needed.

The one sample confidence intervals computed in Chapter 5 all have the same form of

(point estimate)  $\mp$  (error of estimation).

For example; one formula for computing a confidence interval for the population mean is

$$\bar{x} \mp Z \frac{\sigma}{\sqrt{n}}$$

where $\bar{x}$ is the point estimate and $Z \frac{\sigma}{\sqrt{n}}$ is the error of estimation. When the population is relatively small; that is $\frac{n}{N} > 0.05$, the error of estimation given in the above formula is too large. The finite population correction reduces the size of the error of estimation. The corrected error of estimation is given by the formula

$$(i) \quad E_c = E \sqrt{\frac{N - n}{N - 1}}$$

where E is the error of estimation computed from the formulas in Chapter 5, and $E_c$ is the finite population corrected error of estimation. Now the corrected confidence interval becomes

(point estimate)  $\mp$  (finite population corrected  error of estimation);

that is, (point estimate)  $\mp$  $(E_c)$ .

The macro that computes the finite population corrected confidence interval is **Fpc-err.mtb**. (**F**inite **p**opulation **c**orrected **err**or of estimation), and is executed by clicking on *File*, *Other Files*, *Run an Exec ...* Minitab menu bar item.

Click on *File*, *Other Files*, *Run an Exec ...*

In the Run an Exec dialog box: make sure the *Number of times to execute:* box contains the number 1, and then click on the Select File button.

In the Run an Exec dialog box: click on the *Look in:* icon, and then click on the *Data Disc* (if this is not the drive shown). Next click on the desired macro file name to highlight this macro, and click on the Open button.

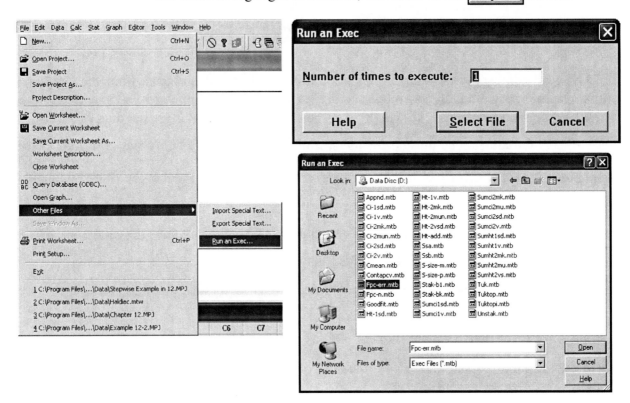

This macro will prompt you for: (1) the left and right endpoints of the one sample confidence interval computed by the Chapter 5 formulas, (2) the sample size (n), and (3) the finite population size (N). The macro will then compute the finite population corrected error of estimation and corresponding confidence interval.

Example A.1: Norwood Electronics purchases transistors in lots of 150. From each lot, 40 are randomly selected for testing, and a 95% confidence interval for the proportion of defectives is computed. From this particular lot, six (6) are defective. Compute the confidence interval.

(continued on the next page)

First, Since y = 6 and (n-y) = 34 are both $\geq$ 5, the one sample confidence interval is computed the formula $\hat{p} \mp Z_\alpha \sqrt{\dfrac{\hat{p}(1-\hat{p})}{n}}$ .

From the Reference Guide in the table with the heading One Sample Confidence Intervals for the **Population Proportion of "Successes"**, and in the Summary Statistics Technique column; use the *Stat , Basic Statistics , 1 Proportion* procedure.

Click on *Stat , Basic Statistics , 1 Proportion ...*

In the 1 Proportion dialog box: make sure the ◉ button to the left of *Summarized data* is selected, and then click inside of the box to the right of *Number of trials:*. In this box erase any previous value and type in 40. Next click inside of the box to the right of *Number of events:*, erase any previous value and type in 6. Then click on the 
$\boxed{\textbf{Options...}}$ button.

In the 1 Proportion - Options dialog box: if the value in the *Confidence level:* box is not 95, erase this value and type 95. Next make sure that the box to the right of *Alternative:* contains *not equal*. If not, click on the down triangle ( $\boxed{\blacktriangledown}$ ), and click on the *not equal* choice. Then make sure that the ☑ box to the left of *Use test and interval based on normal distribution* is checked. Then click on $\boxed{\textbf{OK}}$ .

Back in the 1 Proportion dialog box, click on $\boxed{\textbf{OK}}$ .

The resulting output shown below will appear in the Session Window.

## *Test and CI for One Proportion*

### *Test of p = 0.5 vs p not = 0.5*

| Sample | X | N | Sample p | 95.0 % CI | Z-Value | P-Value |
|--------|---|---|----------|-----------|---------|---------|
| 1 | 6 | 40 | 0.150000 | (0.039344, 0.260656) | -4.43 | 0.000 |

From the Reference Guide in the table with the heading **Finite Population Corrections**; since $\dfrac{n}{N} = \dfrac{40}{150} = 0.2666 > 0.05$, the finite population correction $E_c = E\sqrt{\dfrac{N-n}{N-1}}$ is required. And in the Macro column, the macro to be executed is **Fpc-err.mtb**.

Click on *File , Other Files , Run an Exec ...*

In the Run an Exec dialog box: make sure the *Number of times to execute:* box contains the number 1, and then click on the $\boxed{\textbf{Select File}}$ button.

In the Run an Exec dialog box: click on the *Look in:* icon, and then click on the *Data Disc* (if this is not the drive shown). Next click on the Fpc-err.mtb file name to highlight this macro, and click on the $\boxed{\textbf{Open}}$ button.

(continued on the next page)

This macro will prompt you for: (1) the uncorrected confidence interval endpoints, (2) the sample size (n) and (3) the finite population size (N). Then the macro displays the corrected error of estimation ($E_c$) and the resulting **finite population corrected confidence interval** for the population proportion of "successes." The steps for this macro and resulting output shown below will appear in the Session Window.

### *After the DATA> prompt, enter the LEFT end-point , the RIGHT end-point of the uncorrected confidence interval.*

*DATA>* 0.039344, 0.260656 [ Enter ]

### *After the DATA> prompt, enter the size of the sample.*

*DATA>* 40 [ Enter ]

### *After the DATA> prompt, enter the size of the finite population.*

*DATA>* 150 [ Enter ]

## Data Display

### *The finite population corrected error of estimation =      0.0951*

### *The finite population corrected confidence interval is:*
### *0.0549  to      0.2451*

and so Norwood Electronics is 95% confident that the interval from 0.0549 to 0.2451 contains the proportion of defective transistors in the entire lot of 150 transistors.

In a similar manner, when the population is relatively small, the formulas in Chapter 5 for computing the optimal sample size must be corrected. First compute the optimal sample size (n), and then check if this n over N (the population size) is greater than 0.05 . If so, the finite population corrected optimal sample size is given by the formula

$$\text{(ii)} \quad n_c = \frac{n}{1 + \dfrac{n}{N}}$$

where n is the sample size computed from the formulas in Chapter 5, and $n_c$ is the finite population corrected optimal sample size.

The macro that computes the finite population corrected optimal sample size is **Fpc-n.mtb** (**F**inite **p**opulation **c**orrected sample size (**n**)), and is executed by clicking on the Minitab menu bar item *File , Other Files , Run an Exec ....*

Example A.2:   The administrator of a hospital out-patient clinic wants to estimate the average distance the patients live from the clinic.  He knows that the clinic has a total of 400 patients, but he does not want to take the time and expense to survey every patient.   So he will be satisfied with a 95% confidence interval with an error of estimation of (no more than) ½ mile.  Previous similar studies have indicated that the population standard deviation is 3 miles.

The predetermined confidence level is 95%, and the desired error of estimation is 0.5 .  The standard deviation of 3 obtained from a previous similar study will be used as the "estimate" of σ.

The formula for computing the optimal sample size is $n = \left[\dfrac{Z\sigma}{E}\right]^2$ .  From the Reference Guide in the table with the heading **Determining the Optimal Sample Size Before One Sample Estimation**; the macro to be executed is **S-size-m.mtb** .

Click on *File , Other Files , Run an Exec ...*

In the Run an Exec dialog box:  make sure the *Number of times to execute:* box contains the number 1, and then click on the | **Select File** | button.

In the Run an Exec dialog box: click on the *Look in:* icon, and then click on the *Data Disc* (if this is not the drive shown).   Next click on the S-size-m.mtb file name to highlight this macro, and click on the | **Open** | button.

This macro will prompt you for: (1) the desired confidence level, (2) error of estimation and (3) the best estimate of the population standard deviation.  Then the macro displays the resulting **uncorrected** sample size.  The steps for this macro and resulting output shown next will appear in the Session Window.

**After the DATA> prompt, enter the confidence level.**

**DATA>** 95 | **Enter** |

**After the DATA> prompt, enter the desired Error of Estimation.**

**DATA>** 0.5 | **Enter** |

**After the DATA> prompt, enter the Population Standard Deviation or your best guess of the Population Standard Deviation.**

**DATA>** 3 | **Enter** |

## Data Display

**To compute a 95.0 percent confidence interval for the population mean with a 0.500 error of estimation, the sample size needed is:        139**

(continued on the next page)

Since $\dfrac{n}{N} = \dfrac{139}{400} = 0.3475 > 0.05$, the finite population correction $n_c = \dfrac{n}{1 + \dfrac{n}{N}}$

is required. From the Reference Guide in the table with the heading **Finite Population Corrections**, and in the Macro column; the macro to be executed is **Fpc-n.mtb** .

Click on *File , Other Files , Run an Exec ...*

In the Run an Exec dialog box: make sure the *Number of times to execute:* box contains the number 1, and then click on the | **Select File** | button.

In the Run an Exec dialog box: click on the *Look in:* icon, and then click on the *Data Disc* (if this is not the drive shown). Next click on the Fpc-n.mtb file name to highlight this macro, and click on the | **Open** | button.

This macro will prompt you for the uncorrected sample size (n) and the finite population size (N). Then the macro displays the resulting **finite population corrected sample size** ($n_c$). The steps for this macro and resulting output shown below will appear in the Session Window.

**After the DATA> prompt, enter the uncorrected sample size.**

**DATA>** 139 | **Enter** |

**After the DATA> prompt, enter the size of the finite population.**

**DATA>** 400 | **Enter** |

**The finite population corrected sample size needed is now computing.**

## Data Display

**The finite population corrected sample size needed is:     104**

and so the hospital out-patient clinic administrator would take a random sample of 104 patients in order to satisfy his requirements.

**It is very important to note that once the sample of 104 patients has been selected and a 95% confidence interval has been computed, the finite population correction must still be applied to the resulting confidence interval!   The following example illustrates this.**

Example A.3: The administrator in Example A.2 takes a random sample of 104 from the population of 400 patients and obtains a sample mean distance from the clinic of 14.55 miles and a sample standard deviation of 3.12 miles. Nothing is known about the distribution of these distances. Compute the desired 95% confidence interval.

Since the sample size is greater than 30 and only the sample standard deviation is known, the confidence interval is computed using the formula $\overline{x} \mp Z \dfrac{s}{\sqrt{n}}$ .

From the Reference Guide in the table with the heading **One Sample Confidence Intervals for the Population Mean,** and in the Summary Statistics Technique column; the procedure to compute this confidence interval is given as

*Stat , Basic Statistics , 1-Sample Z ...*

In the 1-Sample Z (Test and Confidence Interval) dialog box: make sure the button to the left of *Summarized data* is selected, and then click inside of the box to the right of *Sample size:*. Now type in 104, the value of the sample size. Next click in the next box down that is to the right of *Mean:* and type in 14.55, the value of the sample mean. Next click inside of the box to the right of *Standard deviation:*, erase any current incorrect value, and type in 3.12, the known value of the sample standard deviation. Make sure that the box to the right of *Test mean:* is empty, and then click on the ⬛ Options... ⬛ button.

In the 1-Sample Z - Options dialog box: if the value in the *confidence level:* box is not the level you want, erase this value and type in 95, the correct confidence level. Then make sure that the box to the right of *Alternative:* contains *not equal*. If not, click on the down triangle ( ⬛▾⬛ ), and click on the *not equal* choice. Then click on ⬛ **OK** ⬛ .

Back in the 1-Sample Z (Test and Confidence Interval) dialog box, click on ⬛ **OK** ⬛ .

The resulting output shown below will appear in the Session Window.

## *One-Sample Z*

### *The assumed standard deviation = 3.12*

| N | Mean | SE Mean | 95% CI |
|-----|---------|---------|----------------------|
| 104 | 14.5500 | 0.3059 | (13.9504, 15.1496) |

Note that the error of estimation is computed as $\left( \overline{x} + Z \dfrac{s}{\sqrt{n}} \right) - \overline{x} = Z \dfrac{s}{\sqrt{n}} = E$ . In this example, E = 15.150 - 14.550 = 0.600 and not the desired 0.5 . This is because the finite population correction has **not** been applied yet, but **must be done** since $\dfrac{n}{N} = \dfrac{104}{400} = 0.26 > 0.05$. The finite population correction is computed using the formula

$$E_c = E \sqrt{\dfrac{N - n}{N - 1}} .$$

(continued on the next page)

From the Reference Guide in the table with the heading **Finite Population Corrections**, and in the Macro column; the macro to be executed is **Fpc-err.mtb**.

Click on *File* , *Other Files* , *Run an Exec* ...

In the Run an Exec dialog box:  make sure the *Number of times to execute:* box contains the number 1, and then click on the ⬚ **Select File** ⬚ button.

In the Run an Exec dialog box: click on the *Look in:* icon, and then click on the *Data Disc* (if this is not the drive shown).  Next click on the Fpc-err.mtb file name to highlight this macro, and click on the ⬚ **Open** ⬚ button.

**After the DATA> prompt, enter the LEFT end-point , the RIGHT end-point of the uncorrected confidence interval.**

*DATA>* 13.9504 , 15.1496  ⬚ **Enter** ⬚

**After the DATA> prompt, enter the size of the sample.**

*DATA>* 104  ⬚ **Enter** ⬚

**After the DATA> prompt, enter the size of the finite population.**

*DATA>* 400  ⬚ **Enter** ⬚

## Data Display

**The finite population corrected error of estimation =      0.5164**

**The finite population corrected confidence interval is:**
**14.0336   to      15.0664**

The hospital administrator is 95% confident that the interval from 14.0336 to 15.0664 miles contains the mean distance that all 400 patients live from the hospital out-patient clinic. Note that <u>after</u> the finite population correction has been applied the corrected error of estimation is 0.5164, and this is very close to the desired 0.5 .  The reason for this slightly larger value is that the sample standard deviation was 3.12 which is slightly larger than 3, the "estimate" of $\sigma$ used in the formula for the sample size in Example A.2 .

# APPENDIX B:

# Reference Guide

## Graphical Display of Data
## High Resolution Graphics

| Graphical Display | MINITAB Procedure |
|---|---|
| Graph a Histogram with the smallest interval's left end point = *l* largest interval's right endpoint = *r* and the class interval's width = *w*. | *Graph , Histogram...* <br> *Simple* <br> Highlight variable and [ Select ] <br> [ OK ] <br> Double click inside the graph <br> Clcik on the *Binning* tab <br> Click on ⊙ to the left of *CutPoint* <br> Click on ⊙ to the left of *Midpoint/CutPoint positions:* <br> Click in box underneath <br> Type *l*:*r* /*w* <br> [ OK ] <br> Optionally edit/add Title, Subtitle, Footnote, Axes Labels and Bar Colors. |
| Graph a two dimensional ( x,y ) plot. | *Graph , Scatterplot...* <br> *Simple* <br> Highlight "y" variable and [ Select ] <br> Highlight "x" variable and [ Select ] <br> [ OK ] <br> Optionally edit/add Title, Subtitle, Footnote, Axes Labels and Plotting Symbol. |
| Graph a Dotplot for one variable. | *Graph , Dotplot...* <br> *One Y Simple* <br> [ OK ] <br> Highlight variable and [ Select ] <br> [ OK ] <br> Optionally edit/add Title, Subtitle, Footnote, Axis Label, Axis Numerical Scaling and Plotting Symbol. |
| Graph Dotplots for two or more variables using the same axis. | *Graph , Dotplot...* <br> *Multiple Y's Simple* <br> [ OK ] <br> Highlight variables and [ Select ] <br> [ OK ] <br> Optionally edit/add Title, Subtitle, Footnote, Axis Labels, Axis Numerical Scaling and Plotting Symbol. |

| Graphical Display | MINITAB Procedure |
|---|---|
| Graph a Bar Chart | *Graph, Bar Chart...*<br>*Simple*<br>OK<br>In the *Categorical variables:* area, highlight the desired variable and Select<br>OK<br>Optionally edit/add Title, Subtitle, Footnote, Axes Labels and Bar Colors. |
| Graph a Pie Chart.. | *Graph , Pie Chart...*<br>Make sure button to left of *Chart data in:* is selected, click in the box to the right, highlight variable and Select<br>OK<br>Optionally edit/add Title, Subtitle, Footnote, Slice Labels, Ordering of the Slices, Combining Small Slices, and Explode Slices.<br>Optionally omit missing data, only at the first time Pie Chart is created.<br>*Graph, Pie Chart...*<br>Data Options...<br>*Group Options*<br>Uncheck box to left of *Include missing as a group*<br>OK |

| Graphical Display | MINITAB Procedure |
|---|---|
| Graph a Box Plot | *Graph, Boxplot...*<br>*One Y Simple*<br>OK<br>Highlight variable(s) and Select<br>Scale...<br>Check box to left of *Transpose value and category scales*<br>OK<br>[ Optional: Click on Multiple Graphs... , click on the circle to the left of *In separate panel of the same graph* and then click on OK ]<br>OK<br>Optionally edit/add Title, Subtitle, Footnote, Axis Label, Axis Numerical Scaling, Box Color and Outlier Symbol. |
| Graph Box Plots for several variables using the same axis. | *Graph, Boxplot...*<br>*One Y Simple*<br>OK<br>Highlight variable and Select<br>Scale...<br>Check box to left of *Transpose value and category scales*<br>OK<br>Optionally edit/add Title, Subtitle, Footnote, Axis Label, Axis Numerical Scaling, Box Color and Outlier Symbol. |

**Graphical Display of Data**
**Stem and Leaf - Character Graph**

| Graphical Display | MINITAB Procedure |
|---|---|
| Graph a Stem-and-Leaf with the class interval's width = *w*. | *Graph , Stem-and-Leaf...*<br>Highlight variable and Select<br>Type value of w into *Increment:* box<br>OK |

**Numerical Descriptive Statistics**

| Statistic to be computed | MINITAB Procedure |
|---|---|
| Sum, Mean, Standard deviation, Minimum, Maximum, Range, Median, Sum of Squares, Total Number of cases, Number of Nonmissing cases or Number of Missing cases | *Calc , Column Statistics ...*<br>Click on ⊙ to the left of the desired *Statistic*<br>    (you may do **only one** statistic at a time)<br>Click in box to right of *Input variable:*<br>Highlight desired variable (**only one** may be chosen)<br>    and  **Select**<br>Type a constant (K#) into the box to the right of<br>    *Store result in:* (Optional)<br>**OK** |
| Number of valid observations, Number of missing observations, Mean, Standard Error of the Mean, Standard Deviation, Minimum, First Quartile, Median, Third Quartile, and Maximum of **one or more** variables (columns). | *Stat, Basic Statistics, Display Descriptive Statistics...*<br>Highlight the **one or more** desired variables<br>    and  **Select**<br>Optionally  **Graphs...**  to add/remove specific<br>    statistics<br>Optionally  **Graphs...**  to graph a histogram and/or<br>    a boxplot<br>**OK** |

# One Sample Confidence Intervals for the Population Mean

| Formula | Raw Data Technique | Summary Statistics Technique |
|---|---|---|
| (i) $\bar{x} \mp Z\dfrac{\sigma}{\sqrt{n}}$ | *Stat , Basic Statistics , 1-Sample Z ...*<br>Make sure the ⦿ to left of *Samples in columns* is filled in, highlight desired variable and [Select]<br>Click in box to right of *Standard deviation:* and type in the population standard deviation<br>Make sure box to to left of □ *Perform hypothesis test* is **un**checked and click on [Options...]<br>Click in box to right of *Confidence level:* and type in confidence level<br>Make sure that the box to the right of *Alternative:* contains *not equal* and [OK] [OK] | *Stat , Basic Statistics , 1-Sample Z ...*<br>Make sure the ⦿ to the left of *Summarized data* is selected<br>Click in box to the right of *Sample size:* and type in sample size.<br>Click in box to right of *Mean:* and type in the value of the sample mean<br>Click inside of the box to the right of *Standard deviation:* and type in the population standard deviation<br>Make sure box to left of □ *Perform hypothesis test* is **un**checked and click on [Options...]<br>Click in box to right of *Confidence level:* and type in confidence level<br>Make sure that box to right of *Alternative:* contains *not equal* and [OK] [OK] |
| (ii) $\bar{x} \mp Z\dfrac{s}{\sqrt{n}}$ | *Calc , Column Statistics ...*<br>Click on ⦿ to left of *Standard deviation*<br>Click in box to right of *Input variable:*, highlight variable and [Select]<br>Click in box to right *Store result in:* and type in constant "k1"<br>[OK]<br>*Stat , Basic Statistics , 1-Sample Z ...*<br>Make sure the ⦿ to left of *Samples in columns* is filled in, highlight desired variable and [Select]<br>Click in box to right of *Standard deviation:* and type in k1<br>Make sure box to left of □ *Perform hypothesis test* is **un**checked and click on [Options...]<br>Click in box to right of *Confidence level:* and type in confidence level<br>Make sure that the box to the right of *Alternative:* contains *not equal* and [OK] [OK] | *Stat , Basic Statistics , 1-Sample Z ...*<br>Make sure the ⦿ to the left of *Summarized data* is selected<br>Click in box to the right of *Sample size:* and type in sample size.<br>Click in box to right of *Mean:* and type in the value of the sample mean<br>Click inside of the box to the right of *Standard deviation:* and type in the sample standard deviation<br>Make sure box to left of □ *Perform hypothesis test* is **un**checked and click on [Options...]<br>Click in box to right of *Confidence level:* and type in confidence level<br>Make sure that box to right of *Alternative:* contains *not equal* and [OK] [OK] |

**One Sample Confidence Intervals for the Population Mean (continued)**

| Formula | Raw Data Technique | Summary Statistics Technique |
|---|---|---|
| (iii) $\bar{x} \mp t\dfrac{s}{\sqrt{n}}$ | *Stat , Basic Statistics , 1-Sample t ...*<br>Make sure the ⊙ to left of *Samples in columns* is filled in, highlight desired variable and [ Select ]<br>Make sure box to left of ☐ *Perform hypothesis test* is **un**checked and click on [ Options... ]<br>Click in box to right of *Confidence level:* and type in confidence level<br>Make sure that the box to the right of *Alternative:* contains *not equal* and [ OK ]<br>[ OK ] | *Stat , Basic Statistics , 1-Sample t ...*<br>Make sure the ⊙ to the left of *Summarized data* is selected<br>Click in box to the right of *Sample size:* and type in sample size.<br>Click in box to right of *Mean:* and type in the value of the sample mean<br>Click inside of the box to the right of *Standard deviation:* and type in the sample standard deviation<br>Make sure box to left of ☐ *Perform hypothesis test* is **un**checked and click on [ Options... ]<br>Click in box to right of *Confidence level:* and type in confidence level<br>Make sure that box to right of *Alternative:* contains *not equal* and [ OK ]<br>[ OK ] |

**One Sample Confidence Intervals for the Population Variance and Standard Deviation**

| Formula | Raw Data Technique | Summary Statistics Technique |
|---|---|---|
| (iv) $\dfrac{(n-1)s^2}{\chi_U^2}$ to $\dfrac{(n-1)s^2}{\chi_L^2}$ | *File, Other Files, Run an Exec...* [ Select File ] *Data Disc* **Ci-1v.mtb** [ Open ] | *File, Other Files, Run an Exec...* [ Select File ] *Data Disc* **Sumci1v.mtb** [ Open ] |
| (v) $\sqrt{\dfrac{(n-1)s^2}{\chi_U^2}}$ to $\sqrt{\dfrac{(n-1)s^2}{\chi_L^2}}$ | *File, Other Files, Run an Exec...* [ Select File ] *Data Disc* **Ci-1sd.mtb** [ Open ] | *File, Other Files, Run an Exec...* [ Select File ] *Data Disc* **Sumci1sd.mtb** [ Open ] |

**One Sample Confidence Interval for the Population Proportion of "Successes"**

| Formula | Raw Data Technique | Summary Statistics Technique |
|---|---|---|
| (vi) $\hat{p} \mp Z\sqrt{\dfrac{\hat{p}(1-\hat{p})}{n}}$ | If necessary, use *Data, Code, Text to Numeric* or *Data, Code, Text to Text* <br><br> *Stat, Basic Statistics, 1 Proportion* <br> Make sure the ◉ to left of *Samples in columns:* is filled in and click in box to the right <br> Highlight desired variable and [ Select ] <br> [ Options... ] <br> Click in box to right of *Confidence level:* and type in the confidence level <br> Make sure *Alternative* is not equal <br> Make sure the ☑ to the left of *Use test and interval based on normal distribution* **is** checked <br> [ OK ] and [ OK ] | *Stat, Basic Statistics, 1 Proportion* <br> Make sure the ◉ to left of *Summarized data* is filled in <br> Click in box to the right of *Number of trials:* and type in the sample size <br> Click in box to the right of *Number of events:* and type in the number of "successes" <br> [ Options... ] <br> Click in box to right of *Confidence level:* and type in the confidence level <br> Make sure *Alternative* is not equal <br> Make sure the ☑ to the left of *Use test and interval based on normal distribution* **is** checked <br> [ OK ] and [ OK ] |

## Determining the Optimal Sample Size Before One Sample Estimation

| Formula | Determine Optimal Sample Size Before Estimating: | Macro |
|---|---|---|
| (vii) $\quad n = \left[\dfrac{Z\sigma}{E}\right]^2$ | The Population Mean | *File, Other Files, Run an Exec...*<br>**Select File**<br>*Data Disc*<br>**S-size-m.mtb**<br>**Open** |
| (viii) $\quad n = p(1-p)\left[\dfrac{Z}{E}\right]^2$ | The Population Proportion of "Successes" | *File, Other Files, Run an Exec...*<br>**Select File**<br>*Data Disc*<br>**S-size-p.mtb**<br>**Open** |

## Finite Population Corrections

| Formula | If $\dfrac{n}{N} > 0.05$, then apply the finite population correction for: | Macro |
|---|---|---|
| (i) $\quad E_c = E\sqrt{\dfrac{N-n}{N-1}}$ | Error of Estimation for a one sample confidence interval | *File, Other Files, Run an Exec...*<br>**Select File**<br>*Data Disc*<br>**Fpc-err.mtb**<br>**Open** |
| (ii) $\quad n_c = \dfrac{n}{1 + \dfrac{n}{N}}$ | Determining the optimal sample size | *File, Other Files, Run an Exec...*<br>**Select File**<br>*Data Disc*<br>**Fpc-n.mtb**<br>**Open** |

# Two Sample Confidence Intervals for The Difference of Two Population Means
## Using Two <u>Independent</u> Samples

| Formula | Raw Data Technique | Summary Statistics Technique |
|---|---|---|
| (i) $(\bar{x}_1 - \bar{x}_2) \mp t\sqrt{\dfrac{s_1^2}{n_1} + \dfrac{s_2^2}{n_2}}$<br><br>("separate variance" formula) | *Stat , Basic Statistics , 2-Sample t ...*<br>Make sure the ⊙ to the left of *Samples in different columns* is filled in, click in box to right of *First:* , click on variable that contains sample 1 data and [Select]<br>Click on variable that contains sample 2 data and [Select]<br>Make sure the □ to the left of *Assume equal variances* is **not** checked<br>[Options...]<br>Click in *Confidence level:* box and type in the desired confidence level<br>Leave the 0.0 in the box to the right of *Test difference:* and make sure that the box to the right of *Alternative:* contains *not equal*<br>[OK] and [OK] | *Stat , Basic Statistics , 2-Sample t ...*<br>Make sure the ⊙ to the left of *Summarized data*, and then click inside of the box on the *First:* row and underneath of *Sample size:* and type in the first sample size. Click in the next box underneath of *Mean:* and type in first sample mean. Next click in the next box underneath of *Standard deviation:* and type in the first sample standard deviation. Then repeat this on the *Second:* row for sample 2.<br>Make sure the □ to the left of *Assume equal variances* box is **not** checked<br>[Options...]<br>Click in *Confidence level:* box and type in the desired confidence level<br>Leave the 0.0 in the *Test difference:* box and make sure that the *Alternative:* box contains *not equal*<br>[OK] and [OK] |
| (ii) $(\bar{x}_1 - \bar{x}_2) \mp t\sqrt{s_p^2\left(\dfrac{n_1 + n_2}{n_1 n_2}\right)}$<br><br>where<br><br>$s_p^2 = \dfrac{(n_1 - 1)s_1^2 + (n_2 - 1)s_2^2}{n_1 + n_2 - 2}$<br><br>("pooled variance" formula) | *Stat , Basic Statistics , 2-Sample t ...*<br>Make sure the ⊙ to the left of *Samples in different columns* is filled in, click in box to right of *First:* , click on variable that contains sample 1 data and [Select]<br>Click on variable that contains sample 2 data and [Select]<br>Click in the ☑ (to fill in) to the left of *Assume equal variances*<br>[Options...]<br>Click in *Confidence level:* box and type in the desired confidence level<br>Leave the 0.0 in the box to the right of *Test difference:* and make sure that the box to the right of *Alternative:* contains *not equal*<br>[OK] and [OK] | *Stat , Basic Statistics , 2-Sample t ...*<br>Make sure the ⊙ to the left of *Summarized data*, and then click inside of the box on the *First:* row and underneath of *Sample size:* and type in the first sample size. Click in the next box underneath of *Mean:* and type in first sample mean. Next click in the next box underneath of *Standard deviation:* and type in the first sample standard deviation. Then repeat this on the *Second:* row for sample 2.<br>Click in the ☑ (to fill in) to the left of *Assume equal variances*<br>[Options...]<br>Click in *Confidence level:* box and type in the desired confidence level<br>Leave the 0.0 in the *Test difference:* box and make sure that the *Alternative:* box contains *not equal*<br>[OK] and [OK] |

594

# Two Sample Confidence Intervals for The Difference of Two Population Means
## Using Two <u>Independent</u> Samples
### (continued)

| Formula | Raw Data Technique | Summary Statistics Technique |
|---|---|---|
| (iii) $(\bar{x}_1 - \bar{x}_2) \mp Z\sqrt{\dfrac{\sigma_1^2}{n_1} + \dfrac{\sigma_2^2}{n_2}}$ | *File, Other Files,* *Run an Exec...*  **[Select File]**  *Data Disc*  **Ci-2mk.mtb**  **[Open]** | *File , Other Files ,* *Run an Exec ...*  **[Select File]**  *Data Disc*  **Sumci2mk.mtb**  **[Open]** |
| (iv) $(\bar{x}_1 - \bar{x}_2) \mp Z\sqrt{\dfrac{s_1^2}{n_1} + \dfrac{s_2^2}{n_2}}$ | *File , Other Files ,* *Run an Exec ...*  **[Select File]**  *Data Disc*  **Ci-2mun.mtb**  **[Open]** | *File, Other Files,* *Run an Exec...*  **[Select File]**  *Data Disc*  **Sumci2mu.mtb**  **[Open]** |

# Two Sample Confidence Intervals for The Difference of Two Population Means
## Using Two <u>Paired</u> Samples

| Formula | Raw Data Technique | Summary Statistics Technique |
|---|---|---|
| (v) $\quad \bar{d} \mp t\dfrac{s_d}{\sqrt{n}}$ | *Stat , Basic Statistics , Paired t ...*<br><br>Click on the circle ◉ to the left of *Samples in columns*, click in the box to the right of *First sample:*, click on the variable containing sample 1 data, and [Select]<br><br>Click on the variable containing sample 2 data, and [Select] button.<br><br>Click on [Options...]<br><br>Click in *Confidence level:* box and type in the desired confidence level . Leave the 0.0 in the box to the right of *Test mean:*. Then make sure that the box to the right of *Alternative:* contains *not equal..* Then click on the [OK] button.<br><br>[OK] | *Stat , Basic Statistics , Paired t ...*<br><br>Click on the circle ◉ to the left of *Summarized data (differences)*. Click in the box to the right of *Sample size:* and type in the common sample size. Next click in box to the right of *Mean:* and type in the sample mean of differences. Next click inside box to the right of *Standard deviation:* and type in the sample standard deviation of the differences<br><br>Click on [Options...]<br><br>Click in *Confidence level:* box and type in the desired confidence level . Leave the 0.0 in the box to the right of *Test mean:*. Then make sure that the box to the right of *Alternative:* contains *not equal..* Then click on the [OK] button.<br><br>[OK] |

# Two Sample Confidence Intervals for The Difference of Two Population Means
## Using Two <u>Paired</u> Samples
### (continued)

| Formula | Raw Data Technique | Summary Statistics Technique |
|---|---|---|
| (vi) $\quad \overline{d} \mp Z\dfrac{s_d}{\sqrt{n}}$ | Name a new column **difference** <br> *Calc , Calculator ...* <br> Click in box to right of *Store result in variable* and *Select* difference <br> Click in box under *Expression:* , click on sample 1 variable, minus button, and sample 2 variable, and ⬚ OK ⬚ <br> *Calc , Column Statistics ...* <br> Click on ⦿ to left of *Standard deviation* <br> Click in the box to the right of *Input variable:* , highlight the **difference** variable and ⬚ Select ⬚ <br> Click in the box to the right of *Store result in:* and type in constant "k1" <br> *Stat , Basic Statistics , 1-Sample Z ...* <br> Click on the circle ⦿ to the left of *Samples in columns* and click in the box below.  Highlight the difference (C3) variable, and click on ⬚ Select ⬚ . Next click inside of the box to the right of *Standard deviation:*, highlight K1and click on ⬚ Select ⬚ button (or just type k1 into this box).  Make sure that the box to the right of *Test mean:* is empty and then click on ⬚ Options... ⬚ <br> Click in *Confidence level:* box and type in the desired confidence level .  Leave the 0.0 in the box to the right of *Test mean:*. Then make sure that the box to the right of *Alternative:* contains *not equal..*   Then click on the ⬚ OK ⬚ button. <br> ⬚ OK ⬚ | *Stat , Basic Statistics , 1-Sample Z ...* <br> Make sure the ⦿ to the left of *Summarized data* is selected <br> Click in box to the right of *Sample size:* and type in common sample size. <br> Click in box to right of *Mean:* and type in the value of the sample mean of the differences <br> Click inside of the box to the right of *Standard deviation:* and type instandard deviation of the differences <br> Make sure box to right of *Test Mean:* is empty and click on ⬚ Options... ⬚ . <br> Click in box to right of *Confidence level:* and type in confidence level <br> Make sure that box to right of *Alternative:* contains *not equal* and ⬚ OK ⬚ |

# Two Sample Confidence Intervals for The Ratio of Two Population Variances and Standard Deviations Using Two <u>Independent</u> Samples

| Formula | Raw Data Technique | Summary Statistics Technique |
|---|---|---|
| (vii) $\dfrac{\left(\dfrac{s_1^2}{s_2^2}\right)}{F_U}$ to $\dfrac{\left(\dfrac{s_1^2}{s_2^2}\right)}{F_L}$ | *File , Other Files ,*<br>*Run an Exec ...*<br>[ **Select File** ]<br>*Data Disc*<br>**Ci-2v.mtb**<br>[ Open ] | *File , Other Files ,*<br>*Run an Exec ...*<br>[ **Select File** ]<br>*Data Disc*<br>**Sumci2v.mtb**<br>[ Open ] |
| (viii) $\sqrt{\dfrac{\left(\dfrac{s_1^2}{s_2^2}\right)}{F_U}}$ to $\sqrt{\dfrac{\left(\dfrac{s_1^2}{s_2^2}\right)}{F_L}}$ | *File , Other Files ,*<br>*Run an Exec ...*<br>[ **Select File** ]<br>*Data Disc*<br>**Ci-2sd.mtb**<br>[ Open ] | *File , Other Files ,*<br>*Run an Exec ...*<br>[ **Select File** ]<br>*Data Disc*<br>**Sumci2sd.mtb**<br>[ Open ] |

**Two Sample Confidence Interval for The Difference of Two Population Proportions of "Successes"**

| Formula | Raw Data Technique | Summary Statistics Technique |
|---|---|---|
| (ix) $(\hat{p}_1 - \hat{p}_2) \mp$ $Z\sqrt{\dfrac{\hat{p}_1(1-\hat{p}_1)}{n_1} + \dfrac{\hat{p}_2(1-\hat{p}_2)}{n_2}}$ | If necessary, use *Data, Code, Text to Numeric* (or *Text to Text* or *Numeric to Numeric* or *Numeric to Text*) <br><br> *Stat, Basic Statistics, 2 Proportions* <br><br> Click on ◉ to the left of *Samples in different columns:* <br> Click in box to the right of *First:*, erase previous variable, click variable containing **first** sample data, and ⬚ Select <br> Click variable containing **second** sample data, and ⬚ Select <br> ⬚ Options... <br> Erase previous value, type in correct confidence level and make sure that the box to the right of *Alternative:* contains *not equal*. <br> ⬚ OK <br> ⬚ OK | *Stat, Basic Statistics, 2 Proportions* <br> Click on ◉ to the left of *Summarized data:* <br> Click in box to the right of *First:* and under *Trials:*, erase previous value and type in **first** sample size. <br> Click in box to the right under *Events:*, erase previous value, and type number of "successes" in **first** sample <br> Repeat for **second** sample on the next row <br> ⬚ Options... <br> Erase previous value, type in correct confidence level and make sure that the box to the right of *Alternative:* contains *not equal*. ⬚ OK <br> ⬚ OK |

## One Sample Hypothesis Tests for the Population Mean

| Formula | Raw Data Technique | Summary Statistics Technique |
|---|---|---|
| (i) $Z = \dfrac{\bar{x} - \mu_0}{\dfrac{\sigma}{\sqrt{n}}}$ | *Stat , Basic Statistics , 1-Sample Z ...* Make sure the button to the left of *Samples in columns* is selected, and highlight desired variable and **Select** Next click inside of the box to the right of *Standard deviation:* and type in the known value of the population standard deviation ($\sigma$). Check the box to the left of ☑ *Perform hypothesis test*, click inside of the box to the right of *Hypothesized mean:*, delete any current value, and type in the specified value of $\mu_0$ given in the null hypothesis ($H_0$:), and then click on the **Options...** button. Ignore the value in the *Confidence level:* box, and then make sure that the box to the right of *Alternative:* contains the correct inequality for your problem (*not equal* or *less than* or *greater than*). If not, click on the down triangle ( ▾ ), and click on the correct choice. Then click on **OK** . **OK** | *Stat , Basic Statistics , 1-Sample Z...* Make sure the button to the left of *Summarized data* is selected, and then click inside of the box to the right of *Sample size:*. Now type in the value of the sample size. Next click in the next box down that is to the right of *Mean:* and type in the value of the sample mean. Next click inside of the box to the right of Standard deviation:, and type in the known value of the population standard deviation ($\sigma$). Check the box to the left of ☑ *Perform hypothesis test*, click inside of the box to the right of *Hypothesized mean:*, delete any current value, and type in the specified value of $\mu_0$ in the null hypothesis($H_0$;), and then click on the **Options...** button. Ignore the value in the *Confidence level:* box, and then make sure that the box to the right of *Alternative:* contains the correct inequality for your problem (*not equal* or *less than* or *greater than*). If not, click on the down triangle ( ▾ ), and click on the correct choice. Then click on **OK** . **OK** . |

# One Sample Hypothesis Tests for the Population Mean

## (continued)

| Formula | Raw Data Technique | Summary Statistics Technique |
|---|---|---|
| (ii) $Z = \dfrac{\overline{x} - \mu_0}{\dfrac{s}{\sqrt{n}}}$ | *Calc , Column Statistics ...*<br><br>Click on ⦿ to left of *Standard deviation*<br><br>Highlight desired variable and \[ **Select** \]<br><br>Click in box to right of *Store result in*, type in k1<br><br>\[ **OK** \]<br><br>*Stat , Basic Statistics , 1-Sample Z ...*<br><br>Make sure the button to the left of *Samples in columns* is selected, and then click inside of the box below.  Now highlight desired variable and \[ **Select** \].<br><br>Click inside of the box to the right of *Standard deviation:*, highlight the K1 constant and click on the \[ **Select** \] button (or just type in k1).<br><br>Check  the box to the left of ☑ *Perform hypothesis test*, click inside of the box to the right of *Hypothesized mean:*, delete any current value, and type in the specified value of $\mu_0$ in the null hypothesis (H$_0$:), and then click on the \[ **Options...** \] button.<br><br>Ignore the value in the *Confidence level:* box, and then make sure that the box to the right of *Alternative:* contains the correct inequality for your problem (*not equal* or *less than* or *greater than*). If not, click on the down triangle ( ▾ ), and click on the correct choice.  Then click on \[ **OK** \] .<br><br>\[ **OK** \] . | *Stat , Basic Statistics , 1-Sample Z...*<br><br>Make sure the ⦿ button to the left of *Summarized data* is selected, and then click inside of the box to the right of *Sample size:* and type in the value of the sample size.<br><br>Click in the next box down that is to the right of *Mean:* and type in the value of the sample mean.<br><br>Click inside of the box to the right of *Standard deviation:* and type in the value of the sample standard deviation.  Check  the box to the left of ☑ *Perform hypothesis test*, click inside of the box to the right of *Hypothesized mean:*, delete any current value, and type in the specified value of $\mu_0$ in the null hypothesis (H$_0$:), and then click on the \[ **Options...** \] button.<br><br>Ignore the value in the *Confidence level:* box , and then make sure that the box to the right of *Alternative:* contains the correct inequality for your problem (*not equal* or *less than* or *greater than*). If not, click on the down triangle ( ▾ ), and click on the correct choice.  Then click on \[ **OK** \] .<br><br>\[ **OK** \] . |

| Formula | Raw Data Technique | Summary Statistics Technique |
|---|---|---|
| (iii) $t = \dfrac{\overline{x} - \mu_0}{\dfrac{s}{\sqrt{n}}}$ | *Stat , Basic Statistics , 1-Sample t ...*<br><br>Make sure the ⦿ button to the left of *Samples in columns* is selected and then click inside of the box below.  Now highlight desired variable and Select<br><br>Check   the box to the left of ☑ *Perform hypothesis test*, click inside of the box to the right of *Hypothesized mean:*, delete any current value, and type in the specified value of $\mu_0$ in the null hypothesis ($H_0$:), and then click on the Options... button.<br><br>Ignore the value in the *Confidence level:* box, and then make sure that the box to the right of *Alternative:* contains the correct inequality for your problem (*not equal* or *less than* or *greater than*).  If not, click on the down triangle ( ▾ ), and click on the correct choice.  Then click on OK .<br><br>OK | *Stat , Basic Statistics , 1 Sample t ...*<br><br>Make sure the ⦿ button to the left of *Summarized data* is selected and then click inside of the box to the right of *Sample size:* and  type in the value of the sample size.<br><br>Click in the next box down that is to the right of *Mean:* and type in the value of the sample mean<br><br>Click in the next box down that is to the right of *Standard deviation:* and type in the value of the sample standard deviation.<br><br>Check   the box to the left of ☑ *Perform hypothesis test*, click inside of the box to the right of *Hypothesized mean:*, delete any current value, and type in the specified value of $\mu_0$ in the null hypothesis ($H_0$:), and then click on the Options... button.<br><br>Ignore the value in the *Confidence level:* box, and then make sure that the box to the right of *Alternative:* contains the correct inequality for your problem (*not equal* or *less than* or *greater than*).  If not, click on the down triangle ( ▾ ), and click on the correct choice.  Then click on OK .<br><br>OK |

## One Sample Hypothesis Test for the Population Variance

| Formula | Raw Data Technique | Summary Statistics Technique |
|---|---|---|
| (iv) $\quad \chi^2 = \dfrac{(n-1)s^2}{\sigma_o^2}$ | *File , Other Files ,*<br>*Run an Exec ...*<br>Select File<br>*Data Disc*<br>**Ht-1v.mtb**<br>Open | *File , Other Files ,*<br>*Run an Exec ...*<br>Select File<br>*Data Disc*<br>**Sumht1v.mtb**<br>Open |

## One Sample Hypothesis Test for the Population Standard Deviation

| Formula | Raw Data Technique | Summary Statistics Technique |
|---|---|---|
| (iv) $\quad \chi^2 = \dfrac{(n-1)s^2}{\sigma_o^2}$ | *File , Other Files ,*<br>*Run an Exec ...*<br>Select File<br>*Data Disc*<br>**Ht-1sd.mtb**<br>Open | *File , Other Files ,*<br>*Run an Exec ...*<br>Select File<br>*Data Disc*<br>**Sumht1sd.mtb**<br>Open |

# One Sample Hypothesis Test for the Population Proportion of "Successes"

| Formula | Raw Data Technique | Summary Statistics Technique |
|---|---|---|
| (v) $Z = \dfrac{\hat{p} - p_0}{\sqrt{\dfrac{p_0(1 - p_0)}{n}}}$ | If necessary, use<br>*Data, Code, Text to Numeric* or<br>*Data, Code, Text to Text* or<br>*Data, Code, Numeric to Numeric* or<br>*Data, Code, Numeric to Text*<br><br>*Stat , Basic Statistics , 1 Proportion*<br>Click on ⦿ to left of *Samples in columns* , click in box to the right, erase any previous variable, click on desired variable and [ **Select** ]<br><br>[ **Options...** ]<br>Ignore the value in the *Confidence level:* box, and then click inside of the box to the right of *Test proportion:*. Delete any current value, and type in the specified value of $p_0$ in the null hypothesis ($H_0$:).<br><br>Make sure that the box to the right of *Alternative:* contains the correct inequality for your problem (*not equal* or *less than* or *greater than*). If not, click on the down triangle ( ▾ ), and click on the correct choice.<br><br>Make sure that the ☑ box to the left of *Use test and interval based on normal distribution* is checked. Then click on [ **OK** ].<br><br>Back in the 1 Proportion dialog box, click on [ **OK** ]. | *Stat , Basic Statistics , 1 Proportion...*<br>Make sure the ⦿ button to the left of *Summarized data* is selected<br>Click inside of the box to the right of *Number of trials:*. and type in the value of the sample size.<br><br>Click in the next box down that is to the right of *Number of events:* and type in the value of the number of "successes" in the sample.<br><br>[ **Options...** ]<br>Ignore the value in the *Confidence level:* box, and then click inside of the box to the right of *Test proportion:*. Delete any current value, and type in the specified value of $p_0$ in the null hypothesis ($H_0$:).<br><br>Make sure that the box to the right of *Alternative:* contains the correct inequality for your problem (*not equal* or *less than* or *greater than*). If not, click on the down triangle ( ▾ ), and click on the correct choice.<br><br>Make sure that the ☑ box to the left of *Use test and interval based on normal distribution* is checked. Then click on [ **OK** ].<br><br>Back in the 1 Proportion dialog box, click on [ **OK** ]. |

# Determining the Power of a Test for One Sample Hypothesis Tests

| Compute the Power of a Test For: | Technique |
|---|---|
| Z-Test of the Population Mean:<br><br>$Z = \dfrac{\bar{x} - \mu_0}{\dfrac{\sigma}{\sqrt{n}}}$ | **If sample size needs to be computed:** *Calc , Column Statistics...*<br><br>In the Column Statistics dialog box: click on the circle to the left of *N nonmissing*, click inside of the *Input variable:* box, click on the variable that contains the sample data, and click on the ⬛ Select ⬛ button. Next click in the box to the **right** of *Store results in:*, and type in k1 as the constant name. Then click on the ⬛ OK ⬛ button. *Stat , Power and Sample Size, 1-Sample Z...*<br><br>Press the ⬛ F3 ⬛ key to clear the contents of this dialog box and reset all options. Click in the box to the right of *Sample sizes:* and type the given sample size or K1. Then click in the box to the right of *Differences:* and type the difference between the $H_a$: and $H_0$: values. **Note that the difference must be <u>positive</u> for a right-tail test (greater than), and the difference must be <u>negative</u> for a left-tail test (less than). The difference may be either positive or negative for a two-tail test (not equal to).**<br><br>Click in the box to the right of *Standard deviation:* type the value of σ<br><br>⬛ Options... ⬛<br><br>In the Power and Sample Size for 1-Sample Z - Options dialog box under the *Alternative Hypothesis* heading, click on the circle that corresponds to the type of alternative for this case. In the box to the right of *Significance level:* will be the default value of 0.05 . If this is nor correct for your problem, erase this value and type in the correct value of α. Optionally you could store the values of the sample size, difference and computed power in three separate columns. If you decide to do this optional storage, you should name the empty columns as "n", "Difference" and "Power" ahead of time. Then click on ⬛ OK ⬛ .<br><br>⬛ OK ⬛ |

| Compute the Power of a Test For: | Technique |
|---|---|
| Z-Test of the Population Mean:<br><br>$Z = \dfrac{\overline{x} - \mu_0}{\dfrac{s}{\sqrt{n}}}$ | **If sample size needs to be computed:**<br><br>*Calc , Column Statistics...*<br><br>In the Column Statistics dialog box: click on the circle to the left of *N nonmissing*, click inside of the *Input variable:* box, click on the variable that contains the sample data, and click on the \| Select \| button. Next click in the box to the **right** of *Store results in:*, and type in k1 as the constant name. Then click on the \| OK \| button.<br><br>**If the sample standard deviation needs to be computed:**<br><br>*Calc , Column Statistics...*<br><br>In the Column Statistics dialog box: click on the circle to the left of *Standard deviation*, click inside of the *Input variable:* box, click on the variable that contains the sample data, and click on the \| Select \| button. Next click in the box to the **right** of *Store results in:*, and type in k2 as the constant name. Then click on the \| OK \| button.<br><br>*Stat , Power and Sample Size, 1-Sample Z...*<br><br>Press the \| F3 \| key to clear the contents of this dialog box and reset all options. Click in the box to the right of *Sample sizes:* and type the given sample size or K1. Click in the box to the right of *Differences:* and type in the $H_a$: - $H_0$: values.<br><br>Click in the box to the right of *Standard deviation:* type in the value of s or K2.<br><br>\| Options... \|<br><br>In the Power and Sample Size for 1-Sample Z - Options dialog box under the *Alternative Hypothesis* heading, click on the circle that corresponds to the type of alternative for this case. In the box to the right of *Significance level:* will be the default value of 0.05 . If this is nor correct for your problem, erase this value and type in the correct value of $\alpha$. Optionally you could store the values of the sample size, difference and computed power in three separate columns. If you decide to do this optional storage, you should name the empty columns as "n", "Difference" and "Power" ahead of time. Then click on \| OK \| .<br><br>\| OK \| |

| Compute the Power of a Test For: | Technique |
|---|---|
| Z-Test of the Population Mean:<br><br>$t = \dfrac{\overline{x} - \mu_0}{\dfrac{s}{\sqrt{n}}}$ | **If sample size needs to be computed:**<br>*Calc , Column Statistics...*<br><br>In the Column Statistics dialog box: click on the circle to the left of *N nonmissing*, click inside of the *Input variable:* box, click on the variable that contains the sample data, and click on the $\boxed{\textbf{Select}}$ button. Next click in the box to the **right** of *Store results in:*, and type in k1 as the constant name. Then click on the $\boxed{\textbf{OK}}$ button.<br><br>**If the sample standard deviation needs to be computed:**<br>*Calc , Column Statistics...*<br><br>In the Column Statistics dialog box: click on the circle to the left of *Standard deviation*, click inside of the *Input variable:* box, click on the variable that contains the sample data, and click on the $\boxed{\textbf{Select}}$ button. Next click in the box to the **right** of *Store results in:*, and type in k2 as the constant name. Then click on the $\boxed{\textbf{OK}}$ button.<br><br>*Stat , Power and Sample Size, 1-Sample t...*<br><br>Press the $\boxed{\textbf{F3}}$ key to clear the contents of this dialog box and reset all options. Click in the box to the right of *Sample sizes:* and type the given sample size or K1. Click in the box to the right of *Differences:* and type in the H$_a$: - H$_0$: values.<br><br>Click in the box to the right of *Standard deviation:* type in the value of s or K2.<br><br>$\boxed{\textbf{Options...}}$<br><br>In the Power and Sample Size for 1-Sample Z - Options dialog box under the *Alternative Hypothesis* heading, click on the circle that corresponds to the type of alternative for this case. In the box to the right of *Significance level:* will be the default value of 0.05 . If this is nor correct for your problem, erase this value and type in the correct value of α. Optionally you could store the values of the sample size, difference and computed power in three separate columns. If you decide to do this optional storage, you should name the empty columns as "n", "Difference" and "Power" ahead of time. Then click on $\boxed{\textbf{OK}}$ .<br><br>$\boxed{\textbf{OK}}$ |

| Compute the Power of a Test For: | Technique |
|---|---|
| Z-Test of the Population Proportion of "Successes": $$Z = \dfrac{\hat{p} - p_0}{\sqrt{\dfrac{p_0(1 - p_0)}{n}}}$$ | **If sample size needs to be computed:** *Calc , Column Statistics...* In the Column Statistics dialog box: click on the circle to the left of *N nonmissing*, click inside of the *Input variable:* box, click on the variable that contains the sample data, and click on the $\boxed{\text{Select}}$ button. Next click in the box to the **right** of *Store results in:*, and type in k1 as the constant name. Then click on the $\boxed{\text{OK}}$ button. <br><br> *Stat , Power and Sample Size, 1 Proportion...* Press the $\boxed{\text{F3}}$ key to clear the contents of this dialog box and reset all options. Click in the box to the right of *Sample sizes:* and type the given sample size or K1. Type the specific $H_a$: value of the proportion into the box to the right of *Alternative values of p:* . Next type the null hypothesized value of the proportion into the box to the right of *Hypothesized p:*, <br><br> $\boxed{\text{Options...}}$ <br><br> In the Power and Sample Size for 1 Proportion - Options dialog box under the *Alternative Hypothesis* heading, click on the circle that corresponds to the type of alternative for this case. In the box to the right of *Significance level:* will be the default value of 0.05 . If this is nor correct for your problem, erase this value and type in the correct value of $\alpha$. Optionally you could store the values of the sample size, difference and computed power in three separate columns. If you decide to do this optional storage, you should name the empty columns as "n", "Difference" and "Power" ahead of time. Then click on $\boxed{\text{OK}}$ . <br><br> $\boxed{\text{OK}}$ |

**Choosing a Sample Size Before One Sample Hypothesis Tests**

| Determine Optimal Sample Size For: | Technique |
|---|---|
| Z-Test of the Population Mean | *Stat , Power and Sample Size, 1-Sample Z...*<br><br>Press the **F3** key to clear the contents of this dialog box and reset all options.<br><br>Click in the box to the right of *Differences:* and type in the $H_a$: - $H_0$: values.<br><br>Click in the box to the right of *Power values:* and type the power of the test. **This must be in decimal form and not as a percent!**<br><br>Click in the box to the right of *Standard deviation:* type the value of $\sigma$<br><br>**Options...**<br><br>Under the *Alternative Hypothesis* heading, click on the circle that corresponds correct alternative.<br><br>In the box to the right of *Significance level:* type in the correct value of $\alpha$. Optionally you may store the values of the sample size, difference and computed power in three separate columns. If you decide to do this, you should name the empty columns as "n", "Difference" and "Power" ahead of time.<br><br>**OK**<br><br>**OK** |
| t-Test of the Population Mean | *Stat , Power and Sample Size, 1-Sample t...*<br><br>Press the **F3** key to clear the contents of this dialog box and reset all options.<br><br>Click in the box to the right of *Differences:* and type in the $H_a$: - $H_0$: values.<br><br>Click in the box to the right of *Power values:* and type the power of the test. **This must be in decimal form and not as a percent!**<br><br>Click in the box to the right of *Standard deviation:* type the value of estimated standard deviation<br><br>**Options...**<br><br>Under the *Alternative Hypothesis* heading, click on the circle that corresponds correct alternative.<br><br>In the box to the right of *Significance level:* type in the correct value of $\alpha$. Optionally you may store the values of the sample size, difference and computed power in three separate columns. If you decide to do this, you should name the empty columns as "n", "Difference" and "Power" ahead of time.<br><br>**OK**<br><br>**OK** |

| Determine Optimal Sample Size For: | Technique |
|---|---|
| Test of the Population Proportion of "Successes" | *Stat , Power and Sample Size, 1 Proportion...*<br><br>Press the F3 key to clear the contents of this dialog box and reset all options.<br><br>Click in the box to the right of *Alternative values of p:* and type value of $H_a$: .**This must be in decimal form!**<br><br>Click in the box to the right of *Power values:* and type the power of the test.<br><br>Click in the box to the right of *Hypothesized p:* type the value of $p_0$ .<br><br>Options...<br><br>Under the *Alternative Hypothesis* heading, click on the circle that corresponds to the correct alternative.<br><br>In the box to the right of *Significance level:* type in the correct value of $\alpha$. Optionally you may store the values of the sample size, difference and computed power in three separate columns. If you decide to do this, you should name the empty columns as "n", "Alternative" and "Power" ahead of time.<br><br>OK<br><br>OK |

# Two Sample Hypothesis Tests for Two Population Means Using Two <u>Independent</u> Samples

| Formula | Raw Data Technique | Summary Statistics Technique |
|---|---|---|
| (i) $\quad t = \dfrac{\bar{x}_1 - \bar{x}_2}{\sqrt{\dfrac{s_1^2}{n_1} + \dfrac{s_2^2}{n_2}}}$ <br><br> ("separate variance" formula) | *Stat , Basic Statistics , 2-Sample-t ...* <br> In the 2-Sample t (Test and Confidence Interval) dialog box: click on the ⊙ to the left of *Samples in different columns*, click in the box to the right of *First:*, click on the variable that contains the data from sample 1, and $\boxed{\text{Select}}$ . The cursor now will be in the box to the right of *Second:*, click on the variable that contains the data from sample 2, and $\boxed{\text{Select}}$ . Make sure that the □ to the left of *equal variances* box is **not** checked. Then click on $\boxed{\text{Options...}}$ . <br><br> Ignore the value in the *confidence level:* box and then click inside of the box to the right of *Test difference:*. If the current value is not 0.0, delete this value and type in 0.0 . Next make sure that the box to the right of *Alternative:* contains the correct inequality for your problem (*not equal* or *less than* or *greater than*). If not, click on the down triangle ( ▾ ), and click on the correct choice. $\boxed{\text{OK}}$ <br> $\boxed{\text{OK}}$ | *Stat , Basic Statistics , 2-Sample t ...* <br> In the 2-Sample t (Test and Confidence Interval) dialog box: you may press the $\boxed{\text{F3}}$ key to clear the contents of this dialog box and reset all options and erase any previous information. Click on the ⊙ to the left of *Summarized data*, and then click inside of the box on the *First:* row and underneath of *Sample size:*. If a previous value is shown, erase this number and type in the value of the first sample size. Click in the next box to the right that is underneath of *Mean:* and type in the value of the first sample mean. Next click inside of the next box to the right that is underneath of *Standard deviation:* and type in the given value of the first sample standard deviation. Then repeat this on the *Second:* row for sample 2. Make sure that the □ to the left of *equal variances* box is **not** checked. Then click on $\boxed{\text{Options...}}$ . <br><br> Ignore the value in the *confidence level:* box and then click inside of the box to the right of *Test difference:*. If the current value is not 0.0, delete this value and type in 0.0 . Next make sure that the box to the right of *Alternative:* contains the correct inequality for your problem (*not equal* or *less than* or *greater than*). If not, click on the down triangle ( ▾ ), and click on the correct choice. $\boxed{\text{OK}}$ <br> $\boxed{\text{OK}}$ |

# Two Sample Hypothesis Tests for Two Population Means Using Two <u>Independent</u> Samples (continued)

| Formula | Raw Data Technique | Summary Statistics Technique |
|---|---|---|
| (ii) $\quad t = \dfrac{\bar{x}_1 - \bar{x}_2}{\sqrt{s_p^2\left(\dfrac{1}{n_1} + \dfrac{1}{n_2}\right)}}$<br><br>where<br><br>$s_p^2 = \dfrac{(n_1 - 1)s_1^2 + (n_2 - 1)s_2^2}{n_1 + n_2 - 2}$<br><br>("pooled variance" formula) | *Stat , Basic Statistics , 2-Sample-t ...*<br>In the 2-Sample t (Test and Confidence Interval) dialog box: click on the ⊙ to the left of *Samples in different columns*, click in the box to the right of *First:*, click on the variable that contains the data from sample 1, and [ **Select** ] . The cursor now will be in the box to the right of *Second:*, click on the variable that contains the data from sample 2, and [ **Select** ] . Make sure that the ☑ to the left of *equal variances* box **is** checked. Then click on [ **Options...** ]<br>Ignore the value in the *confidence level:* box and then click inside of the box to the right of *Test difference:*. If the current value is not 0.0, delete this value and type in 0.0 . Next make sure that the box to the right of *Alternative:* contains the correct inequality for your problem (*not equal* or *less than* or *greater than*). If not, click on the down triangle ( ▾ ), and click on the correct choice. [ **OK** ]<br>[ **OK** ] | *Stat , Basic Statistics , 2-Sample t ...*<br>In the 2-Sample t (Test and Confidence Interval) dialog box: you may press the [ **F3** ] key to clear the contents of this dialog box and reset all options and erase any previous information. Click on the ⊙ to the left of *Summarized data*, and then click inside of the box on the *First:* row and underneath of *Sample size:*. If a previous value is shown, erase this number and type in the value of the first sample size. Click in the next box to the right that is underneath of *Mean:* and type in the value of the first sample mean. Next click inside of the next box to the right that is underneath of *Standard deviation:* and type in the given value of the first sample standard deviation. Then repeat this on the *Second:* row for sample 2. Make sure that the ☑ to the left of *equal variances* box **is** checked. Then click on [ **Options...** ] .<br>Ignore the value in the *confidence level:* box and then click inside of the box to the right of *Test difference:*. If the current value is not 0.0, delete this value and type in 0.0 . Next make sure that the box to the right of *Alternative:* contains the correct inequality for your problem (*not equal* or *less than* or *greater than*). If not, click on the down triangle ( ▾ ), and click on the correct choice. [ **OK** ]<br>[ **OK** ] |

## Two Sample Hypothesis Tests for Two Population Means Using Two <u>Independent</u> Samples
### (continued)

| Formula | Raw Data Technique | Summary Statistics Technique |
|---|---|---|
| (iii) $\quad Z = \dfrac{\bar{x}_1 - \bar{x}_2}{\sqrt{\dfrac{\sigma_1^2}{n_1} + \dfrac{\sigma_2^2}{n_2}}}$ | *File , Other Files ,* <br> *Run an Exec ...* <br> **Select File** <br> *Data Disc* <br> **Ht-2mk.mtb** <br> **Open** | *File , Other Files ,* <br> *Run an Exec ...* <br> **Select File** <br> *Data Disc* <br> **Sumht2mk.mtb** <br> **Open** |
| (iv) $\quad Z = \dfrac{\bar{x}_1 - \bar{x}_2}{\sqrt{\dfrac{s_1^2}{n_1} + \dfrac{s_2^2}{n_2}}}$ | *File , Other Files ,* <br> *Run an Exec ...* <br> **Select File** <br> *Data Disc* <br> **Ht-2mun.mtb** <br> **Open** | *File , Other Files ,* <br> *Run an Exec ...* <br> **Select File** <br> *Data Disc* <br> **Sumht2mu.mtb** <br> **Open** |

## Two Sample Hypothesis Tests for Two Population Means Using Two <u>Paired</u> Samples

| Formula | Raw Data Technique | Summary Statistics Technique |
|---|---|---|
| (v) $\quad t = \dfrac{\overline{d}}{\left(\dfrac{s_d}{\sqrt{n}}\right)}$ | *Stat , Basic Statistics , Paired t ...* <br> In the Paired t (Test and Confidence Intervals): click on the circle ⊙ to the left of *Samples in columns*, click in the box to the right of *First sample:*, click on the variable that contains the data from sample 1, and click on the \| Select \| button. The cursor now will be in the box to the right of *Second:*, click on the variable that contains the data from sample 2, and click on the \| Select \| button. Then click on the \| Options... \| button. <br> In the Paired t - Options dialog box: ignore the value in the *confidence level:* box and then click inside of the box to the right of *Test difference:*. If the current value is not 0.0, delete this value and type in 0.0 . Next make sure that the box to the right of *Alternative:* contains the correct inequality for your problem (*not equal* or *less than* or *greater than*). If not, click on the down triangle ( ▾ ), and click on the correct choice and \| OK \| . <br> \| OK \| . | *Stat , Basic Statistics , Paired t ...* <br> In the Paired t (Test and Confidence Intervals): make sure the ⊙ to the left of *Summarized data (differences)* is selected, and then click inside of the box to the right of *Sample size:*. Type in the value of the common sample size. Click in the next box down that is to the right of *Mean:* and type in the value of the difference sample mean. Click inside of the box to the right of *Standard deviation:*, and type in the difference sample standard deviation. Click on the \| Options... \| button. <br> In the Paired t - Options dialog box: ignore the value in the *confidence level:* box and then click inside of the box to the right of *Test difference:*. If the current value is not 0.0, delete this value and type in 0.0 . Next make sure that the box to the right of *Alternative:* contains the correct inequality for your problem (*not equal* or *less than* or *greater than*). If not, click on the down triangle ( ▾ ), and click on the correct choice and \| OK \| . <br> \| OK \| . |

| Formula | Raw Data Technique | Summary Statistics Technique |
|---|---|---|
| (vi) $\quad Z = \dfrac{\bar{d}}{\left(\dfrac{s_d}{\sqrt{n}}\right)}$ | Name a new, unused column as **d**<br>*Calc , Calculator...*<br>In the Calculator dialog box the cursor will be inside the box to the right of *Store result in variable:*. Highlight the **d** variable and $\boxed{\textbf{Select}}$. Click inside of the box under *Expression:*, click on the variable containing the **first** sample's data, $\boxed{\textbf{Select}}$, click on the minus sign button, click on the variable containing the **second** sample's data, and $\boxed{\textbf{Select}}$. (Or just type in the first sample's column number, followed by a minus sign, and then the second sample's column number.) Click on the $\boxed{\textbf{OK}}$ button.<br>*Calc , Column Statistics...*<br>Click on the ⦿ to the left of *Standard deviation*, click inside of the *Input variable:* box, click on **d**, and $\boxed{\textbf{Select}}$. Click in the box to the right of *Store results in:*, and type in k1 as the constant name. Click on $\boxed{\textbf{OK}}$.<br>*Stat , Basic Statistics , 1-Sample Z...*<br>In the 1-Sample Z (Test and Confidence Interval) dialog box: make sure the button ⦿ to the left of *Samples in columns* is selected, and click inside of the box below. Highlight the **d** variable, and $\boxed{\textbf{Select}}$. Click inside of the box to the right of *Standard deviation:,*, highlight the K1 constant and $\boxed{\textbf{Select}}$ (or just type in k1). Check the box to the left of *Perform hypothesis test*, click inside of the box to the right of *Hypothesized mean:*, delete any current value, and type in 0 (zero), and then click on the $\boxed{\textbf{Options...}}$ button.<br>In the 1-Sample Z - Options dialog box: ignore the value in the *Confidence level:* box, and then make sure that the box to the right of *Alternative:* contains the correct inequality for your problem (*not equal* or *less than* or *greater than*. If not, click on the down triangle ( $\boxed{\blacktriangledown}$ ), and click on the correct choice. Then click on $\boxed{\textbf{OK}}$.<br>$\boxed{\textbf{OK}}$. | *Stat , Basic Statistics , 1-Sample Z...*<br>In the 1-Sample Z (Test and Confidence Interval) dialog box: you may press the $\boxed{\textbf{F3}}$ key to clear the contents of this dialog box and reset all options and erase any previous variables. Make sure the ⦿ button to the left of *Summarized data* is selected, and then click inside of the box to the right of *Sample size:*.<br>Now type in the value of the common sample size. Next click in the next box down that is to the right of *Mean:* and type in the value of the difference sample mean. Next click inside of the box to the right of *Standard deviation:*, erase any current incorrect value, and type in the value of the difference sample standard deviation ($s_d$). Check the box to the left of *Perform hypothesis test*, click inside of the box to the right of *Hypothesized mean:*, delete any current value, and type in 0 (zero) the specified value of $\mu_d$ in the null hypothesis ($H_0$:), and then click on the $\boxed{\textbf{Options...}}$ button.<br>In the 1-Sample Z - Options dialog box: ignore the value in the *Confidence level:* box, and then make sure that the box to the right of *Alternative:* contains the correct inequality for your problem (*not equal* or *less than* or *greater than*. If not, click on the down triangle ( $\boxed{\blacktriangledown}$ ), and click on the correct choice. Then click on $\boxed{\textbf{OK}}$.<br>$\boxed{\textbf{OK}}$. |

## Two Sample Hypothesis Test for Two Population Variances
## and Two Population Standard Deviations Using Two __Independent__ Samples

| Formula | Raw Data Technique | Summary Statistics Technique |
|---|---|---|
| (vii) $\quad F = \dfrac{s_1^2}{s_2^2}$ <br><br> for any of the 3 possible alternatives of < or > or ≠ | *File , Other Files ,* <br> *Run an Exec ...* <br> Select File <br> *Data Disc* <br> **Ht-2vsd.mtb** <br> Open | *File , Other Files ,* <br> *Run an Exec ...* <br> Select File <br> *Data Disc* <br> **Sumht2vs.mtb** <br> Open |
| (vii) $\quad F = \dfrac{s_1^2}{s_2^2}$ <br><br> for **only** the **not equal** alternative | *Stat , Basic Statistics , 2 Variances...* <br> In the 2 Variances dialog box: you may press the F3 key to clear the contents of this dialog box and reset all options and erase any previous variables. Click on the circle to the left of *Samples in different columns*, click in the box to the right of *First:*, click on the variable that contains the data from sample 1, and click on the Select button. The cursor now will be in the box to the right of *Second:*, click on the variable that contains the data from sample 2, and click on the Select button. Then click on OK . | *Stat , Basic Statistics , 2 Variances...* <br> In the 2 Variances dialog box: you may press the F3 key to clear the contents of this dialog box and reset all options and erase any previous information. Click on the circle to the left of *Summarized data*, and then click inside of the box on the *First:* row and underneath of *Sample size:*. If a previous value is shown, erase this number and type in the value of the first sample size. Click in the next box to the right that is underneath of *Variance:* and type in the value of the first sample's variance. Next click inside of the box on the *Second:* row and underneath of *Sample size:* and type in the second sample size. Click in the next box to the right that is underneath of *Variance:* and type in the value of the second sample's variance. Then click on OK . |

# Two Sample Hypothesis Test for Two Population Proportions of "Successes"

| Formula | Raw Data Technique | Summary Statistics Technique |
|---|---|---|
| (viii)<br><br>$Z = \dfrac{\hat{p}_1 - \hat{p}_2}{\sqrt{p^*(1 - p^*)\left(\dfrac{n_1 + n_2}{n_1 n_2}\right)}}$<br><br>where $p^* = \dfrac{Y_1 + Y_2}{n_1 + n_2}$ | If necessary, use<br>*Data, Code, Text to Numeric* or<br>*Data, Code, Text to Text* or<br>*Data, Code, Numeric to Numeric* or<br>*Data, Code, Numeric to Text*<br><br>*Stat, Basic Statistics, 2 Proportions ...*<br>In the 2 Proportions (Test and Confidence Interval) dialog box: make sure the button ⊙ to left of *Samples in different columns* is selected, click inside of the box to the right of *First:*, click on the variable that contains the data from the **first** sample, and click on Select . The cursor will move into the box to the right of *Second:*, click on the variable that contains the data from the **second** sample, and click on Select . Then click on the Options... button.<br>In the 2 Proportions - Options dialog box: ignore the value in the *confidence level:* box and then click inside of the box to the right of *Test difference:* and type in 0.0 . Next make sure that the box to the right of *Alternative:* contains the correct inequality for your problem. Next click in the square ☑ to the left of *Use pooled estimate of p for test:* to check this box, if it is not already checked. OK .<br>OK . | *Stat, Basic Statistics, 2 Proportions ...*<br>In the 2 Proportions (Test and Confidence Interval) dialog box: make sure the button ⊙ to the left of *Summarized data* is selected, and then click inside of the box to the right of *First:* and under *Trials:*. In this box type in the first sample size. Next click inside of the box to the right under *Events:* and type in the number of "successes" in the first sample. Now repeat this for the second sample size and the number of "successes" in the second sample. Then click on the Options... button.<br>In the 2 Proportions - Options dialog box: ignore the value in the *confidence level:* box and then click inside of the box to the right of *Test difference:* and type in 0.0 . Next make sure that the box to the right of *Alternative:* contains the correct inequality for your problem. Next click in the square ☑ to the left of *Use pooled estimate of p for test:* to check this box, if it is not already checked. OK .<br>OK . |

## One-Way Analysis of Variance (ANOVA)
## The Completely Randomized Design

Combine sample data in <u>separate</u> columns into <u>one</u> column.

| Purpose | MINITAB Procedure |
|---|---|
| Combine sample data in <u>separate</u> columns into <u>one</u> new column so as to be able to use the *Stat, ANOVA, One-way* procedure. | Name two **new unused** columns; one as AllData (that will contain the "stacked" data) and the second as Factor.<br><br>*Data , Stack , Columns ...*<br><br>In the Stack Columns dialog box: the cursor will be in the box under the *Stack the following columns:*. Block the columns that contain the original data for each of the samples (hold the ⬚Ctrl⬚ key and click on each variable or drag the mouse over the variables, if consecutive) and click on the ⬚Select⬚ button. Next click on the button to the left of *Column of current worksheet:* and then click inside of the box to its right. Highlight the AllData variable and click on ⬚Select⬚. Then cursor will be inside the box to the right of *Store subscripts in:*, highlight the Factor variable and click on ⬚Select⬚. **If** the columns with the original data have been named, make sure the box to the left of *Use variable names in subscript column* is checked. But if the columns with the original data have **not** been named, click on this box to **un**check it. Click on ⬚OK⬚. |

Compute the residuals.

| Purpose | MINITAB Procedure |
|---|---|
| Compute the <u>residuals</u> and store them in new column. | *Stat , ANOVA , One-way ...*<br><br>In the One-way Analysis of Variance dialog box: the cursor will be in the *Response:* box; click on the variable that contains the stacked data (AllData) and click on ⬚Select⬚. The cursor will move to the *Factor:* box; click on the variable (Factor) that contains the levels of the factor (where the subscripts are stored) and click on ⬚Select⬚. If the square to the left of *Store residuals* is **not checked, click on the square to check this option.** A **new** column to the right of the last column in your worksheet will **automatically** be created **and** be named RESI1. These residual values will be used to check the validity of the assumption that the populations are normally distributed. You may ignore the value in the box to the right of *Confidence level:*. Then click on ⬚OK⬚. |

## One-Way Analysis of Variance (ANOVA)
## The Completely Randomized Design
## (continued)

Checking the Assumptions of One-Way Analysis of Variance where the data is in <u>one</u> column and the Factor level numbers are in a second column

| Assumption | MINITAB Procedure |
|---|---|
| Each population is normally distributed. | *Stat , Basic Statistics , Normality Test* ...<br>Highlight 'RESI1' variable and click on Select<br>Under *Percentile lines*, the button to the left of *None* should be chosen<br>Make sure the ◉ to the left of *Anderson-Darling* is checked<br>Click in the *Title:* box and type in Q-Q Plot (do **not** press Enter )<br>OK |
| The variances of all populations are equal.<br>"homogeneity of variance"<br>Bartlett's test and Levene's Test | *Stat , ANOVA , Test for Equal Variances...*<br>Click on the AllData variable (that contains the stacked data) and Select<br>Click on the Factor variable (that contains the corresponding levels of the stacked data in AllData) and then click on the Select button.<br>ignore the boxes to the right of *Confidence level:* and *Title:* |

One-Way Analysis of Variance where the data is in <u>one</u> column and the Factor level numbers are in a second column

| Null Hypothesis | MINITAB Procedure |
|---|---|
| $H_0: \mu_1 = \mu_2 = \mu_3 = ... = \mu_c$ | *Stat , ANOVA , One-way* ...<br>Click on the variable that contains the stacked data (AllData) and click on Select (to select the *Response:* variable)<br>Click on the variable that contains the level numbers of the factor (Factor) and click on Select (to select the *Factor:* levels)<br>If the residuals have **not** been computed yet, click on the ☑ to the left of *Store residuals*. A new column to the right of the last column in your worksheet will be created, named 'RESI1', and the residuals will be stored in this column.<br>If the residuals **have** already been computed, click on the □ to the left of *Store residuals* to **un**check this option.<br>OK<br>**Note** that since Minitab remembers the previous entries used in a dialog box, the only thing you will actually need to do is to uncheck the *Store residuals* option. |

**One-Way Analysis of Variance (ANOVA)**
**The Completely Randomized Design**
**(continued)**

Multiple Comparisons <u>after</u> the overall null hypothesis $H_0$: $\mu_1 = \mu_2 = \mu_3 = ... = \mu_c$ has been rejected where the data is in the 'AllData' column and the factor level numbers are in the 'Factor' column

| Multiple Comparison Method | MINITAB Procedure |
|---|---|
| **Dunnett's method**. Family error rate is set, and individual rate is computed. For making *control* with all others pairwise comparisons. | *Stat , ANOVA , One-way ...*<br>Click on the AllData variable and click on Select<br>Click on the Factor variable and click on Select<br>If the residuals **have** already been computed, click on the ☐ to the left of *Store residuals* to **un**check this option<br>Click on Comparisons... , click on the ☑ to the left of *Dunnett's* , *family error rate:* , click in the box to the right, type in the desired family error rate, click in the box to the right of *Control group subscript:* , type in the control id name (enclose in quotes) or number and OK<br>OK |
| **Fisher's LSD method**. Individual error rate is set, and family rate is computed. For making <u>all possible</u> pairwise comparisons. | *Stat , ANOVA , One-way ...*<br>Click on the AllData variable and click on Select<br>Click on the Factor variable and click on Select<br>If the residuals **have** already been computed, click on the ☐ to the left of *Store residuals* to **un**check this option<br>Click on Comparisons... , click on the ☑ to the left of *Fisher's* , *individual error rate:* , click in the box to the right, type in the desired individual error rate and OK<br>OK |
| **Tukey's HSD method**. Family error rate is set, and individual rate is computed. For making <u>all possible</u> pairwise comparisons. | *Stat , ANOVA , One-way ...*<br>Click on the AllData variable and click on Select<br>Click on the Factor variable and click on Select<br>If the residuals **have** already been computed, click on the ☐ to the left of *Store residuals* to **un**check this option<br>Click on Comparisons... , click on the ☑ to the left of *Tukey's* , *family error rate:* , click in the box to the right, type in the desired family error rate and OK<br>OK |

**Analysis of Variance (ANOVA)**

**The Randomized Complete Block Design with <u>One</u> Observation per Cell**

Combine sample data in <u>separate</u> columns into <u>one</u> column.

| Purpose | MINITAB Procedure |
|---------|-------------------|
| Combining data from <u>separate</u> columns into <u>one</u> column.<br><br>Stack sample data currently in separate columns (variables) into one new column, C26, and put the Treatment and Block level numbers into C27 and C28. | *File , Other Files , Run an Exec ...*<br><br>Select File<br><br>*Data Disc*<br><br>**Stak-b1.mtb**<br><br>Open |

Compute the residuals.

| Purpose | MINITAB Procedure |
|---------|-------------------|
| Compute the <u>residuals</u> and store them in new column. | *Stat , ANOVA , General Linear Model ...*<br><br>Click on the AllData (C26) variable that contains the stacked data and click on the Select button. Next click inside of the box under the *Model:* heading, hold the Ctrl key while clicking on the Treatment (C27) and Block (C28) variables and click on the Select button. Next click on the Storage... button.<br><br>If the square to the left of *Residuals* is **not checked, click on this square ☑ to check this option**. A new column to the right of the last column in your worksheet will **automatically** be created (usually C29) **and** will be named RESI1. Then click on OK .<br><br>OK . |

## Analysis of Variance (ANOVA)

## The Randomized Complete Block Design with <u>One</u> Observation per Cell

## (continued)

Checking the Assumptions of Two-way Analysis of Variance.

| Assumption | MINITAB Procedure |
|---|---|
| Each population is normally distributed.<br><br>Assumption (1) | *Stat , Basic Statistics , Normality Test ...*<br><br>Highlight 'RESI1' variable and click on [ **Select** ]<br><br>Under the heading of *Percentile lines*, the button to the left of *None* should be chosen.<br><br>Make sure the ⦿ to the left of *Anderson-Darling* is checked<br><br>Click in the *Title:* box and type in Q-Q Plot<br><br>[ **OK** ] |
| The Treatment and Block Effects **are** Additive.<br><br>Assumption (3) | *File , Other Files , Run an Exec ...*<br><br>[ **Select File** ]<br><br>*Data Disc*<br><br>**Ht-add.mtb**<br><br>[ **Open** ] |

**Analysis of Variance (ANOVA)**
**The Randomized Complete Block Design with <u>One</u> Observation per Cell**
**(continued)**
Two-way Analysis of Variance where there is **one** observation per cell

| Null Hypothesis | MINITAB Procedure |
|---|---|
| To test the null hypothesis of equal Treatment effects <br><br> $H_0: \tau_1 = \tau_2 = \tau_3 = ... = \tau_c = 0$ <br> or equivalently <br> $H_0: \mu_{1.} = \mu_{2.} = \mu_{3.} = ... = \mu_{c.} = 0$ | *Stat , ANOVA , General Linear Model ...* <br> Click on the AllData (C26) variable that contains the stacked data and click on the $\boxed{\text{Select}}$ button. Next click inside of the box under the *Model:* heading, hold the $\boxed{\text{Ctrl}}$ key while clicking on the Treatment (C27) and Block (C28) variables and click on the $\boxed{\text{Select}}$ button. Next click on the $\boxed{\text{Storage...}}$ button. <br><br> If the square to the left of *Residuals* **is** checked, click on this square ☐ to **uncheck this option.** Then click on $\boxed{\text{OK}}$ . <br><br> Back in the General Linear Model dialog box: click on $\boxed{\text{OK}}$ .. |

Multiple Comparisons **after** the overall null hypothesis $H_0: \tau_1 = \tau_2 = \tau_3 = ... = \tau_c$ has been rejected
for Two-way Analysis of Variance where there is **one** observation per cell

| Multiple Comparison Method | MINITAB Procedure |
|---|---|
| To compute the Tukey multiple comparison procedure for all pairwise comparisons of $\mu_{i.} = \mu_{j.}$ | *Stat , ANOVA , General Linear Model ...* <br> Click on the AllData (C26) variable and click on $\boxed{\text{Select}}$ . Next click inside of the box under the *Model:* heading, hold the $\boxed{\text{Ctrl}}$ key while clicking on the Treatment (C27) and Block (C28) variables and click on $\boxed{\text{Select}}$ . Click on the $\boxed{\text{Comparisons...}}$ button. <br> Click on the circle ⦿ to the left of *Pairwise comparisons*, and then click in the box under the heading *Terms:*. Now click on the Treatment (C27) variable and click on $\boxed{\text{Select}}$ . Under the heading *Method* if the box to the left of *Tukey* is **not** checked, click on this box ☑ to **check** this option. Next click in the box ☐ to the left of *Confidence interval, with confidence level:* to **uncheck** this option. Now click on the $\boxed{\text{OK}}$ button. <br> Back in the General Linear Model dialog box: click on $\boxed{\text{OK}}$ . |

**Analysis of Variance (ANOVA)**

**The Randomized Complete Block Design with <u>More than One</u> Observation per Cell**

Combine sample data in <u>separate</u> columns into <u>one</u> column.

| Purpose | MINITAB Procedure |
|---|---|
| Stack sample data currently in separate columns (variables) into one new column, C26, and put the Treatment and Block level numbers into C27 and C28. | *File , Other Files , Run an Exec ...*<br><br>Select File<br><br>*Data Disc*<br><br>**Stak-bk.mtb**<br><br>Open |

Compute the residuals.

| Purpose | MINITAB Procedure |
|---|---|
| Compute the <u>residuals</u> and store them in new column. | *Stat , ANOVA , General Linear Model ...*<br><br>Click on the AllData (C26) variable that contains the stacked data and click on the Select button. Next click inside of the box under the *Model:* heading, hold the Ctrl key while clicking on the Treatment (C27) and Block (C28) variables and click on the Select button. Next highlight **only** the Treatment (C27) variable and click on the Select button. Then (using the keyboard) type in an asterisk. Now highlight **only** the Block (C28) variable and click on the Select button. Next click on the Storage... button.<br><br>If the square to the left of *Residuals* is **not checked, click on this square ☑ to check this option**. A new column to the right of the last column in your worksheet will **automatically** be created (usually C29) **and** will be named RESI1. Then click on OK .<br><br>OK . |

**Analysis of Variance (ANOVA)**

**The Randomized Complete Block Design with More than One Observation per Cell**
**(continued)**

Checking the Assumptions of Two-way Analysis of Variance
where there is **more than one** observation per cell.

| Assumption | MINITAB Procedure |
|---|---|
| Each population is normally distributed. Assumption (1) | *Stat , Basic Statistics , Normality Test ...* Highlight 'RESI1' variable and click on \| Select \| Under the heading of *Percentile lines*, the button to the left of *None* should be chosen. Make sure the ⊙ to the left of *Anderson-Darling* is checked Click in the *Title:* box and type in Q-Q Plot \| OK \| |
| The variances of all populations are equal; "homogeneity of variance" Assumption (2)  Bartlett's test and Levene's Test | *Stat , ANOVA , Test for Equal Variances...* Click on the AllData (C26) variable (that contains the stacked data) and click on the \| Select \| button. While holding the \| Ctrl \| key, click on the Treatment (C27) and Block (C28) variables (that contain the corresponding levels of the stacked data in AllData) and then click on the \| Select \| button. Ignore the boxes to the right of *Confidence level:* and *Title:*. Then click on the \| OK \| button. |
| The Treatment and Block Effects **are** Additive. Assumption (3) That is to test the null hypothesis of $H_0$: treatment & block effects **are** additive | Use the p-value for the *Treatmnt* * *Block* interaction term in the resulting Analysis of Variance table. |

# Analysis of Variance (ANOVA)
## The Randomized Complete Block Design with More than One Observation per Cell
## (continued)

Two-way Analysis of Variance. where there is **more than one** observation per cell.

| Null Hypothesis | MINITAB Procedure |
|---|---|
| To test the null hypothesis of equal Treatment effects $H_0: \tau_1 = \tau_2 = \tau_3 = ... = \tau_c = 0$ or equivalently $H_0: \mu_{1.} = \mu_{2.} = \mu_{3.} = ... = \mu_{c.} = 0$ | *Stat , ANOVA , General Linear Model ...* Click on the AllData (C26) variable that contains the stacked data and click on the \| Select \| button. Next click inside of the box under the *Model:* heading, hold the \| Ctrl \| key while clicking on the Treatment (C27) and Block (C28) variables and click on the \| Select \| button. Next highlight **only** the Treatment (C27) variable and click on the \| Select \| button. Then (using the keyboard) type in an asterisk. Now highlight **only** the Block (C28) variable and click on the \| Select \| button. Next click on the \| Storage... \| button. <br><br> If the square to the left of *Residuals* **is** checked, click on this square ☐ to **uncheck this option**. Then click on \| OK \| . <br><br> Back in the General Linear Model dialog box: click on \| OK \| .. |

Multiple Comparisons **after** the overall null hypothesis $H_0: \tau_1 = \tau_2 = \tau_3 = ... = \tau_c$ has been rejected for Two-way Analysis of Variance where there is **more than one** observation per cell

| Multiple Comparison Method | MINITAB Procedure |
|---|---|
| To compute the Tukey multiple comparison procedure for all pairwise comparisons of $\mu_{i.} = \mu_{j.}$ | *Stat , ANOVA , General Linear Model ...* Click on the AllData (C26) variable and click on \| Select \| . Next click inside of the box under the *Model:* heading, hold the \| Ctrl \| key while clicking on the Treatment (C27) and Block (C28) variables and click on \| Select \| . Next highlight **only** the Treatment (C27) variable and click on the \| Select \| button. Then (using the keyboard) type in an asterisk. Now highlight **only** the Block (C28) variable and click on the \| Select \| button. Click on the \| Comparisons... \| button. <br><br> Click on the circle ⦿ to the left of *Pairwise comparisons*, and then click in the box under the heading *Terms:*. Now click on the Treatment (C27) variable and click on \| Select \| . Under the heading *Method* if the box to the left of *Tukey* is **not** checked, click on this box ☑ to **check** this option. Next click in the box ☐ to the left of *Confidence interval, with confidence level:* to **uncheck** this option. Now click on the \| OK \| button. <br><br> Back in the General Linear Model dialog box: click on \| OK \| . |

## One Sample Hypothesis Tests for the Population Median

| Data | Test | MINITAB Procedure |
|---|---|---|
| Measured: **Ordinal**<br>Underlying Distribution: **Ordinal** | **Sign Test**<br>for<br>$H_0$: $M = M_0$ | *Stat , Nonparametrics , 1-Sample Sign...*<br>In the 1-Sample Sign dialog box: you may press the **F3** key to clear the contents of this dialog box and reset all options and erase any previous variables. The variables (columns) will appear in the large box on the left side of this dialog box, click on the variable you want to analyze, and click on the **Select** button. Next click inside of the circle to the left of *Test Median:*, erase any current incorrect value, and type in the given value of the population median ($M_0$). Then make sure that the box to the right of *Alternative:* contains the correct inequality for your problem (*not equal* or *less than* or *greater than*). If not, click on the down triangle ( ▾ ), and click on the correct choice. Then click on **OK** . |
| Measured: **At least Ordinal**<br>Underlying Distribution:<br>**Continuous** | **Wilcoxon Signed-Rank Test**<br>for<br>$H_0$: $M = M_0$ | *Stat , Nonparametrics , 1-Sample Wilcoxon...*<br>In the 1-Sample Wilcoxon dialog box: you may press the **F3** key to clear the contents of this dialog box and reset all options and erase any previous variables. The variables (columns) will appear in the large box on the left side of this dialog box, click on the variable you want to analyze, and click on the **Select** button. Next click inside of the circle to the left of *Test Median:*, erase any current incorrect value, and type in the given value of the population median ($M_0$). Then make sure that the box to the right of *Alternative:* contains the correct inequality for your problem (*not equal* or *less than* or *greater than*). If not, click on the down triangle ( ▾ ), and click on the correct choice. Then click on **OK** . |

## Nonparametric Techniques
## (continued)

## One Sample Confidence Intervals for the Population Median

| Data and Technique | Technique | MINITAB Procedure |
|---|---|---|
| Measured: **Ordinal** <br> Underlying Distribution: **Ordinal** | Based on the **Sign Test** | *Stat , Nonparametrics , 1-Sample Sign...* <br> In the 1-Sample Sign dialog box: you may press the F3 key to clear the contents of this dialog box and reset all options and erase any previous variables. The variables (columns) will appear in the large box on the left side of this dialog box, click on the variable you want to analyze, and click on the Select button. Next click inside of the circle to the left of *Confidence interval*, then click inside of the box to the right of *Level:*, erase any current incorrect value, and type in the correct confidence level. Then click on OK . |
| Measured: **At least Ordinal** <br> Underlying Distribution: **Continuous** | Based on the **Wilcoxon Signed-Rank Test** | *Stat , Nonparametrics , 1-Sample Wilcoxon...* <br> In the 1-Sample Wilcoxon dialog box: you may press the F3 key to clear the contents of this dialog box and reset all options and erase any previous variables. The variables (columns) will appear in the large box on the left side of this dialog box, click on the variable you want to analyze, and click on the Select button. Next click inside of the circle to the left of *Confidence interval*, then click inside of the box to the right of *Level:*, erase any current incorrect value, and type in the correct confidence level. Then click on OK . |

# Nonparametric Techniques
## (continued)

## Two Independent Sample Hypothesis Tests for
## the Difference of Population Medians

| Data | Test | MINITAB Procedure |
|---|---|---|
| Measured: **At least Ordinal**<br>Underlying Distribution:<br>**Continuous** | **Mann-Whitney Test (equivalent to Wilcoxon Rank-Sum Test)** for $H_0: M_1 = M_2$ | *Stat , Nonparametrics , Mann-Whitney...*<br>In the Mann-Whitney dialog box: you may press the $\boxed{F3}$ key to clear the contents of this dialog box and reset all options and erase any previous variables. The variables (columns) will appear in the large box on the left side of this dialog box and the cursor will be inside of the box to the right of *First Sample:*. Click on the variable that contains the data for the first sample, and click on the $\boxed{\text{Select}}$ button. The cursor will now be inside of the box to the right of *Second Sample:*. Click on the variable that contains the data for the second sample, and click on the $\boxed{\text{Select}}$ button. When doing hypothesis testing you may ignore the value inside of the box to the right of *Confidence level:*. Next make sure that the box to the right of *Alternative:* contains the correct inequality for your problem (*not equal* or *less than* or *greater than*). If not, click on the down triangle ( $\boxed{\blacktriangledown}$ ), and click on the correct choice. Then click on $\boxed{\text{OK}}$. |

**Nonparametric Techniques**
**(continued)**

**Two Independent Sample Confidence Intervals for**
**the Difference of Population Medians**

| Data | Technique | MINITAB Procedure |
|---|---|---|
| Measured: **At least Ordinal** Underlying Distribution: **Continuous** | Based on the **Mann-Whitney Test (equivalent to Wilcoxon Rank-Sum Test)** | *Stat , Nonparametrics , Mann-Whitney...* In the Mann-Whitney dialog box: you may press the F3 key to clear the contents of this dialog box and reset all options and erase any previous variables. The variables (columns) will appear in the large box on the left side of this dialog box and the cursor will be inside of the box to the right of *First Sample:*. Click on the variable that contains the data for the first sample, and click on the Select button. The cursor will now be inside of the box to the right of *Second Sample:*. Click on the variable that contains the data for the second sample, and click on the Select button. Next Click inside the box to the right of *Confidence level:*, erase any current incorrect value, and type in the correct confidence level. When doing a confidence interval you may ignore box to the right of *Alternative:*. Then click on OK . |

**Two Paired Sample Hypothesis Tests for**
**the Difference of Population Medians**

| Data | Test | MINITAB Procedure |
|---|---|---|
| Compute Difference Variable  d | | *Calc , Calculator...*<br>In the Calculator dialog box the cursor will be inside the box to the right of *Store result in variable:*. Highlight the new  d  variable and click on the [ Select ] button. Next click inside of the box under *Expression:*, click on the variable containing the **first** sample's data, click on the [ Select ] button, click on the button with the minus sign (-) on it, click on the variable containing the **second** sample's data, and click on the [ Select ] button. (Optionally you may just type in the first sample's column number, followed by a minus sign, and then the second sample's column number.) Then click on [ OK ]. |
| Measured: **Ordinal**<br>Underlying Distribution: **Ordinal** | **Sign Test**<br>for<br>$H_0: M_1 = M_2$<br>or<br>$H_0: M_d = 0$ | *Stat , Nonparametrics , 1-Sample Sign...*<br>In the 1-Sample Sign dialog box: you may press the [ F3 ] key to clear the contents of this dialog box and reset all options and erase any previous variables. The variables (columns) will appear in the large box on the left side of this dialog box, click on  d - the difference variable you want to analyze, and click on the [ Select ] button. Next click inside of the circle to the left of *Test Median:*, erase any current incorrect value, and type in 0 - the given value of the population difference median ($M_d$). Then make sure that the box to the right of *Alternative:* contains the correct inequality for your problem (*not equal* or *less than* or *greater than*). If not, click on the down triangle ( [▼] ), and click on the correct choice. Then click on [ OK ]. |

**Two Paired Sample Hypothesis Tests for**
**the Difference of Population Medians**

| Data | Test | MINITAB Procedure |
|---|---|---|
| Compute Difference Variable  d | | *Calc , Calculator...*<br>In the Calculator dialog box the cursor will be inside the box to the right of *Store result in variable:*. Highlight the new  d  variable and click on the ⬚ Select ⬚ button. Next click inside of the box under *Expression:*, click on the variable containing the **first** sample's data, click on the ⬚ Select ⬚ button, click on the button with the minus sign (-) on it, click on the variable containing the **second** sample's data, and click on the ⬚ Select ⬚ button. (Optionally you may just type in the first sample's column number, followed by a minus sign, and then the second sample's column number.)  Then click on ⬚ **OK** ⬚ . |
| Measured: **At least Ordinal**<br>Underlying Distribution:<br>**Continuous** | **Wilcoxon Signed-Rank Test**<br>for<br>$H_0: M_1 = M_2$<br>or<br>$H_0: M_d = 0$ | *Stat , Nonparametrics , 1-Sample Wilcoxon...*<br>In the 1-Sample Wilcoxon dialog box: you may press the ⬚ **F3** ⬚ key to clear the contents of this dialog box and reset all options and erase any previous variables. The variables (columns) will appear in the large box on the left side of this dialog box, click on  d - the difference variable you want to analyze, and click on the ⬚ Select ⬚ button. Next click inside of the circle to the left of *Test Median:*, erase any current incorrect value, and type in 0 - the given value of the population difference median ($M_d$). Then make sure that the box to the right of *Alternative:* contains the correct inequality for your problem (*not equal* or *less than* or *greater than*).  If not, click on the down triangle ( ⬚▾⬚ ), and click on the correct choice. Then click on ⬚ **OK** ⬚ . |

**Nonparametric Techniques**
**(continued)**

**Two Paired Sample Confidence Intervals for**
**the Difference of Population Medians**

| Data | Technique | MINITAB Procedure |
|---|---|---|
| Compute Difference Variable  d | | *Calc , Calculator...*<br>In the Calculator dialog box the cursor will be inside the box to the right of *Store result in variable:*. Highlight the new  d  variable and click on the [ **Select** ] button. Next click inside of the box under *Expression:*, click on the variable containing the **first** sample's data, click on the [ **Select** ] button, click on the button with the minus sign (-) on it, click on the variable containing the **second** sample's data, and click on the [ **Select** ] button. (Optionally you may just type in the first sample's column number, followed by a minus sign, and then the second sample's column number.)  Then click on [ **OK** ] . |
| Measured: **Ordinal**<br>Underlying Distribution: **Ordinal** | Based on the **Sign Test** | *Stat , Nonparametrics , 1-Sample Sign...*<br>In the 1-Sample Sign dialog box: note that the d variable is already in the *Variables:* box. Next click inside of the circle to the left of *Confidence interval*, click inside of the box to the right of *Level:*, erase any current incorrect value, and type in the correct confidence level. Then click on [ **OK** ] . |

## Nonparametric Techniques
## (continued)

## Two Paired Sample Confidence Intervals for
## the Difference of Population Medians

| Data | Technique | MINITAB Procedure |
|---|---|---|
| Measured: **At least Ordinal** Underlying Distribution: **Continuous** | Based on the **Wilcoxon Signed-Rank Test** | *Calc , Calculator...* In the Calculator dialog box the cursor will be inside the box to the right of *Store result in variable:*. Highlight the new d variable and click on the [ Select ] button. Next click inside of the box under *Expression:*, click on the variable containing the **first** sample's data, click on the [ Select ] button, click on the button with the minus sign (-) on it, click on the variable containing the **second** sample's data, and click on the [ Select ] button. (Optionally you may just type in the first sample's column number, followed by a minus sign, and then the second sample's column number.) Then click on [ OK ]. *Stat , Nonparametrics , 1-Sample Wilcoxon...* In the 1-Sample Wilcoxon dialog box: note that d is already in the *Variables:* box. Next click inside of the circle to the left of *Confidence interval*, click inside of the box to the right of *Level:*, erase any current incorrect value, and type in the correct confidence level. Then click on [ OK ] . |

# Nonparametric Techniques
## (continued)

### One-Way Analysis of Variance; Hypothesis Tests on Population Medians
### Using Multiple Independent Samples
### Mood's Median Test for $H_0$: $M_1 = M_2 = M_3 = ... = M_c$

| Data | MINITAB Procedure |
|---|---|
| Stack the data into Data column and create Factor column | Name two unused columns as Data and Factor. *Data , Stack , Columns ...* In the Stack Columns dialog box: the cursor will be in the box under the *Stack the following columns:*. Block the columns that contain the data for each of the samples (hold the `Ctrl` key and click on each variable or drag the mouse over the variables, if consecutive) and click on the `Select` button. Next click on the button to the left of *Column of current worksheet:* and then click inside of the box to its right. Highlight the stacked data column (Data) and click on `Select` . Then cursor will be inside the box to the right of *Store subscripts in:*, highlight the column (Factor) that contains the sample identification and click on `Select` . **If** the columns with the original data have been named, make sure the box to the left of *Use variable names in subscript column* is checked. But if the columns with the original data have **not** been named, click on this box to **un**check it. Click on `OK` . |
| Measured: **Ordinal**<br>Underlying Distribution: **Ordinal**<br><br>**Mood's Median Test**<br>for $H_0$: $M_1 = M_2 = M_3 = ... = M_c$ | *Stat , Nonparametrics , Mood's Median Test...* In the Mood's Median Test dialog box: you may press the `F3` key to clear the contents of this dialog box and reset all options and erase any previous variables. The cursor will be in the box to the right of *Response:* and the variables (columns) will appear in the large box on the left side of this dialog box; click on the new column (Data) that contains the stacked data, and click on the `Select` button. The cursor will move to the *Factor:* box; click on the variable (Factor) that contains the sample identification information (where the subscripts are stored) and click on `Select` . Then click on `OK` . |

**One-Way Analysis of Variance; Hypothesis Tests on Population Medians**
**Using Multiple Independent Samples**
**Kruskal-Wallis Test for $H_0$: $M_1 = M_2 = M_3 = ... = M_c$**

| Data | MINITAB Procedure |
|---|---|
| Stack the data into Data column and create Factor column | Name two unused columns as Data and Factor.<br>*Data , Stack , Columns ...*<br>In the Stack Columns dialog box: the cursor will be in the box under the *Stack the following columns:*. Block the columns that contain the data for each of the samples (hold the \| Ctrl \| key and click on each variable or drag the mouse over the variables, if consecutive) and click on the \| Select \| button. Next click on the button to the left of *Column of current worksheet:* and then click inside of the box to its right. Highlight the stacked data column (Data) and click on \| Select \|. Then cursor will be inside the box to the right of *Store subscripts in:*, highlight the column (Factor) that contains the sample identification and click on \| Select \|. **If** the columns with the original data have been named, make sure the box to the left of *Use variable names in subscript column* is checked. But if the columns with the original data have **not** been named, click on this box to **un**check it. Click on \| **OK** \|. |
| Measured: **Ordinal**<br>Underlying Distribution: **Ordinal**<br><br>**Kruskal-Wallis Test**<br>for $H_0$: $M_1 = M_2 = M_3 = ... = M_c$ | *Stat , Nonparametrics , Kruskal-Wallis...*<br>In the Kruskal-Wallis dialog box: you may press the \| F3 \| key to clear the contents of this dialog box and reset all options and erase any previous variables. The cursor will be in the box to the right of *Response:* and the variables (columns) will appear in the large box on the left side of this dialog box; click on the new column that contains the stacked data, and click on the \| Select \| button. The cursor will move to the *Factor:* box; click on the variable (Factor) that contains the sample identification information (where the subscripts are stored) and click on \| Select \|. Then click on \| **OK** \|. |

# Nonparametric Techniques
## (continued)

## Analysis of Variance -  The Randomized Complete Block Design; Hypothesis Tests on Population Location Parameters (Medians) Using Multiple Related Samples

## Friedman Test  for $H_0$: $M_1 = M_2 = M_3 = ... = M_c$

| Data | MINITAB Procedure |
|---|---|
| Combining data from <u>separate</u> columns into <u>one</u> column.<br>Stack sample data currently in separate columns (variables) into one new column AllData C26, and put the Treatment and Block level numbers into C27 and C28. | *File , Other Files , Run an Exec ...*<br>**Select File**<br>*Data Disc*<br>**Stak-b1.mtb**<br>**Open** |
| Measured: **Ordinal**<br>Underlying Distribution: **Continuous**<br>One score in each block of each treatment<br>No interaction between treatments and blocks<br><br><br>**Friedman Test**<br>for  $H_0$: $M_1 = M_2 = M_3 = ... = M_c$ | Click on *Stat , Nonparametrics , Friedman...*<br>In the Friedman dialog box: you may press the **F3** key to clear the contents of this dialog box and reset all options and erase any previous variables.  The cursor will be in the box to the right of *Response:* and the variables (columns) will appear in the large box on the left side of this dialog box; click the column that contains the stacked data - usually C26 (AllData), and click on the **Select** button.  The cursor will move to the *Treatment:* box; click on the column that contains the treatment numbers - usually C27 (Treatment),  and click on the **Select** button.  The cursor will move to the *Blocks:* box; click on the column that contains the block numbers - usually C28 (Block),  and click on **Select** .  Then click on **OK** . |

# Chi-Square Tests

### Goodness of Fit Test where data are from a <u>frequency table</u>

| Null Hypothesis | Formula | MINITAB Procedure |
|---|---|---|
| $H_0$: $p_1 = p_{10}$ , $p_2 = p_{20}$ , ... , $p_k = p_{k0}$ | (i) $\chi^2 = \sum_{i=1}^{k} \dfrac{(O_i - E_i)^2}{E_i}$ | Name two columns Category and Observed. Enter the name of each category into the first column and the observed <u>number</u> of occurrences of each outcome into the second column. <br><br> *Stat, Tables, Chi-Square Goodness-of-Fit Test* <br><br> Click on the circle ⊙ to the left of *Observed counts:* and click in the box to its right. Highlight the Observed variable and click on Select . Highlight the Category variable and click on Select . <br><br> Click on the circle ⊙ to the left of *Specific proportions* and in the box underneath contains choose *Input constants.* in the resulting box, enter the corresponding null hypothesized proportions. Click on Graphs... . <br><br> Click in all of the boxes □ to **un**select displaying these graphs. OK <br><br><br> **If $H_0$ is rejected,** <br> *File , Other Files , Run an Exec ...* <br> Select File <br> *Data Disc* <br> **Goodfit.mtb** <br> Open |

# Chi-Square Tests
## (continued)

Goodness of Fit Test where the raw data has **not** been tabulated into a frequency table

| Null Hypothesis | Formula | MINITAB Procedure |
|---|---|---|
| $H_0: p_1 = p_{10}, p_2 = p_{20}, \ldots, p_k = p_{k0}$ | (i) $\chi^2 = \displaystyle\sum_{i=1}^{k} \frac{(O_i - E_i)^2}{E_i}$ | *Stat, Tables, Chi-Square Goodness-of-Fit Test* <br><br> Click on the circle ⦿ to the left of *Categorical data:* and click in the box to its right. Highlight the variable (column) that contains the un-tabulated data and click on [ Select ]. <br><br> Click on the circle ⦿ to the left of *Specific proportions* and in the box underneath contains choose *Input constants.* in the resulting box, enter the corresponding null hypothesized proportions. Click on [ Graphs... ]. <br><br> Click in all of the boxes ☐ to **un**select displaying these graphs. [ OK ] <br><br> **If $H_0$ is rejected,** <br> *File , Other Files , Run an Exec ...* [ Select File ] <br> *Data Disc* <br> **Goodfit.mtb** [ Open ] |

## Chi-Square Tests
## (continued)

Test of Independence where data are from a   r (rows) by c (columns)   <u>contingency table</u>

| Null Hypothesis | Formula | MINITAB Procedure |
|---|---|---|
| $H_0$: two variables are independent | (ii)  $\chi^2 = \sum_{i=1}^{r} \sum_{j=1}^{c} \frac{\left(O_{i,j} - E_{i,j}\right)^2}{E_{i,j}}$ | Enter the data in the "rxc" table into "r" rows of columns C1 to Cc<br>*Stat , Tables , Chi-Square Test ...*<br>Hold [ **Ctrl** ] key, click on and block the "c" columns that contain the data (usually C1 to Cc), click [ **Select** ] and then on [ **OK** ]<br>**If $H_0$ is rejected, do post-hoc analysis**<br><br>*File , Other Files , Run an Exec ...*<br>[ **Select File** ]<br>*Data Disc*<br>**Contapcv.mtb**<br>[ **Open** ] |

Test of Independence where the raw data has **<u>not</u>** been tabulated into a contingency table

| Null Hypothesis | Formula | MINITAB Procedure |
|---|---|---|
| $H_0$: two variables are independent | (ii)  $\chi^2 = \sum_{i=1}^{r} \sum_{j=1}^{c} \frac{\left(O_{i,j} - E_{i,j}\right)^2}{E_{i,j}}$ | *Stat, Tables, Cross Tabulation and Chi-Square ...*<br>Click on the row variable that contains the raw data and [ **Select** ]<br>Click in the box to the right of *For columns:* , click on the column variable that contains the raw data and [ **Select** ].  Then [ **Chi-Square...** ]<br>Click on the boxes ☑ to the left of *Chi-Square Analysis* , *Expected Cell Counts* , and *Each cell's contribution to the Chi-Square statistic.*  Then click on [ **OK** ]<br>Click on [ **Options...** ]<br>Click on the circle ◉ to the left of *No variables,* and then click on [ **OK** ]<br>[ **OK** ] |

# Simple Linear Regression and Correlation

| Purpose | MINITAB Procedure |
|---|---|
| Examine the relationship between the X and Y variables. Graphically check if X and Y are linearly related; i.e., assumption (1). | *Graph , Scatterlot ...*<br>*Simple* graph should be highlighted. Click on the [ OK ] button.<br>Click on the desired Y variable and click on the [ Select ] button.<br>Click on the desired X variable and click on the [ Select ] button.<br>Then click on the [ OK ] button. |
| Check for outliers | *Stat , Regression , Regression ...*<br>If **new** problem, press [ F3 ] to clear previous information<br>Click on the Y variable for the *Response:* and [ Select ]<br>Click on the X variable for the *Predictors:* and [ Select ]<br>[ OK ] |
| Check the validity of assumption (1); i.e., test<br>$H_0$: X and Y are **not** linearly related<br>$H_a$: X and Y **are** linearly related | Use the values of the F test statistic and the p-value in the *Analysis of Variance* table that is in the *Regression* output. |
| Compute the Residuals | *Stat , Regression , Regression ...*<br>If **continuing** a problem, do **not** press [ F3 ]<br>Y & X variables should be in *Response:* & *Predictors:* boxes<br>[ Storage... ] Click on the ☑ to the left of *Residuals* and then click on [ OK ] . A **new** column numbered 1 more than the highest existing column number will be created, named RESI1, and the residuals will be stored in this column and click on [ OK ]<br>.<br>[ OK ] |

| Purpose | MINITAB Procedure |
|---|---|
| Graphically check if the variances of all subpopulations are equal; i.e., assumption (2), by graphing the residuals against the X values. | *Graph , Scatterplot...*<br>*Simple* graph should be highlighted.  Click on the $\boxed{\text{OK}}$ button.<br>Highlight RESI1 (Residual) variable and $\boxed{\text{Select}}$<br>Highlight X variable and $\boxed{\text{Select}}$<br>$\boxed{\text{OK}}$ |
| Check the validity of assumption (2); i.e., test<br>$H_0$:  all $\sigma^2_{y.x}$ are equal<br>$H_a$:  $\sigma^2_{y.x}$ are in a megaphone shape | Name three new columns as Sorted X, Corres R and Factor<br>*Data , Sort...*<br>Hold $\boxed{\text{Ctrl}}$ , click on X and RESI1 (Residual) variables, $\boxed{\text{Select}}$<br>Click in box right of *Sort by column:*, click on X variable, $\boxed{\text{Select}}$<br>Click on the circle ⊙ to the left of *Column(s) of current worksheet:*<br>Click in box under *Store sorted column(s) in:* , hold $\boxed{\text{Ctrl}}$ , click on<br>    Sorted X and Corresp R variables, $\boxed{\text{Select}}$<br>$\boxed{\text{OK}}$<br>*Data , Code , Numeric to Text...*<br>Click on Sorted X variable and $\boxed{\text{Select}}$<br>Click in *Into columns:* box, click on Factor variable, $\boxed{\text{Select}}$<br>Click in first *Original values* box and type in adjusted  min : $m_1$<br>Click in first *New:* box and type in Lo<br>Click in second *Original values* box and type in adjusted  $m_2$ : max<br>Click in second *New:* box and type in Hi<br>$\boxed{\text{OK}}$<br>*Stat , ANOVA , Test for Equal Variances...*<br>Click on Corresp R variable and $\boxed{\text{Select}}$<br>Click on Factor variable and $\boxed{\text{Select}}$<br>$\boxed{\text{OK}}$ |
| Graphically and numerically verify assumption (3), that each subpopulation is normally distributed by graphing a Q-Q plot and testing the hypothesis<br>$H_0$: subpops. of Y are normal<br>$H_a$: subpops. of Y are not normal | *Stat , Basic Statistics , Normality Test ...*<br>$\boxed{\text{F3}}$ to clear any previous information<br>Click on the RESI1 variable and $\boxed{\text{Select}}$<br>Under *Percentile lines*, Click on the circle ⊙ the left of *None*.<br>Make sure the ⊙ to the left of *Anderson-Darling* is checked<br>Click in the *Title:* box and type in Q-Q Plot (do **not** press $\boxed{\text{Enter}}$ )<br>$\boxed{\text{OK}}$ |

| Purpose | MINITAB Procedure |
|---|---|
| Compute the predicted value and a prediction interval(s) for the Y value(s) of a new object(s), when this object's X value(s) is known to be $x_0$. | *Stat , Regression , Regression ...* <br> Y & X variables should be in *Response:* & *Predictors:* boxes <br> **Storage...** <br> Click on the □ to the left of *Residuals* to **un**check this option and then click on the **OK** button. <br> **Options...** <br> Click in the box below *Prediction intervals for new observations*; <br> (a) type in the new object's known X value ($x_0$) or <br> (b) highlight Xo Values column and click on the **Select** button. <br> **If also computing prediction intervals(s)**, then click in the box to the right of *Confidence level* , erase current value and type in desired confidence level <br> Click on **OK** <br> **OK** |
| Compute the Pearson Product Moment Coefficient of Correlation (linear) between two variables and test the hypothesis <br> $H_0: \rho = 0$ <br> $H_a: \rho \neq 0$ | *Stat , Basic Statistics , Correlation ...* <br> **F3** to clear any previous information <br> Hold the **Ctrl** key and click on the X and Y variables and click on **Select** <br> **OK** |
| Compute the Pearson Product Moment Coefficient of Correlation (linear) among several variables. | *Stat , Basic Statistics , Correlation ...* <br> **F3** to clear any previous information <br> Hold the **Ctrl** key and click on each of the variables and click on **Select** <br> Click on the □ to left of *Display p values* to **un**check this option <br> (unless you want to do multiple hypothesis testing on the $\rho$) <br> **OK** |

# Multiple Linear Regression

| Purpose | MINITAB Procedure |
|---|---|
| Examine the relationship among the Y and the set of $X_1, X_2, \ldots, X_k$ variables. | *Graph , Matrix Plot...*<br><br>In the Matrix Plots dialog box: the *Matrix of plots Simple* graph should be highlighted.  Next click on the **OK** button.<br><br>In the Matrix Plots - Matrix of Plots Simple: you may need to press the **F3** key to clear any previous information.  The cursor will be in the box under the *Graph variables:* heading.  Hold the **Ctrl** key and click on each of the "predictor" (X) variables, and then click on **Select** .  Now highlight the "response" (Y) variable and click on **Select** .  Then click on **Matrix Options...** .<br><br>In the Matrix Plot - Options dialog box: under the *Matrix Display* heading, click on the circle to the left of *Lower left*, and under the *Variable Label Placement* heading, click on the circle to the left of *Boundary*.  Then click on the **OK** button.<br><br>Back in Matrix Plots - Matrix of Plots Simple: click on **OK** . |
| Check for outliers | *Stat , Regression , Regression ...*<br><br>In the Regression dialog box, if this is a **new** problem, press the **F3** key to clear any previous information from all Regression dialog boxes.  The cursor should be in the box to the right of the *Response:* heading; click on the "response" (Y) variable and click on the **Select** button.  The cursor will move down to the *Predictors:* box; hold the **Ctrl** key and click on each of the "predictor" (X) variables, and then click on the **Select** button.  Then click on **OK** . |
| Check the validity of assumption (1); i.e., test<br><br>$H_0$: $X_1, X_2, \ldots, X_k$ and Y are **not** linearly related<br><br>$H_a$: $X_1, X_2, \ldots, X_k$ and Y **are** linearly related | Use the values of the F test statistic and the p-value in the *Analysis of Variance* table that is in the *Regression* output. |

| Purpose | MINITAB Procedure |
|---------|-------------------|
| Compute the Fitted Y Values: $\hat{y}$ and the Residuals: ( y - $\hat{y}$ ) | *Stat , Regression , Regression ...*<br><br>In the Regression dialog box, the cursor should be in the box to the right of the *Response:* heading; click on the "response" (Y) variable and click on the  Select  button. The cursor will move down to the *Predictors:* box; hold the  Ctrl  key and click on each of the "predictor" (X) variables, and then click on the  Select  button. Next click on the  Storage...  button. Note that since Minitab remembers the information in the dialog boxes from the previous time, you will only need to click on the  Storage...  button.<br><br>In the Regression - Storage dialog box, click in the squares to the left of *Residuals* and to the left of *Fits* to check these two options. No other options should be checked. Then click on  OK . Two new columns automatically will be created and named FITS1 and RESI1.<br><br>Back in the Regression dialog box, click on  OK . |
| Graphically check if the variances of all subpopulations are equal; i.e., assumption (2), by graphing the fitted Y values ( $\hat{y}$ ) against the residuals. | *Graph , Scatterplot ...*<br><br>In the Scatterplots dialog box: the *Simple* graph should be highlighted. Next click on the  OK  button.<br><br>In the Scatterplot - Simple dialog box: the cursor will be in the box on the first line under the *Y variables* heading; click on the RESI1 variable and click on the  Select  button. The cursor will move to the box in the first line under the *X variables* heading; click on the FITS1 variable and click on the  Select  button. Then click on the  OK  button.<br><br>It is desirable to label the X axis with the name of "y hat" and to label the Y axis as "Residuals". |

| Purpose | MINITAB Procedure |
|---|---|
| Check the validity of assumption (2); i.e., test $H_0$: all $\sigma^2_{y.x}$ are equal $H_a$: $\sigma^2_{y.x}$ are in a megaphone shape | *Data , Sort...* Highlight the FITS1 column only and [Select] . Then highlight the RESI1 column only and [Select] . **It is important that these two variables be entered in this order.** Next click inside the box to the right of the first *By column:* heading, click on the FITS1 variable, and [Select] . Next click on the circle to the left of *Column(s) of current worksheet:*, and then click inside of the box under this heading. inside of the box under the *Store sorted column(s) in:* heading, hold the [Ctrl] key and click on the Sorted Fit and Corresp R variables to highlight them both. **It is important that these two variables be entered in this order.** Then click on [Select] . Now click on [OK] .<br><br>*Stat , Basic Statistics , Describe Statistics* Highlight the Sorted X variable, click on the [Select] button, and then click on the [Statistics...] button.<br><br>Click to uncheck all boxes **except** for the *Minimum , Maximum* and *N nonmissing* statistics, and click on [OK] . [OK]<br><br>*Data , Code , Numeric to Text...* Click on Sorted Fit variable and [Select] Click in *Into columns:* box, click on Factor variable, [Select] Click in first *Original values* box and type in adjusted min : $m_1$ Click in first *New:* box and type in Lo Click in second *Original values* box and type in adjusted $m_2$ : max Click in second *New:* box and type in Hi [OK]<br><br>*Stat , ANOVA , Test for Equal Variances...* In the Test for Equal Variances dialog box: the cursor will be in the box to the right of *Response:*. Click on the Corresp R variable and [Select] . The cursor will move to the large box to the right of *Factors:*, click on the Factor variable and [Select] . You may ignore the boxes to the right of *Confidence level:* and *Title:*. Then click on the [OK] button. |

**Multiple Linear Regression  (continued)**

| Purpose | MINITAB  Procedure |
|---|---|
| Graphically and numerically verify assumption (3), that each subpopulation is normally distributed by graphing a Q-Q plot and testing the hypothesis <br> $H_0$: subpops. of Y are normal <br> $H_a$: subpops. of Y are not normal | *Stat , Basic Statistics , Normality Test ...* <br> `F3` to clear any previous information <br> Click on the RESI1 variable and `Select` <br> Make sure the ◉ to the left of *Anderson-Darling* is checked <br> Click in the *Title:* box and type in Q-Q Plot (do **not** press the `Enter` key) <br> `OK` |
| Compute the predicted value and a prediction interval for the Y value of a new object, when this object's $(X_1, X_2, ... , X_k)$ values are known to be $(x_{10}, x_{20}, ... , x_{k0})$. | *Stat , Regression , Regression ...* <br> Y & X1, X2, ... , Xk  variables should be in *Response:* and the *Predictors:* boxes <br> `Storage...` <br> Click on the □ to the left of *Fits* and to the left of *Residuals* to **un**check this option and then click on `OK` <br> `Options...` <br> Click in the box below *Prediction intervals for new observations*; <br> (a) type in the new object's known X1, X2, ... , Xk values ($x_{10}$, $x_{20}$, ... , $x_{k0}$ ), or <br> (b) highlight X1o Values, X2o Values, ... Xko Values columns and click on `Select` . <br> **If also computing prediction intervals(s)**, then click in the box to the right of *Confidence level* , erase current value and type in desired confidence level <br> Click on `OK` <br> `OK` |
| Use Stepwise Regression to choose a *best* set of "predictor" variables. <br><br> Then compute the Estimated Regression Line of Y on these *best* set of $X_i$ "predictor" variables, check assumptions, and compute point and interval predictions. | *Stat , Regression , Stepwise ...* <br> If **new** problem, press `F3` to clear previous information <br> Click on the Y variable for the *Response:* and `Select` <br> Hold the `Ctrl` key and click each of the k potential $X_i$ variables for the *Predictors:* and `Select` <br> `OK` <br><br> Then continue with the Multiple Linear Regression Analysis with Y as the "Response" variable, and the specific $X_i$ variables identified by the *Stepwise* procedure as the "predictors". |

647

# INDEX